Ford Taurus & Mercury Sable Automotive Repair Manual

by Ken Layne and John H Haynes
Member of the Guild of Motoring Writers

Models covered:

Ford Taurus and Mercury Sable
1996 through 2007

Does not include information specific to SHO or E85 models

(36075 - 11S20)

ABCDE
FGHIJK
LMNOP
QRS

3

Haynes Publishing Group
Sparkford Nr Yeovil
Somerset BA22 7JJ England

Haynes North America, Inc
861 Lawrence Drive
Newbury Park
California 91320 USA

Acknowledgements

Wiring diagrams originated exclusively for Haynes North America, Inc. by Valley Forge Technical Information Services.

© **Haynes North America, Inc. 1998, 2000, 2001, 2004, 2005, 2014**

With permission from J.H. Haynes & Co. Ltd.

A book in the Haynes Automotive Repair Manual Series

Printed in the U.S.A.

ISBN-10: 1-62092-144-8
ISBN-13: 978-1-62092-144-9

Library of Congress Control Number: 2014954205

Contents

Haynes mechanic, author and photographer with 1997 Taurus

About this manual

Its purpose

The purpose of this manual is to help you get the best value from your vehicle. It can do so in several ways. It can help you decide what work must be done, even if you choose to have it done by a dealer service department or a repair shop; it provides information and procedures for routine maintenance and servicing; and it offers diagnostic and repair procedures to follow when trouble occurs.

We hope you use the manual to tackle the work yourself. For many simpler jobs, doing it yourself may be quicker than arranging an appointment to get the vehicle into a shop and making the trips to leave it and pick it up. More importantly, a lot of money can be saved by avoiding the expense the shop must pass on to you to cover its labor and overhead costs. An added benefit is the sense of satisfaction and accomplishment that you feel after doing the job yourself.

Using the manual

The manual is divided into Chapters. Each Chapter is divided into numbered Sections, which are headed in bold type between horizontal lines. Each Section consists of consecutively numbered paragraphs.

At the beginning of each numbered Section you will be referred to any illustrations which apply to the procedures in that Section. The reference numbers used in illustration captions pinpoint the pertinent Section and the Step within that Section. That is, illustration 3.2 means the illustration refers to Section 3 and Step (or paragraph) 2 within that Section.

Procedures, once described in the text, are not normally repeated. When it's necessary to refer to another Chapter, the reference will be given as Chapter and Section number. Cross references given without use of the word "Chapter" apply to Sections and/or paragraphs in the same Chapter. For example, "see Section 8" means in the same Chapter.

References to the left or right side of the vehicle assume you are sitting in the driver's seat, facing forward.

Even though we have prepared this manual with extreme care, neither the publisher nor the author can accept responsibility for any errors in, or omissions from, the information given.

NOTE

A **Note** provides information necessary to properly complete a procedure or information which will make the procedure easier to understand.

CAUTION

A **Caution** provides a special procedure or special steps which must be taken while completing the procedure where the Caution is found. Not heeding a Caution can result in damage to the assembly being worked on.

WARNING

A **Warning** provides a special procedure or special steps which must be taken while completing the procedure where the Warning is found. Not heeding a Warning can result in personal injury.

Introduction

This manual covers the second generation of Taurus and Sable models, introduced in 1996. Taurus and Sable models are available as four-door sedans and station wagons. The available engines are:

A 3.0-liter (182-cid) V6, called the "Vulcan" engine. The Vulcan V6 is a two-valve-per-cylinder, pushrod, overhead-valve (OHV) engine. Flexible-fuel versions of the Vulcan engine are available that run on gasoline and methanol-blend fuel or gasoline and ethanol-blend fuel.

A 3.0-liter (181-cid) overhead camshaft (OHC) V6, called the "Duratec" engine. The Duratec V6 is a four-valve-per-cylinder engine.

A 3.4-liter (207-cid) overhead-cam V8 engine, available in Taurus SHO models only through 1999. The SHO V8 is a 4-valve-per-cylinder engine.

Unique features of the SHO V8 and the flexible-fuel Vulcan V6 engines are not covered by this manual.

All models have a fifth-generation electronic engine control system (EEC-V) with second-generation onboard diagnostic (OBD-II) capabilities. All engines have electronically controlled multiport fuel injection and direct (distributorless) ignition systems. OBD-II monitors engine and emission control system operation for malfunctions. The malfunction indicator lamp (MIL) on the instrument panel (also called the CHECK ENGINE lamp) will light if a component malfunction occurs.

Power from the engine is transferred through a four-speed, electronically controlled automatic transaxle and final drive assembly to the front wheels. Front driveaxles carry power from the transaxle to the front wheels.

Suspension is independent in the front, with MacPherson struts (combination coil springs and shock absorber struts) and lower control arms to locate the spindle assembly at each wheel. The rear suspension has independent control arms on each side with coil springs and shock absorbers. Sedans use a MacPherson-type strut, and station wagons have separate springs and shock absorbers.

The steering gear is a power-assisted rack-and-pinion type, mounted to the sub-frame.

The brakes are disc at the front and either drum or disc at the rear, with vacuum assist as standard equipment. An Anti-lock Brake System (ABS) is optional on all models.

Vehicle identification numbers

Modifications are a continuing and unpublicized process in vehicle manufacturing. Your individual vehicle identification number (VIN) and major component identification numbers often are necessary to identify proper diagnostic and repair procedures, as well as correct replacement parts.

Vehicle Identification Number (VIN)

This very important identification number is stamped on a plate attached to the dashboard inside the windshield on the driver's side of the vehicle **(see illustration)**. The VIN also appears on the vehicle certificate of title and the vehicle registration certificate. The VIN contains information such as where and when the vehicle was manufactured, the body style or trim level, the individual serial number, and most importantly, the model year and the engine code.

VIN engine and model year codes

Two very important pieces of information in the VIN are the engine code and the model year code. Counting from the left, the engine code letter is the 8th digit, and the model year code letter is the 10th digit.

On the models covered by this manual the engine codes are:

U .... 3.0L (182-cid) OHV V6
S .... 3.0L (181-cid) OHC V6

On the models covered by this manual the model year codes are:

T 1996
V 1997
W 1998
X 1999
Y 2000
1 2001
2 2002
3 2003
4 2004
5 2005
6 2006
7 2007

Vehicle Certification Label

The vehicle certification label is attached to the driver's side (left front) door or door pillar **(see illustration)**. Information on this label includes the name of the manufacturer, the month and year of production, and information on the options with which it is equipped. This label is especially useful for matching the color and type of paint for repair work.

Engine identification number

A label with the engine code and build date is on the valve cover. The engine number also is stamped on a machined pad on the outside of the engine block.

Automatic transmission identification number

The automatic transaxle ID number is on a label attached to top of the torque converter housing area of the transaxle case.

Vehicle Emissions Control Information label

This label is found in the engine compartment. See Chapter 6 for more information on this label.

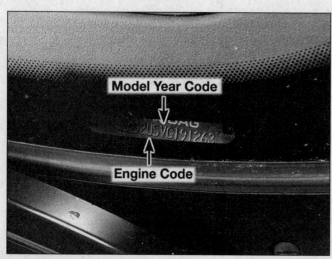

The VIN is visible through the windshield on the driver's side

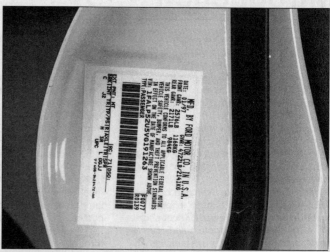

The Vehicle Certification label is on the driver's side door

Buying parts

Replacement parts are available from many sources, which generally fall into one of two categories - authorized dealer parts departments and independent retail auto parts stores. Our advice concerning these parts is as follows:

Retail auto parts stores: Good auto parts stores will stock frequently needed components which wear out relatively fast, such as clutch components, exhaust systems, brake parts, tune-up parts, etc. These stores often supply new or reconditioned

parts on an exchange basis, which can save a considerable amount of money. Discount auto parts stores are often very good places to buy materials and parts needed for general vehicle maintenance such as oil, grease, filters, spark plugs, belts, touch-up paint, bulbs, etc. They also usually sell tools and general accessories, have convenient hours, charge lower prices and can often be found not far from home.

Authorized dealer parts department: This is the best source for parts which are

unique to the vehicle and not generally available elsewhere (such as major engine parts, transmission parts, trim pieces, etc.).

Warranty information: If the vehicle is still covered under warranty, be sure that any replacement parts purchased - regardless of the source - do not invalidate the warranty!

To be sure of obtaining the correct parts, have engine and chassis numbers available and, if possible, take the old parts along for positive identification.

Maintenance techniques, tools and working facilities

Maintenance techniques

There are a number of techniques involved in maintenance and repair that will be referred to throughout this manual. Application of these techniques will enable the home mechanic to be more efficient, better organized and capable of performing the various tasks properly, which will ensure that the repair job is thorough and complete.

Fasteners

Fasteners are nuts, bolts, studs and screws used to hold two or more parts together. There are a few things to keep in mind when working with fasteners. Almost all of them use a locking device of some type, either a lockwasher, locknut, locking tab or thread adhesive. All threaded fasteners should be clean and straight, with undamaged threads and undamaged corners on the

hex head where the wrench fits. Develop the habit of replacing all damaged nuts and bolts with new ones. Special locknuts with nylon or fiber inserts can only be used once. If they are removed, they lose their locking ability and must be replaced with new ones.

Rusted nuts and bolts should be treated with a penetrating fluid to ease removal and prevent breakage. Some mechanics use turpentine in a spout-type oil can, which works quite well. After applying the rust penetrant, let it work for a few minutes before trying to loosen the nut or bolt. Badly rusted fasteners may have to be chiseled or sawed off or removed with a special nut breaker, available at tool stores.

If a bolt or stud breaks off in an assembly, it can be drilled and removed with a special tool commonly available for this purpose. Most automotive machine shops can perform

this task, as well as other repair procedures, such as the repair of threaded holes that have been stripped out.

Flat washers and lockwashers, when removed from an assembly, should always be replaced exactly as removed. Replace any damaged washers with new ones. Never use a lockwasher on any soft metal surface (such as aluminum), thin sheet metal or plastic.

Fastener sizes

For a number of reasons, automobile manufacturers are making wider and wider use of metric fasteners. Therefore, it is important to be able to tell the difference between standard (sometimes called U.S. or SAE) and metric hardware, since they cannot be interchanged.

All bolts, whether standard or metric, are sized according to diameter, thread pitch and length. For example, a standard 1/2 - 13 x 1 bolt is 1/2 inch in diameter, has 13 threads per inch and is 1 inch long. An M12 - 1.75 x 25 metric bolt is 12 mm in diameter, has a thread pitch of 1.75 mm (the distance between threads) and is 25 mm long. The two bolts are nearly identical, and easily confused, but they are not interchangeable.

In addition to the differences in diameter, thread pitch and length, metric and standard bolts can also be distinguished by examining the bolt heads. To begin with, the distance across the flats on a standard bolt head is measured in inches, while the same dimension on a metric bolt is sized in millimeters (the same is true for nuts). As a result, a standard wrench should not be used on a metric bolt and a metric wrench should not be used on a standard bolt. Also, most standard bolts have slashes radiating out from the center of the head to denote the grade or strength of the bolt, which is an indication of the amount of torque that can be applied to it. The greater the number of slashes, the greater the strength of the bolt. Grades 0 through 5 are commonly used on automobiles. Metric bolts have a property class (grade) number, rather than a slash, molded into their heads to indicate bolt strength. In this case, the higher the number, the stronger the bolt. Property class numbers 8.8, 9.8 and 10.9 are commonly used on automobiles.

Strength markings can also be used to distinguish standard hex nuts from metric hex nuts. Many standard nuts have dots stamped into one side, while metric nuts are marked with a number. The greater the number of dots, or the higher the number, the greater the strength of the nut.

Metric studs are also marked on their ends according to property class (grade). Larger studs are numbered (the same as metric bolts), while smaller studs carry a geometric code to denote grade.

It should be noted that many fasteners, especially Grades 0 through 2, have no distinguishing marks on them. When such is the case, the only way to determine whether it is standard or metric is to measure the thread pitch or compare it to a known fastener of the same size.

Standard fasteners are often referred to as SAE, as opposed to metric. However, it should be noted that SAE technically refers to a non-metric fine thread fastener only. Coarse thread non-metric fasteners are referred to as USS sizes.

Grade 1 or 2　　**Grade 5**　　**Grade 8**

Bolt strength marking (standard/SAE/USS; bottom - metric)

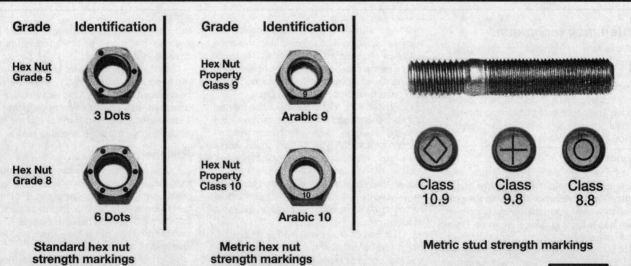

Grade	Identification		Grade	Identification
Hex Nut Grade 5	3 Dots		Hex Nut Property Class 9	Arabic 9
Hex Nut Grade 8	6 Dots		Hex Nut Property Class 10	Arabic 10

Class 10.9　　Class 9.8　　Class 8.8

Standard hex nut strength markings　　**Metric hex nut strength markings**　　**Metric stud strength markings**

Since fasteners of the same size (both standard and metric) may have different strength ratings, be sure to reinstall any bolts, studs or nuts removed from your vehicle in their original locations. Also, when replacing a fastener with a new one, make sure that the new one has a strength rating equal to or greater than the original.

Tightening sequences and procedures

Most threaded fasteners should be tightened to a specific torque value (torque is the twisting force applied to a threaded component such as a nut or bolt). Overtightening the fastener can weaken it and cause it to break, while undertightening can cause it to eventually come loose. Bolts, screws and studs, depending on the material they are made of and their thread diameters, have specific torque values, many of which are noted in the Specifications at the beginning of each Chapter. Be sure to follow the torque recommendations closely. For fasteners not assigned a specific torque, a general torque value chart is presented here as a guide. These torque values are for dry (unlubricated) fasteners threaded into steel or cast iron (not aluminum). As was previously mentioned, the size and grade of a fastener determine the amount of torque that can safely be applied to it. The figures listed here are approximate for Grade 2 and Grade 3 fasteners. Higher grades can tolerate higher torque values.

Fasteners laid out in a pattern, such as cylinder head bolts, oil pan bolts, differential cover bolts, etc., must be loosened or tightened in sequence to avoid warping the component. This sequence will normally be shown in the appropriate Chapter. If a specific pattern is not given, the following procedures can be used to prevent warping.

Metric thread sizes	Ft-lbs	Nm
M-6	6 to 9	9 to 12
M-8	14 to 21	19 to 28
M-10	28 to 40	38 to 54
M-12	50 to 71	68 to 96
M-14	80 to 140	109 to 154
Pipe thread sizes		
1/8	5 to 8	7 to 10
1/4	12 to 18	17 to 24
3/8	22 to 33	30 to 44
1/2	25 to 35	34 to 47
U.S. thread sizes		
1/4 - 20	6 to 9	9 to 12
5/16 - 18	12 to 18	17 to 24
5/16 - 24	14 to 20	19 to 27
3/8 - 16	22 to 32	30 to 43
3/8 - 24	27 to 38	37 to 51
7/16 - 14	40 to 55	55 to 74
7/16 - 20	40 to 60	55 to 81
1/2 - 13	55 to 80	75 to 108

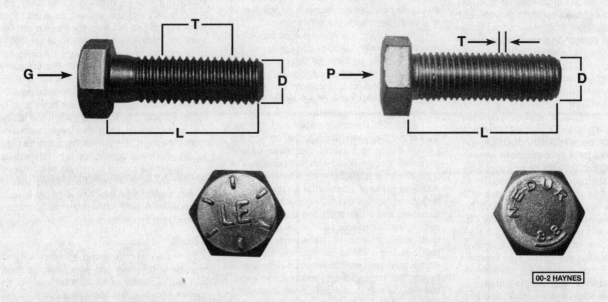

00-2 HAYNES

Standard (SAE and USS) bolt dimensions/grade marks

G   Grade marks (bolt strength)
L   Length (in inches)
T   Thread pitch (number of threads per inch)
D   Nominal diameter (in inches)

Metric bolt dimensions/grade marks

P   Property class (bolt strength)
L   Length (in millimeters)
T   Thread pitch (distance between threads in millimeters)
D   Diameter

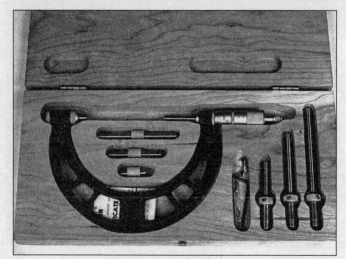

Micrometer set

Dial indicator set

Initially, the bolts or nuts should be assembled finger-tight only. Next, they should be tightened one full turn each, in a criss-cross or diagonal pattern. After each one has been tightened one full turn, return to the first one and tighten them all one-half turn, following the same pattern. Finally, tighten each of them one-quarter turn at a time until each fastener has been tightened to the proper torque. To loosen and remove the fasteners, the procedure would be reversed.

Component disassembly

Component disassembly should be done with care and purpose to help ensure that the parts go back together properly. Always keep track of the sequence in which parts are removed. Make note of special characteristics or marks on parts that can be installed more than one way, such as a grooved thrust washer on a shaft. It is a good idea to lay the disassembled parts out on a clean surface in the order that they were removed. It may also be helpful to make sketches or take instant photos of components before removal.

When removing fasteners from a component, keep track of their locations. Sometimes threading a bolt back in a part, or putting the washers and nut back on a stud, can prevent mix-ups later. If nuts and bolts cannot be returned to their original locations, they should be kept in a compartmented box or a series of small boxes. A cupcake or muffin tin is ideal for this purpose, since each cavity can hold the bolts and nuts from a particular area (i.e. oil pan bolts, valve cover bolts, engine mount bolts, etc.). A pan of this type is especially helpful when working on assemblies with very small parts, such as the carburetor, alternator, valve train or interior dash and trim pieces. The cavities can be marked with paint or tape to identify the contents.

Whenever wiring looms, harnesses or connectors are separated, it is a good idea to identify the two halves with numbered pieces of masking tape so they can be easily reconnected.

Gasket sealing surfaces

Throughout any vehicle, gaskets are used to seal the mating surfaces between two parts and keep lubricants, fluids, vacuum or pressure contained in an assembly.

Many times these gaskets are coated with a liquid or paste-type gasket sealing compound before assembly. Age, heat and pressure can sometimes cause the two parts to stick together so tightly that they are very difficult to separate. Often, the assembly can be loosened by striking it with a soft-face hammer near the mating surfaces. A regular hammer can be used if a block of wood is placed between the hammer and the part. Do not hammer on cast parts or parts that could be easily damaged. With any particularly stubborn part, always recheck to make sure that every fastener has been removed.

Avoid using a screwdriver or bar to pry apart an assembly, as they can easily mar the gasket sealing surfaces of the parts, which must remain smooth. If prying is absolutely necessary, use an old broom handle, but keep in mind that extra clean up will be necessary if the wood splinters.

After the parts are separated, the old gasket must be carefully scraped off and the gasket surfaces cleaned. Stubborn gasket material can be soaked with rust penetrant or treated with a special chemical to soften it so it can be easily scraped off. A scraper can be fashioned from a piece of copper tubing by flattening and sharpening one end. Copper is recommended because it is usually softer than the surfaces to be scraped, which reduces the chance of gouging the part. Some gaskets can be removed with a wire brush, but regardless of the method used, the mating surfaces must be left clean and smooth. If for some reason the gasket surface is gouged, then a gasket sealer thick enough to fill scratches will have to be used during reassembly of the components. For most applications, a non-drying (or semi-drying) gasket sealer should be used.

Hose removal tips

Warning: *If the vehicle is equipped with air conditioning, do not disconnect any of the A/C hoses without first having the system depressurized by a dealer service department or a service station.*

Hose removal precautions closely parallel gasket removal precautions. Avoid scratching or gouging the surface that the hose mates against or the connection may leak. This is especially true for radiator hoses. Because of various chemical reactions, the rubber in hoses can bond itself to the metal spigot that the hose fits over. To remove a hose, first loosen the hose clamps that secure it to the spigot. Then, with slip-joint pliers, grab the hose at the clamp and rotate it around the spigot. Work it back and forth until it is completely free, then pull it off. Silicone or other lubricants will ease removal if they can be applied between the hose and the outside of the spigot. Apply the same lubricant to the inside of the hose and the outside of the spigot to simplify installation.

As a last resort (and if the hose is to be replaced with a new one anyway), the rubber can be slit with a knife and the hose peeled from the spigot. If this must be done, be careful that the metal connection is not damaged.

If a hose clamp is broken or damaged, do not reuse it. Wire-type clamps usually weaken with age, so it is a good idea to replace them with screw-type clamps whenever a hose is removed.

Tools

A selection of good tools is a basic requirement for anyone who plans to maintain and repair his or her own vehicle. For the owner who has few tools, the initial investment might seem high, but when compared to the spiraling costs of professional auto maintenance and repair, it is a wise one.

To help the owner decide which tools are needed to perform the tasks detailed in this manual, the following tool lists are offered: *Maintenance and minor repair,*

Dial caliper

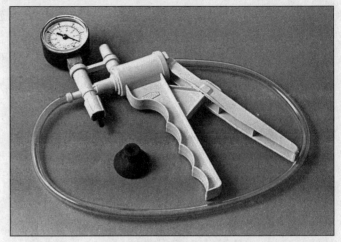

Hand-operated vacuum pump

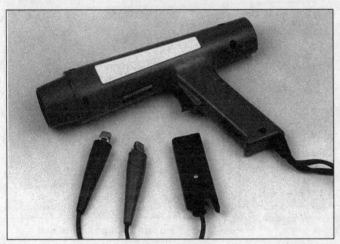

Timing light

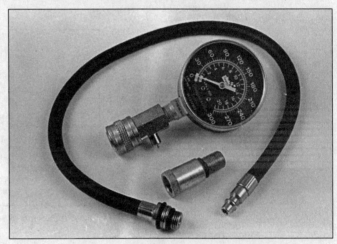

Compression gauge with spark plug hole adapter

Damper/steering wheel puller

General purpose puller

Hydraulic lifter removal tool

Repair/overhaul and *Special*.

The newcomer to practical mechanics should start off with the *maintenance and minor repair* tool kit, which is adequate for the simpler jobs performed on a vehicle. Then, as confidence and experience grow, the owner can tackle more difficult tasks, buying additional tools as they are needed.

Eventually the basic kit will be expanded into the *repair and overhaul* tool set. Over a period of time, the experienced do-it-yourselfer will assemble a tool set complete enough for most repair and overhaul procedures and will add tools from the special category when it is felt that the expense is justified by the frequency of use.

Maintenance and minor repair tool kit

The tools in this list should be considered the minimum required for performance of routine maintenance, servicing and minor repair work. We recommend the purchase of combination wrenches (box-end and open-

Valve spring compressor

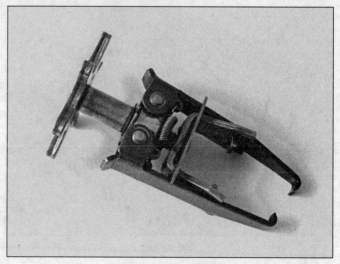

Valve spring compressor

Ridge reamer

Piston ring groove cleaning tool

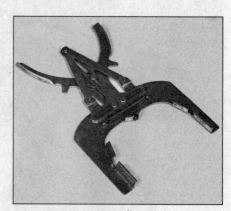

Ring removal/installation tool

end combined in one wrench). While more expensive than open end wrenches, they offer the advantages of both types of wrench.

> Combination wrench set (1/4-inch to
>   1 inch or 6 mm to 19 mm)
> Adjustable wrench, 8 inch
> Spark plug wrench with rubber insert
> Spark plug gap adjusting tool
> Feeler gauge set
> Brake bleeder wrench
> Standard screwdriver (5/16-inch x
>   6 inch)
> Phillips screwdriver (No. 2 x 6 inch)
> Combination pliers - 6 inch
> Hacksaw and assortment of blades
> Tire pressure gauge
> Grease gun
> Oil can
> Fine emery cloth
> Wire brush
> Battery post and cable cleaning tool
> Oil filter wrench
> Funnel (medium size)
> Safety goggles
> Jackstands (2)
> Drain pan

Note: *If basic tune-ups are going to be part of routine maintenance, it will be necessary to purchase a good quality stroboscopic timing*

light and combination tachometer/dwell meter. Although they are included in the list of special tools, it is mentioned here because they are absolutely necessary for tuning most vehicles properly.

Repair and overhaul tool set

These tools are essential for anyone who plans to perform major repairs and are in addition to those in the maintenance and minor repair tool kit. Included is a comprehensive set of sockets which, though expensive, are invaluable because of their versatility, especially when various extensions and drives are available. We recommend the 1/2-inch drive over the 3/8-inch drive. Although the larger drive is bulky and more expensive, it has the capacity of accepting a very wide range of large sockets. Ideally, however, the mechanic should have a 3/8-inch drive set and a 1/2-inch drive set.

> Socket set(s)
> Reversible ratchet
> Extension - 10 inch
> Universal joint
> Torque wrench (same size drive as
>   sockets)
> Ball peen hammer - 8 ounce
> Soft-face hammer (plastic/rubber)

Ring compressor

> Standard screwdriver (1/4-inch x 6 inch)
> Standard screwdriver (stubby -
>   5/16-inch)
> Phillips screwdriver (No. 3 x 8 inch)
> Phillips screwdriver (stubby - No. 2)
> Pliers - vise grip
> Pliers - lineman's
> Pliers - needle nose
> Pliers - snap-ring (internal and external)
> Cold chisel - 1/2-inch

Cylinder hone

Brake hold-down spring tool

Scribe
Scraper (made from flattened copper
   tubing)
Centerpunch
Pin punches (1/16, 1/8, 3/16-inch)
Steel rule/straightedge - 12 inch
Allen wrench set (1/8 to 3/8-inch or
   4 mm to 10 mm)
A selection of files

Wire brush (large)
Jackstands (second set)
Jack (scissor or hydraulic type)
Note: *Another tool which is often useful is an
electric drill with a chuck capacity of 3/8-inch
and a set of good quality drill bits.*

Special tools

The tools in this list include those which
are not used regularly, are expensive to buy,
or which need to be used in accordance with
their manufacturer's instructions. Unless
these tools will be used frequently, it is not
very economical to purchase many of them.
A consideration would be to split the cost
and use between yourself and a friend or
friends. In addition, most of these tools can
be obtained from a tool rental shop on a temporary basis.

This list primarily contains only those
tools and instruments widely available to the
public, and not those special tools produced
by the vehicle manufacturer for distribution to
dealer service departments. Occasionally,
references to the manufacturer's special tools
are included in the text of this manual. Generally, an alternative method of doing the job
without the special tool is offered. However,

sometimes there is no alternative to their use.
Where this is the case, and the tool cannot be
purchased or borrowed, the work should be
turned over to the dealer service department
or an automotive repair shop.

Valve spring compressor
Piston ring groove cleaning tool
Piston ring compressor
Piston ring installation tool
Cylinder compression gauge
Cylinder ridge reamer
Cylinder surfacing hone
Cylinder bore gauge
Micrometers and/or dial calipers
Hydraulic lifter removal tool
Balljoint separator
Universal-type puller
Impact screwdriver
Dial indicator set
*Stroboscopic timing light (inductive
   pick-up)*
Hand operated vacuum/pressure pump
Tachometer/dwell meter
Universal electrical multimeter
Cable hoist
*Brake spring removal and installation
   tools*
Floor jack

Torqur angle gauge

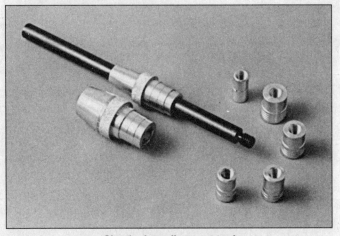

Clutch plate alignment tool

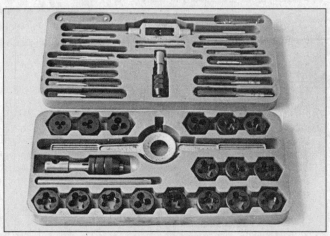

Tap and die set

Buying tools

For the do-it-yourselfer who is just starting to get involved in vehicle maintenance and repair, there are a number of options available when purchasing tools. If maintenance and minor repair is the extent of the work to be done, the purchase of individual tools is satisfactory. If, on the other hand, extensive work is planned, it would be a good idea to purchase a modest tool set from one of the large retail chain stores. A set can usually be bought at a substantial savings over the individual tool prices, and they often come with a tool box. As additional tools are needed, add-on sets, individual tools and a larger tool box can be purchased to expand the tool selection. Building a tool set gradually allows the cost of the tools to be spread over a longer period of time and gives the mechanic the freedom to choose only those tools that will actually be used.

Tool stores will often be the only source of some of the special tools that are needed, but regardless of where tools are bought, try to avoid cheap ones, especially when buying screwdrivers and sockets, because they won't last very long. The expense involved in replacing cheap tools will eventually be greater than the initial cost of quality tools.

Care and maintenance of tools

Good tools are expensive, so it makes sense to treat them with respect. Keep them clean and in usable condition and store them properly when not in use. Always wipe off any dirt, grease or metal chips before putting them away. Never leave tools lying around in the work area. Upon completion of a job, always check closely under the hood for tools that may have been left there so they won't get lost during a test drive.

Some tools, such as screwdrivers, pliers, wrenches and sockets, can be hung on a panel mounted on the garage or workshop wall, while others should be kept in a tool box or tray. Measuring instruments, gauges, meters, etc. must be carefully stored where they cannot be damaged by weather or impact from other tools.

When tools are used with care and stored properly, they will last a very long time. Even with the best of care, though, tools will wear out if used frequently. When a tool is damaged or worn out, replace it. Subsequent jobs will be safer and more enjoyable if you do.

How to repair damaged threads

Sometimes, the internal threads of a nut or bolt hole can become stripped, usually from overtightening. Stripping threads is an all-too-common occurrence, especially when working with aluminum parts, because aluminum is so soft that it easily strips out.

Usually, external or internal threads are only partially stripped. After they've been cleaned up with a tap or die, they'll still work. Sometimes, however, threads are badly damaged. When this happens, you've got three choices:

1) *Drill and tap the hole to the next suitable oversize and install a larger diameter bolt, screw or stud.*

2) *Drill and tap the hole to accept a threaded plug, then drill and tap the plug to the original screw size. You can also buy a plug already threaded to the original size. Then you simply drill a hole to the specified size, then run the threaded plug into the hole with a bolt and jam nut. Once the plug is fully seated, remove the jam nut and bolt.*

3) *The third method uses a patented thread repair kit like Heli-Coil or Slimsert. These easy-to-use kits are designed to repair damaged threads in straight-through holes and blind holes. Both are available as kits which can handle a variety of sizes and thread patterns. Drill the hole, then tap it with the special included tap. Install the Heli-Coil and the hole is back to its original diameter and thread pitch.*

Regardless of which method you use, be sure to proceed calmly and carefully. A little impatience or carelessness during one of these relatively simple procedures can ruin your whole day's work and cost you a bundle if you wreck an expensive part.

Working facilities

Not to be overlooked when discussing tools is the workshop. If anything more than routine maintenance is to be carried out, some sort of suitable work area is essential.

It is understood, and appreciated, that many home mechanics do not have a good workshop or garage available, and end up removing an engine or doing major repairs outside. It is recommended, however, that the overhaul or repair be completed under the cover of a roof.

A clean, flat workbench or table of comfortable working height is an absolute necessity. The workbench should be equipped with a vise that has a jaw opening of at least four inches.

As mentioned previously, some clean, dry storage space is also required for tools, as well as the lubricants, fluids, cleaning solvents, etc. which soon become necessary.

Sometimes waste oil and fluids, drained from the engine or cooling system during normal maintenance or repairs, present a disposal problem. To avoid pouring them on the ground or into a sewage system, pour the used fluids into large containers, seal them with caps and take them to an authorized disposal site or recycling center. Plastic jugs, such as old antifreeze containers, are ideal for this purpose.

Always keep a supply of old newspapers and clean rags available. Old towels are excellent for mopping up spills. Many mechanics use rolls of paper towels for most work because they are readily available and disposable. To help keep the area under the vehicle clean, a large cardboard box can be cut open and flattened to protect the garage or shop floor.

Whenever working over a painted surface, such as when leaning over a fender to service something under the hood, always cover it with an old blanket or bedspread to protect the finish. Vinyl covered pads, made especially for this purpose, are available at auto parts stores.

Booster battery (jump) starting

Booster battery (jump) starting

Observe the following precautions when using a booster battery to start a vehicle:

a) *Before connecting the booster battery, make sure the ignition switch is in the Off position.*

b) *Ensure that all electrical equipment (lights, heater, wipers etc.) are switched off.*

c) *Make sure that the booster battery is the same voltage as the discharged battery in the vehicle.*

d) *If the battery is being jump started from the battery in another vehicle, the two vehicles MUST NOT TOUCH each other.*

e) *Make sure the transaxle is in Neutral (manual transaxle) or Park (automatic transaxle).*

f) *Wear eye protection when jump starting a vehicle.*

Connect one jumper lead between the positive (+) terminals of the two batteries. Connect the other jumper lead first to the negative (-) terminal of the booster battery, then to a good engine ground on the vehicle to be started **(see illustration)**. Attach the lead at least 18 inches from the battery, if possible. Make sure that the jumper leads will not contact the fan, drivebelt of other moving parts of the engine.

Start the engine using the booster battery and allow the engine idle speed to stabilize. Disconnect the jumper leads in the reverse order of connection.

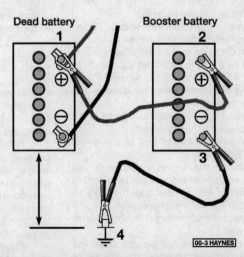

Make the booster battery cable connections in the numerical order shown (note that the negative cable of the booster battery is NOT attached to the negative terminal of the dead battery)

Jacking and towing

Jacking

Warning: *The jack supplied with the vehicle should only be used for changing a tire or placing jackstands under the frame. Never work under the vehicle or start the engine while this jack is being used as the only means of support.*

When one of the front wheels is off the ground, the transaxle alone will not keep the vehicle from slipping off the jack, even if it is in park. Always be sure that the parking brake is securely set.

The vehicle should be on level ground. Place the shift lever in park. Block the wheel diagonally opposite the wheel being changed. Set the parking brake.

Remove the spare tire and jack from stowage. Remove the wheel cover as follows: **Caution:** *On some models the wheel cover is retained by a bolt in its center. Do not try to pry the wheel cover off the wheel without removing the center bolt that is under the center ornament of the cover.*

Carefully pry the center ornament off the wheel cover with the lug wrench.

Remove the center bolt of the wheel cover, if equipped.

Remove the wheel cover with the tapered end of the lug wrench by inserting and twisting the handle and then prying against the back of the wheel cover.

Loosen the wheel lug nuts about 1/4 to 1/2 turn each.

Place the scissors-type jack under the side of the vehicle and adjust the jack height until it fits in the notch in the vertical rocker panel flange nearest the wheel to be changed. There is a front and rear jacking

Place the jack so it engages the notch in the rocker panel nearest the wheel to be raised

point on each side of the vehicle **(see illustration).**

Turn the jack handle clockwise until the tire clears the ground. Remove the wheel lug nuts and pull the wheel off. Replace it with the spare.

Install the wheel lug nuts with the beveled edges facing in. Tighten them snugly. Don't attempt to tighten them completely until the vehicle is lowered, or it could slip off the jack. Turn the jack handle counterclockwise to lower the vehicle. Remove the jack and tighten the lug nuts in a diagonal pattern.

Reinstall the wheel cover and, if equipped, the center bolt. Be sure the cover is secure; then reinstall the center ornament.

Stow the tire, jack, and wrench. Unblock the wheels.

Towing

The manufacturer recommends that your vehicle be transported on a flatbed carrier. If it is necessary to tow your vehicle with only one end raised, the wheels at the other end should be on a towing dolly.

If your vehicle is towed with the rear wheels raised and a towing dolly is unavailable, the steering wheel must be clamped in the straight ahead position with a special device designed for use during towing. The ignition key must be off - but not locked - since the steering lock mechanism isn't strong enough to hold the front wheels straight while towing.

If your vehicle must be towed with all four wheels on the ground in an emergency, speeds must not exceed 35 mph and the distance must not exceed 50 miles. Before towing, check the transmission fluid level (see Chapter 1). If the level is below the HOT line on the dipstick, add fluid or use a towing dolly. Release the parking brake, put the transmission in neutral and turn the ignition key off.

Equipment specifically designed for towing should be used. It should be attached to the main structural members of the vehicle, not to the bumpers or brackets or suspension components.

Safety is a major consideration when towing and all applicable state and local laws must be obeyed. A safety chain system must be used at all times. Remember that power steering and power brakes will not work with the engine off.

Automotive chemicals and lubricants

A number of automotive chemicals and lubricants are available for use during vehicle maintenance and repair. They include a wide variety of products ranging from cleaning solvents and degreasers to lubricants and protective sprays for rubber, plastic and vinyl.

Cleaners

Carburetor cleaner and choke cleaner is a strong solvent for gum, varnish and carbon. Most carburetor cleaners leave a dry-type lubricant film which will not harden or gum up. Because of this film it is not recommended for use on electrical components.

Brake system cleaner is used to remove brake dust, grease and brake fluid from the brake system, where clean surfaces are absolutely necessary. It leaves no residue and often eliminates brake squeal caused by contaminants.

Electrical cleaner removes oxidation, corrosion and carbon deposits from electrical contacts, restoring full current flow. It can also be used to clean spark plugs, carburetor jets, voltage regulators and other parts where an oil-free surface is desired.

Demoisturants remove water and moisture from electrical components such as alternators, voltage regulators, electrical connectors and fuse blocks. They are non-conductive and non-corrosive.

Degreasers are heavy-duty solvents used to remove grease from the outside of the engine and from chassis components. They can be sprayed or brushed on and, depending on the type, are rinsed off either with water or solvent.

Lubricants

Motor oil is the lubricant formulated for use in engines. It normally contains a wide variety of additives to prevent corrosion and reduce foaming and wear. Motor oil comes in various weights (viscosity ratings) from 0 to 50. The recommended weight of the oil depends on the season, temperature and the demands on the engine. Light oil is used in cold climates and under light load conditions. Heavy oil is used in hot climates and where high loads are encountered. Multi-viscosity oils are designed to have characteristics of both light and heavy oils and are available in a number of weights from 5W-20 to 20W-50.

Gear oil is designed to be used in differentials, manual transmissions and other areas where high-temperature lubrication is required.

Chassis and wheel bearing grease is a heavy grease used where increased loads and friction are encountered, such as for wheel bearings, balljoints, tie-rod ends and universal joints.

High-temperature wheel bearing grease is designed to withstand the extreme temperatures encountered by wheel bearings in disc brake equipped vehicles. It usually contains molybdenum disulfide (moly), which is a dry-type lubricant.

White grease is a heavy grease for metal-to-metal applications where water is a problem. White grease stays soft under both low and high temperatures (usually from -100 to +190-degrees F), and will not wash off or dilute in the presence of water.

Assembly lube is a special extreme pressure lubricant, usually containing moly, used to lubricate high-load parts (such as main and rod bearings and cam lobes) for initial start-up of a new engine. The assembly lube lubricates the parts without being squeezed out or washed away until the engine oiling system begins to function.

Silicone lubricants are used to protect rubber, plastic, vinyl and nylon parts.

Graphite lubricants are used where oils cannot be used due to contamination problems, such as in locks. The dry graphite will lubricate metal parts while remaining uncontaminated by dirt, water, oil or acids. It is electrically conductive and will not foul electrical contacts in locks such as the ignition switch.

Moly penetrants loosen and lubricate frozen, rusted and corroded fasteners and prevent future rusting or freezing.

Heat-sink grease is a special electrically non-conductive grease that is used for mounting electronic ignition modules where it is essential that heat is transferred away from the module.

Sealants

RTV sealant is one of the most widely used gasket compounds. Made from silicone, RTV is air curing, it seals, bonds, waterproofs, fills surface irregularities, remains flexible, doesn't shrink, is relatively easy to remove, and is used as a supplementary sealer with almost all low and medium temperature gaskets.

Anaerobic sealant is much like RTV in that it can be used either to seal gaskets or to form gaskets by itself. It remains flexible, is solvent resistant and fills surface imperfections. The difference between an anaerobic sealant and an RTV-type sealant is in the curing. RTV cures when exposed to air, while an anaerobic sealant cures only in the absence of air. This means that an anaerobic sealant cures only after the assembly of parts, sealing them together.

Thread and pipe sealant is used for sealing hydraulic and pneumatic fittings and vacuum lines. It is usually made from a Teflon compound, and comes in a spray, a paint-on liquid and as a wrap-around tape.

Chemicals

Anti-seize compound prevents seizing, galling, cold welding, rust and corrosion in fasteners. High-temperature ant-seize, usually made with copper and graphite lubricants, is used for exhaust system and exhaust manifold bolts.

Anaerobic locking compounds are used to keep fasteners from vibrating or working loose and cure only after installation, in the absence of air. Medium strength locking compound is used for small nuts, bolts and screws that may be removed later. High-strength locking compound is for large nuts, bolts and studs which aren't removed on a regular basis.

Oil additives range from viscosity index improvers to chemical treatments that claim to reduce internal engine friction. It should be noted that most oil manufacturers caution against using additives with their oils.

Gas additives perform several functions, depending on their chemical makeup. They usually contain solvents that help dissolve gum and varnish that build up on carburetor, fuel injection and intake parts. They also serve to break down carbon deposits that form on the inside surfaces of the combustion chambers. Some additives contain upper cylinder lubricants for valves and piston rings, and others contain chemicals to remove condensation from the gas tank.

Miscellaneous

Brake fluid is specially formulated hydraulic fluid that can withstand the heat and pressure encountered in brake systems. Care must be taken so this fluid does not come in contact with painted surfaces or plastics. An opened container should always be resealed to prevent contamination by water or dirt.

Weatherstrip adhesive is used to bond weatherstripping around doors, windows and trunk lids. It is sometimes used to attach trim pieces.

Undercoating is a petroleum-based, tar-like substance that is designed to protect metal surfaces on the underside of the vehicle from corrosion. It also acts as a sound-deadening agent by insulating the bottom of the vehicle.

Waxes and polishes are used to help protect painted and plated surfaces from the weather. Different types of paint may require the use of different types of wax and polish. Some polishes utilize a chemical or abrasive cleaner to help remove the top layer of oxidized (dull) paint on older vehicles. In recent years many non-wax polishes that contain a wide variety of chemicals such as polymers and silicones have been introduced. These non-wax polishes are usually easier to apply and last longer than conventional waxes and polishes.

Conversion factors

Length (distance)

Inches (in)	X	25.4	= Millimetres (mm)	X 0.0394	= Inches (in)
Feet (ft)	X	0.305	= Metres (m)	X 3.281	= Feet (ft)
Miles	X	1.609	= Kilometres (km)	X 0.621	= Miles

Volume (capacity)

Cubic inches (cu in; in^3)	X	16.387	= Cubic centimetres (cc; cm^3)	X 0.061	= Cubic inches (cu in; in^3)
Imperial pints (Imp pt)	X	0.568	= Litres (l)	X 1.76	= Imperial pints (Imp pt)
Imperial quarts (Imp qt)	X	1.137	= Litres (l)	X 0.88	= Imperial quarts (Imp qt)
Imperial quarts (Imp qt)	X	1.201	= US quarts (US qt)	X 0.833	= Imperial quarts (Imp qt)
US quarts (US qt)	X	0.946	= Litres (l)	X 1.057	= US quarts (US qt)
Imperial gallons (Imp gal)	X	4.546	= Litres (l)	X 0.22	= Imperial gallons (Imp gal)
Imperial gallons (Imp gal)	X	1.201	= US gallons (US gal)	X 0.833	= Imperial gallons (Imp gal)
US gallons (US gal)	X	3.785	= Litres (l)	X 0.264	= US gallons (US gal)

Mass (weight)

Ounces (oz)	X	28.35	= Grams (g)	X 0.035	= Ounces (oz)
Pounds (lb)	X	0.454	= Kilograms (kg)	X 2.205	= Pounds (lb)

Force

Ounces-force (ozf; oz)	X	0.278	= Newtons (N)	X 3.6	= Ounces-force (ozf; oz)
Pounds-force (lbf; lb)	X	4.448	= Newtons (N)	X 0.225	= Pounds-force (lbf; lb)
Newtons (N)	X	0.1	= Kilograms-force (kgf; kg)	X 9.81	= Newtons (N)

Pressure

Pounds-force per square inch (psi; lbf/in^2; lb/in^2)	X	0.070	= Kilograms-force per square centimetre (kgf/cm^2; kg/cm^2)	X 14.223	= Pounds-force per square inch (psi; lbf/in^2; lb/in^2)
Pounds-force per square inch (psi; lbf/in^2; lb/in^2)	X	0.068	= Atmospheres (atm)	X 14.696	= Pounds-force per square inch (psi; lbf/in^2; lb/in^2)
Pounds-force per square inch (psi; lbf/in^2; lb/in^2)	X	0.069	= Bars	X 14.5	= Pounds-force per square inch (psi; lbf/in^2; lb/in^2)
Pounds-force per square inch (psi; lbf/in^2; lb/in^2)	X	6.895	= Kilopascals (kPa)	X 0.145	= Pounds-force per square inch (psi; lbf/in^2; lb/in^2)
Kilopascals (kPa)	X	0.01	= Kilograms-force per square centimetre (kgf/cm^2; kg/cm^2)	X 98.1	= Kilopascals (kPa)

Torque (moment of force)

Pounds-force inches (lbf in; lb in)	X	1.152	= Kilograms-force centimetre (kgf cm; kg cm)	X 0.868	= Pounds-force inches (lbf in; lb in)
Pounds-force inches (lbf in; lb in)	X	0.113	= Newton metres (Nm)	X 8.85	= Pounds-force inches (lbf in; lb in)
Pounds-force inches (lbf in; lb in)	X	0.083	= Pounds-force feet (lbf ft; lb ft)	X 12	= Pounds-force inches (lbf in; lb in)
Pounds-force feet (lbf ft; lb ft)	X	0.138	= Kilograms-force metres (kgf m; kg m)	X 7.233	= Pounds-force feet (lbf ft; lb ft)
Pounds-force feet (lbf ft; lb ft)	X	1.356	= Newton metres (Nm)	X 0.738	= Pounds-force feet (lbf ft; lb ft)
Newton metres (Nm)	X	0.102	= Kilograms-force metres (kgf m; kg m)	X 9.804	= Newton metres (Nm)

Vacuum

Inches mercury (in. Hg)	X	3.377	= Kilopascals (kPa)	X 0.2961	= Inches mercury
Inches mercury (in. Hg)	X	25.4	= Millimeters mercury (mm Hg)	X 0.0394	= Inches mercury

Power

Horsepower (hp)	X	745.7	= Watts (W)	X 0.0013	= Horsepower (hp)

Velocity (speed)

Miles per hour (miles/hr; mph)	X	1.609	= Kilometres per hour (km/hr; kph)	X 0.621	= Miles per hour (miles/hr; mph)

Fuel consumption*

Miles per gallon, Imperial (mpg)	X	0.354	= Kilometres per litre (km/l)	X 2.825	= Miles per gallon, Imperial (mpg)
Miles per gallon, US (mpg)	X	0.425	= Kilometres per litre (km/l)	X 2.352	= Miles per gallon, US (mpg)

Temperature

Degrees Fahrenheit = (°C x 1.8) + 32

Degrees Celsius (Degrees Centigrade; °C) = (°F - 32) x 0.56

*It is common practice to convert from miles per gallon (mpg) to litres/100 kilometres (l/100km), where mpg (Imperial) x l/100 km = 282 and mpg (US) x l/100 km = 235

Safety first!

Regardless of how enthusiastic you may be about getting on with the job at hand, take the time to ensure that your safety is not jeopardized. A moment's lack of attention can result in an accident, as can failure to observe certain simple safety precautions. The possibility of an accident will always exist, and the following points should not be considered a comprehensive list of all dangers. Rather, they are intended to make you aware of the risks and to encourage a safety conscious approach to all work you carry out on your vehicle.

Essential DOs and DON'Ts

DON'T rely on a jack when working under the vehicle. Always use approved jackstands to support the weight of the vehicle and place them under the recommended lift or support points.

DON'T attempt to loosen extremely tight fasteners (i.e. wheel lug nuts) while the vehicle is on a jack - it may fall.

DON'T start the engine without first making sure that the transmission is in Neutral (or Park where applicable) and the parking brake is set.

DON'T remove the radiator cap from a hot cooling system - let it cool or cover it with a cloth and release the pressure gradually.

DON'T attempt to drain the engine oil until you are sure it has cooled to the point that it will not burn you.

DON'T touch any part of the engine or exhaust system until it has cooled sufficiently to avoid burns.

DON'T siphon toxic liquids such as gasoline, antifreeze and brake fluid by mouth, or allow them to remain on your skin.

DON'T inhale brake lining dust - it is potentially hazardous (see *Asbestos* below).

DON'T allow spilled oil or grease to remain on the floor - wipe it up before someone slips on it.

DON'T use loose fitting wrenches or other tools which may slip and cause injury.

DON'T push on wrenches when loosening or tightening nuts or bolts. Always try to pull the wrench toward you. If the situation calls for pushing the wrench away, push with an open hand to avoid scraped knuckles if the wrench should slip.

DON'T attempt to lift a heavy component alone - get someone to help you.

DON'T *rush or take unsafe shortcuts to finish a job.*

DON'T allow children or animals in or around the vehicle while you are working on it.

DO wear eye protection when using power tools such as a drill, sander, bench grinder, etc. and when working under a vehicle.

DO keep loose clothing and long hair well out of the way of moving parts.

DO make sure that any hoist used has a safe working load rating adequate for the job.

DO get someone to check on you periodically when working alone on a vehicle.

DO carry out work in a logical sequence and make sure that everything is correctly assembled and tightened.

DO keep chemicals and fluids tightly capped and out of the reach of children and pets.

DO remember that your vehicle's safety affects that of yourself and others. If in doubt on any point, get professional advice.

Steering, suspension and brakes

These systems are essential to driving safety, so make sure you have a qualified shop or individual check your work. Also, compressed suspension springs can cause injury if released suddenly - be sure to use a spring compressor.

Airbags

Airbags are explosive devices that can **CAUSE** injury if they deploy while you're working on the vehicle. Follow the manufacturer's instructions to disable the airbag whenever you're working in the vicinity of airbag components.

Asbestos

Certain friction, insulating, sealing, and other products - such as brake linings, brake bands, clutch linings, torque converters, gaskets, etc. - may contain asbestos or other hazardous friction material. Extreme care must be taken to avoid inhalation of dust from such products, since it is hazardous to health. If in doubt, assume that they do contain asbestos.

Fire

Remember at all times that gasoline is highly flammable. Never smoke or have any kind of open flame around when working on a vehicle. But the risk does not end there. A spark caused by an electrical short circuit, by two metal surfaces contacting each other, or even by static electricity built up in your body under certain conditions, can ignite gasoline vapors, which in a confined space are highly explosive. Do not, under any circumstances, use gasoline for cleaning parts. Use an approved safety solvent.

Always disconnect the battery ground (-) cable at the battery before working on any part of the fuel system or electrical system. Never risk spilling fuel on a hot engine or exhaust component. It is strongly recommended that a fire extinguisher suitable for use on fuel and electrical fires be kept handy in the garage or workshop at all times. Never try to extinguish a fuel or electrical fire with water.

Fumes

Certain fumes are highly toxic and can quickly cause unconsciousness and even death if inhaled to any extent. Gasoline vapor falls into this category, as do the vapors from some cleaning solvents. Any draining or pouring of such volatile fluids should be done in a well ventilated area.

When using cleaning fluids and solvents, read the instructions on the container carefully. Never use materials from unmarked containers.

Never run the engine in an enclosed space, such as a garage. Exhaust fumes contain carbon monoxide, which is extremely poisonous. If you need to run the engine, always do so in the open air, or at least have the rear of the vehicle outside the work area.

The battery

Never create a spark or allow a bare light bulb near a battery. They normally give off a certain amount of hydrogen gas, which is highly explosive.

Always disconnect the battery ground (-) cable at the battery before working on the fuel or electrical systems.

If possible, loosen the filler caps or cover when charging the battery from an external source (this does not apply to sealed or maintenance-free batteries). Do not charge at an excessive rate or the battery may burst.

Take care when adding water to a non maintenance-free battery and when carrying a battery. The electrolyte, even when diluted, is very corrosive and should not be allowed to contact clothing or skin.

Always wear eye protection when cleaning the battery to prevent the caustic deposits from entering your eyes.

Household current

When using an electric power tool, inspection light, etc., which operates on household current, always make sure that the tool is correctly connected to its plug and that, where necessary, it is properly grounded. Do not use such items in damp conditions and, again, do not create a spark or apply excessive heat in the vicinity of fuel or fuel vapor.

Secondary ignition system voltage

A severe electric shock can result from touching certain parts of the ignition system (such as the spark plug wires) when the engine is running or being cranked, particularly if components are damp or the insulation is defective. In the case of an electronic ignition system, the secondary system voltage is much higher and could prove fatal.

Hydrofluoric acid

This extremely corrosive acid is formed when certain types of synthetic rubber, found in some O-rings, oil seals, fuel hoses, etc. are exposed to temperatures above 750-degrees F (400-degrees C). The rubber changes into a charred or sticky substance containing the acid. *Once formed, the acid remains dangerous for years. If it gets onto the skin, it may be necessary to amputate the limb concerned.*

When dealing with a vehicle which has suffered a fire, or with components salvaged from such a vehicle, wear protective gloves and discard them after use.

Troubleshooting

Contents

Engine

1 Engine will not rotate when attempting to start

1   Battery terminal connections loose or corroded. Check the cable terminals at the battery; tighten cable clamp and clean off corrosion as necessary (see Chapter 1).
2   Battery discharged or faulty. If the cable ends are clean and tight on the battery posts, turn the ignition key on and switch on the headlights or windshield wipers. If they won't run, the battery is discharged.
3   Automatic transmission not engaged in park (P) or Neutral (N).
4   Broken, loose or disconnected wires in the starting circuit. Inspect all wires and connectors at the battery, starter relay, and ignition switch (on steering column).
5   Starter motor pinion jammed in driveplate ring gear. Remove starter (Chapter 5) and inspect pinion and driveplate (Chapter 2).
6   Starter relay faulty (Chapter 5).
7   Starter motor faulty (Chapter 5).
8   Ignition switch faulty (Chapter 12).
9   Engine seized. Try to turn the crankshaft with a large socket and breaker bar on the pulley bolt.
10 Transmission range (TR) sensor out of adjustment or defective (Chapter 6).

2 Engine rotates but will not start

1   Fuel tank empty.
2   Fuel pump shutoff switch (inertia switch) has been activated by a vehicle impact. Locate the shutoff switch in the right-hand side of the trunk (sedan) or behind the service panel on the right-hand side of the cargo area (wagon). Press the switch button and try to start the engine again.
3   Battery discharged (engine rotates slowly).
4   Battery terminal connections loose or corroded.
5   Fuel not reaching fuel injectors. Check for clogged fuel filter or lines and defective fuel pump. Also be sure the tank vent lines aren't clogged (Chapter 4).
6   Low cylinder compression. Check as described in Chapter 2.
7   Water in fuel. Drain tank and fill with new fuel.
8   Broken, loose, or disconnected wires at the ignition coil assembly or faulty coil (Chapter 5).
9   Dirty or clogged fuel injectors (Chapter 4).
10 Wet or damaged ignition components (Chapters 1 and 5).
11 Damaged or disconnected crankshaft position sensor (Chapter 6).
12 Worn, faulty, or incorrectly gapped spark plugs (Chapter 1).
13 Broken, loose, or disconnected wires in the starting circuit (see previous Section).

14 Timing chain failure or wear affecting valve timing (Chapter 2).
15 Fuel injection or engine control system failure (Chapters 4 and 6).

3 Starter motor operates without turning engine

1   Starter pinion or drive mechanism sticking. Remove the starter (Chapter 5) and inspect.
2   Starter pinion or driveplate teeth worn or broken. Remove the inspection cover and inspect.

4 Engine hard to start when cold

1   Battery discharged or low. Check as described in Chapter 1.
2   Fuel not reaching the fuel injectors. Check the fuel filter, lines and fuel pump (Chapters 1 and 4).
3   Defective spark plugs (Chapter 1).
4   Defective engine coolant temperature sensor (Chapter 6).
5   Fuel injection or engine control system malfunction (Chapters 4 and 6).

5 Engine hard to start when hot

1   Air filter dirty (Chapter 1).
2   Fuel not reaching the fuel injectors. Check for clogged fuel lines.
3   Bad engine ground connection.
4   Defective engine coolant temperature sensor (Chapter 6).
5   Fuel injection or engine control system malfunction (Chapters 4 and 6).

6 Starter motor noisy or engages roughly

1   Starter pinion or driveplate teeth worn or broken. Remove torque converter housing lower cover plate, if so equipped, to inspect.
2   Starter motor mounting bolts loose or missing.

7 Engine starts but stops immediately

1   Loose or damaged wire harness connections at coil assembly or alternator.
2   Intake manifold vacuum leaks. Make sure all mounting bolts and nuts are tight and all vacuum hoses connected to the manifold are attached properly and in good condition.
3   Insufficient fuel pressure (see Chapter 4).
4   Fuel injection or engine control system malfunction (Chapters 4 and 6).

8 Engine lopes while idling or idles roughly

1   Vacuum leaks. Check mounting bolts at the intake manifold for tightness. Make sure that all vacuum hoses are connected and in good condition. Use a stethoscope or a length of fuel hose held against your ear to listen for vacuum leaks while the engine is running. A hissing sound will be heard. A soapy water solution will also detect leaks. Check the intake manifold gasket surfaces.
2   Leaking EGR valve or plugged PCV valve (see Chapters 1 and 6).
3   Air filter clogged (Chapter 1).
4   Fuel pump not delivering enough fuel (Chapter 4).
5   Leaking head gasket. Check cylinder compression (Chapter 2).
6   Timing chain worn (Chapter 2).
7   Camshaft lobes worn (Chapter 2).
8   Valves burned or otherwise leaking (Chapter 2).
9   Ignition system not operating properly (Chapters 1 and 5).
10 Fuel injection or engine control system malfunction (Chapters 4 and 6).

9 Engine misses at idle

1   Spark plugs faulty, dirty, or not gapped properly (Chapter 1).
2   Faulty spark plug wires (Chapter 1).
4   Short circuits in ignition, coil, or spark plug wires.
5   Clogged fuel filter or dirt in fuel. Remove the fuel filter (Chapter 1) and inspect.
6   Vacuum leaks at intake manifold or hose connections.
7   Incorrect idle speed (Chapter 4).
8   Low or uneven cylinder compression. Check as described in Chapter 2.
9   Fuel injection or engine control system malfunction (Chapters 4 and 6).

10 High idle speed

1   Idle air control problem (Chapter 4).
2   Sticking throttle linkage (Chapter 4).
3   Vacuum leaks at intake manifold or hose connections. Check as described in Section 8.
4   Fuel injection or engine control system malfunction (Chapters 4 and 6).

11 Battery will not hold a charge

1   Alternator drivebelt defective or not adjusted properly (Chapter 1).
2   Battery cables loose or corroded (Chapter 1).
3   Alternator not charging properly (Chapter 5).
4   Loose, broken or faulty wires in the

charging circuit (Chapter 5).
5   Short circuit causing a continuous drain on the battery.
6   Battery defective internally.

12   Alternator light stays on

1   Fault in alternator or charging circuit (Chapter 5).
2   Alternator drivebelt defective or not properly adjusted (Chapter 1).

13   Alternator light does not come on when key is turned on

1   Faulty bulb (Chapter 12).
2   Defective alternator (Chapter 5).
3   Fault in the printed circuit, dash wiring, or bulb holder (Chapter 12).

14   Engine misses throughout driving speed range

1   Fuel filter clogged or dirt in the fuel system. Check the fuel filter (Chapter 1) or have the fuel injection system cleaned.
2   Fouled or incorrectly gapped spark plugs (Chapter 1).
3   Defective spark plug wires (Chapter 1).
4   Emission system components faulty (Chapter 6).
5   Low or uneven cylinder compression pressures. Check as described in Chapter 2.
6   Weak or faulty ignition coil assembly (Chapter 5).
7   Weak or faulty ignition system (Chapter 5).
8   Vacuum leaks at intake manifold or vacuum hoses (see Section 8).
9   Dirty or clogged fuel injectors (Chapter 4).
10   Leaky EGR valve (Chapter 6).
11   Fuel injection or engine control system malfunction (Chapters 4 and 6).

15   Hesitation or stumble during acceleration

1   Ignition system not operating properly (Chapter 5).
2   Dirty or clogged fuel injectors (Chapter 4).
3   Low fuel pressure. Check for proper operation of the fuel pump and for restrictions in the fuel filter and lines (Chapter 4).
4   Fuel injection or engine control system malfunction (Chapters 4 and 6).

16   Engine stalls

1   Idle speed incorrect (Chapter 4).
2   Fuel filter clogged or water and dirt in the fuel system (Chapter 1).
3   Emission system components faulty (Chapter 6).
4   Faulty or incorrectly gapped spark plugs (Chapter 1). Also check the spark plug wires (Chapter 1).
5   Vacuum leak at the intake manifold or vacuum hoses.
6   Fuel injection or engine control systems malfunction (Chapters 4 and 6).

17   Engine lacks power

1   Dirty or incorrectly gapped spark plugs (Chapter 1).
2   Air filter dirty (Chapter 1).
3   Faulty ignition coil(s) (Chapter 5).
4   Brakes binding (Chapters 1 and 10).
5   Automatic transmission fluid level incorrect, causing slippage (Chapter 1).
6   Fuel filter clogged or dirt in the fuel system (Chapters 1 and 4).
7   EGR system not working properly (Chapter 6).
8   Use of substandard fuel. Fill tank with proper octane fuel.
9   Low or uneven cylinder compression pressures. Check as described in Chapter 2.
10   Vacuum leak at intake manifold or vacuum hoses.
11   Dirty or clogged fuel injectors (Chapters 1 and 4).
12   Fuel injection or engine control system malfunction (Chapters 4 and 6).
13   Restricted exhaust system (Chapter 4).

18   Engine backfires

1   EGR system not functioning properly (Chapter 6).
3   Vacuum leak.
4   Damaged valve springs or sticking valves (Chapter 2).
5   Vacuum leak at the intake manifold or vacuum hoses.

19   Engine surges while holding accelerator steady

1   Vacuum leak at the intake manifold or vacuum hoses.
2   Intake air leak (Chapter 4).
3   Restricted air filter (Chapter 1).
4   Fuel pump or pressure regulator defective (Chapter 4).
5   Fuel injection or engine control system malfunction (Chapters 4 and 6).

20   Engine pings or knocks when under load

1   Incorrect grade of fuel. Fill tank with fuel of the proper octane rating.
2   EGR system not working properly (Chapter 6).
3   Carbon buildup in combustion chambers. Remove cylinder heads and clean combustion chambers (Chapter 2).
4   Incorrect spark plugs (Chapter 1).
5   Fuel injection or engine control system malfunction (Chapters 4 and 6).
6   Restricted exhaust system (Chapter 4).

21   Engine diesels (continues to run) after being turned off

1   Idle speed too high (Chapter 4).
2   Incorrect spark plug heat range (Chapter 1).
3   Vacuum leak at the intake manifold or vacuum hoses (see Section 8).
4   Carbon buildup in combustion chambers. Remove the cylinder heads and clean the combustion chambers (Chapter 2).
5   Valves sticking (Chapter 2).
6   EGR system not working properly (Chapter 6).
7   Fuel injection or engine control system malfunction (Chapters 4 and 6).
8   Check for causes of overheating (Section 27).

22   Low oil pressure

1   Improper grade of oil.
2   Oil pump worn or damaged (Chapter 2).
3   Engine overheating (refer to Section 27).
4   Clogged oil filter (Chapter 1).
5   Clogged oil strainer (Chapter 2).
6   Oil pressure gauge not working properly (Chapter 2).

23   Excessive oil consumption

1   Loose oil drain plug.
2   Loose bolts or damaged oil pan gasket (Chapter 2).
3   Loose bolts or damaged front cover gasket (Chapter 2).
4   Front or rear crankshaft oil seal leaking (Chapter 2).
5   Loose bolts or damaged valve cover gasket (Chapter 2).
6   Loose oil filter (Chapter 1).
7   Loose or damaged oil pressure switch (Chapter 2).
8   Pistons and cylinders excessively worn (Chapter 2).
9   Piston rings not installed correctly on pistons (Chapter 2).
10   Worn or damaged piston rings (Chapter 2).
11   Intake or exhaust valve oil seals worn or damaged (Chapter 2).
12   Worn or damaged valve stems or guides (Chapter 2).
13   Faulty or incorrect PCV valve allowing too much crankcase airflow.

24 Excessive fuel consumption

1   Dirty or clogged air filter element (Chapter 1).
2   Incorrect idle speed (Chapter 4).
3   Low tire pressure or incorrect tire size (Chapter 10).
4   Inspect for binding brakes.
5   Fuel leakage. Check all connections, lines and components in the fuel system (Chapter 4).
6   Dirty or clogged fuel injectors (Chapter 4).
7   Fuel injection or engine control system malfunction (Chapters 4 and 6).
8   Thermostat stuck open or not installed.
9   Improperly operating transmission.

25 Fuel odor

1   Fuel leakage. Check all connections, lines and components in the fuel system (Chapter 4).
2   Fuel tank overfilled. Fill only to automatic shutoff.
3   Charcoal canister filter in evaporative emission control system clogged (Chapter 1).
4   Vapor leaks from evaporative emission control system lines (Chapter 6).

26 Miscellaneous engine noises

1   A strong dull noise that becomes more rapid as the engine accelerates indicates worn or damaged crankshaft bearings or an unevenly worn crankshaft. To pinpoint the trouble spot, remove the spark plug wire from one plug at a time and crank the engine over. If the noise stops, the cylinder with the removed plug wire indicates the problem area. Replace the bearing or service or replace the crankshaft (Chapter 2).
2   A similar (yet slightly higher pitched) noise to the crankshaft knocking described in the previous Step, that becomes more rapid as the engine accelerates, indicates worn or damaged connecting rod bearings (Chapter 2). The procedure for locating the problem cylinder is the same as described in Step 1.
3   An overlapping metallic noise that increases in intensity as the engine speed increases, yet diminishes as the engine warms up indicates abnormal piston and cylinder wear (Chapter 2). To locate the problem cylinder, use the procedure described in Step 1.
4   A rapid clicking noise that becomes faster as the engine accelerates indicates a worn piston pin or piston pin hole. This sound will happen each time the piston hits the highest and lowest points in the stroke (Chapter 2). The procedure for locating the problem piston is described in Step 1.
5   A metallic clicking noise coming from the water pump indicates worn or damaged water pump bearings or pump. Replace the water pump with a new one (Chapter 3).
6   A rapid tapping sound or clicking sound that becomes faster as the engine speed increases indicates "valve tapping." This can be identified by holding one end of a section of hose to your ear and placing the other end at different spots along the valve cover. The point where the sound is loudest indicates the problem valve. If the pushrod and rocker arm components are in good shape, you likely have a collapsed valve lifter. Changing the engine oil and adding a high-viscosity oil treatment will sometimes cure a stuck lifter problem. If the problem persists, the lifters, pushrods and rocker arms must be removed for inspection (see Chapter 2).
7   A steady metallic rattling or rapping sound coming from the area of the timing chain cover indicates a worn or damaged timing chain. Service or replace the chain and related components (Chapter 2).

Cooling system

27 Overheating

1   Insufficient coolant in system (Chapter 1).
2   Drivebelt defective or not adjusted properly (Chapter 1).
3   Radiator core blocked or radiator grille dirty and restricted (Chapter 3).
4   Thermostat faulty (Chapter 3).
5   Cooling fan not functioning properly (Chapter 3).
6   Radiator cap not maintaining proper pressure. Have cap pressure tested by a repair shop.
7   Defective water pump (Chapter 3).
8   Improper grade of engine oil.
9   Inaccurate temperature gauge (Chapter 12).

28 Overcooling

1   Thermostat faulty (Chapter 3).
2   Inaccurate temperature gauge (Chapter 12).

29 External coolant leakage

1   Deteriorated or damaged hoses. Loose clamps at hose connections (Chapter 1).
2   Water pump seals defective. If this is the case, water will drip from the weep hole in the water pump body (Chapter 3).
3   Leakage from radiator core or expansion tank. This will require the radiator to be professionally repaired (see Chapter 3 for removal procedures).
4   Leakage from the coolant reservoir or expansion tank.
5   Engine drain plugs or water jacket core plugs leaking (see Chapters 1 and 2).
6   Leak from coolant temperature switch (Chapter 3).
7   Leak from damaged gaskets or small cracks (Chapter 2).

30 Internal coolant leakage

Note: *Internal coolant leaks can usually be detected by examining the oil. Check the dipstick and inside the rocker arm cover for water deposits and an oil consistency like that of a milkshake.*
1   Leaking cylinder head gasket. Have the system pressure tested or remove the cylinder head (Chapter 2) and inspect.
2   Cracked cylinder bore or cylinder head. Dismantle engine and inspect (Chapter 2).
3   Loose cylinder head bolts (tighten as described in Chapter 2).

31 Abnormal coolant loss

1   Overfilling system (Chapter 1).
2   Coolant boiling away due to overheating (see causes in Section 27).
3   Internal or external leakage (see Sections 29 and 30).
4   Faulty radiator cap. Have the cap pressure tested.
5   Cooling system being pressurized by engine compression. This could be due to a cracked head or block or a leaking head gaskets. Have the system tested at a shop for combustion gas in the coolant.

32 Poor coolant circulation

1   Inoperative water pump. Pinch the top radiator hose closed with your hand while the engine is idling, then release it. You should feel a surge of coolant if the pump is working properly (Chapter 3).
2   Restriction in cooling system. Drain, flush and refill the system (Chapter 1). If necessary, remove the radiator (Chapter 3) and have it reverse flushed or professionally cleaned.
3   Loose water pump drivebelt (Chapter 1).
4   Thermostat sticking (Chapter 3).
5   Insufficient coolant (Chapter 1).

33 Corrosion

1   Excessive impurities in the water. Soft, clean water is recommended.
2   Insufficient antifreeze solution (refer to Chapter 1 for the proper ratio of water to antifreeze).
3   Infrequent flushing and draining of system. Flush the cooling system at the specified intervals as listed in (Chapter 1).

Automatic transmission

Note: *Because of the complexity of the automatic transmission, it's difficult for the home mechanic to properly diagnose and service. For problems other than the following, the vehicle should be taken to a reputable mechanic.*

34   Fluid leakage

1   Automatic transmission fluid is a deep red color, and fluid leaks should not be confused with engine oil which can easily be blown by airflow to the transmission.
2   To pinpoint a leak, first remove all dirt and grime from the transmission. Degreasing agents or steam cleaning will achieve this. With the underside clean, drive the vehicle at low speeds so the airflow will not blow the leak far from its source. Raise the vehicle and determine where the leak is located. Common areas of leakage are:

a) *Fluid pan: tighten mounting bolts or replace pan gasket as necessary (Chapter 1).*
b) *Rear extension: tighten bolts or replace oil seal as necessary.*
c) *Filler pipe: replace the rubber oil seal where pipe enters transmission case.*
d) *Transmission oil lines: tighten fittings where lines enter transmission case or replace lines.*
e) *Vent pipe: transmission overfilled or water in fluid (see checking procedures, Chapter 1).*
f) *Vehicle speed sensor: replace the O-ring where speed sensor enters transmission case.*

35   General shift mechanism problems

Chapter 7 deals with checking and adjusting the shift linkage on automatic transmissions. Common problems which may be caused by out-of-adjustment linkage are:

a) *Engine starting in gears other than P (park) or N (Neutral).*
b) *Indicator pointing to a gear other than the one actually engaged.*
c) *Vehicle moves with transmission in P (Park) position.*

36   Transmission will not downshift with the accelerator pedal pressed to the floor

Chapter 7 deals with adjusting the throttle valve cable to enable the transmission to downshift properly.

37   Engine will start in gears other than Park or Neutral

Chapter 7 deals with adjusting the neu-tral-start switch installed on automatic transmissions.

38   Transmission slips, shifts roughly, is noisy or has no drive in forward or reverse gears

1   There are many possible causes for the above problems, but the home mechanic should concern himself only with one possibility: fluid level.
2   Before taking the vehicle to a shop, check the fluid level and condition as described in Chapter 1. Add fluid, if necessary, or change the fluid and filter if needed. If problems persist, have a professional diagnose the transmission.

Driveaxles

Note: *Refer to Chapter 8, unless otherwise specified, for service information.*

39   Clicking noise on turns

Worn or damaged outer constant-velocity (CV) joint. Check for leaking or otherwise damaged boots. Repair as necessary (Chapter 8).

40   Knock or clunk when accelerating after coasting

Worn or damaged outer constant-velocity (CV) joint. Check for leaking or otherwise damaged boots. Repair as necessary (Chapter 8).

41   Shudder or vibration during acceleration

1   Incorrect universal joint angle. Have checked and correct as necessary (Chapter 8).
2   Worn, sticking, or damaged CV joint. Repair or replace as necessary (Chapter 8).

Brakes

Note: *Before assuming a brake problem exists, make sure the tires are in good condition and inflated properly, the front end alignment is correct, and the vehicle is not loaded with weight unequally. All service procedures for the brakes are in Chapter 9, unless otherwise noted.*

42   Vehicle pulls to one side during braking

1   Defective, damaged, or oil-contaminated brake pad on one side. Inspect as described in Chapter 1. Refer to Chapter 9 if replacement is required.
2   Excessive wear of brake pad material or disc on one side. Inspect and repair as necessary.
3   Loose or disconnected front suspension components. Inspect and tighten all bolts securely (Chapters 1 and 10).
4   Defective front brake caliper. Remove caliper and inspect for stuck piston or damage.
5   Scored or out-of-round disc.

43   Noise (high-pitched squeal)

1   Brake pads worn out. This noise comes from the wear sensor rubbing against the disc. Replace pads with new ones immediately!
2   Glazed or contaminated pads.
3   Dirty or scored disc.
4   Bent caliper support.

44   Excessive brake pedal travel

1   Partial brake system failure. Inspect entire system (Chapter 1) and correct as required.
2   Insufficient fluid in master cylinder. Check and add fluid (Chapter 1). Bleed system if necessary.
3   Air in system. Bleed system.
4   Defective master cylinder.

45   Brake pedal feels spongy when depressed

1   Air in brake lines. Bleed the brake system.
2   Deteriorated rubber brake hoses. Inspect all system hoses and lines. Replace parts as necessary.
3   Master cylinder mounting nuts loose. Inspect master cylinder bolts or nuts and tighten them securely.
4   Master cylinder faulty.
5   Clogged reservoir cap vent hole.
6   Deformed rubber brake lines.
7   Poor quality brake fluid. Bleed entire system and fill with new approved fluid.

46   Excessive effort required to stop vehicle

1   Power brake booster not operating properly.
2   Excessively worn brake pads. Check and replace if necessary.
3   One or more caliper pistons seized or sticking. Inspect and rebuild as required.
4   Brake pads contaminated with oil or grease. Inspect and replace as required.
5   Worn or damaged master cylinder or calipers. Check particularly for frozen pistons.

47 Pedal travels to the floor with little resistance

Little or no fluid in the master cylinder reservoir caused by leaking caliper pistons or loose, damaged or disconnected brake lines. Inspect entire system and repair as necessary.

48 Brake pedal pulsates during braking

1   Wheel bearings damaged, worn or out of adjustment.
2   Caliper not sliding properly due to improper installation or obstructions. Remove and inspect.
3   Disc not within specifications. Check for excessive lateral runout and incorrect parallelism. Have the discs resurfaced or replace them with new ones.

49 Brakes drag (indicated by sluggish engine performance or wheels being very hot after driving)

1   Pushrod adjustment incorrect at the brake pedal or power booster.
2   Obstructed master cylinder compensator. Replace the master cylinder.
3   Master cylinder piston seized in bore. Replace master cylinder.
4   Caliper piston sticking. Replace or overhaul caliper.
5   Piston cups in master cylinder or caliper deformed. Replace master cylinder or overhaul/replace caliper.
6   Parking brake will not release.
7   Clogged or internally split brake lines.
8   Wheel bearings defective.
9   Brake pedal height improperly adjusted.

50 Rear brakes lock up under light brake application

1   Tire pressures too high.
2   Tires excessively worn (Chapter 1).
3   Defective proportioning valve.

51 Rear brakes lock up under heavy brake application

1   Tire pressures too high.
2   Tires excessively worn (Chapter 1).
3   Front brake pads contaminated with oil, mud or water. Clean or replace the pads.
4   Front brake pads excessively worn.
5   Defective proportioning valve.

Suspension and steering

Note: *All service procedures for the suspension and steering systems are in Chapter 10, unless otherwise noted.*

52 Vehicle pulls to one side

1   Tire pressures uneven (Chapter 1).
2   Defective tire (Chapter 1).
3   Excessive wear in suspension or steering components (Chapter 1).
4   Front end alignment incorrect.
5   Front brakes dragging.
6   Wheel bearings defective (Chapter 1).

53 Shimmy, shake or vibration

1   Tire or wheel out of balance or out of round.
2   Wheel bearings loose, worn or out of adjustment (Chapter 1).
3   Shock absorbers or suspension components worn or damaged (Chapter 10).
4   Wheel lug nuts loose.

54 Excessive pitching or rolling around corners or during braking

1   Defective shock absorbers. Replace as a set.
2   Broken or weak springs or other suspension components.
3   Worn or damaged stabilizer bar or bushings.

55 Wandering or general instability

1   Improper tire pressures.
2   Incorrect front end alignment.
3   Worn or damaged steering linkage or suspension components.
4   Improperly adjusted steering gear.
5   Out-of-balance wheels.
6   Loose wheel lug nuts.
7   Worn rear shock absorbers.
8   Fatigued or damaged rear springs.

56 Excessively stiff steering

1   Lack of fluid in the power steering fluid reservoir (Chapter 1).
2   Incorrect tire pressures (Chapter 1).
3   Lack of balljoint lubrication (Chapter 1).
4   Front end out of alignment.
5   Steering gear out of adjustment or lacking lubrication.
6   Improperly adjusted wheel bearings.
7   Worn or damaged steering gear.
8   Interference of steering column with turn signal switch.
9   Low tire pressures.
10   Worn or damaged balljoints.
11   Worn or damaged tie-rod ends.

57 Excessive play in steering

1   Loose wheel bearings (Chapter 1).
2   Excessive wear in suspension bushings (Chapter 1).
3   Steering gear improperly adjusted.
4   Steering gear mounting bolts loose.
5   Worn steering gear.
6   Worn tie-rod ends.

58 Lack of power assistance

1   Steering pump drivebelt worn or loose (Chapter 1).
2   Fluid level low (Chapter 1).
3   Hoses or pipes restricting the flow. Inspect and replace parts as necessary.
4   Air in power steering system. Bleed system.
5   Defective power steering pump.

59 Steering wheel fails to return to straight-ahead position

1   Incorrect front end alignment.
2   Tire pressures low.
3   Steering column out of alignment.
4   Worn, damaged, or defective steering gear.
5   Worn or damaged balljoint.
6   Worn or damaged tie-rods ends.
7   Lack of fluid in power steering pump.

60 Steering effort not the same in both directions (power system)

1   Leaks in steering gear.
2   Clogged fluid passage in steering gear.

61 Noisy power steering pump

1   Insufficient oil in pump.
2   Clogged hoses or oil filter in pump.
3   Loose pulley.
4   Improperly adjusted drivebelt (Chapter 1).
5   Defective pump.

62 Miscellaneous noises

1   Improper tire pressures.
2   Insufficiently lubricated balljoint or steering linkage.
3   Loose or worn steering gear, steering linkage, or suspension parts.
4   Defective shock absorber.
5   Defective wheel bearing.
6   Worn or damaged suspension bushings.
7   Damaged spring.
8   Loose wheel nuts.
9   Worn or damaged rear shock absorber mounting bushing.

63 Excessive tire wear (not specific to one area)

1   Incorrect tire pressures.
2   Tires out of balance.
3   Wheels damaged. Inspect and replace as necessary.
4   Suspension or steering components worn (Chapter 1).
5   Front end alignment incorrect.
6   Lack of proper tire rotation. See maintenance schedule in Chapter 1.

64 Excessive tire wear on outside edge

1   Incorrect tire pressure.
2   Excessive speed in turns.
3   Front end alignment incorrect.

65 Excessive tire wear on inside edge

1   Incorrect tire pressure.

2   Front end alignment incorrect.
3   Loose or damaged steering components (Chapter 1).

66 Tire tread worn in one place

1   Tires out of balance.
2   Damaged or buckled wheel. Inspect and replace if necessary.
3   Defective tire.

Chapter 1
Tune-up and routine maintenance

Contents

Specifications

Recommended lubricants and fluids

Note: *Listed here are manufacturer recommendations at the time this manual was written. Manufacturers occasionally upgrade their fluid and lubricant specifications, so check with your local auto parts store for current recommendations.*

Engine oil	
Type	API "certified for gasoline engines"
Viscosity	See accompanying chart
Fuel	Unleaded gasoline, 87 octane (minimum)
Engine coolant	50:50 mixture of ethylene glycol antifreeze and water
Brake fluid	DOT 3 heavy-duty brake fluid
Power steering fluid	MERCON automatic transmission fluid
Automatic transaxle fluid	MERCON V automatic transmission fluid
Chassis grease	SAE NLGI no.2 chassis grease

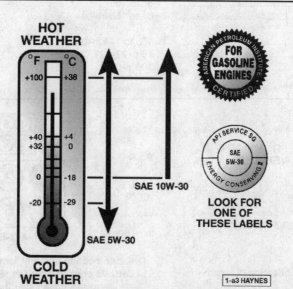

HOT WEATHER

FOR GASOLINE ENGINES — AMERICAN PETROLEUM INSTITUTE — CERTIFIED

°F °C
+100 +38
+40 +4
+32 0
0 -18
-20 -29

SAE 10W-30

SAE 5W-30

COLD WEATHER

API SERVICE SG
SAE 5W-30
ENERGY CONSERVING II

LOOK FOR ONE OF THESE LABELS

Recommended engine oil viscosity

1-a3 HAYNES

Capacities*

Engine oil (with filter change)
    OHV engine (all years).. 4.5 qts
    OHC engine
        2003 and earlier.. 5.8 qts
        2004 to 2005.. 6.5 qts
Fuel tank
    1996 to 1999 .... 16.0 gal
    2000 and later .... 18.0 gal
Cooling system
    OHV engine .... 11.6 qts
    OHC engine .... 10.6 qts
Automatic transaxle (total fill - see Section 25 for drain and refill requirements)
    AX4S .... 12.2 qts
    AX4N/4F50N .... 13.4 qts

All capacities approximate. Add as necessary to bring to appropriate level.

General

Radiator cap pressure rating
    1996 to 1999 .... 16 psi
    2000 and later .... 12.9 to 18 psi
Disc brake pad thickness (minimum) .... 1/8 inch

Ignition system

Spark plug Type and Gap
    OHV engine.. Motorcraft AGSF32PM (original)/AGSF-32FM (current)
        or equivalent @ 0.042 to 0.046 inch

    OHC engine
        1996 to 2002... Motorcraft AWSF-32F or equivalent @ 0.052 to 0.056 inch
        2003 and later... Motorcraft AGSF-32FM or equivalent @ 0.054 inch
Firing order
    All engines... 1-4-2-5-3-6

Torque specifications   **Ft-lbs** (unless otherwise noted)

Note: *One foot-pound (ft-lb) of torque is equivalent to 12 inch-pounds (in-lbs) of torque. Torque values below approximately 15 ft-lbs are expressed in inch-pounds, since most foot-pound torque wrenches are not accurate at these smaller values.*

Drivebelt tensioner bolt
    OHV engines
        1996 through 2000 35
        2001 and later... 18
    OHC engines.. 18
Water pump drivebelt tensioner bolt... 89 in-lbs
Wheel lug nuts .... 85 to 105
Spark plugs .... 84 to 168 in-lbs
Oil pan drain plug
    OHV engine .... 108 to 144 in-lbs
    OHC engine .... 16 to 22
Automatic transaxle pan bolts.. 106 in-lbs

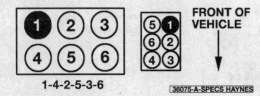

1-4-2-5-3-6

Cylinder location and coil terminal identification diagram -
3.0L OHV V6 engine

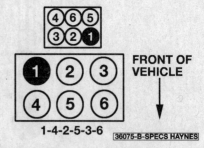

1-4-2-5-3-6

Cylinder location and coil terminal identification diagram - 3.0L
OHC V6 engines through 1999. 2000 and later 3.0L OHC V6
engines have individual coils at each spark plug

Typical engine compartment components (3.0L OHV V6 engine)

1	Engine drivebelt	5	Battery	10	Engine oil dipstick
2	Automatic transaxle dipstick (not visible)	6	Power distribution box	11	Power steering fluid reservoir
3	Brake master cylinder reservoir	7	Ignition coil pack and spark plug wires	12	Cooling system expansion tank
4	Air filter housing	8	Engine oil filler cap	13	Cooling system pressure cap
		9	Spark plugs (left bank)	14	Windshield washer fluid reservoir

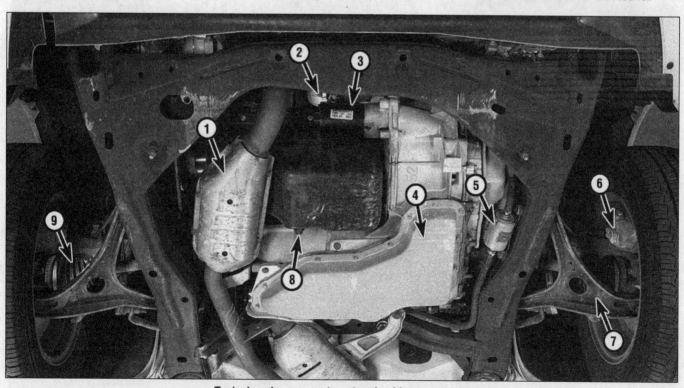

Typical engine compartment underside components

1	Catalytic converter	4	Transaxle fluid pan	7	Lower control arm
2	Oil filter	5	Power steering fluid filter	8	Engine oil drain plug
3	Starter motor	6	Front brake caliper	9	Driveaxle

Typical rear underside components

1	Muffler	7	Gas tank
2	Evaporative emission canister	8	Load sensing proportioning valve (sedan models only)
3	Evaporative emission canister hoses	9	Suspension strut rod
4	Fuel filter	10	Brake caliper
5	Rear suspension control arm	11	Rear strut assembly
6	Sway bar bushing		

1 Maintenance schedule

The following maintenance intervals are based on the assumption that the vehicle owner will be doing the maintenance or service work, rather than having a dealer service department or other repair shop do the work. Although the time and mileage intervals are loosely based on factory recommendations, most have been shortened to ensure, for example, that such items as lubricants and fluids are checked and changed at intervals that promote maximum engine and driveline service life. Also, many of the maintenance procedures may be performed more often than recommended in the following schedule if the owner wants to keep his or her vehicle in peak condition at all times and maintain the vehicle's highest ultimate resale value. We encourage such owner initiative.

When the vehicle is new it should be serviced initially by a factory-authorized dealer service department to protect the factory warranty.

Every 250 miles or weekly, whichever comes first

Check the engine oil level (Section 4)
Check the engine coolant level (Section 4)
Check the windshield washer fluid level (Section 4)
Check the brake fluid level (Section 4)
Check the tires and tire pressures (Section 5)

Every 3000 miles or 3 months, whichever comes first

All items listed above, plus:
Check the power steering fluid level (Section 6)
Check the automatic transaxle fluid level (Section 7)
Change the engine oil and oil filter (Section 8)

Every 6000 miles or 6 months, whichever comes first

All items listed above, plus:
Check and service the battery (Section 9)
Inspect and replace, if necessary, the windshield wiper blades (Section 10)
Rotate the tires (Section 11)
Check the seatbelt operation (Section 12)

Every 15,000 miles or 12 months, whichever comes first

All items listed above, plus:
Inspect and replace, if necessary, all underhood hoses; (Section 13)

Inspect the cooling system (Section 14)
Check the fuel system (Section 15)
Inspect the steering and suspension components (Section 16)
Inspect the brakes (Section 17) ·
Replace the passenger compartment air filter if equipped (Section 18)

Every 30,000 miles or 24 months, whichever comes first

Check the engine drivebelts (Section 19)
Inspect and replace, if necessary, the ignition system components (Section 20)
Replace the engine air filter (Section 21)*
Check the PCV valve (Section 22)
Replace the fuel filter (Section 23)
Inspect the exhaust system (Section 24)
Change the automatic transaxle fluid and filter (Section 25)**
Service the cooling system (drain, flush and refill) (Section 26)

Every 60,000 miles or 48 months, whichever comes first

Replace the spark plugs (Section 27)

Replace every 15,000 miles if is the vehicle is driven in dusty areas.
**If the vehicle is operated in continuous stop-and-go driving or in mountainous areas, change at 15,000 miles.*

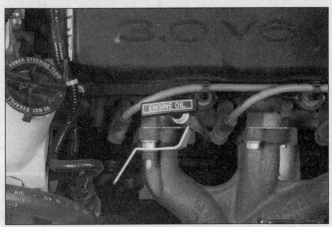

4.2 The oil dipstick is located on the forward side of the engine

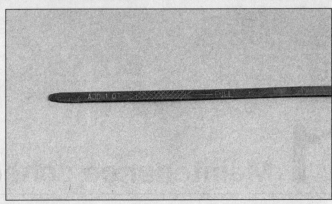

4.4 The oil level should be at or near the FULL mark on the dipstick - If it isn't, add enough oil to bring the level near the FULL mark

2   Introduction

This Chapter will help the home mechanic maintain the Taurus or Sable for maximum performance, economy, safety and reliability.

Included is a master maintenance schedule, followed by procedures specifically for each item on the schedule. Visual checks, adjustments, component replacement, and other helpful items are included. Refer to the **accompanying illustrations** of the engine compartment and the underside of the vehicle for the locations of various components.

Servicing the vehicle in accordance with the mileage and time maintenance schedule and the step-by-step procedures will result in a planned maintenance program that should produce a long and reliable service life. Remember that it is a comprehensive plan, so maintaining some items but not others at the specified intervals will not produce the same results.

As you service the vehicle, you will discover that many of the procedures can - and should - be grouped together because of the nature of the particular procedure you're performing or because of the close proximity of two otherwise unrelated components to one another.

For example, if the vehicle is raised for chassis lubrication, you should inspect the exhaust, suspension, steering and fuel systems while you're under the vehicle. When you're rotating the tires, it makes good sense to check the brakes since the wheels are already removed. Finally, let's suppose you have to borrow or rent a torque wrench; you might as well check the torque of as many critical fasteners as time allows.

The first step in this maintenance program is to prepare yourself before the actual work begins. Read through all the procedures you're planning to do, then gather up all the parts and tools needed. If it looks like you might run into problems during a particular job, seek advice from a mechanic or an experienced do-it-yourselfer.

3   Tune-up general information

The term tune-up is used in this manual to represent a combination of individual operations rather than one specific procedure.

If the routine maintenance schedule is followed closely from the time the vehicle is new and frequent checks are made of fluid levels and high-wear items as suggested throughout this manual, the engine will be kept in relatively good condition and the need for additional work will be minimized.

More likely than not, however, there will be times when the engine is running poorly due to lack of regular maintenance. This is even more likely if a used vehicle, which has not received regular and frequent maintenance, is purchased. In such cases, an engine tune-up will be needed outside of the regular routine maintenance intervals.

The first step in any tune-up or diagnostic procedure to help correct a poor running engine is a cylinder compression check. A compression check (see Chapter 2) will help determine the condition of internal engine components and should be used as a guide for tune-up and repair procedures. If a compression check indicates serious internal engine wear, a conventional tune-up will not improve the performance of the engine and would be a waste of time and money. Because of its importance, the compression check should be done by someone with the right equipment and the knowledge to use it properly.

The following procedures are those most often needed to bring a generally poor running engine back into a proper state of tune.

Minor tune-up

Check all engine related fluids (Section 4)
Clean, inspect and test the battery
  (Section 9)
Check all underhood hoses (Section 13)
Check the cooling system (Section 14)
Check the drivebelt (Section 19)
Inspect the spark plug wires (Section 20)
Check the air filter (Section 21)

Major tune-up

All items listed under Minor tune-up, plus . . .

Check the fuel system (Section 15)
Replace the spark plug wires (Section 20)
Replace the air filter (Section 21)
Replace the PCV valve (Section 22)
Replace the fuel filter (Section 23)
Replace the spark plugs (Section 27)
Check the charging system (Chapter 5)

4   Fluid level checks (every 250 miles or weekly)

1   Fluids are an essential part of the lubrication, cooling, brake and windshield washer systems. Because the fluids gradually become depleted or contaminated during normal operation of the vehicle, they must be periodically replenished. See *Recommended lubricants and fluids* at the beginning of this Chapter before adding fluid to any of the following components. **Note:** *The vehicle must be on level ground when fluid levels are checked.*

Engine oil

Refer to illustrations 4.2, 4.4 and 4.6

2   The oil level is checked with a dipstick, which is mounted on the left side of the engine block at the front of the engine compartment **(see illustration)**. The dipstick extends through a metal tube down into the oil pan.

3   The oil level should be checked before the vehicle has been driven, or about 15 minutes after the engine has been shut off. If the oil is checked immediately after driving the vehicle, some of the oil will remain in the upper part of the engine, resulting in an inaccurate reading on the dipstick.

4   Pull the dipstick out of the tube and wipe all the oil from the end with a clean rag or paper towel. Insert the clean dipstick all the way back into the tube and pull it out again. Note the oil at the end of the dipstick. At its highest point, the level should be above the ADD 1 QT mark, within the hatched

4.6 Remove the twist-off cap and add oil through the oil filler opening in the valve cover

4.9 The cooling system expansion tank is located at the right front corner of the engine compartment

marked section of the dipstick (see illustration).

5   Do not allow the level to drop below the ADD 1 QT mark or oil starvation may cause engine damage. Conversely, overfilling the engine (adding oil above the FULL mark) may cause oil-fouled spark plugs, oil leaks or oil seal failures.

6   To add oil, remove the filler cap from the valve cover (see illustration). After adding oil, wait a few minutes to allow the level to stabilize, then pull out the dipstick and check the level again. Add more oil if required. Install the filler cap and tighten it by hand only.

7   Checking the oil level is an important preventive maintenance step. A consistently low oil level indicates oil leakage through damaged seals, defective gaskets, or past worn rings or valve guides. If the oil looks milky or has water droplets in it, a cylinder head gasket may be blown or a head or the block may be cracked. The engine should be checked immediately. The condition of the oil should also be checked. Whenever you check the oil level, slide your thumb and index finger up the dipstick before wiping off the oil. If you see small dirt or metal particles clinging to the dipstick, the oil should be changed (see Section 8).

Engine coolant

Refer to illustration 4.9
Warning: *Do not allow antifreeze to contact your skin or painted surfaces of the vehicle. Flush contaminated areas immediately with plenty of water. Don't store new coolant or leave old coolant lying around where it's accessible to children or pets. They may be attracted by its sweet smell. Ingestion of even a small amount of coolant can be fatal! Wipe up garage floor and drip pan spills immediately. Keep antifreeze containers covered and repair cooling system leaks as soon as they're noticed.*

8   All vehicles covered by this manual have a pressurized coolant recovery system. A pressurized plastic expansion tank is located

at the front of the engine compartment and connected by a hose to the radiator. As the engine heats up during operation, the expanding coolant fills the tank. The Taurus and Sable models covered by this manual do not have traditional radiator caps. The pressurized cap of the expansion tank is point at which the cooling system is filled and the coolant level checked.

9   Check the coolant level in the expansion tank regularly. **Warning:** *Do not remove the pressure cap on the expansion tank until the engine has completely cooled. The level in the expansion tank varies with the temperature of the engine. When the engine is cold, the coolant level should be within the COLD FILL RANGE marked on the bottle. Once the engine has warmed up, the level should be at or near the top of that range. If it isn't, allow the engine to cool, then remove the cap from the expansion tank and add a 50:50 mixture of ethylene glycol antifreeze and water (see illustration).*

10   Drive the vehicle and recheck the coolant level. Don't use rust inhibitors or additives. If only a small amount of coolant is required to bring the system up to the proper level, water can be used. However, repeated additions of water will dilute the antifreeze and water mixture. To maintain the proper ratio of antifreeze and water, always top up the coolant level with the correct mixture. An empty plastic milk jug or bleach bottle makes an excellent container for mixing coolant.

11   If the coolant level drops consistently, there may be a leak in the system. Inspect the radiator, hoses, filler cap, drain plugs and water pump (see Section 14). If no leaks are noted, have the cooling system pressure tested by a garage or radiator shop with the necessary equipment.

12   If you have to remove the expansion tank cap, wait until the engine has cooled completely, then wrap a thick cloth around the cap and turn it to the first stop. Loosen it slowly, stopping if you hear a hissing noise. If coolant or steam escapes, let the engine cool longer, then remove the cap.

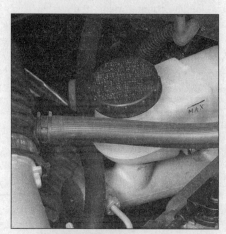

4.15 The brake fluid level should be near the MAX mark on the translucent plastic reservoir

13   Check the condition of the coolant. It should be relatively clear. If it's brown or rust colored, the system should be drained, flushed and refilled. Even if the coolant appears to be normal, the corrosion inhibitors wear out, so it must be replaced at the specified intervals.

Brake fluid

Refer to illustration 4.15
Warning: *Brake fluid can harm your eyes and damage painted surfaces, so use extreme caution when handling or pouring it. Do not use brake fluid that has been standing open or is more than one year old. Brake fluid absorbs moisture from the air, which can cause a dangerous loss of braking effectiveness.*

14   The brake fluid level is checked by looking through the plastic reservoir on the master cylinder. The master cylinder is mounted on the front of the power booster unit in the left (driver's side) rear corner of the engine compartment.

15   The fluid level should be between the MAX and MIN lines on the side of the reservoir (see illustration).

4.22 The windshield washer filler cap is located directly behind the cooling system expansion tank on the right side of the engine compartment - the washer reservoir is mounted under the fender well

16   If the fluid level is low, wipe the top of the reservoir and the cap with a clean rag to prevent contamination of the system as the cap is unscrewed.

17   Add only the specified brake fluid to the reservoir. (Refer to *Recommended lubricants and fluids* at the front of this Chapter or your owner's manual.) Mixing different types of brake fluid can damage the system. Fill the reservoir to the MAX line.

18   While the reservoir cap is off, check the master cylinder reservoir for contamination. If rust, dirt or water is present, the system should be flushed and refilled by a repair shop.

19   After filling the reservoir to the proper level, make sure the cap is seated to prevent fluid leakage and contamination.

20   The fluid level in the master cylinder will drop slightly as the disc brake pads wear down during normal operation. If the brake fluid level drops consistently, check the entire system for leaks immediately. Examine all brake lines, hoses and connections, along with the calipers, wheel cylinders and master cylinder (see Section 17).

21   If you discover the reservoir empty or nearly empty when you check the fluid level, the brake system should be bled (see Chapter 9).

Windshield washer fluid

Refer to illustration 4.22

22   Windshield washer fluid is stored in a plastic reservoir located under the right front (passenger's side) fender, directly behind the coolant expansion tank **(see illustration)**.

23   In milder climates, plain water can be used in the reservoir, but it should be kept no more than 2/3 full to allow for expansion if the water freezes. In colder climates, use windshield washer system antifreeze, available at any auto parts store, to lower the freezing point of the fluid. Mix the antifreeze with water according to the manufacturer's direc-

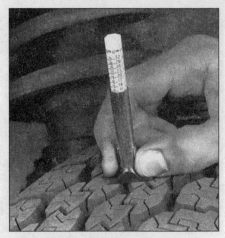

5.2 Use a tire tread depth indicator to check tire wear - they are available at auto parts stores and service stations and cost very little

tions on the container. **Caution:** *Do not use cooling system antifreeze, it will damage the vehicle's paint.*

5   Tire and tire pressure checks (every 250 miles or weekly)

Refer to illustrations 5.2, 5.3, 5.4a, 5.4b and 5.8

1   Periodic inspection of the tires may

UNDERINFLATION

CUPPING

Cupping may be caused by:

● Underinflation and/or mechanical irregularities such as out-of-balance condition of wheel and/or tire, and bent or damaged wheel.
● Loose or worn steering tie-rod or steering idler arm.
● Loose, damaged or worn front suspension parts.

OVERINFLATION

INCORRECT TOE-IN OR EXTREME CAMBER

FEATHERING DUE TO MISALIGNMENT

5.3 This chart will help you determine the condition of the tires, the probable causes of abnormal wear, and the corrective action necessary

5.4a If a tire loses air on a steady basis, check the valve stem core first to make sure it's snug (special inexpensive wrenches are commonly available at auto parts stores)

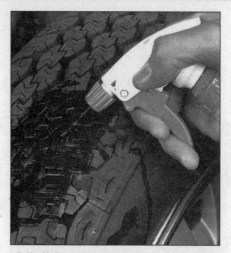

5.4b If the valve stem core is tight, raise the corner of the vehicle with the low tire and spray a soapy water solution onto the tread as the tire is turned slowly - leaks will cause small bubbles to appear

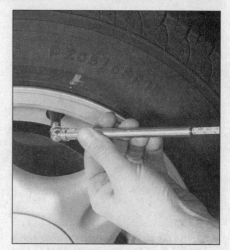

5.8 To extend the life of the tires, check the air pressure at least once a week with an accurate gauge (don't forget the spare)

spare you the inconvenience of being stranded with a flat tire. It can also provide you with vital information regarding possible problems in the steering and suspension systems before major damage occurs.

2   All tires have 1/2-inch-wide bands that appear within the tread when tread depth reaches 1/16-inch, but they don't appear until the tires are worn out. Tread wear can be monitored with a simple, inexpensive tread depth indicator (**see illustration**).

3   Note any abnormal tread wear (**see illustration**). Tread pattern irregularities such as cupping, flat spots, and more wear on one side than the other indicate front end alignment or balance problems. If any of these conditions are noted, take the vehicle to a tire shop or garage to correct the problem.

4   Look closely for cuts, punctures and embedded nails or tacks. Sometimes a tire will hold air pressure for a short time or leak down very slowly after a nail has embedded itself in the tread. If a slow leak persists, check the valve stem core to make sure it is tight (**see illustration**). Examine the tread for an object that may have embedded itself in the tire or for a "plug" that may have begun to leak. (Radial tire punctures are repaired with a plug that is installed in a puncture). If a puncture is suspected, it can be verified by spraying a solution of soapy water onto the puncture area (**see illustration**). The soapy solution will bubble if there is a leak. Unless the puncture is unusually large, a tire shop or service station can usually repair the tire.

5   Carefully inspect the inner sidewall of each tire for evidence of brake fluid leakage. If you see any, inspect the brakes immediately.

6   Correct air pressure adds miles to the life of the tires, improves gas mileage, and enhances overall ride quality. Tire pressure cannot be accurately estimated by looking at a tire. A tire pressure gauge is essential. Keep

an accurate gauge in the glove compartment. The pressure gauges attached to the nozzles of air hoses at gas stations are often inaccurate.

7   Always check tire pressure when the tires are cold. Cold, in this case, means the vehicle has not been driven over a mile in the three hours preceding a tire pressure check. A pressure rise of four to eight pounds is not uncommon once the tires are warm.

8   Unscrew the valve cap protruding from the wheel or hubcap and push the gauge firmly onto the valve stem (**see illustration**). Note the reading on the gauge and compare the figure to the recommended tire pressure shown on the tire placard on the driver's door. Be sure to reinstall the valve cap to keep dirt and moisture out of the valve stem mechanism. Check all four tires and, if necessary, add enough air to bring them up to the recommended pressure.

9   Don't forget to keep the spare tire inflated to the specified pressure (refer to your owner's manual or the decal attached to the right door pillar). Note that the pressure recommended for the temporary (mini) spare is higher than for the tires on the vehicle.

6   Power steering fluid level check (every 3000 miles or 3 months)

Refer to illustrations 6.5a, 6.5b and 6.5c

1   Check the power steering fluid level periodically to avoid steering system problems, such as damage to the pump. **Caution:** *DO NOT hold the steering wheel against either stop (extreme left or right turn) for more than five seconds. If you do, the power steering pump could be damaged.*

2   The power steering pump is on the right side (passenger's side) of the engine compartment, toward the front. On OHV engines,

the pump reservoir is an integral part of the pump and has a twist-off cap with a fluid level dipstick. On OHC engines, the pump reservoir is mounted on the right strut tower, remote from the pump. This reservoir has fluid level graduations on its side to visually inspect the MIN and MAX fluid levels.

3   Park the vehicle on level ground and apply the parking brake.

4   Run the engine until it has reached normal operating temperature. With the engine at idle, turn the steering wheel left and right several times to get any air out of the system. On OHV engines, shut the engine off, remove the cap by turning it counterclockwise, wipe the dipstick clean, and reinstall the cap. Make sure it is seated.

5   Remove the cap again and note the fluid level. It must be between the dipstick arrows in the FULL HOT range on the OHV engines (**see illustrations**). For OHC engines, fluid level should be between the MIN and MAX marks on the side of the reservoir.

6.5a A dipstick is used to check the power steering fluid level on OHV engines

6.5b The dipstick is marked on both sides so the fluid can be checked hot . . .

6.5c . . . or cold

7.4 The automatic transaxle dipstick (arrow) is located at the rear of the engine compartment

6   Add small amounts of fluid until the level is correct. **Caution:** *Do not overfill the reservoir. If too much fluid is added, remove the excess with a clean syringe or suction pump.*
7   If additional fluid is required, pour the specified type directly into the reservoir, using a funnel to prevent spills. Reinstall the cap and dipstick.
8   If the reservoir requires frequent fluid addition, check the pump, the steering gear, and all hoses and fittings for leaks.

7   Automatic transaxle fluid level check (every 3000 miles or 3 months)

Refer to illustrations 7.4 and 7.6
1   The automatic transaxle fluid level should be carefully maintained. Low fluid level can lead to slipping or loss of drive, and overfilling can cause foaming and loss of fluid. Either condition can damage the transaxle.
2   Because transaxle fluid expands as it heats up, the fluid level should be checked only when the transaxle is warm (at normal operating temperature). If the vehicle has just

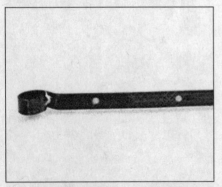

7.6 Check the fluid with the transaxle at normal operating temperature - the level should be kept in the cross-hatched area - don't add fluid if the level is anywhere in this area

been driven over 20 miles (32 km), the transaxle can be considered warm. **Caution:** *If the vehicle has just been driven for a long time at high speed or in city traffic in hot weather, or if it has been pulling a trailer, an accurate fluid level reading cannot be obtained.* Allow the transaxle to cool down for about 30 minutes. You also can check the transaxle fluid level when the transaxle is cold. If the vehicle has not been driven for over five hours and the fluid is about room temperature (70 to 95 degrees F), the transaxle is cold. It is best, however, to check the fluid level with the transaxle warm to ensure accurate results.
3   Immediately after driving the vehicle, park it on a level surface, set the parking brake, and start the engine. While the engine is idling, depress the brake pedal and move the selector lever through all the gear ranges, beginning and ending in Park.
4   Locate the automatic transaxle dipstick at the left rear of the engine compartment, just below the brake fluid reservoir **(see illustration)**.
5   With the engine still idling in Park, pull the dipstick from the tube, wipe it off with a clean rag, push it all the way back into the tube and withdraw it again, then note the fluid level.
6   If the transaxle is warm, the fluid level should be in the operating temperature range (in the cross-hatched area) **(see illustration)**. If the level is low, slowly add the specified automatic transaxle fluid through the dipstick tube. Use a funnel to prevent spills.
7   Add just enough fluid to fill the transaxle to the proper level. It takes about one pint to raise the level from the low mark to the high mark when the fluid is hot, so add the fluid a little at a time and keep checking the level until it's correct.
8   The condition of the fluid should also be checked along with the level. If the fluid is black or a dark reddish-brown, or if it smells burned, it should be changed (see Section 25). If you are in doubt about its condition, purchase some new fluid and compare the two for color and smell.

8   Engine oil and filter change (every 3000 miles or 3 months)

Refer to illustrations 8.2, 8.7, 8.12 and 8.16
1   Frequent oil changes are the most important preventive maintenance procedures that can be done by the home mechanic. As engine oil ages, it becomes diluted and contaminated, which leads to premature engine wear.
2   Make sure that you have all the necessary tools before you begin this procedure **(see illustration)**. You should also have plenty of rags or newspapers to mop up oil spills.
3   Access to the oil drain plug and filter will be improved if the vehicle can be lifted on a hoist, driven onto ramps, or supported by jackstands.
4   If you haven't changed the oil on this car before, get under it and locate the oil drain plug and the oil filter. The exhaust components will be warm as you work, so note how they are routed to avoid touching them when you are under the vehicle.
5   Start the engine and allow it to reach normal operating temperature - oil and sludge will flow out more easily when warm. If new oil, a filter or tools are needed, use the car to go get them and warm up the engine and oil at the same time. Park on a level surface and shut off the engine when it's warmed up. Remove the oil filler cap from the valve cover.
6   Raise the vehicle and support it on jackstands. Make sure it is safely supported! **Warning:** *Do not work under a vehicle supported only by a bumper, hydraulic, or scissors-type jack. Always use jackstands.*
7   Being careful not to touch the hot exhaust components, position a drain pan under the plug in the bottom of the engine, then remove the plug **(see illustration)**. It's a good idea to wear a rubber glove while unscrewing the plug the final few turns to avoid being scalded by hot oil.

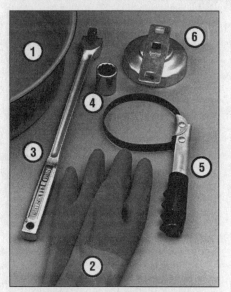

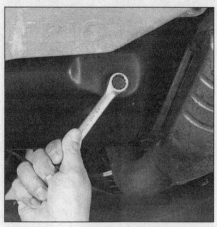

8.7 Use a proper size box-end wrench or socket to remove the oil drain plug and avoid rounding it off

8.12 The oil filter is located at the front side of the engine and is accessible from underneath the car - the oil filter is usually on very tight and will require a filter wrench to remove it - Install the new filter hand-tight, a filter wrench should not be necessary

8.2 These tools are required when changing the engine oil and filter

1   *Drain pan* - *fairly shallow in depth, but wide to prevent spills*
2   *Rubber gloves* - *When removing the drain plug and filter, you will get oil on your hands. The gloves will prevent burns*
3   *Breaker bar* - *Sometimes the oil drain plug is tight, and a long breaker bar is needed to loosen it*
4   *Socket* – *To be used with the breaker bar or a ratchet (must be the correct size to fit the drain plug - six-point preferred)*
5   *Filter wrench* - *This is a metal band-type wrench, which requires clearance around the filter to be effective*
6   *Filter wrench* - *This type fits on the bottom of the filter and can be turned with a ratchet or breaker bar. Different-sized wrenches are available for different types of filters*

8   It may be necessary to move the drain pan slightly as oil flow slows to a trickle. Inspect the old oil for metal particles.
9   After all the oil has drained, wipe off the drain plug with a clean rag. Any small metal particles clinging to the plug would immediately contaminate the new oil.
10   Clean the area around the drain plug opening, reinstall the plug, and tighten it securely but don't strip the threads.
11   Move the drain pan into position under the oil filter.
12   Loosen the oil filter by turning it counterclockwise with a filter wrench **(see illustration)**.
13   Be prepared for oil to spill out of the canister as it's loosened.
14   Once the filter is loose, use your hands to unscrew it from the block. Just as the filter is detached from the block, immediately tilt the open end up to prevent the oil inside the filter from spilling out.
15   Using a clean rag, wipe off the mounting

8.16 Lubricate the oil filter gasket with clean engine oil before installing the filter on the engine

surface on the block. Also, make sure that none of the old gasket remains stuck to the mounting surface. It can be removed with a scraper if necessary.
16   Compare the old filter with the new one to make sure they are the same type. Put some engine oil on the rubber gasket of the new filter and screw it into place **(see illustration)**. Overtightening the filter will damage the gasket, so a filter wrench should not be necessary for installation. Normally a filter should be tightened 3/4-turn after the gasket contacts the block, but be sure to follow the directions on the filter or container.
17   Remove all tools and materials from under the vehicle, being careful not to spill the oil in the drain pan, then lower the vehicle.
18   Add new oil to the engine through the oil filler cap. Use a funnel to prevent oil from spilling onto the top of the engine. Pour four quarts of fresh oil into the engine. Wait a few minutes to allow the oil to drain into the pan, then check the level on the dipstick (see Section 4 if necessary). If the oil level is in the OK range (hatched area), install the filler cap.
19   Start the engine and run it for about a

minute. While the engine is running, look under the vehicle and check for leaks at the oil pan drain plug and around the oil filter. If either one is leaking, stop the engine and tighten the plug or filter slightly.
20   Wait a few minutes, then recheck the level on the dipstick. Add oil as necessary to bring the level into the OK range.
21   During the first few trips after an oil change, make it a point to check frequently for leaks and proper oil level.
22   The old oil drained from the engine cannot be reused in its present state and should be discarded. Oil reclamation centers, auto repair shops and gas stations will normally accept the oil, which can be recycled. After the oil has cooled, it can be drained into a container (plastic jugs or bottles, etc.) for transport to a disposal site.

9   Battery check, maintenance and charging (every 6000 miles or 6 months)

Refer to illustrations 9.1, 9.6a, 9.6b, 9.7a and 9.7b
Warning: *Certain precautions must be followed when checking and servicing the battery. Hydrogen gas, which is highly flammable, is always present in the battery cells, so keep lighted tobacco and all other open flames and sparks away from the battery. The electrolyte inside the battery is dilute sulfuric acid, which will cause injury if splashed on your skin or in your eyes. It will also ruin clothes and painted surfaces. When removing the battery cables, always disconnect the negative cable first and connect it last.*

1   A routine preventive maintenance program for the battery in your vehicle is the only way to ensure quick and reliable starts. But

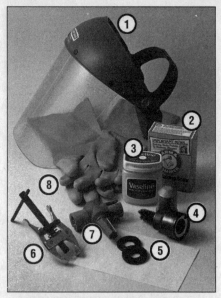

9.1 Tools and materials required for battery maintenance

1   *Face shield or safety goggles - When removing corrosion with a brush, the acidic particles can easily fly up into your eyes*

2   *Baking soda - A solution of baking soda and water can be used to neutralize corrosion*

3   *Petroleum jelly - A layer of this on the battery posts will help prevent corrosion*

4   *Battery post and cable cleaner - This wire brush cleaning tool will remove all traces of corrosion from the battery posts and cable clamps*

5   *Treated felt washers - Placing one of these on each post, directly under the cable clamps, will help prevent corrosion*

6   *Puller - Sometimes the cable clamps are very difficult to pull off the posts, even after the nut or bolt has been completely loosened. This tool pulls the clamp straight up and off the post without damage*

7   *Battery post and cable cleaner - Here is another cleaning tool, which is a slightly different version of number 4 above, but it does the same thing*

8   *Rubber gloves - Another safety item to consider when servicing the battery; remember that's acid inside the battery.*

before performing any battery maintenance, make sure that you have the proper equipment to work safely around the battery **(see illustration)**.

2   Several other precautions should be taken whenever battery maintenance is performed. Before servicing the battery, always turn the engine and all accessories off and disconnect the cable from the negative terminal of the battery.

3   The battery produces hydrogen gas, which is both flammable and explosive. Never create a spark, smoke or light a match

9.6a Battery terminal corrosion usually appears as light, fluffy powder

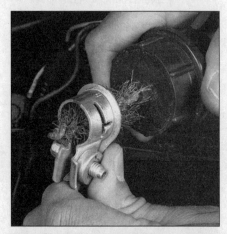

9.7a When cleaning the cable clamps, be sure to remove all corrosion (the inside of the clamp is tapered to match the taper on the post, so don't remove too much material)

around the battery. Always charge the battery in a ventilated area.

4   Electrolyte contains poisonous and corrosive sulfuric acid. Do not allow it to get in your eyes, on your skin, or on your clothes. Never ingest it. Wear protective safety glasses when working near the battery. Keep children away from the battery.

5   Note the external condition of the battery. If the positive terminal and cable clamp on your car's battery has a rubber protector, make sure that it's not torn or damaged. It should completely cover the terminal. Look for any corroded or loose connections, cracks in the battery case or cover, or loose hold-down clamps. Also check the entire length of each cable for cracks and frayed conductors.

6   If corrosion (which looks like white, fluffy deposits) is evident, particularly around the terminals **(see illustration)**, remove the battery for cleaning. Loosen the cable clamp bolts with a wrench - being careful to remove the ground cable first - and slide them off the terminals **(see illustration)**. Then disconnect

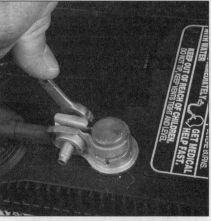

9.6b Removing the cable from a battery post with a wrench - sometimes special battery pliers are required for this procedure if corrosion has caused deterioration of the nut hex (always remove the ground cable first and hook it up last!)

9.7b Regardless of the type of tool used on the battery posts, a clean, shiny surface should be the result

the hold-down clamp bolt and nut, remove the clamp, and lift the battery from the engine compartment.

7   Clean the cable clamps thoroughly with a battery brush or a terminal cleaner and a solution of warm water and baking soda **(see illustration)**. Wash the terminals and the top of the battery with the same solution but make sure that the solution doesn't get into the battery. When cleaning the cables, terminals and battery top, wear safety goggles and rubber gloves to prevent any solution from coming in contact with your eyes or hands. Wear old clothes too. Even diluted, sulfuric acid splashed onto clothes will burn holes in them. If the terminals are extensively corroded, clean them up with a terminal cleaner **(see illustration)**. Thoroughly wash all cleaned areas with plain water.

8   Make sure that the battery tray is in good condition and the hold-down clamp bolts are tight. If the battery is removed from

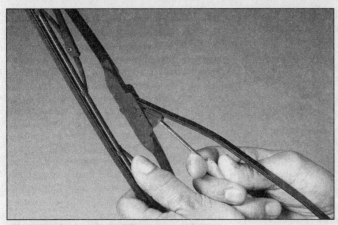

10.4 Turn the blade at an angle from the wiper arm, then push the lockpin with a screwdriver to release the blade - pull the blade down toward the windshield to remove it from the arm

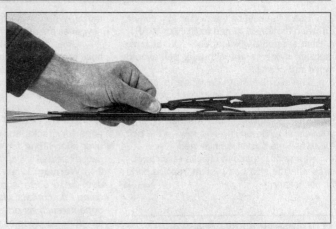

10.5 Use needle-nose pliers to compress the rubber element, then slide the element out - slide the new element in and lock the blade assembly into the notches of the wiper element

the tray, make sure no parts remain in the bottom of the tray when the battery is reinstalled. When reinstalling the hold-down clamp bolts, do not overtighten them.

9   Information on removing and installing the battery is in Chapter 5. Information on jump starting is at the front of this manual. For more detailed battery checking procedures, refer to the *Haynes Automotive Electrical Manual*.

Cleaning

10   Remove corrosion on the hold-down components, battery case and surrounding areas with a solution of water and baking soda. Thoroughly rinse all cleaned areas with plain water.

11   Any metal parts of the vehicle damaged by corrosion should be covered with a zinc-based primer, then painted.

Charging

Warning: *When batteries are being charged, hydrogen gas, which is very explosive and flammable, is produced. Do not smoke or allow open flames near a charging or a recently charged battery. Wear eye protection when near the battery during charging. Also, make sure the charger is unplugged before connecting or disconnecting the battery from the charger.*

12   Slow-rate charging is the best way to restore a battery that's discharged to the point where it will not start the engine. It's also a good way to maintain the battery charge in a vehicle that's only driven a few miles between starts. Maintaining the battery charge is particularly important in the winter when the battery must work harder to start the engine and electrical accessories that drain the battery are in greater use.

13   It's best to use a one- or two-ampere battery charger (sometimes called a "trickle" charger). They are the safest and put the least strain on the battery. They are also the least expensive. For a faster charge, you can use a higher amperage charger, but rapid boost charges that claim to restore the power

of the battery in one to two hours are hardest on the battery and can damage batteries not in good condition. This type of charging should only be used in emergency situations.

14   The average time necessary to charge a battery should be listed in the instructions that come with the charger. As a general rule, a trickle charger will charge a battery in 12 to 16 hours.

10 Windshield wiper blade inspection and replacement (every 6000 miles or 6 months)

Refer to illustrations 10.4 and 10.5

1   Inspect the windshield wiper and blade assembly periodically for damage, loose components, and cracked or worn blades.

2   Road film can build up on the wiper blades and affect their efficiency, so they should be washed regularly with a mild detergent solution.

3   If the wiper blade elements are cracked, worn or warped, or no longer clean adequately, replace them with new ones.

4   Lift the arm assembly away from the glass for clearance, press on the release lever, then slide the wiper blade assembly out of the hook in the end of the arm **(see illustration)**.

5   Use needle-nose pliers to compress the blade element, then slide the element out of the frame and discard it **(see illustration)**.

6   Installation is the reverse of removal.

11 Tire rotation (every 6000 miles or 6 months)

Refer to illustration 11.4

1   The tires should be rotated at the specified intervals and whenever uneven wear is noticed. Since the vehicle will be raised and the tires removed anyway, check the brakes also (see Section 17).

2   Raise the car on a hoist or support it on

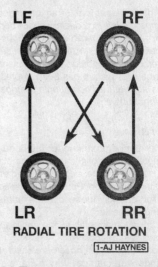

RADIAL TIRE ROTATION

1-AJ HAYNES

11.4 The recommended tire rotation pattern for these vehicles

jackstands to get all four wheels off the ground. Make sure the vehicle is safely supported!

3   Refer to the information in *Jacking and towing* at the front of this manual for the proper procedure to follow when raising the vehicle and changing a tire. If the brakes must be checked, don't apply the parking brake.

4   Radial tires must be rotated in a specific pattern **(see illustration)**. If your vehicle has a compact spare tire, don't include it in the rotation pattern.

5   After the rotation is finished, check and adjust the tire pressures as necessary and be sure to check the wheel lug nut tightness.

12 Seatbelt check (every 6000 miles or 6 months)

1   Check seatbelts, buckles, latch plates, and guide loops for damage and signs of wear.

2   See if the seat belt reminder light comes on when the key is turned to RUN or START. A chime should also sound. On passive restraint systems, the shoulder belt should move into position.

3   The seat belts are designed to lock up during a sudden stop or impact, yet allow free movement during normal driving. Make sure the retractors return the belt against your chest while driving and rewind the belt fully when the buckle is unlatched.

4   If any of the above checks reveal problems with the seat belt system, replace parts as necessary.

13   Underhood hose check and replacement (every 15,000 miles or 12 months)

Warning: *Replacement of air conditioning hoses must be left to a dealer service department or air conditioning shop that has the equipment to depressurize the system safely. Never remove air conditioning components or hoses until the system has been depressurized. Do not vent air conditioning refrigerant to the atmosphere.*

General

1   High temperatures under the hood can cause deterioration of the rubber and plastic hoses used for engine, accessory, and emission system operation. Periodically inspect all hoses for cracks, loose clamps, material hardening and leaks.

2   Information specific to the cooling system hoses is in Section 14.

3   Most (but not all) hoses are secured to the fittings with clamps. Where clamps are used, check to be sure they haven't lost their tension, allowing the hose to leak. If clamps aren't used, make sure the hose has not expanded or hardened where it slips over the fitting, allowing it to leak.

PCV system hose

4   To reduce hydrocarbon emissions, crankcase blow-by gas is vented through the PCV valve in the valve cover to the intake manifold through a rubber hose on most models. The blow-by gases mix with incoming air in the intake manifold before being burned in the combustion chambers.

5   Check the PCV hose for cracks, leaks and other damage. Disconnect it from the valve cover and the intake manifold and check the inside for obstructions. If it's clogged, replace it.

Vacuum hoses

6   It's quite common for vacuum hoses, especially those in the emission system, to be color coded or identified by colored stripes molded into them. Various systems require hoses with different wall thickness, collapse resistance, and temperature resis-

tance. When replacing hoses, be sure the new ones are made of the same material.

7   Often the only effective way to check a hose is to remove it completely from the vehicle. If more than one hose is removed, be sure to label the hoses and fittings to ensure correct installation.

8   When inspecting vacuum hoses, be sure to check any plastic T-fittings. Inspect the fittings for cracks and the hose where it fits over each fitting for distortion, which could cause leakage.

9   **Warning:** *When probing with the vacuum hose stethoscope, be careful not to come into contact with moving engine components such as drivebelts, the cooling fan, etc. A small piece of vacuum hose (1/4-inch inside diameter) can be used as a stethoscope to detect vacuum leaks. Hold one end of the hose to your ear and probe around vacuum hoses and fittings, listening for the "hissing" sound of a vacuum leak.*

Fuel hose

Warning: *Gasoline is extremely flammable, so take extra precautions when you work on any part of the fuel system. Don't smoke or allow open flames or bare light bulbs near the work area, and don't work in a garage where a natural gas appliance (such as a water heater or clothes dryer) with a pilot light is present. Since gasoline is carcinogenic, wear latex gloves when there's a possibility of being exposed to fuel, and, if you spill any fuel on your skin, wash it off immediately with soap and water. Mop up any spills immediately, do not store fuel-soaked rags where they could ignite. The fuel system is under constant pressure, so if any fuel lines are to be disconnected, the fuel system pressure must be relieved first (see Chapter 4 for more information). When you do any kind of work on the fuel system, wear safety glasses and have a Class B fire extinguisher on hand.*

10   The fuel lines are usually under pressure so if any fuel lines are to be disconnected, be prepared to catch spilled fuel. Refer to Chapter 4 for the fuel system pressure relief procedure. **Warning:** *Your vehicle is fuel injected and you must relieve the fuel system pressure before servicing the fuel lines.*

11   Check all flexible fuel lines for deterioration and chafing. Check especially for cracks near fittings and in areas where the hose bends, such as where a hose attaches to the fuel pump, fuel filter, and fuel injection rail.

12   When replacing a hose, use only hose that is specifically designed for your fuel injection system.

13   Spring-type clamps are sometimes used on fuel return or vapor lines. These clamps often lose their tension over a period of time, and can be "sprung" during removal. Replace all spring-type clamps with screw clamps whenever a hose is replaced. Some fuel lines use spring-lock type couplings, which require a special tool to disconnect. See Chapter 4 for more information on these type of couplings.

Metal lines

14   Sections of steel tubing are often used for fuel lines between the fuel pump and the fuel injection unit. Check carefully to make sure the line isn't bent, crimped or cracked.

15   If a section of metal fuel line must be replaced, use seamless steel tubing only. Copper and aluminum tubing cannot withstand vibration caused by the engine.

16   Check the metal brake lines where they enter the master cylinder and brake proportioning valve for cracks in the lines and loose fittings. Any sign of brake fluid leakage calls for an immediate thorough inspection of the brake system.

14   Cooling system check (every 15,000 miles or 12 months)

Refer to illustration 14.4

Note: *The cooling systems on Taurus and Sable vehicles use a expansion tank, which is referred to as a "coolant reservoir" in some owner's manuals but which is more than a traditional overflow reservoir. The expansion tank is pressurized when the engine is warm for correct cooling system operation and to remove any air that might be trapped in the system. The radiators in these cars do not have conventional pressure caps. The expansion tank has the pressure-relief cap for the system.*

1   Many major engine failures can be caused by a faulty cooling system. The cooling system also is important in prolonging transaxle life because it cools the automatic transaxle fluid.

2   The engine must be cold for the cooling system check, so perform the following procedure before the vehicle is driven for the day or after it has been shut off for at least three hours.

3   Remove the pressure-relief cap from the expansion tank at the right side of the engine compartment. Clean the cap thoroughly, inside and out, with clean water. The presence of rust or corrosion in the expansion tank means the coolant should be changed (see Section 26). The coolant inside the expansion tank should be relatively clean and transparent. If it's rust colored, drain the system and refill it with new coolant.

4   Carefully check the radiator hoses and the heater hoses **(see illustration)**. Inspect each coolant hose along its entire length. Replace any hose that is cracked, swollen or deteriorated. Cracks will show up better if the hose is squeezed. Pay close attention to hose clamps that secure the hoses to cooling system components. Hose clamps can pinch and puncture hoses, resulting in coolant leaks. Some hoses are hidden from view so sometimes you'll have to trace a coolant leak.

5   Make sure that all hose connections are tight. A leak in the cooling system will usually show up as white or rust colored deposits on the area adjoining the leak. If wire-type clamps are used on the hoses, it may be a

Check for a chafed area that could fail prematurely.

Check for a soft area indicating the hose has deteriorated inside.

Overtightening the clamp on a hardened hose will damage the hose and cause a leak.

Check each hose for swelling and oil-soaked ends. Cracks and breaks can be located by squeezing the hose.

14.4 Hoses, like drivebelts, can fail at the worst possible time. To prevent the inconvenience of a blown radiator or heater hose, inspect them carefully as shown here

good idea to replace them with screw-type clamps.

6   Clean the front of the radiator and air conditioning condenser with compressed air, if available, or a soft brush. Remove all bugs, leaves, etc. embedded in the radiator fins. Be very careful not to damage the cooling fins or cut your fingers on them.

7   If the coolant level has been dropping consistently and no leaks are detectable, have the cooling system pressure checked at a garage.

15 Fuel system check (every 15,000 miles or 12 months)

Refer to illustrations 15.3 and 15.5

Warning 1: *Gasoline is extremely flammable, so take extra precautions when you work on*

15.3 The inline fuel filter is located underneath the car, ahead of the right rear tire - Inspect the for lines leakage and damage

any part of the fuel system. Don't smoke or allow open flames or bare light bulbs near the work area, and don't work in a garage where a natural gas appliance (such as a water heater or clothes dryer) with a pilot light is present. Since gasoline is carcinogenic, wear latex gloves when there's a possibility of being exposed to fuel, and, if you spill any fuel on your skin, wash it off immediately with soap and water. Mop up any spills immediately and do not store fuel-soaked rags where they could ignite. When you perform any kind of work on the fuel system, wear safety glasses and have a Class B fire extinguisher on hand. The fuel system is under constant pressure, so, before any lines are disconnected, the fuel system pressure must be relieved. See Chapter 4 for more information.
Warning 2: *Your vehicle is fuel injected, so you must relieve the fuel system pressure before servicing fuel system components. The fuel system pressure relief procedure is in Chapter 4.*

1   If you smell gasoline while driving or after the vehicle has been sitting in the sun, inspect the fuel system immediately.

2   Remove the gas filler cap and inspect it for damage and corrosion. The gasket should have an unbroken sealing imprint. If the gasket is damaged, install a new cap.

3   Inspect the fuel supply and return lines for cracks. Make sure that the connections between the fuel lines and the fuel injection system and between the fuel lines and the inline fuel filter are tight **(see illustration)**.

4   Because some parts of the fuel system - the tank and part of the fuel supply and return lines, for example - are underneath the car, you can inspect them more easily with the vehicle raised on a hoist. If that's not possible, raise the vehicle and support it on jackstands.

5   With the vehicle raised and safely supported, inspect the gas tank and filler neck for punctures, cracks and other damage **(see illustration)**. The connection between the filler neck and the tank is particularly critical.

15.5 Inspect the fuel tank filler tube and hose, for leakage and damage - also check the hose clamps for tightness

Sometimes a rubber filler neck will leak because of loose clamps or deteriorated rubber. Inspect all fuel tank mounting brackets and straps to be sure that the tank is securely attached to the vehicle. **Warning:** *Do not, under any circumstances, try to repair a fuel tank (except rubber components). A welding torch or any open flame can easily cause fuel vapors inside the tank to explode.*

6   Carefully check all rubber hoses and metal lines leading away from the fuel tank. Check for loose connections, deteriorated hoses, crimped lines and other damage. Repair or replace damaged sections as necessary (see Chapter 4).

16 Steering and suspension check (every 15,000 miles or 12 months)

Refer to illustrations 16.6, 16.9a, 16.9b, 16.9c, 16.11 and 16.14
Note: *The steering linkage and suspension components should be checked periodically. Worn or damaged suspension and steering linkage components can result in excessive and abnormal tire wear, poor ride quality and vehicle handling, and reduced fuel economy. For detailed illustrations of the steering and suspension components, refer to Chapter 10.*

Suspension strut check

1   Park the car on level ground, turn the engine off and set the parking brake. Check the tire pressures.

2   Push down at one corner of the car, then release it while noting the movement of the body. It should stop moving and come to rest in a level position within one or two bounces.

3   If the car continues to move up and down or if it fails to return to its original position, a worn or weak strut assembly is probably the reason.

4   Repeat the above check at each of the three remaining corners.

5   Raise the car and support it securely on jackstands.

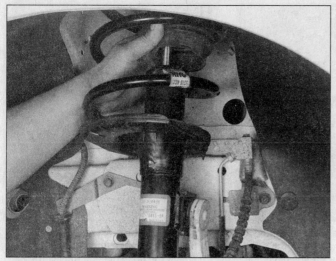

16.6 Check the struts for leakage where the rod goes into the cylinder

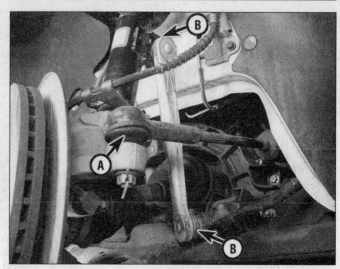

16.9a Inspect the tie rod ends (A) and the stabilizer bar links (B) for damaged grease seals

16.9b Check the steering gear boots for cracks and leaking steering fluid

16.9c Check the stabilizer bar bushings (arrow) for damage or deterioration at the front and the rear of the vehicle

16.11 With the steering wheel in the lock position and the vehicle raised, grasp the front tire as shown and try to move it back-and-forth - if any play is noted, check the steering gear mounts and the tie rod ends for looseness

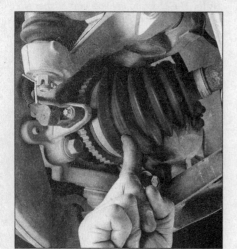

16.14 Inspect the driveaxle boots for damage and deterioration - don't overlook the inner boots on both driveaxles - although harder to inspect, they are just as susceptible to damage and deterioration

6   Check the struts for fluid leakage **(see illustration)**. A light film of fluid is no cause for concern. Make sure that any fluid noted is from the struts and not from some other source. If leakage is noted, replace the struts as a set.

7   Check the struts to be sure that they are securely mounted and undamaged. If damage or wear is noted, replace the struts as a set (front or rear).

8   If the struts must be replaced, refer to Chapter 10 for the procedure.

Steering and suspension check

9   Inspect the steering system components for wear and damage. Look for damaged seals, boots and bushings and leaks of any kind **(see illustrations)**.

10   Clean the lower end of the steering knuckle. Have an assistant grasp the lower edge of the tire and move the wheel in and out while you look for movement at the steering knuckle-to-control arm balljoint. If there is

any movement the suspension balljoint must be replaced.

11   Grasp each front tire at the front and rear edges, push in at the front, pull out at the rear and feel for play in the steering system. If any freeplay is noted, check the steering gear mounts and the tie rod ends for looseness **(see illustration)**.

12   Additional steering and suspension system information and illustrations are in Chapter 10.

Driveaxle boot check

13   Damaged or deteriorated rubber boots can cause serious damage to the CV joints.

14   The rubber boots must be kept clean so wipe them off before inspection. Check the four boots (two on each axle) for deterioration, cracks, holes, and damaged clamps **(see illustration)**. If boots are damaged or deteriorated, they must be replaced.

17.6 You will find an inspection hole like this in each caliper - place a ruler across the hole to determine the thickness of the pad material for both inner and outer pads

17.11 Check along the brake hoses and at each fitting for deterioration and cracks

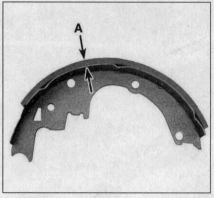

17.13 If the lining is bonded to the brake shoe, measure the lining thickness from the outer surface of the shoe to the surface of the lining at the thinnest point, as shown here. If the lining is riveted to the shoe, measure the lining thickness from the rivet heads

17   Brake check (every 15,000 miles or 12 months)

Warning: *The dust created by the brake system may contain asbestos, which is harmful to your health. Never blow it out with compressed air and don't inhale any of it. Wear an approved filtering mask when working on the brakes. Do not, under any circumstances, use petroleum-based solvents to clean brake parts. Use brake system cleaner or denatured alcohol only.*
Note: *For detailed photographs of the brake system, refer to Chapter 9.*
1   In addition to the specified intervals, the brakes should be inspected every time the wheels are removed or whenever a defect is suspected.
2   Any of the following symptoms could indicate a potential brake system defect: The vehicle pulls to one side when the brake pedal is depressed; the brakes make squealing or dragging noises when applied; brake pedal travel is excessive; the pedal pulsates; brake fluid leaks, usually onto the inside of the tire or wheel.
3   Loosen the wheel lug nuts.
4   Raise the vehicle and place it securely on jackstands.
5   Remove the wheels (see *Jacking and towing* at the front of this book, or your owner's manual, if necessary).

Disc brakes
Refer to illustrations 17.6 and 17.11
6   There are two pads (an outer and an inner) in each caliper. The pads are visible through inspection holes in each caliper **(see illustration)**.
7   Check the pad thickness by looking at each end of the caliper and through the inspection hole in the caliper body. If the lining material is less than the thickness listed in this Chapter's Specifications, replace the pads. **Note:** *The lining material is riveted or bonded to a metal backing plate and the metal plate is not included in this measurement.*
8   If it is difficult to determine the exact thickness of the remaining pad material by the

above method, or if you are concerned about the condition of the pads, remove the calipers, then remove the pads from the calipers for further inspection (refer to Chapter 9).
9   Once the pads are removed from the calipers, clean them with brake cleaner and measure them with a ruler or a vernier caliper.
10   Measure the rotor thickness with a micrometer to make sure that it still has service life remaining. If any rotor is thinner than the specified minimum thickness, replace it (refer to Chapter 9). Even if the rotor has service life remaining, check its condition. Look for scoring, gouging and burned spots. If these conditions exist, remove the rotor and have it resurfaced (see Chapter 9).
11   Before installing the wheels, check all brake lines and hoses for damage, wear, deformities, cracks, corrosion, leakage, bends and twists, particularly the rubber hoses at the calipers **(see illustration)**. Check the clamps for tightness and the connections for leakage. Make sure that all hoses and lines are clear of sharp edges, moving parts, and the exhaust system. If any of the above conditions are noted, repair, reroute or replace the lines and fittings as necessary (see Chapter 9).

Drum brakes
Refer to illustrations 17.13 and 17.15
12   Refer to Chapter 9 and remove the rear brake drums.
13   Check the thickness of the lining on each brake shoe **(see illustration)**. If the lining is less than the thickness listed in this Chapter's Specifications, replace the brake shoes. **Note:** *Keep in mind that the lining material is riveted or bonded to a metal backing plate and the metal portion is not included in this measurement.* Also replace the brake shoes if the lining is cracked, glazed, or contaminated by grease, oil, or brake fluid (see Chapter 9).
14   Check the shoe return and hold-down springs and the adjusting mechanism for damage, deterioration, and incorrect installation. Worn or damaged springs may let the brake linings drag on the drums and wear prematurely.
15   Carefully pull back the wheel cylinder boots and check for leakage **(see illustra-**

tion). Replace the cylinder if you find brake fluid behind a boot (see Chapter 9).
16   Inspect the brake drums for cracks, scoring, deep scratches, and hard spots caused by overheating. Remove small imperfections with emery cloth. Take the drums to a machine shop to be refinished if they are deeply scratched or scored. Replace the drums if they are cracked, overheated, of worn beyond the maximum diameter cast on their outer surfaces. (see Chapter 9).
17   Refer to Chapter 9 and reinstall the drums.

Brake booster check
18   Sit in the driver's seat and perform the following tests.
19   With the brake fully depressed, start the engine. The pedal should move down a little when the engine starts.
20   With the engine running, depress the brake pedal several times. The travel distance should not change.
21   Depress the brake, stop the engine and hold the pedal in for about 30 seconds. The

17.15 Carefully peel back the wheel cylinder dust boot and check for leaking fluid indicating that the cylinder must be replaced

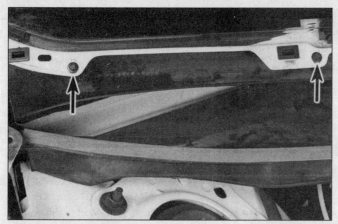

18.3a Remove the screws from the cowl inner panel

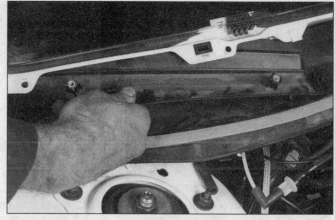

18.3b Then slide the cover toward the center of the vehicle and remove it from the cowl

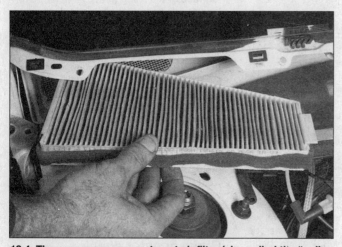

18.4 The passenger compartment air filter (also called the "pollen filter") is located under the cowl on the passenger's side of the vehicle

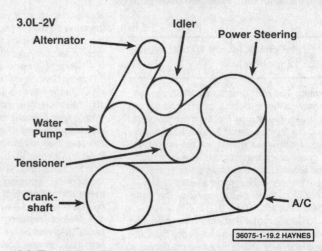

19.2 The routing diagram for the serpentine belt is usually on the fan shroud. This one is for the OHV engine

pedal should neither sink nor rise.

22   Restart the engine, run it for about a minute and turn it off. Then firmly depress the brake several times. The pedal travel should decrease with each application.

23   If your brakes do not operate as described when these tests are performed, the brake booster has failed. Refer to Chapter 9 for the removal procedure.

Parking brake

24   Depress the parking brake pedal to apply the brakes. Verify that the pedal travels five to seven notches when applied and that the car will not move with the brakes applied. The parking brakes on these vehicles require periodic adjustment. For more adjustment procedures on the parking brake, see Chapter 9.

18   Passenger compartment air filter replacement (1997 and later) (every 15,000 miles or 12 months)

Refer to illustrations 18.3a, 8.3b and 18.4

1   The passenger compartment air filter is

an option on 1997 and later vehicles. It removes airborne dust and pollen from the passenger compartment ventilation airflow. The filter is located in front of the windshield, under the cowl vent screen on the passenger side of the car. Open the hood to begin the filter replacement.

2   Rotate and remove the four pushpins from the cowl vent screen. Then remove the push-on clips.

3   Remove the two screws that retain the cowl top inner panel shield, then remove the shield. Slide it toward the center of the car to remove it easily **(see illustrations)**.

4   Remove the filter **(see illustration)**.

5   Installation is the reverse of removal.

19   Drivebelt check and replacement (every 30,000 miles or 24 months)

Refer to illustrations 19.2, 19.4, 19.5 and 19.6

1   All Taurus and Sable engines use a single, serpentine (V-ribbed) drivebelt for all engine-driven accessories which is located at the front of the engine on the passenger's side of the vehicle. The serpentine drivebelt is

a durable, long-lived component, but eventually it will wear out. Although the belt should be inspected at the recommended intervals, replacement may not be necessary for more than 100,000 miles.

2   The drivebelt part number and routing around the accessory pulleys will vary, depending on the accessories installed on your car. Most cars have a drivebelt routing decal on the upper radiator panel or underside of the hood to help during drivebelt installation **(see illustration)**. If the decal is damaged or missing, make a sketch of drivebelt routing before removing the old belt. This can save time and frustration during belt replacement.

Inspection

3   With the engine off, open the hood and locate the drivebelt at the front of the engine. Using your fingers (and a flashlight, if necessary), move along the belt and check for cracks and separation of the belt plies. Inspect both sides of the belt, which means you will have to twist the belt to check the underside. Also check for fraying and glazing, which gives the belt a shiny appearance. Small cracks in the V-groove side of the belt are

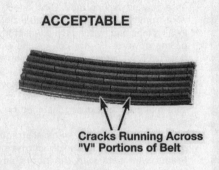

ACCEPTABLE

Cracks Running Across
"V" Portions of Belt

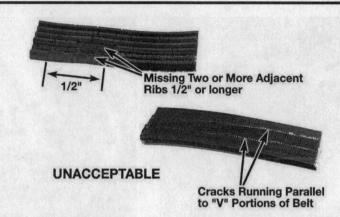

1/2"

Missing Two or More Adjacent
Ribs 1/2" or longer

UNACCEPTABLE

Cracks Running Parallel
to "V" Portions of Belt

19.4 Small cracks in the underside of a V-ribbed belt are acceptable - lengthwise cracks, or missing pieces that cause the belt to make noise, are cause for replacement

normal. Replace the belt if your inspection reveals large cracks, separated plies, missing chunks or glazing of the belt surfaces.

4   Check the ribs on the underside of the belt. They should all be the same depth, with none of the surface uneven **(see illustration)**.

5   The tension of the belt is automatically adjusted by the belt tensioner and does not require any adjustments. Drivebelt wear can be checked by looking at the wear indicator marks on the side of the tensioner body. Locate the belt tensioner at the front of the engine, then find the tensioner operating marks **(see illustration)**. If the indicator mark is outside the MIN - MAX range, replace the belt.

Replacement

Accessory drivebelts

6   To replace the drivebelt, use a 15 mm wrench on the bolt that holds the tensioner pulley **(see illustration)**. To relieve belt tension, rotate the tensioner away from the drivebelt.

7   Remove the belt from the auxiliary components and carefully release the tensioner.

8   Route the new belt over the various pulleys, again rotating the tensioner to allow the belt to be installed then release the belt tensioner. Make sure the belt fits properly into the pulley grooves. The drivebelt must be completely engaged.

Water pump drivebelt on 2001 and later OHC engines

Note: *Overhead Camshaft (OHC) Duratec engines are equipped with a water pump and drivebelt located on the opposite side of the engine from the accessory drivebelt.*

Models without belt tensioner

Refer to illustration 19.10

9   The water pump drivebelt is located at the left end of the engine and is driven by a pulley attached to the end of the front cylinder bank exhaust camshaft. The belt and pulley are protected by a cover. The belt is of a unique design, called a "stretchy belt," which provides tension without the use of a mechanical tensioner.

10   Disconnect the cable from the negative terminal of the battery (see Chapter 5). Remove the cover from over the pulley. Insert a length of flexible material such as a leather or plastic strap under the belt at the pulley at the end of the camshaft, then have an assistant rotate the engine (clockwise) by using a socket and breaker bar on the crankshaft pulley bolt, while you feed the remover strap between the belt and the pulley **(see illustration)**. Pull the strap quickly to force the belt from the pulley on the camshaft. **Caution:** *Do not use hard plastic or metal tools to pry the belt off; it can be easily damaged.* **Note:** *If the belt is not going to be re-used, you can simply cut it off.* **Note:** *It will be necessary to remove the fender splash shield to access the crankshaft pulley bolt (see Chapter 11).*

11   Route the new belt under the water pump pulley, then over the pulley on the camshaft, and have your assistant rotate the engine again; the belt should pop over the pulley on the camshaft. Make sure the belt is positioned properly on both pulleys.

12   Reinstall the cover and tighten the fasteners securely.

Models with a belt tensioner

13   Remove the water pump pulley cover.

14   Rotate the drivebelt tensioner clockwise and remove the belt.

15   Installation is the reverse of removal.

19.5 Belt wear indicator marks are located on the side of the tensioner body - when the belt reaches the maximum wear mark it must be replaced

19.6 Rotate the tensioner arm to relieve belt tension

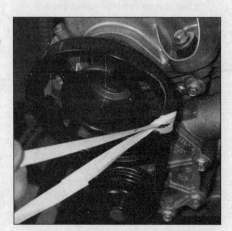

19.10 Feed the remover strap between the belt and the pulley

20.5 Use a plug wire removal tool to disconnect the wires from the plugs. Pull only on the boot, not on the wire itself

21.2 Release the clips (arrows) that hold the air filter housing halves together

20 Ignition system component check and replacement (every 30,000 miles or 24 months)

Refer to illustrations 20.5 and 20.9

Spark plug wires

Note 1: *Ford recommends that every time a spark plug wire is disconnected from a spark plug or the coil, silicone dielectric compound (a white grease available at auto parts stores) should be applied to the inside of each boot before reconnection. Use a small standard screwdriver to coat the entire inside surface of each boot with a thin layer of the compound.*

Note 2: *2000 and later model 3.0L OHC engines have six individual coils, one mounted over each spark plug. Since they do not have a coil pack as in previous models, they do not have spark plug wires.*

1   Inspect the spark plug wires at the same time new spark plugs are installed and replace the plug wires if necessary. It is best

20.9 Remove each spark plug wire from the ignition coil pack - check for looseness, damage, corrosion or deterioration

practice to replace spark plug wires as a matched set, but individual wires can be replaced in an emergency.

2   One easy way to identify bad wires is to look at them while the engine is running. In a dark, well-ventilated garage, start the engine and look at each plug wire. (Be careful not to contact with any moving engine parts.) If there is a break in the wire, you will see arcing or a small spark at the damaged area. If arcing is noticed, replace the wires.

3   Another way to check the plug wires, is to check for continuity between the ends of each plug wire with an ohmmeter. Typically there should be approximately 5000 ohms of resistance per foot on each plug wire. If the plug wire has an open or has too much resistance it should be replaced.

4   Inspect the spark plug wires one at a time, beginning with the spark plug for the number one cylinder to prevent confusion (the cylinder toward the right rear of the engine compartment). Label each original plug wire with a piece of tape marked with the cylinder number. Reinstall the plug wires in the correct order for proper engine operation.

5   Disconnect the plug wire from the first spark plug. A removal tool can be used (**see illustration**), or you can grab the wire boot, twist it slightly and pull the wire free. Do not pull on the wire itself, only on the rubber boot.

6   Push the wire and boot back onto the end of the spark plug. The wire terminal and the boot should fit snugly. If not, detach the wire and boot once more and use a pair of pliers to carefully crimp the metal connector inside the wire boot until it connects securely.

7   Using a clean rag, wipe the entire length of the wire to remove built-up dirt and grease.

8   When the wire is clean, check for burns, cracks and other damage. Do not bend the wire sharply or you might break the conductor.

9   Spark wires are secured to the coil pack assembly by locking tabs. Disconnect each wire from the coil pack by squeezing the locking tabs and twisting the connector while pulling upward. Do not pull on the wire or boot without squeezing the locking tabs. Check the wire terminal for corrosion and a tight fit (**see illustration**). Reinstall the wire.

10   Inspect each spark plug wire, making sure that each is securely fastened on each end.

11   If new spark plug wires are required, purchase a set for your specific engine model. Precut wire sets with the boots already installed are available. Remove and replace the wires one at a time to avoid mix-ups in the firing order. If a mix-up occurs, refer to the Specifications at the beginning this Chapter.

Ignition coil pack

12   Remove dirt and grease from the coil pack with a clean, dry cloth.

13   Inspect the coil pack for cracks, damage and carbon tracking. If damage exists refer to Chapter 5 for the replacement procedure.

21 Air filter replacement (every 30,000 miles or 24 months)

Refer to illustrations 21.2 and 21.3

1   Purchase a new filter element for your specific engine.

2   Release the retaining clips to remove the air filter cover (**see illustration**). Move the cover to side, being careful not to stretch or kink the wiring for the mass airflow sensor.

3   Remove the filter element (**see illustration**).

4   Place the new air filter element in the housing and reinstall the cover.

5   The remainder of the installation is the reverse of removal.

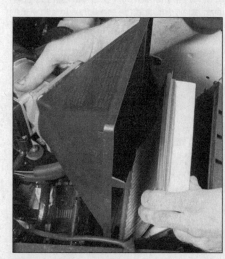

21.3 Carefully pull the inner housing cover inward, toward the engine, and remove the filter

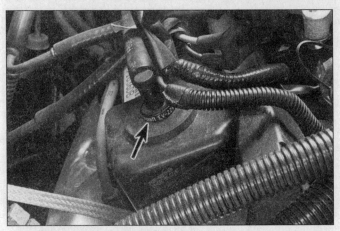

22.1 The PCV valve on OHV engines is located in the rear valve cover (arrow), toward the right side of the engine compartment

22.2 With the engine running at idle, remove the PCV valve and verify that vacuum can be felt at the end of the valve

22   Positive crankcase ventilation (PCV) valve check (every 30,000 miles or 24 months)

Refer to illustrations 22.1 and 22.2

Note: *To maintain efficient operation of the PCV system, clean the hoses and check the PCV valve at the intervals recommended in the maintenance schedule. For additional information on the PCV system, refer to Chapter 6.*

1   On OHV engines, the PCV valve is located in the rear valve cover, toward the right side of the engine compartment **(see illustration)**. On OHC engines, the PCV valve is installed in an oil separator tube, attached to the lower part of the intake manifold.

2   Start the engine and allow it to idle, then disconnect the PCV valve from the valve cover or intake manifold and feel for vacuum at the end of the valve **(see illustration)**. If vacuum is felt, the PCV valve and system are working properly (see Chapter 6 for additional PCV system information).

3   If no vacuum is felt, remove the valve and check for vacuum at the hose. If vacuum

is present at the hose but not at the valve, replace the valve. If no vacuum is felt at the hose, check for a plugged or cracked hose between the PCV valve and the intake plenum. Also inspect the hose for damage, wear and deterioration. Make sure it fits snugly on the fittings.

4   Check the rubber grommet in the valve cover, intake manifold, or oil separator for cracks and distortion. If it's damaged, replace it.

5   If the PCV valve is clogged, the hose also is probably plugged. If the hose is restricted, replace it.

6   If necessary, install a new PCV valve.

23   Fuel filter replacement (every 30,000 miles or 24 months)

Refer to illustration 23.4

Warning: *Gasoline is extremely flammable, so be very careful when you work on any part of the fuel system. Don't smoke or allow open flames or bare light bulbs near the work area, and don't work in a garage where a natural gas appliance (such as a water heater or clothes dryer) with a pilot light is present. Since gasoline is carcinogenic, wear latex gloves when there's a possibility of being exposed to fuel. If you spill any fuel on your skin, wash it off immediately with soap and water. Mop up any spills immediately and do not store fuel-soaked rags where they could ignite. When you perform any kind of work on the fuel system, wear safety glasses and have a Class B fire extinguisher on hand.*

1   The inline fuel filter is mounted under the car on the right side, in front of the gas tank.

2   Raise the vehicle and support it securely on jackstands. Inspect the fittings at both ends of the filter to see if they're clean. If more than a light coating of dust is present, clean the fittings before proceeding.

3   Refer to Chapter 4 and relieve the fuel system pressure.

4   Disconnect the hairpin-type fuel line fitting retainers from the filter by carefully pry-

ing upward with a small screwdriver **(see illustration)**. Separate the fuel line from the connector nipples on both ends of the filter.

5   After the lines are detached, check the fittings for damage and distortion. If they were damaged in any way during removal, new ones must be used when the lines are reattached to the new filter (if new clips are packaged with the filter, be sure to use them in place of the originals).

6   Remove the filter from the bracket and install the new fuel filter in the same direction, being careful to note the direction of the flow arrow on the filter. It should point toward the engine.

7   The rubber grommets in the fuel filter bracket are electrically conductive to minimize electrostatic charge buildup in the fuel system. If you replace the filter bracket, use the original grommets or new ones that meet the Ford original-equipment specification.

8   Carefully push each fuel line onto the fittings on the filter until the line is seated. Then attach the hairpin clips and make sure the fuel line is securely fastened to the fuel filter.

9   Start the engine and check for fuel leaks.

24   Exhaust system check (every 30,000 miles or 24 months)

Refer to illustrations 24.2a, 24.2b, 24.3a, 24.3b and 24.4

1   With the engine cold (at least three hours after the car has been driven), check the complete exhaust system from the engine to the end of the tailpipe. Ideally, the inspection should be done with the vehicle on a hoist to permit unrestricted access. If a hoist isn't available, raise the vehicle and support it securely on jackstands.

2   The exhaust system on Taurus and Sable models is a complicated, welded assembly that has two catalytic converters, a Y-pipe that bolts to the manifolds, a muffler, a tail pipe and the associated brackets. Inspect the exhaust flanges that attach to both manifolds and the

23.4 Use a small screwdriver to pry off the fuel line fitting retaining clips at both ends of the filter

24.2a Check the exhaust flanges at both manifolds for exhaust leaks - also be sure that the nuts are securely tightened

24.2b These are some of the brackets that attach the Y-pipe to the engine and body - inspect all brackets for looseness and damage

24.3a Heatshields (arrow) protect the underbody of the car from high temperatures - be sure they are installed tightly

brackets that mount the Y-pipe to the engine and body **(see illustrations)**.
3   Inspect heat shields and pipe brackets for looseness and damage **(see illustrations)**.

24.3b These vehicles have many brackets to secure the exhaust system - check all for looseness and damage

24.4 Check the rubber insulators on exhaust brackets for damage and deterioration

4   Check the exhaust pipes and connections for evidence of leaks, severe corrosion and damage. Make sure that all brackets and hangers are in good condition and tight **(see illustration)**.
5   At the same time, inspect the underside of the body for holes, corrosion, open seams, etc. that may allow exhaust gases to enter the passenger compartment. Seal all body openings with silicone or body putty.
6   Rattles and other noises can often be traced to the exhaust system, especially the mounts and hangers. Try to move the pipes, muffler and catalytic converters. If the components can come in contact with the body or suspension parts, secure the exhaust system with new mounts.
7   Check the running condition of the engine by inspecting inside the end of the tailpipe. The exhaust deposits here are an indication of the engine state of tune. If the pipe is black and sooty or coated with white deposits, the engine may need a tune-up, including a thorough fuel system inspection and service.

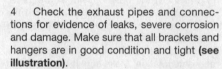

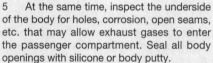

25.6 Remove all but two of the transaxle pan bolts, then pry the pan free of the gasket and allow the fluid to drain

25 Automatic transaxle fluid and filter change (every 30,000 miles or 24 months)

Refer to illustrations 25.6, 25.7, 25.9a, 25.9b and 25.10
1   The transaxle fluid should be drained and replaced at the specified intervals. Because the fluid will remain hot long after driving, do this job only after the engine and transaxle have cooled completely. **Note:** *The transaxle fluid capacities in this Chapter's Specifications are for complete refill, including the torque converter. Draining the fluid as described here will not drain the torque converter, which holds 4 to 5 quarts. Therefore, do not fill the transaxle with the total amount of fluid listed in this Chapter's Specifications. Follow the instructions at the end of this procedure and check the fluid level on the dipstick several times.*
2   Before beginning work, purchase the specified transaxle fluid (*see Recommended lubricants and fluids at the front of this Chapter*), a new filter and gaskets. Never reuse the old filter or gasket.
3   Other tools necessary for this job include jackstands to support the vehicle in a raised position, a drain pan that holds at least eight quarts, newspapers, and clean rags.
4   Raise the vehicle and support it securely on jackstands.
5   With the drain pan in place, remove all of the transaxle pan mounting bolts except the rear corners. Loosen those two bolts about three turns but leave them in place to support the pan.
6   Carefully pry the transaxle pan loose with a screwdriver and allow the fluid to drain **(see illustration)**. Don't nick or otherwise damage the pan or transaxle gasket surfaces or leaks could develop.
7   Remove the remaining bolts, pan and gasket. Carefully clean the gasket surface of the transaxle to remove all traces of the old gasket and sealant **(see illustration)**.

25.7 Be sure to clean all traces of the old gasket from the pan before installing a new one

25.9a Grasp the filter with two hands, then pull straight down to separate it from the transaxle

25.9b Pry out the old filter seal - be careful not to nick or gouge the seal mating surface

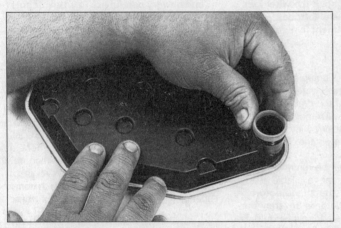

25.10 Install a new filter seal on the transaxle filter

26.4 The radiator drain fitting is located at the lower left corner of the radiator (arrow)

8   Drain the rest of the fluid from the pan, clean it with solvent, and dry it thoroughly. If you dry the pan with a cloth, be sure to remove all traces of lint, which could clog the valve body after reassembly.

9   Remove the old filter and the filter seal from the transaxle **(see illustrations)**.

10   Install a new O-ring seal on the new filter **(see illustrations)** and install the new filter in the transaxle.

11   Make sure the gasket surface on the transaxle pan is clean, then install a new gasket. Put the pan in place against the transaxle and install the bolts. Working around the pan, tighten each bolt a little at a time until the final torque figure listed in this Chapter's Specifications is reached. Don't overtighten the bolts.

12   Lower the vehicle and add four quarts of automatic transaxle fluid through the filler tube (see Section 7).

13   With the transaxle in Park and the parking brake set, run the engine at a fast idle, but don't race it.

14   Move the gear selector through each range and back to Park. Check the fluid level. Add fluid if needed to reach the correct level.

15   Check under the vehicle for leaks during the first few trips.

26 Cooling system servicing (draining, flushing and refilling) (every 30,000 miles or 24 months)

Refer to illustrations 26.4 and 26.5

Warning: *Do not allow antifreeze to contact your skin or painted surfaces of the vehicle. Rinse off spills immediately with plenty of water. Antifreeze is highly toxic if ingested. Never leave antifreeze lying around in an open container or in puddles on the floor, children and pets may be attracted by it's sweet smell and may drink it. Check with local authorities about disposing of used antifreeze. Many communities have collection centers which will see that antifreeze is disposed of safely.*

1   The cooling system should be drained, flushed with clean water, and refilled periodically to replenish the antifreeze mixture and prevent rust and corrosion. When the cooling system is serviced, all hoses and the radiator cap should be checked and replaced if necessary.

Draining

2   Apply the parking brake and block the wheels. If the vehicle has just been driven, allow the engine to cool before beginning this procedure.

3   When the engine is completely cool, remove the pressure relief cap on the expansion tank.

4   Move a large container under the radiator drain to catch the coolant. The drain fitting is located at the bottom left side (driver's side) of the radiator **(see illustration)**. A pair of pliers may be required to open the drain fitting.

5   After the coolant stops flowing out of

26.5 The block drain plugs (arrow) are generally located about one to two inches above the oil pan rail. There is one on each side of the engine block

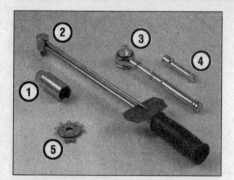

27.2 Tools required for changing spark plugs

1 **Spark plug socket** - This will have special padding inside to protect the spark plugs' porcelain insulator
2 **Torque wrench** - Although not mandatory, using this tool is the best way to ensure the plugs are tightened properly
3 **Ratchet** - Standard hand tool to fit the spark plug socket
4 **Extension** - Depending on model and accessories, you may need special extensions and universal joints to reach one or more of the plugs
5 **Spark plug gap gauge** - This gauge for checking the gap comes in a variety of styles. Make sure the gap for your engine is included

the radiator, move the container under the engine block drain plugs and allow the coolant in the block to drain **(see illustration)**. The block drain plugs are small pipe plugs with internal hexheads. Each bank of a V-type engine has a separate drain plug, but you may not be able to reach the drain for the rear bank in these vehicles. If not, opening the drain in one bank should be empty the block satisfactorily.
6   While the coolant is draining, check the condition of the radiator hoses, heater hoses and clamps. Refer to Section 13 if necessary.
7   Replace any damaged clamps or hoses. Refer to Chapter 3 for replacement procedures.

27.5a Spark plug manufacturers recommend using a wire-type gauge when checking the gap. If the wire does not slide between the electrodes with a slight drag, adjustment is required

Flushing

8   When the system is completely drained, flush the radiator with fresh water from a hose until water runs clear at the drain. The flushing action of the water will remove most sediment from the radiator but will not remove rust and scale from the engine and radiator tube surfaces.
9   These deposits can be removed by the chemical action of a cleaner available at auto parts stores. Follow the manufacturer's instructions. If the radiator is severely corroded, damaged or leaking, it should be removed (see Chapter 3) and taken to a radiator repair shop.

Refilling

10   Close and tighten the radiator drain. Install and tighten the block drain plugs.
11   Place the heater temperature control in the maximum heat position.
12   Slowly add new coolant (a 50:50 mixture of water and antifreeze) to the expansion tank until it is full up to the FULL HOT mark.
13   Leave the pressure relief cap off and run

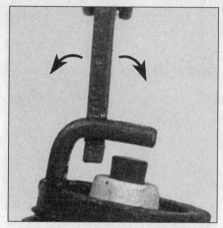

27.5b To change the gap, bend the side electrode only, as indicated by the arrows, and be very careful not to crack or chip the porcelain insulator around the center electrode

the engine in a well-ventilated area until the thermostat opens (coolant will begin flowing through the radiator and the upper radiator hose will become hot).
14   Turn the engine off and let it cool. Add more coolant mixture to bring the level back up to the FULL HOT mark on the expansion tank.
15   Squeeze the upper radiator hose to expel air, then add more coolant mixture if necessary. Replace the pressure relief cap.
16   Start the engine, allow it to reach normal operating temperature, and check for leaks.

27 Spark plug check and replacement (every 60,000 miles or 48 months)

Refer to illustrations 27.2, 27.5a, 27.5b, 27.7, 27.9, 27.11a and 27.11b
Note: *On vehicles equipped with 3.0L DOHC engines, it may be necessary to remove the upper intake manifold for access to the spark plugs near the firewall.*
1   On OHV engines, the spark plugs are in

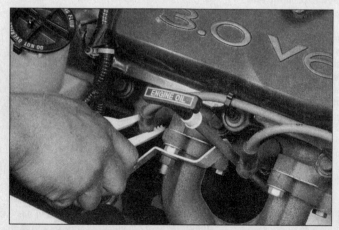

27.7 When removing the spark plug wires, pull only on the boot and twist it back and forth

27.9 Use a spark plug socket and a ratchet to remove and install the spark plugs

27.11a Apply a thin film of antiseize compound to the spark plug threads to prevent damage to the cylinder head

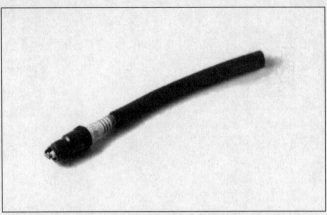

27.11b A length of 3/8-inch ID rubber hose will save time and prevent damaged threads when installing the spark plugs

the cylinder heads, below the valve covers. On OHC engines, the spark plugs are accessible through the valve covers, between the camshafts.

2   The basic tools for spark plug replacement are a spark plug socket that fits onto a ratchet (spark plug sockets are padded inside to prevent damage to the porcelain insulators on the plugs), various extensions, and a gap gauge to check and adjust the gaps on the new plugs (see illustration). A special plug wire removal tool is available for separating the wire boots from the spark plugs, but it isn't absolutely necessary. A torque wrench should be used to tighten the new plugs.

3   The best approach when replacing the spark plugs is to purchase the new ones in advance, adjust them to the proper gap, and replace the plugs one at a time. When buying the new spark plugs, be sure to obtain the correct plug type for your particular engine. This information is in the Specifications Section a the beginning of this Chapter, on the emission control information label under the hood, or in the car owner's manual. If differences exist between the plug specified on the emission label, Specifications Section, or in the owner's manual, assume that the emission label is correct.

4   Let the engine cool completely before trying to remove any of the plugs. OHC engines have aluminum cylinder heads, which can be damaged if the spark plugs are removed when the engine is hot. While you are waiting for the engine to cool, check the

new plugs for defects and adjust the gaps.

5   Check the gap by inserting the proper thickness gauge between the electrodes at the tip of the plug (see illustration). The gap between the electrodes should be as specified on the emission control information label. The wire gauge should just slide between the electrodes with a slight drag. If the gap is incorrect, use the adjuster on the gauge body to bend the curved side electrode slightly until the specified gap is obtained (see illustration). If the side electrode is not exactly over the center electrode, bend it with the adjuster until it is. Check for cracks in the porcelain insulator. If any are found, do not use the plug.

6   On 1996 through 1999 model OHC engines, disconnect the wiring harness from the ignition coil pack, remove the four coil hold-down screws, and remove the coil pack for access to the spark plugs in cylinders 1, 2, and 3 (the rear bank). On 2000 and later model OHC engines, each spark plug has its own coil. Remove the screws securing the individual ignition coil for each plug, then set the coil aside.

7   With the engine cool, remove the spark plug wire from one spark plug. Pull only on the boot at the end of the wire, do not pull on the wire (see illustration). Use a plug wire removal tool if available.

8   If compressed air is available, use it to blow any dirt or foreign material away from the spark plug hole. A bicycle pump will also work. The idea is to eliminate the possibility of debris falling into the cylinder as the spark

plug is removed.

9   Place the spark plug socket over the plug and remove the plug from the engine by turning it counterclockwise (see illustration).

10   Compare the spark plug to those shown in the photos on the inside back cover to get an indication of the general running condition of the engine.

11   Apply a small amount of antiseize compound to the spark plug threads (see illustration). Take care not to get any anti-seize on the porcelain or the electrodes of the plug. Install one of the new plugs into the hole until you can no longer turn it with your fingers, then tighten it with a torque wrench (if available) or the ratchet. It is a good idea to slip a short length of rubber hose over the end of the plug to use as a tool to thread it into place (see illustration). The hose will grip the plug well enough to turn it, but will start to slip if the plug begins to cross-thread in the hole. This will prevent damaged threads and the accompanying repair costs.

12   Before pushing the spark plug wire onto the end of the plug, inspect it following the procedures in Section 20.

13   Attach the plug wire to the new spark plug, again using a twisting motion on the boot until it is seated on the spark plug.

14   Repeat the procedure for the remaining spark plugs, replacing them one at a time to prevent mixing up the spark plug wires.

15   On 1996 to 1999 OHC engines, reinstall the ignition coil pack, or reconnect the individual coils on 2000 and later OHC engines.

Notes

Chapter 2 Part A
Overhead valve (OHV) engine

Contents

Specifications

General

Cylinder numbers - drivebelt end (right) to transaxle end (left)	
Rear bank	1-2-3
Front bank	4-5-6
Firing order	1-4-2-5-3-6
Compression pressure	Lowest cylinder within 15 psi of highest cylinder; 100 psi minimum
Timing chain deflection	6 degrees
Collapsed tappet gap (nominal)	0.085 to 0.185 inch

1-4-2-5-3-6

Cylinder location and coil
terminal identification

Camshaft

Lobe lift	
1996 to 1999 (intake and exhaust)	0.260 inch
2000 and later	
Intake	0.251 inch
Exhaust	0.264 inch
Maximum lobe lift wear	0.005 inch

Torque specifications

Ft lbs (unless otherwise specified)

Note: *One foot-pound (ft-lb) of torque is equivalent to 12 inch-pounds (in-lbs) of torque. Torque values below approximately 15 ft-lbs are expressed in inch-pounds, since most foot-pound torque wrenches are not accurate at these smaller values.*

Alternator brace-to-upper manifold bolts and nuts	108 to 168 in-lbs
Alternator-to-bracket bolt	27
Alternator-to-cylinder head bolt	35
Camshaft position sensor bolt	17
Camshaft sprocket-to-camshaft bolt	37 to 51
Camshaft thrust plate bolts	88 in-lbs
Connecting rod cap nuts	23 to 28
Crankshaft damper-to-crankshaft bolt	93 to 121
Crankshaft position sensor bolts	
1996 to 1999	45 to 61 in-lbs
2000 and later	89 in-lbs
Crankshaft pulley-to-damper bolts	30 to 44
Cylinder head bolts	
1996 to 1998	
Step 1	52 to 66
Step 2	Loosen 360 degrees (1 turn)
Step 3	34 to 40
Step 4	63 to 73
1999	
Step 1	35 to 39
Step 2	Loosen 360 degrees (1 turn)
Step 3	20 to 24
Step 4	Tighten an additional 85 to 90 degrees
Step 5	Tighten an additional 85 to 90 degrees

Torque specifications (continued)

Ft lbs (unless otherwise specified)

Note: *One foot-pound (ft-lb) of torque is equivalent to 12 inch-pounds (in-lbs) of torque. Torque values below approximately 15 ft-lbs are expressed in inch-pounds, since most foot-pound torque wrenches are not accurate at these smaller values.*

Cylinder head bolts (continued)	
2000 and later	
Step 1	37
Step 2	Loosen 360 degrees (1 turn)
Step 3	22
Step 4	Tighten an additional 90 degrees
Step 5	Tighten an additional 90 degrees
Driveplate-to-crankshaft bolts	54 to 64
EGR tube connector-to-exhaust manifold	30 to 34
EGR tube-to-EGR valve and exhaust manifold	26 to 47
EGR valve-to-upper intake manifold bolts	15 to 22
Engine front cover-to-block bolts	15 to 22
Engine anti-roll strut brace and strut bolts (2000 and later models)	35
Engine and transaxle support bracket-to-transaxle bolts	40 to 53
Engine and transaxle support (engine mount)-to-bracket bolt	57 to 76
Engine and transaxle support (engine mount)-to-subframe bolts	57 to 76
Exhaust manifold bolts and studs	
1996 to 1999	15 to 18
2000 and later	
Step 1	89 in-lbs
Step 2	16
Exhaust Y-pipe-to-exhaust manifold nuts	25 to 34
Front engine support (engine mount)-to-engine block bolts	48 to 55
Front engine support (engine mount)-to-subframe bolt	57 to 76
Front subframe-to-body bolts	57 to 75
Ignition coil bracket-to-cylinder head bolts	30 to 40
Intake manifold-to-cylinder head bolts	
1996 to 1999	
Step 1	15 to 22
Step 2	20 to 23
2000 and later	
Step 1	132 in-lbs
Step 2	24
Oil pan-to-block bolts	89 to 123 in-lbs
Oil pump-to-engine block bolt	30 to 40
Power steering bracket-to-cylinder head bolt	30 to 40
Rocker arm pivot-to-cylinder head bolts	
Step 1	72 to 132 in-lbs
Step 2	20 to 28
Upper intake manifold-to-lower intake manifold bolts and studs	
1996 to 1999	15 to 22
2000	
Step 1	15
Step 2	18
2001 and later	
Step 1	hand-tight
Step 2	89 in-lbs
Valve cover screws or studs	89 to 123 in-lbs
Valve lifter guide plate-to- block bolts	89 to 123 in-lbs
Water outlet-to-intake manifold bolts	89 to 123 in-lbs
Water pump pulley-to-hub bolts	15 to 22
Water pump-to-front cover bolts	71 to 106 in-lbs

1   General Information

Refer to illustrations 1.1a, 1.1b and 1.1c

This part of Chapter 2 covers in-vehicle repairs for the 3.0 liter overhead valve V6 engine **(see illustrations)**. This version of the 3.0L V6 engine features a cast iron engine block and cast iron cylinder heads. The camshaft is located in the engine block and the valves (two valves per cylinder) are actuated by pushrods and rocker arms.

All information on engine removal and installation, as well as engine block and cylinder head overhaul, is in Part C of Chapter 2.

The following repair procedures are based on the assumption that the engine is installed in the vehicle. If the engine has been removed and mounted on a stand, many of the steps in this part of Chapter 2 will not apply.

The Specifications in this part of Chapter 2 apply only to the procedures in this part. Part C contains other specifications for cylinder head and engine block service.

2   Repair operations possible with the engine in the vehicle

Many major repairs can be accomplished without removing the engine from the vehicle. Clean the engine compartment and the exterior of the engine with a pressure washer or degreaser solvent before beginning work. Cleaning the engine and engine compartment will make repairs easier and help to keep dirt out of the engine.

It may help to remove the hood for bet-

1.1a Front view of the 3.0L overhead valve V6 engine

1.1b Left-hand bank view of the 3.0L overhead valve V6 engine

1.1c Right-hand bank view of the 3.0L overhead valve V6 engine

3.6a Mark the TDC line on the crankshaft damper with white paint to help align it with the pointer on the front cover (arrow)

ter access to the engine (refer to Chapter 11, if necessary.)

If the engine has vacuum, exhaust, oil, or coolant leaks that indicate the need for gasket replacement, repairs can usually be accomplished with the engine in the vehicle. The intake and exhaust manifold gaskets, the engine front cover gasket, the oil pan gasket, crankshaft oil seals, and cylinder head gaskets are all accessible with the engine in the vehicle.

Exterior engine components, such as the intake and exhaust manifolds, the oil pan, the water pump, the starter motor, the alternator, and many fuel system components also can be serviced with the engine installed.

Because the cylinder heads can be removed without removing the engine, valve train components can be serviced with the engine in the vehicle. The timing chain and sprockets also can be replaced without removing the engine. However, because of space limitations, the camshaft <u>cannot</u> be removed with the engine in the vehicle.

In some cases - caused by a lack of equipment - pistons, piston rings, connecting rods, and rod bearings can be replaced with the engine in the vehicle. This is not recommended, however, because of the cleaning and preparation that must be done to the components involved.

3 Top Dead Center (TDC) for number one piston - locating

Refer to illustrations 3.6a and 3.6b
Note: *Although this engine does not have a distributor, timing marks on the crankshaft damper and a stationary pointer on the engine front cover will help you to locate Top Dead Center (TDC) for cylinders 1 and 5.*

1 Top dead center (TDC) is the highest point in the cylinder that each piston reaches as it travels upward when the crankshaft turns. Each piston reaches TDC on the compression stroke and on the exhaust stroke, but TDC usually refers to piston position on the compression stroke.

2 Positioning one or more pistons at TDC is an essential part of many procedures such as rocker arm removal, valve adjustment, and timing chain replacement.

3 To place any piston at TDC, turn the crankshaft using one of the methods described below. When you look at the front of the engine (right side of the engine compartment), crankshaft rotation is clockwise.
Warning: *Before using any of the following methods to turn the crankshaft, be sure the transmission is in park. Also disconnect the ignition wiring harness connector from the*

side of the coil pack assembly.

a) *The best way to turn the crankshaft is to use a large socket and breaker bar on the crankshaft damper bolt on the front of the crankshaft.*

b) *You also can use a remote starter switch connected to the S (switch) and B (battery) terminals of the starter relay. Operate the remote switch in short intervals until the piston is close to TDC. Then use a socket and breaker bar for the final rotation to TDC.*

c) *If an assistant is available to operate the ignition switch in short intervals, you can rotate the crankshaft until the piston is close to TDC. Then use a socket and breaker bar for the final rotation to TDC.*

4 Remove the spark plug from number 1 cylinder and install a compression gauge in its place.

5 Rotate the crankshaft by one of the methods described in step 3, above, until a compression reading is indicated on the gauge. The piston should be approaching TDC.

6 While observing the timing marks, complete the rotation with a socket and breaker bar until the timing marks align **(see illustration)**. If you go past TDC, rotate the engine backwards (counterclockwise) until the timing marks indicate that the piston is before

3.6b The graduations on the crankshaft damper (arrow) indicate that the engine is Before Top Dead Center (BTDC) in the view shown here

4.4 The forward valve cover is shown here with the spark plug wires removed for clarity. Removing the coil assembly will provide more room for valve cover removal

TDC **(see illustration)**. Then rotate the crankshaft clockwise until the marks align. Final rotation should always be clockwise to remove slack from the timing chain and ensure that the piston is truly at TDC.

7   After locating TDC for number one piston, TDC can be located for the remaining cylinders by rotating the crankshaft clockwise in 120-degree increments and following the firing order (i.e. 120-degrees rotation from no. 1 TDC places no. 4 at TDC, another 120-degrees rotation places no. 2 at TDC, etc.).

4   Valve covers - removal and installation

Note: *The valve covers have integral (built-in) gaskets that should last the life of the engine. If the valve covers are removed, they can be reinstalled with the original gaskets and a small amount of RTV sealant.*

Removal

Refer to illustrations 4.4, 4.5 and 4.6

1   Disconnect the cable from the negative battery terminal.

2   Disconnect the spark plug wires from the spark plugs.

3   Remove the ignition wiring and coil bracket from the forward valve cover and move it out of the way.

4   Remove the forward (left-hand) valve cover as follows **(see illustration)**:

 a) *Disconnect the PCV hose and remove the oil filler cap.*

 b) *Remove the engine sensor harness brackets from the valve cover studs. Then remove the sensor harness retaining nuts and move the harness out of the way.*

5   Remove the rear (right-hand) valve cover as follows **(see illustration)**:

 a) *Remove the upper intake manifold (see Section 7).*

 b) *Place a shop towel over the lower intake manifold to keep out dirt, small tools, and stray lockwashers.*

 c) *Loosen the nut on the lower tube that connects the EGR valve to the exhaust manifold. Rotate the tube out of the way.*

 d) *If you are replacing the valve cover with a new one, remove the PCV valve for use in the new cover.*

 e) *Remove the engine sensor harness brackets from the valve cover studs. Then remove the sensor harness retaining nuts and move the harness out of the way.*

6   Remove the valve cover bolts and studs, noting their locations, and carefully slide a sharp, thin-bladed knife between the valve cover and the cylinder head at the point where the intake manifold mates to the cylinder head at two places on each valve cover **(see illustration)**. **Caution:** *Be careful not to cut the valve cover gasket. Cut only the RTV sealant loose from the cylinder head and be sure that the sealant does not pull the gasket out of the valve cover.*

7   If necessary, remove the gasket from the valve cover.

Installation

8   Be sure all bolt and stud threads are clean. You can oil the threads with one or two drops of clean engine oil to aid installation.

4.5 Place a clean shop towel over the lower intake manifold while removing and reinstalling the rear valve cover

4.6 Use a sharp knife, scraper, and thin chisel to cut the beads of RTV sealant at the joints where the intake manifold meets the cylinder heads

5.2a Remove the bolt and pivot from each rocker arm to be removed

5.2b To remove just a pushrod, loosen the rocker arm bolt and turn the rocker to the side for pushrod access

9   Clean the valve cover gasket channel with a clean, dry shop towel and use a suitable solvent to remove any traces of RTV sealant.

10   **Caution:** *Be sure the gasket is installed and aligned correctly in the valve cover channel; it should lie flat in the channel. If installed incorrectly, the gasket may leak oil.* Place the gasket in the channel and align the fastener holes. Hold the head of each fastener and slide the gasket over each fastener to hold it in place.

11   Before applying RTV sealant, clean the sealing surfaces with denatured alcohol. Then apply a bead of RTV sealant at the step, or joint, where the intake manifold meets the cylinder head at two places on each side.

12   Lower the valve cover straight down onto the cylinder head and install the bolts and studs. Working from the center out in a spiral pattern, tighten the bolts to the torque listed in this Chapter's Specifications.

13   The remainder of installation is the reverse of removal.

5   Rocker arms and pushrods - removal, inspection and installation

Removal

Refer to illustrations 5.2a, 5.2b and 5.3

1   Refer to Section 4 and remove the valve covers as required.

2   Remove the rocker arm retaining bolt for each rocker arm to be removed **(see illustration)**; then remove the rocker arm and pivot. If you are removing more that one rocker arm, place each one, along with its bolt and pivot, in a numbered container so that each one can be installed in its original location. (An old egg carton works well; so does a cardboard box with holes punched in it.) If you are removing only the pushrods, loosen each rocker arm bolt just enough to rotate the rocker to the side for pushrod removal **(see illustration)**.

3   Remove the pushrods and place each in a numbered holder so that each one can be installed in its original location **(see illustration)**.

Inspection

Refer to illustration 5.5

4   Inspect each rocker arm, pushrod, and pivot for excessive wear, cracks, or other damage. Ensure that the hole in the pushrod end of each rocker arm is open.

5   Inspect each rocker arm pivot area for excessive wear and galling **(see illustration)**. If any rocker arm is badly worn, cracked, damaged or galled, replace the rocker arm and pivot as a matched pair.

6   Roll each pushrod across a piece of plate glass to see if it's bent. Replace any bent pushrod; do not try to straighten it.

Installation

7   Lubricate the lower ends of the pushrods with clean engine oil; then install them in their original locations. Be sure each pushrod seats completely in its valve lifter.

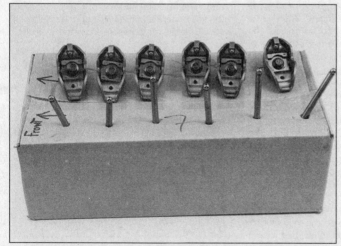

5.3 Store the rocker arms, pushrods, and other valve train components in a numbered container so they can be reinstalled in their original locations

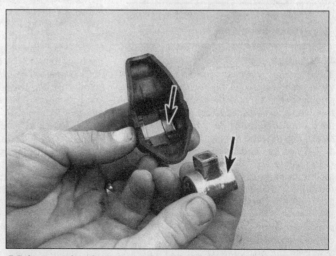

5.5 Inspect the pivot areas of each rocker arm and pivot for wear and damage. If a rocker arm or pivot must be replaced, replace both as a matched pair

6.3 An air hose adapter that screws into the spark plug hole in a cylinder is available from many parts stores

6.6 After compressing the valve spring, you can remove the valve keepers with a magnet or needle-nose pliers - don't drop them

6.8 Pull the seal (arrow) off the valve guide with a pair of pliers

8   Lubricate the upper ends of the push-rods, the valve stems, and the rocker arm pivots with clean engine oil. Then install the rocker arms, pivots and bolts but do not fully tighten the bolts.

9   Be sure that each rocker arm pivot is fully seated on the cylinder head and that the rocker arm contacts the pivot correctly. Then check to be sure that each pushrod is seated properly in the rocker arm and the valve lifter. **Caution:** *Do not tighten the rocker arm bolts for any cylinder until the piston in that cylinder is at TDC on the compression stroke. Tightening a rocker arm bolt with a valve open may damage valve train components.*

10   Refer to Section 3 and rotate the engine to TDC of the compression stroke for number 1 cylinder. Tighten the number 1 cylinder rocker arm bolts to the torque listed in this Chapter's Specifications.

11   Rotate the crankshaft so that each successive cylinder in the firing order is at TDC; then tighten the rocker arm bolts for that cylinder.

12   The remainder of installation is the reverse of removal. Refer to Section 4 and reinstall the valve covers and upper intake manifold, as required.

6   Valve springs, retainers and seals - replacement

Refer to illustrations 6.3, 6.6, 6.8 and 6.17
Note: *Broken valve springs and defective valve stem seals can be replaced without removing the cylinder heads. Two special tools and a compressed air source are needed for this job. Read this Section carefully and rent or buy the tools before starting the job.*

1   Refer to Section 3 and rotate the crankshaft to TDC on the compression stroke for the cylinder to be serviced. Disconnect the cable from the negative battery terminal.

2   Refer to Sections 4 and 5 and remove the valve covers and rocker arms, as required. Remove the spark plugs from all cylinders to be serviced.

3   With the piston at TDC, install a compressed air adapter in the spark plug hole of the first cylinder to be serviced and connect

an air hose to the adapter **(see illustration)**.
Note: *Air hose adapters are available from many auto parts stores, or some compression gauges have similar screw-in adapters that may work with the quick-disconnect coupling from your air hose.*

4   Remove the rocker arm bolt, pivot, rocker arm and pushrod for the valve to be serviced. If all valve seals are to be replaced, refer to Section 5 and remove all rocker arms and pushrods.

5   **Caution:** *Compressed air may force the piston down in the cylinder and cause the crankshaft to rotate unexpectedly. Be sure to remove the wrench from the crankshaft damper bolt to avoid damage before applying compressed air.* Apply approximately 90- to 110-psi compressed air to the cylinder to hold the valves against their seats. Air pressure must remain applied continuously until instructed to release it. Failure of air pressure to hold the valves closed indicates valve or seat damage that will require removal of the cylinder head for repair.

6   Stuff shop rags into the cylinder head holes near the valve to keep tools and small parts from falling into the engine. Then use a valve spring compressor to compress the valve spring **(see illustration)**. **Note:** *Several types of valve spring compressors are available. One kind, shown here, grips the valve spring coils and presses on the retainer as the knob is turned. Another kind uses the rocker arm bolt for leverage. Both types work quite well, but the lever type is usually cheaper.*

7   Remove the valve keepers and the retainer; release the spring compressor pressure and remove the spring.

8   Use locking pliers to grip the valve seal on the valve guide and remove the seal from the guide **(see illustration)**.

9   Wrap two or three turns of tape around the top of the valve stem so the valve won't fall into the combustion chamber, Then release the air pressure.

10   Inspect the valve stem for damage and rotate the valve in its guide to check for bind-

ing or eccentric movement of the stem that indicates a bent valve.

11   Move the valve up and down in its guide to check for binding. If the stem binds, either the valve or the guide is damaged. Any damage to the valve or its guide requires removal of the cylinder head for repair.

12   Reapply air pressure to the cylinder to hold the valves closed. Then remove the tape from the valve stem.

13   Lubricate the valve stem with clean engine oil and apply a small amount of grease to the tip of the valve stem.

14   **Note:** *If using original-equipment valve stem seals, intake seals have a silver band; exhaust seals have a red band.* Install a new valve stem seal, using a deep socket to press it onto the valve guide. Be sure that the seal is fully seated against the cylinder head.

15   Place the valve spring and retainer over the valve stem.

16   Use the spring compressor to compress the valve spring.

17   Apply a small dab of grease to the valve keepers **(see illustration)** and install the keepers in the valve stem groove.

18   Carefully release the spring compressor and verify that the keepers are fully seated in the valve stem and the valve spring retainer.

19   Release air pressure from the cylinder,

6.17 A small dab of heavy grease on the valve keepers will hold them in place on the valve stem as the spring is released

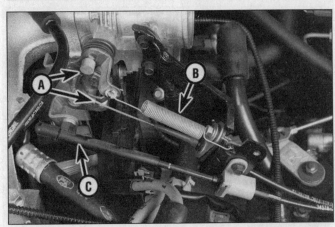

7.2a Disconnect the accelerator (throttle) cable (A), the throttle spring (B), and the cruise-control cable (C) . . .

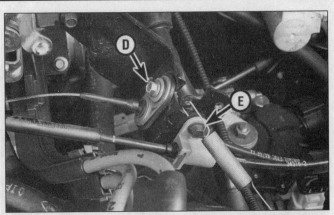

7.2b . . . use a small socket or box wrench to disconnect the guides (bushings) for the accelerator cable (D) and the cruise-control cable (E) from the bracket

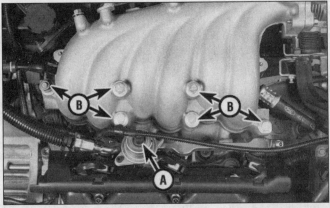

7.4 Disconnect the vacuum line from the fuel pressure regulator (A) - to remove the upper manifold, remove the bolts (B) - 1996 to 2000 models have six bolts, 2001 models have only four bolts

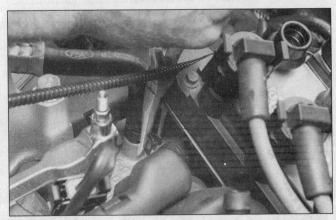

7.8 Disconnect the cooling system hose from the lower manifold

disconnect the air hose, and remove the adapter.

20 Repeat this procedure for each cylinder in which you plan to replace valve seals.

21 Refer to Sections 4 and 5 and reinstall the rocker arms, pushrods, and the valve covers as required. Reinstall the spark plugs and reconnect the spark plug wires.

22 Connect the negative battery cable, start the engine and check for oil leaks and unusual noises.

7 Intake manifold - removal and installation

Note: *The overhead valve V6 uses a two-piece intake manifold. The upper section is the air intake plenum and contains the throttle body. The lower section holds the fuel injectors and the fuel rail.*

Removal

Upper manifold

Refer to illustrations 7.2a, 7.2b, 7.4, 7.8, 7.9, and 7.14

Warning: *Gasoline is extremely flammable, so take extra precautions when you work on any part of the fuel system. Don't smoke or allow open flames or bare light bulbs near the work area. Don't work in a garage where a gas appliance (such as a water heater or clothes dryer) is present. Since gasoline is carcinogenic, wear latex gloves when there's a possibility of being exposed to fuel. If you spill any fuel on your skin, wash it off immediately with soap and water. Mop up any spills immediately; do not store fuel-soaked rags where they could ignite. The fuel system is under constant pressure, so if any fuel lines are to be disconnected, the fuel system pressure must be relieved first (see Chapter 4 for more information). When you do any kind of work on the fuel system, wear safety glasses and have a Class B fire extinguisher on hand.*

1 Refer to Chapter 4 and relieve fuel system pressure and remove the intake air duct assembly. Disconnect the cable from the negative battery terminal.

2 Remove the accelerator (throttle) cable shield from the cable bracket; remove the throttle spring; then disconnect the accelerator cable and the cruise control cable from the throttle lever **(see illustrations)**. Refer to Chapter 4 for more details on disconnecting the accelerator cable and the cruise control cable.

3 Remove two throttle cable bracket bolts from the throttle body; then remove the bracket and move it out of the way.

4 Disconnect the vacuum hose from the fuel pressure regulator **(see illustration)**.

5 Completely loosen the nut that holds the EGR valve to the exhaust manifold tube. Then disconnect the EGR backpressure transducer hoses from the EGR valve and exhaust manifold tube.

6 Remove the PCV hose, the evaporative emission tube, and various vacuum hoses from underneath the upper intake manifold. Tag the hoses to identify them for reconnection later.

7 Disconnect the engine wiring harness from the Idle Air Control (IAC) valve, the Throttle Position (TP) sensor, the EGR transducer, and the EGR vacuum solenoid. Tag the wires to identify them for reconnection later.

8 Refer to Chapter 3 and drain the cooling system. Then disconnect the hose from the expansion tank at the lower intake manifold fitting **(see illustration)**.

9 Remove the alternator brace. Then remove the engine wiring harness bracket and the spark plug wire bracket from the throttle body and move the harness out of the

7.9 Remove the spark plug wire bracket (arrows) from the throttle body

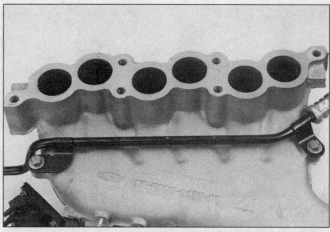

7.14 The tube for the cooling system expansion tank is attached to the bottom of the upper intake manifold

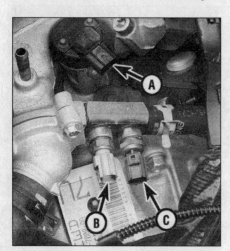

7.17 Disconnect the camshaft position sensor (A), the engine coolant temperature sensor (B), and the coolant temperature sender (C), along with the ignition coil pack (not shown)

7.18 Disconnect the each fuel injector and cover the lower manifold openings with a shop towel until you are ready to remove the manifold

7.21 Remove the spark plug wire retainers from the valve cover stud bolts

way **(see illustration)**.

10   If equipped, remove the intake manifold support from the throttle body and the rear (right-hand) cylinder head.

11   Remove the upper intake manifold bolts and stud nuts **(see illustration 7.4)**; then lift the upper manifold from the lower manifold. Discard the upper intake manifold gasket.

12   If necessary, refer to Chapter 6 and remove the EGR valve, EGR backpressure transducer, and the EGR vacuum solenoid from the manifold.

13   If required, remove the throttle body and the Idle Air Control (IAC) valve from the upper intake manifold.

14   If required, remove the tube for the expansion tank from the bottom of the upper intake manifold **(see illustration)**.

Lower manifold

Refer to illustrations 7.17, 7.18 and 7.21

15   Remove the PCV hose from the valve cover. Remove the upper intake manifold as

described previously.

16   Refer to Chapter 4 and disconnect the fuel line connectors from the fuel rail. Mark the locations of all vacuum lines and disconnect them.

17   Disconnect the engine wiring harness from the Camshaft Position (CMP) sensor, the Engine Coolant Temperature (ECT) sensor, the ignition coil pack assembly, and the coolant temperature sender **(see illustration)**. Tag the wires to identify them for reconnection later.

18   Disconnect the engine wiring harness from the valve cover stud bolts. Then carefully disconnect the wiring harness connectors from each fuel injector and move the harness out of the way **(see illustration)**. Tag the wires to identify them for reconnection later.

19   Disconnect the upper radiator hose from the hose connection on the lower manifold. Twist the hose carefully to free it from the manifold.

20   Disconnect the heater hoses and move them out of the way.

21   Disconnect the spark plug wires from the plugs and remove the spark plug wire retainers from the valve cover stud bolts **(see illustration)**.

22   Refer to Chapter 6 and remove the Camshaft Position (CMP) sensor.

23   Remove the ignition coil pack assembly from the front (left-hand) cylinder head.

24   Refer to Section 4 and remove the valve covers.

25   Loosen the retaining bolt for the intake valve rocker arm pivot on cylinder number 3 (rear, left - nearest to the brake booster). rotate the rocker arm off the pushrod and away from the top of the valve stem; remove the pushrod.

26   Remove the eight lower intake manifold bolts with a Torx-head socket **(see illustration 7.38)**. **Note:** *You can remove the lower intake manifold with the fuel injectors and fuel rail installed, even though the lower manifold is shown here with the fuel rail removed for clarity.*

27   Before trying to remove the intake manifold, break the seal between the manifold and the block. Insert a prybar between the lower

7.30 Scrape the old gasket from the cylinder heads

7.34 Apply RTV sealant to the four corners where the cylinder heads join the block

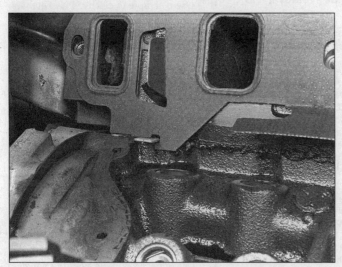

7.35 Align the locking tabs on the gaskets

7.38 Lower intake manifold bolt TIGHTENING sequence

manifold and the block in the area between the radiator hose connection and the transaxle and carefully pry upward. **Caution:** *Be very careful when prying on aluminum engine components. Aluminum is soft and gouges and cracks easily. Cracked or severely gouged components may require replacement.*

28   Lift the lower manifold off the block.

Installation

Lower manifold

Refer to illustrations 7.30, 7.34, 7.35 and 7.38

29   Lightly oil all bolt and stud threads with clean engine oil before installation.

30   Place a large, clean shop towel in the engine valley (above the valve lifters) to catch any gasket scrapings and other debris. Then carefully scrape old gasket material off the cylinder head surfaces **(see illustration)**. Similarly remove old gasket material from the lower manifold, use a sharp plastic or hardwood scraper to avoid gouging the soft aluminum surface.

31   Clean the mating surfaces of the cylin-

der heads, block, and lower manifold with acetone, lacquer thinner or brake system cleaner. After cleaning remove the shop towel from the engine valley.

32   If installing a new lower intake manifold, transfer the radiator hose connection, heater hose elbow, thermostat, and all sensors to the new manifold. Use new gaskets where required.

33   If removed, install the fuel rail and fuel injectors in accordance with Chapter 4.

34   Apply a 1/4-inch bead of RTV sealant to the joints, or intersections, of both cylinder heads and the engine block in the four corners of the engine **(see illustration)**.

35   Place the lower intake manifold gasket on the cylinder heads and align the tabs on the manifold gasket with slots in the cylinder head gaskets **(see illustration)**.

36   Install the front and rear manifold end seals and secure with retainers, if equipped.

37   Carefully place the lower intake manifold on the engine and align the manifold bolt holes with the holes in the cylinder heads. Do not disturb the RTV sealant.

38   Install bolts 1, 2, 3, and 4; tighten them

hand-tight. Install the remaining bolts and tighten all the bolts, following the recommended tightening sequence, in two stages to the torque listed in this Chapter's Specifications **(see illustration)**.

39   Refer to Section 5 and reinstall the pushrod and rocker arm for the number 3 intake valve. Be sure the valve is fully closed before tightening the rocker arm bolt to the torque listed in this Chapter's Specifications.

40   The remainder of installation is the reverse of removal.

Upper manifold

Refer to illustrations 7.44 and 7.47

41   If removed, install the lower intake manifold as described previously.

42   Lightly oil all bolt and stud threads with clean engine oil before installation.

43   Inspect and clean all sealing surfaces of the upper and lower intake manifolds and the throttle body. **Caution:** *Be very careful when scraping on aluminum engine components. Aluminum is soft and gouges easily. Severely gouged components may require replacement.*

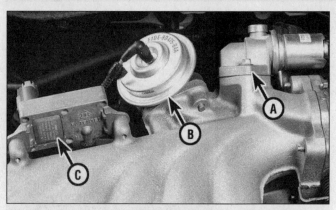

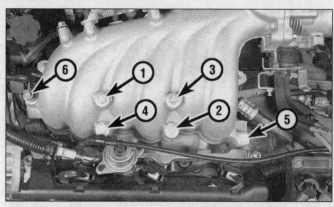

7.44 Install the IAC valve (A), the EGR valve (B), the EGR backpressure transducer (C), and the EGR vacuum solenoid (to the left of the transducer, not shown)

7.47 Upper intake manifold tightening sequence - 1996 to 2000 models

44   If removed, reinstall the IAC valve and the throttle body (see illustration).

45   Guide studs are recommended to align the upper manifold for installation. Obtain four bolts, slightly longer than the manifold bolts (or cut the heads off spare manifold bolts) and cut a screw slot in the top of each bolt. Install the guide studs in four holes in the lower manifold.

46   If removed, install the EGR valve, transducer, and vacuum solenoid on the upper manifold (see illustration 7.44).

47   Install a new gasket over the guide studs in the lower manifold. Carefully install the upper manifold over the guide studs on the lower manifold. Remove the guide studs and install the manifold bolts. Tighten the bolts in sequence to the torque listed in this Chapter's Specifications (see illustration). On 2001 model engines, there are only four bolts, tighten the inner bolts first, then the end bolts.

48   Reinstall all other components in the reverse order of removal.

49   Refer to Chapter 3 and refill the engine cooling system.

50   Start and run the engine and check for vacuum, exhaust and coolant leaks.

51   If the throttle body was removed, adjust the engine minimum idle speed as described in Chapter 6.

8   Exhaust manifolds - removal and installation

Rear (right-hand) manifold
Removal
Refer to illustrations 8.2 and 8.3

Note: *The exhaust headpipe is a welded assembly of two catalytic converters and the headpipes for both banks of the engine - this assembly is referred to as the Y-pipe.*

1   Disconnect the cable from the negative battery terminal and remove the intake air duct assembly if necessary for access to the exhaust manifold.

2   Remove the nut that holds the EGR valve to the exhaust manifold tube (see illustration). Then disconnect the EGR backpressure transducer hoses from the EGR valve and exhaust manifold tube.

3   Remove three bolts from the exhaust manifold heat shield and remove the shield (see illustration).

4   Disconnect the exhaust Y-pipe from the manifold outlet.

5   Remove the six manifold bolts and remove the manifold and gasket from the engine. Discard the old gasket.

Installation
6   Use a scraper to clean old gasket material from the mating surfaces of the rear cylinder head and the manifold.

7   Lightly oil all bolt and stud threads with clean engine oil before installation.

8   If you are replacing the manifold, remove the EGR tube from the old manifold and install it in the new one (see illustration 8.2).

9   Place a new manifold gasket and the manifold on the cylinder head and install the six bolts. Tighten the bolts to the torque listed in this Chapter's Specifications.

10   The remainder of installation is the reverse of removal.

11   Start and run the engine and check for exhaust leaks.

Front (left-hand) manifold
Removal
Refer to illustration 8.13

12   Disconnect the cable from the negative battery terminal.

13   Remove the engine oil dipstick tube bracket (see illustration). Then remove the engine wiring harness retainer from the dipstick tube bracket and remove the dipstick and tube. On 2000 and later models, disconnect the power steering pressure hose from the power steering pump.

8.2 Disconnect the EGR tube from the EGR valve at the nut (arrow). Loosening or removing the tube from the manifold may aid manifold removal

8.3 Remove three bolts (arrows) from the exhaust manifold heat shield

8.13 Remove the nut for the dipstick bracket (arrow) and withdraw the dipstick tube from the engine block

9.15 After removing the cylinder head bolts, pry the cylinder head loose at a point where the gasket surfaces won't be damaged

9.16a To remove the rear cylinder head, remove the intake manifold brace . . .

9.16b . . . and the ground strap

14   Disconnect the exhaust headpipe from the manifold outlet.
15   Note the position of the stud bolt and remove the six manifold bolts and remove the manifold and gasket from the engine. Discard the old gasket.

Installation

16   Use a scraper to clean old gasket material from the mating surfaces of the front cylinder head and the manifold.
17   Lightly oil all bolt and stud threads with clean engine oil before installation.
18   Place a new manifold gasket and the manifold on the cylinder head and install the six bolts. Be sure to install the stud bolt in its correct location for the dipstick bracket **(see illustration 8.13)**. Tighten the bolts to the torque listed in this Chapter's Specifications.
19   The remainder of installation is the reverse of removal. On 2000 and later models, use a new Teflon seal when reattaching the power steering hose to the power steering pump.
20   Start and run the engine and check for exhaust leaks.

9   Cylinder heads - removal and installation

Warning: *Wait until the engine is completely cool before beginning this procedure.*

Removal

Preliminary steps

Note: *Cylinder heads can be removed individually for service, but the following preliminary steps are required for removal of either, or both, cylinder heads.*
1   Refer to Chapter 4 and relieve fuel system pressure.
2   Refer to Chapter 1 and remove the spark plugs and spark plug wires for the cylinder head to be removed.
3   Rotate the crankshaft to position the number 1 piston at TDC on the compression stroke (see Section 3). Disconnect the cable from the negative battery terminal.

4   Refer to Chapter 1 and drain the cooling system and engine oil.
5   Remove the valve covers (see Section 4).
6   Remove the upper and lower intake manifolds (see Section 7). **Note:** *Regardless of which cylinder head is being removed, the pushrod for the intake valve of cylinder number 3 must be removed to remove the lower intake manifold (see Section 7).*
7   Remove the exhaust manifolds (see Section 8).

Front (left-hand) cylinder head

Refer to illustration 9.15
8   Disconnect the alternator electrical connectors and move the wiring harness out of the way
9   Refer to Chapter 1 and remove the drivebelt.
10   Remove the drivebelt tensioner.
11   Remove the alternator and the alternator brackets.
12   Unbolt the power steering pump and pump bracket from the engine. Remove the long studs that secure the bracket. Separate the pump and its bracket from the engine as an assembly and move it out of the way. Secure the pump upright so that it will not leak fluid.
13   Loosen the rocker arm retaining bolts just enough to rotate the rocker arms to the side for pushrod removal.
14   Remove the pushrods and place each in a numbered holder so that each one can be installed in its original location. Remove and discard the cylinder head bolts. **Note:** *Torque-to-yield bolts cannot be reused. New bolts must be used when the cylinder head is installed.*
15   Use a prybar or a large screwdriver to break the cylinder head loose from the gasket **(see illustration)**. Pry on a heavy portion of the cylinder head casting and block to avoid damage. Remove the cylinder head and discard the old gasket.

Rear (right-hand) cylinder head

Refer to illustrations 9.16a and 9.16b
16   Remove the intake manifold support brace and the ground strap **(see illustrations)**. Then follow the preceding steps 13 through 15 to remove the cylinder head.

Installation

Refer to illustrations 9.22 and 9.24
17   Inspect and clean all sealing surfaces of the cylinder heads, the upper and lower intake manifolds, and the exhaust manifolds. If possible, use a sharp plastic or hardwood scraper to avoid gouging the aluminum surfaces of the intake manifolds. **Caution:** *Be very careful when scraping on aluminum engine components. Aluminum is soft and gouges easily. Severely gouged components may require replacement.*
18   If you have to scrape or clean cylinder head surfaces still attached to the engine, place a large, clean shop towel in the engine valley (above the valve lifters) to catch any gasket scrapings and other debris. Then carefully scrape old gasket material off the cylinder head surfaces.
19   Use a suitable solvent to remove all gasket material from the cylinder heads, block, and lower manifold. After cleaning remove the shop towel from the engine valley.
20   Lightly oil all bolt and stud threads with clean engine oil before installation.
21   Inspect the two cylinder head locating dowels in each bank of the engine block; replace if damaged.
22   Align a new cylinder head gasket with

9.22 Place the cylinder head gasket over the dowels in the block. Be sure any mark such as UP or FORWARD is oriented correctly

9.24 Cylinder head bolt TIGHTENING sequence

10.5 Mark the pulley and the crankshaft damper so that the pulley
can be reinstalled in the same relative position

the dowels in the block and place the gasket on the block; note any markings for UP or FORWARD **(see illustration)**. On 2000 and later models, the front of the gaskets is marked with a "V-notch".

23   Align the cylinder head with the dowels in the block and install the cylinder head on the block.

24   Install new cylinder head bolts and following the recommended tightening sequence, tighten them in four steps to the torque listed in this Chapter's Specifications **(see illustration)**. *Caution: Torque-to-yield bolts cannot be reused. New bolts must be used when the cylinder head is installed.*

25   Install the pushrods and rocker arms for each cylinder (see Section 5). Rotate the crankshaft so that each successive cylinder in the firing order is at TDC; then tighten the rocker arm bolts for that cylinder.

26   Refer to Chapter 1 and install the drivebelt.

27   Install the exhaust manifolds (see Section 8).

28   Install the upper and lower intake manifolds (see Section 7).

29   Install the valve covers (see Section 4) and refer to Chapter 1 to reinstall the spark plugs and spark plug wires.

30   Refer to Chapter 4 to connect the fuel lines.

31   Refill the engine with oil, then fill and bleed the cooling system (see Chapter 1). Start the engine and check for leaks.

10 Crankshaft pulley, damper, and front oil seal - removal and installation

Removal

Refer to illustrations 10.5, 10.6 and 10.7

1   Disconnect the cable from the negative battery terminal.

2   Refer to Chapter 1 and remove the drivebelt.

3   Raise the vehicle and support it on jackstands.

4   Remove the right front wheel and the plastic inner fender liner, if equipped.

5   Mark the crankshaft and the pulley so that the pulley can be reinstalled in the same position **(see illustration)**. Then remove the four bolts that secure the crankshaft pulley to the crankshaft and remove the pulley.

6   Using a suitable puller, remove the crankshaft damper **(see illustration)**. *Caution: Use a puller designed to remove a crankshaft damper. Such a puller has bolts that screw into the pulley bolt holes in the center hub of the damper. Do not use a gear puller or any puller that grips the outer circumference of the damper. Such a puller will*

10.6 Use a puller designed to remove a
crankshaft damper - DO NOT use a
gear puller

damage the damper.

7   Using a suitable seal puller, remove the crankshaft front seal from the engine front cover **(see illustration)**. Note the orientation of the sealing lip so that the new seal will be installed in the same direction.

Installation

Refer to illustrations 10.9a, 10.9b, 10.9c and 10.10

8   Inspect the front cover and the damper

10.7 Pry the front oil seal out of the cover - be very careful not to
scratch the crankshaft

10.9a A seal driver is an economical investment to make the job
easier and faster

10.9b Carefully drive in the new seal

10.9c If you don't have a seal driver, use a large socket

10.10 Installing the crankshaft damper with an installation tool

seal surface for nicks, burrs, or other roughness that could damage the new seal. Correct as necessary.

9 Lubricate the new seal with clean engine oil and install it in the engine front cover with a suitable seal driver (see illustrations). Be sure that the lip of the seal faces inward. If a seal driver is unavailable, carefully tap the seal into place with a large socket and hammer (see illustration).

10 Apply RTV sealant to the keyway and inner bore of the damper and lubricate the outer sealing surface of the damper with clean engine oil. Then align the damper keyway with the crankshaft key and install the damper with a suitable tool (available at auto parts stores) (see illustration). If such a tool is unavailable, start the damper onto the crankshaft with a soft-faced mallet and finish the installation by tightening the retaining bolt. Tighten the bolt to the torque listed in this Chapter's Specifications.

11 Reinstall the remaining components in the reverse order of removal.

12 Connect the negative battery cable, start the engine and check for oil leaks.

11 Engine front cover - removal and installation

Warning: *Wait until the engine is completely cool before beginning this procedure.*

Removal

Refer to illustrations 11.3, 11.11 and 11.12

1 Disconnect the cable from the negative battery terminal.

2 Refer to Chapter 3 and drain the cooling system. On 2000 and later models, remove the coolant expansion tank.

3 Loosen the four water pump pulley bolts while the drivebelt is still installed (see illustration). **Note:** *On 2000 and later models, remove the engine strut brace (above the alternator), and the engine anti-roll torque arm (one bolt at each end).*

4 Refer to Chapter 1 and remove the drivebelt. Then remove the drivebelt tensioner.

5 Remove the lower radiator hose and the heater hose from the pump.

6 Remove the crankshaft pulley and damper (see Section 10).

7 Disconnect the wiring harness from the crankshaft position (CKP) sensor, mounted on the front cover and move the harness out of the way (see illustration 11.3). If the front cover is to be replaced, remove the CKP sensor for installation in the new cover.

8 Raise the vehicle and support it on jackstands.

9 **Caution:** *Do not cut the front portion of the oil pan gasket and try to reseal it with a small portion cut from a new gasket. Such attempts are usually unsuccessful and will leak oil.* Remove the oil pan (see Section 14). Discard the old oil pan gasket and clean the gasket surfaces of the pan and the block.

10 Remove the water pump pulley bolts and the pulley.

11 Remove the bolts that secure the front cover to the engine (see illustration). Don't remove the smaller bolts - these retain the water pump to the front cover. The pump and cover can be removed as a unit by leaving

11.3 To remove the front cover, first remove the water pump pulley bolts (A) and pulley, the heater hose (B), and the wiring harness for the crankshaft position sensor (C)

11.11 Location of the front cover-to-engine block bolts (arrows)

11.12 Tap the front cover lightly with a soft-faced mallet to loosen it. You can remove the cover and water pump as an assembly

11.15 The two dowels on the front of the engine (arrows) will hold the cover gasket in place during installation

in the reverse order of removal. Refill the engine with oil, then fill and bleed the cooling system (see Chapter 1).

26   Start the engine and check for oil leaks.

12   Timing chain and sprockets - removal and installation

Warning: *Wait until the engine is completely cool before beginning this procedure.*

Removal

Refer to illustrations 12.7 and 12.8

1   Rotate the crankshaft to position the number 1 piston at TDC on the compression stroke (see Section 3). Disconnect the cable from the negative battery terminal.

2   Refer to Chapter 3 and drain the cooling system.

3   Refer to Chapter 1 and remove the drivebelt and the drivebelt tensioner.

4   Remove the lower radiator hose and the heater hose.

5   Remove the crankshaft pulley and damper (see Section 10).

6   Remove the front engine cover (see Section 11) and the oil pan (see Section 14).

7   Verify that the camshaft timing marks are aligned to indicate that the number 1 piston at TDC on the compression stroke **(see illustration)**.

8   Remove the camshaft sprocket retaining bolt and washer **(see illustration)**.

9   Slide both the camshaft sprocket and the crankshaft sprocket, along with the chain, forward and remove them as an assembly.

Installation

Refer to illustration 12.11a and 12.11b

10   Inspect and clean all sealing surfaces of the engine front cover and the block. **Caution:** *Be very careful when scraping on aluminum engine components. Aluminum is soft and gouges easily. Severely gouged components may require replacement.*

these bolts in place.

12   Carefully remove the front cover and water pump as an assembly from the engine **(see illustration)**.

Installation

Refer to illustration 11.15

13   **Caution:** *Be very careful when scraping on aluminum engine components. Aluminum is soft and gouges easily. Severely gouged components may require replacement.* Inspect and clean all sealing surfaces of the engine front cover and the block.

14   Inspect the front oil seal installed in the front cover for wear or damage; replace it if necessary.

15   Place a new gasket over the locating dowels on the front of the engine **(see illustration)**.

16   If available, place a seal-protecting sleeve over the front of the crankshaft. If such a sleeve is not available, lubricate the end of the crankshaft with clean engine oil and be very careful when sliding the seal over the end of the crankshaft.

17   Loosely install the four bolts that attach the water pump pulley and install the front cover and water pump onto the engine as an assembly.

18   Apply Teflon pipe sealant to the front cover bolts threaded into the engine water jackets to prevent coolant leakage. Lightly oil the remaining bolt threads with clean engine oil before installation.

19   Install the front cover bolts and tighten them to the torque listed this Chapter's Specifications.

20   Install the oil pan with a new gasket (see Section 14).

21   Hand-tighten the water pump pulley bolts.

22   Install the crankshaft damper and pulley (see Section 10).

23   If the CKP sensor was removed, install it and connect the wiring harness.

24   Install the drivebelt tensioner and the drivebelt; then tighten the water pump pulley bolts to the torque listed in this Chapter's Specifications.

25   Install the remainder of the components

12.7 With the no. 1 piston at TDC, the camshaft and crankshaft sprocket timing marks should align (arrows)

12.8 Remove the camshaft sprocket bolt

12.11a Align the timing marks on the camshaft sprocket and the crankshaft sprocket (arrows) . . .

12.11b . . . then slide the sprockets and timing chain onto the camshaft and crankshaft

13.8a Remove the bolts from the lifter guide plate (arrows) . . .

13.8b . . . and remove six lifter guides

11 Align the timing marks on the camshaft and crankshaft sprockets and slide both sprockets and the chain onto the engine as an assembly **(see illustrations)**. Be sure the sprockets are fully seated on the camshaft and the crankshaft.

12 Install the camshaft sprocket bolt and tighten it to the torque listed in this Chapter's Specifications. Lubricate the chain and sprockets with fresh engine oil. **Caution:** *The camshaft sprocket bolt has a drilled hole for timing chain lubrication. If the bolt is damaged, do not replace it with a standard, undrilled bolt or the engine will be damaged.*

13 Inspect the front oil seal installed in the front cover for wear or damage; replace it if necessary.

14 Install the front cover (see Section 11), the oil pan with a new gasket (see Section 15), and the crankshaft damper and pulley (see Section 10).

15 Install the remainder of the components in the reverse order of removal. Refill the engine with oil, then fill and bleed the cooling system (see Chapter 1).

16 Start the engine and check for oil leaks.

13 Valve lifters - removal, inspection and installation

Note: *Before replacing a valve lifter for noisy operation, be sure that the noise does not come from improper valve-to-rocker arm clearance or from worn pushrods or rocker arms.*

Removal

Refer to illustrations 13.8a, 13.8b, 13.10a, 13.10b, and 13.11

1 Rotate the crankshaft to position the number 1 piston at TDC on the compression stroke (see Section 3). Disconnect the cable from the negative battery terminal.

2 Refer to Chapter 3 and drain the cooling system.

3 Refer to Chapter 1 and remove the drivebelt and the drivebelt tensioner.

4 Refer to Chapter 4 and relieve fuel system pressure.

5 Remove the valve covers (see Section 4).

6 Remove the upper and lower intake manifolds (see Section 7). **Note:** *The pushrod for the intake valve of cylinder number 3 must*

be removed to remove the lower intake manifold (see Section 7).

7 Remove the rocker arms and pushrods for the lifters to be replaced.

8 Remove the valve lifter guide plate from the engine valley. Then remove the six individual lifter guides **(see illustrations)**.

9 Before removing any lifter, make a small paint mark at one point on the upper rim of the lifter. This will be an orientation mark when you reinstall the lifter. The overhead valve engine has roller-type valve lifters, which must be reinstalled in their original positions in the lifter bores. The axis of the lifter roller must be parallel to the camshaft, and the lifter roller should not be reversed end for end in its bore.

10 Remove the lifters to be replaced. If a lifter is stuck in its bore, use a magnet to lift it upward; then grasp it with your fingers. Sometimes spraying light penetrating lubricant, such as WD40, on the lifter while moving it up and down will free it for removal. If any lifter is severely stuck, you may have to use a special removal tool (available at most auto parts stores) **(see illustrations)**. **Caution:** *Do not use pliers to remove a lifter stuck in its bore unless you intend to discard the lifter.*

13.10a Remove the lifters with a magnet

13.10b If the lifters are stuck in their bores, a removal tool that grips the inside circumference of the lifter should do the job

13.11 Store the lifters in a numbered container so they can be reinstalled in their original bores

13.14 Check the pushrod seat in each lifter (arrow) for wear

13.15 Inspect each roller closely for wear and flat spots

14.4 To measure cam lobe lift, secure a dial indicator to the head next to each valve (one at a time) - position the dial indicator plunger tip against the rocker arm, directly above the pushrod

11   If you plan to reuse the lifters, place each one in a numbered container so that it can be reinstalled in its original location **(see illustration)**.

Inspection

Refer to illustrations 13.14 and 13.15

12   Thoroughly clean each lifter in cleaning solvent and wipe dry with a clean, lint-free towel.

13   Inspect the lifter body for scoring and galling. Replace any lifter that is badly worn, but check the lifter bore in the engine for similar wear before installing a new lifter. Damage to the lifter bore will require engine removal and disassembly for machine work.

14   Check the pushrod seat in each lifter for wear **(see illustration)**.

15   Inspect the lifter roller for flat spots and spin the roller on its axle to verify free rotation **(see illustration)**. If a roller has a flat spot or is badly worn, the camshaft may require replacement. If the roller doesn't rotate freely, replace the lifter.

Installation

16   Liberally apply clean engine oil or engine assembly lubricant to the lifter bores, the lifter bodies, and the rollers. Engine assembly lubricant is desired, it will stick to lifter and camshaft surfaces longer and provide more protection at startup.

17   If you are reinstalling the old lifters, insert each in its original bore. Use the paint mark made in step 9 to position the lifter correctly. If you are installing new lifters, insert each one in a lifter bore, being careful to keep each roller axis parallel with the camshaft.

18   Install the remainder of the components in the reverse order of removal. Refill the engine with oil, then fill and bleed the cooling system (see Chapter 1).

19   Start the engine and check for leaks.

14   Camshaft lobe lift - check

Refer to illustration 14.4

1   In order to determine the extent of cam lobe wear, the lobe lift should be checked

prior to camshaft removal. Since the camshaft cannot be removed with the engine in the vehicle, removal and installation is covered in Part C.

2   Remove the valve cover(s) (see Section 4).

3   Position the number one piston at TDC on the compression stroke (see Section 3).

4   Beginning with the valves for the number one cylinder, mount a dial indicator on the engine and position the plunger against the top surface of the first rocker arm. The plunger should be directly above and in line with the pushrod **(see illustration). Note:** A more accurate measurement can be obtained by removing the rocker arm and placing the indicator plunger directly against the tip of the pushrod.

5   Zero the dial indicator, then very slowly turn the crankshaft in the normal direction of rotation until the indicator needle stops and begins to move in the opposite direction. The point at which it stops indicates maximum cam lobe lift.

6   Record this figure for future reference, then reposition the piston at TDC on the compression stroke.

7   Move the dial indicator to the other number one cylinder rocker arm and repeat the check. Be sure to record the results for each valve.

8   Repeat the same check for the remaining valves. Since each piston must be at TDC on the compression stroke for this procedure, work from cylinder-to-cylinder following the firing order (see Section 3).

9   After the check is complete, compare the results to the Specifications. If camshaft lobe lift is less than specified, cam lobe wear has occurred and a new camshaft should be installed (refer to Chapter 2C).

15   Oil pan - removal and installation

Removal

Refer to illustration 15.8

1   Disconnect the cable from the negative battery terminal.

2   Remove the engine oil dipstick.

3   Raise the vehicle and support it on jack-stands.

4   Refer to Chapter 1 to drain the oil and remove the oil filter.

5   Refer to Chapter 5 and remove the starter motor.

6   If the engine has an electronic oil level sensor installed in the oil pan, disconnect the wiring harness from the sensor and move the harness out of the way.

7   Disconnect the wiring from all four exhaust oxygen sensors.

8   Remove the two exhaust oxygen sensors installed upstream (ahead of) the two catalytic converters **(see illustration)**. These sensors must be removed to remove the converter and Y-pipe assembly from the vehicle. The downstream sensors can be left in place.

9   Refer to Chapter 4 and remove the exhaust Y-pipe and catalytic converter assembly from both exhaust manifolds.

10   Remove the rear engine cover plate from the torque converter housing.

11   Remove the oil pan bolts and remove the oil pan from the engine. The oil pan gasket usually holds the oil pan to the bottom of the block after the bolts are removed. If the pan is hard to remove, tap it gently with a rubber mallet. Lower the pan carefully to avoid snagging the internal pan baffle or the oil pump screen and tube.

Installation

Refer to illustration 15.12

12   Thoroughly clean the oil pan with solvent and remove all traces of the old gasket from the pan and the lower surface of the block **(see illustration)**. As a final cleaning step, wipe the gasket surfaces of the pan and the block with denatured alcohol to help gasket sealing. **Caution:** *Be very careful when scraping on aluminum engine components. Aluminum is soft and gouges easily. Severely gouged components may require replacement.*

13   Apply a 1/4-inch bead of RTV sealant to the junction of the rear main bearing cap and the block and to the joint where the front cover meets the block.

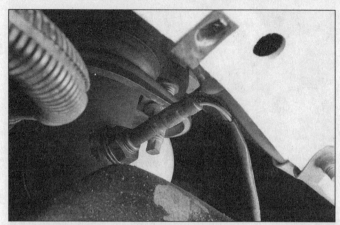

15.8 Remove the upstream oxygen sensor from each branch of the Y-pipe to remove the Y-pipe and converter assembly from the vehicle

15.12 The one-piece pan gasket should peel off easily, but be sure to remove all traces of old gasket and sealant

16.7 Oil pump mounting bolt and locating pin (arrows)

17.1 Punch a small hole in the seal, thread a self-tapping screw into the hole, then pry out on the screw head - be careful not to scratch the crankshaft

14   Locate the oil pan gasket in its proper position on the oil pan and secure it to the oil pan with gasket adhesive.

15   Lightly oil all bolt and stud threads with clean engine oil before installation.

16   Position the oil pan on the engine block and install the bolts. Don't let the sealant dry before oil pan installation.

17   Tighten the bolts to the torque listed in this Chapter's Specifications. Then loosen all bolts and retorque to specifications. Do not overtighten the bolts, or the gasket will leak.

18   Install the remainder of the components in the reverse order of removal. Refill the engine with oil and install a new oil filter (see Chapter 1).

19   Start the engine and check for leaks.

16 Oil pump - removal and installation

Removal

Refer to illustration 16.7

1   Disconnect the cable from the negative battery terminal.

2   Remove the engine oil dipstick.

3   Raise the vehicle and support it on jack-stands.

4   Refer to Chapter 1 to drain the oil and remove the oil filter.

5   Refer to Chapter 5 and remove the starter motor.

6   Remove the oil pan (see Section 15).

7   Remove the oil pump bolts and the pump from the bottom of the engine **(see illustration)**. If you're replacing the pump, be sure to remove the oil pump intermediate shaft from the old pump.

Installation

8   Insert the oil pump intermediate shaft into the hex drive hole in the pump until the shaft retaining ring clicks into place.

9   Prime the pump by pouring oil into the pickup tube and turning the pump by rotating the shaft.

10   Position the pump on the locating pins at the rear of the engine and install the bolts. Tighten the bolts to the torque listed in this Chapter's Specifications.

11   Install the oil pan (see Section 15) and install the remainder of the components in the reverse order of removal. Refer to Chapter 1 and fill the engine with fresh engine oil.

12   Connect the negative battery cable, start the engine and check for leaks.

17 Crankshaft rear oil seal - replacement

Refer to illustrations 17.1 and 17.5

Note: *The overhead valve V6 crankshaft has a one-piece rear oil seal. The seal can be replaced with the engine in the vehicle, but the transaxle must be removed as explained in Chapter 7, and the driveplate must be removed as explained in Chapter 2C.*

1   Using a sharp awl, punch one hole into the rear oil seal metal surface between the seal lip and the block **(see illustrations)**. Thread a self-tapping screw into the hole, then pry outward on the screw head to remove the seal. **Caution:** *Be careful not to*

17.5 If a seal installation tool isn't available, tap the new seal in with a drift punch and hammer

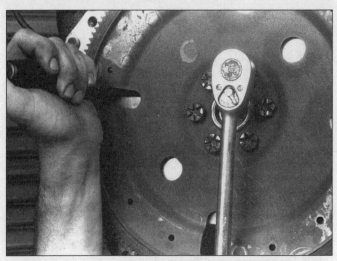

18.4 Insert a screwdriver or prybar through one of the holes in the driveplate to keep it from turning while loosening the bolts

nick the crankshaft or the rear of the block or seal leakage may occur.
2   Thoroughly lubricate the new oil seal and the crankshaft journal with fresh engine oil.
3   Place the new seal on a crankshaft seal installation tool (available at auto parts stores).
4   Position the new seal and the tool on the rear of the engine and alternately tighten the tool bolts to seat the new seal squarely in the seal bore. The sealing lip of the new seal will be very stiff - make sure the entire circumference of the seal lip seats properly on the crankshaft.
5   If the seal installation tool is not available, carefully tap the seal into place with a blunt drift punch and hammer until it is seated evenly in the block **(see illustration).** Regardless of the installation method you use, the rear face of the seal must be within 0.005 inch of the rear face of the block and even all the way around.

18   Driveplate - removal and installation

Removal

Refer to illustration 18.4
1   Disconnect the cable from the negative terminal of the battery.
2   Remove the transaxle (see Chapter 7).
3   Apply alignment marks on the crankshaft flange and driveplate to ensure correct alignment on installation.
4   Remove the bolts retaining the driveplate to the crankshaft. Use a flywheel/driveplate holding tool (available at auto parts stores) or wedge a screwdriver or prybar through one of the holes in the driveplate to keep it from turning while you loosen the bolts **(see illustration).**
5   Remove the driveplate.

Installation

6   Position the driveplate on the crankshaft flange, aligning the marks made during removal. Align the bolt holes; note that some models may have a staggered bolt pattern to ensure correct installation.
7   Install the bolts and tighten them in a crossing pattern to the torque listed in this Chapter's Specifications.
8   Install the transaxle (see Chapter 7).

19   Engine mounts - inspection and replacement

Note: *The manufacturer identifies the mounts at the right side of the engine compartment as "front" mounts. Similarly, the manufacturer refers to the forward mount as the "left-hand" mount and the rear mount (closest to the firewall) as the "right-hand" mount. The "rear"*

19.6a The forward (left-hand) lower stud is accessible through the bottom of the subframe

19.6b The rear (right-hand) lower stud is accessible through the bottom of a bracket

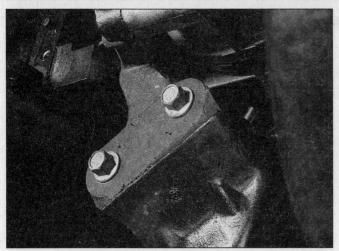

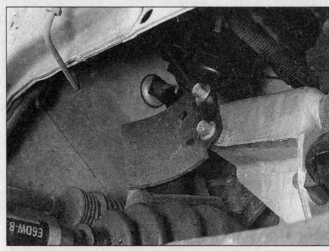

19.8 The two forward (left-hand) through-bolts are accessible through the right fender-well

19.9 These are the two rear (right-hand) through-bolts

engine and transaxle mount is toward the left side of the engine compartment. Removal and replacement of the rear (left side) engine and transaxle mount are covered in Chapter 7.

Inspection

Warning: *Do not work or place any part of your body under the vehicle when it is supported only by a jack. Jack failure could result in severe injury or death.*

1   You can inspect the engine mounts for damage or deterioration without removing the engine.

2   Disconnect the cable from the negative battery terminal. Raise the vehicle and support it on jackstands. Remove the inner liner from the right front fenderwell, if necessary, for better access to the front mounts.

3   Place a hydraulic floor jack under the engine oil pan with a block of wood between the jack and the pan to protect the pan.

4   Slowly and carefully raise the jack slightly to take the engine weight off the engine mounts.

5   Inspect the mounts for damage, deterioration or separation. Use a flashlight to inspect the mounts closely. Sometimes a rubber insulator that is separated from a bracket or bolt will not be apparent until engine weight is removed from the mount.

Replacement

Refer to illustrations 19.6a, 19.6b, 19.8 and 19.9

6   Remove the lower nuts that hold the left and right front mounts to the right-hand side of the vehicle subframe **(see illustrations)**.

7   Raise the engine with the jack enough to fully unload the mounts.

8   Remove the two bolts that secure the forward (left-hand) mount to the air condition-

ing compressor bracket and remove the forward mount **(see illustration)**.

9   Remove the two bolts that secure the rear (right-hand) mount to the transaxle case bracket and remove the rear mount **(see illustration)**.

10   Attach the new forward (left-hand) mount to the air conditioning compressor bracket with two bolts. Tighten the bolts to the torque listed in this Chapter's Specifications.

11   Attach the new rear (right-hand) mount to the transaxle case with two bolts. Tighten the bolts to the torque listed in this Chapter's Specifications.

12   Slowly and carefully lower the hydraulic jack until the engine weight is removed from the jack.

13   Install the two nuts that hold the left and right front mounts to the right-hand side of the vehicle subframe. Tighten the nuts to the torque listed in this Chapter's Specifications.

Notes

Chapter 2 Part B
Overhead camshaft (OHC) engine

Contents

Specifications

General

Cylinder numbers - drivebelt end (right) to transaxle end (left)	
Rear bank	1-2-3
Front bank	4-5-6
Firing order	1-4-2-5-3-6
Compression pressure	Lowest cylinder within 15 psi of highest cylinder; 100 psi minimum
Timing chain deflection	6 degrees

Camshafts

Lobe lift (intake and exhaust)	0.188 inch
Journal diameter	1.060 to 1.061 inches
Bearing inside diameter	1.062 to 1.063 inches
Journal-to-bearing oil clearance	
Standard	0.001 to 0.003 inch
Service limit	0.0047
Endplay	
Standard	0.001 to 0.0064 inch
Service limit	0.0075 inch

Hydraulic lash adjuster

Diameter	0.6290 to 0.6294 inch
Lash adjuster-to-bore clearance	
Standard	0.007 to 0.0027 inch
Service limit	0.0006 inch

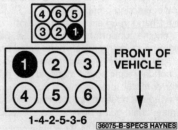

FRONT OF VEHICLE

1-4-2-5-3-6

36075-B-SPECS HAYNES

Cylinder location and coil terminal identification diagram - 3.0L OHC V6 engines through 1999. 2000 and later 3.0L OHC V6 engines have individual coils at each spark plug

Oil pump

Inner rotor-to-outer rotor tip clearance	0.0024 to 0.0071 inch
Endplay	0.0012 to 0.0035 inch

Torque specifications*

Ft-lbs (unless otherwise indicated)

Note: *One foot-pound (ft-lb) of torque is equivalent to 12 inch-pounds (in-lbs) of torque. Torque values below approximately 15 ft-lbs are expressed in inch-pounds, since most foot-pound torque wrenches are not accurate at these smaller values.*

Accessory drive crankshaft pulley bracket nuts	15 to 22
Accessory drive crankshaft pulley-to-crankshaft damper	
1996 to 1999, bolts	30 to 44
2000 and later, nut (reverse thread)	74
Air conditioning compressor bolts	15 to 22
Air conditioning compressor brace bolts	15 to 22
Air conditioning compressor bracket nuts	
Step 1	18
Step 2	Tighten an additional 90 degrees
Alternator bolt	15 to 22
Camshaft journal cap bolts	71 to 106 in-lbs
Crankshaft damper-to-crankshaft bolt	
Step 1	88
Step 2	Loosen one full turn (360 degrees)
Step 3	35 to 39
Step 4	Tighten an additional 90 degrees
Crankshaft pulley-to-damper	70 to 77
Crankshaft pulley bracket nuts	15 to 22
Cylinder head bolts	
Step 1	28 to 31
Step 2	Tighten an additional 90 degrees
Step 3	Loosen one full turn (360 degrees)
Step 4	28 to 31
Step 5	Tighten an additional 90 degrees
Step 6	Tighten an additional 90 degrees
Drivebelt idler pulley nut	15 to 22
Driveplate-to-crankshaft bolts	54 to 64
EGR valve bolt	15 to 22
EGR valve-to-exhaust manifold tube nuts	26 to 33
Engine front cover bolts	15 to 22
Engine-to-transaxle	25 to 33
Engine and transaxle support nuts	84 in-lbs
Exhaust manifold nuts	13 to 16
Front subframe-to-body bolts	57 to 75
Idle air control valve bolts	71 to 106 in-lbs
IMRC actuator bolts (1996 to 1999)	71 to 106 in-lbs
Lower intake manifold bolts	71 to 106 in-lbs
Oil filter adapter-to-engine bolt	12 to 17
Oil pan baffle nuts	15 to 22
Oil pan bolts	15 to 22
Oil pan-to-transaxle bolts	25 to 33
Oil pump screen cover and tube bolts	71 to 106 in-lbs
Oil pump screen cover and tube nut	15 to 22
Oil pump-to-engine block bolts	71 to 106 in-lbs
Oil separator bolts	71 to 106 in-lbs
Oxygen sensor-to-exhaust manifold	26 to 34
Power steering pump bolts	71 to 106 in-lbs
Right-hand (rear) and left-hand (front)	
engine support through bolt	75 to 102
Right-hand (rear) and left-hand (front) engine support	
(engine mount)-to-subframe bolts	30 to 41
Secondary air injection manifold tube nut	28 to 30
Starter motor retaining nuts	15 to 22
Thermostat housing bracket retaining bolts	71 to 106 in-lbs
Timing chain guide bolts	15 to 22
Timing chain tensioner bolts	15 to 22
Transaxle oil cooler line nuts	18 to 22
Transaxle support bracket retaining bolt	15 to 22

Torque specifications*

	Ft-lbs (unless otherwise indicated)
Transaxle support bracket-to-oil pan retaining nuts and stud bolts	71 to 106 in-lbs
Upper front engine support (engine mount) bracket nuts	
Step 1	84 in-lbs
Step 2	52 to 70
Upper intake manifold bolts	71 to 106 in-lbs
Valve cover bolts	71 to 106 in-lbs

* **Note:** *Refer to Chapter 2, Part C for additional torque specifications.*

1 General information

This part of Chapter 2 covers in-vehicle repairs for the 3.0 liter Overhead Camshaft (OHC) V6 engine. This version of the 3.0L V6 engine features an aluminum engine block and aluminum cylinder heads with dual overhead camshafts and four valves per cylinder.

All information on engine removal and installation, as well as engine block and cylinder head overhaul, is in Part C of Chapter 2.

The following repair procedures are based on the assumption that the engine is installed in the vehicle. If the engine has been removed and mounted on a stand, many of the steps in this part of Chapter 2 will not apply.

The Specifications in this part of Chapter 2 apply only to the procedures in this part. Part C contains other specifications for cylinder head and engine block service.

In this chapter, "left" and "right" are used to describe locations on the engine. These directions are in relation to the vehicle overall from the position of sitting in the driver's seat. So, "left" means the driver's side, and "right" means the passenger's side of the vehicle.

2 Repair operations possible with the engine in the vehicle

Many major repairs can be done without removing the engine from the vehicle. Clean the engine compartment and the exterior of the engine with a pressure washer or degreaser solvent before doing any work. Cleaning the engine and engine compartment will make repairs easier and help to keep dirt out of the engine.

It may help to remove the hood for better access to the engine. (Refer to Chapter 11, if necessary.)

If the engine has vacuum, exhaust, oil, or coolant leaks that indicate the need for gasket replacement, repairs can usually be done with the engine in the vehicle. The intake and exhaust manifold gaskets, the timing cover gasket, the oil pan gasket, crankshaft oil seals, and cylinder head gaskets are all accessible with the engine in the vehicle.

Exterior engine components, such as the intake and exhaust manifolds, the oil pan, the water pump, the starter motor, the alternator, and many fuel system components also can be serviced with the engine installed.

Because the cylinder heads can be removed without pulling the engine, valve train components can be serviced with the engine in the vehicle. The timing chain and sprockets also can be replaced without removing the engine, although clearance is very limited.

In some cases - caused by a lack of equipment - pistons, piston rings, connecting rods, and rod bearings can be replaced with the engine in the vehicle. This is not recommended, however, because of the cleaning and preparation that must be done to the parts involved.

3 Top Dead Center (TDC) for piston number one - locating

Refer to illustration 3.6
Note: *Although this engine does not have a distributor, timing marks on the crankshaft damper and a stationary pointer on the engine front cover will help you to locate Top Dead Center (TDC) for cylinders 1 and 5.*

1 Top Dead Center (TDC) is the highest point in the cylinder that each piston reaches as it travels upward when the crankshaft turns. Each piston reaches TDC on the compression stroke and on the exhaust stroke, but TDC usually refers to piston position on the compression stroke.

2 Positioning one or more pistons at TDC is an essential part of many procedures such as rocker arm removal, valve adjustment, and timing chain replacement.

3 To place any piston at TDC, turn the crankshaft using one of the methods described below. When you look at the front of the engine (right side of the engine compartment), crankshaft rotation is clockwise. **Warning:** *Before using any of the following methods to turn the crankshaft, be sure the transmission is in park. Also disconnect the ignition wiring harness connector from the side of the coil pack assembly.*

a) *The best way to turn the crankshaft is to use a socket and breaker bar on the crankshaft damper bolt on the front of the crankshaft.*
b) *You also can use a remote starter switch connected to the S (switch) and B (battery) terminals of the starter relay. Operate the remote switch in short intervals until the piston is close to TDC. Then use a socket and breaker bar for the final rotation to TDC.*

c) *If an assistant is available to operate the ignition switch in short intervals, you can rotate the crankshaft until the piston is close to TDC. Then use a socket and breaker bar for the final rotation to TDC.*

4 Remove the spark plug from number 1 cylinder and install a compression gauge in its place.

5 Rotate the crankshaft by one of the methods described in step 3, until a compression reading is indicated on the gauge. The piston should be approaching TDC.

6 Continue turning the crankshaft with a socket and breaker bar until the keyway in the crankshaft damper is at the 11 o'clock position and the notch is aligned with the TDC mark on the front cover **(see illustration)**. At this point number one cylinder is at TDC on the compression stroke. If the marks aligned but there was no compression, the piston was on the exhaust stroke. Continue rotating the engine until compression is indicated.

7 If you go past TDC, rotate the engine backwards (counterclockwise) until the timing marks indicate that the piston is before TDC. Then rotate the crankshaft clockwise until the marks align. Final rotation should always be clockwise to remove slack from the timing chains and ensure that the piston is truly at TDC.

8 After the number one piston is at TDC on the compression stroke, TDC for any of the remaining cylinders can be located by turning the crankshaft and following the firing

3.6 To position the number 1 piston at TDC, position the crankshaft pulley keyway (A) at 11 o'clock and align the mark on the pulley (B) with the mark (C) on the engine front cover

order (refer to the Specifications). Divide the crankshaft pulley into three equal sections with chalk marks at three points, each indicating 120 degrees of crankshaft rotation. For example, rotating the engine 120 degrees past TDC for number 1 piston will place the engine at TDC for cylinder number 4 (see Chapter 2A).

4   Valve covers - removal and installation

Refer to illustrations 4.1, 4.5, 4.6a, 4.6b and 4.9

Front (left-hand) valve cover

1   Remove the plastic shield from the front of the engine, if so equipped. Disconnect the crankcase ventilation tube from the front (left-hand) valve cover **(see illustration)**. Remove the tube from the vehicle.
2   On 1996 to 1999 models, remove the upper intake manifold (see Section 5).
3   Remove the fuel injector wiring brackets from the front valve cover studs. If necessary, disconnect the injector wires from the injectors. Move the wiring out of the way.
4   Disconnect the spark plug wires from the spark plugs on the front (left-hand) cylin-

der bank. Remove the spark plug wire bracket from the valve cover and lay the wires out of the way. If necessary, disconnect and remove the coolant expansion tank hose. Disconnect or remove any other wires, hoses or brackets that will interfere with valve cover removal. **Note:** *On 2000 and later models, remove the individual coils by disconnecting the electrical connector, removing the one bolt at each coil, then twisting as you pull up to remove the coil.*
5   Loosen the valve cover fasteners gradually **(see illustration)** and evenly until all are loose. Remove the valve cover fasteners and lift the valve cover off the engine.
6   Remove and discard the valve cover gaskets and spark plug tube seals **(see illustrations)**. Install new gaskets and seals during reassembly.
7   Inspect the valve cover and cylinder head sealing surfaces for nicks or other damage. Clean the sealing surfaces with a clean solvent and a shop towel.
8   Install new valve cover gaskets into the cover. Make sure the gaskets are properly seated in their grooves.
9   Apply a 5/16-inch bead of RTV sealant at the locations shown **(see illustration)**.
10   Lower the valve cover into position, making sure that the gaskets stay in place. Install the cover fasteners and tighten them

4.1 Disconnect and remove the crankcase ventilation tube from the front valve cover (arrow)

gradually and evenly to the torque listed in this Chapter's Specifications.
11   Reconnect the coolant expansion tank hose and wiring. Attach the spark plug wire bracket to the valve cover and connect the spark plug wires to the spark plugs.
12   Install the upper intake manifold on 1996 to 1999 models (see Section 5).
13   Reconnect the crankcase ventilation tube to the valve cover.

4.5 Loosen the valve cover fasteners (arrows) gradually and evenly

4.6a Remove and discard the old valve cover gasket - it must be replaced during assembly to prevent leakage

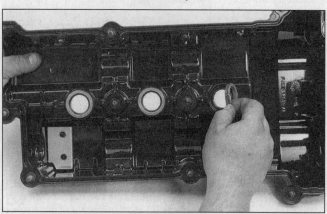

4.6b Remove and discard the spark plug tube seals from the valve cover

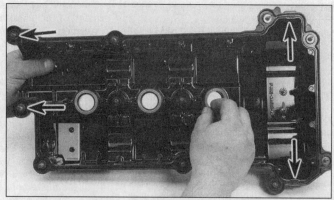

4.9 Apply a 5/16-inch bead of RTV sealant to the locations shown (arrows) - be sure the new spark plug tube seals are securely in position before installing the cover

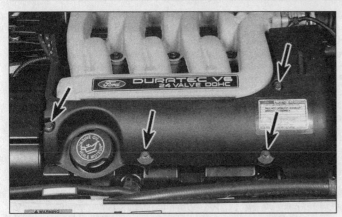

5.3 Remove the bolts and lift the plastic shield off of the front valve cover and water pump pulley

5.4 Unplug the connector from the Mass Airflow (MAF) sensor

Rear (right-hand) valve cover

14   Remove the upper intake manifold (see Section 5).

15   On 1996 to 1999 models, disconnect the spark plug wires from the spark plugs and ignition coil pack. Remove the spark plug wire holding bracket. On 2000 and later models, disconnect and remove the individual ignition coils from each spark plug (refer to Step 4).

16   Refer to Chapter 5 and remove the ignition coil pack on 1996 to 1999 models.

17   Disconnect the fuel injection wires from the injectors. Lay the injector wiring harness out of the way.

18   Remove or disconnect any other wires, hoses or brackets that will interfere with valve cover removal.

19   Loosen the valve cover fasteners gradually and evenly, until all fasteners are loose **(see illustration 4.5)**. Then, unscrew and remove the fasteners. Lift the valve cover off the cylinder head.

20   Inspect the valve cover and cylinder head sealing surfaces for nicks or other damage. Clean the sealing surfaces with clean solvent and a shop towel.

21   Remove and discard the valve cover gaskets and spark plug tube seals **(see illustrations 4.6a and 4.6b)**. Install new gaskets and seals during reassembly.

22   Apply a 5/16-inch bead of RTV sealant to the two locations where the valve cover and engine front cover contact **(see illustration 4.9)**.

23   Install new gaskets on the valve cover. Make sure the gaskets are properly seated in their grooves. Lower the valve cover into place, making sure the gaskets are still in place.

24   Install the valve cover fasteners and tighten them gradually and evenly to the torque listed in this Chapter's Specifications.

25   Reinstall all wiring harnesses and brackets.

26   Reinstall the ignition coil pack.

27   Reattach the spark plug wire bracket. Connect the spark plug wires to the spark plugs, or replace the individual coils on 2000 and later models.

28   Install the upper intake manifold (see Section 5).

5   Intake manifold - removal and installation

Warning: *The fuel system pressure must be relieved before disconnecting any fuel lines (see Chapter 4 for more information). Gasoline is extremely flammable, so take extra precautions when you work on any part of the fuel system. Don't smoke or allow open flames or bare light bulbs near the work area. Don't work in a garage where a natural gas appliance (such as a water heater or clothes dryer) with a pilot light is present. Since gasoline is carcinogenic, wear latex gloves when there's a possibility of being exposed to fuel. If you spill any fuel on your skin, wash it off immediately with soap and water. Mop up any spills immediately; do not store fuel-soaked rags where they could ignite. When you do any kind of work on the fuel system, wear safety glasses and have a Class B fire extinguisher on hand.*

Upper intake manifold

Removal

Refer to illustrations 5.3, 5.4, 5.10a, 5.10b, 5.12, 5.13 and 5.16

1   Disconnect the cable from the negative battery terminal.

2   On 1996 to 1999 models, remove the cowl vent screen and windshield wiper.

3   Remove the plastic shield from the front of the engine, if so equipped **(see illustration)**.

4   Disconnect the connector from the Mass Airflow (MAF) sensor **(see illustration)**.

5   Pry back the clips securing the air filter housing cover. Refer to Chapter 1 and remove the air filter housing cover and lift out the filter element.

6   Disconnect air bypass hose and PCV hoses from the air cleaner duct.

7   Loosen the clamps and remove the air cleaner duct from the MAF sensor and throttle body inlet.

8   Disconnect the Intake Air Temperature (IAT) sensor connector on the side of the intake air inlet tube.

9   Remove the fasteners securing the air filter housing and remove the housing.

10   Pry off the clip securing the throttle and speed control cables to the mounting bracket, then disconnect the cables **(see illustrations)** and remove the throttle cable mounting bracket.

11   Disconnect the vacuum hose from the Exhaust Gas Recirculation (EGR) valve. Refer to Chapter 6 and remove the two bolts securing the EGR valve and remove the valve. Remove and discard the EGR valve gasket. The EGR valve may possibly remain attached

5.10a Pry off the throttle and speed control cable retaining clip . . .

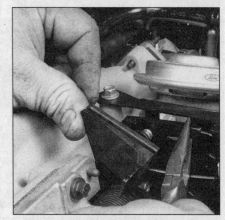

5.10b . . . then disconnect the cables

to the exhaust manifold tube. If not, remove the EGR valve from the tube. On 2000 and later models, remove the EVR (EGR vacuum regulator).

12   Disconnect the Idle Air Control (IAC) valve electrical connector **(see illustration)**.

13   Disconnect the vacuum lines from the upper intake manifold **(see illustration)**. Dis-

5.12 Disconnect the Idle Air Control (IAC) electrical connector

connect the electrical connector from the Throttle Position sensor (TP).

14   Disconnect the vacuum hoses and electrical connector from the EGR vacuum regulator (EVR).

15   Disconnect the PCV hose from the upper intake manifold.

16   Loosen the upper intake manifold bolts in the sequence shown **(see illustration)**. Remove and discard the upper intake manifold gaskets.

Installation

Refer to illustration 5.19

Caution: *Be very careful when scraping on aluminum engine parts. Aluminum is soft and gouges easily. Severely gouged parts may require replacement.*

17   If the gasket was leaking, have the mating surfaces checked for warpage at an automotive machine shop. Check carefully around the mounting points of components such as the IAC valve and the EGR pipe. Replace the manifold if it is cracked or badly warped.

18   Install a new gasket. If the mating surfaces are clean and flat, a new gasket will ensure the joint is sealed. Don't use any kind of silicone sealant on any part of the fuel sys-

tem or intake manifold.

19   Locate the upper manifold on the lower manifold and install the fasteners. Tighten the fasteners in three or four steps in the sequence shown **(see illustration)** to the torque listed in this Chapter's Specifications. On 2000 and later models, the intake manifold is made of composite material, do not over-torque the fasteners.

20   Install the remaining parts in the reverse order of removal. Tighten all fasteners to the torque listed in this Chapter's Specifications.

21   Before starting the engine, check the accelerator cable for correct adjustment and the throttle linkage for smooth operation.

22   When the engine is fully warm, check for fuel and vacuum leaks. Road test the vehicle and check for proper operation of all components.

Lower intake manifold

Removal

Refer to illustrations 5.26, 5.27, 5.29, 5.30 and 5.31

Warning: *The fuel system pressure must be relieved before disconnecting any fuel lines (see Chapter 4 for more information). Gasoline*

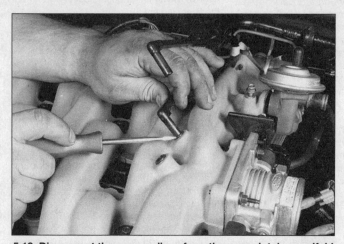

5.13 Disconnect the vacuum lines from the upper intake manifold

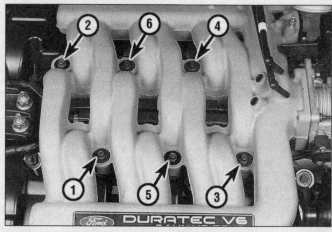

5.16 Loosen the upper intake manifold bolts in the sequence shown

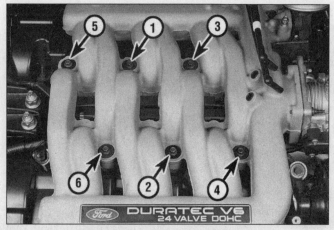

5.19 Tighten the upper intake manifold bolts in the sequence shown

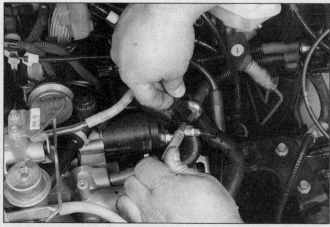

5.26 Remove the safety clip from the spring-lock coupling

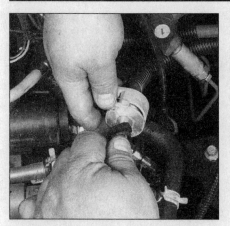

5.27 Disconnect the fuel line using a spring-lock coupling disconnect tool

5.29 Disconnect the Coolant Temperature Sensor (CTS), located above the starter motor

5.30 Disconnect the electrical connector and vacuum hose from the EGR backpressure transducer (arrow)

is extremely flammable, so take extra precautions when you work on any part of the fuel system. Don't smoke or allow open flames or bare light bulbs near the work area. Don't work in a garage where a natural gas appliance (such as a water heater or clothes dryer) with a pilot light is present. Since gasoline is carcinogenic, wear latex gloves when there's a possibility of being exposed to fuel. If you spill any fuel on your skin, wash it off immediately with soap and water. Mop up any spills immediately; do not store fuel-soaked rags where they could ignite. When you do any kind of work on the fuel system, wear safety glasses and have a Class B fire extinguisher on hand.

23   Refer to Chapter 4 and relieve the fuel pressure.

24   Disconnect the cable from the negative battery terminal.

25   Remove the upper intake manifold.

26   Remove the safety clips from the fuel line spring-lock connector **(see illustration)**.

27   Place the spring-lock coupling disconnect tool (see Chapter 4) around the spring-lock coupling **(see illustration)**. Close the tool and push it firmly into the open side of the coupling. Separate the coupling and remove the disconnect tool.

28   Disconnect the fuel injection electrical

connectors from the fuel injectors. Move the injector wiring harness out of the way.

29   Disconnect the Coolant Temperature Sensor (CTS) on 1996 to 1999 models **(see illustration)**. The sensor is located above the starter motor.

30   Disconnect the vacuum hose and electrical connector from the EGR backpressure transducer on 1996 to 1999 models **(see illustration)**.

31   Disconnect the vacuum hose from the fuel pressure regulator **(see illustration)** and on 2000 and later models, remove the regulator. **Caution:** *On 1996 to 1999 models, don't loosen, bend or damage the Intake Manifold Runner Control (IMRC) cable bracket when disconnecting the IMRC cable.*

32   Disconnect the IMRC actuator rod from the stud and bracket (1996 to 1999 models).

33   Disconnect the spark plug wires from the spark plugs in the forward cylinder bank (cylinders 4, 5, and 6) and move the wires out of the way (1996 to 1999 models).

34   To prevent warpage, loosen the eight lower manifold bolts gradually and evenly in the reverse of the tightening sequence until all are loose **(see illustration 5.39)**. Then, remove the bolts.

35   Lift the lower intake manifold off the

engine. Remove and discard the manifold gaskets.

36   Carefully clean all gasket material from the manifold and cylinder head mating surfaces. Don't nick, scratch or gouge the sealing surfaces. **Caution:** *Be very careful when scraping on aluminum engine parts. Aluminum is soft and gouges easily. Severely gouged parts may require replacement.* Inspect all parts for cracks or other damage. If the manifold gaskets were leaking, have the mating surfaces checked for warpage at an automotive machine shop and resurfaced if necessary.

Installation

Refer to illustration 5.39

37   Install new lower intake manifold gaskets on the cylinder heads. Make sure the locating pins on the gaskets are facing down and are properly engaged with the locating holes in the cylinder heads.

38   Place the lower manifold into position on the cylinder heads. Make sure the gaskets are not dislodged.

39   Install the lower manifold bolts. Tighten the bolts gradually and evenly, in the sequence shown **(see illustration)**, to the torque listed in this Chapter's Specifications.

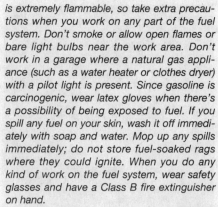

5.31 Disconnect the vacuum hose from the fuel pressure regulator (arrow)

5.39 Lower intake manifold bolt TIGHTENING sequence

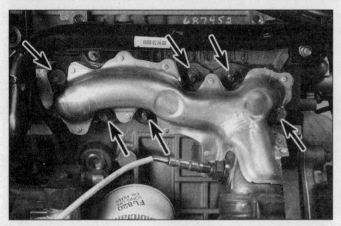

6.4 Remove the exhaust manifold fasteners (arrows) to remove the manifold

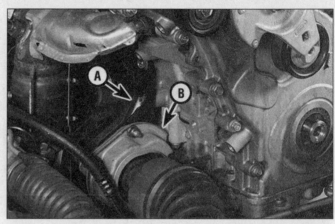

6.15 Remove the bracket (A) from the driveaxle support bearing (B) and engine block (shown with engine removed for clarity)

40   The remainder of installation is the reverse of the removal procedure. Tighten the fasteners to the torque listed in this Chapter's Specifications.

---

6   Exhaust manifolds - removal and installation

Note: *The exhaust headpipe is a welded assembly of two catalytic converters and the headpipes for both banks of the engine and is referred to as the Y-pipe. To remove either manifold, the Y-pipe should be disconnected (or at least loosened) from both manifolds.*

Front (left-hand) exhaust manifold

Refer to illustration 6.4
Warning: *The engine and exhaust system must be completely cool before performing this procedure.*
1   Disconnect the cable from the negative battery terminal. Also disconnect the electrical connector for the oxygen sensor.
2   Refer to Chapter 4 and disconnect the exhaust Y-pipe from the front (left-hand) manifold or remove the complete Y-pipe assembly.
3   If necessary for additional clearance, drain the cooling system and remove the radiator lower hose.
4   Remove the six nuts securing the exhaust manifold **(see illustration)**. Remove and discard the manifold gasket. **Note:** *On some models it may be necessary to remove the splash shield beneath the radiator in order to better access the lower exhaust manifold bolts.*
5   Using a scraper, remove all old gasket material and carbon deposits from the manifold and cylinder head mating surfaces. **Caution:** *Be very careful when scraping on aluminum engine parts. Aluminum is soft and gouges easily. Severely gouged parts may require replacement. If the gasket was leaking, have the manifold checked for warpage at an automotive machine shop and resurfaced if necessary.*

6   Install a new manifold gasket over the cylinder head studs. Lightly oil all bolt and stud threads with clean engine oil before installation. Install the manifold and install the nuts.
7   Tighten the nuts in three or four steps, in a spiral pattern starting with the center fasteners, to the torque listed in this Chapter's Specifications.
8   The remainder of installation is the reverse of the removal procedure. If drained, refer to Chapter 3 and refill the cooling system. Start and run the engine and check for exhaust leaks.

Rear (right-hand) exhaust manifold

Refer to illustrations 6.15 and 6.16
9   Disconnect the cable from the negative battery terminal. Remove the intake air duct assembly if necessary for access to the exhaust manifold. On 2000 and later models, remove the cowl grille.
10   Refer to Chapter 5 and remove the alternator and alternator mounting bracket (1996 to 1999 models).
11   Remove the upper intake manifold (see Section 6) and the ignition coil pack (1996 to 1999 models).
12   Raise the vehicle and support it securely on jackstands.
13   Refer to Chapter 4 and disconnect the exhaust Y-pipe from the rear manifold or remove the complete Y-pipe assembly.
14   Remove the right front wheel.
15   Remove the bracket that attaches the right driveaxle support bearing to the engine block on 1996 to 1999 models **(see illustration)**. Remove the bracket from the support bearing and the block. On 2000 and later models, remove the nut at the rear powertrain mount and raise the engine with an engine hoist or support cradle until there's clearance to remove the manifold. **Caution:** *Never work underneath the engine when it is supported solely by a hydraulic jack.*
16   Disconnect the EGR tube from the exhaust manifold. Then, remove the six exhaust manifold mounting nuts and remove

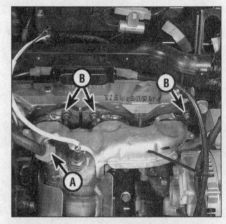

6.16 Disconnect the EGR tube (A) then remove the manifold mounting nuts (B) - the three lower nuts are not visible

the manifold from the engine **(see illustration)**. Remove and discard the manifold gasket.
17   Using a scraper, remove all gasket material and carbon deposits from the exhaust manifold and cylinder head mating surfaces. **Caution:** *Be very careful when scraping on aluminum engine parts. Aluminum is soft and gouges easily. Severely gouged parts may require replacement. If the gasket was leaking, have the manifold checked for warpage at an automotive machine shop and resurfaced if necessary.*
18   Install a new manifold gasket over the cylinder head studs. Lightly oil all bolt and stud threads with clean engine oil before installation. Install the manifold and install the nuts.
19   Tighten the nuts in three or four steps, in a spiral pattern starting with the center fasteners, to the torque listed in this Chapter's Specifications.
20   Complete the remaining installation by reversing the removal procedure. If drained, refer to Chapter 3 and refill the cooling system. Lower the vehicle to the ground, start and run the engine and check for exhaust leaks.

7.6 To keep the crankshaft from turning, remove the driveplate access cover and engage ring gear teeth with a large screwdriver or pry bar

7.9 Loosen and remove the crankshaft damper bolt

7.10 Remove the crankshaft damper with a bolt-type puller

7.13 Install the crankshaft front seal (arrow) flush with the front cover surface

7 Crankshaft pulley, damper and front oil seal - removal and installation

Removal

Refer to illustrations 7.6, 7.9 and 7.10

1   Disconnect the cable from the negative battery terminal.
2   Refer to Chapter 1 and remove the drivebelt.
3   Loosen the right front wheel lug nuts. Raise the vehicle and support it securely on jackstands.
4   Remove the right front wheel.
5   Remove the plastic inner fender liner (splash shield).
6   Remove the driveplate access cover and hold the ring gear teeth with a large screwdriver or pry bar to prevent the crankshaft from turning **(see illustration)**.
7   Remove the nuts that secure the pulley bracket to the engine front cover. Remove the pulley and bracket from the engine.
8   The crankshaft pulley screws into the crankshaft damper with a left-hand thread;

turn the crankshaft pulley clockwise to loosen and remove it.
9   Remove the crankshaft damper retaining bolt (it has conventional, right-hand threads) **(see illustration)**.
10   Using a suitable puller, remove the crankshaft damper **(see illustration)**. **Caution:** *Use a puller designed to remove a crankshaft damper. Such a puller has bolts that screw into the holes in the center of the damper. Do not use a gear puller or any puller that grips the outer circumference of the damper. Such a puller will destroy the damper.*
11   Using a suitable seal puller, remove the crankshaft front seal from the engine front cover. Note the orientation of the sealing lip so that the new seal will be installed in the same direction.

Installation

Refer to illustration 7.13

12   Inspect the front cover and the damper seal surface for nicks, burrs, or other roughness that could damage the new seal. Correct as necessary.
13   Lubricate the new seal with clean engine oil and install it in the engine front cover with

a suitable seal driver. Be sure that the lip of the seal faces inward. If a seal driver is unavailable, carefully tap the seal into place with a large socket and hammer until it's flush with the front cover surface **(see illustration)**.
14   Apply RTV sealant to the keyway and inner bore of the damper and lubricate the outer sealing surface of the damper with clean engine oil. Then align the damper keyway with the crankshaft key and install the damper with a suitable damper installation tool (available at auto parts stores). If such a tool is unavailable, start the damper onto the crankshaft with a soft-faced mallet and finish the installation by tightening the retaining bolt. Tighten the bolt to the torque listed in this Chapter's Specifications.
15   Install the crankshaft pulley and bracket assembly, tightening the pulley by rotating it counterclockwise (left-hand threads), to the torque listed in this Chapter's Specifications. **Caution:** *Turning the crankshaft counterclockwise can cause the timing chains to bind and damage the chains, sprockets and tensioners. If you need to turn the crankshaft, turn it only clockwise.* Tighten the bracket nuts to the torque listed in this Chapter's Specifications.

8.12 Disconnect the camshaft position sensor (A) and the crankshaft position sensor (B)

8.16 Remove the cover fasteners - note the locations of all studs and bolts for installation reference

16   Reinstall the remaining parts in the reverse order of removal. Tighten the wheel lug nuts to the torque listed in the Chapter 1 Specifications.

17   Connect the negative battery cable, start the engine and check for oil leaks.

8   Engine front cover - removal and installation

Note: *Because of a lack of clearance, this procedure is very difficult with the engine installed in the vehicle. If major engine work is being performed, it may be easier to remove the engine from the vehicle (see Chapter 2C).*

Removal

Refer to illustrations 8.12, 8.16 and 8.17

1   Disconnect the cable from the negative battery terminal.

2   Refer to Chapter 1 and drain the engine oil.

3   Refer to Chapter 1 and remove the drivebelt.

4   Remove the valve covers (see Section 4).

5   Refer to Chapter 5 and remove the alternator and alternator mounting bracket.

6   Remove the crankshaft pulley and damper (see Section 7).

7   Disconnect the low-coolant-level sensor electrical connector. Then drain the cooling system (see Chapter 1) and remove the coolant expansion tank (see Chapter 3).

8   Loosen the bolts that secure the power steering pulley to the power steering pump. Don't remove the bolts.

9   Refer to Chapter 10 and remove the power steering pump pulley, power steering pump, and pump mounting bracket.

10   Refer to Chapter 3 and remove the water pump.

11   Raise the front of the vehicle and support it securely on jackstands. Remove the right front wheel.

12   Disconnect the electrical connectors and remove the camshaft position sensor and the crankshaft position sensor **(see illustration)**.

13   Remove the oil pan (see Section 13).

14   If necessary, loosen the air conditioning compressor mounting bolts and move the compressor aside as required for access to the engine cover. **Warning:** *The air conditioning system is under high pressure. Do not disconnect the hoses from the compressor.* Remove or disconnect any remaining wires, hoses, clamps, or brackets that will interfere

with engine cover removal. On 2000 and later models, disconnect and remove the engine's electric cooling fan for clearance.

15   Remove the drivebelt tensioner.

16   Loosen the engine cover fasteners gradually and evenly; then remove the fasteners **(see illustration). Note:** *Draw a sketch of the engine cover and cover fasteners. Identify the location of all stud bolts for installation in their original locations.*

17   Remove the front cover **(see illustration)**.

18   Remove and discard the cover-to-cylinder block gaskets.

Installation

Refer to illustration 8.21

19   Inspect and clean all sealing surfaces of the engine front cover and the block. **Caution:** *Be very careful when scraping on aluminum engine parts. Aluminum is soft and gouges easily. Severely gouged parts may require replacement.*

20   If necessary, replace the crankshaft seal in the front cover.

21   Apply a bead of RTV sealant approximately 1/8 inch wide at the locations shown **(see illustration)**.

22   Install a new front cover gasket on the engine block. Make sure the gasket fits over

8.17 Lift off the front cover

8.21 Apply a bead of RTV sealant at the locations shown

9.2 With the crankshaft keyway at 11 o'clock and the marks on the backside of the timing sprockets aligned, the number 1 cylinder is at TDC on the compression stroke

9.4a Remove the bolts securing the rear timing chain tensioner and remove the tensioner . . .

the alignment dowels.

23 Install the front cover and cover fasteners. Make sure the fasteners are in their original locations. Tighten the fasteners by hand until the cover is contacting the block and cylinder heads around its entire periphery.

24 Following a crossing pattern, tighten the cover fasteners to the torque listed in this Chapter's Specifications.

25 Install the drivebelt and tensioner. Tighten the tensioner pulley to the torque listed in this Chapter's Specifications.

26 Install the oil pan (see Section 13).

27 Install the crankshaft damper and pulley (see Section 7).

28 Connect the wiring harness connectors to the camshaft and crankshaft position sensors. Secure the wiring harnesses with the clamps.

29 Refer to Chapter 10 and install the power steering pump and hoses.

30 Reinstall the remaining parts in the reverse order of removal.

31 Refer to Chapter 1 and fill the crankcase with the recommended oil; fill the power steering reservoir with the correct fluid; and refill the cooling system.

32 Connect the negative battery cable, start the engine and check for leaks. Check all fluid levels.

9 Timing chains, tensioners, and chain guides - removal, inspection, and installation

Note: *Because of a lack of clearance, this procedure is very difficult with the engine installed in the vehicle. If major engine work is being performed, it may be easier to remove the engine from the vehicle (see Chapter 2C).*

Removal

** CAUTION **

The timing system is complex. Severe engine damage will occur if you make any mistakes. Do not attempt this procedure unless you are highly experienced with this type of repair. If you are at all unsure of your abilities, consult an expert. Double-check all your work and be sure everything is correct before you attempt to start the engine.

Refer to illustrations 9.2, 9.4a, 9.4b, 9.5, 9.6, 9.7, 9.8a, 9.8b and 9.10.

1 Remove the engine front cover (see Section 8). Slide the crankshaft position sensor trigger wheel off the crankshaft.

2 Install the crankshaft pulley retaining bolt into the crankshaft. Then use a wrench on the bolt to turn the crankshaft clockwise and place the crankshaft keyway at the 11 o'clock position. Verify TDC by observing the index marks on the backside of the camshaft sprockets. If the number 1 cylinder is at TDC, the index marks will be aligned **(see illustration)**. If not, turn the crankshaft exactly one full turn and again position the

crankshaft keyway at 11 o'clock. **Caution:** *Turning the crankshaft counterclockwise can cause the timing chains to bind and damage the chains, sprockets and tensioners. Turn the crankshaft only clockwise.*

3 Recheck the marks on the sprockets; if they are aligned and the keyway is at 11 o'clock, the number 1 cylinder is at TDC on the compression stroke. Continue to turn the crankshaft clockwise until the keyway is at the 3 o'clock position, which will set the camshafts on the rear cylinder head in their "neutral" position.

4 Remove the two bolts securing the timing chain tensioner for the rear chain. Remove the tensioner, then remove the tensioner arm **(see illustrations)**. Mark all parts that will be reused so they can be reinstalled in their original locations.

5 Lift the rear timing chain from the sprockets and remove the chain **(see illustration)**.

9.4b . . . then slide the tensioner arm off its pivot

9.5 Lift the rear timing chain off the sprockets and remove the chain

9.6 Remove the bolts securing the rear timing chain guide; then remove the guide

9.7 Remove the rear timing chain sprocket from the crankshaft

9.8a Remove the bolts that secure the front timing chain tensioner; then remove the tensioner . . .

6   Remove the bolts securing the rear chain guide and remove the guide **(see illustration)**.
7   Slide the crankshaft sprocket for the rear timing chain off the crankshaft **(see illustration)**.
8   Rotate the crankshaft 1-2/3 turns clockwise, until the keyway is in the 11 o'clock position, setting the camshafts in the front cylinder head in their neutral position. Remove the front timing chain tensioner mounting bolts. Remove the tensioner and tensioner arm **(see illustrations)**.
9   Lift the front timing chain off the sprockets and remove the chain.
10   Remove the chain guide mounting bolts and remove the front chain guide **(see illustration)**. If necessary, slide the crankshaft sprocket for the front timing chain off the crankshaft.

Inspection

Note: *Do not mix parts from the front and rear timing chains and tensioners. Keep the parts separate.*
11   Clean all parts with clean solvent. Dry with compressed air.
12   Inspect the chain tensioners and tensioner arms for excessive wear or other damage.

13   Inspect the timing chain guides for deep grooves, excessive wear, or other damage.
14   Inspect the timing chain for excessive wear or damage.
15   Inspect the camshaft and crankshaft sprockets for chipped or broken teeth, excessive wear, or damage.
16   Replace any component that is in questionable condition.

Installation

> ### ** CAUTION **
>
> Before starting the engine, carefully rotate the crankshaft by hand through at least two full revolutions (use a socket and breaker bar on the crankshaft pulley center bolt). If you feel any resistance, STOP! There is something wrong - most likely, valves are contacting the pistons. You must find the problem before proceeding. Check your work and see if any updated repair information is available.

Refer to illustration 9.28
17   The timing chain tensioners must be fully compressed and locked in place before

chain installation. To prepare the chain tensioners for installation:

a)   *Insert a small screwdriver into the access hole in the tensioner and release the pawl mechanism.*
b)   *Compress the plunger into the tensioner housing until the plunger tip is below the plate on the pawl.*
c)   *Hold the plunger in the compressed position and rotate the plunger one-half turn so the plunger can be removed. Remove the plunger and plunger spring.*
d)   *Drain the oil from the tensioner housing and plunger.*
e)   *Lubricate the tensioner housing, spring and plunger with clean engine oil. Insert the plunger spring into the tensioner housing. Install the plunger into the housing and push it in until fully compressed. Then, turn the plunger 180 degrees and use a small screwdriver to push back the pawl mechanism into contact with the plunger.*
f)   *With the plunger compressed, insert a 1/16-inch drill bit or a straightened paper clip into the small hole above the pawl mechanism to hold the plunger in place.*
g)   *Repeat this procedure for the other tensioner.*

9.8b . . . and remove the tensioner arm

9.10 Remove the bolts securing the front timing chain guide and remove the guide

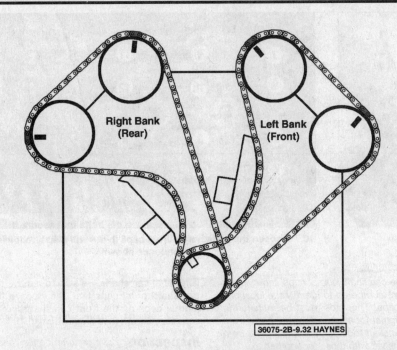

36075-2B-9.32 HAYNES

9.28 Location of the number 1 TDC with crankshaft keyway at 11 o'clock - although not visible, the painted link on the left bank (front) chain (crankshaft sprocket) is located in the same position as the right bank (rear) chain (crankshaft sprocket)

18 If removed, install the crankshaft sprocket for the front timing chain. Make sure the crankshaft keyway is still at 11 o'clock.

19 Look at the index marks on the backside of the front bank exhaust and intake camshaft sprockets. The marks should be facing each other **(see illustration 9.2)**. If not, reposition the camshafts to align the index marks. **Caution:** *The timing chains have three links that are a different color than the rest of the links. When installed, the colored links on the chain must be aligned with the index marks on the camshaft and crankshaft sprockets* **(see illustration 9.32).**

20 Install the front timing chain guide. Tighten the mounting bolts to the torque listed in this Chapter's Specifications.

21 Install the front timing chain around the camshaft and crankshaft sprockets. Make sure the index marks on the sprockets are aligned and the colored links of the chain are aligned with the marks on the camshaft and crankshaft sprockets.

22 Install the front tensioner arm over its pivot dowel. Seat the tensioner arm firmly on the cylinder head and block.

23 Install the front timing chain tensioner assembly **(see illustrations 9.8a and 9.8b)**. Be sure the tensioner plunger is fully compressed and locked in place. Tighten the tensioner mounting bolts to the torque listed in this Chapter's Specifications. Verify that the colored links of the timing chain are aligned with the index marks on the camshaft and crankshaft sprockets, the index marks on the camshaft sprockets are facing each other, and the crankshaft keyway is at 11 o'clock. If not, remove the timing chain and repeat the installation procedure.

24 Rotate the crankshaft clockwise until the crankshaft keyway is in the 3 o'clock position. This will correctly position the pistons for installation of the rear timing chain.

25 Install the crankshaft sprocket for the rear timing chain on the crankshaft **(see illustration 9.7)**.

26 Install the rear timing chain guide. Tighten the mounting bolts to the torque listed in this Chapter's Specifications.

27 Position the camshaft marks on the rear (right bank) sprockets, with the exhaust camshaft sprocket mark at the 12 o'clock position and the intake camshaft sprocket mark at the 3 o'clock position (advanced settings) **Caution:** *The timing chains have three links that are a different color than the rest of the links. When installed, the colored links on the chain must be aligned with the index marks on the camshaft and crankshaft sprockets* **(see illustration 9.28).**

28 Install the rear timing chain around the camshaft and crankshaft sprockets **(see illustration)**. Make sure the index marks on the camshaft sprockets are facing each other and that the colored links of the chain are aligned with the index marks on the front of the camshaft and crankshaft sprockets.

29 Install the rear tensioner arm over its pivot dowel. Seat the tensioner arm firmly on the cylinder head and block.

30 Install the rear timing chain tensioner. Be sure the tensioner plunger is fully compressed and locked in place. Tighten the tensioner mounting bolts to specification **(see illustrations 9.4a and 9.4b)**. Verify that the colored links of the timing chain are aligned

with the index marks on the camshaft and crankshaft sprockets, and the crankshaft keyway is at 3 o'clock. If not, remove the timing chain and repeat the installation procedure.

31 Remove the drill bits or wires (locking pins) from the timing chain tensioners.

32 Rotate the crankshaft clockwise to the 11 o'clock position or the Number 1 TDC position. Verify the timing marks on the camshafts sprockets and the crankshaft sprocket. **Note:** *Verify that all the camshaft marks are in the correct positions and the crankshaft keyway is in the 11 o'clock position. The colored links will not be aligned after rotating the engine away from the TDC number 1 position.*

33 Install the crankshaft position sensor trigger wheel on the crankshaft. Make sure the orange paint stripe on the trigger wheel is aligned with the crankshaft key.

34 Install the engine front cover (see Section 8).

35 Reinstall the remaining parts in the reverse order of removal.

36 Refer to Chapter 1 and fill the crankcase with the recommended oil; fill the power steering reservoir with the correct fluid; and refill and bleed the cooling system.

37 Connect the negative battery cable, start the engine and check for leaks. Check all fluid levels.

10 Camshafts, hydraulic lash adjusters and rocker arms - removal inspection, and installation

Removal

Refer to illustrations 10.6, 10.7, 10.12 and 10.13

1 Remove the valve covers and engine front cover as described in Sections 4 and 8. **Note:** *If only one camshaft requires removal, only remove the timing chain attached to that camshaft.*

2 Install the crankshaft damper bolt into the crankshaft so the crankshaft can be rotated with a wrench. **Caution:** *Turning the crankshaft counterclockwise can cause the timing chains to bind and damage the chains, sprockets and tensioners. Turn the crankshaft only clockwise.*

3 Turn the crankshaft clockwise until the crankshaft keyway is at the 11 o'clock position and the index marks on the backside of the rear timing chain sprockets are facing each other **(see illustration 9.2)**. With the keyway at 11 o'clock and the sprocket index marks aligned, the number 1 piston is at TDC on the compression stroke.

4 Turn the crankshaft clockwise 120 degrees until the keyway is at the 3 o'clock position. This locates the rear (right-hand) camshafts in the neutral position (base circle).

5 Remove the rear timing chain tensioner (see Section 9).

10.6 Remove the camshaft thrust caps

10.7 Loosen the camshaft journal caps in several steps, following the sequence shown

6   The camshaft thrust caps are next to the timing sprockets. Remove the bolts securing the thrust caps **(see illustration)** then remove the caps. The camshaft thrust caps and journal caps fit on dowels in the cylinder head. It may be necessary to tap the caps lightly with a soft-faced mallet to loosen them. **Caution:** *The camshaft thrust caps must be removed before the journal caps are removed to prevent damage to the thrust caps, the camshaft, or the cylinder head.*

7   Following the sequence shown **(see illustration)**, gradually loosen the bolts that secure the camshaft caps to the cylinder head. Loosen the bolts seven to eight turns in several steps, but do not completely remove the bolts.

8   Remove the rear (right-hand) timing chain tensioner arm and rear (right-hand) timing chain. Then remove the timing chain guide and the timing chain crankshaft sprocket, if necessary (see Section 9).

9   Mark the positions of the rocker arms so they can be reinstalled in their original locations.

10   Finish removing the bolts and remove the camshaft caps. It may be necessary to tap the caps lightly with a soft-faced mallet to loosen them from the locating dowels. **Cau-**

tion: *The camshaft journal caps and cylinder heads are numbered to identify the locations of the caps. The caps must be installed in their original locations. Keep all parts from each camshaft together; never mix parts from one camshaft with those for another.*

11   Mark the intake and exhaust camshafts to prevent reinstalling them in the wrong locations. Then lift the rear (right-hand) camshafts straight up and out of the cylinder head.

12   Remove the rocker arms **(see illustration)**.

13   Place the rocker arms in a suitable container so they can be separated and identified **(see illustration)**.

14   If necessary, lift the hydraulic lash adjusters from their bores in the cylinder head. Identify and separate the adjusters so they can be reinstalled in their original locations.

15   To place the front (left-hand) camshafts in the neutral position (base circle) turn the crankshaft two turns (clockwise) until the crankshaft keyway is at 11 o'clock and the index marks on the timing sprockets are facing each other.

16   Remove the timing chain for the front (left-hand) cylinder bank (see Section 9).

17   Repeat steps 5 to 14 to remove the front

(left-hand) camshafts. Be sure to remove the camshaft thrust caps first, then loosen the journal caps on the front camshafts in the sequence shown **(see illustration 10.7)**.

Inspection

Refer to illustrations 10.18, 10.21, 10.22a, 10.22b, 10.23, 10.24 and 10.25

18   Check each hydraulic lash adjuster for excessive wear, scoring, pitting, or an out-of-round condition **(see illustration)**. Replace as necessary.

19   Measure the outside diameter of each adjuster at the top and bottom of the adjuster. Then take a second set of measurements at a right angle to the first; if any measurement is significantly different from the others, the adjuster is tapered or out of round and must be replaced. If the necessary equipment is available, measure the diameter of the lash adjuster and the inside diameter of the corresponding cylinder head bore. Subtract the diameter of the lash adjuster from the bore diameter to obtain the oil clearance. Compare the measurements obtained to those given in this Chapter's Specifications. If the adjusters or the cylinder head bores are excessively worn, new adjusters or a new

10.12 Remove the rocker arms (arrows)

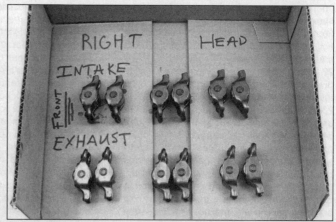

10.13 Place all the parts in a container so they can be separated and identified for installation in their original locations

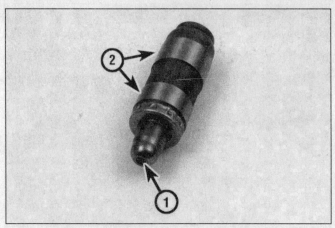

10.18 Inspect the lash adjusters for signs of excessive wear or damage, such as pitting, scoring or signs of overheating (bluing or discoloration), where the tip contacts the rocker arm (1) and the side surfaces that contact the bore in the cylinder head (2)

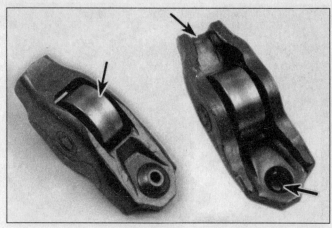

10.20 Check the roller surface (left arrow) of the rocker arm and the areas where the valve stem and lash adjuster contact the rocker arm (right arrows)

10.21 Check the cam lobes for pitting, excessive wear, and scoring. If scoring is excessive, as shown here, replace the camshaft

10.22a Measure the camshaft lobe height (greatest dimension) . . .

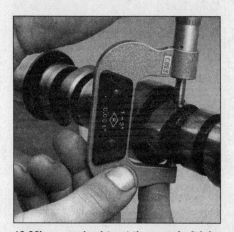

10.22b . . . and subtract the camshaft lobe base circle diameter (smallest dimension) to obtain the lobe lift specification

cylinder head, or both, may be required. If the valve train is noisy, particularly if the noise persists after a cold start, you can suspect a faulty hydraulic adjuster.

20   Inspect the rocker arms for signs of wear or damage. The areas of wear are the tip that contacts the valve stem, the socket that contacts the lash adjuster and the roller that contacts the camshaft (see illustration).

21   Examine the camshaft lobes for scoring, pitting, galling (wear due to rubbing), and evidence of overheating (blue, discolored areas). Look for flaking of the hardened surface layer of each lobe (see illustration). If any such wear is evident, replace the camshaft.

22   Calculate the camshaft lobe lift by measuring the lobe height and the diameter of the base circle of the lobe (see illustrations). Subtract the base circle measurement from the lobe height to determine the lobe lift. If the lobe lift is less than that listed in this Chapter's Specifications the camshaft lobe is worn and should be replaced.

23   Inspect the camshaft bearing journals and

the cylinder head bearing surfaces for pitting or excessive wear. If any such wear is evident, replace the component concerned. Using a micrometer, measure the diameter of each camshaft bearing journal at several points (see illustration). If the diameter of any journal is less than specified, replace the camshaft.

24   To check the bearing journal oil clearance, remove the rocker arms and hydraulic lash adjusters (if not already done), use a suitable solvent and a clean lint-free rag to clean all bearing surfaces, then install the camshafts and bearing caps with a piece of

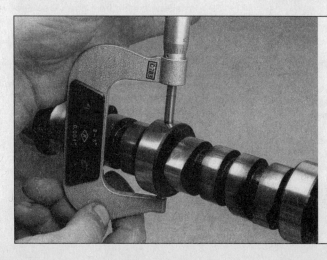

10.23 Measure each journal diameter with a micrometer. If any journal is less than the specified minimum, replace the camshaft

10.24 Lay a strip of Plastigage on each camshaft journal, in line with the camshaft

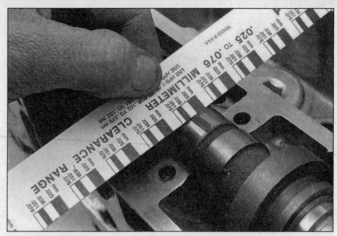

10.25 Compare the width of the crushed Plastigage to the scale on the package to determine the journal oil clearance

Plastigage across each journal **(see illustration)**. Tighten the bearing cap bolts to the specified torque. Don't rotate the camshafts.

25   Remove the bearing caps and measure the width of the flattened Plastigage with the Plastigage scale **(see illustration)**. Scrape off the Plastigage with your fingernail or the edge of a credit card. Don't scratch or nick the journals or bearing caps.

26   If the oil clearance of any bearing is worn beyond the specified service limit, install a new camshaft and repeat the check. If the clearance is still excessive, replace the cylinder head.

27   To check camshaft endplay, remove the hydraulic lash adjusters, clean the bearing surfaces carefully, and install the camshafts and bearing caps. Tighten the bearing cap bolts to the specified torque, then measure the endplay using a dial indicator mounted on the cylinder head so that its tip bears on the camshaft end.

28   Lightly but firmly tap the camshaft fully toward the gauge, zero the gauge, then tap the camshaft fully away from the gauge and note the gauge reading. If the measured end-play is at or beyond the specified service limit, install a new camshaft thrust cap and repeat the check. If the clearance is still excessive, the camshaft or the cylinder head must be replaced.

Installation

Refer to illustration 10.37

29   Make sure the crankshaft keyway is at the 11 o'clock position.

30   Lubricate the rocker arms and hydraulic lash adjusters with engine assembly lubricant or fresh engine oil. Install the front (left-hand) adjusters into their original bores, then install the rocker arms in their correct locations.

31   Similarly lubricate the front (left-hand) camshafts and install them in their correct locations.

32   Install the front (left-hand) camshaft journal caps in their correct locations. Install the journal cap bolts and tighten by hand until snug. Then, install the front (left-hand)

camshaft thrust caps and bolts. Tighten the bolts in four to five steps, following the sequence shown **(see illustration 10.37)** to the torque listed in this Chapter's Specifications.

33   Install the front timing chain sprocket on the crankshaft. Then install the front timing chain guide, the chain, and the tensioner (see Section 9).

34   Turn the crankshaft two full turns and position the crankshaft keyway at 3 o'clock.

35   Lubricate the rear (right-hand) rocker arms and hydraulic lash adjusters with engine assembly lubricant or fresh engine oil. Install the adjusters into their original bores, then install the rocker arms in their correct locations.

36   Similarly lubricate the rear (right-hand) camshafts and install them in their correct locations.

37   Install the rear (right-hand) camshaft journal caps in their correct locations. Install the journal cap bolts and tighten by hand until snug. Then, install the rear (right-hand) camshaft thrust caps and bolts. Tighten the bolts in four to five steps, following the sequence shown **(see illustration)** to the torque listed in this Chapter's Specifications.

38   Install the rear timing chains (see Section 9).

39   Install the engine front cover (see Section 8).

40   Reinstall the remaining parts in the reverse order of removal.

41   Refer to Chapter 1 and fill the crankcase with the recommended oil; fill the power steering reservoir with the correct fluid; and refill the cooling system.

42   Connect the negative battery cable, start the engine and check for leaks. Check all fluid levels.

11   Cylinder heads - removal and installation

Warning: *Wait until the engine is completely cool before beginning this procedure.*

Note: *The following instructions describe the steps necessary to remove both cylinder heads. If only one cylinder head requires removal, disregard the steps for the other cylinder head. If both cylinder heads must be removed, you must remove both timing chains, camshafts and rocker arms. If just the rear cylinder head requires removal, you only need to remove the timing chain, camshafts, and rocker arms from the rear cylinder head; the front can remain installed. However, if just the front cylinder head must be removed, you must first remove the rear timing chain for access to the front chain. In this case, the rear camshafts and rocker arms can remain installed.*

Removal

Refer to illustrations 11.9, 11.10 and 11.11

1   Disconnect the cable from the negative battery terminal.

2   Refer to Chapter 1 and drain the cooling system.

3   Remove the upper and lower intake manifolds (see Section 5) and valve covers (see Section 4).

4   Refer to Chapter 1 and drain the engine oil. Remove the oil pan (see Section 12).

5   Remove the engine front cover (see Section 8).

6   Remove the timing chains, camshafts, rocker arms and lash adjusters as necessary (see Section 10).

7   If removing the rear cylinder head, remove the oxygen sensor from the rear exhaust manifold, using a socket designed for this purpose (see Chapter 6).

8   Disconnect the EGR valve backpressure transducer hoses from the tube that connects the EGR valve to the rear exhaust manifold.

9   Disconnect the electrical connector from the EGR backpressure transducer **(see illustration)**.

10   Remove the EGR valve tube from the rear exhaust manifold **(see illustration)**.

11   Remove any hoses or electrical connectors from the coolant bypass tube. Remove

10.37 Camshaft journal cap TIGHTENING sequence

11.9 Disconnect the electrical connector from the EGR backpressure transducer (arrow)

the two fasteners securing the coolant bypass tube **(see illustration)**. Then remove the tube. **Note:** *The rear cylinder head can be removed with the exhaust manifold and EGR valve backpressure transducer still attached.*

12   Loosen each cylinder head bolt, one turn at a time, following the reverse order of the tightening sequence **(see illustration 11.26a)**. When all cylinder head bolts are loose, remove and discard the bolts. New torque-to-yield cylinder head bolts must be used during installation.

13   Remove the cylinder head from the engine block and place it on a workbench. **Caution:** *If the cylinder head sticks to the block, pry only on a casting protrusion to prevent damaging the mating surfaces.* Remove and discard the cylinder head gasket. If necessary, remove the exhaust manifold from the cylinder head.

14   To remove the front cylinder head, remove the water pump. Remove the two nuts securing the tube attached to the lower radiator hose. Remove the tube from the front cylinder head.

15   If still installed, remove the coolant

bypass tube **(see illustration 11.11)**.

16   Remove the dipstick tube.

17   Loosen each cylinder head bolt, one turn at a time, following the reverse order of the sequence shown in **illustration 11.26a**. When all cylinder head bolts are loose, remove and discard the bolts. New torque-to-yield cylinder head bolts must be used during installation.

18   Remove the cylinder head from the engine block and place it on a workbench. **Caution:** *If the cylinder head sticks to the block, pry only on a casting protrusion to prevent damaging the mating surfaces.* Remove and discard the cylinder head gasket. If necessary, remove the exhaust manifold from the cylinder head.

Installation

Refer to illustrations 11.26a and 11.26b

19   The mating surfaces of the cylinder head and the block must be perfectly clean before installing the cylinder head. Clean the surfaces with a scraper, but be careful not to gouge the aluminum. **Caution:** *Be very careful when scraping on aluminum engine parts.*

Aluminum is soft and gouges easily. Severely gouged parts may require replacement.

20   Check the mating surfaces of the block and the cylinder head for nicks, deep scratches, and other damage. If slight, they can be removed carefully with a file; if excessive, machining may be the only alternative to replacement.

21   If you suspect warpage of the cylinder head gasket surface, use a straightedge to check it for distortion. Refer to Part C of this Chapter, if necessary.

22   Clean the mating surfaces of the cylinder head and block with a clean shop towel and solvent as needed.

23   Ensure that the two locating dowels are in position in the cylinder block and that all cylinder head bolt holes are free of oil, corrosion, or other contamination.

24   Install new cylinder head gaskets on the block, over the locating dowels.

25   Carefully install the cylinder heads. Use caution when lowering the cylinder heads onto the cylinder block to prevent damage to the cylinder heads or block. Make sure the cylinder heads fit properly over the locating

11.10 Remove the EGR tube (arrow) from the rear exhaust manifold

11.11 Remove the coolant bypass tube (arrow) from the engine and lay it aside

11.26a Cylinder head TIGHTENING sequence

11.26b An angle gauge is required to properly tighten the torque-to-yield cylinder head bolts

dowels in the block.

26   Install new cylinder head bolts and turn down by hand until snug. **Caution:** *The cylinder head bolts are the torque-to-yield type and are stretched during tightening. Therefore, the original bolts must be discarded and new bolts installed during assembly.* Using a torque wrench and an angle gauge, tighten the cylinder head bolts in the sequence shown to the torque listed in this Chapter's Specifications **(see illustrations)**. **Note:** *The method used for the cylinder head bolt tightening procedure is referred to as the "torque angle" or "torque-to-yield" method; follow the procedure exactly. Tighten the bolts using a torque wrench, then use a breaker bar and a special torque angle adapter (available at auto parts stores) to tighten the bolts the required angle.*

27   Install the rest of the parts in the reverse order of removal. Tighten fasteners to the torque values listed in this Chapter's Specifications.

28   Refer to Chapter 1 and fill the engine with fresh engine oil, then fill and bleed the cooling system.

29   Start the engine and check for leaks.

12 Oil pan - removal and installation

Removal

Refer to illustrations 12.6 and 12.7

1   Disconnect the cable from the negative battery terminal.

2   Refer to Chapter 1 and drain the engine oil. Reinstall the oil drain plug and tighten it to the torque listed in the Chapter 1 Specifications, using a new gasket if necessary.

3   Raise the vehicle and support it securely on jackstands.

4   Refer to Chapter 4 and remove the exhaust Y-pipe and converter assembly from the vehicle.

5   Remove the transaxle support bracket from the oil pan.

6   Remove the bolts that secure the oil pan to the transaxle **(see illustration)**.

7   Remove the driveplate access cover **(see illustration)**.

8   Remove the oil pan fasteners and remove the oil pan. Note the location of any stud bolts.

9   Remove and discard the oil pan gasket. If necessary, remove the fasteners that secure the oil screen and pickup tube and remove the screen and tube assembly.

10   Thoroughly clean the oil pan and cylinder block mating surfaces using lacquer thinner or acetone. The surfaces must be free of any residue that will keep the sealant from adhering properly. Clean the oil pan inside and out with solvent and dry with compressed air.

Installation

11   If removed, install a new O-ring seal onto the oil pickup tube. Install the tube and screen assembly and tighten the retaining fasteners to the torque listed in this Chapter's Specifications. Use a new self-locking nut to secure the pickup tube support bracket. Tighten the nut to the torque listed in this Chapter's Specifications.

12   Install a new gasket on the oil pan. Apply a 1/8-inch bead of RTV sealant to the oil pan gasket in the area of the engine front cover-to-cylinder block parting line.

13   Install the oil pan, being careful not to dislodge the pan gasket. Install the pan bolts

12.6 Remove the bolts (arrows) that secure the oil pan to the transaxle

12.7 Remove the driveplate access cover to locate the two rear oil pan bolts - one bolt shown (arrow)

13.3 Remove the oil pump retaining bolts (arrows) and pull the oil pump off the crankshaft

13.4 To disassemble the oil pump, remove the screws securing the pump cover to the pump body

and tighten by hand. Be sure to install any stud bolts in the locations noted during removal. Install the oil pan-to-transaxle bolts. Firmly push the oil pan against the transaxle and tighten the pan-to-transaxle bolts snugly. Then, tighten the oil pan bolts, gradually and evenly, to the torque listed in this Chapter's Specifications.

14 The remainder of installation is the reverse of removal, noting the following items:

a) Tighten all fasteners to the torque values listed in this Chapter's Specifications.
b) Always replace any self-locking nuts disturbed on removal.
c) Refer to Chapter 1 and fill the engine with fresh engine oil. Install a new oil filter.
d) Refill and bleed the cooling system (see Chapter 1).
e) Start the engine and check for leaks.

13 Oil pump - removal, inspection and installation

Note: *Because of the difficulty of removing the oil pump, this job is best done as part of complete engine overhaul with the engine out of the vehicle.*

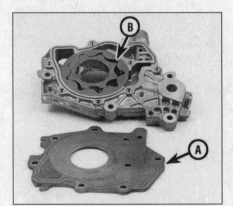

13.5 Remove the pump cover (A) and noting any identification marks on the rotors, remove the inner and outer rotors (B) from the pump body

Removal

Refer to illustration 13.3

1 Remove the oil pan and oil screen and pickup tube assembly (see Section 12).
2 Remove the engine front cover (see Section 8), timing chains and crankshaft sprockets (see Section 9).
3 Loosen each of the four oil pump mounting bolts one turn. Then, gradually and evenly, loosen each bolt in several steps. When all bolts are loose, remove the bolts and oil pump **(see illustration)**.

Inspection

Refer to illustrations 13.4 and 13.5

4 Remove the oil pump cover from the oil pump body **(see illustration)**.
5 Note any identification marks on the rotors and withdraw the rotors from the pump body **(see illustration)**.
6 Thoroughly clean and dry the components.
7 Inspect the rotors for obvious wear or damage. If either rotor, the pump body or the cover is scored or damaged, the complete oil pump assembly must be replaced.
8 Temporarily install the rotors into the pump body and check the rotor tip clearance and endplay as follows:

a) Rotate the inner rotor until a rotor lobe tip aligns with a lobe tip on the outer rotor. using a feeler gauge, measure the clearance between the rotor tips.
b) Place a precision straightedge across the pump cover mounting surface. using a feeler gauge measure the clearance between the rotors and the straightedge - this the pump endplay.
c) Compare your measurements with the values listed in this Chapter's Specifications. If any clearance is excessive, replace the pump assembly.

9 If the oil pump components are in acceptable condition, dip the rotors in clean engine oil and install them into the pump body with any identification marks positioned as noted during disassembly.

10 install the cover and tighten the screws securely.

Installation

11 Rotate the oil pump inner rotor so it aligns with the flats on the crankshaft. Install the oil pump over the crankshaft and fit it firmly against the cylinder block.
12 Install the oil pump bolts and tighten by hand until snug. Tighten the bolts gradually and evenly to the torque listed in this Chapter's Specifications.
13 Install the remainder of the components in the reverse order of removal. Tighten the fasteners to the torque values listed in this Chapter's Specifications.
14 Refer to Chapter 1 and fill the engine with fresh engine oil. Install a new oil filter. Refill and bleed the cooling system.
15 Start the engine and check for leaks.

14 Crankshaft rear oil seal - replacement

Refer to Chapter 2, Part A for the crankshaft rear oil seal replacement procedure.

15 Driveplate - removal and installation

This procedure is essentially the same as for the OHV engine. Refer to part A and follow the procedure outlined there. However, use the bolt torque listed in this Chapter's Specifications.

16 Engine mounts - inspection and replacement

This procedure is essentially the same as for the OHV engine. Refer to part A and follow the procedure outlined there. However, use the bolt torque listed in this Chapter's Specifications.

Notes

Chapter 2 Part C
General engine overhaul procedures

Contents

Specifications

General

Oil pressure (engine hot at 2500 rpm)	40 to 60 psi
Cylinder head warpage limit	0.003 inch (in any 6 inches), 0.006 inch overall
Compression pressure	Lowest cylinder within 15 psi of highest cylinder; 100 psi minimum

OHV engine

Cylinder bore

Diameter	3.504 inches
Out-of-round limit	0.002 inch
Taper limit	0.002 inch

Valves and related components

Valve face angle	44 degrees
Seat angle	45 degrees
Minimum valve margin width	1/32 inch
Stem diameter	
1996 to 1999	
Intake	0.3134 to 0.3126 inch
Exhaust	0.3129 to 0.3121 inch
2000 and later	
Intake	0.2744 to 0.2752 inch
Exhaust	0.2740 to 0.2748 inch

OHV engine (continued)

Valves and related components (continued)

Stem-to-guide clearance
Intake .... 0.001 to 0.0028 inch
Exhaust .... 0.0015 to 0.0033 inch
Valve spring
Free length .... 1.84 inches
Installed height
1996 to 1999 .... 1.58 inches
2000 and later .... 1.650 to 1.736 inches
Valve lifter diameter .... 0.874 inch
Lifter-to-bore clearance
Standard .... 0.0007 to 0.0027 inch
Service limit .... 0.005 inch

Camshaft

Lobe lift
1996 to 1999 (intake and exhaust) .... 0.260 inch
2000 and later
Intake .... 0.251 inch
Exhaust .... 0.264 inch
Maximum lobe lift wear .... 0.005 inch
Journal diameter .... 2.0074 to 2.0084 inches
Journal-to-bearing oil clearance .... 0.001 to 0.003 inch
Endplay
Standard .... 0.001 to 0.003 inch
Service limit .... 0.005 inch

Crankshaft and connecting rods

Connecting rod journal
Diameter .... 2.1253 to 2.1261 inches
Taper and out-of-round limit .... 0.0003 inch
Bearing oil clearance
Desired .... 0.001 to 0.0014 inch
Allowable .... 0.00086 to 0.0027 inch
Connecting rod side clearance (endplay)
Standard .... 0.006 to 0.014 inch
Service limit (maximum) .... 0.014 inch
Main journal
Diameter* .... 2.5190 to 2.5198 inches
Taper and out-of-round limit .... 0.0003 inch
Main bearing oil clearance
Desired .... 0.001 to 0.0014 inch
Allowable .... 0.00086 to 0.0027 inch
Crankshaft endplay .... 0.004 to 0.008 inch

*Note: *The crankshaft journals can't be machined more than 0.010 inch under the standard dimension.*

Pistons and rings

Piston diameter
Coded red .... 3.5024 to 3.5031 inches
Coded blue .... 3.5035 to 3.5041 inches
Coded yellow .... 3.5045 to 3.5051 inches
Piston-to-bore clearance .... 0.0014 to 0.0022 inch
Service limit (maximum) .... 0.003 inch
Piston ring end gap
Top compression ring .... 0.010 to 0.020 inch
Bottom compression ring .... 0.010 to 0.020 inch
Oil ring .... 0.010 to 0.049 inch
Piston ring side clearance
1996 to 1999 .... 0.0012 to 0.0031 inch
2000 and later .... 0.0016 to 0.0037 inch

Torque specifications   **Ft-lbs** (unless otherwise specified)

Main bearing cap bolts .... 56 to 62
Connecting rod cap nuts .... 23 to 28

Note: *Refer to Chapter 2, Part A for additional torque specifications.*

OHC engine

Cylinder bore
Diameter
- Grade 1 .... 3.50393 to 3.504323 inches
- Grade 2 .... 3.504323 to 3.504717 inches
- Grade 3 .... 3.504717 to 3.50511 inches

Out-of-round
- Standard .... 0.0005 inch
- Service limit .... 0.0007 inch
- Taper .... 0.008 inch

Valves and related components
Intake valve
- Seat angle .... 44.75 degrees
- Valve face angle .... 45.5 degrees
- Stem diameter .... 0.2350 to 0. 2358 inch
- Valve stem-to-guide clearance .... 0.0007 to 0.027 inch

Exhaust valve
- Seat angle .... 44.75 degrees
- Valve face angle .... 45.5 degrees
- Stem diameter .... 0.2343 to 0.2350 inch
- Valve stem-to-guide clearance .... 0.0017 to 0.037 inch

Valve springs
- Free length .... 1.84 inches
- Installed height .... 1.57 inches

Hydraulic lash adjuster
- Diameter .... 0.6290 to 0.6294 inch
- Lash adjuster-to-bore clearance
  - Standard .... 0.0007 to 0.0027 inch
  - Service limit .... 0.0006 inch

Crankshaft and connecting rods
Crankshaft
- Endplay .... 0.004 to 0.009 inch
- Runout to rear face of block .... 0.001 inch

Connecting rod journal
- Diameter .... 1.967 to 1.968 inches
- Bearing oil clearance .... 0.001 to 0.0025 inch
- Taper and out-of-round limit .... 0.0006 inch
- Side clearance (endplay)
  - Standard .... 0.0039 to 0.0118 inch
  - Service limit .... 0.0137 inch

Main bearing journal
- Diameter .... 2.467 to 2.479 inches
- Bearing oil clearance
  - Desired .... 0.0009 to 0.0001 inch
  - Allowable .... 0.0009 to 0.0019 inch
- Taper and out-of-round limit .... 0.0006 inch

Pistons and rings
Piston diameter
- Coated, grade 1 .... 3.5035 to 3.5043 inches
- Coated, grade 2 .... 3.5039 to 3.5048 inches
- Coated, grade 3 .... 3.5043 to 3.5051 inches
- Uncoated, grade 1 .... 3.50275 to 3.50314 inches
- Uncoated, grade 2 .... 3.50306 to 3.50362 inches
- Uncoated, grade 3 .... 3.50432 to 3.50511 inches

Piston-to-bore clearance .... 0.0004 to 0.0009 inch

Piston ring end gap
- Compression ring, top .... 0.0039 to 0.0098 inch
  - Service limit .... 0.0196 inch
- Compression ring, bottom .... 0.0106 to 0.0165 inch
  - Service limit .... 0.0255 inch
- Oil ring .... 0.0055 to 0.0255 inch
  - Service limit .... 0.0354 inch

Piston ring side clearance
- Compression ring (top) .... 0.0015 to 0.0029 inch
- Compression ring (bottom) .... 0.0015 to 0.0033 inch
- Service limit .... 0.0039 inch maximum
- Oil ring .... Snug fit

Torque specifications *

	Ft-lbs
Connecting rod cap bolts **	
Step 1	30 to 33
Step 2	Tighten an additional 90 degrees
Crankshaft main bearing support bolts **	
Step 1 (fasteners 1 through 8)	17 to 20
Step 2 (fasteners 9 through 16)	28 to 31
Step 3 (fasteners 1 through 16)	Tighten an additional 90 degrees
Step 4 (fasteners 17 through 22)	15 to 22

* Note: *Refer to Chapter 2, Part B for additional torque specifications.*

** Note: *Connecting rod cap bolts and crankshaft main bearing support bolts 1 through 16 are torque-to-yield bolts and must be replaced. Do not reuse torque-to-yield bolts.*

1   General information

This part of Chapter 2 contains the general overhaul procedures for the cylinder heads and internal engine components. The information ranges from advice about preparation for an overhaul and the purchase of replacement parts to detailed, step-by-step procedures for removal, inspection and installation of internal engine components.

The following Sections are based on the assumption that the engine is removed from the vehicle. For information on in-vehicle engine repair, as well as removal and installation of external components, see Parts A and B of this Chapter and Section 7 of this Part.

The specifications in this Part are only those necessary for the inspection and overhaul procedures which follow. Refer to Parts A and B for additional specifications.

It's not always easy to determine when, or if, an engine should be overhauled because a number of factors must be considered. High mileage does not necessarily indicate that an overhaul is needed, and low mileage does not preclude the need for an overhaul. Frequency of servicing is probably the most important consideration. An engine that has had regular and frequent oil and filter changes, as well as other required maintenance, should give thousands of miles of reliable service. Conversely, a neglected engine may require an overhaul very early in its life.

Excessive oil consumption indicates that piston rings or valve guides need attention. Make sure that oil leaks are not responsible before deciding that the rings or guides are bad, however. Test the cylinder compression (Section 3) or have a leakdown test performed by an experienced tune-up technician to determine the work required.

If the engine is making obvious knocking or rumbling noises, the connecting rod or main bearings are probably at fault. To accurately test oil pressure, see Section 2. If the pressure is extremely low, the oil pump or crankshaft bearings are probably worn out.

Loss of power, rough running, excessive valve train noise and high fuel consumption may also point to the need for an overhaul, especially if they are all present at the same time. If a complete tune-up does not remedy the situation, major mechanical work is the only solution.

An engine overhaul involves restoring the internal parts to the specifications of a new engine. During an overhaul, the piston rings are replaced and the cylinder walls are reconditioned (rebored and honed). If a rebore is done, new pistons are required. The main bearings, connecting rod bearings, and camshaft bearings are replaced with new ones and, if necessary, the crankshaft may be reground to restore the journals. Generally, the valves are serviced as well, since they are usually in less-than-perfect condition at this point. The end result should be a like-new engine that will give many trouble-free miles.

Critical cooling system components such as the hoses, the drivebelts, the thermostat and the water pump must be replaced when an engine is overhauled. The radiator should be checked carefully to ensure that it isn't clogged or leaking. Some engine rebuilding shops will not honor their engine warranty unless you have the radiator replaced or professionally cleaned. If in doubt, replace it with a new one. Also, we do not recommend overhauling the oil pump; always install a new one when an engine is rebuilt.

Before beginning the engine overhaul, read the entire procedure to familiarize yourself with the scope and requirements of the job. Overhauling an engine is not difficult, but it is time consuming. Plan on the vehicle being tied up for at least two weeks, especially if parts must be taken to a machine shop for repair or reconditioning. Check on availability of parts and obtain any necessary special tools and equipment in advance. Most work can be done with typical hand tools, but several precision measuring tools are required for inspecting parts to determine if they must be replaced. Often an automotive machine shop will inspect and measure parts for you and offer advice about reconditioning and replacement.

Always wait until the engine has been completely disassembled and all components, especially the engine block, have been inspected before deciding what service and repairs must be performed by an automotive machine shop. Because the block's condition

2.2 The oil pressure sending unit on the OHV engine is located at the rear of the engine block, just ahead of the transaxle (arrow). The sender on the OHC V6 is on the forward side of the block, just above the oil filter

will be the major factor when determining whether to overhaul the original engine or buy a rebuilt one, never purchase parts or have machine work done on other components until the block has been thoroughly inspected. As a general rule, time is the primary cost of an overhaul, so it does not pay to install worn or substandard parts.

As a final note, to ensure maximum life and minimum trouble from a rebuilt engine, everything must be assembled with care in a spotlessly clean environment.

2   Oil Pressure check

Refer to illustration 2.2

1   Low engine oil pressure can be a sign of an engine in need of rebuilding. A "low oil pressure" indicator (often called an "idiot light") is not a test of the oiling system. Such indicators only come on when the oil pressure is dangerously low. Even a factory oil pressure gauge in the instrument panel is only a relative indication, although much better for driver information than a warning light. A better test is with a mechanical (not electrical) oil pressure gauge. When used in conjunction with an accurate tachometer, an

3.5 Disconnect the primary circuit connector (arrow) from the coil pack to disable the ignition

3.6 A compression gauge with a threaded fitting for the spark plug hole is better than one that requires hand pressure to maintain the seal - open the throttle valve as far as possible during the compression check

engine's oil pressure performance can be compared to the manufacturers Specifications.

2   Locate the oil pressure indicator sending unit (see illustration).

3   Remove the oil pressure sending unit and install a fitting which will allow you to directly connect your hand-held, mechanical oil pressure gauge. Use Teflon tape or sealant on the threads of the adapter and the fitting on the end of your gauge's hose.

4   Connect an accurate tachometer to the engine, according to the tachometer manufacturer's instructions.

5   Check the oil pressure with the engine running (full operating temperature) at the specified engine speed, and compare it to this Chapter's Specifications. If it's extremely low, the bearings and/or oil pump are probably worn out.

3   Cylinder compression check

Refer to illustrations 3.5 and 3.6

1   A compression check will indicate the mechanical condition of the upper end of your engine (pistons, rings, valves, head gaskets). Specifically, it can tell you if the compression is down because of leakage caused by worn piston rings, defective valves and seats, or a blown head gasket. **Note:** *The engine must be at normal operating temperature for this check and the battery must be fully charged.*

2   Begin by cleaning the area around the spark plugs before you remove them (compressed air works best for this). This will keep dirt from getting into the cylinders as the compression check is being done.

3   Remove all of the spark plugs from the engine (see Chapter 1).

4   Block the throttle wide open.

5   Disable the ignition by disconnecting the

primary wiring connector from the coil pack assembly (see illustration).

6   Install the compression gauge in the number one spark plug hole, crank the engine for at least four compression strokes, and watch the gauge (see illustration). The compression should build up quickly in a healthy engine. Low compression on the first stroke, followed by gradually increasing pressure on successive strokes, indicates worn piston rings. A low compression reading on the first stroke, which does not build up during successive strokes, indicates leaking valves or a blown head gasket. (A cracked head could also be the cause.) Record the highest gauge reading obtained.

7   Repeat the procedure for the remaining cylinders and compare the results to the specifications. Generally, the lowest cylinder compression reading should be at least 75 percent of the highest cylinder reading. Use the minimum and maximum values listed in the chart.

8   Add some engine oil (about three squirts from a plunger-type oil can) to each cylinder, through the spark plug hole, and repeat the test.

9   If the compression increases after the oil is added, the piston rings are definitely worn. If the compression does not increase significantly, the leakage is occurring at the valves or head gasket. Leakage past the valves may be caused by burned valve seats or faces or by warped, cracked or bent valves.

10   If two adjacent cylinders have equally low compression, there is a strong possibility that the head gasket between them is blown. The appearance of coolant in the combustion chambers or the crankcase would verify this condition.

11   If the compression is unusually high, the combustion chambers are probably coated with carbon deposits. If that is the case, the cylinder heads should be removed and decarbonized.

12   If compression is way down or varies greatly between cylinders, it would be a good idea to have a leakdown test performed by an automotive repair shop. This test will pinpoint exactly where the leakage is occurring and how severe it is.

4   Vacuum gauge diagnostic checks

Refer to illustration 4.5

1   A vacuum gauge provides valuable information about what is going on in the engine at a low cost. You can check for worn rings or cylinder walls, leaking head or intake manifold gaskets, vacuum leaks in the intake manifold, restricted exhaust, stuck or burned valves, weak valve springs, improper valve timing, and ignition problems. Vacuum gauge readings are easy to misinterpret, however, so they should be used in conjunction with other tests to confirm the diagnosis.

2   Both the absolute readings and the rate of needle movement are important for accurate interpretation. Most gauges measure vacuum in inches of mercury (in-Hg). The following references to vacuum assume the diagnosis is being performed at sea level. As elevation increases (or atmospheric pressure decreases), the reading will decrease. For every 1,000 foot increase in elevation above approximately 2000 feet, the gauge readings will decrease about one inch of mercury.

3   Connect the vacuum gauge directly to intake manifold vacuum, not to ported (throttle body) vacuum. Be sure no hoses are left disconnected during the test or false readings will result. **Note:** *Do not disconnect engine sensors or vacuum solenoids to connect the vacuum gauge. Disconnected engine control components can affect engine operation and produce abnormal vacuum gauge readings.*

4   Before you begin the test, warm the engine up completely. Block the wheels and set the parking brake. With the transmission in Park, start the engine and allow it to run at normal idle speed. **Warning:** *Carefully inspect the fan blades for cracks or damage before starting the engine. Keep your hands and the vacuum gauge clear of the fan and do not stand in front of the vehicle or in line with the fan when the engine is running.*

5   Read the vacuum gauge; an average, healthy engine should normally produce about 17 to 22 inches of vacuum with a fairly steady gauge needle at idle. Refer to the following vacuum gauge readings and what they indicate about the engine's condition **(see illustration)**.

6   A low steady reading usually indicates a leaking intake manifold gasket. this could be at one of the cylinder heads, between the upper and lower manifolds, or at the throttle body. Other possible causes are a leaky vacuum hose or incorrect camshaft timing.

7   If the reading is 3 to 8 inches below normal and it fluctuates at that low reading, suspect an intake manifold gasket leak at an intake port or a faulty fuel injector.

8   If the needle regularly drops about two to four inches at a steady rate, the valves are probably leaking. Perform a compression check or leakdown test to confirm this.

9   An irregular drop or downward flicker of the needle can be caused by a sticking valve or an ignition misfire. Perform a compression check or leakdown test and inspect the spark plugs to identify the faulty cylinder.

10   A rapid needle vibration of about four inches at idle combined with exhaust smoke indicates worn valve guides. Perform a leakdown test to confirm this. If the rapid vibration occurs with an increase in engine speed, check for a leaking intake manifold gasket or head gasket, weak valve springs, burned valves, or ignition misfire.

11   A slight fluctuation - one inch up and down - may mean ignition problems. Check all the usual tune-up items and, if necessary, run the engine on an ignition analyzer.

12   If there is a large fluctuation, perform a compression or leakdown test to look for a weak or dead cylinder or a blown head gasket.

13   If the needle moves slowly through a wide range, check for a clogged PCV system or intake manifold gasket leaks.

14   Check for a slow return of the gauge to a normal idle reading after revving the engine by quickly snapping the throttle open until the engine reaches about 2,500 rpm and let it shut. Normally the reading should drop to near zero, rise about 5 inches above normal idle reading, and then return to the previous idle reading. If the vacuum returns slowly and doesn't peak when the throttle is snapped shut, the rings may be worn. If there is a long delay, look for a restricted exhaust system (often the muffler or catalytic converter). One way to check this is to temporarily disconnect the exhaust ahead of the suspected part and repeat the test.

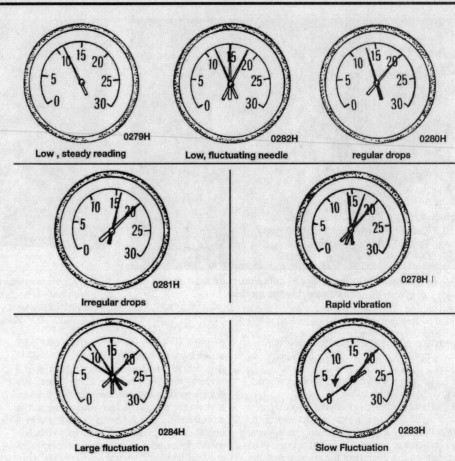

Low , steady reading　　Low, fluctuating needle　　regular drops

Irregular drops　　　　　　　　　　Rapid vibration

Large fluctuation　　　　　　　　　Slow Fluctuation

4.5 Typical vacuum gauge diagnostic readings

5   Engine removal - methods and precautions

If you have decided that an engine must be removed for overhaul or major repair work, several preliminary steps should be taken.

Locating a suitable work area is extremely important. A shop is, of course, the best place to work. Adequate work space, along with storage space for the vehicle, will be needed. If a shop or garage is not available, at the very least a flat, level, clean work surface made of concrete or asphalt is required.

Cleaning the engine compartment and engine before beginning the removal procedure will help keep tools clean and organized.

An engine hoist or A-frame will be needed. Make sure that the equipment is rated in excess of the combined weight of the engine and its accessories. Safety is of primary importance, considering the potential hazards involved in lifting the engine out of the vehicle.

If the engine is being removed by a novice, a helper should be available. Advice and aid from someone more experienced would also be helpful. There are many instances when one person cannot simultaneously perform all of the operations required

when lifting the engine out of the vehicle.

Plan the operation ahead of time. Arrange for, or obtain, all the tools and equipment you will need before beginning the job. Besides an engine hoist, some of the equipment necessary for safe and easy engine removal and installation are a heavy duty floor jack, complete sets of wrenches and sockets as described in the front of this manual, wooden blocks, and plenty of rags and cleaning solvent for mopping up spilled oil, coolant and gasoline. If you have to rent the hoist, make sure that you arrange for it in advance and perform beforehand all of the operations possible without it. This will save you money and time.

Plan for the vehicle to be out of use for a considerable amount of time. A machine shop will be required to perform some of the work which the do-it-yourselfer can't accomplish without special equipment. These shops often have a busy schedule, so it is wise to consult them before removing the engine to accurately estimate the time required to rebuild or repair components that may need work.

If your vehicle is air conditioned, determine ahead of time whether or not you can unbolt the air conditioning compressor and position it out of the way with the hoses connected. Similarly, determine if you have enough clearance for engine removal with air

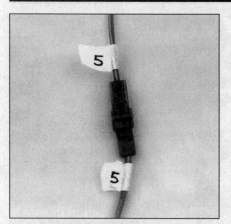

6.7 Label each wire before unplugging the connector

conditioning lines connected to the condenser and other system components or whether you will have to remove any air conditioning hoses and tubing. If air conditioning components must be removed for engine removal, have the air conditioning system discharged by an automotive air conditioning shop before starting work on the engine. Discharging air conditioning refrigerant to the atmosphere is illegal in most states and dangerous as well. Observe the **Warning** in Section 6 about discharging the air conditioning system.

Always use extreme caution when removing and installing the engine. Serious injury can result from careless actions. Plan ahead, take your time and a job of this nature, although major, can be accomplished successfully.

6   Engine - removal and installation

Warning 1: *The air conditioning system is under high pressure. DO NOT loosen any fittings or remove any components until after the system has been discharged. Air conditioning refrigerant should be properly discharged into an EPA-approved container at a dealer service department or an automotive air conditioning repair facility. Always wear eye protection when disconnecting air conditioning system fittings.*

Warning 2: *Your vehicle is fuel injected and you must relieve the fuel system pressure before disconnecting any fuel lines. Gasoline is extremely flammable, so take extra precautions when you work on any part of the fuel system. Don't smoke or allow open flames or bare light bulbs near the work area. Don't work in a garage where a natural gas appliance (such as a water heater or clothes dryer) with a pilot light is present. Since gasoline is carcinogenic, wear latex gloves when there's a possibility of being exposed to fuel. If you spill any fuel on your skin, wash it off immediately with soap and water. Mop up any spills immediately; do not store fuel-soaked rags where they could ignite. The fuel system is under constant pressure, so if any fuel lines are to be disconnected, the fuel system pres-*

sure must be relieved first (see Chapter 4 for more information). When you do any kind of work on the fuel system, wear safety glasses and have a Class B fire extinguisher on hand.
Warning 3: *Do not place any part of your body under the vehicle or the engine when the engine is supported only by a hoist. Keep your hands out of the engine compartment, away from areas between the engine and the body when raising or lowering the engine.*

Removal
Refer to illustrations 6.7, 6.21 and 6.27

1   Cover the fenders, cowl, and front grille area with fender covers or old blankets. Refer to Chapter 11 and remove the hood.

2   Refer to Chapter 4 and relieve fuel system pressure. Then disconnect the cable from the negative battery terminal.

3   Refer to Chapter 3 and drain the cooling system.

4   Remove the intake air duct assembly.

5   Refer to Chapter 1 and to either Part A or B of Chapter 2 (depending on the engine in your vehicle) and remove upper engine components that are easier to remove with the engine in the vehicle or that may interfere with engine removal. Some accessories and engine components can make engine removal awkward if left in place; others could be damaged when lifting the engine. Such components include the upper and lower intake manifolds, ignition coils and spark plug wires, the drivebelt, and various hoses and wires. Depending on the engine-lifting equipment you are using, it may be easier to remove the cylinder heads before removing the engine. If you don't remove the heads, you should not have to remove valve covers or other cylinder head parts. Similarly, the front cover, water pump, and crankshaft pulley can be left in place for engine removal.

6   Loosen, but do not remove the spark plugs if you are removing the engine with the heads installed. Loosening the plugs will relieve compression if you have to rotate the crankshaft; leaving the plugs in place will keep dirt out of the cylinders.

7   To ensure correct reinstallation, label and then disconnect the vacuum lines, emission system hoses, electrical connectors, ground straps, wiring harnesses, throttle and cruise control linkage, and fuel lines that would interfere with engine removal. Pieces of masking tape with numbers or letters on them work well **(see illustration)**. If there's any possibility of confusion, make a sketch of the engine compartment and clearly label the lines, hoses and wires.

8   Raise the vehicle and support it on jackstands. Remove both front wheels.

9   Label and detach all cooling system and heater hoses from the engine.

10   Disconnect the transaxle oil cooler lines from the transaxle cooler and from the radiator. Then refer to Chapter 3 and remove the cooling fan, shroud, and radiator; refer to Chapter 7 and remove the transaxle cooler.

11   Refer to Chapter 10 and unbolt the power steering pump. If the pump bracket is

mounted on studs, remove them from the front cylinder head. Leave the lines and hoses attached and keep the pump upright in the engine compartment. Use wire or rope to hold it out of the way.

12   On air conditioned models, remove the compressor mounting bolts and move the compressor out of the way. Observe the **Warning** at the beginning of this Section and the precautions in Section 5 about discharging air conditioning systems. Refer to Chapter 3 for additional instructions on air conditioning component removal.

13   Refer to Chapter 1 and to Part A or B of Chapter 2 (depending on your engine) and remove the drivebelt and the water pump. This will provide more clearance for engine removal and make the job easier.

14   Refer to Chapter 5 and remove the alternator and starter motor.

15   Refer to Chapter 4 for instructions on exhaust system removal. It is usually easier and faster to unbolt the exhaust Y-pipe assembly from the manifolds and remove the engine with the manifolds attached. Depending on the accessories on your vehicle and the engine-lifting equipment you are using, however, it may be easier to remove the exhaust manifolds from the cylinder heads before removing the engine.

16   Refer to Chapter 2 Part A and remove the engine mounts on the right side of the vehicle. Also refer to Chapter 7 and remove the engine and transaxle mount on the left side.

17   Position a hydraulic jack under the transaxle with a block of wood between the jack and the transaxle pan to protect the pan. Raise the jack until the wooden block just contacts the transaxle. **Note:** *The transaxle must be supported when the engine is out of the vehicle. This can be done with a jack underneath the transaxle or with a support fixture resting on the fenders or on the cowl and radiator bulkhead and supporting the transaxle from above. Such a fixture can be rented from a tool rental company or fabricated from lumber or steel tubing.*

18   Remove the bolts securing the top of the transaxle case to the engine (including one stud on the OHV V6) and then remove the lower transaxle-to-engine bolts. On the OHV V6, remove the lower torque converter cover from the lower front of the transaxle case.

19   Working through the starter motor opening, remove the four nuts that secure the torque converter to the engine driveplate. Use a large screwdriver on the driveplate ring gear to rotate the engine and remove all four nuts.

20   If the vehicle is still raised on jackstands, you may want to install the front wheels and lower the vehicle to the ground at this point. If the engine lifting equipment you are using allows you to remove the engine while the vehicle is on jackstands, it may be easier to leave the vehicle on the stands. If you lower the vehicle, use a hydraulic jack to maintain support for the engine and transaxle.

6.21 Use a prybar or a large screwdriver and pry the engine from the transaxle bellhousing

6.27 Use long, high-strength bolts (arrows) to hold the engine on the engine stand - make sure they are tight before lowering the hoist and placing the entire weight of the engine on the stand

21   Use a prybar or large screwdriver to carefully separate the engine from the transaxle case **(see illustration)**.

22   Attach an engine sling or a length of sturdy chain to the engine and then to the engine hoist. Usually the easiest and best lifting points are the ends of the cylinder heads. Depending on the kind of lifting equipment you are using, bolt the sling or chain to diagonally opposite ends of the heads. You may be able to buy or rent a special sling to make this job easier. **Warning:** *On 2000 and later model engines, do not attach a sling or chains to the fabricated exhaust manifolds or the plastic upper intake manifold. The components could break, possibly causing injury.*

23   **Warning:** *Do not place any part of your body under the vehicle or the engine when the engine is supported only by a hoist. Keep your hands out of the engine compartment, away from areas between the engine and the body when raising or lowering the engine.* Roll the hoist into position and connect the sling or chain to it. Take up the slack in the sling or chain, but don't lift the engine yet.

24   Recheck to be sure nothing is still connecting the engine to the transaxle or vehicle. Disconnect anything still remaining.

25   Raise the engine slightly. Carefully work it forward to separate it from the transaxle. Be sure the torque converter stays in the transaxle (clamp a pair of vise grips to the transaxle housing to keep the converter from sliding out). Slowly raise the engine out of the engine compartment. Check carefully to make sure nothing is hanging up.

26   Remove the driveplate from the engine crankshaft.

27   Mount the engine on an engine stand **(see illustration)**.

28   Once the engine is removed, support the transaxle as explained previously.

Installation

29   Check the engine and transaxle mounts. If they're worn or damaged, replace them.

30   Carefully lower the engine into the engine compartment. Make sure the engine mounts line up.

31   Guide the torque converter onto the crankshaft driveplate following the procedure in Chapter 7. Don't pull the converter away from the transaxle; let the engine move back against the transaxle.

32   Install the transaxle-to-engine bolts and tighten them securely. **Caution:** *Do not use the bolts to force the transaxle and engine together.*

33   Reinstall the remaining components in the reverse order of removal.

34   Add coolant and oil. Run the engine and check for leaks and proper operation of all accessories; then install the hood and test drive the vehicle.

7   Engine rebuilding alternatives

The do-it-yourselfer has several options when performing an engine overhaul. The decision to replace the engine block, the piston and connecting rod assemblies, and crankshaft, and the cylinder heads depends on a number of factors. The most important consideration is the condition of the block. Other considerations are cost, access to machine shop facilities, parts availability, time required to complete the project, and the mechanical experience and skills of the do-it-yourselfer. Some of the rebuilding alternatives include:

Individual parts - If inspection reveals that the engine block and most engine components are in reusable condition, purchasing individual parts may be the most economical alternative. The block, crankshaft, heads, and piston and rod assemblies should all be inspected carefully. Even if the block shows little wear, the cylinder bores should be surface honed.

Crankshaft kit - This rebuild package consists of a reground crankshaft and a matched set of pistons and connecting rods. The pistons will already be installed on the rods, and piston rings and the necessary bearings will be included in the kit. These kits

are commonly available for standard cylinder bores and for engine blocks that have been bored to a regular oversize.

Short block - A short block consists of an engine block with a crankshaft, camshaft and timing chain (for an overhead-valve engine with the camshaft in the block), new oil pump, and piston and rod assemblies already installed. All new bearings are installed, and all clearances will be correct. The existing cylinder heads and upper valve train components and external parts can be bolted to the short block with little or no machine shop work necessary.

Long block - A long block consists of a short block plus new or reconditioned cylinder heads and all valve train components. All components are installed with new bearings, seals and gaskets used throughout. The installation of manifolds and external parts is all that is necessary.

Used Engine – Money can often be saved by purchasing a complete used engine from an auto wrecking yard. Make sure you get the same year and model engine, that the donor vehicle's mileage is low, and that the wrecking yard offers a warranty on the used engine.

Give careful thought to which alternative is best for you and discuss the situation with local automotive machine shops, auto parts dealers, or parts store countermen before ordering or purchasing replacement parts.

8   Engine overhaul - disassembly sequence

Caution: *The cylinder head bolts on all models, as well as the connecting rod bolts and the large main bearing support bolts on the OHC engine, are torque-to-yield bolts and are not reusable. A predetermined stretch of the bolt gives the even clamping load needed to seal the cylinders properly. Once removed they must be replaced.*

1   It's much easier to disassemble and work on the engine if it's mounted on an engine stand. A stand can often be rented quite cheaply from an equipment rental company. Before you mount the engine on a stand, remove the driveplate from the crankshaft.

2   If a stand isn't available, it's possible to disassemble the engine with it blocked up on the floor. Be extra careful not to tip or drop the engine when working without a stand.

3   If you're going to obtain a rebuilt engine, all external components must come off first to be transferred to the replacement engine, just as they will if you're doing a complete engine overhaul yourself. These include:

> Alternator and brackets
> Starter motor (already removed)
> Emissions and engine control components
> All engine control sensors
> Spark plug wires and spark plugs (new plugs and wires are recommended for a new or rebuilt engine)
> Thermostat housing (install a new thermostat if one is not supplied with the new engine)
> Water pump (a new or rebuilt pump is recommended if not already supplied with a rebuilt engine)
> Fuel injection and other fuel system components
> Intake and exhaust manifolds
> Oil filter (replace)
> Engine mounts
> Driveplate
> Crankshaft damper and pulley

4   When you remove external engine components, pay close attention to details that may be helpful or important during installation. Note the installed position of gaskets, seals, spacers, pins, brackets, washers, bolts and other small items.

5   If you're obtaining a short block as described previously, the cylinder heads, will have to be removed as well. See *Engine rebuilding alternatives* for additional information about the different possibilities to be considered.

6   If you're planning a complete overhaul, the engine must be disassembled and the components removed in the following order:

> Driveplate (if not already removed)
> Valve covers
> Intake manifolds
> Exhaust manifolds
> Rocker arms and pushrods (OHV V6 engine)
> Camshafts, rocker arms and lash adjusters (OHC V6 engine)
> Valve lifters (OHV V6 engine)
> Crankshaft vibration damper
> Timing chain cover
> Timing chains, sprockets, guides and tensioners
> Camshaft (OHV V6 engine)
> Cylinder heads
> Oil pan
> Oil pump (replace)

> Piston and connecting rod assemblies
> Crankshaft and main bearings (replace bearings)

7   Before beginning the disassembly and overhaul, make sure the following items are available. Also, refer to *the engine overhaul reassembly sequence* for a list of tools and materials needed for engine reassembly.

> Common hand tools
> Small cardboard boxes and plastic bags for storing parts
> Gasket scraper
> Ridge reamer
> Vibration damper puller
> Micrometers
> Telescoping gauges
> Dial indicator set
> Valve spring compressor
> Cylinder surfacing hone
> Piston ring groove cleaning tool
> Electric drill motor
> Tap and die set (inch sizes and metric)
> Wire brushes
> Oil gallery brushes
> Cleaning solvent

9   Cylinder head - disassembly

Refer to illustrations 9.1, 9.2 and 9.3

Note: *New and rebuilt cylinder heads are commonly available for most engines at dealerships and auto parts stores. Because some specialized tools are necessary for the disassembly and inspection, and replacement parts may not be readily available, it may be more practical and economical for the home mechanic to purchase replacement heads rather than taking the time to disassemble, inspect and recondition the originals.*

1   Cylinder head disassembly involves removal of the intake and exhaust valves and related components. On a OHV V6 engine, remove the rocker arms and related parts as explained in Chapter 2, Part A, if not already removed. On a OHC V6, you must remove the camshafts and timing chains for access to the cylinder head bolts in order to remove the heads. After the camshafts are removed

9.1 A small plastic bag, with an appropriate label, can be used to store the valve train components so they can be kept together and reinstalled in their original positions

from a OHC engine, the rocker arms and hydraulic lash adjusters can be lifted out of the head. Label the parts or store them separately **(see illustration)** so they can be reinstalled in their original locations.

2   Compress the springs on the first valve with a spring compressor and remove the keepers **(see illustration)**. Carefully release the valve spring compressor and remove the retainer, the spring and the spring seat (if used).

3   Pull the valve out of the head, then remove the oil seal from the guide. If the valve binds in the guide (won't pull through), push it back into the head and deburr the area around the keeper groove with a fine file or whetstone **(see illustration)**.

4   Repeat the procedure for the remaining valves. Remember to keep all the parts for each valve together so they can be reinstalled in the same locations.

5   Once the valves and related components have been removed and stored in an organized manner, the head should be thoroughly cleaned and inspected. If you are doing a complete engine overhaul, finish the engine disassembly before beginning the cylinder head cleaning and inspection.

9.2 Use a valve spring compressor to compress the spring, then remove the keepers from the valve stem with needle-nose pliers or a magnet

9.3 If the valve won't pull through the guide, deburr the edge of the stem end and the area around the top of the keeper groove with a file or whetstone

10.12 Check the cylinder head gasket surface for warpage by trying to slip a feeler gauge under the straightedge (see this Chapter's Specifications for the maximum warpage allowed and use a feeler gauge of that thickness)

10.14 Lay the head on its edge, pull each valve out about 1/16 inch, set up a dial indicator with the probe touching the valve stem, move the valve back-and-forth and measure its movement

10   Cylinder head - cleaning and inspection

1   Thorough cleaning of the cylinder heads and related valve train components, followed by a detailed inspection, will let you to decide how much valve service must be done during the engine overhaul. **Note:** *If the engine was severely overheated, the cylinder head is probably warped* (see Step 12).

Cleaning

2   Scrape all traces of old gasket material and sealing compound off the sealing surfaces of the heads and the intake and exhaust manifolds. Special gasket removal solvents that soften gaskets and make removal easier are available at auto parts stores. **Caution:** *Be very careful when scraping on aluminum engine parts. Aluminum is soft and gouges easily. Severely gouged parts may require replacement.*

3   Remove all built-up scale from the coolant passages.

4   Run a stiff wire brush through the various holes to remove deposits that may have formed in them.

5   Run an appropriate-sized tap into each of the threaded holes to remove corrosion and thread sealant that may be present. If compressed air is available, use it to clear the holes of debris produced by this operation. **Warning:** *Wear eye protection when using compressed air!*

6   Clean the exhaust manifold stud threads, if equipped.

7   Clean the cylinder head with solvent and dry it thoroughly. Compressed air will speed the drying process and ensure that all holes and recessed areas are clean. **Note:** *Decarbonizing chemicals are available and may be useful when cleaning cylinder heads and valve train parts. They are very caustic and must be used with caution. Be sure to follow*

the instructions on the container.

8   Clean the valvetrain components with solvent and dry them thoroughly (don't mix them up during the cleaning process). If available, use compressed air to speed the drying process and to clean out the oil passages.

9   Clean all the valve springs, spring seats, keepers and retainers with solvent and dry them thoroughly. Work with the components from one valve at a time to avoid mixing up the parts.

10   Scrape off any heavy deposits that may have formed on the valves; then use a motorized wire brush to remove deposits from the valve heads and stems. Again, make sure the valves don't get mixed up.

Inspection

Note: *Perform all of the following inspection procedures before concluding that machine shop work is required. Make a list of the items that need attention.*

Cylinder head

Refer to illustrations 10.12 and 10.14

11   Carefully inspect the head for cracks, evidence of coolant leakage, and other damage. If cracks are found, check with an automotive machine shop about repair. If repair isn't possible, obtain a new cylinder head.

12   Using a straightedge and feeler gauge, check the head gasket mating surface for warpage **(see illustration)**. Check the head both straight across and corner to corner. If the warpage exceeds the limit listed in this Chapter's Specifications, the head can be resurfaced at an automotive machine shop. If one head is resurfaced, the other head should be resurfaced the same amount. Also, if the heads are resurfaced, the intake manifold flanges may require surfacing.

13   Examine the valve seats in each combustion chamber. If they're pitted, cracked or burned, the head will require valve service that is beyond the scope of the home mechanic.

14   Check the valve stem-to-guide clearance by measuring the lateral movement of the valve stem with a dial indicator attached securely to the head **(see illustration)**. The valve must be in the guide and approximately 1/16-inch off the seat. The total valve stem movement indicated by the gauge needle must be divided by two to obtain the actual clearance. After this is done, if there's still some doubt regarding the condition of the valve guides, they should be checked by an machine shop. (The cost should be minimal).

Valves

Refer to illustrations 10.15 and 10.16

15   Carefully inspect each valve face for uneven wear, deformation, cracks, pits and burned areas **(see illustration)**. Check the valve stem for scuffing and galling and the neck for cracks. Rotate the valve and check for any obvious indication that it's bent. Look for pits and excessive wear on the end of the stem. Any of these conditions indicates the need for valve service by an automotive machine shop.

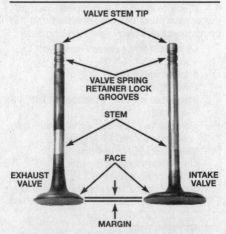

10.15 Check the valve for damage or wear at the indicated areas

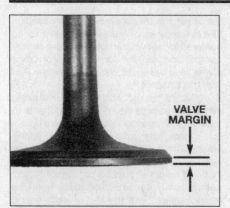

10.16 The margin width on each valve must be as specified (if no margin exists, the valve cannot be reused)

10.17 Measure the free length of each valve spring with a dial or vernier caliper

10.18 Check each valve spring for squareness; if it's out-of-square it should be replaced

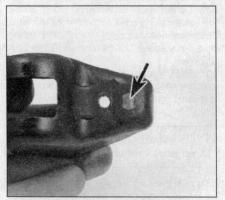

10.22a On OHV V6 engines, check the rocker arms where the pushrod rides (arrow) . . .

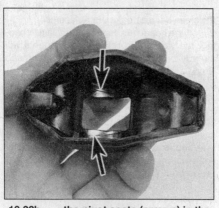

10.22b . . . the pivot seats (arrows) in the top of the rocker arm . . .

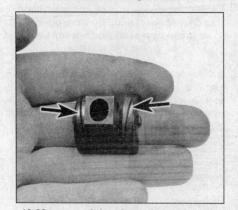

10.22c . . . and the pivots themselves for wear and galling (arrows)

16   Measure the margin width on each valve **(see illustration)**. Replace any valve with a margin narrower than 1/32 inch.

Valve components

Refer to illustrations 10.17 and 10.18

17   Check each valve spring for wear on the ends and pits. Measure the free length and compare it to the Specifications **(see**

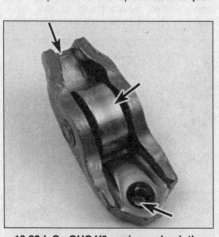

10.22d On OHC V6 engines, check the rocker arms for wear at the valve stem end, the roller, and the pocket that contacts the lash adjuster (arrows)

illustration). Any springs that are shorter than specified have sagged and should not be reused. The tension of all springs should be checked with a special fixture before deciding that they're suitable for use in a rebuilt engine (take the springs to an automotive machine shop for this check).

18   Stand each spring on a flat surface and check it for squareness **(see illustration)**. If any of the springs are distorted or sagged, replace all of them with new parts.

19   Check the spring retainers and keepers for obvious wear and cracks. Any questionable parts should be replaced with new ones because extensive damage will occur if they fail during engine operation.

Rocker arm components

Refer to illustrations 10.22a, 10.22b, 10.22c and 10.22d

20   Clean all the parts thoroughly. Make sure all oil passages are open.

21   Check the rocker arm faces (the areas that contact the pushrod ends, or lash adjusters, and the valve stems) for pits, wear, galling, score marks and rough spots.

22   Check the rocker arm pivot contact areas and seats. Look for cracks in each rocker arm and bolt **(see illustrations)**.

23   Inspect the pushrod ends for scuffing and excessive wear. Roll each pushrod on a

flat surface - such as a piece of plate glass - to determine if it's bent.

24   Any damaged or excessively worn parts must be replaced with new ones.

25   If inspection indicates that the valve components are in generally poor condition and worn beyond the limits specified, which is usually the case in an engine that's being overhauled, reassemble the valves in the cylinder head and refer to Section 11 for valve servicing recommendations.

11   Valves - servicing

1   Because of the complex nature of the job and the special tools and equipment needed, servicing of the valves, the valve seats, and the valve guides - commonly known as a valve job - should be done by a professional.

2   The home mechanic can remove and disassemble the head, do the initial cleaning and inspection, then reassemble and deliver it to a dealer service department or an automotive machine shop for the actual service work. Doing the inspection will enable you to see the condition of the head and valve train components and will ensure that you know what work and new parts are required when dealing with a machine shop.

12.3a On OHV V6 engines with the type of seal shown, use a hammer and a seal installer (or a deep socket, as shown here) to drive the seal onto the valve guide - umbrella-type seals don't need to be driven into place

3　A dealer service department or a machine shop will remove the valves and springs; recondition or replace the valves and valve seats; recondition or replace the valve guides; check and replace the valve springs, spring retainers and keepers; replace the valve seals with new ones; reassemble the valve components and make sure the installed spring height is correct. The cylinder head gasket surface will also be resurfaced if it's warped.

4　After the valve job has been done, the head will be in like-new condition. When the head is returned, be sure to clean it again before installation on the engine to remove any metal particles and abrasive grit that may still be present from the valve service or head resurfacing operations. Use compressed air, if available, to blow out all the oil holes and passages.

12　Cylinder head - reassembly

Refer to illustrations 12.3a, 12.3b, 12.7a, 12.7b and 12.9

1　Whether or not the head was sent to a machine shop for valve servicing, make sure

12.7a Apply a small dab of grease to each keeper as shown here before installation to hold them in place on the valve stem as the spring is released

12.3b Installing a valve stem seal on a OHC V6 engine

it's clean before beginning reassembly.

2　If the head was sent out for valve servicing, the valves and related components will already be in place. Begin reassembly with Step 9.

3　On all engines, lubricate and install the valves, then install new seals on each of the valve guides. Using a valve seal installer or a hammer and deep socket, gently tap each seal into place until it's seated on the guide **(see illustrations)**. Don't twist or cock the seals during installation or they will not seat properly on the valve stems.

4　On OHC engines, reinstall the hydraulic lash adjusters.

5　Beginning at one end of the head, lubricate and install the first valve. Liberally apply clean engine oil to the valve stem.

6　Place the spring seat over the valve guide and set the valve spring, retainer and sleeve (if used) in place.

7　Apply a small dab of grease to each keeper to hold it in place **(see illustration)**. Compress the springs with a valve spring compressor and carefully install the keepers in the upper groove **(see illustration)**; then slowly release the compressor and make sure the keeper seats properly. **Note:** *When*

12.7b Compress the springs with a valve spring compressor and position the keepers in the upper groove, then slowly release the compressor and make sure the keepers seat properly

the camshafts are not on the cylinder head on OHC V6 engines, only the type of valve spring compressor shown can be used; the factory compressor uses the camshafts for leverage and is used during disassembly only (see Part B of this Chapter).

8　Repeat the procedure for the remaining valves. Be sure to return the components to their original locations; don't mix them up.

9　Check the assembled valve spring height with a dial or vernier caliper. If the head was sent out for service work, the installed height should be correct; but don't automatically assume that it is. Take the measurement from the top of each spring seat to the bottom of the retainer **(see illustration)**. If the assembled height is greater than this Chapter's Specifications, shims can be added under the spring to correct it. **Caution:** *Do not install valve spring shims unless the valve spring assembled height exceeds Specifications. Incorrect use of valve spring shims may cause coil binding and valve train damage.*

10　Apply grease to the rocker arm faces and the seats, then install the rocker arms and seats on the cylinder head studs.

13　Camshaft and bearings (OHV engine) - removal and inspection

Note: *On the OHV engine, the camshaft can be removed only after the engine has been removed from the vehicle. The following instructions assume that the rocker arms, pushrods, valve lifters, timing chain and camshaft position sensor/synchronizer assembly have been removed.*

Removal

Refer to illustrations 13.2 and 13.3

1　Before removing the camshaft, check the camshaft end play with a dial indicator aligned with the front of the camshaft. Insert a camshaft sprocket bolt and use it to pull the camshaft fore and aft. If the play is greater than specified, replace the thrust plate with a new one when the camshaft is reinstalled.

12.9 Valve spring installed height is the distance from the spring seat on the head to the bottom of the spring retainer

13.2 Remove the screws retaining the camshaft thrust plate (arrows)

13.3 Carefully withdraw the camshaft from the engine block - avoid nicking the bearings with the lobes

13.5 Measure the camshaft journal diameters to check for wear or out-of-round conditions

2   Remove the camshaft thrust plate bolts **(see illustration)**.
3   Carefully pull the camshaft out. Support the cam so the lobes don't nick or gouge the bearings as it's withdrawn **(see illustration)**.

Inspection

Refer to illustrations 13.5, 13.6a and 13.6b
4   After the camshaft has been removed, clean it with solvent and dry it, then inspect the bearing journals for uneven wear, pitting and evidence of seizure. If the journals are damaged, the bearing inserts in the engine block are probably damaged as well. Both the camshaft and bearings will have to be replaced. Replacement of the camshaft bearings requires special tools and techniques which place it beyond the scope of the home mechanic. The engine block will have to be taken to an automotive machine shop for this procedure.
5   Measure the bearing journals with a micrometer to determine whether they are excessively worn or out-of-round **(see illustration)**.
6   Measure the camshaft lobe height (greatest dimension), then subtract the measurement of the base circle (smallest dimension) to determine the lobe lift **(see illustrations)**.
7   Inspect the camshaft lobes for heat dis-

coloration, score marks, chipped areas, pitting and uneven wear. If the lobes are in good condition and if the lobe lift measurements are as specified, you can reuse the camshaft, although replacement of the camshaft is recommended during an engine overhaul.

14   Pistons and connecting rods - removal

Refer to illustrations 14.1, 14.3, 14.4, 14.6, 14.7 and 4.8
Note: *Before removing the piston and connecting rod assemblies, remove the cylinder heads, the oil pan and the oil pump by referring to the appropriate Sections in Chapter 2, Part A or B, depending which engine is being overhauled.*
1   Use your fingernail to feel if a ridge has formed at the upper limit of ring travel (about 1/4-inch down from the top of each cylinder). If carbon deposits or cylinder wear have produced ridges, they must be completely removed with a special tool **(see illustration)**. Follow the manufacturer's instructions provided with the tool. Failure to remove the ridges before attempting to remove the piston and rod assemblies may damage the

13.6a To calculate lobe lift after the camshaft has been removed, measure the lobe height . . .

pistons. **Note:** *Do not let the tool cut into the ring travel area more than 1/32-inch.*
2   After the cylinder ridges have been removed, turn the engine upside-down so the crankshaft is facing up.
3   Before removing the connecting rods, check the rod endplay with a dial indicator or with feeler gauges **(see illustration)**. Slide them between the first connecting rod and the crankshaft throw until the play is

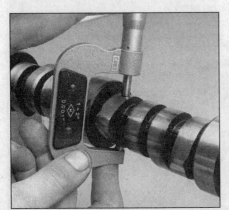

13.6b . . . then measure the camshaft base circle (smallest diameter) and subtract the base circle from the lobe height

14.1 A ridge reamer is required to remove the ridge from the top of each cylinder before removing the pistons

14.3 Check the connecting rod side clearance (endplay) with a dial indicator or a feeler gauge

14.4 Mark the rod bearing caps in order from the front of the engine to the rear. Use a set of number stamps or make one mark for the front cap, two on the second, and so on

14.6 Remove the rod cap and the bearing insert together

14.7 Place a short length of plastic or rubber hose or tubing over the bolt threads to protect the crankshaft and the cylinder walls as you remove the rod

removed. The endplay is equal to the feeler gauge thickness. If the endplay exceeds the service limit, new connecting rods will be required. If new rods (or a new crankshaft) are installed, the endplay may fall under the specified minimum. If it does, the rods will have to be machined to restore it. Consult a machine shop for advice. Repeat the procedure for the remaining connecting rods.

4   Check the connecting rods and caps for identification marks. If they aren't plainly marked, use a small centerpunch, number-stamping die **(see illustration)**, or scribe to make the appropriate number of indentations, or marks, on each rod and cap (1, 2, 3, etc., depending on the engine type and cylinder number).

5   Loosen each of the connecting rod cap nuts one-half turn at a time until they can be removed by hand.

6   Remove the connecting rod cap and bearing insert **(see illustration)**. Don't drop the bearing insert out of the cap.

7   If the rod bolts are inserted into the top side of the big end of the rod, put a short

length of plastic or rubber hose over the bolt threads to protect the crankshaft and the cylinder walls as you remove the rod **(see illustration)**.

8   Remove the bearing insert and push the connecting rod and piston assembly out through the top of the engine. Use a wooden or plastic hammer handle to push on the upper bearing surface in the connecting rod **(see illustration)**. Be careful to avoid hitting the crankshaft journal with the end of the connecting rod. If resistance is felt, double-check to be sure that all of the ridge was removed from the cylinder.

9   Repeat the procedure for the remaining cylinders.

10   After removal, reassemble the connecting rod caps and bearing inserts in their respective connecting rods and install the cap nuts finger tight. Leave the old bearing inserts in place until reassembly to protect the rod bearing surfaces from kicks or gouges.

11   Don't separate the pistons from the connecting rods (see Section 19 for additional information).

15 Crankshaft - removal

Refer to illustrations 15.1 and 15.3

Note: *The crankshaft can be removed only after the engine has been removed from the vehicle. The following instructions assume that the driveplate, vibration damper, timing chains, oil pan, oil pump, pistons and connecting rods have already been removed.*

1   Before starting to remove the crankshaft, check the endplay. Mount a dial indicator with the stem in line with the crankshaft and just touching the end of the crankshaft **(see illustration)**.

2   Push the crankshaft all the way to the rear and zero the dial indicator. Next, pry the crankshaft to the front as far as possible and check the reading on the dial indicator. The distance that it moves is the endplay. If it's greater than limit listed in this Chapter's Specifications, check the crankshaft thrust surfaces for wear. If no wear is evident, new main bearings should correct the endplay.

3   If a dial indicator isn't available, feeler gauges can be used. Gently pry or push the

14.8 Use a hammer handle to drive the piston and connecting assembly down and out of the cylinder block, being very careful not to nick the crankshaft on the way out

15.1 Checking crankshaft endplay with a dial indicator

15.3 Checking crankshaft endplay with a feeler gauge

15.5a Mark the main bearing caps in order from the front to the rear of the engine

crankshaft all the way to the front of the engine. Slip feeler gauges between the crankshaft and the front face of the thrust main bearing to determine the clearance **(see illustration)**.

4 Main bearing removal and installation are quite different on the OHV and the OHC engines. The OHV engine has traditional main bearing caps, while the OHC engine has a separate one-piece integral main bearing support section.

OHV engine

Refer to illustrations 15.5a and 15.5b

Note: *The thrust bearing on the OHV V6 engine is the number three main bearing. It has an upper and lower thrust bearing shell.*

5 On a OHV V6, check the main bearing caps to see if they're marked to indicate their locations **(see illustration)**. They should be numbered consecutively from the front of the engine to the rear. If they aren't, mark them with number-stamping dies or a center-punch. Main bearing caps have cast arrows that point to the front of the engine **(see illustration)**.

6 Loosen the main bearing cap bolts one-quarter turn at a time each, until they can be removed by hand. Note if any studs are used and make sure they're returned to their original locations when the crankshaft is reinstalled.

7 Gently tap the caps with a soft-face hammer; then separate them from the engine block. If necessary, use the bolts as levers to remove the caps. Try not to drop the bearing inserts if they come out with the caps.

8 Carefully lift the crankshaft out of the engine. It may help to have an assistant available because the crankshaft is quite heavy. With the bearing inserts in place in the engine block and main bearing caps, return the caps to their correct locations on the engine block and tighten the bolts finger tight.

OHC engine

Refer to illustration 15.9

Note: *The thrust bearing on the OHC V6 engine is the number four lower main bearing. A semicircular thrust washer is installed in the engine block to align with the lower thrust bearing and absorb crankshaft endplay.*

9 The one-piece main bearing support of the OHC V6 engine is attached to the upper crankcase, or block, with 22 bolts: 16 of which are torque-to-yield bolts. Remove the bolts in the sequence shown **(see illustration)**. **Note:** *Mark the location of the stud bolts so they can be returned to their original locations.*

10 Gently tap the main bearing support with a rubber mallet; then lift the main bearing support from the engine block. Try not to drop the bearing inserts if they come out with

15.5b The arrows on the main bearing caps point toward the front of the engine (drivebelt end)

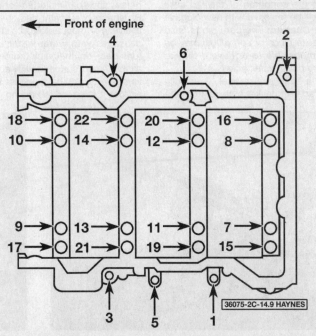

15.9 Remove the main bearing support bolts in this sequence. Bolts 7 through 22 are torque-to-yield bolts and should not be reused

16.1a A hammer and a large punch can be used to knock the core plugs sideways in their bores

16.1b Pull the core plugs from the block with pliers

the support section.

11   Carefully lift the crankshaft out of the engine. It may help to have an assistant available because the crankshaft is quite heavy. With the bearing inserts in place in the block and the main bearing support, reinstall the main bearing support on the block and tighten the bolts finger tight.

16   Engine block - cleaning

Refer to illustrations 16.1a, 16.1b, 16.8 and 16.10

1   Using the wide end of a punch **(see illustration)** tap in on the outer edge of the core plug to turn the plug sideways in its bore. Then, using a pair of pliers, pull the core plug from the block **(see illustration)**. Don't worry about the condition of the old core plugs; they will be replaced with new plugs at reassembly. **Caution:** *The core plugs (also known as freeze plugs or soft plugs) may be difficult or impossible to retrieve if they're driven into the block water jackets.*

2   Using a gasket scraper, carefully remove all traces of gasket material from the

engine block. **Caution:** *Be very careful when scraping on aluminum engine parts. Aluminum is soft and gouges easily. Severely gouged parts may require replacement.*

3   Remove the main bearing caps on a OHV engine or the main bearing support on a OHC engine and separate the bearing inserts from the caps and the block (Section 15). Tag the bearings with their numbers and indicate whether each insert was in the cap or the block; then set them aside.

4   Remove all of the threaded oil gallery plugs from the block. The plugs are usually very tight; they may have to be drilled out and the holes retapped. Use new plugs when the engine is reassembled.

5   If the engine is extremely dirty take it to a machine shop to be steam cleaned or cleaned in commercial cleaning equipment.

6   After the block is returned, clean all oil holes and oil galleries one more time. Brushes specifically designed for this are available at most auto parts stores. Flush the passages with warm water until the water runs clear, dry the block thoroughly, and wipe all machined surfaces with a light, rust-preventive oil. If you have access to compressed air, use it to speed the drying process and to

blow out all the oil holes and galleries. **Warning:** *Wear eye protection when using compressed air.*

7   If the block isn't extremely dirty or sludged up, you can do an adequate cleaning job with hot soapy water and a stiff brush. Take plenty of time and do a thorough job. Regardless of the cleaning method used, be sure to clean all oil holes and galleries very thoroughly, dry the block completely and coat all machined surfaces with light oil.

8   The threaded holes in the block must be clean to ensure accurate torque readings during reassembly. Run the proper size tap into each of the holes to remove rust, corrosion, thread sealant or sludge and restore damaged threads **(see illustration)**. If possible, use compressed air to clear the holes of debris from this operation. Now is a good time to clean the threads on the head bolts and the main bearing cap bolts as well.

9   Reinstall the main bearing caps or main bearing support and tighten all bolts finger tight.

10   Coat the sealing edges of the new core plugs with Permatex no. 2 sealant, or equivalent, and install them in the block **(see illustration)**. Make sure they're driven in straight

16.8 All bolt holes in the block - particularly the main bearing cap and head bolt holes - should be cleaned and restored with a tap - be sure to remove debris from the holes after this is done

16.10 You can use a large socket on an extension to drive the new core plugs into their bores

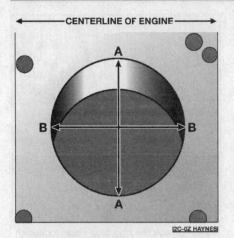

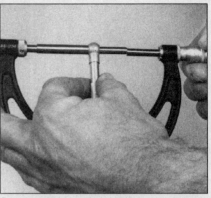

17.4c Then measure the gauge with a large micrometer to determine the bore size

17.4a Measure the diameter of each cylinder at a right angle to the engine centerline (A), and parallel to engine centerline (B). Out-of-round is the difference between A and B; taper is the difference between A and B at the top of the cylinder and A and B at the bottom of the cylinder

17.4b The ability to "feel" when the telescoping gauge is at the correct point will be developed over time, so work slowly and repeat the check until you're satisfied the bore measurement is accurate

and seated properly, or leakage could result. Special tools are available for this purpose, but a large socket, with an outside diameter that will just slip into the core plug, a 1/2-inch drive extension and a hammer will work as well.

11   Apply sealant that doesn't harden (such as Permatex no. 2 or Teflon pipe sealant) to the new oil gallery plugs and thread them into the holes in the block. Tighten the plugs securely.

12   If the engine isn't going to be reassembled right away, cover it with a large plastic trash bag to keep it clean.

17   Engine block - inspection

Refer to illustrations 17.4a, 17.4b and 17.4c

1   Before inspecting the block, clean it as described in Section 16.

2   Check the block for cracks, rust and corrosion. Look for stripped threads in the threaded holes. It's also a good idea to have the block checked for hidden cracks by an automotive machine shop that has the special equipment to do this. If defects are found, have the block repaired, if possible, or replaced.

3   Check the cylinder bores for scuffing and scoring.

4   Check the cylinders for taper and out-of-round conditions as follows (**see illustrations**).

5   Measure the diameter of each cylinder at the top (just under the ridge area), center and bottom of the cylinder bore, parallel to the crankshaft axis.

6   Next measure each cylinder diameter at the same three locations perpendicular to the crankshaft axis.

7   The taper of the cylinder is the differ-

ence between the bore diameter at the top of the cylinder and the diameter at the bottom. The out-of-round specification of the cylinder bore is the difference between the parallel and perpendicular readings. Compare your results to those listed in this Chapter's Specifications.

8   Repeat the procedure for the remaining cylinders.

9   If the cylinder walls are badly scuffed or scored, or if they're out of round or tapered beyond the limits in this Chapter's Specifications, have the block rebored and honed at a machine shop. If a rebore is done, oversize pistons and rings will be required.

10   If the cylinders are in reasonably good condition and not worn outside of the limits, and if the piston-to-cylinder clearances can be maintained properly, then they don't have to be rebored. Honing is all that's necessary (see Section 18).

18   Cylinder honing

Refer to illustrations 18.3a and 18.3b

1   Before engine reassembly, the cylinder bores must be honed so the new piston rings will seat correctly and provide the best possible combustion chamber seal. **Note:** *If you don't have the tools or don't want to tackle the honing operation, most automotive machine shops will do it for a reasonable fee.*

2   Before honing the cylinders, install the main bearing caps or main bearing support and tighten the bolts to the torque in this Chapter's Specifications. Make sure you use only the original main cap bolts, not the new ones for final assembly.

3   Two types of cylinder hones are commonly available: the flex hone or "bottle brush" type, and the more traditional surfacing hone with spring-loaded stones. Both will do the job, but for the less experienced mechanic the "bottle brush" hone should be easier to use. You'll also need some

18.3a A "bottle brush" hone will produce better results if you've never honed cylinders before

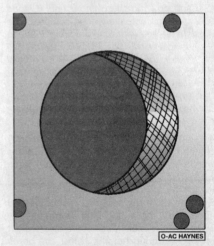

18.3b The cylinder hone should leave a smooth, crosshatch pattern with the lines intersecting at approximately a 60-degree angle

kerosene or honing oil, rags and an electric drill motor. Proceed as follows:

a) *Mount the hone in the drill motor, compress the stones and slip it into the first cylinder* (**see illustration**). *Be sure to wear safety goggles or a face shield!*

19.4a The piston ring grooves can be cleaned with a special tool, as shown here . . .

19.4b . . . or a section of a broken ring

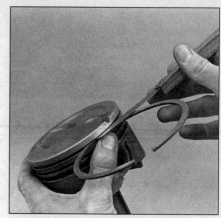

19.10 Check the ring side clearance with a feeler gauge at several points around the groove

b) *Lubricate the cylinder with plenty of honing oil, turn on the drill and move the hone up and down in the cylinder at a pace that will produce a fine crosshatch pattern on the cylinder walls. Ideally, the crosshatch lines should intersect at approximately a 60-degree angle* **(see illustration)**. *Be sure to use plenty of lubricant and don't take off any more material than is absolutely necessary to produce the desired finish.* **Note:** *Piston ring manufacturers may specify a smaller crosshatch angle than the traditional 60-degrees. Read and follow any instructions included with the new rings.*

c) *Don't withdraw the hone from the cylinder while it's running. Instead, shut off the drill and continue moving the hone up and down in the cylinder until it stops rotating completely, then compress the stones and withdraw the hone. If you're using a "bottle brush" hone, stop the drill motor, then turn the chuck in the normal direction of rotation by hand while withdrawing the hone from the cylinder.*

d) *Wipe the oil out of the cylinder and repeat the procedure for the remaining cylinders.*

4   After the honing is complete, slightly chamfer the top edges of the cylinder bores with a small file so the rings won't catch when the pistons are installed. Be careful not to nick the cylinder walls with the file.

5   The entire engine block must be washed again very thoroughly with warm, soapy water to remove all traces of the abrasive grit produced during honing. **Note:** *The bores can be considered clean when a lint-free, white cloth - dampened with clean engine oil - used to wipe them out doesn't pick up any more honing residue. Honing residue will appear as gray areas on the cloth. Be sure to run a brush through all oil holes and galleries and flush them with running water.*

6   After rinsing, dry the block and apply a coat of light rust-preventive oil to all machined surfaces. Wrap the block in a plastic trash bag to keep it clean and set it aside until reassembly.

19   Pistons and connecting rods - inspection

Refer to illustrations 19.4a, 19.4b, 19.10 and 19.11

1   Before inspection, the pistons and connecting rods must be cleaned and the original piston rings removed from the pistons. **Note:** *Always use new piston rings when the engine is reassembled.*

2   Using a piston ring installation tool, carefully remove the rings from the pistons **(see illustration 23.11)**. Be careful not to nick or gouge the pistons in the process.

3   Scrape all traces of carbon from the top of the piston. A hand-held wire brush or a piece of fine emery cloth can be used once most of the deposits have been scraped away. **Caution:** *Do not, under any circumstances, use a wire brush mounted in a drill motor to remove deposits from the pistons. The piston material is soft and will be eroded by the wire brush.*

4   Use a piston ring groove cleaning tool to remove carbon deposits from the ring grooves. If a tool isn't available, a piece broken off the old ring will do the job **(see illustrations)**. Be very careful to remove only the carbon deposits. Don't remove any metal and do not nick or scratch the sides of the ring grooves.

5   After the deposits are removed, clean the piston and rod assemblies with solvent and dry them with compressed air (if available). Be sure the oil return holes in the back sides of the ring grooves are clear.

6   If the pistons and cylinder walls aren't damaged or worn excessively, and if the engine block is not rebored, new pistons won't be necessary. Normal piston wear appears as even vertical wear on the piston thrust surfaces and slight looseness of the top ring in its groove. New piston rings, however, should always be used when an engine is rebuilt.

7   Carefully inspect each piston for cracks around the skirt, at the pin bosses, and at the ring lands.

8   Look for scoring and scuffing on the thrust faces of the skirt, holes in the piston crown and burned areas at the edge of the crown. If the skirt is scored or scuffed, the engine may have been suffering from overheating or abnormal combustion, which caused excessively high operating temperatures. The cooling and lubrication systems should be checked thoroughly. A hole in the piston crown is an indication that abnormal combustion (preignition) was occurring. Burned areas at the edge of the piston crown are usually evidence of spark knock (detonation). If any of these problems exist, the causes must be corrected or the damage will occur again. The causes may include intake air leaks, incorrect fuel-air mixture, incorrect ignition timing, and EGR system malfunctions.

9   Corrosion of the piston, in the form of small pits, indicates that coolant is leaking into the combustion chamber or the crankcase. Again, the cause must be corrected, or the problem may persist in the rebuilt engine.

10   Measure the piston ring side clearance by laying a new piston ring in each ring groove and slipping a feeler gauge in beside

19.11 Measure the piston diameter at a 90-degree angle to the piston pin and in line with it

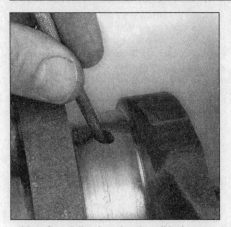

20.1 Carefully chamfer the oil holes so sharp edges won't gouge or scratch the new bearings

20.2 Use a wire or stiff plastic bristle brush to clean the oil passages in the crankshaft

it **(see illustration)**. Check the clearance at three or four locations around each groove. Be sure to use the correct ring for each groove; they are different. If the side clearance is greater than the figure in this Chapter's Specifications, new pistons are needed.

11 Check the piston-to-bore clearance by measuring the bore (Section 17) and the piston diameter. Make sure the pistons and bores are correctly matched. Measure the piston across the skirt, at both a 90-degree angle to the piston pin and in line with the piston pin **(see illustration)**. Subtract the piston diameter from the bore diameter to obtain the clearance. If it's greater than specified, the block will have to be rebored and new pistons and rings installed.

12 Check the piston-to-rod clearance by twisting the piston and rod in opposite directions. Any noticeable play indicates excessive wear, which must be corrected. The piston and rod assemblies should be taken to an automotive machine shop to have the pistons and rods resized and new pins installed.

13 If the pistons must be removed from the connecting rods for any reason, they must be

taken to a machine shop. While they are there have the connecting rods checked for bend and twist. Automotive machine shops have special equipment for these jobs. **Note:** *Unless new pistons or connecting rods must be installed, do not disassemble the pistons and connecting rods.*

14 Check the connecting rods for cracks and other damage. Temporarily remove the rod caps, lift out the old bearing inserts, wipe the rod and cap bearing surfaces clean and inspect them for nicks, gouges and scratches. After checking the rods, replace the old bearings, slip the caps into place and tighten the nuts finger tight. **Note:** *If the engine is being rebuilt because of a connecting rod knock, be sure to install new rods.*

20 Crankshaft - inspection

Refer to illustrations 20.1, 20.2, 20.5 and 20.7

1 Remove all burrs from the crankshaft oil holes with a stone or file **(see illustration)**.
2 Clean the crankshaft with solvent and dry it with compressed air (if available). Be

sure to clean the oil holes with a stiff brush **(see illustration)** and flush them with solvent.
3 Check the main and connecting rod bearing journals for uneven wear, scoring, pits and cracks.
4 Check the rest of the crankshaft for cracks and other damage. It is strongly recommended that the crankshaft be Magnafluxed at an automotive machine shop to look for hidden cracks.
5 Using a micrometer, measure the diameter of the main and connecting rod journals and compare the results to this Chapter's Specifications **(see illustration)**. By measuring the diameter at a number of points around each journal's circumference, you'll be able to determine whether or not the journal is out of round. Take the measurement at each end of the journal, near the crank throws, to determine if the journal is tapered.
6 If the crankshaft journals are damaged, tapered, out of round, or worn beyond the limits in the Specifications, have the crankshaft reground by a machine shop. Be sure to use the correct size bearing inserts if the crankshaft is reground.
7 Check the oil seal journals at each end of the crankshaft for wear and damage. If the seal has worn a groove in the journal, or if it's nicked or scratched **(see illustration)**, the new seal may leak when the engine is reassembled. In some cases, an automotive machine shop may be able to repair the journal by pressing on a thin sleeve. If repair isn't feasible, a new crankshaft should be installed.
8 Refer to Section 21 and examine the main and rod bearing inserts.

21 Main and connecting rod bearings - inspection

Refer to illustration 21.1

1 Even though the main and connecting rod bearings should be replaced with new ones during the engine overhaul, the old

20.5 Measure the diameter of each crankshaft journal at several points to detect taper and out-of-round conditions

20.7 If the seals have worn grooves in the crankshaft journals, or if the seal contact surfaces are nicked or scratched, the new seals will leak

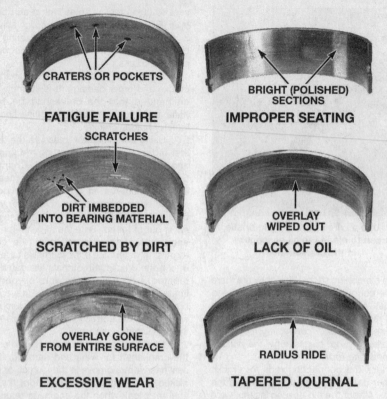

FATIGUE FAILURE
CRATERS OR POCKETS

IMPROPER SEATING
BRIGHT (POLISHED) SECTIONS

SCRATCHED BY DIRT
SCRATCHES
DIRT IMBEDDED INTO BEARING MATERIAL

LACK OF OIL
OVERLAY WIPED OUT

EXCESSIVE WEAR
OVERLAY GONE FROM ENTIRE SURFACE

TAPERED JOURNAL
RADIUS RIDE

21.1 Typical bearing failures

bearings should be examined closely because they may reveal valuable information about the condition of the engine **(see illustration)**.

2   Bearing failure occurs because of lack of lubrication, the presence of dirt or other foreign particles, overloading the engine, and corrosion. Regardless of the cause of bearing failure, it must be corrected before the engine is reassembled to prevent it from happening again.

3   When examining the bearings, remove them from the engine block, the main bearing caps, the connecting rods and the rod caps and lay them out on a clean surface in the same position as their location in the engine. This will enable you to match any bearing problems with the corresponding crankshaft journal.

4   Dirt and other foreign particles get into the engine in several ways. Dirt may be left in the engine during assembly, or it may pass through filters or the PCV system. It may get into the oil and from there into the bearings. Metal chips from machining operations and normal engine wear are often present. Abrasives are sometimes left in engine components after reconditioning, especially when parts are not thoroughly cleaned. Whatever the source, these foreign objects often end up embedded in the soft bearing material and are easily recognized. Large particles will not embed in the bearing and will score or gouge the bearing and journal. The best prevention for this cause of bearing failure is to clean all parts thoroughly and keep everything spot-

lessly clean during engine assembly. Frequent and regular engine oil and filter changes are also recommended.

5   Lack of lubrication (or lubrication breakdown) has a number of interrelated causes. Excessive heat (which thins the oil), overloading (which squeezes the oil from the bearing face), and oil leakage or throw off (from excessive bearing clearances, worn oil pump or high engine speeds) all contribute to lubrication breakdown. Blocked oil passages, which usually result from misaligned oil holes in a bearing shell, also will starve a bearing of oil and destroy it. When lack of lubrication causes bearing failure, the bearing material is wiped or extruded from the steel backing of the bearing. Temperatures may increase to the point where the steel backing turns blue from overheating.

6   Driving habits also can affect bearing life. Low speed operation in too high a gear (lugging the engine) puts very high loads on bearings, which tends to squeeze out the oil film. These loads cause the bearings to flex, which produces fine cracks in the bearing face (fatigue failure). Eventually the bearing material will loosen in pieces and tear away from the steel backing. Short-trip driving leads to corrosion of bearings because the engine does not warm up enough to drive off the condensed water and corrosive gases. These byproducts collect in the engine oil, forming acid and sludge. As the oil is carried to the engine bearings, the acid attacks and corrodes the bearing material.

7   Incorrect bearing installation during

engine assembly also will lead to bearing failure. Tight fitting bearings leave insufficient bearing oil clearance and will result in oil starvation. Dirt or foreign particles trapped behind a bearing insert result in high spots on the bearing, which lead to failure.

22 Engine overhaul - reassembly sequence

1   Before engine reassembly, make sure you have all the necessary new parts, gaskets and seals. These include new torque-to-yield head bolts, rod bolts, and main bearing bolts where required. Then be sure you have the following items on hand:

Common hand tools
A 1/2-inch drive torque wrench
A 3/8-inch drive torque wrench (inch-pound. measurement)
Piston ring installation tool
Piston ring compressor
Vibration damper installation tool
Short lengths of rubber or plastic hose or tubing to fit over connecting rod bolts on OHV V6 engines)
Plastigage
Feeler gauges
A fine-tooth file
New engine oil
Engine assembly lube or grease
Gasket sealant
Thread-locking compound

2   To save time and avoid problems, reassemble the engine in the following general order:

OHV engine

New camshaft bearings (should be done by a machine shop)

Piston rings
Crankshaft and main bearings
Piston and connecting rod assemblies
Oil pump
Oil pan
Camshaft
Valve lifters
Timing chain and sprockets
Timing chain cover
Cylinder heads
Rocker arms and pushrods
Exhaust manifolds
Valve covers
Driveplate

OHC engine

Piston rings
Crankshaft, main bearings, and main bearing support
Piston and connecting rod assemblies
Oil pump
Oil pan
Cylinder heads
Hydraulic valve lash adjusters
Rocker arms
Camshafts and sprockets
Camshaft caps
Timing chains

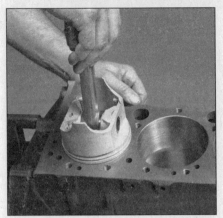

23.3 When checking piston ring end gap, the ring must be square in the cylinder bore - push the ring down with the top of a piston as shown

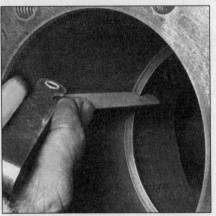

23.4 With the ring square in the cylinder, measure the end gap with a feeler gauge

23.8a Installing the spacer, or expander, in the oil control ring groove . . .

Timing chain guides and tensioners
Timing chain cover
Exhaust manifolds
Valve covers
Driveplate

23 Piston rings - installation

Refer to illustrations 23.3, 23.4, 23.8a, 23.8b and 23.11

1   Before installing the new piston rings, check the ring end gaps. It's assumed that the piston ring side clearance has been checked and verified (Section 19).

2   Lay out the piston and connecting rod assemblies and the new ring sets so the ring sets will be matched with the same piston and cylinder during the end gap measurement and engine assembly.

3   Insert the top (number one) ring into the first cylinder and square it up with the cylinder walls by pushing it in with the top of the piston **(see illustration)**. The ring should be near the bottom of the cylinder, at the lower limit of ring travel.

4   To measure the end gap, slip feeler gauges between the ends of the ring until a gauge equal to the gap width is found **(see illustration)**. The feeler gauge should slide between the ring ends with a slight amount of drag. Compare the measurement to this Chapter's Specifications. If the gap is larger or smaller than specified, double-check to make sure you have the correct rings before proceeding. If there is any doubt contact the parts store where the rings were purchased, to verify that the correct ring set is being used.

5   Excess end gap isn't critical unless it's greater than 0.040-inch. Again, double-check to make sure you have the correct rings for your engine.

6   Repeat the procedure for each ring that will be installed in the first cylinder and for each ring in the remaining cylinders. Remember to keep rings, pistons and cylinders matched up.

23.8b . . . followed by the side rails - DO NOT use a piston ring installation tool when installing the oil ring side rails

7   Once the ring end gaps have been checked, and corrected if necessary, the rings can be installed on the pistons.

8   The oil control ring (lowest one on the piston) is usually installed first. It's composed of three separate components. Slip the spacer or expander into the groove **(see illustration)**. Next, install the lower side rail. Don't use a piston ring installation tool on the oil ring side rails, as they may be damaged. Instead, place one end of the side rail into the groove between the spacer or expander and the ring land, hold it firmly in place and slide a finger around the piston while pushing the rail into the groove **(see illustration)**. Next, install the upper side rail in the same manner.

9   After the three oil ring components have been installed, check to make sure that both the upper and lower side rails can be turned smoothly in the ring groove.

10   The number two (middle) ring is installed next. It's usually stamped with a mark which must face up, toward the top of the piston. **Note:** *Always follow the instructions printed on the ring package or box - different manufacturers may require different approaches. Do not mix up the top and middle rings, as they have different cross-sections.*

11   Use a piston ring installation tool and make sure the identification mark is facing

23.11 Installing the compressor rings with a ring expander - the mark (arrow) must face up

the top of the piston, then slip the ring into the middle groove on the piston **(see illustration)**. Don't expand the ring any more than necessary to slide it over the piston.

12   Install the number one (top) ring in the same manner. Make sure the mark is facing up. Be careful not to confuse the number one and number two rings.

13   Repeat the procedure for the remaining pistons and rings.

24 Crankshaft installation and main bearing oil clearance check

Caution: *The large main bearing support bolts on the OHC engine are torque-to-yield bolts and are not reusable. Once removed they must be replaced with new bolts. During clearance checks using Plastigage, use the old bolts and tighten them to specifications; use new bolts for final assembly.*

1   Crankshaft installation is the first step in engine reassembly. It is assumed at this point that the engine block and crankshaft have been cleaned, inspected and repaired or reconditioned.

2   Position the engine with the bottom facing up.

3   On a OHV V6 engine, remove the main bearing cap bolts and lift out the caps. Lay them out in the proper order to ensure correct installation. On a OHC V6, remove the main bearing support.

4   If they're still in place, remove the original bearing inserts from the block and the main bearing caps. Wipe the bearing surfaces of the block and caps with a clean, lint-free cloth. They must be kept spotlessly clean.

Main bearing oil clearance check

Refer to illustrations 24.11 and 24.15

5   Before permanently installing the crankshaft, check the main bearing oil clearance as directed in the following steps.

6   Clean the backs of the new main bearing inserts and lay one in each main bearing saddle in the block. If one of the bearing inserts from each set has a large groove in it, make sure the grooved insert is installed in the block. Lay the other bearing from each set in the corresponding main bearing cap or in the main bearing support. Be sure the tab on the bearing insert fits smoothly into the notch in the block or cap. **Caution:** *The oil holes in the block must line up with the oil holes in the bearing insert. Do not hammer the bearing into place and don't nick or gouge the bearing faces. No lubrication should be used at this time.*

7   On the OHV engine, install the flanged thrust bearing in the third cap and saddle. On the OHC engine, install the flanged thrust bearing in the number four (rear) bearing location of the main bearing support.

8   Carefully clean the faces of the bearings in the block and the crankshaft main bearing journals with a clean, lint-free cloth.

9   Check or clean the oil holes in the crankshaft. Dirt here can go only one way: straight to the new bearings.

10   When you're sure the crankshaft is clean, carefully lay it in position in the main bearings.

11   Cut several pieces of the appropriate-size Plastigage slightly shorter than the width of the main bearings and place one piece on each crankshaft main bearing journal, parallel with the journal axis **(see illustration)**.

12   On OHV engines, clean the faces of the bearings in the caps and install the caps in their correct positions with the arrows pointing toward the front of the engine (see Section 15). On OHC engines, place the main bearing support assembly into position. Don't disturb the Plastigage. On OHC engines, use the old main bearing support bolts for the oil clearance check, saving the new bolts for final installation.

13   On OHV engines, starting with the center main and working out toward the ends, tighten the main bearing cap bolts to the torque listed in this Chapter's Specifications. Don't rotate the crankshaft at any time during this operation. On OHC engines, tighten the main bearing support bolts, following the recommended tightening sequence **(see**

24.11 Lay the Plastigage strips (arrow) on the main bearing journals, parallel to the crankshaft centerline

illustration 23.40) to the torque listed in this Chapter's Specifications.

14   Remove the bolts and carefully lift off the main bearing caps or main bearing support assembly. Keep them in order. Don't disturb the Plastigage or rotate the crankshaft. If any of the main bearing caps are difficult to remove, tap them gently from side to side with a soft-faced hammer to loosen them.

15   Compare the width of the crushed Plastigage on each journal to the scale printed on the Plastigage envelope to determine the main bearing oil clearance **(see illustration)**. Check the Specifications to make sure it's correct.

16   If the clearance is not as specified, the bearing inserts may be the wrong size, which means different ones will be required. Before deciding that different inserts are needed, make sure that no dirt or oil was between the bearing inserts and the caps or block when the clearance was measured. Also check the block and the main bearing caps for dirt or metal burrs that could keep the cap from seating firmly on the block. If the Plastigage was wider at one end than the other, the journal may be tapered (see Section 20).

17   Carefully scrape all traces of the Plastigage off the main bearing journals and the bearing faces. Use your fingernail or the edge of a plastic card. Don't nick or scratch the bearing faces.

18   Carefully lift the crankshaft out of the engine.

Final crankshaft installation

OHV engine

19   Clean the bearing faces in the block; then apply a thin, uniform layer of engine assembly lube or clean engine oil to each of the bearing surfaces. Be sure to coat the thrust faces as well as the journal face of the thrust bearing.

20   Make sure the crankshaft journals are clean; then lay the crankshaft back in place in the block.

21   Clean the faces of the bearings in the caps; then apply lubricant to them.

22   Install the caps in their respective posi-

24.15 Compare the width of the crushed Plastigage to the scale on the envelope to determine the main bearing oil clearance - always measure at the widest point of the Plastigage. Be sure to use the correct scale; standard and metric ones are provided

tions with the arrows pointing toward the front of the engine.

23   Install the main cap bolts.

24   Tighten all, except the thrust bearing cap bolts (cap number 3) to the torque listed in this Chapter's Specifications.

25   Tighten the thrust bearing cap bolts finger tight.

26   Pry the crankshaft forward. While holding pressure on the crankshaft, pry the thrust bearing cap backward. Forcing these two in opposite directions against each other will align the thrust bearing surfaces.

27   While keeping forward pressure on the crankshaft, tighten all main bearing cap bolts to the torque listed in this Chapter's Specifications.

28   Rotate the crankshaft several times by hand to check for any obvious binding.

29   As a final step, check the crankshaft endplay with a feeler gauge or a dial indicator (see Section 14). The endplay should be correct if the crankshaft thrust faces aren't worn or damaged and new bearings have been installed.

30   Thoroughly lubricate the new rear oil seal and the crankshaft journal with fresh engine oil.

31   Place the new seal on a crankshaft seal installation tool (Ford T99L-6701-A, or equivalent).

32   Position the new seal and the tool on the rear of the engine and alternately tighten the tool bolts to seat the new seal squarely in the seal bore. The sealing lip of the new seal will be very stiff. Slide it carefully over the crankshaft and lubricate both the seal and the crankshaft liberally with clean oil during installation.

33   If the seal installation tool is not available, carefully tap the seal into place with a blunt drift punch and hammer until it is seated evenly in the block. Regardless of the installation method you use, the rear face of the seal must be within 0.005 inch of the rear face of the block and even all the way around.

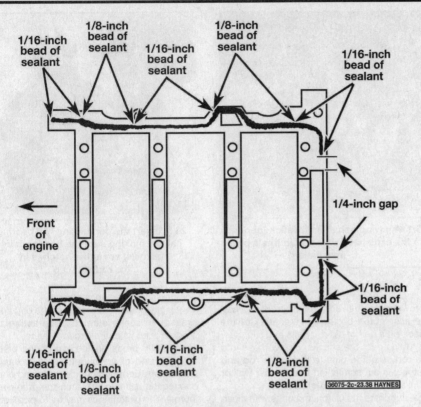

24.38 Apply sealant to the lower surface of the engine block and install the main bearing support within four minutes

OHC engine

Refer to illustrations 24.38 and 24.40
Caution: *The main bearing support bolts 1 through 16 on the OHC V6 engine are torque-to-yield bolts and are not reusable. A predetermined stretch of the bolt, calculated by the manufacturer, gives the added rigidity required with this cylinder block. Once* removed these bolts must be replaced with new bolts. Bolts 17 through 22 are reusable. During clearance checks using Plastigage, use the old bolts and torque to Specifications, but use only new bolts for final assembly.
Note: *Main bearings for the OHC V6 must be selected individually, with their sizes based on the inside diameter of each main bearing*

24.40 Main bearing support bolt TIGHTENING sequence for the OHC V6 engine

web in the assembled engine block and the outside diameter of each crankshaft journal. This selection should be done by an automotive engine machine shop or a Ford parts dealer.

34 Install the upper main bearings and the upper crankshaft thrust washer in the engine block. Be sure that all oil holes are clear and properly aligned and that the bearings seat correctly in the block.

35 Lubricate the upper bearings and the crankshaft journals with fresh engine oil or assembly lubricant. Then carefully place the crankshaft in the block.

36 Install the lower main bearings in the main bearing support. Be sure that all oil holes are clear and properly aligned and that the bearings seat correctly in the crankcase. Then lubricate the lower bearings with fresh engine oil or assembly lubricant.

37 Clean the mating surfaces of the engine block and the main bearing support with a clean, lint-free cloth and denatured alcohol. Be sure that all grease, dirt, and traces of old sealant are removed and that the surfaces are dry.

38 Apply a 1/16-inch and a 1/8-inch bead of RTV sealant to the lower surface of the engine block as shown **(see illustration)**. **Note:** *The main bearing support must be installed and the bolts torqued to final specifications within four minutes of applying the sealer.*

39 Align the main bearing support with the eight alignment dowels in the engine block and install it on the block.

40 Install new torque-to-yield bolts in locations 1 through 16. Tighten all bolts and studs to 27 to 44 inch-pounds in the sequence shown **(see illustration)**. **Note:** *Do not rotate the crankshaft until all bolts are tightened to their final torque specifications.*

41 Push the crankshaft rearward and then use a screwdriver or small prybar to lightly seat the thrust washer forward.

42 Tighten all bolts and studs to the torque listed in this Chapter's Specifications in the sequence shown **(see illustration 24.40)**.

43 Rotate the crankshaft several times by hand to check for any obvious binding.

44 Clean any residual sealer from inside the engine with a clean, lint-free cloth.

45 Lubricate the crankshaft flange and rear oil seal inside diameter with fresh engine oil or assembly lubricant.

46 Place the new seal on a crankshaft seal installation tool and adapter (Ford T82L-6701-A and T91P-6701-A, or equivalent).

47 Position the new seal and the tool on the rear of the engine and alternately tighten the tool bolts to seat the new seal squarely in the seal bore. The sealing lip of the new seal will be very stiff. Slide it carefully over the crankshaft and lubricate both the seal and the crankshaft liberally with clean oil during installation. When installed, the rear face of the seal should be flush with the rear face of the block and even all the way around.

48 Install a dial indicator on the engine and check crankshaft endplay again.

25 Camshaft (OHV engine) - installation

Installation

Refer to illustration 25.1

1   Lubricate the camshaft bearing journals and cam lobes with moly-base grease or engine assembly lube **(see illustration)**.

2   Slide the camshaft into the engine. Support the cam near the engine block and be careful not to scrape or nick the bearings.

3   Apply moly-base grease or engine assembly lube to both sides of the thrust plate, then position it on the engine block with the oil grooves in (against the engine block). Install the bolts and tighten them to the torque listed in this Chapter's Specifications.

26 Pistons and connecting rods - installation and rod bearing oil clearance check

Caution: *The connecting rod bolts on the OHC V6 engine are all torque-to-yield bolts and are not reusable. Once removed they must be replaced with new bolts. During clearance checks using Plastigage, use the old bolts and tighten them to specifications; use new bolts for final assembly.*

1   Before installing the piston and connecting rod assemblies, the cylinder walls must be perfectly clean, the top edge of each cylinder must be chamfered, and the crankshaft must be in place.

2   Remove the cap from the number one connecting rod (refer to the marks made during removal). Remove the original bearing inserts and wipe the bearing surfaces of the connecting rod and cap with a clean, lint-free cloth. They must be spotlessly clean.

Connecting rod bearing oil clearance check

Refer to illustrations 26.3, 26.5, 26.7, 26.10, 26.12, 26.14 and 26.18

3   Clean the back side of the new upper bearing insert; then lay it in place in the connecting rod **(see illustration)**. Make sure the tab on the bearing fits into the notch in the rod. Don't hammer the bearing insert into place and be very careful not to nick or gouge the bearing face. Don't lubricate the bearing at this time.

4   Clean the back side of the other bearing insert and install it in the rod cap. Again, make sure the tab on the bearing fits into the notch in the cap, and don't apply any lubricant. It's very important that the mating surfaces of the bearing and connecting rod be perfectly clean and oil free when they're assembled.

5   Position the piston ring gaps at intervals around the piston **(see illustration)**.

6   On OHV engines, install the connecting rod bolts in the lower ends of the rods and slip a section of plastic or rubber hose over each bolt.

25.1 Apply camshaft installation lubricant to the camshaft lobes and journals prior to installation

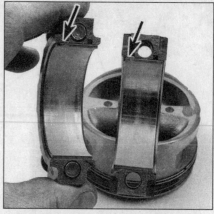

26.3 Insert the connecting rod bearing halves, making sure the bearing tabs (arrows) are in the notches in the rod and cap

7   OHC engines use cap bolts that are screwed into the rod after the rod and cap are assembled on the crankshaft. Cut the heads off a pair of old rod bolts and slip plastic tubing over the shanks. Screw these into the rod as guide pins to install the rod and piston without scratching the cylinder wall or crankshaft **(see illustration)**.

8   Lubricate the piston and rings with clean engine oil and attach a piston ring compressor to the piston. Leave the skirt protruding about 1/4-inch to guide the piston into the cylinder. The rings must be compressed until they're flush with the piston.

9   Rotate the crankshaft until the number one connecting rod journal is at bottom dead center (BDC) and apply a coat of engine oil to the cylinder walls.

10   With the arrow or notches on top of the piston facing the front of the engine **(see illustration)**, gently insert the piston and rod assembly into the number one cylinder bore and rest the bottom edge of the ring

compressor on the engine block.

11   Lightly tap the top edge of the ring compressor to make sure it's contacting the block around its entire circumference.

12   Gently press on the top of the piston with the end of a wooden hammer handle **(see illustration)** while guiding the end of the connecting rod into place on the crankshaft journal. The piston rings may try to pop out of the ring compressor just before entering the cylinder bore, so keep some downward pressure on the ring compressor. Work slowly, and if any resistance is felt as the piston enters the cylinder, stop immediately. Find out what's hanging up and fix it before proceeding. Do not, for any reason, force the piston into the cylinder. You might break a ring or the piston. Remove the guide pins from the rod or the plastic tubing from the rod bolts.

13   Once the piston and rod assembly is installed, the connecting rod bearing oil clearance must be checked before the rod cap is permanently installed.

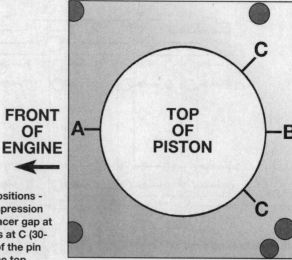

26.5 Ring end gap positions - align the bottom compression ring and the oil ring spacer gap at A, the oil ring side rails at C (30-degrees either side of the pin centerline), and the top compression ring at B

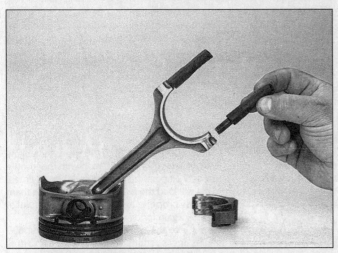

26.7 Cut the heads off two old rod bolts to use as rod installation guides - put rubber hose over them to protect the cylinder wall and the crankshaft

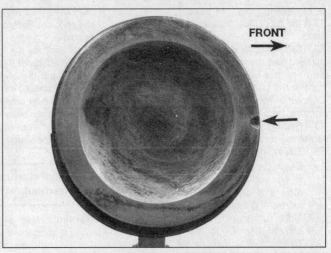

26.10 When installing the pistons, be sure the mark on the piston crown (arrow) faces the front of the engine (drivebelt end)

14   Cut a piece of the appropriate-sized Plastigage slightly shorter than the width of the connecting rod bearing and lay it on the number one connecting rod journal, parallel with the journal axis **(see illustration)**.

15   Clean the connecting rod cap bearing face and install the rod cap. Make sure the mating mark on the cap is on the same side as the mark on the connecting rod.

16   Install the nuts or bolts and tighten them to the torque listed in this Chapter's Specifications. **Note:** *Use a thin-wall socket to avoid erroneous torque readings that can result if the socket is wedged between the rod cap and nut or bolt. If the socket wedges itself between the nut and the cap, lift up on it slightly until it no longer contacts the cap. Do not rotate the crankshaft at any time during this operation.*

17   Remove the nuts or bolts and detach the rod cap, being very careful not to disturb the Plastigage.

18   Compare the width of the crushed Plastigage to the scale printed on the Plastigage envelope to determine the oil clearance **(see illustration)**. Compare it to the Specifications.

19   If the clearance is not as specified, the bearing inserts may be the wrong size (which means different ones will be required). Before deciding that different inserts are needed, make sure that no dirt or oil was between the bearing inserts and the connecting rod or cap when the clearance was measured. Check the mating surfaces of the rod and cap for dirt or metal burrs that could keep the cap from seating firmly on the rod. Also, recheck the journal diameter. If the Plastigage was wider at one end than the other, the journal may be tapered (refer to Section 20).

Final connecting rod installation

20   Carefully scrape all traces of the Plastigage material off the rod journal and bearing face. Be very careful not to scratch the bearing. Use your fingernail or the edge of a

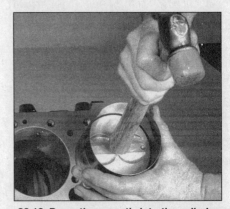

26.12 Press them gently into the cylinder bore with the end of a wooden or plastic hammer handle

plastic card.

21   Make sure the bearing faces are perfectly clean, then fresh engine oil or assembly lubricant to both of them. You'll have to push the piston into the cylinder to expose the face

26.14 Lay the Plastigage strips on each rod bearing journal, parallel to the crankshaft centerline

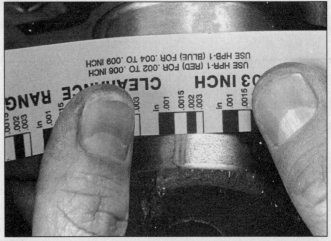

26.18 Measure the width of the crushed Plastigage to determine the rod bearing oil clearance - be sure to use the correct scale; standard and metric ones are provided

of the bearing insert in the connecting rod. (Slip the protective hoses over the rod bolts first.)

22   Slide the connecting rod back into place on the journal, remove the protective hoses from the rod bolts, install the rod cap, and tighten the bolts to the torque listed in this Chapter's Specifications. **Caution:** *On OHC engines, install new rod bolts.*

23   Repeat the entire procedure for the remaining piston and rod assemblies.

24   The important points to remember are:

a) *Keep the back sides of the bearing inserts and the insides of the connecting rods and caps perfectly clean when assembling them.*

b) *Make sure you have the correct piston and rod assembly for each cylinder.*

c) *The notches or mark on the piston must face the front of the engine.*

d) *Lubricate the cylinder walls with clean oil.*

e) *Lubricate the bearing faces when installing the rod caps after the oil clearance has been checked.*

25   After all the piston and rod assemblies are installed, rotate the crankshaft several times by hand to check for any obvious binding.

26   As a final step, check the connecting rod endplay. Refer to Section 14 for this procedure.

27   Compare the measured endplay to the Specifications. If it was correct before disassembly and the original crankshaft and rods were reinstalled, it should still be right. If new rods or a new crankshaft were installed, the endplay may be wrong. If so, the rods will have to be removed and taken to an automotive machine shop for resizing.

27   Initial startup and break-in after overhaul

Warning: *Have a fire extinguisher handy when starting the engine for the first time.*

1   After the engine is installed in the vehicle, double-check the engine oil and coolant levels.

2   With the spark plugs out of the engine and the ignition system disabled by disconnecting the primary connector at the coil pack, crank the engine until oil pressure registers on the gauge or the light goes out.

3   Install the spark plugs, connect the plug wires, and connect the primary circuit connector to the coil pack.

4   Start the engine. It may take a few moments for the fuel system to build up pressure, but the engine should start without a much effort.

5   After the engine starts, allow it to warm up to normal operating temperature. While the engine is warming up, thoroughly check for fuel, oil and coolant leaks.

6   Shut the engine off and recheck the engine oil and coolant levels.

7   Drive the vehicle to an area with no traffic, accelerate from 30 to 50 mph, then allow the vehicle to slow to 30 mph with the throttle closed. Repeat the procedure 10 or 12 times. This will load the piston rings and cause them to seat properly against the cylinder walls. Check again for oil and coolant leaks.

8   Drive the vehicle gently for the first 500 miles (no sustained high speeds) and frequently check the oil level. It is not unusual for an engine to use oil during the break-in period.

9   After approximately 500 to 600 miles, change the oil and filter.

10   For the next few hundred miles, drive the vehicle normally. Do not pamper it or abuse it.

11   After 2000 miles, change the oil and filter again and consider the engine broken in.

Chapter 3
Cooling, heating and air conditioning systems

Contents

Specifications

Thermostat (all engines)	
1996 to 1999	
Opening temperature	193 to 200 degrees F
Fully open temperature	224 degrees F
2000 and later	
Opening temperature	175 to 188 degrees F
Fully open temperature	210 to 220 degrees F
Expansion tank pressure cap	
Specified cap pressure	16 to 18 psi
Test pressure	20 psi
Refrigerant type	R-134a
Refrigerant capacity	34.0 ounces
Refrigerant oil type	Polyalkylene glycol (PAG)
Refrigerant oil capacity	7.0 ounces

Torque specifications   Ft-lbs (unless otherwise indicated)

Note: *One foot-pound (ft-lb) of torque is equivalent to 12 inch-pounds (in-lbs) of torque. Torque values below approximately 15 ft-lbs are expressed in inch-pounds, since most foot-pound torque wrenches are not accurate at these smaller values.*

Thermostat housing bolts	
OHV engine	89 to 124 in-lbs
OHC engine	71 to 106 in-lbs
Water pump bolts	
OHV engine	
Large-diameter bolts (M6)	15 to 22
Small-diameter bolts (M8	71 to 106 in-lbs
OHC engine	
1996 to 2000	
Water pump/housing assembly-to-engine stud-bolts	22
Water pump-to-stud nuts	18
2001 and later, three bolts	
Step 1	89 in-lbs
Step 2	Tighten an additional 90 degrees
Water pump pulley-to-hub bolts (OHV engine only)	15 to 22
Drivebelt tensioner bolts	See Chapter 1
Idler pulley bolt	35

1   General information

The cooling systems on these models use a expansion tank, which is referred to as a "coolant reservoir" in some owner's manuals but which is more than a traditional overflow reservoir. The expansion tank is pressurized when the engine is warm for correct cooling system operation and to remove any air that might be trapped in the system. The radiators in these vehicles do not have conventional pressure caps. The system is pressurized by the pressure cap on the expansion tank, which increases the boiling point of the coolant.

The cooling system also contains the radiator, a thermostat, two temperature-controlled electric cooling fans, and a belt-driven water pump.

The radiator cooling fans are mounted in a shroud on the engine side of the radiator. The fans operate in unison at high and low speeds. Fan speed is controlled by the powertrain control module (PCM) and two relays to keep the engine in the desired operating-temperature range.

The pressurized expansion tank is a plastic reservoir on the right side of the engine compartment. When the engine thermostat is closed, coolant flows through the expansion tube and hose from the lower radiator hose to the expansion tank. When the thermostat is open, coolant flows through both the small hose from the top of the radiator outlet tank and through the expansion tube and hose from the engine to the expansion tank. **Warning** *Never open the expansion tank when the engine is running because there is a danger of injury from steam or scalding water.*

Coolant circulates through the lower radiator hose to the water pump, where it is forced through the water passages in the cylinder block. The coolant then travels up into the cylinder heads, circulates around the combustion chambers and valve seats, travels out of the cylinder head past the open thermostat into the upper radiator hose and back into the radiator. When the minimum operating temperature is reached, the thermostat begins to open and lets coolant return to the radiator.

The left side of the radiator contains an oil cooler for the automatic transmission fluid.

The heating system works by directing air through the heater core, which is like a small radiator mounted behind the dash. Hot engine coolant heats the core, over which air passes to the interior of the vehicle through a system of ducts. Temperature is controlled by mixing heated air with fresh air, using a system of flapper doors in the ducts and a heater motor.

Air conditioning is an optional accessory, consisting of an evaporator located under the dash, a condenser in front of the radiator, an accumulator-drier in the engine compartment and a belt-driven compressor mounted on the engine.

3.7 Disconnect the radiator hose from the thermostat housing (OHV engine)

2   Antifreeze - general information

Warning: *Do not allow antifreeze to contact your skin or painted surfaces of the vehicle. Rinse off spills immediately with plenty of water. Antifreeze is highly toxic if ingested. Never leave antifreeze lying around in an open container or in puddles on the floor; children and pets may be attracted by its sweet smell and may drink it. Check with local authorities about disposing of used antifreeze. Many communities have collection centers which will see that antifreeze is disposed of safely.*

Note: *Nontoxic antifreeze is now manufactured and available at local auto parts stores, but even this type should be disposed of properly.*

The cooling system should be filled with a water and ethylene glycol antifreeze solution which will prevent freezing down to at least -20 degrees F, or lower in very cold climates. The coolant mixture also protects against corrosion and increases the coolant boiling point. The OHC engine has an aluminum block and heads. The OHV engine has an iron block and heads, but many aluminum parts, such as the water pump and the front cover. The manufacturer recommends that only coolant that is safe for aluminum engine components be used.

The cooling system should be drained, flushed and refilled as specified in the Maintenance Schedule (see Chapter 1)..

Before adding antifreeze to the system, check all hose connections. Antifreeze can leak through very small openings.

The exact mixture of antifreeze to water which you should use depends on the local climate conditions. The mixture should contain at least 50-percent antifreeze, but should never contain more than 70-percent antifreeze.

3   Thermostat - check and replacement

Warning: *The engine must be completely cool when this procedure is performed.*

3.8 Remove the thermostat housing from the lower intake manifold (OHV engine)

Note: *Do not drive the vehicle without a thermostat. The electronic engine control system will not operate properly, and emissions and fuel economy will suffer.*

Check

1   Before condemning the thermostat, check the coolant level, drivebelt tension and temperature gauge (or light) operation.

2   If the engine takes a long time to warm up, the thermostat is probably stuck open. Replace the thermostat.

3   If the engine runs hot, check the temperature of the upper radiator hose. If the hose isn't hot, the thermostat is probably stuck shut. Replace the thermostat.

4   If the upper radiator hose is hot, it means the coolant is circulating and the thermostat is open. Refer to the *Troubleshooting* section at the front of this manual for the cause of overheating.

5   If an engine has been overheated, you may find damage such as leaking head gaskets, scuffed pistons, and warped or cracked cylinder heads.

Replacement

OHV engine

Refer to illustrations 3.7, 3.8 and 3.9

6   Drain coolant from the radiator until the coolant level is below the thermostat housing on the engine (See Chapter 1).

7   Disconnect the upper radiator hose from the thermostat housing **(see illustration)**.

8   Remove the three thermostat housing bolts and the housing. The thermostat should come out with the housing **(see illustration)**.

9   Make orientation marks on the housing and on the thermostat before separating the two. Then remove the thermostat and the gasket from the housing **(see illustration)**. Note that the thermostat is not round and will fit into the housing only in one position. For reference, the "jiggle valve," or small pin, on the thermostat must be toward the top of the housing.

10   Position a new gasket and a new thermostat on the thermostat housing. Be sure that the thermostat is properly oriented as

3.9 Note the position of the thermostat in the housing. The thermostat and the housing opening are not round, and the thermostat will fit in only one position

described above. Check the old thermostat to verify the position.

11   Note that the thermostat spring goes into the engine intake manifold, not toward the radiator hose. **Caution:** *Do not install the thermostat backward or it will not open. Serious engine overheating may result.*

12   Install the thermostat housing and the three bolts. Tighten the bolts to the torque listed in this Chapter's Specifications.

13   Connect the upper radiator hose to the thermostat housing and fill the cooling system with the coolant mixture listed in the Chapter 1 Specifications.

14   Start the engine and check for leaks. Let the engine warm up so that the thermostat opens; then stop the engine and top up the expansion tank to the FULL COLD mark.

OHC engine

15   Drain coolant from the radiator until the coolant level is below the lower coolant inlet housing on the engine (see Chapter 1).

16   Raise the vehicle and support it on jackstands.

17   Disconnect the lower radiator hose from the coolant inlet housing.

18   Remove the two coolant inlet housing bolts and the housing. Then remove the thermostat and the O-ring from the thermostat housing (upper coolant inlet housing).

19   Install a new thermostat and O-ring into

the thermostat housing with the spring up. **Caution:** *Do not install the thermostat backward or it will not open. Serious engine overheating may result.* Then install the lower coolant inlet housing and reconnect the radiator hose.

20   Lower the vehicle to the ground and fill the cooling system with the coolant mixture listed in this Chapter's Specifications.

21   Start the engine and check for leaks. Let the engine warm up so that the thermostat opens; then stop the engine and top up the expansion tank to the FULL COLD mark.

---

4   Engine cooling fan and circuit - check, removal and installation

Warning 1: *The models covered by this manual have Supplemental Restraint Systems (SRS), known as airbags. To avoid accidental deployment of the airbag and possible injury, always disconnect the battery ground (negative) cable, then the positive battery cable and wait two minutes before working near any of the impact sensors, steering column, or instrument panel (see Chapter 12). Do not use any electrical test equipment on any of the airbag system wires or tamper with them in any way.*

Warning 2: *Do not work with your hands near the fan any time the engine is running or when the ignition key is in the RUN position. The fan can start at any time the key is in RUN, even with the engine off.*

Check

Refer to illustrations 4.5 and 4.8

1   All models have a pair of two-speed electric fans, mounted in a shroud attached to the back of the radiator.

2   Fan operation is controlled by the powertrain control module (PCM) and a pair of relays for high-speed and low-speed operation. On 1996 and 1997 models, the fan relays are in the constant control relay module (CCRM), along with fuel pump and air conditioning relays (see Chapter 12 for more information regarding the CCRM). On 1998 and later mod-

els, the fans are controlled by individual low- and high-speed relays in the engine compartment relay panel. The coolant temperature sensor (CTS) signals the PCM of engine temperature, and the PCM energizes the low-speed or the high-speed relay as required.

3   If the fans operate continuously, the fault could be either of the relays or the CTS. Refer to Chapter 6 for diagnosis of the sensor.

4   Warm the engine until the instrument panel gauge indicates the high side of normal. The fans should come on. If not, check the cooling fan fuse in the fuse panel (see Chapter 12 for fuse locations).

5   If the fuse is OK, disconnect the electrical connectors from the electric fan motors **(see illustration).**

6   Connect a voltmeter to a chassis ground and probe the connector at the gray/red wire on 1996 and 1997 models or the red/orange wire on 1998 and later models. If the engine is hot and the temperature gauge shows above normal, there should be battery voltage at this wire.

7   Check the circuit ground by switching your meter to the ohms scale. Ground one side of the meter and probe the other side at the black wire terminal of the fan connector. Resistance should be no more than 5 ohms. If resistance is high, trace the black ground wire to the chassis.

8   If there is no power at the terminals in Step 6, check that power is being supplied to the relay. On 1996 and 1997 models, the CCRM is mounted near the battery **(see illustration).** On 1998 and later models, the relays are in the engine compartment relay panel.

Removal and installation

Refer to illustration 4.12

9   Leave the electrical connector disconnected from the fan motor. Then disconnect the plastic clips holding the wiring harness to the fan shroud and move the harness away from the fans.

10   Remove the single bolt from the fan assembly to be removed **(see illustration 4.5, arrow B).**

11   Then lift the fan assembly out of the shroud.

4.5 Disconnect the connector (A) from the fan motor and check for power under hot conditions with a voltmeter - to remove the cooling fan and motor from the fan shroud, remove the bolt (B)

4.8 The CCRM (arrow) on 1996 and 1997 models is located near the battery

4.12 Remove the metal clip and deburr the motor shaft (if necessary) to pull the fan from the motor

5.1 Remove the three hoses from the expansion tank, mounted inside the right front fender

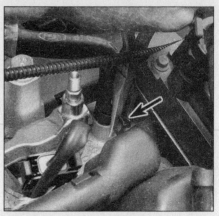

5.6 Use long-nosed pliers to remove the hose clamp from one end of the expansion tube (arrow)

12   To remove the fan blade from the motor, take off the metal clip and slide the fan off the motor shaft **(see illustration)**. If the fan does not slide off easily, check the shaft for burrs and remove any with a fine file.
13   Installation is the reverse of removal.

5   Radiator, expansion tank, and expansion tube - removal and installation

Warning 1: *The engine must be completely cool when this procedure is performed.*
Warning 2: *The models covered by this manual have Supplemental Restraint Systems (SRS), known as airbags. To avoid accidental deployment of the airbag and possible injury, always disconnect the battery ground (negative) cable, then the positive battery cable and wait two minutes before working near any of the impact sensors, steering column, or instrument panel (see Chapter 12). Do not use any electrical test equipment on any of the airbag system wires or tamper with them in any way.*

Expansion tank

Refer to illustration 5.1
1   Drain the cooling system (see Chap-

ter 1), then disconnect the three hoses from the expansion tank **(see illustration)**.
2   Remove the bolts and the expansion tank.
3   Before installation, wash the expansion tank inside and out with soapy water and a long brush if necessary.
4   Installation is the reverse of removal.
5   Refill the system as described in Chapter 1 and check for leaks. Check the coolant level in the expansion tank after the engine has warmed up and cooled down.

Expansion tube (OHV engine only)

Refer to illustrations 5.6, 5.7 and 5.8
6   The expansion tube on the OHV engine passes underneath the upper intake manifold and is attached to the lower intake manifold near the ignition coil pack. Begin by releasing the hose clamp near the ignition coil **(see illustration)**.
7   Then remove the hose clamp at the drivebelt end of the engine **(see illustration)**.
8   With thin open-end wrenches, you may be able to remove the two small capscrews that hold the expansion tube to the bottom of the upper intake manifold **(see illustration)**. If not, refer to Chapter 2A and remove the

upper intake manifold.
9   Installation is the reverse of removal.
10   Refill the system as described in Chapter 1 and check for leaks. Check coolant level in the expansion tank after the engine has warmed up and cooled down.

Radiator

Refer to illustrations 5.13, 5.18a, 5.18b and 5.19
11   Refer to Chapter 5 and remove the battery and the battery tray.
12   On a 1996 or 1997 model, remove the CCRM from its mounting clip and move the module and the attached wiring harness out of the way **(see illustration 4.8)**.
13   Mark and remove the hood latch **(see illustration)**.
14   Raise the vehicle and support it on jackstands.
15   Refer to Chapter 11 and remove the bumper on 1996 through 1998 models.
16   Remove the radiator splash shield.
17   Refer to the warnings in Section 2 about antifreeze and drain the cooling system. Dispose of drained coolant at a disposal center; don't pour it down a drain.
18   Remove the 15 bolts and 2 clips that hold the upper radiator support bulkhead on 1996

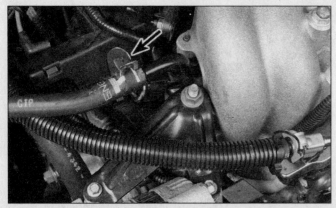

5.7 The other end of the expansion tube is connected to a hose by a similar clamp (arrow). The other end of this hose is connected to the bottle

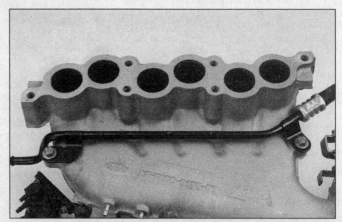

5.8 For clarity, here is a view of the expansion tube attached to the upper manifold with the manifold removed from the engine

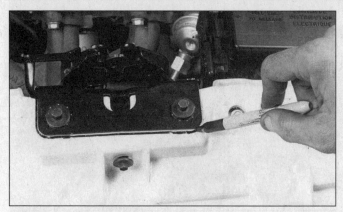

5.13 Draw a line around the hood latch so you can reinstall it in the right location; then remove it

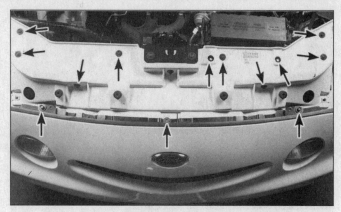

5.18a Remove the 13 bolts indicated by the arrows (and two more which are not shown) . . .

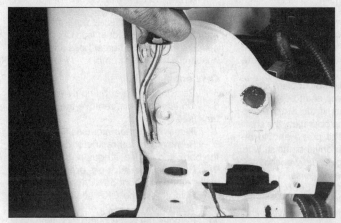

5.18b . . . then pry off the two clips and remove the upper radiator support bulkhead

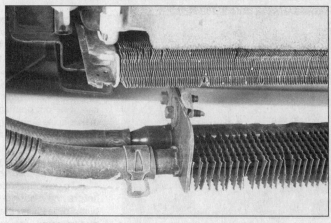

5.19 If equipped, remove the power steering cooler

through 1998 models **(see illustrations)**. On 1999 and later models, remove the two bolts securing the condenser to the radiator assembly (from the engine compartment).

19   If equipped, remove the power steering cooler **(see illustration)**.

20   Remove the upper and lower radiator hoses.

21   Using a special tool, available at auto parts stores, disconnect the the transaxle cooler lines from the radiator.

22   Remove the transaxle cooler bracket and move the cooler out of the way.

23   Remove the two lower condenser-to-radiator bolts.

24   Remove the lower radiator screws and remove the radiator from the bottom of the car. On some models, the lower radiator bracket must be unbolted and removed.

25   Installation is the reverse of removal.

26   Refill the system as described in Chapter 1 and check for leaks. Check coolant level in the expansion tank after the engine has warmed up and cooled down.

---

6   Coolant temperature sending unit - check and replacement

Warning: *Wait until the engine is completely cool before beginning this procedure.*

Check

Refer to illustration 6.1

1   The temperature sending unit that operates the instrument panel gauge has a single-wire brown connector **(see illustration)**. The Coolant Temperature Sensor (CTS) has a two-wire gray connector and is an input to the PCM (computer). Check and replacement of the CTS is covered in Chapter 6.

2   If the instrument panel gauge indicates overheating, check the coolant level in the system. Make sure the wiring between the gauge and the sending unit is secure and all fuses are intact.

3   To test the temperature sending unit, disconnect the electrical connector and connect an ohmmeter between the sending unit terminal and an engine ground. When the engine is cold, resistance should be close to 275 ohms. As the engine warms up, the sending unit resistance should drop and at full operating temperature should read 18 to 20 ohms.

Replacement

4   Drain coolant from the radiator until the coolant level is below the thermostat housing (See Chapter 1).

5   To replace the sending unit, disconnect the electrical connector, unscrew the unit from the engine, and install the replacement. **Caution:** *be careful not to crack the plastic connector on the sensor when installing it.* Use sealant on the threads.

6   Refill the system as described in Chapter 1 and check for leaks. Check coolant level in the expansion tank after the engine has warmed up and cooled down.

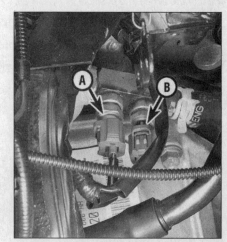

6.1 The connector for the Coolant Temperature Sensor (CTS) is gray (A). The sending unit connector (B) is brown

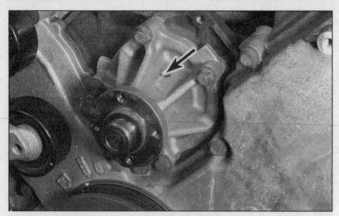

7.2 If coolant is leaking from the weep hole (arrow), the water pump must be replaced

8.11a The OHV engine water pump is secured to the engine by 12 bolts (arrows) of two different diameters

8.11b If necessary after removing all bolts, tap the pump gently with a soft-faced mallet to free it from the front cover

7   Water pump - check

Refer to illustration 7.2
Warning: *The models covered by this manual have Supplemental Restraint Systems (SRS), known as airbags. To avoid accidental deployment of the airbag and possible injury, always disconnect the battery ground (negative) cable, then the positive battery cable and wait two minutes before working near any of the impact sensors, steering column, or instrument panel (see Chapter 12). Do not use any electrical test equipment on any of the airbag system wires or tamper with them in any way.*
1   Water pump failure can cause overheating and serious engine damage. There are three ways to check the operation of the water pump while it's installed on the engine. If any one of the following quick checks indicates water pump problems, the pump should be replaced immediately.
2   A seal protects the water pump shaft bearing from contamination by engine coolant. If this seal fails, a weep hole in the water pump snout will leak coolant **(see illustration)** (An inspection mirror can be used to look at the underside of the pump if the hole isn't on top). If the weep hole is leaking, shaft

bearing failure will follow. Replace the water pump immediately. A small amount of gray discoloration around the weep hole is normal. A wet area or heavy brown deposits indicate the pump seal has failed.
3   Besides contamination by coolant after a seal failure, the water pump shaft bearing can also wear out prematurely. If the water pump makes noise during engine operation, the shaft bearing has failed and the pump should be replaced. Do not confuse drivebelt noise with bearing noise. Loose or glazed drivebelts may emit a high-pitched squealing noise.
4   To identify excessive bearing wear before the bearing fails, grasp the water pump pulley (with the drivebelt removed) and try to force it up and down or from side to side. If you can move the pulley either horizontally or vertically, the bearing is nearing the end of its service life. Replace the water pump.

8   Water pump - removal and installation

Warning: *The models covered by this manual have Supplemental Restraint Systems (SRS), known as airbags. To avoid accidental deployment of the airbag and possible injury, always disconnect the battery ground (negative) cable, then the positive battery cable and wait two minutes before working near any of the impact sensors, steering column, or instrument panel (see Chapter 12). Do not use any electrical test equipment on any of the airbag system wires or tamper with them in any way.*

Removal
Refer to illustrations 8.11a and 8.11b
Warning: *Wait until the engine is completely cool before starting this procedure.*
1   Disconnect the battery ground (negative) cable.
2   Refer to Chapter 1 and drain the cooling system.

OHV engines and 1996 through 2000 OHC engines
3   With the drivebelt installed, loosen the

water pump pulley bolts. Remove the drivebelt and the drivebelt tensioner (see Chapter 1).
4   Disconnect the heater hose and the inlet hose from the water pump.

OHV engines
5   Remove the water pump pulley.
6   On later models, remove the expansion tank (see Section 5).
7   Remove the alternator (see Chapter 5).
8   Remove the roll restrictor bracket from the body and engine, if equipped.
9   Remove the support brace from the water pump and front cover, if equipped.
10   Disconnect the CKP sensor connector (see Chapter 6).
11   Remove the water pump mounting bolts **(see illustration)** and separate the water pump from the front cover **(see illustration)**.

OHC engines
12   Remove the air conditioning compressor support bracket.
13   Remove the water pump mounting nuts and separate the water pump from the engine front cover.

2001 and later OHC engines
Note: *2001 and later Overhead Camshaft (OHC) Duratec engines are equipped with a water pump and drivebelt located on the opposite side of the engine from the accessory drivebelt.*
14   Remove the air filter housing (see Chapter 4).
15   Remove the battery and the battery tray (see Chapter 5).
16   Remove the water pump belt (see Chapter 1).
17   Disconnect the heater hose from the bottom of the water pump. Be sure to have a pan positioned under the engine/transaxle for coolant spillage.
18   Remove the upper radiator hose, the heater hose and the thermostat hose (see Chapter 3).
19   Disconnect the ECT sensor connector, remove the bracket bolt and position the harness aside.
20   Remove the water pump bolts and separate the pump from the housing.

9.5 The blower motor resistor assembly is mounted on the evaporator case, under the right side of the dash

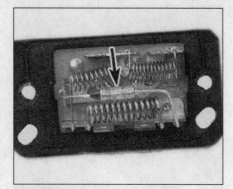

9.6 The resistor assembly contains a thermal limiter (arrow)

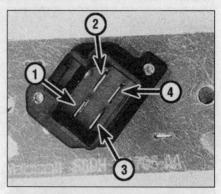

9.7 Test the resistor assembly with an ohmmeter for continuity

Installation

21   Clean all gasket or sealant material from the water pump, the engine front cover, or the block.

22   Place a new gasket on the water pump and coat it on both sides with RTV sealant.

23   On OHV engines, install the water pump onto the engine and tighten the bolts to the torque listed in this Chapter's Specifications.

24   On OHC engines, install the pump on the pump housing and tighten the bolts to the torque listed in this Chapter's Specifications, then install the pump/housing assembly on the engine and install the nuts, tightening them to the torque listed in this Chapter's Specifications.

25   The rest of installation is the reverse of removal.

26   Refill the system as described in Chapter 1 and check for leaks. Check coolant level in the expansion tank after the engine has warmed up and cooled down.

9   Heater and air conditioning blower motor circuit check

Refer to illustrations 9.5, 9.6, 9.7 and 9.8

Warning: *The models covered by this manual have Supplemental Restraint Systems (SRS), known as airbags. To avoid accidental deployment of the airbag and possible injury, always disconnect the battery ground (negative) cable, then the positive battery cable and wait two minutes before working near any of the impact sensors, steering column, or instrument panel (see Chapter 12). Do not use any electrical test equipment on any of the airbag system wires or tamper with them in any way.*

Note: *The blower motor is switched on the ground side of the circuit.*

1   Check the fuses and all connections in the circuit for looseness and corrosion. Make sure the battery is fully charged.

2   With the transmission in Park and the parking brake securely set, turn the ignition switch ON. It isn't necessary to start the vehicle.

3   Locate the electrical connector at the blower motor and inspect it, making sure it is tight and not corroded. Backprobe the con-

nector with a test light or voltmeter. There should be battery voltage at one of the terminals. If not, there is an open in the circuit between the power distribution box and the blower motor.

4   Refer to the wiring diagrams in Chapter 12 and, leaving the blower motor connector connected, ground the wire that runs from the blower motor to the blower motor switch and resistor. If the motor now runs, there is a problem in the blower switch, resistor assembly or wiring between them. If the motor does not run, it is faulty. Replace it.

5   The blower motor resistor assembly is located on the evaporator housing under the dash on the right side, near the blower motor **(see illustration)**. Refer to Chapter 11 for the glove box removal procedure for access to the blower and blower motor resistor. There are three resistor elements on the resistor board to provide low and medium blower speeds (high speed bypasses the resistor). The blower operates continuously when the ignition switch is on and the mode switch is in any position other than off.

6   A thermal limiter resistor is integrated into the circuit to prevent heat damage to the components **(see illustration)**. If the thermal limiter circuit has been opened because of excessive heat, it should be replaced only with the identical replacement part. Do not replace the blower resistor with a resistor that does not have the thermal limiter.

7   With the resistor assembly removed from the car, inspect the limiter for damage, indicated by the material melting out of the limiter. Check the resistor block for continuity between all terminals **(see illustration)**. Resistance between terminals 3 and 4 should be approximately 1.3 to 1.5 ohms; resistance between terminals 2 and 4 should be 1.8 to 2.0 ohms, and resistance between terminals 1 and 4 should be 2.3 to 2.5 ohms. If any resistor element does not pass the test, replace the resistor assembly.

8   If the blower operates, but not at all speeds and you have already checked the blower resistor, refer to Section 11 and remove the heater and air conditioning control panel. Disconnect the electrical connector from the back of the blower speed switch and test the terminals for continuity **(see**

9.8 Check the blower speed switch for continuity

illustration). In the Medium 1 position, there should be continuity between terminals B and D; in Medium 2 position, there should be continuity between terminals B, C and D; and in HI position, there should be continuity between terminals B, A and C . If any switch position is open, replace switch.

10   Heater and air conditioning blower motor - removal and installation

Refer to illustration 10.2

Warning: *The models covered by this manual have Supplemental Restraint Systems (SRS), known as airbags. To avoid accidental deployment of the airbag and possible injury, always disconnect the battery ground (negative) cable, then the positive battery cable and wait two minutes before working near any of the impact sensors, steering column, or instrument panel (see Chapter 12). Do not use any electrical test equipment on any of the airbag system wires or tamper with them in any way.*

1   On all models, remove the pushpins securing the lower insulator panel below the glove box area. On some 1999 and later models, the instrument panel mounting screws may have to be removed and the panel pulled back to allow clearance for removal of the blower motor (see Section 12).

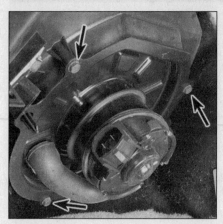

10.2 Remove the three blower motor retaining screws (arrows) to remove the motor

11.3 Two pieces of heavy wire, bent into "U" shapes can be used to release the retaining clips and remove the control assembly

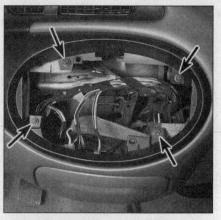

12.6 Remove these screws (arrows) and unclip the heater/air conditioning control assembly finish panel

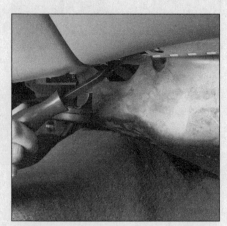

12.9 Pry down at the push-in fasteners and remove this plastic panel

Disconnect the blower motor electrical connector from the motor.

2　Remove the three blower motor retaining screws and remove the motor from the evaporator housing **(see illustration)**.

3　If you are replacing the blower motor, transfer the fan wheel to the new motor at this time. It is attached to the blower motor shaft with a push-nut. Being careful not to crack the push-nut, grasp it with pliers and pull it off or pry it off with a small screwdriver. To reinstall the nut, simply push it onto the shaft.

4　The remainder of the installation is the reverse of removal.

11　Heater and air conditioning control assembly - removal and installation

Warning: *The models covered by this manual have Supplemental Restraint Systems (SRS), known as airbags. To avoid accidental deployment of the airbag and possible injury, always disconnect the battery ground (negative)*

cable, then the positive battery cable and wait two minutes before working near any of the impact sensors, steering column, or instrument panel (see Chapter 12). Do not use any electrical test equipment on any of the airbag system wires or tamper with them in any way.

Removal
Refer to illustration 11.3

1　Disconnect the battery ground (negative) cable.

2　Insert special removal tools or pieces of bent heavy wire into the holes in the control panel faceplate.

3　Apply a light spreading force on the tools to pull the control assembly out of the instrument panel **(see illustration)**.

4　Disconnect the electrical connectors, vacuum harness, and temperature control cable. When disconnecting the vacuum lines, be careful to avoid cracking the plastic connectors and causing a vacuum leak.

5　Refer to Section 9 for electrical tests of the blower motor speed switch.

6　Installation is the reverse of removal.

12　Instrument panel and heater core - removal and installation

Warning: *The models covered by this manual have Supplemental Restraint Systems (SRS), known as airbags. To avoid accidental deployment of the airbag and possible injury, always disconnect the battery ground (negative) cable, then the positive battery cable and wait two minutes before working near any of the impact sensors, steering column, or instrument panel (see Chapter 12). Do not use any electrical test equipment on any of the airbag system wires or tamper with them in any way.*

Instrument panel
Refer to illustrations 12.6, 12.9, 12.10, 12.15, 12.17, 12.20, 12.22, 12.23, 12.24, 12.25, 12.26 and 12.27

1　Take the vehicle to a dealer service

department or automotive air conditioning shop and have the air conditioning system discharged.

2　Disconnect the negative battery cable from the battery.

3　Refer to Chapter 1 and drain the cooling system.

4　Remove the center console assembly (see Chapter 11)

5　Remove the heater/air conditioning control assembly (see Section 11).

6　Remove the screws and unclip the heater/air conditioning control assembly finish panel **(see illustration)**.

7　Remove the headlight switch and pry out the headlight switch finish panel and the trunk release button finish panel (if equipped) (see Chapter 12). Unplug the electrical connectors for the switch and button and remove them.

8　Remove the instrument cluster assembly (see Chapter 12).

9　Pry down at the plastic push-in fasteners to remove the plastic panel beneath the passenger's side of the instrument panel **(see illustration)**.

10　Disconnect the electrical and vacuum connectors from the heater/air conditioning assembly and the blower motor **(see illustration)**.

11　Remove the screws below the glove box door.

12　Open the glove box door and squeeze each side of the glove box liner until the limit pins pop out. Remove the glove box assembly from the vehicle.

13　Remove the screws and pry off the glove box finish panel.

14　Remove the metal clip from behind the dash at the brake release handle assembly. Disconnect the brake release cable end from the release arm, then slide the cable housing out of the bracket. Pull on the brake release handle and slide the handle and cable assembly straight out of the dash.

15　Remove the bulb holder assemblies from the instrument panel frame **(see illustration)**.

16　Remove the two screws from the bot-

12.10 Once the panel is removed, these electrical and vacuum fasteners are exposed (arrows)

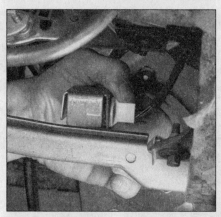

12.15 Disconnect all the bulb holder assemblies from the instrument panel frame

12.17 Disconnect all electrical connectors from the steering column

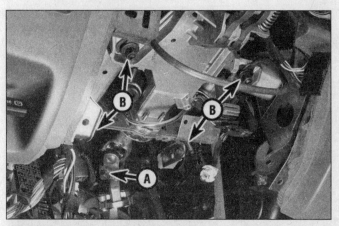

12.20 Remove the pinch bolt (A), then unscrew the four steering column mounting nuts (B). The lower left nut is hidden from view in this photo

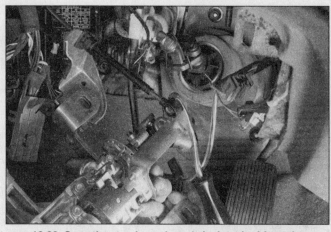

12.22 Once the steering column is is detached from the instrument panel, unclip this cable

tom of the trim panel directly beneath the steering column and unclip the trim panel.

17   Disconnect all electrical connectors from the steering column assembly **(see illustration)**.

18   Turn the ignition key to the LOCK position and verify the steering wheel is locked in position and cannot rotate. **Caution:** *Failure to lock the steering column at this time will result in damage to the airbag's "clockspring" connection. Do not unlock the steering column until it is back in place and attached to the intermediate shaft.*

19   Remove the steering wheel (see Chapter 12).

20   Mark the position relationship of the steering column U-joint to the intermediate shaft, then remove the U-joint pinch bolt **(see illustration)**.

21   Remove the four nuts that secure the steering column, lower the column down and slide it off the intermediate shaft.

22   Pry the cable off at the base of the steering column **(see illustration),** then release the cable housing from its bracket on the steering column assembly.

23   Unscrew the diagnostic connector from the lower instrument panel frame **(see illustration).**

24   Remove the instrument panel frame screws at either side of the glove box opening **(see illustration).**

12.23 Remove the screws and detach the diagnostic connector from the lower instrument panel frame

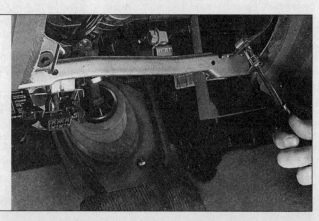

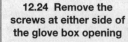

12.24 Remove the screws at either side of the glove box opening

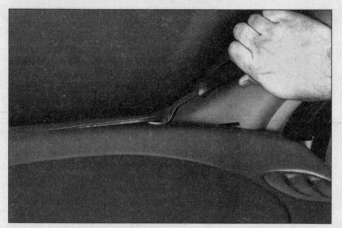

12.25 Pry up and remove the finish panel at the base of the windshield

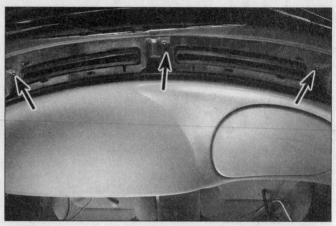

12.26 Once the finish panel is removed, these three instrument panel attachment screws will be exposed (arrows)

12.27 There are two instrument panel attachment screws at either end of the dash, beneath covers that can be pried off

12.32 Disconnect the heater hoses (arrows) from the heater core inlet and outlet tubes in the engine compartment. Plug the tubes to prevent spilling coolant on the carpet

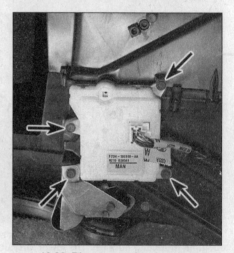

12.33 Disconnect the electrical connector, remove the screws (arrows) and detach the blend door actuator

12.34 Disengage the spring from the heater core cover

25   Carefully pry up and remove the finish panel at the base of the windshield **(see illustration)**.

26   Remove the three attachment screws at the top of the instrument panel **(see illustration)**.

27   Open the front doors and pry off the trim panels at the left and right ends of the instrument panel **(see illustration)** and remove the two screws at each end.

28   Check carefully that there are no more electrical connectors or other parts still connected to the instrument panel assembly.

29   Gently lift the instrument panel assembly up and back, then remove the panel assembly through one of the doors. If the panel does not lift out easily, check to make sure there are no other fasteners or components still attached.

30   Installation is the reverse of removal.

Heater core

Refer to illustrations 12.32, 12.33, 12.34, 12.35, 12.37a, 12.37b and 12.38

Warning: *The air conditioning system is under high pressure. Do not loosen any fit-* tings or remove any components until the system has been discharged. Air conditioning refrigerant should be properly discharged into an EPA-approved container at a dealer service department or an automotive air conditioning repair facility. Always wear eye protection when disconnecting air conditioning system fittings.

Caution: *To prevent damage to the carpet from spilled coolant, it is best to cover the carpet area around the heater core with an old blanket or towels.*

31   Remove the instrument panel (refer to Steps 1 through 30). On 2000 and later models, remove the passenger-side cowl vent screen.

32   Disconnect the heater hoses from the heater core inlet and outlet tubes at the firewall in the engine compartment **(see illustration)**. Plug the heater core tubes or use a length of hose and blow residual coolant out of the core to keep from spilling any on the carpet.

33   Remove the four screws and remove the blend door actuator from the evaporator housing **(see illustration)**.

34   Disengage the spring from the heater core cover **(see illustration)**. **Caution:** *The short lever is very brittle and will break if you try to bend it.*

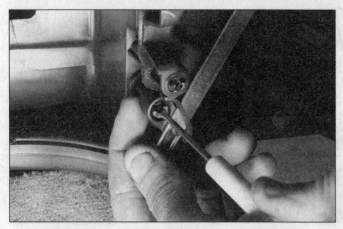

12.35 Remove the short lever from the temperature control door shaft

12.37a Remove the three screws (arrows) . . .

35   Gently depress the locking ramp and remove the short lever from the temperature control door shaft **(see illustration)**.

36   Rotate the temperature control door shaft downward and remove the long metal link from the pin at its lower end.

37   Remove the three screws from the heater core cover **(see illustration)**, then lift up on the lever and remove the cover and gasket from the housing **(see illustration)**.

38   Remove the heater core **(see illustration)**.

39   Transfer the foam seal to the new heater core and install the new core in the housing.

40   The rest of installation is the reverse of removal.

41   Refill the cooling system as described in Chapter 1 and check for leaks. Check coolant level in the expansion tank after the engine has warmed up and cooled down. Have the air conditioning system charged and check for proper operation of the system.

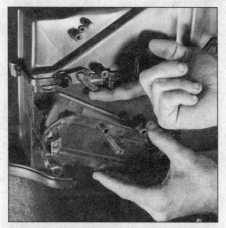

12.37b . . .then lift up on the lever and remove the heater core cover

12.38 Slowly remove the heater core, being careful not to spill coolant

---

13   Air conditioning and heating system - check and maintenance

Warning: *The air conditioning system is under high pressure. Do not loosen any fittings or remove any components until the system has been discharged. Air conditioning refrigerant should be properly discharged into an EPA-approved container at a dealer service department or an automotive air conditioning repair facility. Always wear eye protection when disconnecting air conditioning system fittings.*

1   Perform the following maintenance steps regularly to ensure that the air conditioner continues to operate at peak efficiency.

a) *Check the condition of the drivebelt (Chapter 1).*

b) *Check the condition of the hoses. Look for cracks, hardening and deterioration.* **Warning:** *Do not replace air conditioning hoses until the system has been discharged by a dealer or air conditioning shop.*

c) *Check the fins of the condenser for leaves, bugs and other foreign material. Use a soft brush and compressed air to remove them.*

d) *Check the wiring harness for correct routing, broken wires, and damaged insulation. Make sure the harness connections are clean and tight.*

e) *Maintain the correct refrigerant charge.*

2   Operate the air conditioning for about 10 minutes at least once a month. This is particularly important during the winter because long-term nonoperation can cause hardening of the internal seals.

3   Because of the complexity of the air conditioning system and the special equipment required to work on it, troubleshooting should be left to a professional technician. One probable cause for poor cooling that can be determined by the home mechanic is low refrigerant charge. If the system loses its cooling ability, the following procedure will help you pinpoint the cause.

Check

4   Warm the engine to normal operating temperature.

5   Place the air conditioning temperature selector at the coldest setting and turn the blower on to the highest setting. Open the doors to make sure the air conditioning system doesn't cycle off as soon as it cools the passenger compartment.

6   After the system reaches operating temperature, feel the two pipes connected to the evaporator at the firewall.

7   The pipe (thinner tubing) leading from the condenser outlet to the evaporator should be cold, and the evaporator outlet line (the thicker tubing that leads back to the compressor) should be slightly colder. If the evaporator outlet is considerably warmer than the inlet, the system needs a charge.

8   Insert a thermometer in the center air distribution duct on the instrument panel while operating the air conditioning system. The temperature of the outlet air should be 35 to 40 degrees F below the ambient air temperature (down to approximately 40 degrees F). If the ambient (outside) air temperature is over 100 degrees F, the duct air temperature may be 60 to 70 degrees F; but generally the air conditioning is 35 to 40 degrees F cooler than the ambient air. If the air isn't as cold as it used to be, the system probably needs a charge. Further inspection or testing of the system is beyond the scope of the home mechanic and should be left to a professional.

13.10 A charging kit for R-134a systems is available at most auto parts stores. It must say R-134a (not R-12) and so must the 12-ounce can of refrigerant

13.11 Charge the air conditioning system through the low-side port only. Do not try to connect the hose to the high-side port

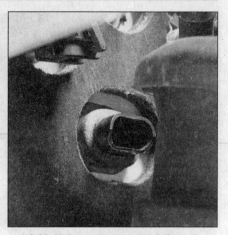

13.20 If the evaporator drain hose is blocked, moisture will accumulate in the evaporator housing and cause a musty smell

Adding refrigerant

Refer to illustrations 13.10 and 13.11

9   All models covered by this manual use refrigerant R-134a. When recharging or replacing air conditioning components, use only refrigerant, refrigerant oil, and seals compatible with this system. The seals and compressor oil used with older R-12 refrigerant are not compatible with the components in this system.

10   Buy an automotive charging kit at an auto parts store **(see illustration)**. A charging kit includes a 14-ounce can of R-134a refrigerant, a tap valve and a short section of hose that can be attached between the tap valve and the system low-side service port. Because one can of refrigerant may not be enough to charge the system to the proper level, it's a good idea to buy a couple of additional cans. Try to find at least one can that contains red refrigerant dye. If the system is leaking, the red dye will leak out with the refrigerant and help you pinpoint the location of the leak.

11   Follow the manufacturer's instructions and connect the charging kit to the low-side service port near the firewall **(see illustration)**. **Warning:** *Wear protective eye wear when working with pressurized refrigerant cans.* Following the manufacturer's instructions, close the valve handle on the charging hose and screw the valve onto the refrigerant can. Make sure that the O-ring or rubber seal inside the threaded portion of the kit is in place. Remove the dust cap from the low-side charging port and attach the quick-connect fitting on the kit hose **(see illustration)**. **Warning:** *DO NOT connect the charging hose to the system high side! The fittings on the charging kit are designed to fit only on the low side of the system.*

12   Warm the engine to normal operating temperature and turn on the air conditioning. Keep the charging kit hose away from the drivebelt and other moving parts. **Warning:** *Never add more than two cans of refrigerant*

to the system. Turn the valve handle on the kit until the stem pierces the can, then back the handle out to release the refrigerant. You should be able to hear the rush of gas. Add refrigerant to the low side of the system until both the outlet and the evaporator inlet pipe feel about the same temperature. Allow stabilization time between each addition. The can may frost up, slowing the procedure. Wet a shop towel with hot water and wrap it around the bottom of the can to keep it from frosting.

13   Put your thermometer back in the center register and verify that the output air is getting colder.

14   When the can is empty, close the valve and disconnect the hose from the low-side port. Replace the port dust cap.

15   Remove the charging kit from the can and store the kit for future use with the piercing valve in the up position to prevent accidentally piercing the can on the next use.

Heating systems

Refer to illustration 13.20

16   If the air coming out of the heater vents isn't hot, the problem could be any of the following:

a) *The thermostat is stuck open, preventing the engine coolant from warming up enough to carry heat to the heater core. Replace the thermostat (Section 3).*

b) *A heater hose is blocked, preventing coolant flow through the heater core. Feel both heater hoses at the firewall. They should be hot. If one is cold, there is an obstruction in one of the hoses or in the heater core, or the heater control valve is shut. Detach the hoses and backflush the heater core with a water hose. If the heater core is clear but circulation is blocked, remove the two hoses and flush them with a water hose. If flushing fails to remove the blockage from the heater core, the core must be replaced. (Section 12).*

c) *The temperature control door inside the heater/air-conditioning box is stuck or*

not operating properly. This problem is best diagnosed by a dealer service department or other qualified shop.

17   If the blower motor speed does not correspond to the setting of the blower switch, the problem could be a bad fuse, circuit, control panel or blower resistor (Section 10).

18   If there isn't any air coming out of the vents:

a) *Turn on the ignition and the blower switch. Listen for the motor at the heating and air conditioning outlet .*

b) *If you can't hear the motor and have already verified that the blower switch and the blower motor resistor are good, the blower motor is probably bad (Section 10).*

19   If the carpet under the heater core is damp, or if antifreeze vapor or steam is coming through the vents, the heater core is leaking. Remove it (Section 12) and install a new unit. (Most radiator shops will not repair a leaking heater core.)

20   Inspect the evaporator drain hose at the bottom of the firewall **(see illustration)**. Make sure it is not clogged. If there is a humid mist coming from the system ducts, this hose may be plugged with leaves or road debris.

Eliminating air conditioning odors

Refer to illustration 13.24

21   Unpleasant odors that often develop in air conditioning systems are caused by the growth of a fungus, usually on the surface of the evaporator core. The warm, humid environment is a perfect breeding ground for mildew.

22   The evaporator core on most vehicles is hard to access, and dealership service departments have a lengthy procedure to eliminate the fungus by opening the evaporator case and using a powerful disinfectant and rinse on the core until the fungus is gone. You can service your own system at home, but it takes something much stronger than basic household germ-killers or deodorizers.

13.24 Remove the blower resistor and spray disinfectant through the hole (arrow) onto the evaporator core to destroy mildew that causes air conditioning odors

14.4 Disconnect the electrical connector (left arrow) at the A/C cycling switch on the accumulator-drier. The nut and stud (right arrow) hold the drier to the vehicle body

23   Aerosol disinfectants for automotive air conditioning systems are available in most auto parts stores, but the most effective treatments are also the most expensive. The basic procedure for using these sprays is to start by running the system in the recirculation mode for 10 minutes with the blower on its highest speed. Use the highest heat mode to dry out the system. Keep the compressor from engaging by disconnecting the wiring connector at the compressor (Section 15).

24   The disinfectant can usually comes with a long spray hose. Remove the blower motor resistor (Section 10), point the nozzle inside the hole and spray, according to the manufacturer's recommendations **(see illustration)**. Try to cover the whole surface of the evaporator core by aiming the spray up, down and sideways. Follow the manufacturer's recommendations for the length of spray and waiting time between applications.

25   After the evaporator is cleaned, the best way to prevent the mildew from returning is to make sure your evaporator housing drain tube is clear **(see illustration 13.20)**.

14   Air conditioning accumulator-drier - removal and installation

Removal

Refer to illustrations 14.4, 14.5a and 14.5b

Warning: *The air conditioning system is under high pressure. Do not loosen any fittings or remove any components until the system has been discharged. Air conditioning refrigerant should be properly discharged into an EPA-approved container at a dealer service department or an automotive air conditioning repair facility. Always wear eye protection when disconnecting air conditioning system fittings.*

Caution: *Cap or plug any open refrigerant lines when components are removed from the system. Open lines allow air, moisture, and dirt to enter the system, which can dam-*

age new parts and harm system performance.
Note: *Special spring-lock coupling tools are required to release the connectors used on the refrigerant lines. They are available in a set at auto parts stores.*

1   The accumulator-drier stores refrigerant and removes moisture from the system. When any major air conditioning component (compressor, condenser, or evaporator) is replaced, or the system has been apart and exposed to air for any time, the accumulator-drier must be replaced.

2   Have the air conditioning system discharged by a dealer service department or an automotive air conditioning shop.

3   Remove the mounting bolts for the cooling system expansion tank and disconnect and cap the two upper hoses on the bottle. Move the expansion tank out of the way for access to the accumulator-drier. On 2001 and later models, remove the two bolts and remove the engine's anti-roll arm (near the expansion tank) and its mounting bracket.

4   Disconnect the electrical connector on the air conditioning cycling switch on top of the accumulator-drier **(see illustration)**.

5   On 1996 to 1999 models, disconnect the refrigerant inlet line from the evaporator at the firewall. Then disconnect the outlet line at the accumulator-drier. On 2000 and later models, both inlet and outlet lines are disconnected at the drier with spring-lock couplings. Remove the metal clips first, then use spring-lock coupling tools to disconnect the two lines **(see illustrations)**. To disconnect a fitting, close the two halves of the tool over the connection and push the tool towards the garter spring to expand the spring to release its hold. While the spring is expanded and the tool is still in place, pull in opposite directions on the two lines to separate the connection. Cap or plug the open lines immediately. Use a 3/4-inch coupling tool on the evaporator line and a 5/8-inch tool on the drier line.

6   Remove the nut from the mounting bracket and slide the accumulator-drier assembly up and out of the mounting bracket **(see illustration 14.4)**. **Note:** *On some models, a nut and/or stud must be removed to remove an air-conditioning hose mounting bracket to allow the freedom to pull out the accumulator-drier.*

14.5a Pull off the metal clip at each connection . . .

14.5b . . . and use the spring-lock coupling tool to separate the line connections

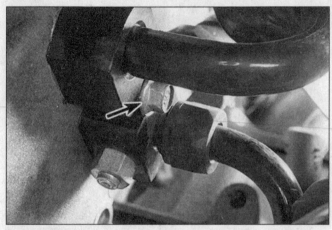

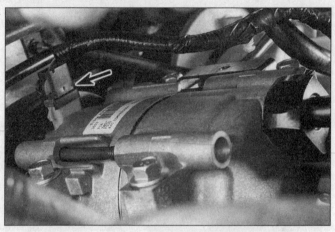

15.4 Remove this bolt (arrow) and detach the refrigerant lines from the compressor

15.5a Disconnect the compressor clutch (arrow) and . . .

Installation

7   If you are replacing the accumulator-drier, drain the refrigerant oil from the old accumulator-drier. (Drill two 1/2-inch holes in the bottom of the old drier to be sure all of the oil drains out.) Add the same amount plus two ounces of clean refrigerant oil to the new accumulator, but do not exceed 7 ounces. This maintains the correct oil level in the system after the repairs are completed.

8   Place the new accumulator-drier into position, tighten the mounting bracket screw lightly, still allowing the accumulator drier to be turned to align the line connections.

9   Install the inlet and outlet lines. Lubricate the O-rings using clean refrigerant oil and reconnect the lines. Now tighten the clamp bolt securely and reconnect the electrical connector.

10   Reinstall the coolant expansion tank.

11   Have the system evacuated, recharged, and leak tested by a dealer service department or an air conditioning service facility.

---

15   Air conditioning compressor - removal and installation

Warning: *The air conditioning system is under high pressure. Do not loosen any fittings or remove any components until the system has been discharged. Air conditioning refrigerant should be properly discharged into an EPA-approved container at a dealer service department or an automotive air conditioning repair facility. Always wear eye protection when disconnecting air conditioning system fittings.*

Caution: *Cap or plug any open refrigerant lines when components are removed from the system. Open lines allow air, moisture, and dirt to enter the system, which can damage new parts and harm system performance.*

Note 1: *Special spring-lock coupling tools are required to release the connectors used on the refrigerant lines. They are available in a set at auto parts stores. See Section 14 for tool description and use.*

Note 2: *Whenever a compressor is replaced, the accumulator-drier also must be replaced and the evaporator orifice tube should be replaced by an air conditioning service shop if the system contains any dirt or debris.*

Removal

OHV engine

Refer to illustrations 15.4, 15.5a and 15.5b

1   Have the air conditioning system discharged by a dealer service department or an automotive air conditioning shop.

2   Disconnect the battery ground (negative) cable and remove the engine drivebelt. (See Chapter 1.)

3   Remove the right-hand cooling fan (Section 4). On 2000 and later models, disconnect the power steering hose from the pump and remove the nut securing the hose to the front exhaust manifold. Set the hose aside.

4   Remove the refrigerant manifold (and tubing) from the rear of the compressor **(see illustration)**.

5   Disconnect the electrical connectors at the compressor clutch and at the pressure cutoff switch **(see illustrations)**.

6   Disengage the wiring harness from the compressor bracket and move the harness aside.

7   Remove the compressor mounting bolts. **Note:** *On 2000 and later models, the top-left-hand mounting bolt must come out with the compressor.*

8   Remove the compressor from its bracket. Drain the refrigerant oil from the compressor and measure it in a graduated container.

OHC engine

9   Take the vehicle to a dealer service department or automotive air conditioning shop and have the air conditioning system discharged.

10   Remove the battery and remove the drivebelt. (See Chapter 1.)

11   Refer to Chapter 1 and drain the cooling system.

12   Disconnect the lower radiator hose from the radiator and from the thermostat housing.

15.5b . . . the pressure cutoff switch (arrow)

Move the hose aside. On 2000 and later models, disconnect the coolant hoses and remove the metal coolant pipe along the front of the engine.

13   Remove the two lower bolts that hold the compressor to its bracket.

14   Remove the upper radiator support (Section 5).

15   Remove both the left-hand and right-hand fans (section 4).

16   Remove the 4 bolts that hold the fan shroud to the subframe and push the shroud forward.

17   Remove the refrigerant manifold (and tubing) from the rear of the compressor **(see illustration 15.4)**.

18   Disconnect the electrical connectors at the compressor clutch and at the pressure cutoff switch **(see illustrations 15.5a and 15.5b)**.

19   Disengage the wiring harness from the compressor bracket and move the harness aside. On 2000 and later models, disconnect the heated oxygen sensor electrical connector.

20   Remove the 2 upper compressor mounting bolts.

15.24 Use new O-rings (arrows), lubricated with refrigerant oil, when reattaching the manifold to the compressor

21   Remove the compressor from its bracket. Drain the refrigerant oil from the compressor and measure it in a graduated container.

Installation

Refer to illustration 15.24

22   If the compressor is being replaced, drain any shipping oil that may be in the new compressor.

23   If the amount of refrigerant oil drained from the old compressor was 3 ounces or less, add a total of 6 ounces of new oil to the new compressor. If the amount drained was more than 5 ounces, add that amount of new oil, and if the drained amount was between 3 and 5 ounces, add that amount plus an extra ounce to the new compressor.

24   Installation procedures are the reverse of those for removal. When installing the refrigerant line manifold to the compressor, use new O-rings and lubricate them with clean refrigerant oil **(see illustration)**.

25   After the compressor is installed, have the system evacuated, recharged and leak tested by a dealer service department or an air conditioning service shop.

---

16   Air conditioning condenser - removal and installation

Warning 1: *The models covered by this manual have Supplemental Restraint Systems (SRS), known as airbags. To avoid accidental deployment of the airbag and possible injury, always disconnect the battery ground (negative) cable, then the positive battery cable and wait two minutes before working near any of the impact sensors, steering column, or instrument panel (see Chapter 12). Do not use any electrical test equipment on any of the airbag system wires or tamper with them in any way.*

Warning 2: *The air conditioning system is under high pressure. Do not loosen any fittings or remove any components until the system has been discharged. Air conditioning refrigerant should be properly discharged into an EPA-approved container at a dealer service department or an automotive air conditioning repair facility. Always wear eye protection when disconnecting air conditioning system fittings.*

Caution: *Cap or plug any open refrigerant lines when components are removed from the system. Open lines allow air, moisture, and dirt to enter the system, which can damage new parts and harm system performance.*

Note: *Special spring-lock coupling tools are required to release the connectors used on the refrigerant lines. They are available in a set at auto parts stores. See Section 14 to see how they are used.*

Removal

Caution: *Whenever a condenser is replaced, the accumulator-drier also must be replaced and the evaporator orifice tube should be replaced by an air conditioning service shop if the system contains any dirt or debris.*

1   Have the air conditioning system discharged by a dealer service department or an automotive air conditioning shop.

2   Remove the 2 screws that hold the top of the condenser to the radiator.

3   Raise the vehicle, support it on jackstands, refer to Chapter 11, and remove the radiator splash shield (lower air deflector).

4   Remove the two nuts and one screw that hold the power steering cooler (if equipped) to the A/C condenser and move the cooler out of the way.

5   Disconnect the condenser outlet tube (to the evaporator) and the inlet tube and manifold (from the compressor). On some models, they are disconnected by removing a nut at an aluminum block-type connector. On other models, spring-lock coupling tools will be required (see Section 14 for information on using spring-lock coupling tools).

6   Remove the remaining two screws that hold the condenser to the radiator.

7   Lift the condenser off the support brackets on the radiator and lower it out the bottom of the vehicle.

Installation

8   If the condenser is being replaced with a new one, transfer the brackets and mounts from the old unit to the new one.

9   Before installation, check the brackets and mounts for wear or damage. Replace them if necessary.

10   When replacing the condenser add one ounce of refrigerant oil to the condenser before reassembly to maintain the correct oil level in the system.

11   Installation is the reverse of removal. When installing hoses and fittings that have O-rings, use new O-rings and lubricate them with clean refrigerant oil.

12   After the condenser is installed have the system evacuated, charged, and leak tested by a dealer service department or an air conditioning service shop.

Notes

Chapter 4
Fuel and exhaust systems

Contents

Specifications

Fuel pressure

Fuel system pressure
  1996 through 1999 models (at idle)
    Vacuum hose attached .... 30 to 45 psi
    Vacuum hose detached .... 40 to 50 psi
  2000 models (key On, engine not running) .... 30 to 45 psi
  2001 models (key On, engine not running) .... 35 to 65 psi
  2002 and later models (key On, engine not running)
    3.0L OHV engine .... 39 to 65 psi
    3.0L OHC engine .... 39 to 55 psi
    3.0L OHC flexible fuel vehicle .... 30 to 65 psi
Fuel system hold pressure (after 5 minutes) .... less than 5 psi loss from indicated operating pressure
Fuel pump pressure (maximum) .... 65 psi
Injector resistance
  1996 through 1999 models .... 11 to 18 ohms
  2000 models
    3.0L OHC flexible fuel engines .... 13.8 to 15.2 ohms
    3.0L OHV and 3.0L OHC engine .... 11 to 18 ohms
  2001 models
    3.0L OHV engine .... 8.5 to 15.5 ohms
    3.0L OHV engine .... 10.3 to 17.3 ohms
  2002 and later models
    3.0L OHV and 3.0L OHC flexible fuel engines .... 11.4 to 12.6 ohms
    3.0L OHC engine .... 13.1 to 14.5 ohms

Torque specifications

Ft-lbs (unless otherwise indicated)

Note: *One foot-pound (ft-lb) of torque is equivalent to 12 inch-pounds (in-lbs) of torque. Torque values below approximately 15 ft-lbs are expressed in inch-pounds, since most foot-pound torque wrenches are not accurate at these smaller values.*

Throttle body mounting nuts
  OHV V6 engine
    1996 to 1998 .... 15 to 22
    1999
      Bolt .... 71 to 106 in-lbs
      Nuts .... 45 to 61 in-lbs
    2000 and later, all .... 89 in-lbs
  OHC V6 engine
    1996 to 1999 .... 71 to 106 in-lbs
    2000 and later .... 89 in-lbs

1   General information

Sequential Multiport Fuel Injection (SFI) system

The fuel system consists of the Powertrain Control Module (PCM), the Constant Control Relay Module (CCRM) (1996 and 1997 models), the Inertia Fuel Shutoff (IFS) switch, the Fuel Pump Driver Module (FPDM) (2002 and later models), the fuel tank, the electric in-tank fuel pump/fuel level sensor, the fuel rail pressure sensor (2000 and later models), the fuel pressure regulator, the fuel rail and injectors, the air filter housing and the throttle body. For a more detailed description of the fuel injection system, refer to Section 11.

The Constant Control Relay Module (CCRM) (1996 and 1997) is located in the engine compartment and incorporates the fuel pump relay and the Powertrain Control Module (PCM) relay. The fuel pump relay (1998 and later models) is located in the fuse/relay center in the engine compartment. The fuel pressure regulator is mounted in different locations depending on the year. On 1996 through 1999 models, the fuel pressure regulator is on the fuel rail. On 2001 and 2002 models, the regulator is on the fuel pump assembly. 2002 and later models use a Fuel Pump Driver Module (FPDM) to regulate the fuel pressure electronically, instead of using a fuel pressure regulator. The PCM controls the fuel pressure by controlling the duty cycle of the FPDM, which in turn controls the speed of the fuel pump by modulating the voltage to the fuel pump.

1996 through 1999 models are equipped with a return-type fuel system. Excess fuel is returned from the fuel rail back to the fuel tank by way of a fuel return line. 2000 and later models are equipped with a returnless fuel system; 2000 and 2001 models are equipped with a Mechanical Returnless Fuel system (MRFS) and 2002 and later models are equipped with an Electronic Returnless Fuel system (ERFS).

Fuel pump circuit

The fuel pump relay is equipped with a primary and secondary voltage circuit. The primary circuit is controlled by the PCM and the secondary circuit is linked directly to battery voltage from the ignition switch. With the ignition switch ON (engine not running), the PCM will ground the relay for one second. During cranking, the PCM grounds the fuel pump relay as long as it receives reference pulses from the Camshaft Position (CMP) sensor (see Chapter 6). If there are no reference pulses, the fuel pump will shut off after two or three seconds.

Inertia Fuel Shutoff (IFS) switch

The Inertia Fuel Shutoff (IFS) switch disables the fuel pump circuit in the event of a collision. The IFS switch is located in the luggage compartment behind the trunk trim

panel. When an impact of sufficient force occurs, the switch opens the fuel pump circuit, thereby stopping the flow of fuel. Once the IFS switch is open, you must manually reset it (see Section 2).

Fuel pump

Return-type fuel system (1996 through 1999)

Fuel is circulated from the fuel tank to the fuel injection system and back to the fuel tank through a pair of metal lines running along the underside of the vehicle. An electric fuel pump is located inside the fuel tank. The return system routes fuel in excess of the engine's requirements back to the fuel tank through a separate return line. The fuel pump will operate as long as the engine is running or cranking and the PCM is receiving ignition reference pulses from the electronic ignition system.

Returnless Fuel system (2000 and later)

Fuel is circulated from the fuel tank to the fuel injection system through a metal line running along the underside of the vehicle. An electric fuel pump/fuel level sensor is located inside the fuel tank. The fuel pump/fuel level sensor assembly consists of the pump, the fuel level sensor, an inlet filter (sometimes referred to as a *sock* or *strainer*), a check valve to maintain pressure after the pump is shut off and a pressure relief valve to protect the pump from over-pressurization in the event of a blocked fuel line.

Mechanical returnless fuel system (MRFS) - 2000 and 2001 models

This system incorporates the fuel pressure regulator as an integral component of the fuel pump/fuel level sending unit that is located in the fuel tank. This system bleeds off excess fuel directly at the fuel pressure regulator in the tank.

Electronic returnless fuel system (ERFS) - 2002 and later models

What sets this fuel system apart from conventional in-tank pumps is its variable speed capability. The PCM controls fuel pressure by controlling the speed (rpm) of the pump. The PCM alters the fuel pressure by controlling the duty cycle of the Fuel Pump Driver Module (FPDM), which in turn controls the speed of the fuel pump by modulating the voltage to the fuel pump.

Exhaust system

The exhaust system includes the exhaust manifolds, the catalytic converters, the mufflers and the exhaust pipes connecting all of these components together.

The catalytic converters, which are installed in the exhaust system, are emission-control devices that reduce the three principal tailpipe pollutants: hydrocarbons (HC), carbon monoxide (CO) and oxides of nitrogen (NOx). For more information about how catalysts work, refer to Chapter 6.

2   Fuel pressure relief procedure

Refer to illustrations 2.1 and 2.5

Warning: *Gasoline is extremely flammable, so take extra precautions when you work on any part of the fuel system. Don't smoke or allow open flames or bare light bulbs near the work area, and don't work in a garage where a gas-type appliance (such as a water heater or a clothes dryer) is present. Since gasoline is carcinogenic, wear latex gloves when there's a possibility of being exposed to fuel, and, if you spill any fuel on your skin, rinse it off immediately with soap and water. Mop up any spills immediately and do not store fuel-soaked rags where they could ignite. The fuel system is under constant pressure, so, if any fuel lines are to be disconnected, the fuel pressure in the system must be relieved first. When you perform any kind of work on the fuel system, wear safety glasses and have a Class B type fire extinguisher on hand.*

Note: *After the fuel pressure has been relieved. it's a good idea to lay a shop towel over any fuel connection to be disassembled, to absorb the residual fuel that may leak out when servicing the fuel system.*

1   The fuel pump switch (sometimes called the "inertia switch") which shuts off fuel to the engine in the event of a collision, affords a simple and convenient means by which fuel pressure can be relieved before servicing fuel injection components. The inertia switch is located in the right side of the trunk behind the trim panel **(see illustration)**.

2   Unplug the inertia switch electrical connector.

3   Start the engine and allow it to run until it stops. This should take only a few seconds.

4   The fuel system pressure is now relieved. Before working on any fuel system components, disconnect the cable from the negative terminal of the battery.

5   When you're finished working on the fuel system, simply plug the electrical connector back into the switch and reconnect the battery. If the inertia switch was popped (activated) during this procedure, push the reset button on the top of the switch **(see illustration)**.

3   Fuel pump operation and fuel pressure - check

Warning: *Gasoline is extremely flammable, so take extra precautions when you work on any part of the fuel system. See the* **Warning** *in Section 2.*

Note 1: *You will need a fuel pressure gauge and adapter set (fuel line fittings) for the fuel pressure test.*

Note 2: *The fuel pump operates whenever the engine is cranking or running and the PCM is receiving ignition reference pulses (a tachometer signal) from the ignition system. If the PCM stops receiving the ignition reference pulses, it will turn off the pump after two or three seconds.*

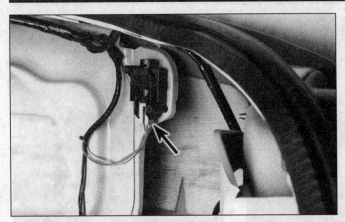

2.1 The inertia switch is located in the trunk. Disconnect the electrical connector (arrow) to disable the fuel pump

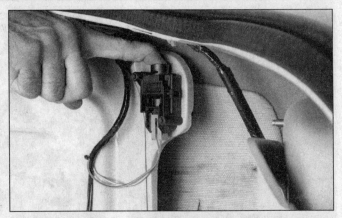

2.5 If necessary, push the reset button after connecting the inertia switch to energize the fuel pump

Note 3: *After the fuel pressure has been relieved, it's a good idea to place a shop towel under any fuel connection to be disassembled, to absorb the residual fuel that may leak out.*

Fuel pump operation

Refer to illustration 3.3

Note: *The fuel pump relay on 1996 and 1997 models is part of the constant control relay module (CCRM), which is an integrated module that contains the EEC power relay, the air conditioning relay, the engine fan relays, and the fuel pump relay. The CCRM is a sealed unit, located near the battery, and the relays cannot be serviced or replaced separately. The CCRM was eliminated from 1998 models, and the fuel pump relay, along with the EEC power relay, is in the power distribution box in the engine compartment.*

1   If the fuel system does not deliver the proper amount of fuel, or any fuel at all, check the simplest thing first. Press the reset button on the inertia switch in the trunk **(see illustration 2.5)**. Then, check fuel pump operation as follows:

2   Remove the fuel filler cap. Have an assistant turn the ignition key on (engine not running) while you listen at the fuel filler opening. You should hear the whirring sound of the pump running, which should last for a couple seconds.

3   If you don't hear anything, check the fuel pump fuse in the engine compartment power distribution box **(see illustration)**. If the fuse is blown, replace it and see if it blows again. If it does, trace the fuel pump circuit for a short.

4   If the fuse is not blown, check the relay operation by following the check procedure in Chapter 12.

5   Listen at the fuel filler opening again. If you now hear the pump whirring, the relay or its control circuit is faulty. **Note:** *Because the CCRM on 1996 and 1997 models is expensive, you might want to have it tested by a dealership service department or other qualified repair shop before buying a new one.*

6   If there is still no whirring sound, there is a problem in the fuel pump circuit from the

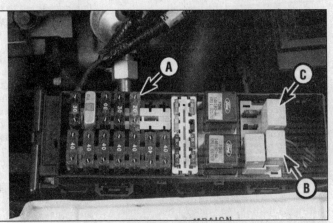

3.3 The 20-amp fuel pump fuse is number 10 (A) in the power distribution box. On a 1998 model, you can swap the fuel pump relay (B) with the EEC power relay (C) to check fuel pump operation. You can't run the engine, however, with a defective relay in the EEC relay position

relay to the fuel pump, a defective fuel pump relay, or a defective fuel pump.

7   With the ignition on, check for battery voltage to the fuel pump relay connector and the power relay connector in the CCRM harness connector (1996 and 1997) or at the battery positive (B+) terminals in the power distribution box (1998 and later). If battery voltage is not present, have the CCRM or the relay tested at a dealership service department or other qualified repair shop.

Fuel pump pressure check

Refer to illustration 3.9

Note: *Before proceeding, obtain a fuel pres-*

sure gauge capable of measuring fuel pressure well above the specified operating range of the fuel system you're going to test. You will also need fittings suitable for connecting the gauge onto the fuel rail (early models) or into the fuel system between the fuel delivery line and the fuel rail (late models).

8   Relieve the fuel system pressure (see Section 2).

9   In addition to a fuel pressure gauge capable of reading fuel pressure in excess of 65 psi, you'll need a hose and an adapter suitable for connecting the gauge onto the fuel rail (early models) or into the fuel system between the fuel delivery line and the fuel rail (late models) **(see illustration)**.

3.9 A typical fuel pressure gauge with hoses and fittings suitable for connecting to the fuel rail

3.10 Connect a fuel pressure gauge to the test port on the fuel rail

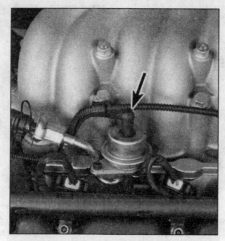

3.12 Check fuel pressure with the vacuum line connected to the pressure regulator (arrow) and with the line disconnected

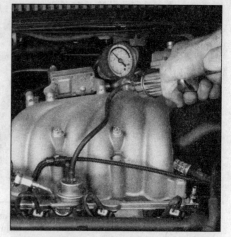

3.15 Connect a vacuum pump to the fuel pressure regulator and check fuel pressure with vacuum applied and with no vacuum applied

Return-type fuel system (1996 through 1999)

Refer to illustrations 3.10, 3.12 and 3.15

10   Remove the cap from the fuel pressure test port and attach a fuel pressure gauge **(see illustration)**. If you don't have the correct adapter for the test port, remove the Schrader valve and connect the gauge hose to the fitting, using a hose clamp.

11   Start the engine.

12   Check the fuel pressure at idle. Compare your readings with the values listed in this Chapter's Specifications. Disconnect the vacuum hose from the fuel pressure regulator and watch the fuel pressure gauge - the fuel pressure should jump up considerably as soon as the hose is disconnected **(see illustration)**. If it doesn't, check for a vacuum signal to the fuel pressure regulator (see Step 17).

13   If the fuel pressure is low, pinch the fuel return line shut and watch the gauge. If the pressure doesn't rise, the fuel pump is defective or there is a restriction in the fuel feed line. If the pressure rises sharply, replace the pressure regulator. **Note:** *If the vehicle is equipped with a nylon fuel return line (or fuel lines made up of steel or other rigid material), it will be necessary to install a special fuel testing harness between the fuel rail and the return line. This can be made up from compatible fuel line connectors (available at a dealer parts department and some auto parts stores), fuel hose and hose clamps.*

14   If the fuel pressure is too high, turn the engine off. Disconnect the fuel return line and blow through it to check for a blockage. If there is no blockage, replace the fuel pressure regulator.

15   Hook up a hand-held vacuum pump to the port on the fuel pressure regulator **(see illustration)**.

16   Read the fuel pressure gauge with vacuum applied to the fuel pressure regulator and also with no vacuum applied. The fuel pressure should decrease as vacuum increases (and

increase as vacuum decreases).

17   Connect a vacuum gauge to the pressure regulator vacuum hose. Start the engine and check for vacuum. If there isn't vacuum present, check for a clogged hose or vacuum port. If the amount of vacuum is adequate, replace the fuel pressure regulator.

18   Turn the ignition switch to OFF, wait five minutes and recheck the pressure on the gauge. Compare the reading with the hold pressure listed in this Chapter's Specifications. If the hold pressure is less than specified:

  a) *The fuel lines may be leaking.*
  b) *The fuel pressure regulator may be allowing the fuel pressure to bleed through to the return line.*
  c) *A fuel injector (or injectors) may be leaking.*
  d) *The fuel pump may be defective.*

Returnless fuel system (2000 and later)

Note: *Some models are equipped with a fuel pressure test port on the fuel rail. Follow the fuel pressure gauge installation procedure in Step 10 but follow the fuel pressure testing procedure for the returnless fuel systems.*

19   Disconnect the quick-connect fitting at the connection between the fuel delivery hose and the fuel rail (see Section 4).

20   Using the proper spring-lock connectors, tee into the fuel pressure gauge between the fuel delivery hose and the fuel rail. Note that some models may be equipped with a Schrader valve located on the fuel rail that allows easy attachment of the fuel pressure gauge **(see illustration 3.10)**.

21   Turn off all the accessories, then start the engine and let it idle. The fuel pressure should be within the operating range listed in this Chapter's Specifications. If the pressure reading is within the specified range, the system is operating correctly.

22   If the fuel pressure is higher than specified, then the pump, the Fuel Pump Driver

Module (FPDM), the Powertrain Control Module (PCM) or the circuit connecting these components is probably defective. Checking this circuit is beyond the scope of the home mechanic, so have the circuit checked by a professional.

23   If the fuel pressure is lower than specified, inspect the fuel delivery lines and hoses for an obstruction or a kink. Also inspect all fuel delivery line and hose quick-connect fittings for leaks. Replace the fuel filter (see Chapter 1) and re-check the pressure. If the lines, hoses, connections and the fuel filter are all in good shape, remove the fuel pump/ fuel level sensor assembly (see Section 6) and inspect the fuel pump inlet strainer for restrictions. If everything else is okay, replace the fuel pump (see Section 6).

24   Turn the ignition switch to OFF, wait five minutes and recheck the pressure on the gauge. Compare the reading with the hold pressure listed in this Chapter's Specifications. If the hold pressure is less than specified:

  a) *The fuel delivery line or a quick-connect fitting might be leaking.*
  b) *A fuel injector (or injectors) may be leaking.*
  c) *The fuel pump might be defective.*

25   After the testing is complete, relieve the fuel pressure (see Section 2), remove the fuel pressure gauge and reconnect the fuel delivery line to the fuel rail (see Section 4).

4   Fuel lines and fittings - replacement

Warning 1: *Gasoline is extremely flammable, so take extra precautions when you work on any part of the fuel system. See the* **Warning** *in Section 2.*

Warning 2: *Before disconnecting any fuel lines, relieve the fuel system pressure (see Section 2).*

1   The manufacturer uses three kinds of

4.3 A hairpin clip, push-connect fitting (arrow)

4.8 An assembled push-connect fitting with a duck-bill clip

4.11 Remove the safety clamp

fuel line fittings, or connectors:

- "Hairpin" push-connect fittings on 3/8- and 5/16-inch diameter lines
- "Duck-bill" push-connect fittings on 1/4-inch diameter lines
- Spring-lock fittings used on the engine fuel rail

The procedure for releasing each type of fitting is different. The push-connect hairpin and duck-bill clips should be replaced whenever a fitting is disassembled. Disconnect all fittings from any fuel system component before loosening the component for removal.

3/8- and 5/16-inch push-connect fittings (hairpin clip)

Refer to illustration 4.3

2   Inspect the visible internal parts of the fitting for dirt. If more than a light coating of dust is present, clean the fitting before disassembly. The seals in the fitting will stick to the fuel line over a period of time. Twist the fitting on the line, then push and pull the fitting until it moves freely.

3   Remove the hairpin clip from the fitting by bending the shipping tab down until it clears the body. Then, using only your hands, spread each leg about 1/8-inch to disengage the body and push the legs through the fitting. Do not use any tools for this part of the procedure. Finally, pull lightly on the triangular end of the clip and work it clear of the line and fitting. A small screwdriver may help for final removal **(see illustration)**.

4   Grasp the fitting and hose and pull it straight off the line.

5   Do not reuse the original clip in the fitting; install a new clip at reassembly.

6   Before reinstalling the fitting on the line, wipe the line end with a clean cloth. Inspect the inside of the fitting to ensure that it is free of dirt.

7   To reinstall the fitting on the line, align the fitting and line and push the fitting into place. When the fitting is engaged, you will hear a definite click. Pull on the fitting to ensure that

it is completely engaged. To install the new clip, insert it into any two adjacent openings in the fitting with the triangular portion of the clip pointing away from the fitting opening **(see illustration 4.3)**. Push the clip in carefully by hand until the legs are locked on the outside of the fitting.

1/4-inch push-connect fittings (duck-bill clip)

Refer to illustrations 4.8, 4.11 and 4.12

8   The duck-bill clip fitting consists of a body, spacers, O-rings, and the retaining clip **(see illustration)**. The clip holds the fitting securely in place on the line. Use one of the two following methods to disconnect this kind of fitting.

9   Before disconnecting the fitting, check the visible internal parts of the fitting for dirt. If more than a light coating of dust is present, clean the fitting before disassembly.

10   The seals in the fitting will stick to the fuel line over a period of time. Twist the fitting on the line, then push and pull the fitting until it moves freely.

11   Remove the safety clamp from the fuel line **(see illustration)**.

12   The preferred way to disconnect the fitting requires a special tool, which is available at most auto parts stores. To disengage the line from the fitting, align the slot in the tool with either tab on the clip, 90-degrees from the slots on the side of the fitting, and insert the tool **(see illustration)**. This disengages the duck-bill clip from the line. **Note:** *Some fuel lines have a secondary bead that aligns with the outer surface of the clip. The bead can make tool insertion difficult. If necessary, use the alternative disassembly method described below.*

13   Holding the tool and the line with one hand, pull the fitting off. Only moderate effort is necessary if the clip is properly disengaged. The use of anything other than your hands should not be necessary.

14   After disassembly, inspect and clean the line sealing surface of the fitting. Also inspect

the inside of the fitting and the line for any parts that may have been dislodged from the fitting. Any loose parts should be immediately reinstalled. (Use the line to insert the parts into the fitting.)

15   The alternative disassembly procedure requires a pair of small adjustable with a jaw width of 3/16-inch or less.

16   Align the jaws of the pliers with the openings in the side of the fitting and compress the part of the retaining clip that engages the body of the fitting. This disengages the clip from the body. (Often one side of the clip will disengage before the other; both sides must be disengaged.)

17   Pull the fitting off the line. Only moderate effort is necessary if the clip is properly disengaged. The use of anything other than your hands should not be necessary.

18   After disassembly, inspect and clean the line and the fitting according to step 14 above.

19   The retaining clip will remain on the line. Disengage the clip from the line bead to remove it. Do not reuse the retaining clip; install a new one at reassembly.

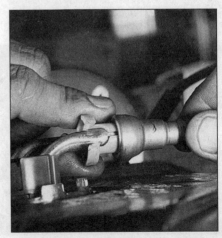

4.12 Push the disconnect tool into the fitting

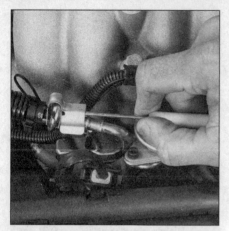

4.24 Pry off the safety clip . . .

4.25 . . . place the spring-lock coupling tool around the coupling . . .

4.26 . . . push the tool into the opening to expand the spring and release the female fitting, then pull the fitting apart

20   Before reinstalling the fitting, wipe the line end with a clean cloth. Check the inside of the fitting to make sure that it's free of dirt.
21   To reinstall the fitting, align it with the line and push it into place. When the fitting is engaged, you will hear a definite click. Pull on the fitting to ensure that it is fully engaged.
22   Install the new replacement clip by inserting one of the serrated edges on the duck bill into one of the openings. Push on the other side until the clip snaps into place.

Spring-lock couplings - disassembly and reassembly

Refer to illustrations 4.24, 4.25 and 4.26
23   The fuel supply and return lines on the engine fuel rail have spring-lock couplings instead of plastic push-connect fittings. The male end of the spring-lock coupling, with two O-rings, is inserted into a flared female fitting. The coupling is secured by a garter spring, which prevents disengagement by gripping the flared end of the female fitting. Clip-on covers over the fittings provide additional security. Special tools are required to disconnect the fittings, but they simply snap together by hand for assembly.
24   Remove the clip-on cover **(see illustration)**.

25   Open the spring-lock coupling tool and place it around the fitting **(see illustration)**. Then close it.
26   Push the tool into the opening around the garter spring to expand the spring and disengage the female half of the fitting **(see illustration)**. Then pulling the fitting apart.
27   Inspect the coupling for a missing or damaged spring or O-rings. If either O-ring is damaged, replace both O-rings.
28   To reassemble the fitting, insert the male half into the female half and push them together until the garter spring is engaged.

5   Fuel tank - removal and installation

Note: *The fuel tanks used in these models are not repairable.*
Warning: *Gasoline is extremely flammable, so take extra precautions when you work on any part of the fuel system. See the* **Warning** *in Section 2. If the fuel tank is removed from the vehicle, it should not be placed where sparks or open flames could ignite any fumes coming out of the tank. Be especially careful inside a garage where any appliance with a pilot light is located because the pilot light*

could cause an explosion.
Note: *Don't begin this procedure until the gauge indicates that the tank is empty or nearly empty. If the tank must be removed when it is full, siphon any remaining fuel from the tank before removal.*
Warning: *Do not start the siphoning action by mouth. Use a siphoning kit, available from most auto parts stores.*

Removal

Refer to illustrations 5.5, 5.6 and 5.7
1   If the fuel gauge on the instrument panel reads above "E" (empty), siphon the residual fuel out before removing the tank.
2   Relieve the fuel pressure (Section 2).
3   Disconnect the cable from the negative terminal of the battery.
4   Raise the vehicle and support it on jackstands.
5   Remove the three bolts that secure the fuel filler neck and the fuel tank filler pipe retainer **(see illustration)**. These are accessible from inside the fuel filler door, on the outside of the car. Disconnect any braces between the fuel filler tube and the car body.
6   Disconnect the fuel lines and vapor lines **(see illustration)**.
7   Disconnect the electric fuel pump and

5.5 Remove the bolts (arrows) from the fuel filler neck

5.6 Disconnect the fuel filler hoses and vent lines and hoses from the tank

5.7 Disconnect the electrical connector from the fuel pump harness

6.6 Use a hammer and a brass punch or wooden dowel to turn the locking ring

sending unit electrical connector **(see illustration)**. A small screwdriver may help to release the connector locking tabs.

8   Disconnect the plastic push-connect fitting at the upper right rear corner of the tank. (This connects the evaporative emission shut-off valve to the evaporative emission tube.)

9   Place a floor jack under the tank with a block of wood between the jack pad and the tank. Raise the jack until it's supporting the tank.

10   Remove the bolts from the rear end of the fuel tank support straps. The straps are hinged at the front and will swing down and out of the way.

11   Lower the tank far enough to unplug the fuel tank pressure sensor and any vapor lines or other wire harness connectors that may be hard to reach when the tank is installed.

12   Slowly lower the jack while steadying the tank. Remove the tank from the car.

Installation

13   Refer to Section 6 to remove and install the fuel pump or sending unit.

14   Installation is the reverse of removal. Clean engine oil can be used as an assembly aid when pushing the fuel filler neck back into the tank.

15   Make sure the fuel tank heat shields, if equipped, are assembled correctly onto the

fuel tank before reinstalling the tank in the vehicle.

16   Tape any hoses and wires that pass over the top of the tank to the tank in their correct locations so that they aren't pinched between the tank and the car body when the tank is lifted into position.

17   Carefully angle the fuel tank filler neck into the filler pipe assembly and lift the tank into place.

18   Lower the car to the ground, reconnect the battery ground cable, fill the fuel tank with at least 10 gallons of gasoline, start the engine and check thoroughly for fuel leaks.

6   Fuel pump - removal and installation

Refer to illustrations 6.6, 6.7, 6.9a, 6.9b, 6.10 and 6.11

Warning 1: *Gasoline is extremely flammable, so take extra precautions when you work on any part of the fuel system. See the* **Warning** *in Section 2.*

Warning 2: *Do not start the siphoning action by mouth. Use a siphoning kit, available from most auto parts stores.*

Note: *Don't begin this procedure until the gauge indicates that the tank is empty or*

nearly empty. If the tank must be removed when it is full, siphon any remaining fuel from the tank before removal.

1   If the fuel gauge on the instrument panel reads above "E" (empty), siphon the residual fuel out before removing the tank.

2   Relieve the fuel pressure (Section 2).

3   Disconnect the battery ground (negative) cable.

4   Raise the vehicle and support it on jackstands.

5   Remove the fuel tank from the vehicle (see Section 5).

6   Using a brass punch or wood dowel, tap the lock-ring counterclockwise until it's loose **(see illustration)**.

7   Lift the fuel pump assembly out of the tank until the locking tabs are accessible. Reach through the opening and squeeze the tabs together. Then remove the pump assembly from the tank **(see illustration)**.

8   Remove the old lock-ring gasket and discard it.

9   If you're planning to reinstall the original fuel pump assembly, remove the strainer **(see illustrations)** by prying it off with a screwdriver, wash it with carburetor cleaner spray, then push it back into place on the pump. If you're installing a new pump and sending unit, the assembly will include a new strainer.

10   To separate the fuel pump from the

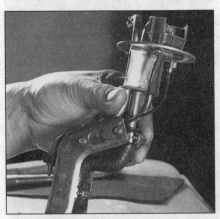

6.7 Carefully angle the fuel pump out of the fuel tank without damaging the fuel strainer

6.9a Remove the C-clip from the base of the fuel pump . . .

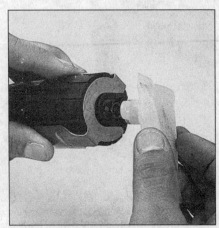

6.9b . . . then separate the strainer from the fuel pump

assembly, remove the clamp and disconnect the electrical connector from the fuel pump **(see illustration)**.

11   Remove the fuel pump mounting screws **(see illustration)**.

12   Clean the fuel pump mounting flange and the tank mounting surface and seal ring groove.

13   Installation is the reverse of removal.

Be careful not to damage the float rod and hoses.

14   Align the pump assembly with the tank retainer and push the assembly into the retainer. You will hear a distinct click when the two tabs on the pump engage the tank retainer. Pull on the assembly to be sure it is engaged securely.

15   Install the pump assembly sender plate.

Ensure that the locating keys are in the keyways and that the O-ring is in place.

16   The rest of installation is the reverse of removal. Apply a thin coat of heavy grease to the new seal ring to hold it in place during assembly.

17   Lower the car to the ground, reconnect the battery ground cable, fill the fuel tank with at least 10 gallons of gasoline, start the engine and check thoroughly for fuel leaks.

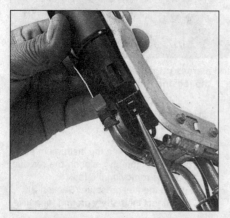

6.10 Disconnect the fuel pump electrical connector from the fuel pump

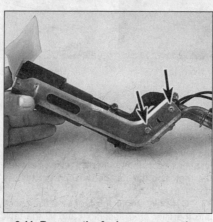

6.11 Remove the fuel pump mounting screws (arrows)

7   Fuel level sending unit - check

Refer to illustrations 7.3 and 7.6

1   Raise the car and support it on jackstands.

2   Disconnect the electrical connector for the fuel level sending unit.

3   Use an ohmmeter to check the resistance between the connector terminals attached to the sender **(see illustration)**. These usually are the yellow-white and black/yellow wires, but trace the wires to the sender to be sure. Use the 200-ohm scale on the ohmmeter.

4   With the fuel tank completely full, the resistance should be about 160 ohms. With the fuel tank nearly empty, the resistance of the sending unit should be about 15 ohms.

5   If the readings are incorrect, replace the sending unit.

6   You can check the sending unit more accurately by removing it from the fuel tank and checking its resistance while moving the float arm up and down **(see illustration)**. Refer to Sections 5 and 6 for instructions on removing the fuel tank and the fuel pump.

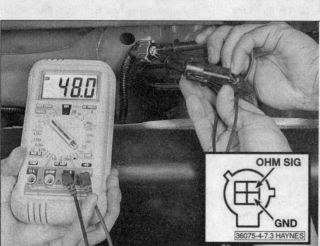

7.3 Use an ohmmeter to probe the terminals of the fuel sending unit to check the resistance

OHM SIG

GND

36075-4-7.3 HAYNES

8   Air cleaner housing - removal and installation

Refer to illustrations 8.1, 8.2, 8.5 and 8.6

1   Refer to Chapter 1 and remove the air filter from the air cleaner housing **(see illustration)**.

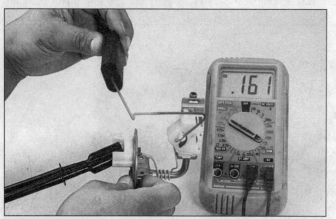

7.6 You can check the fuel level sending unit more accurately with the assembly on the bench. Move the float from "empty" to "full" and check for a smooth change in resistance between these positions

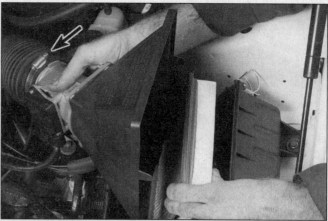

8.1 Remove the air filter. Then loosen the clamp (arrow) that holds the air duct to the MAF sensor housing

8.2 Loosen the clamp (A) and disconnect the IAT sensor (B) to remove the air duct from the throttle body

8.5 Disconnect the crankcase ventilation hoses (arrow)

8.6 Remove the mounting bolts (A) from the air cleaner housing. If necessary to replace parts, remove the MAF sensor nuts (B) from the air cleaner

2   Disconnect the wiring harness from the mass airflow (MAF) sensor and the intake air temperature (IAT) sensor **(see illustration)**.

3   Loosen the clamp the holds the air intake duct to the MAF sensor and separate the duct from the sensor housing **(see illustration 8.1)**.

4   Loosen the clamp the holds the air intake duct to the throttle body and remove the air intake duct **(see illustration 8.2)**.

5   Disconnect the crankcase ventilation hoses from the air duct **(see illustration)**.

6   Remove the bolts that hold the air cleaner housing to the car body **(see illustration)**.

7   Disconnect the intake resonator tube from the air cleaner inlet by pushing in at the top and bottom tube surfaces and pulling the air cleaner outward away from the tube.

8   If necessary after removing the air cleaner housing, remove the four nuts that secure the MAF sensor housing to the air cleaner housing **(see illustration 8.6)**.

9   Refer to Chapter 11 and remove the left front fender splash shield.

10   Disconnect and relocate any electrical devices between the battery and the air intake resonator tube that would interfere with tube removal.

11   Remove the nuts and bolts securing the resonator tube to the car body and remove the tube.

12   If necessary, remove the air cleaner outlet tube from the air cleaner housing by loosening the tube clamp.

13   Reassembly and installation are the reverse of removal. Install a new air filter, if needed, during reassembly.

9   Accelerator cable - removal and installation

Removal

Refer to illustrations 9.2, 9.4, 9.6, 9.7, 9.9 and 9.10

1   If necessary for access, remove the air intake duct (Section 9).

2   Remove the two bolts and the cable splash shield at the throttle body **(see illustration)**. Disconnect the throttle return spring.

3   Disconnect the accelerator cable snap-in nylon bushing from the accelerator pedal arm inside the car.

4   Remove the bolt that holds the cable housing to the bracket at the throttle body **(see illustration)**.

5   Remove the cable housing from the firewall under the dash panel by removing two screws and pushing outward from inside the car.

6   Unwind the cable from the semicircular part of the throttle lever at the throttle body and detach the cable end from the lever **(see illustration)**.

9.2 Remove the splash shield to expose the accelerator cable (A) and the cruise control cable (B)

9.4 Remove the cable housing bolt from the bracket

9.6 Disengage the accelerator cable end from the throttle lever by twisting until the flattened nylon cable end aligns with the slot

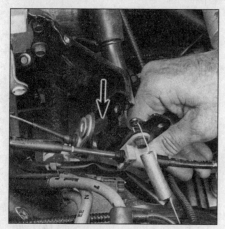

9.7 Slide the cable housing out of the slot in the bracket (arrow)

9.9 Remove the cruise control cable bolt from the bracket (arrow)

9.10 Disconnect the cruise control cable from the throttle lever

7   Remove the cable from the slot in the cable bracket **(see illustration)**.
8   Remove the accelerator cable through the firewall from the engine compartment.
9   Remove the cruise control cable housing bolt from the cable bracket **(see illustration)**.
10   Disconnect the cruise control cable from the throttle lever **(see illustration)**.

Installation

11   Installation is the reverse of removal. Be sure the cables are routed correctly and that the accelerator cable housing seats completely in the firewall.
12   Apply sealant around the accelerator cable housing at the engine compartment side of the firewall to prevent water from entering the passenger compartment.
13   Measure the accelerator cable freeplay by firmly gripping the cable and pushing it down from the cable housing. There should be a slight amount of slack that will allow cable freeplay.
14   The cable must move freely and smoothly. If it binds or does not move, replace the cable assembly.

10   Throttle body - removal and installation

Removal

Refer to illustrations 10.2 and 10.3

1   Disconnect the IAT sensor connector and the crankcase ventilation hoses from the air intake duct (Section 8). Then remove the duct and the accelerator cable and cruise control cable from the throttle body (Section 9).
2   Remove the accelerator cable bracket from the throttle body **(see illustration)**.
3   Disconnect the throttle position (TP) sensor connector **(see illustration)**.
4   On an OHV engine, remove the spark plug wire retainer from the two lower fasteners for the throttle body **(see illustration 10.3)**. Move the wires and the retainer out of

10.2 Remove the two bolts (arrows) that secure the cable bracket to the throttle body

the way.
5   Remove the bolts and stud bolts from the throttle body and note their locations for correct reinstallation. Remove the throttle body from the upper intake manifold and discard the gasket.
6   Clean old gasket material from the throttle body and the intake manifold. Use a scraper as necessary. **Caution:** *Be very careful when scraping on aluminum engine parts. Aluminum is soft and gouges easily. Severely gouged parts may require replacement.*
7   Install a new gasket on the intake manifold and reinstall the throttle body.
8   Install the rest of the parts in the reverse order of removal.

11   Fuel injection system - general information

The sequential fuel injection (SFI) system used on Taurus and Sable vehicles is a multipoint fuel injection system that is an integral part of the EEC-V engine control system. The EEC-V powertrain control module (PCM) receives inputs from various engine sensors to compute the fuel flow required to

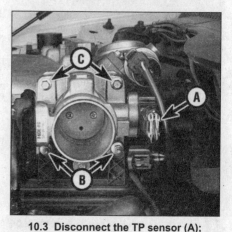

10.3 Disconnect the TP sensor (A); remove the spark plug wire retainer (B); then remove the other bolts (C) to remove the throttle body

maintain the optimum air/fuel ratio throughout the entire engine operating range. The PCM sends output commands to the fuel injectors to meter the required quantity of fuel. The system automatically senses and compensates for changes in altitude, load, and speed.

The electric in-tank fuel pump forces fuel through metal and plastic lines and an inline fuel filter to the fuel rail. The SFI system uses a single high-pressure pump inside the tank.

The fuel pressure regulator maintains a constant fuel pressure at the injector nozzles. The regulator is on the fuel rail, downstream from the fuel injectors. Excess fuel passes through the regulator and returns to the fuel tank through a fuel return line.

On the SFI system, each injector is energized once every other crankshaft revolution in sequence with engine firing order. The period of time that the injectors are energized is called "on-time" or "pulse width" and is controlled by the PCM. Air entering the engine is sensed by airflow, pressure, and temperature sensors. The outputs of these sensors are processed by the PCM, which determines the needed injector pulse width and sends a command to each injector to meter the exact quantity of fuel.

12 Fuel injection system - check

Refer to illustrations 12.7, 12.8 and 12.9

Warning: *Gasoline is extremely flammable, so take extra precautions when you work on any part of the fuel system. See the* **Warning** *in Section 2.*

1   Check all electrical connectors - especially ground connections - for the system. Loose connectors and poor grounds can cause at least half of all engine control system problems.

2   Verify that the battery is fully charged because the powertrain control module (PCM) and sensors cannot operate properly without adequate supply voltage.

3   Refer to Chapter 1 and check the air filter element. A dirty or partially blocked filter will reduce performance and economy.

4   Check fuel pump operation (Section 3). If the fuel pump fuse is blown, replace it and see if it blows again. If it does, refer to Chapter 12 and the wiring diagrams and look for a grounded wire in the harness to the fuel pump.

5   Inspect the vacuum hoses connected to the intake manifold for damage, deterioration and leakage.

6   Remove the air intake duct from the throttle body and check for dirt, carbon, varnish, or other residue in the throttle body, particularly around the throttle plate. If it's dirty, refer to Chapter 6 and troubleshoot the PCV and EGR systems for the cause of excessive varnish buildup. An extremely dirty throttle body requires replacement. **Caution:** *The throttle bodies on these engines have a protective coating on their bores, throttle plates, and shafts. Do not try to clean the throttle body; you may damage the coating and do more harm than good.*

7   With the engine running, place an automotive stethoscope against each injector, one at a time, and listen for a clicking sound that indicates operation **(see illustration)**. If you don't have a stethoscope, you can place the tip of a long screwdriver against the injector and listen through the handle.

8   If an injector does not seem to be operating electrically (not clicking), purchase a special injector test light (sometimes called a "noid" light) and install it into the injector wiring harness connector **(see illustration)**. Start the engine and see if the noid light flashes. If it does, the injector is receiving proper voltage. If it doesn't flash, further diagnosis is necessary. You might want to have it checked by a dealership service department or other qualified repair shop.

9   With the engine off and the fuel injector electrical connectors disconnected, measure the resistance of each injector with an ohmmeter **(see illustration)**. Check the specifications at the beginning of this chapter for the correct resistance.

10   Refer to Section 13 and Chapter 6 for other system checks.

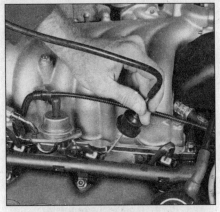

12.7 Use a stethoscope or screwdriver to determine if the injectors are operating electrically. They should make a steady clicking sound that rises and falls as engine speed changes

13 Fuel rail, injectors, and pressure regulator - removal, inspection, and installation

Refer to illustrations 13.3, 13.5, 13.7a, 13.7b, 13.8, 13.9, 13.11a, 13.11b and 13.14

Warning: *Gasoline is extremely flammable, so take extra precautions when you work on any part of the fuel system. See the* **Warning** *in Section 2.*

Note: *Refer to Chapter 6 for test and replacement procedures for the throttle position (TP) sensor.*

Removal

1   Relieve the fuel pressure (Section 2).

2   Disconnect the cable from the negative terminal of the battery.

3   Refer to Chapter 2A or 2B and remove the upper intake manifold. Place a clean shop cloth over the openings in the lower manifold to keep things from falling in **(see illustration)**.

4   Disconnect the electrical connectors

13.3 Cover the manifold openings and disconnect the electrical connectors from the injectors

12.8 Install the fuel injector test light, or "noid light," into the fuel injector wiring harness connector and see if it blinks when the engine is cranking or running

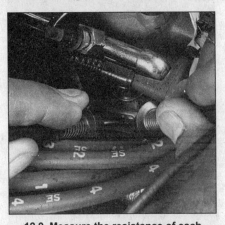

12.9 Measure the resistance of each injector. It should be within specifications

from the fuel injectors **(see illustration 13.3)**.

5   Using the spring-lock coupler tool, or equivalent, disconnect the fuel supply and (on 1999 and earlier models) return lines from the fuel rail **(see illustration)**. Refer to Section 4 for details on disconnecting fuel lines.

6   On 1999 and earlier models, disconnect

13.5 Remove the safety clip from the fuel fitting (A) and disconnect the regulator vacuum line (B)

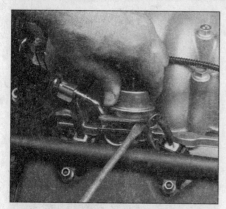

13.7a Remove the regulator

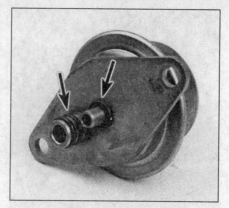

13.7b Replace the regulator
O-rings (arrows)

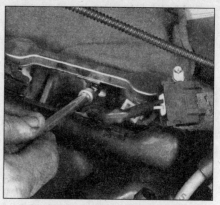

13.8 Remove the four screws that secure
the fuel rail to the manifold

13.9 Carefully lift the fuel rail upward to
remove it from the engine

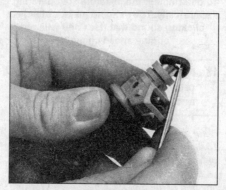

13.11a Remove the O-ring from the top of
the fuel injector . . .

13.11b . . . then remove the lower O-ring
from the injector

the vacuum line from the fuel pressure regulator (**see illustration 13.5**). Note: *Some pressure regulators are secured by a retainer clip; others are secured by two screws.*

7   On 1999 and earlier models, remove the regulator (**see illustration**). You may have to pry it out gently to release the O-ring seal. Remove and replace the two O-ring seals on the bottom of the regulator (**see illustration**).

8   Remove the four fuel rail retaining screws (two on each side) (**see illustration**).

9   Carefully lift the fuel rail upward to remove it from the engine (**see illustration**). The injectors may come off with the fuel rail, or they may stay in the intake manifold.

10   Use a rocking, side-to-side motion to remove the injectors from the fuel rail or from the intake manifold.

11   Remove the O-rings from the injectors

(**see illustrations**). Inspect each injector for obvious damage or dirt at the fuel-metering tip. Handle the injectors carefully and avoid touching the fuel-metering tips.

12   Inspect the pressure regulator and all fittings on the fuel rail for damage or dirt. Clean, repair, or replace parts as required.

Installation

13   Install new O-rings on the pressure regulator and on both ends of each injector (**see illustrations 13.7b, 13.11a and 13.11b**). Lightly lubricate the O-rings with fresh engine oil.

14   Place the fuel rail over each of the injectors and seat the injectors into the fuel rail (**see illustration**). Ensure that the injectors are well seated in the fuel rail assembly.

15   Secure the fuel rail assembly with the

four retaining screws.

16   Install the rest of the parts in the reverse order of removal.

17   Connect the battery ground cable, start the engine, and check thoroughly for fuel leakage.

14 Idle Air Control (IAC) valve - check and replacement

Refer to illustration 14.5

Warning: *Gasoline is extremely flammable, so take extra precautions when you work on any part of the fuel system. See the* **Warning** *in Section 2.*

Caution: *The throttle bodies on these engines have a protective coating on their bores, throttle plates, and shafts. Do not try to clean the throttle body; you may damage the coating and do more harm than good.*

1   The Idle Air Control (IAC) valve controls engine idle speed by regulating the amount of air that bypasses the throttle valve at closed throttle. The IAC valve is mounted on the upper intake manifold, just downstream from the throttle body. It is controlled by voltage pulses from the PCM. The IAC valve within the body moves in or out to allow more or less intake air into the engine to maintain the computer-controlled idle speed. To increase airflow, the PCM opens the IAC valve and allows more air to bypass the throttle. To decrease

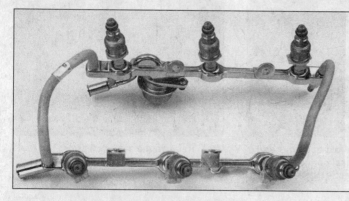

13.14 You can
place the injectors
in the fuel rail, as
shown here, or
install them in the
manifold and fit the
rail to the tops
of the injectors

14.5 The IAC valve is fastened to the upper intake manifold by two small capscrews (arrows)

16.2a This is the forward O2 sensor, upstream from the catalytic converter

16.2b This is the rear O2 sensor, upstream from the catalytic converter

airflow, the PCM moves the valve plunger (or pintle) toward the closed position.

2   The minimum idle speed is set at the factory and cannot be adjusted.

3   To check IAC valve operation, disconnect the IAC valve electrical connector. Then turn the ignition key on but do not start the engine.

4   Using a voltmeter set on dc volts, place the red meter lead on the red wire at the connector and the black meter lead on the white/blue wire. The meter should read approximately 10.5 to 12.5 volts. This indicates that the IAC valve is receiving the proper signal from the PCM.

5   To remove the valve, remove the two attaching screws from the upper intake manifold **(see illustration)**.

6   Remove the valve and discard the gasket.

7   Place a new gasket on the IAC valve, install the valve, tighten the screws, and connect the electrical connector to the valve.

15   Intake manifold runner control (IMRC) system (1996 to 1999 OHC V6 engine) - general information

The intake manifold runner control (IMRC) system on the OHC engine controls the intake airflow by opening or closing secondary butterfly valves in the manifold runners to the intake valves. By closing the butterflies to the secondary intake valves under 3000 rpm, the intake runners are effectively lengthened to increase low-speed torque and improve driveability. Above 3000 rpm the butterfly valves open to shorten the intake runners and increase high-speed performance. The butterfly valves are controlled by the IMRC electric actuator and cable assembly. The actuator, in turn, is controlled by the PCM.

The IMRC system is difficult to check and requires a special scan tool for diagnostic access to the PCM. Have the system tested by a dealer service department or other quali-

fied repair shop.

The IMRC actuator is mounted on the rear valve cover and connected by a cable to the lever on the lower intake manifold. Neither the actuator, the cable, nor the lever assembly is adjustable. Be careful when disconnecting the cable to be sure it does not bind nor become kinked.

16   Exhaust system - removal and installation

Warning 1: *Do not work on exhaust system components until the system has cooled completely. Catalytic converters operate at very high temperature and retain heat long after other exhaust components have cooled. Be careful working around the catalytic converters to avoid serious burns.*
Warning 2: *When working under the vehicle, be sure it is securely supported on jackstands.*
Warning 3: *If you do decide to do exhaust system repairs at home, be sure to wear safety goggles to protect your eyes from metal chips and other debris. Also wear gloves to protect your hands.*

The exhaust system is made up of two exhaust manifolds, a welded one-piece assembly of two catalytic converters and the exhaust headpipe, four exhaust oxygen sensors, an exhaust pipe, and one or two mufflers. Exhaust components are attached to the car by assorted brackets and hangers. If any of the parts are improperly installed, excessive noise and vibration will be transmitted to the body.

Inspect the exhaust system regularly to keep it safe and quiet. Look for any damaged or bent parts, open seams, holes, loose connections, excessive corrosion, or other defects which could allow exhaust fumes to enter the car. Deteriorated exhaust system parts should not be repaired; they should be replaced.

If the exhaust system parts are badly corroded or rusted, a cutting torch may be required to remove them. The convenient way to do this is to have a muffler shop remove

the corroded sections with a torch. If you want to save money by doing it yourself, and you don't have a welding outfit with a cutting torch, cut off the old parts with a hacksaw. If you have compressed air, pneumatic cutting chisels also can be used.

Follow these general guidelines to make exhaust system repair easier:

a) *If possible, work from the back to the front when removing exhaust system components.*
b) *Apply penetrating oil to the exhaust system fasteners to make them easier to remove.*
c) *Use new gaskets, hangers, and clamps when installing exhaust systems components.*
d) *Apply antiseize compound to the threads of all exhaust system fasteners during reassembly.*
e) *Allow enough clearance between newly installed parts and all points on the underbody to avoid overheating the floor pan and possibly damaging the interior carpet and insulation. Pay particularly close attention to the catalytic converter and heat shield.*

Dual converter Y-pipe

Refer to illustrations 16.2a, 16.2b, 16.4, 16.5 and 16.6
Note: *The exhaust headpipe on these cars is a welded assembly of two catalytic converters and the headpipes for both banks of the engine. The manufacturer calls it the "dual converter Y-pipe," or simply the Y-pipe. The Y-pipe assembly must be removed for other service work, such as oil pan removal. Refer to Chapter 6 for more information about the catalytic converters.*

1   Raise the vehicle and support it on jackstands.

2   Disconnect the wiring connectors from the four exhaust oxygen (O2) sensors **(see illustrations)**. O2 sensors are installed upstream and downstream from both catalytic converters.

3   Remove the O2 sensors from the head-

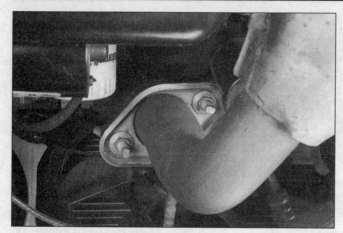

16.4 Remove the nuts that secure the headpipes to the
exhaust manifolds

16.5 Remove the exhaust brackets from the transaxle (arrows)

pipes as follows to get the Y-pipe assembly
out of the car:
a) *On a Vulcan V6 engine, remove the
upstream O2 sensors from each headpipe, just below each exhaust manifold.
The downstream sensors can stay in
place.*
b) *On a Duratec V6 engine, remove all four
O2 sensors.*

4   Remove the nuts that secure the front
and rear headpipes to the exhaust manifold
studs (see illustration).
5   Remove the nuts and bolts from the catalytic converter brackets at the transaxle (see
illustration).
6   Remove the nuts and bolts at the flange
connection of the Y-pipe assembly to the
exhaust system flex tube (see illustration).
7   Remove the Y-pipe assembly from the
car. You may want an assistant to help you
because the pipe assembly is heavy and awkward.
8   Install new gaskets at all exhaust system joints during reinstallation. If the nuts and
bolts are corroded, it's a good idea to replace

them also.
9   Install the rest of the parts in the reverse
order of removal. Start the engine, and check
for exhaust leaks.

Exhaust flex tube, exhaust pipe, brackets, hangers and mufflers

Refer to illustrations 16.6, 16.14a and 16.14b
Note 1: *The exhaust pipes and mufflers
on these cars also are welded assemblies,
joined to the forward Y-pipe assembly by a
flex tube under the middle of the car. Models
with Vulcan V6 engines have a single muffler at the left rear of the car; models with
Duratec V6 engines have two mufflers.*
Note 2: *Because removal and installation procedures for the original-equipment
exhaust pipe and muffler assembly require
separation of the rear lower control arms and
struts to get the muffler and pipe out as one
piece, it may be more efficient to have a muffler shop cut the old parts out of the car and
weld in replacements.*

10   Raise the car and support it on
jackstands.
11   Remove the nuts and bolts at the flange
connection of the Y-pipe assembly to the flex
tube (see illustration 16.6).
12   Remove the U-bolt clamp at the rear of
the flex tube and remove the flex tube from
the car.
13   If you plan to install an original-equipment welded assembly, refer to Chapter 10
and separate the rear ball joints from the control arms on the right or left side, as required.
14   Support the muffler and exhaust pipe
assembly with suitable stands and remove
the exhaust pipe brackets and hangers from
the bottom of the car (see illustration).
15   Remove the muffler and exhaust pipe
assembly from the car.
16   Install new gaskets at all exhaust system
joints during reinstallation. If nuts and bolts
are corroded, it's a good idea to replace them
also.
17   Install the rest of the parts in the reverse
order of removal. Start the engine, and check
for exhaust leaks.

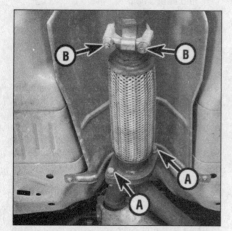

16.6 Remove the fasteners at the Y-pipe
flange (A). To remove the flex tube,
remove the U-bolt clamp (B)

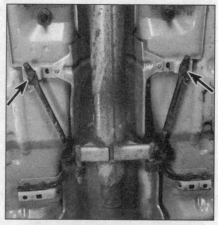

16.14a Remove the exhaust pipe
bracket fasteners, near the center of the
underbody (arrows)

16.14b Lift the pipe and the rubber
insulators off the brackets near the rear
wheels (arrow)

Chapter 5
Engine electrical systems

Contents

Specifications

General

Firing order	1-4-2-5-3-6
Cylinder numbers - drivebelt end (right) to transaxle end (left)	
Rear bank	1-2-3
Front bank	4-5-6

Ignition coil resistance

Primary resistance	0.5 ohm
Secondary resistance	13,600 ohms

Ignition timing

	Not adjustable

Alternator

Brush length	
New	1/2 inch
Minimum	1/4 inch
Current output (amperes)	
Rated maximum	130
Test, at 2000 rpm	
1996 to 1999 models	87 psi at 2000 rpm
2000 and later models	58 or higher at 2000 rpm

Starter motor

Minimum cranking voltage	9.6
Cranking current draw	130 to 220 amperes

1   General information

The engine electrical systems are the ignition, charging, and starting systems. Because of their engine-related functions, these components - along with the battery - are considered separately from chassis electrical systems such as the lights, instruments, and power accessories.

Be very careful when working on the engine electrical components. They are easily damaged if checked, connected, or handled improperly. The alternator is driven by an engine drivebelt that can cause serious injury if your hands, hair or clothes become tangled in it with the engine running. Both the starter and alternator are connected directly to the battery and could arc or cause a fire if mishandled, overloaded, or shorted.

Don't disconnect the battery cables while the engine is running. Correct polarity must be maintained when connecting battery cables from another source, such as another vehicle, during jump starting. Always disconnect the negative cable first and connect it last or the battery may be shorted by the tool used to loosen the cable clamps.

Additional safety related information on the engine electrical systems can be found in *Safety first* near the front of this manual. Refer to those safety precautions before beginning any operation in this Chapter.

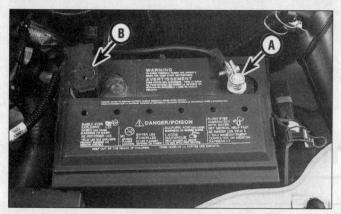

2.1 Disconnect the battery cables: negative first (A), then positive (B)

2.2 Remove the bolt and the wedge that holds the base of the battery to the tray

2   Battery - removal and installation

Refer to illustrations 2.1, 2.2 and 2.4

1   Disconnect both cables from the battery terminals **(see illustration)**. **Warning:** *Always disconnect the negative cable first and connect it last, or the battery may be shorted by the tool used to loosen the cable clamps.* Unclip the rubber cover on the positive cable and fold it forward for access to the terminal.

2   Remove the bolt and hold-down wedge from the battery tray **(see illustration)**.

3   Lift out the battery. Use a battery lifting strap that attaches to the battery posts to lift the battery safely and easily.

4   If necessary for access to other components, remove the bolts that secure the battery tray to the car body **(see illustration)**.

5   Installation is the reverse of removal. **Warning:** *When connecting the battery cables, always connect the positive cable first and the negative cable last to avoid a short circuit caused by the tool used to tighten the cable clamps.*

3   Battery - emergency jump starting

Refer to the *Booster battery (jump) starting* procedure at the front of this manual.

4   Battery cables - check and replacement

1   Periodically inspect the entire length of each battery cable for damage, cracked or burned insulation and corrosion. Poor battery cable connections can cause starting problems and decreased engine performance.

2   Check the cable-to-terminal connections at the ends of the cables for cracks, loose wire strands and corrosion. The presence of white, fluffy deposits under the insulation at the cable terminal connection is a sign that the cable is corroded and should be replaced. Check the terminals for distortion, missing mounting bolts and corrosion.

3   When replacing the cables, always disconnect the negative cable first and hook it up last or the battery may be shorted by the tool used to loosen the cable clamps. Even if only the positive cable is being replaced, be sure to disconnect the negative cable from the battery first.

4   Disconnect and remove the cable **(see illustration 2.1)**. Make sure the replacement cable is the same length and diameter.

5   Clean the threads of the fasteners at the starter motor for the positive cable and at the engine or chassis ground connection for the negative cable. Remove all dirt, rust and corrosion to ensure a clean connection. Apply a light coat of petroleum jelly to the threads to prevent future corrosion.

6   Attach the cable to the starter motor or the ground connection, as appropriate, and tighten the fasteners securely.

7   Before connecting the new cable to the battery, make sure that it reaches the battery post without having to be stretched. Clean the battery posts thoroughly and apply a light coat of petroleum jelly to prevent corrosion.

8   Connect the positive cable first, followed by the negative cable.

5   Ignition system - general information

Most models covered by this manual have distributorless ignition systems (DIS) and employ a coil pack assembly which consists of three coils. Each coil supplies ignition voltage to two cylinders. Duratec (OHC) engines from 2000 on have individual coils for each spark plug.

The ignition system consists of the ignition coil pack assembly, a crankshaft position (CKP) sensor, the Powertrain Control Module (PCM), and the spark plugs and spark plug wires. These systems do not have a separate ignition module. All ignition timing and control functions are performed by the PCM.

The ignition coil pack contains three separate coils. All coils receive battery positive (B+) voltage on one wire of the four-wire connector. The PCM controls the ground side of each coil primary circuit individually to

2.4 Remove the four mounting bolts for the battery tray

deliver secondary ignition voltage to two cylinders simultaneously.

The PCM fires one coil for each pair of cylinders that are at top dead center (TDC) at the same time. These cylinder pairs are called companion cylinders, or "running mates." One cylinder is at TDC on the compression stroke, while the other is at TDC on the exhaust stroke. The spark in the cylinder at TDC on the compression stroke ignites the air-fuel mixture to produce power. The spark in the cylinder at TDC on the exhaust stroke is wasted. Therefore, this kind of system is called a "waste-spark" system.

Each waste-spark DIS coil is in series with its two spark plugs. As the coil fires, secondary current creates a high-voltage spark across the gaps of both plugs. One plug fires with the traditional forward polarity of an ignition system: negative (–) to positive (+). The other plug fires with opposite polarity: positive (+) to negative (–). Thus, one plug always fires with what has always been called "reversed polarity." The voltage capacity of a DIS coil is high enough, however, to ensure that the available voltage is always high enough to fire the plug with reversed polarity when it is on the compression stroke.

The CKP sensor is mounted on the engine front cover and triggered by a trigger wheel on the front of the crankshaft. The trigger wheel has 35 evenly spaced teeth and one gap where a 36th tooth would be. The

6.3 To use a spark tester, disconnect a spark plug wire, clip the tester to a convenient ground (like a valve cover bolt), and operate the starter. If enough voltage is present to fire the plug, sparks will be visible between the electrode tip and the tester body

6.6 The coil pack gets battery positive (B+) voltage on the white/blue wire (arrow); it should be approximately 12 volts with the key on and more than 10 volts while cranking

gap lets the CKP sensor signal the PCM when the crankshaft is 90 degrees before TDC for cylinders 1 and 5. the PCM then computes actual TDC or any number of degrees before or after TDC. The CKP sensor is a magnetic pickup, or variable reluctance, sensor that produces a direct-current (dc) sine wave voltage signal. The sensor does the job of a distributor pickup in a distributor-type electronic ignition. Besides providing information on crankshaft position, the CKP sensor delivers the engine speed signal to the PCM. Refer to Chapter 6 for more information on the PCM and the CKP sensor.

On Duratec engines, the "coil-on-plug" system uses an individual coil for each cylinder, mounted directly over the spark plug, and controlled by the PCM. When the engine is first cranked over, the PCM will fire two cylinders at once, one on compression and one as a waste spark, just like the coil-pack. However, once the engine starts, cylinders are only fired one at a time, on their compression stroke.

Base ignition timing is normally 10±2 degrees before top dead center (BTDC), but it cannot be checked or adjusted.

6 Ignition system - general operating check

Refer to illustrations 6.3 and 6.6

1 A spark tester (or "calibrated ignition tester") is a spark plug body with a shortened center electrode and a small clamp welded to the metal shell. They are sold at most auto parts stores, and two kinds are available. One kind of spark tester has a short center electrode extending from the insulator and is intended for use on breaker-point and older electronic ignitions. The other kind does not have a visible center electrode and is for use on DIS and other high-voltage ignition systems. Be sure to use the high-voltage spark tester on these systems.
2 If the engine cranks but won't start, disconnect the spark plug wire (or coil-on-plug coil) from any spark plug and attach it to the spark tester.

3 Clip the tester to a bolt or metal bracket on the engine **(see illustration)**, crank the engine and watch the end of the tester to see if consistent, bright, well-defined sparks occur.
4 If sparks occur, enough voltage is reaching the plug to fire it. Repeat the test at the other plug wires to verify spark availability for all cylinders.
5 If voltage is available, but the engine still does not start, the plugs may be fouled or one or more plug wires may be open or grounded. Remove the spark plugs and check them as described in Chapter 1 or install new ones. Check for a bad spark plug wire by swapping wires.
6 If no sparks or intermittent sparks occur, check for battery voltage to the ignition coil pack on the white/blue wire at the 4-wire coil connector **(see illustration)**. Check for a bad spark plug wire by swapping wires. Check the coil pack as explained in Section 7. A few sparks followed by no spark is the same as no spark at all.
7 Be sure the ground wire between one mounting bolt of the coil pack and the intake manifold on an OHC V6 engine is not loose or broken. If this wire is defective, the coils may not fire.

8 Refer to Chapter 6 and check the operation of the CKP sensor.
9 If all the components and the ignition system checks are correct, have the system diagnosed by an experienced driveability technician.

7 Ignition coil pack - check and replacement

Check

Refer to illustrations 7.1 and 7.2

1 With the ignition off, disconnect the 4-wire connector from the coil. Connect an ohmmeter between pin 4 on the coil connector (the pin that connects to the white/blue wire) and each of the other three pins in sequence **(see illustration)**. The primary resistance should be as listed in this Chapter's Specifications. If resistance is out of limits for any one of the individual coils, the complete coil pack must be replaced. On 2000 and later OHC engines, if any individual coil-on-plug coils fails to produce a spark in the test in Section 6, replace that coil.
2 Connect an ohmmeter between the secondary terminals **(see illustration)** (the one

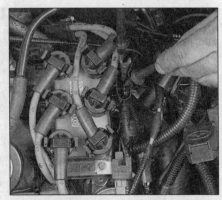

7.1 Check the coil primary resistance by connecting an ohmmeter between terminal 4 and each of the other three terminals on the coil connector in sequence

7.2 Check the coil secondary resistance by connecting an ohmmeter between the secondary terminals for each of the coils in the assembly

that the spark plug wires connect to) of each coil in the coil pack. Coil secondary terminals are paired as follows:

a) *coil 1 = cylinders 1 and 5*
b) *coil 2 = cylinders 3 and 4*
c) *coil 3 = cylinders 2 and 6*

3   Cylinder numbers are marked on the coil pack, and spark plug wires are numbered for each cylinder. The secondary resistance should be as listed in this Chapter's Specifications. If not, replace the coil.

Replacement

Refer to illustrations 7.6 and 7.7

4   Disconnect the battery ground (negative) cable.
5   Disconnect the ignition coil pack electrical connector.
6   Disconnect all the spark plug wires by squeezing the locking tabs and twisting while pulling **(see illustration)**. Do not pull on the wires.
7   Remove the four bolts that secure the coil pack to the engine and disconnect the radio interference capacitor **(see illustration)**. On OHV engines, the coil pack is on a bracket attached to the forward cylinder head. On OHC engines, the coil pack is mounted on the rear valve cover, and a small ground wire is connected from one mounting bolt to the intake manifold.
8   Installation is the reverse of the removal procedure with the following additions:

a) *Before installing the spark plug wire connector into the ignition coil, coat the entire interior of the rubber boot with silicone dielectric compound.*
b) *Insert each spark plug wire into the proper terminal of the ignition coil. Push the wire into the terminal and make sure the boots are fully seated and both locking tabs are engaged properly.*
c) *Remember to connect the radio interference capacitor on all engines and the ground wire between the coil pack and the manifold on an OHC engine.*

7.6 Squeeze the locking tabs on the spark plug wire boots to remove them from the coil pack

8   Charging system - general information and precautions

Refer to illustration 8.1

The charging system consists of the alternator, the voltage regulator, a charge indicator or warning lamp on the instrument panel, the battery, a megafuse in the alternator output circuit, a 30-ampere fuse in the field circuit, and the wiring between all the components. The charging system supplies electrical power for the ignition system, the lights, the radio, the electronic control systems and all other electrical components on the car.

The alternator generates alternating current (ac) that is rectified to direct current (dc) to charge the battery and supply power to other electrical systems. The alternator is driven by a drivebelt at the front of the engine.

The voltage regulator limits the alternator charging voltage by regulating the current supplied to the alternator field circuit. The regulator is a solid-state electronic assembly mounted on the rear of the alternator.

7.7 Remove the four bolts (one at each corner) that secure the coil and disconnect the radio interference capacitor (arrow)

The megafuse is a 175-ampere fuse between the alternator and the battery. It is mounted in the engine compartment power distribution box **(see illustration)** and serves as the main circuit protection device for the entire vehicle electrical system. The power distribution box also contains the 30-ampere fuse for the alternator field circuit.

The drivebelt, battery, wires and connections should be inspected at the intervals listed in Chapter 1.

Be very careful when making any circuit connections and note the following:

a) *Never start the engine with a battery charger connected.*
b) *Always disconnect both battery cables before using a battery charger: negative cable first, positive cable last.*

9   Charging system - check

Refer to illustration 9.2

1   If the charging system malfunctions, don't immediately assume that the alternator

8.1 The power distribution box in the engine compartment holds the megafuse (A) and the 30-ampere field circuit fuse (B), hidden just behind a relay in this view

9.2 Battery voltage should be about 12 volts with the engine off. With the engine running, regulated voltage should be 14 to 15 volts

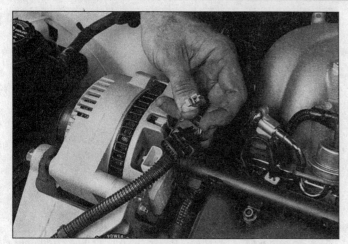

10.2 The black 3-wire connector attaches to the regulator; the gray single-wire connector plugs into the stator terminal at the top of the alternator; the red output wire is not shown in this view

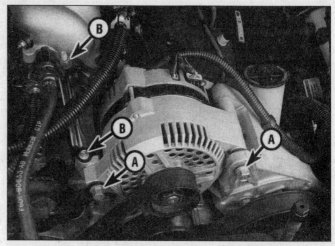

10.3 Remove the drivebelt, then remove the two mounting bolts (A) and the alternator brace fasteners (B)

is causing the problem. First check the following items:

a) *Ensure that the battery cable connections at the battery are clean and tight.*

b) *If the battery is not a maintenance-free type, check the electrolyte level and specific gravity. If the electrolyte level is low, add clean, mineral-free tap water. If the specific gravity is low, charge the battery.*

c) *Check the alternator wiring and connections.*

d) *Check the drivebelt condition and tension (Chapter 1).*

e) *Check the alternator mounting bolts for looseness.*

f) *Run the engine and check the alternator for abnormal noise.*

2   Use a voltmeter to check the battery voltage with the engine off. It should be approximately 12 volts **(see illustration)**.

3   Start the engine and check the battery voltage again. It should now be approximately 14 to 15 volts.

4   If the voltage reading is less than the specified charging voltage, check the 30-ampere fuse and the 175-ampere megafuse in the engine compartment power distribution box. If either fuse is blown replace it. If the fuses are OK, replace the voltage regulator.

5   If the voltage reading is more than the specified charging voltage, replace the voltage regulator.

6   Some models have an ammeter on the instrument panel that indicates charge or discharge. With all electrical equipment on and the engine idling, the gauge needle may show a discharge condition. At fast idle or normal driving speeds, the needle should stay on the charge side of the gauge. The state of charge of the battery determines the amount of charging current shown by the ammeter. (The lower the battery state of charge, the farther the needle should move toward the charge side.)

7   Some models have a voltmeter on the instrument panel that indicates battery voltage with the key on and engine off and alternator charging voltage when the engine is running.

8   The charge lamp on the instrument panel lights with the key on and engine not running and should go out when the engine runs.

9   If the ammeter or voltmeter does not show a charge when it should, or the alternator light remains on, there is a fault in the system. Before inspecting the brushes or replacing the voltage regulator or the alternator, check the battery condition, alternator belt tension, and electrical cable connections.

10   If replacing the regulator doesn't restore voltage to the specified range, the problem may be in the alternator. Have the alternator tested by an automotive electrical specialist.

10   Alternator - removal and installation

Refer to illustrations 10.2 and 10.3
Note: *The alternator on the OHV V6 engine is mounted on the top of the engine, toward the front of the engine compartment. This is the installation shown in the following instructions. The alternator on the OHC V6 engine is mounted below the rear cylinder bank of the engine, at the rear of the engine compartment. Access may be easier through the right front fenderwell or from underneath the car.*

1   Disconnect the battery ground (negative) cable.

2   Disconnect the electrical connectors from the alternator **(see illustration)**. The output wire is secured by a nut on the output terminal.

3   Refer to Chapter 1 and remove the drivebelt **(see illustration)**.

4   On 1996 to 2001 OHV V6, remove the two alternator mounting bolts and the alternator brace **(see illustration 10.3)**. On 2002 and later OHV V6, remove the alternator three top mounting bolts. On an OHC V6, remove the two bolts and one stub bolt that secure the alternator to the bracket. On 2000 and later OHC engines, the crankshaft pulley must be removed first for clearance (see Chapter 2B).

5   Installation is the reverse of removal.

6   After the alternator is installed, install the drivebelt and reconnect the ground cable to the negative terminal of the battery.

11   Voltage regulator and alternator brushes - replacement

Refer to illustrations 11.2, 11.3, 11.4 and 11.8
Note: *The models covered by this manual use two types of alternators. One has an external voltage regulator and brush holder assembly, mounted on the rear of the alternator (that is the design shown in the following procedure). The other alternator design has an internal regulator, and the alternator must be opened for regulator replacement.*

1   Remove the alternator (Section 10) and place it on a clean workbench.

2   Remove the four voltage regulator mounting screws **(see illustration)**.

11.2 To detach the voltage regulator and brush holder assembly, remove the four screws

11.3 Lift the assembly from the alternator

11.4 To remove the brushes, remove the rubber plugs from the two brush lead screws and remove both screws (arrows)

3   Remove the regulator and brush holder assembly from the alternator **(see illustration)**.
4   Remove the rubber plugs and use a Torx screwdriver to remove the brush lead retaining screws and nuts to separate the brush leads from the holder **(see illustration)**.
5   Note the relationship of the brushes to the brush holder and remove both brushes. Don't lose the springs.
6   If you're installing new brushes into the old regulator, insert them into the brush holder. Make sure the springs are properly compressed and the brushes are properly inserted into the brush holder. If you're installing a new voltage regulator, it is best to install new brushes, as well.
7   Install the brush lead retaining screws and nuts.
8   Insert a short piece of wire, like a paper clip, through the hole in the voltage regulator **(see illustration)** to hold the brushes in the retracted position during regulator installation.
9   Carefully install the regulator. Make sure the brushes don't hang up on the rotor.
10   Install the voltage regulator screws and tighten them securely.
11   Remove the wire or paper clip.
12   Install the alternator (Section 10).

12 Starting system - general information and precautions

The starting system comprises the starter motor (with a solenoid), the battery, the ignition switch, the transmission range sensor and connecting wires. Most models also have a starter relay.
Turning the ignition key to the Start position actuates the starter through the starter control circuit and the solenoid. The transmission range (TR) sensor in the starter control circuit takes the place of the neutral start switch used on older vehicles. The TR

sensor prevents operation of the starter unless the shift lever is in Neutral or Park.
The 1996-97 models with OHV V6 engines do not have a starter relay in the control circuit, but 1996-97 models with the OHC V6 include a starter relay. All 1998 and later models have a starter relay, which is in the engine compartment power distribution box.
Never operate the starter motor for more than 15 seconds at a time without pausing to allow it to cool for at least two minutes. Excessive cranking can cause overheating, which can damage the starter.

13 Starter motor and circuit - test

Refer to illustration 13.6
Note: *Before diagnosing starter problems, make sure the battery is fully charged.*
1   If the starter motor doesn't turn at all when the ignition switch is operated, make sure the shift lever is in Neutral or Park.
2   Make sure the battery is charged and that all cables at the battery and starter solenoid terminals are secure. Also check the battery ground cable connection to the engine or body.
3   If the starter motor spins but the engine doesn't turn over, the drive assembly in the starter motor is slipping and the starter motor must be replaced (Section 14).
4   If the starter motor doesn't operate at all but the starter solenoid operates (clicks) when the switch is actuated, the problem is with either the battery, the starter solenoid, or the starter motor connections.
5   If the starter solenoid doesn't click when the ignition switch is actuated, either the starter solenoid circuit is open or the solenoid itself is defective. Check the starter solenoid circuit (see the wiring diagrams at the end of this book) or replace the solenoid (Section 15).
6   To check the starter solenoid circuit, remove the push-on connector from the solenoid "S" terminal **(see illustration)**. Make

11.8 Before installing the voltage regulator and brush holder, insert a paper clip as shown to hold the brushes in place during installation. After installation, pull the paper clip out

sure that the connection is clean and secure.
7   If the solenoid connections are good, check the operation of the solenoid. Put the transmission in Park and remove the push-on connector from the solenoid "S" terminal. Connect a jumper wire or remote starter switch between the battery positive terminal and the exposed "S" terminal on the solenoid. If the starter motor now operates, the starter solenoid is OK. The problem is in the ignition switch, the transmission range (TR) sensor, or in the starting circuit wiring. Inspect for open or loose connections.
8   If the starter motor still doesn't operate, replace the solenoid (Section 15).
9   If the starter motor cranks the engine very slowly, make sure the battery is fully charged and all terminal connections are clean and tight. Then check the connections at the starter solenoid and battery ground. Eyelet terminals should not be easily rotated by hand. If the engine is partially seized, or has high-viscosity oil in it in cold weather, it will crank slowly.

13.6 Connect a jumper wire or preferably a remote starter switch from the solenoid "S" terminal (arrow) to battery positive voltage. The solenoid should engage, and the motor should operate.

14.4 Remove the starter bolts (arrows) and remove the starter from the bellhousing

10   Check the starter circuit. Consult the wiring diagrams at the end of Chapter 12. Check the condition of the TR sensor.
11   Check the operation of the starter relay, if equipped. Check for battery voltage to the relay and correct operation of the relay. Refer to Chapter 12 for additional information on the locations of relays and how to test them.
12   If the car has an anti-theft system, refer to Chapter 12 and check the circuit and the control module for shorts or damaged components.

14 Starter motor - removal and installation

Refer to illustration 14.4
Note: *The models covered by this manual use two different starter motors that are electrically identical but different in their mounting arrangements. Starters on OHV V6 engines are mounted to the front of the transaxle bellhousing by two bolts. Starters on OHC V6 engines are mounted to the side of the transaxle bellhousing. All starter motors are permanent-magnet motors with electrical connections only for the solenoid and the motor armature. The motors are not repairable except for solenoid replacement.*
1   Disconnect the battery ground (negative) cable.
2   Raise the vehicle and support it securely on jackstands. On 2000 and later models, remove the push-pins and the splash shield below the radiator.
3   Disconnect the large cable from the terminal on the solenoid and disconnect the solenoid "S" terminal.
4   Remove the starter motor mounting bolts **(see illustration)** and remove the starter from the engine.
5   If necessary, turn the wheels to one side for access to the starter.
6   Installation is the reverse of removal.

15 Starter solenoid - replacement

1   Remove the starter from the engine (Section 14).
2   Remove the motor brush connector from the solenoid "M" terminal.
3   Remove the solenoid mounting bolts and separate the solenoid from the starter body.
4   Installation is the reverse of removal.

Notes

Chapter 6
Emissions and engine control systems

Contents

1   General information

Refer to illustrations 1.3 and 1.7

The emissions control systems on the models covered by this manual are an integral part of the overall electronic engine control system. The engine control system on these vehicles is the manufacturer's fifth generation of engine controls, called EEC-V. The EEC-V system also includes all the government-required diagnostic features of the second generation of onboard diagnostic systems, or OBD-II.

At the center of the EEC-V and OBD-II operations is the Powertrain Control Module (PCM), or onboard computer. On older vehicles, engine control computers were called electronic control modules or electronic control units. The name PCM is a standard term now used by all auto manufacturers as part of the standard requirements of OBD-II. Powertrain Control Module is particularly appropriate because the PCM controls not only engine operation, but also the automatic transmission.

The PCM receives engine operating

1.3 Typical emission and engine control system component locations (OHV V6 engine shown, others similar)

1	EGR vacuum solenoid	
2	Fuel pressure regulator	
3	EGR backpressure sensor	
4	EGR valve	
5	Idle Air Control (IAC) valve	
6	Throttle body and Throttle Position Sensor (TPS)	
7	Crankcase ventilation tube	
8	Intake Air Temperature (IAT) sensor	
9	Mass Airflow (MAF) sensor	
10	Air filter housing	
11	Battery	
12	Power distribution box (fuses and relays)	
13	Ignition coil pack	
14	Spark plugs and wires	
15	Fuel injectors	

information as input signals from a number of sensors **(see illustration)** and provides output commands to actuators such as the ignition coil, the fuel injectors, and various solenoids and relays for the engine and transmission. Other emission controls included in the overall engine control system are:

- Positive crankcase ventilation (PCV)
- Evaporative emission controls
- Secondary air injection
- Exhaust gas recirculation (EGR)
- Two catalytic converters

The sections in this chapter include general descriptions, test procedures, and component replacement procedures (when practical) for most of the EEC-V system sensors and actuators, as well as other emission control devices. Refer to Chapter 4 for more information on the fuel and exhaust systems and to Chapter 5 for information on the ignition system. Also refer to Chapter 1 for scheduled maintenance operations that relate to emission control and engine performance.

The information in this chapter is intended to be economically practical and within the capabilities of the home mechanic. The diagnosis and service of some engine and emission control functions and driveability problems requires specialized tools, equipment and training. If checking and servicing become too difficult or require special test equipment, consult a dealer service department or other qualified repair shop.

Although engine and emission control systems are very sophisticated on late-model vehicles, you can perform many checks and do most of the regular maintenance at home with common tune-up and hand tools and relatively inexpensive meters. Because of the Federally mandated warranty that covers the emission control system, check with a dealer about warranty coverage before working on any emission-related systems. After the warranty has expired, you may wish to perform some of the component checks and replacement procedures in this Chapter to save money. Remember, the most frequent cause of emission and driveability problems is a loose or broken vacuum hose or wire, so always check the hose and wiring connections first.

Pay close attention to any special precautions given in this Chapter. Remember that illustrations of various systems may not exactly match the system installed on the vehicle you're working on because of

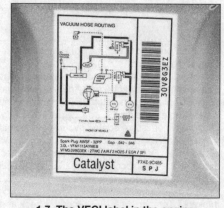

1.7 The VECI label in the engine compartment identifies the emission control devices on a particular engine and includes a vacuum hose routing diagram

changes made by the manufacturer during production or from year to year.

A Vehicle Emission Control Information (VECI) label is located in the engine compartment **(see illustration)**. This label contains emission-control and engine tune-up specifications and adjustment information. It also includes a vacuum hose routing diagram for emission-control components. When servicing the engine or emission systems, always check the VECI label in your vehicle. The VECI label always takes precedence over information in manuals.

2 EEC-V sensors and actuators - general information

Information sensors

Note: *The sensors listed below send input voltage signals to the PCM, which tell the PCM about various engine and vehicle operating conditions. Sensor checks, removal and replacement procedures are given in more detail in later sections of this chapter.*

1 **Heated Oxygen sensors (HO2S)** - The HO2S generates a voltage signal that varies with the difference between the oxygen content of the exhaust and the oxygen in the surrounding air. Exhaust oxygen sensors have been the principal feedback sensors used by engine control systems to calculate air/fuel ratios for more than 20 years.

The models covered by this manual have four HO2S, two upstream sensors installed just ahead of each catalytic converter and two downstream sensors installed after each catalytic converter. Upstream HO2S provide the input signals that the PCM uses for fuel control. Downstream sensors do not affect fuel control; the PCM compares the downstream HO2S signal with the upstream HO2S signal for each branch of the exhaust system to monitor catalyst operation.

2 **Crankshaft position (CKP) sensor** - The CKP sensor is a magnetic pickup, or variable-reluctance, sensor mounted on the engine front cover and triggered by a toothed wheel on the front of the crankshaft. The trigger wheel has 35 evenly spaced teeth and one gap where a 36th tooth would be. The gap lets the CKP sensor signal the PCM when the crankshaft is 60 degrees before TDC for cylinders 1 and 5. The PCM then computes actual TDC or any number of degrees before or after TDC and uses this information to control ignition spark advance. The CKP sensor produces a direct-current (DC) sine wave voltage signal. The sensor does the job of a distributor pickup in a distributor-type electronic ignition. It provides information on crankshaft position and the engine speed signal to the PCM.

3 **Camshaft position (CMP) sensor** - The CMP sensor on the OHV V6 engine is a Hall-effect sensor, mounted where the ignition distributor was located on older versions of this engine. The OHV CMP sensor produces a square-wave voltage signal. The CMP sensor on the OHC V6 engine is a magnetic pickup, or variable-reluctance, sensor, mounted on the forward left side of the forward cylinder head, below the valve cover, and triggered by a special tooth on the exhaust camshaft. The OHC CMP sensor

produces a direct-current (DC) sine wave voltage signal. The PCM uses either kind of CMP signal to identify number 1 cylinder and to time the sequential fuel injection.

4 **Engine coolant temperature (ECT) sensor** - The ECT is a variable-resistance thermistor that is threaded into a coolant passage. It monitors engine coolant temperature and sends the PCM a voltage signal that affects PCM control of the fuel mixture, ignition timing, and EGR operation.

5 **Intake Air Temperature (IAT) sensor** - The IAT also is a variable-resistance thermistor. It is installed in the air intake duct and provides the PCM with intake air temperature information. The PCM uses this information to control fuel flow, ignition timing, and EGR system operation.

6 **Throttle Position Sensor (TPS)** - The TPS is a variable-resistance potentiometer, mounted on the side of the throttle body and connected to the throttle shaft. It senses throttle movement and position, then transmits a voltage signal to the PCM. This signal enables the PCM to determine when the throttle is closed, in a cruise position, or wide open.

7 **Mass airflow (MAF) sensor** - The MAF sensor is mounted in the air cleaner intake passage and measures the mass of the air entering the engine. Air/fuel ratios are calculated by weight, or mass (which are equivalent on the surface of the earth). Therefore, measuring the molecular mass of the intake airflow is the most accurate way for the PCM to compute the required air/fuel ratio. The MAF sensor, along with the IAT sensor, provide mass airflow and air temperature information for the most precise fuel metering.

8 **Knock sensor** - The knock sensor is piezoresistive microphone that detects the sound of engine detonation, or "pinging." The PCM uses the input signal from the knock sensor to recognize detonation and retard spark advance to avoid engine damage. The knock sensor is used only on the OHC V6; it is mounted in the forward side of the engine block, near the oil filter.

9 **Vehicle speed sensor (VSS)** - The vehicle speed sensor is a pickup coil, or variable-reluctance sensor, mounted in the transaxle. It provides a DC sine wave signal (similar to other pickup coil sensors such as the CKP sensor) to the PCM to indicate vehicle speed.

10 **EGR backpressure sensor** - The EGR backpressure sensor is a differential-pressure, strain-gauge sensor that sends a voltage signal to the PCM that is proportional to the EGR pressure drop across the metering orifice in the EGR tube. The PCM uses this as a feedback signal to monitor the rate and flow of exhaust gas recirculation into the intake system.

11 **Fuel tank pressure sensor** - The fuel tank pressure sensor is part of the evaporative emission control system, which is an integral part of the EEC-V system and controlled by the PCM. The fuel tank pressure sensor monitors vapor pressure in the tank

and sends a proportional voltage signal to the PCM. The PCM uses this information to turn on and off the purge valves and solenoids of the evaporative emission system.

12 **Power steering pressure (PSP) switch** - The PSP sensor is a hydraulic pressure switch in the power steering system. When the switch closes, the PCM receives an input signal that causes it to maintain engine speed under high steering loads during parking. This switch signal also causes the PCM to increase transaxle hydraulic line pressure during low-speed vehicle maneuvers.

13 **Brake On-Off (BOO) switch** - This switch is a normally open switch, also called the "cruise control brake switch." When the driver applies the brakes, the switch closes and signals the PCM to disengage the cruise control and change fuel metering and spark advance during deceleration. On 1998 models, this switch is called the Brake Pedal Position (BPP) switch.

14 **Additional transaxle sensors** - In addition to the sensors listed above that affect transaxle operation, the PCM receives input signals from the following sensors inside the transaxle or connected to it: (a) the turbine shaft speed sensor, (b) the transmission fluid temperature sensor, and (c) the transmission range sensor.

Output actuators

Note: *The actuators and other output control devices listed below receive commands from the PCM or provide electric power to different subsystems and components. Actuator checks and removal and replacement procedures are given in more detail in later sections of this chapter.*

15 **EEC power relay** - The main EEC power relay is activated by the ignition switch and supplies battery power to the PCM and the EEC-V system when the switch is in the Start or Run position. On 1996 and 1997 models, the EEC power relay is part of the Constant Control Relay Module (CCRM). On 1998 and later models, the power relay is in the power distribution box in the engine compartment. Refer to Chapter 12 or your owner's manual for more information on relay location.

16 **Fuel pump relay** - The fuel pump relay is activated by the PCM with the ignition switch in the Start or Run position. When the ignition switch is turned on, the relay is activated to supply initial line pressure to the system. On 1996 and 1997 models, the fuel pump relay is part of the Constant Control Relay Module (CCRM). On 1998 and later models, the fuel pump relay is in the power distribution box in the engine compartment. For more information on fuel pump check and replacement, refer to Chapter 4.

17 **Fuel injectors** - The PCM opens the fuel injectors individually in firing order sequence. The PCM also controls the time the injector is open, called the "pulse width." The pulse width of the injector (measured in

milliseconds) determines the amount of fuel delivered. For more information on the fuel delivery system and the fuel injectors, including injector replacement, refer to Chapter 4.

18   **Ignition coil pack** - The Distributorless Ignition System (DIS) is controlled directly by the PCM. No separate ignition module is used. Battery positive voltage is supplied on a single wire to the ignition coil pack. The PCM controls the ground side of each coil individually in the coil pack to fire the spark plugs with the correct ignition timing. Refer to Chapter 5 for more information on the ignition coil pack.

19   **Idle air control (IAC) valve** - The IAC allows air to bypass the throttle plate and is mounted on the throttle body or on the intake manifold next to the throttle body. The IAC valve opening and the resulting airflow is controlled by the PCM. Refer to Chapter 4 for more information on the IAC valve.

20   **EGR vacuum solenoid** - The EGR vacuum solenoid is controlled by the PCM to regulate the opening of the vacuum-operated EGR valve.

21   **Secondary air injection pump** - The secondary air injection system supplies air to the exhaust manifolds to aid catalytic converter warm-up and operation. The secondary air pump is an electric pump, controlled by the PCM.

22   **Canister purge valve** - The evaporative emission canister purge valve is a solenoid valve, operated by the PCM to purge the fuel vapor canister and route fuel vapor to the intake manifold for combustion.

23   **Canister vent solenoid** - The evaporative emission canister vent solenoid is operated by the PCM during the OBD-II evaporative emission monitor (see Section 3) and during an emission test of the evaporative system.

---

3   Onboard diagnostic system (OBD-II) and diagnostic trouble codes

OBD-II system general description

Refer to illustration 3.1

The U.S. Environmental Protection Agency (EPA) and the California Air Resources Board (CARB) are the government agencies primarily responsible for the second generation of onboard diagnostic systems, known as OBD-II. Auto manufacturers started to introduce OBD-II systems on some 1994 models, and they became standard on 1996 and later vehicles. OBD-II systems differ from earlier onboard diagnostic systems in the following major ways:

a) *Specific programmed self-tests, called "system monitors," that let the PCM test the operation of subsystems and components.*

b) *A standard list of basic system operating data, called system "parameters," transmitted by the PCM to a diagnostic scan tool.*

c) *A standardized library of diagnostic trouble codes (DTC) used by all carmakers.*

d) *A standardized diagnostic connector, called a data link connector (DLC), used by all auto manufacturers.*

Onboard diagnostic systems before OBD-II had a wide variety of test capabilities, operating parameter information (or lack of it), and trouble code displays. No two auto manufacturers provided exactly the same kind of information. OBD-II is an attempt to standardize diagnostic capabilities worldwide and to ensure that all vehicles provide minimum basic information to promote more accurate repairs and more reliable emission control. Although all auto manufacturers must meet the basic requirements of OBD-II, they also are free to provide enhanced diagnostic capabilities of their own design for their vehicle electronic systems. OBD-II is not an electronic control system, nor is it separate from any vehicle's engine management system. Rather, OBD-II is a set of diagnostic requirements that each auto manufacturer must incorporate into its particular electronic control system.

OBD-II System Monitors

The OBD-II system "monitors" are self-tests programmed into the EEC-V PCM. An OBD-II system can perform up to 11 emission system monitor tests. Three of these monitors run continuously whenever the vehicle is being operated. They are: misfire detection, fuel system monitoring, and comprehensive component monitoring. The PCM performs other monitors, known as noncontinuous monitors, once per trip. These are: catalytic converter, evaporative emissions, secondary air, oxygen sensor, oxygen sensor heater, and EGR system monitors. The PCM also may have a monitor test for the air conditioning system to detect refrigerant leakage.

Monitor tests occur during a key-on, engine-run, key-off cycle when certain operating conditions, or enabling criteria, are met. Test criteria include information such as elapsed time since startup, engine speed, throttle position, engine coolant temperature, and vehicle speed. Any driving cycle that includes an emission monitor test is called a trip. Clearing DTC memory following repairs also clears monitor results from memory.

The PCM starts, directs, processes, and communicates the results of monitor tests using a software program called the "diagnostic executive," or simply the "executive." The diagnostic executive performs the emission monitor tests on each vehicle trip. Specific driving requirements must be met to start and finish each monitor. Often, the executive must delay completion of a monitor because not all criteria are met. The executive can delay a monitor for several reasons.

Delays fall into three categories: (1) suspended, (2) pending, and (3) conflicting.

A test can be suspended when another test with a higher priority takes precedence. All of the emission self-tests are prioritized, and the executive may suspend a low-priority monitor so that one with higher priority can run. The executive only runs some secondary tests after the system passes certain primary tests. When the secondary tests are delayed, awaiting primary test results, they are pending. Conflicts also can occur as different monitors use the same circuits or components. In such cases, the executive requires each test to finish before allowing another to begin.

The diagnostic executive conducts three types of tests: (1) passive, (2) active, and (3) intrusive. A passive test monitors a system or component without affecting its operation. If a passive test fails, an active test will start. During an active test, the PCM sends a test signal on the suspect circuit so that it can evaluate the response. Active testing does not disable the component or suspend control system operation. Intrusive tests do affect engine performance and emissions, and the executive performs these tests only after the passive and active tests both fail.

When a monitor test ends, a pass or fail report is recorded in PCM memory by the diagnostic executive. Most monitor failures do not set a DTC and light the MIL unless failure occurs during two consecutive trips. When checking monitor test status with a scan tool, the scan tool display can read complete or not complete, supported or not supported.

Misfire monitor

Poor cylinder combustion that causes engine misfire also causes an increase of HC emissions in the exhaust. The excess HC that results from a misfire also can overload the catalytic converters and accelerate their deterioration. The OBD-II system checks for, and alerts the driver, of an engine misfire that could damage the converter or raise emissions above standards.

Whenever a cylinder misfires, combustion pressure drops momentarily and slows down the piston. Because this retarded piston movement also slows the crankshaft, the CKP sensor can detect engine misfire. The CKP signal of a running engine produces a predictable waveform with evenly spaced peaks. When a misfire slows the crankshaft, it interrupts the even spacing of the waveform cycles. By comparing the CKP and CMP sensor signals, the PCM also can determine which cylinder misfired.

To prevent a false DTC from occurring from conditions that mimic a misfire, such as excessive driveline vibration caused by rough roads, the monitor maintains a misfire counter for each cylinder, which records the number of misfires that occurred during the past 200 and 1000 crankshaft revolutions. Whenever the monitor reports a misfire, the diagnostic executive program checks all of the cylinder misfire counters. A DTC sets only if one or more of the counters has significantly more misfire counts than the others.

OBD-II has two categories of misfire: those that can damage the catalytic converter, and those that can cause exhaust emissions to exceed federal standards by more than 50 percent. The executive sets a DTC immediately and flashes the MIL if the monitor detects misfire in more than 15 percent of the cylinder firings during 200 crankshaft revolutions. This is a type A misfire. A less serious type B misfire, is one in which two percent of the cylinder firing opportunities misfire during 1000 crankshaft revolutions. The executive sets a DTC and lights the MIL if a type B misfire occurs during two consecutive trips.

Fuel system monitor

The EEC-V system uses two fuel control parameters: short-term fuel trim (STFT) and long-term fuel trim (LTFT). The OBD-II diagnostic executive monitors how well the PCM is regulating the air/fuel mixture. The fuel-trim values indicate how much fuel is being added to, or removed from, the mixture to keep the engine running at peak efficiency. Fuel-trim factors are a PCM response based on feedback from the HO2S and other system inputs. Short-term fuel trim responds immediately to a change in operating conditions; long-term fuel trim reacts more slowly in response to general trends.

The fuel system monitor will detect when fuel trim is operating at the limits and can no longer compensate for operating conditions that lead to an overly rich or lean air/fuel mixtures. The OBD-II fuel system monitor measures fuel trim as a percentage. A fuel system monitor failure must occur on two consecutive trips before a DTC sets and the MIL lights.

Comprehensive component monitor

The comprehensive component monitor checks PCM input and output signals for malfunctions affecting any component or circuit not evaluated by another monitor. Typically, the PCM looks for open or short circuits and for out-of-range values. Additionally, "rationality" tests check input signals, and "functionality" tests check output circuits to compare signals from one device with those of another.

Catalytic converter monitor

The PCM uses signals from two heated oxygen sensors (HO2S), one upstream and the other downstream from each catalytic converter, to evaluate converter operation. By comparing voltage signals of the downstream HO2S and the upstream HO2S, the PCM calculates how much oxygen each catalyst retains. With a good catalyst, a voltage signal from the downstream HO2S will have little switching activity, while the voltage signal from the upstream HO2S crosses the midpoint of the operating range vigorously. The more that downstream HO2S activity

matches that of the upstream HO2S, the greater the degree of converter deterioration.

Oxygen sensor monitor

This monitor runs several tests by evaluating data from the heater circuit reference signals from each sensor. The upstream (pre-catalyst) HO2S monitor checks for high and low threshold voltage and switching frequency. Switching frequency, or cross-counts, is the number of times the signal voltage crosses the midpoint of the sensor signal range during a specific time. An HO2S monitor also evaluates sensor response by measuring the time required to perform a lean-to-rich and a rich-to-lean transition. The PCM compares test results to previously stored values. Because downstream (postcatalyst) O2S voltage fluctuations are slight and the signal seldom crosses the midpoint of the range, the monitor samples voltage level under lean and rich operation. During rich-running conditions, the monitor looks for a fixed, low-voltage signal from the downstream sensor. During lean conditions, the monitor looks for downstream HO2S voltage to stay high and steady. The diagnostic executive lights the MIL to alert the driver of a malfunction, if an HO2S monitor fails on two consecutive trips.

Evaporative emission system monitor

The OBD-II evaporative emission system monitor checks for canister purge volume and leakage. Most systems use a solenoid-operated purge valve to vent vapors from the charcoal canister to the intake manifold during cruising. Typically, the PCM closes the system to atmospheric pressure and opens the purge valve to begin an evaporative monitor test. A pressure sensor on the fuel tank sends information to the PCM on how fast vacuum increases in the system. The PCM uses this pressure sensor feedback to calculate purge flow rate. To perform a vapor leak test, the PCM closes the purge valve to create a sealed system. Any leakage in the system will cause pressure to drop, and this pressure change is reported to the PCM by the pressure sensor. An evaporative failure must occur on two consecutive trips before a DTC sets and the MIL lights.

EGR system monitor

The EGR monitor tests EGR flow and determines if the system is operating efficiently. To do this, the PCM opens and closes the EGR valve while monitoring the amount of change in the EGR sensor voltage signal. The monitor then calculates EGR system efficiency by comparing these live samples to values in the lookup tables that correspond to exhaust gas flow. If the EGR efficiency level does not meet the programmed standard in two consecutive trips, the MIL lights and a DTC sets.

Secondary air injection monitor

The secondary air injection monitor sev-

eral tests to evaluate the rate of airflow and the operation and efficiency of the diverter valve. The monitor also tests electric pump operation and measures the amount of air the pump is delivering to the exhaust. The upstream HO2S for each cylinder bank detects the excess oxygen from the air pump system. The air injection monitor has a low priority, however, and the diagnostic executive puts it in a pending status until all of the HO2S monitor tests pass. Like most other monitors, a secondary air monitor DTC only sets after failure on two consecutive trips.

Freeze frame

Freeze frame is an OBD-II PCM feature that records all related sensor and actuator activity on the PCM data stream whenever an emission fault is detected and a DTC is set. After it is created, the freeze frame is stored in PCM memory where it can be retrieved for later analysis on a scan tool. This ability to look at the circuit conditions and values when a fault occurs is a valuable tool when troubleshooting an intermittent problem.

Drive Cycles

For a complete test of the EEC-V system, the engine must be running at normal operating temperature; but some initial tests can be done on a cold engine. For some procedures, such as troubleshooting a no-start problem, you must start with a cold engine. Other examples include problems that only occur when the engine is cold or operating in open loop. Often, you can check engine operation immediately after a cold start and then monitor engine performance as it goes into closed loop.

Before it will allow an emissions certification test, the PCM must receive a pass from all of the onboard monitors. These monitors test the integrity of emission system components at various speeds, loads, and temperatures during normal driving conditions. With an onboard monitor test suspended, pending, or conflicting, the vehicle must be driven through a specific drive cycle to perform all of the emission control monitor checks. The system must complete and pass all of the monitors.

These warm-up conditioning procedures are an important part of EEC-V troubleshooting. You can view data parameter values on a scan tool during the drive cycle, and a DTC will set if a fault occurs. Look for unusual circuit activity, such as high or low signals, voltage dropouts, and a lack of switching. When you spot a problem on one circuit, also look for unusual activity on related circuits. After all repairs are made, retest to verify that the problem is gone and then clear the DTC memory. Code clearing is a scan tool function that resets all monitors.

Malfunction indicator lamp

Although it may still be labeled CHECK ENGINE, the warning lamp on the instrument panel is called the malfunction indicator lamp (MIL) in an OBD-II system. The PCM lights

3.27 The data link connector (DLC) is located under the instrument panel (arrow), near the steering column

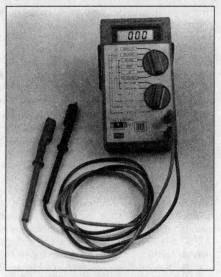

3.29 Digital multimeters can be used to test all types of circuits. Because of their high impedance, they are more accurate than analog meters for measuring voltage in low-voltage computer circuits

3.30 Scanners like these are designed for the home mechanic and are more affordable than professional equipment. Many are compatible with OBD-II systems

the MIL when an emission control malfunction occurs or when a system or component fails one of the OBD-II self-test monitors as described previously. Other EEC-V system problems also may light the MIL, but not all diagnostic trouble codes (DTC) cause the MIL to light. That is, you may find a DTC stored in the PCM memory with no indication on the MIL.

Unlike the CHECK ENGINE lamp on older vehicles, the MIL on an OBD-II system will not always turn off when an intermittent problem goes away. If the PCM detects an emission control problem on two consecutive trips and lights the MIL, it will stay lit until the problem is fixed, the system passes the related self-test monitor, and the MIL is turned off by a scan tool. Additionally, DTC's cannot be made to flash on the MIL as was possible with some diagnostic systems on older vehicles.

Data link connector

Refer to illustration 3.27

Another standardized component required by OBD-II is the 16-pin data link connector (DLC) located under the driver's side of the instrument panel **(see illustration)**. This DLC replaces the variety of diagnostic connectors used by auto manufacturers before OBD-II. Diagnostic information can be obtained through the DLC only by using a scan tool that is compatible with OBD-II.

Diagnostic equipment

Refer to illustrations 3.29 and 3.30

Some diagnostic equipment for engine and emission control systems costs several thousands of dollars and is not practical for the home mechanic. Several equipment companies, however, are building more and more electronic test equipment that is intended for the do-it-yourself mechanic and is available at economical prices. Much of this equipment can be purchased for just a few hundred dollars and some for less than $100.

Digital multimeter

A digital volt-ohm-ammeter, or multime-

ter, is necessary instead of an analog meter for several reasons. An analog meter cannot display voltage, ohms, or amperage measurements in increments of hundredths and thousandths of a unit. When working with electronic systems, which are usually very low-voltage circuits, this kind of precise reading is most important. Another good reason for the digital multimeter is its high input impedance. The digital multimeter has high-resistance internal circuitry of 10 million ohms or more. Because a voltmeter is connected in parallel with the circuit when testing, none of the voltage being measured should drop across the parallel path of the meter. If you are measuring a low-voltage circuit, such as the HO2S signal voltage, a fraction of a volt is a significant amount when diagnosing a problem. Many digital multimeters with all the necessary capabilities for late-model vehicle electronic systems are available for less than $100 **(see illustration)**.

Scan tool

A hand-held scan tool, or scanner, is a small test computer that communicates with the vehicle PCM. Scanners originally were intended for professional driveability technicians and cost several thousand dollars. Today, several equipment companies are building more economical scanners for the home mechanic. Many of these relatively economical scan tools are compatible with OBD-II systems **(see illustration)**.

An OBD-II scan tool communicates with the vehicle PCM and reads DTC's, as well as system operating parameters. Basic OBD-II diagnostic capabilities consist of reading standard DTC's and the basic list of operating parameters. These are called "generic OBD-II tests" and usually are available from any scan tool compatible with OBD-II. Some scan tools also include advanced OBD-II

tests for specific carmakers' systems. If you are considering the purchase of a scanner, be sure that it has at least the generic OBD-II capabilities. Then consider whether it has advanced OBD-II capabilities for your vehicle and decide if the price justifies its usefulness. Many scanners can be revised, or updated, with interchangeable cartridges. Others can be reprogrammed easily and economically by the tool distributor.

Diagnostic trouble codes (DTC)

This OBD-II system uses the same library of standardized DTC's used in other manufacturers OBD-II systems, worldwide. The OBD-II DTC's are five-digit, alphanumeric codes. Each DTC begins with a letter, such as P for powertrain. The second digit is either a 0 if the code is a generic, or universal code, used by all auto manufacturers or a 1 if it is unique manufacturer's code. The last three digits indicate the subsystem and circuit or component where the fault has been detected.

OBD-II DTC's can only be read from the PCM memory through the DLC, using a scan tool that is compatible with OBD-II. The DTC's cannot be flashed on the MIL or displayed in any way other than through an OBD-II scan tool.

Clearing codes

To clear a DTC from the PCM memory, connect an OBD-II scan tool to the DLC and follow the tool manufacturer's instructions. Remember that the MIL cannot be turned off for an emission-related DTC until the system passes the appropriate OBD-II self-test monitor.

Do not disconnect the battery to clear the DTC's. It won't work, but it will erase stored operating parameters from the PCM memory and cause the engine to run roughly for some time while the PCM relearns the information.

OBD-II Trouble Codes

Code	Probable cause
P0102	Mass Airflow (MAF) sensor circuit low input
P0103	Mass Airflow (MAF) sensor circuit high input
P0106	Barometric Pressure sensor circuit performance
P0107	Barometric Pressure sensor circuit low voltage
P0108	Barometric Pressure sensor circuit high voltage
P0109	Barometric Pressure sensor circuit intermittent
P0112	Intake Air Temperature (IAT) sensor circuit low input
P0113	Intake Air Temperature (IAT) sensor circuit high input
P0117	Electronic Coolant Temperature (ECT) sensor circuit low input
P0118	Electronic Coolant Temperature (ECT) sensor circuit high input
P0121	In range Throttle Position Sensor (TPS) fault
P0122	Throttle Position Sensor (TPS) circuit low input
P0123	Throttle Position Sensor (TPS) circuit high input
P0125	Insufficient coolant temperature
P0127	Intake Air temperature sensor "A" circuit
P0131	Upstream heated O2 sensor circuit low voltage (Bank 1)
P0133	Upstream heated O2 sensor circuit slow response (Bank 1)
P0135	Upstream heated O2 sensor heater circuit fault (Bank 1)
P0136	Downstream heated O2 sensor fault (Bank 1)
P0141	Downstream heated O2 sensor heater circuit fault (Bank 1)
P0151	Upstream heated O2 sensor circuit low voltage (Bank 2)
P0153	Upstream heated O2 sensor circuit slow response (Bank 2)
P0155	Upstream heated O2 sensor heater circuit fault (Bank 2)
P0156	Downstream heated O2 sensor fault (Bank 2)
P0161	Downstream heated O2 sensor heater circuit fault (Bank 2)
P0171	System Adaptive fuel too lean (Bank 1)
P0172	System Adaptive fuel too rich (Bank 1)
P0174	System Adaptive fuel too lean (Bank 2)
P0175	System Adaptive fuel too rich (Bank 2)
P0176	Flexible Fuel sensor "A" circuit
P0181	Engine Fuel Temperature sensor "A" circuit range
P0182	Engine Fuel Temperature sensor "A" circuit low input
P0183	Engine Fuel Temperature sensor "A" circuit high input
P0186	Engine Fuel Temperature sensor "B" circuit range
P0187	Engine Fuel Temperature sensor "B" circuit low input
P0188	Engine Fuel Temperature sensor "B" circuit high input
P0190	Fuel Rail Pressure sensor circuit performance
P0191	Injector Pressure sensor system performance
P0192	Injector Pressure sensor circuit low input
P0193	Injector Pressure sensor circuit high input
P0300	Random misfire
P0301	Cylinder no. 1 misfire detected
P0302	Cylinder no. 2 misfire detected
P0303	Cylinder no. 3 misfire detected
P0304	Cylinder no. 4 misfire detected
P0305	Cylinder no. 5 misfire detected
P0306	Cylinder no. 6 misfire detected
P0320	Ignition Engine Speed input circuit performance
P0325	Knock sensor circuit fault
P0326	Knock sensor circuit performance
P0330	Knock sensor 2 circuit malfunction
P0331	Knock sensor 2 range
P0340	Camshaft Position sensor circuit malfunction
P0350	Ignition coil primary/secondary circuit malfunction
P0351	Ignition coil no. 1 primary circuit fault
P0352	Ignition coil no. 2 primary circuit fault
P0353	Ignition coil no. 3 primary circuit fault
P0354	Ignition coil no. 4 primary circuit fault
P0355	Ignition coil no. 5 primary circuit fault
P0356	Ignition coil no. 6 primary circuit fault

OBD-II Trouble Codes (continued)

Code	Probable cause
P0400	EGR flow fault
P0401	EGR insufficient flow detected
P0402	EGR excessive flow detected
P0411	Secondary Air Injection system upstream flow
P0412	Secondary Air Injection system circuit malfunction
P0420	Catalyst system efficiency below threshold (Bank 1)
P0421	Catalyst system efficiency below threshold (Bank 1)
P0430	Catalyst system efficiency below threshold (Bank 2)
P0431	Catalyst system efficiency below threshold (Bank 2)
P0442	EVAP small leak detected
P0443	EVAP VMV circuit fault
P0451	FTP sensor circuit noisy
P0452	EVAP fuel tank pressure sensor low input
P0453	EVAP fuel tank pressure sensor high input
P0455	EVAP Control system leak detected, very small leak
P0457	EVAP Control system leak detected, fuel filler cap loose/off
P0460	Fuel Level sensor circuit malfunction
P0500	VSS malfunction
P0501	VSS range
P0502	VSS intermittent
P0505	IAC valve system fault
P0552	Power Steering Pressure sensor circuit malfunction
P0553	Power Steering Pressure sensor circuit malfunction
P0602	Control Module programming error
P0603	PCM Keep Alive Memory test error
P0605	PCM Read Only Memory test error
P0703	Brake switch circuit input malfunction
P0720	Output Shaft Speed sensor, insufficient input

4   Powertrain Control Module (PCM) - replacement

Refer to illustration 4.2

Caution: *To avoid electrostatic discharge damage to the PCM, handle the PCM only by its case. Do not touch the electrical terminals during removal and installation. If available, ground yourself to the vehicle with a anti-static ground strap, available at computer supply stores.*

Note: *The PCM is a highly reliable component and rarely requires replacement. Because the PCM is the most expensive part of the EEC-V system, you should be absolutely positive it has failed before replacing it. If in doubt, have the system tested by an experienced driveability technician.*

1   Disconnect the cable from the negative terminal of the battery.

2   The PCM is installed in the firewall, or cowl between the engine compartment and the passenger compartment on the right (passenger) side of the vehicle. Disconnect the electrical connector retaining bolt and two PCM retaining nuts from the engine compartment side **(see illustration)**.

3   Carefully slide the PCM out of its mounting bracket from the engine compartment side.

4   Installation is the reverse of removal.

5   After installing a replacement PCM (or reinstalling the original one), start the engine and let it idle for 2 to 4 minutes. Then drive the car through a stop-and-go and highway-cruising drive cycle to reset the OBD-II system monitors and the PCM adaptive memory.

4.2 Remove the connector retaining bolt (A) and two nuts (B) from the PCM mounting studs

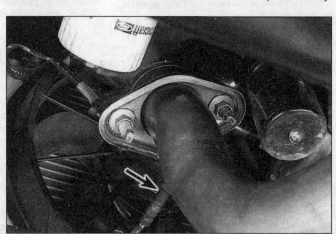

5.1a This is the upstream HO2S (arrow) in the forward exhaust pipe . . .

5.1b . . . and this is the upstream HO2S (arrow) in the rear exhaust pipe

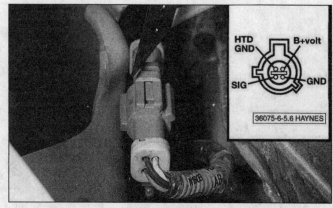

5.6 Test the HO2S circuits at the sensor connector

5 Heated oxygen sensor (HO2S) - check and replacement

General description and check

Refer to illustrations 5.1a, 5.1b, and 5.6

Note: *If the following tests indicate that a sensor is good, and not the cause of a driveability problem or DTC, check the wiring harness and connectors between the sensor and the PCM for an open or short circuit. If no problems are found, have the vehicle checked by a dealer service department or other qualified repair shop.*

1   Because of OBD-II catalyst monitoring requirements, the EEC-V system on these models has four heated oxygen sensors (HO2S), two in each exhaust pipe at the inlet and outlet of each catalytic converter. The oxygen in the exhaust reacts with the HO2S to produce a voltage output that varies from 0.1 volt (high oxygen, lean mixture) to 0.9 volt (low oxygen, rich mixture). The upstream HO2S in each branch of the exhaust system provides a feedback signal to the PCM that indicates the amount of leftover oxygen in the exhaust **(see illustrations)**. The PCM monitors this variable voltage continuously to determine the required fuel injector pulse width and to control the engine air/fuel ratio. A mixture ratio of 14.7 parts air to 1 part fuel is the ideal ratio for minimum exhaust emissions, as well as the best combination of fuel economy and engine performance. Based on HO2S signals, the PCM tries to maintain this air/fuel ratio of 14.7:1 at all times.

2   The downstream HO2S in each branch of the exhaust system has no effect on PCM control of the air/fuel ratio. These sensors are identical to the upstream sensors and operate in the same way. The PCM uses their signals, however, for the OBD-II catalyst monitor described in Section 3. A downstream HO2S will produce a more slowly fluctuating voltage signal that reflects the lower oxygen content in the postcatalyst exhaust.

3   An HO2S produces no voltage when it is below its normal operating temperature of about 600-degrees F. During this warm-up period, the PCM operates in an open-loop

fuel control mode. It does not use the HO2S signal as a feedback indication of residual oxygen in the exhaust. Instead, the PCM controls fuel metering based on the inputs of other sensors and its own programs.

4   Proper operation of an HO2S depends on four conditions:

a) *Electrical - The low voltages generated by the sensor require good, clean connections which should be checked whenever a sensor problem is suspected or indicated.*

b) *Outside air supply - The sensor needs air circulation to the internal portion of the sensor. Whenever the sensor is installed, make sure the air passages are not restricted.*

c) *Proper operating temperature - The PCM will not react to the sensor signal until the sensor reaches approximately 600-degrees F. This factor must be considered when evaluating the performance of the sensor.*

d) *Unleaded fuel - Unleaded fuel is essential for proper operation of the sensor.*

5   The OBD-II system can detect several different HO2S problems and set DTC's to indicate the specific fault. If an OBD-II scan tool is not available, have the codes read by a dealer service department or other qualified driveability technician with the necessary equipment. When an HO2S fault occurs that sets a DTC, the PCM will disregard the HO2S signal voltage and revert to open-loop fuel control as described previously. **Note:** *Refer to the wiring diagrams in Chapter 12 to identify circuit functions by wire color coding for the following tests.* **Caution:** *The HO2S is very sensitive to excessive circuit loads and circuit damage of any kind. For safest testing, install jumper wires in the HO2S connector to connect your voltmeter. If jumper wires aren't available, carefully backprobe the wires in the connector shell with straight pins or similar devices. Do not puncture the HO2S wires or try to backprobe the sensor itself. Use only a digital voltmeter to test an HO2S.*

6   Turn the ignition on but do not start the engine. Connect your voltmeter negative (-) lead to a good ground and the positive (+)

lead to the SIG wire at the HO2S connector **(see illustration)**. The meter should read approximately 400 to 450 millivolts (0.40 to 0.45 volt). If it doesn't, trace and repair the circuit from the sensor to the PCM.

7   Start the engine and let it warm up to normal operating temperature; again check the HO2S signal voltage.

a) *Voltage from an upstream sensor should range from 100 to 900 millivolts (0.1 to 0.9 volt) and switch actively between high and low readings.*

b) *Voltage from a downstream sensor should also read between 100 to 900 millivolts (0.1 to 0.9 volt) but it should not switch actively. The downstream HO2S voltage may stay toward the center of its range (about 400 millivolts) or stay for relatively longer periods of time at the upper or lower limits of the range.*

8   Also check the battery voltage supply to the HO2S heating circuits. Move the voltmeter negative (-) lead to the HTR GND terminal and the positive (+) lead to the B+Volt terminal of the sensor connector **(see illustration 5.6)**. With the ignition on, the meter should read more than 10 volts. Battery voltage is supplied to the sensors through a relay for only about three seconds when the engine is not running. Have an assistant turn the ignition on while you read the voltmeter. Refer to the wiring diagrams in Chapter 12 for more information on the circuits and relays.

Replacement

9   The exhaust pipe contracts when cool, and the HO2S may be hard to loosen when the engine is cold. To make sensor removal easier, start and run the engine for a minute or two; then shut it off. Be careful not to burn yourself during the following procedure. Also observe these guidelines when replacing an HO2S.

a) *The sensor has a permanently attached pigtail and electrical connector which should not be removed from the sensor. Damage or removal of the pigtail or electrical connector can harm operation of the sensor.*

b) *Keep grease, dirt and other contaminants away from the electrical connector and the louvered end of the sensor.*

6.1a CKP sensor location on an OHV V6 engine. The timing marks and pointer are for locating number 1 cylinder TDC, not for checking ignition timing

6.1b CKP sensor location (arrow) on an OHC V6 engine

7.2a The CMP sensor (arrow) on an OHV V6 is a Hall-effect switch, mounted where the distributor was installed on older engines

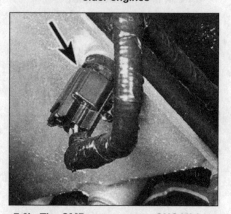

7.2b The CMP sensor on an OHC V6 is a pickup coil, installed in the end of the forward cylinder head

c) *Do not use cleaning solvents of any kind on the oxygen sensor.*

d) *Do not drop or roughly handle the sensor.*

10   Raise the vehicle and place it securely on jackstands.

11   Disconnect the electrical connector from the sensor.

12   Using a suitable wrench, unscrew the sensor from the exhaust manifold.

13   Anti-seize compound must be used on the threads of the sensor to aid future removal. The threads of most new sensors will be coated with this compound. If not, be sure to apply anti-seize compound before installing the sensor.

14   Install the sensor and tighten it securely.

15   Lower the vehicle and reconnect the electrical connector for the sensor.

6   Crankshaft position (CKP) sensor - check and replacement

General description and check

Refer to illustrations 6.1a and 6.1b

Note: *If the following tests indicate that a sensor is good, and not the cause of a driveability problem or DTC, check the wiring harness and connectors between the sensor and the PCM for an open or short circuit. If no problems are found, have the vehicle checked by a dealer service department or other qualified repair shop.*

1   The crankshaft position CKP) sensor is mounted on the engine front cover, next to a toothed trigger wheel. On an OHV V6 engine, the CKP sensor is on the outside of the cover **(see illustration)**. On an OHC V6 engine, the CKP sensor is installed through the side of the front cover on the lower side, toward the firewall **(see illustration)**. The trigger wheel has 35 evenly spaced teeth and one gap where a 36th tooth would be. The gap lets the CKP sensor signal the PCM when the crankshaft is 60-degrees before TDC for cylinders 1 and 5. The PCM then computes actual TDC or any number of degrees before

or after TDC and uses this information to control ignition spark advance. The CKP sensor also provides the engine speed signal to the PCM and is part of the misfire monitor circuit described in Section 3.

2   The OBD-II system can detect different CKP sensor problems and set DTC's to indicate the specific fault. If an OBD-II scan tool is not available, have the codes read by a dealer service department or a qualified driveability technician with the necessary equipment.

3   Disconnect the CKP sensor connector and turn the ignition On but do not start the engine. Use a voltmeter to check for voltage between the sensor connector and ground as shown on the wiring diagrams. Approximately 1.5 volts should be present on one of the sensor wires with the key on and the engine off.

4   Disable the fuel system as described in the fuel pressure relief section of Chapter 4 (this will enable the engine to be cranked over without it starting). Connect a voltmeter to the CKP sensor, set the meter on the AC scale, and check for voltage pulses as you crank the engine. **Caution:** *Keep voltmeter leads away from the drivebelt and rotating engine parts while cranking the engine.*

5   If no pulsing voltage signal is produced, replace the crankshaft sensor.

Replacement

6   Be sure the ignition is off and disconnect the sensor electrical connector.

7   Remove the retaining bolts and remove the sensor from the engine cover **(see illustrations 6.1a or 6.1b)**.

8   Installation is the reverse of removal.

7   Camshaft position (CMP) sensor - check and replacement

General description

Refer to illustrations 7.2a and 7.2b

Note: *If the following tests indicate that a sensor is good, and not the cause of a driveability problem or DTC, check the wiring harness and connectors between the sensor and*

the PCM for an open or short circuit. If no problems are found, have the vehicle checked by a dealer service department or other qualified repair shop.

1   The camshaft position (CMP) sensor sends a voltage signal pulse to the PCM that indicates when the number 1 piston is approaching TDC on the compression stroke. The PCM uses this signal to synchronize and sequence the fuel injectors.

2   The CMP sensor on the OHV V6 engine is a Hall-effect switch, mounted on the top of the engine where the distributor was installed on earlier versions of this engine **(see illustration)**. The CMP sensor on the OHC V6 engines is a magnetic pickup, or variable-reluctance, sensor, mounted on the left side of the forward cylinder head, below the valve cover, and triggered by a special tooth on the exhaust camshaft **(see illustration)**.

OHV V6 engine

Check

3   Turn the ignition On but do not start the engine. Refer to the wiring diagrams in Chapter 12 and identify the battery positive (B+) terminal of the CMP connector. Backprobe the wire for this terminal with your voltmeter posi-

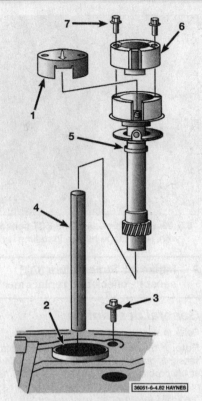

7.10 Exploded view of the CMP sensor and drive assembly with the alignment tool

1   *Alignment tool*
2   *Engine block*
3   *Hold-down clamp and bolt*
4   *Oil pump intermediate shaft*
5   *Drive assembly*
6   *CMP sensor*
7   *Bolt*

tive (+) lead; the reading should be more than 10 volts. If it isn't, trace and repair the circuit between the CMP sensor and the PCM.

4   Move the voltmeter positive (+) lead to the sensor signal terminal of the connector and crank the engine. The meter should show a pulsing DC-voltage reading of approximately 5 volts, once for each sensor revolution.

5   If the CMP sensor doesn't produce a pulsating voltage signal but battery voltage is present in Step 3, refer to the wiring diagrams and check the sensor ground connection. If the ground is OK, then replace the sensor.

Replacement

Refer to illustrations 7.10 and 7.14

6   The CMP sensor is mounted on a drive unit. If you are replacing only the CMP sensor, remove the sensor screws, detach it from the drive assembly, and install the new sensor. You do not have to remove the drive assembly from the engine. Many engine repair procedures, however, require removal of the drive assembly. In these cases, you must time the drive assembly when you reinstall it. This procedure requires a special tool to align the sensor properly. Read the entire

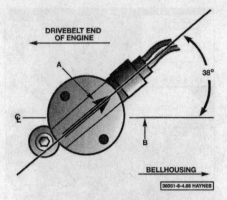

7.14 With the housing seated on the engine block, the arrow on the tool (A) must point 38-degrees counterclockwise from the engine centerline (B)

procedure and obtain the necessary tool before beginning.

7   Refer to Chapter 2A and position the number 1 piston at TDC.

8   Disconnect the battery ground (negative) cable.

9   Mark the relative position of the CMP sensor electrical connector so the assembly can be oriented properly during installation. (This is necessary only if the drive assembly will be removed.) Disconnect the electrical connector from the CMP sensor. Remove the screws and remove the sensor from the drive assembly.

10   To remove the drive assembly, remove the bolt and hold-down clamp and lift the drive out of the engine. Remove the oil pump intermediate shaft along with the CMP sensor drive **(see illustration)**.

11   Place the alignment tool onto the drive assembly and align the vane of the synchronizer with the radial slot in the tool.

12   Turn the tool on the drive assembly until the boss on the tool engages the notch on the drive housing.

13   Transfer the oil pump intermediate shaft onto the drive assembly. Lubricate the gear, the thrust washer, and the lower bearing of the drive with clean engine oil.

14   Insert the assembly into the engine so that the drive gear engages the camshaft gear and the oil pump shaft engages the pump. Then rotate the sensor assembly so that the arrow on the tool points 38-degrees counterclockwise from the engine centerline **(see illustration)**. This should be the orientation point for the connector that you marked before removing the sensor drive assembly.

15   Check the position of the electrical connector on the sensor to make sure it is aligned with the mark you made during removal. If it isn't oriented correctly, do not rotate the drive assembly to reposition it. Doing so will result in the fuel system being out of time with the engine and possible engine damage. If the connector is not oriented properly, repeat the installation procedure.

16   Install the hold-down clamp and bolt

7.22 Working on the bench, pass a metal object close to the tip of the CMP sensor and see if an AC voltage is produced

and tighten it securely. Remove the positioning tool.

17   Install the CMP sensor and tighten the screws securely.

18   Connect the sensor electrical connector and reconnect the battery ground cable.

OHC V6 engine

Check

Refer to illustration 7.22

19   Disconnect the CMP sensor connector and turn the ignition On but do not start the engine. Use a voltmeter to check for voltage between the sensor connector and ground as shown on the wiring diagrams. Approximately 1.5 volts should be present on one of the sensor wires with the key on and the engine off.

20   Connect a voltmeter to the CMP sensor, set the meter on the AC scale, and check for voltage pulses as you crank the engine. **Caution:** *Keep the voltmeter leads away from the drivebelt and rotating engine parts while cranking the engine.*

21   If no pulsing voltage signal is produced, replace the CMP sensor.

22   As an alternative, you can remove the CMP sensor from the engine and test it as follows:

a)   *Remove the CMP sensor from the engine and place it on a workbench.*

b)   *Connect the voltmeter to both terminals of the CMP sensor and set the meter on the AC-voltage scale. Pass a steel object across the tip of the sensor and look for voltage pulses on the meter (see illustration).*

c)   *If no pulsing voltage signal is produced, replace the camshaft sensor.*

Replacement

23   Disconnect the electrical connector from the sensor.

24   Remove the retaining screw and remove then CMP sensor from the cylinder head **(see illustration 7.2b)**.

25   Installation is the reverse of removal.

8.2 The ECT sensor (arrow) has a two-wire connector, and the plastic shell is usually gray (OHV engine shown)

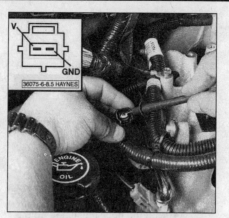

8.5 Check the open-circuit voltage from the PCM to the ECT sensor connector with the ignition On and the engine not running - it should be approximately 5 volts

8.6 Wrap the threads of the ECT sensor with Teflon tape before installing it

8   Engine Coolant Temperature (ECT) sensor - check and replacement

General description

Refer to illustration 8.2

Note: *If the following tests indicate that a sensor is good, and not the cause of a driveability problem or DTC, check the wiring harness and connectors between the sensor and the PCM for an open or short circuit. If no problems are found, have the vehicle checked by a dealer service department or other qualified repair shop.*

1   The coolant sensor is a thermistor, which is a variable resistor that changes its resistance as temperature changes. The sensor is installed in the engine cooling system to sense coolant temperature. As coolant temperature increases, sensor resistance decreases and vice versa. The PCM uses this information to compute the engine operating temperature. A problem in the ECT sensor circuit will set a trouble code. The fault may be in the circuit wiring or connections or in the sensor itself.

2   These engines have two almost identical coolant temperature sensor units **(see illustration)**. One is the sender for the instrument panel temperature gauge, the other is the

9.1 The IAT sensor is located in air intake duct

ECT sensor for the EEC-V system. The temperature sender for the instrument panel gauge has a single-wire connector and has a tan or brown plastic body, the ECT sensor has a two-wire connector and the sensor itself has a gray plastic body.

Check

Refer to illustration 8.5

Note: *Before condemning an ECT sensor, check the coolant level in the system.*

3   Disconnect the ECT sensor and use an ohmmeter to measure resistance across the two terminals of the sensor. At 65 degrees F, resistance should be approximately 40,500 ohms.

4   Next, start the engine and warm it up until it reaches operating temperature. The resistance should be lower. For example, at 180 to 220-degrees F resistance should be 3,800 to 1,840 ohms.

5   If the resistance values of the sensor are correct, refer to the wiring diagrams in Chapter 12 and check the voltage from the PCM to the disconnected sensor connector **(see illustration)**. The open-circuit voltage should be approximately 5 volts.

Replacement

Refer to illustration 8.6

Warning: *Wait until the engine is completely cool before performing this procedure.*

6   Before installing the new sensor, wrap the threads with Teflon sealing tape to prevent leakage and thread corrosion **(see illustration)**.

7   Unscrew the ECT sensor from the engine. Install the new sensor as quickly as possible to minimize coolant loss. Tighten the sensor securely and reconnect the electrical connector.

8   Check the coolant level as described in Chapter 1, adding some, if necessary. Start the engine and allow it to reach normal operating temperature, then check for coolant leaks. Check the coolant level in the expansion tank after the engine has warmed up and then cooled down again.

9   Intake Air Temperature (IAT) sensor - check and replacement

General description

Refer to illustration 9.1

Note: *If the following tests indicate that a sensor is good, and not the cause of a driveability problem or DTC, check the wiring harness and connectors between the sensor and the PCM for an open or short circuit. If no problems are found, have the vehicle checked by a dealer service department or other qualified repair shop.*

1   Like the ECT sensor, the IAT sensor is a thermistor that changes resistance as temperature changes. The sensor is installed in the intake air duct to sense air temperature **(see illustration)**. As temperature increases, sensor resistance decreases and vice versa. The PCM uses this information to compute the intake temperature and fine tune fuel metering. A problem in the IAT sensor circuit will set a trouble code. The fault may be in the circuit wiring or connections or in the sensor itself.

Check

2   With the engine cool, disconnect the IAT sensor and use an ohmmeter to measure resistance across the two terminals of the sensor. For example, at 68-degrees F the resistance should be approximately 37,300 ohms.

3   Next, start the engine and warm it up until it reaches operating temperature. Turn the engine off, disconnect the sensor and measure the resistance again. It should be lower. If the sensor resistance doesn't change as described, replace it.

4   If the resistance values of the sensor are correct, refer to the wiring diagrams in Chapter 12 and check the voltage from the PCM to the disconnected sensor. The open-circuit voltage should be approximately 5 volts.

Replacement

5   Carefully remove the IAT sensor from the air intake duct. Be careful not to damage any of the plastic parts.

6   Install and connect the new sensor.

10.1 The TPS has a three-wire connector (arrow). Refer to the wiring diagrams to identify the connector terminal functions

10.2 With the TPS connected (arrow), backprobe the wire terminals with a voltmeter to test sensor operation (refer to the wiring diagrams at the end of this manual for terminal designations). You can check reference voltage with the sensor either connected or disconnected

10 Throttle Position Sensor (TPS) - check and replacement

General description

Refer to illustration 10.1

Note: *If the following tests indicate that a sensor is good, and not the cause of a driveability problem or DTC, check the wiring harness and connectors between the sensor and the PCM for an open or short circuit. If no problems are found, have the vehicle checked by a dealer service department or other qualified repair shop.*

1   The Throttle Position Sensor (TPS) is a variable-resistance potentiometer, mounted on the side of the throttle body and connected to the throttle shaft **(see illustration)**. It senses throttle movement and position, then transmits a voltage signal to the PCM. This signal enables the PCM to determine when the throttle is closed, in a cruise position, or wide open. A defective TPS can cause surging, stalling, rough idle and other

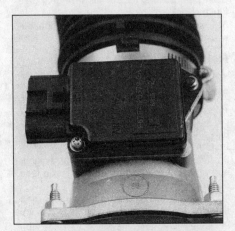

11.1 Disconnect the air inlet duct, remove the nuts, and separate the MAF sensor from the air cleaner housing. The plastic sensor body and the metal duct are an inseparable assembly

driveability problems because the PCM thinks the throttle is moving when it is not. The OBD-II system can detect several different TPS problems and set trouble codes to indicate the specific fault. If an OBD-II scan tool is not available, have the codes read by a dealer service department or other qualified repair shop.

Check

Refer to illustration 10.2

2   Do not disconnect the sensor connector from the sensor for these tests **(see illustration)**.

3   Refer to the wiring diagrams in Chapter 12 and backprobe the signal terminal of the sensor connector with the positive (+) lead of your voltmeter. Backprobe the ground terminal with the meter negative (-) lead.

4   Turn the ignition On but do not start the engine. The meter should read less than 1.0 volt with the throttle closed.

5   Open the throttle (or have a helper depress the accelerator) until the throttle is wide open. The voltmeter reading should increase smoothly and steadily to approximately 5.0 volts.

6   Also, check the TPS reference voltage. Insert the voltmeter positive (+) probe into the reference voltage terminal of the connector and the negative (-) probe into the ground terminal. With the ignition On but the engine not running, the meter should read 5.0 ± 0.1 volts. **Note:** *If TPS-related driveability problems continue but these general tests don't indicate a TPS fault, have the sensor tested with an oscilloscope by an experienced driveability technician. A TPS often develops a voltage signal dropout of such short duration that it can't be seen on a voltmeter. The PCM can see such a signal fault and a driveability problem will result.*

Replacement

7   The TPS is not adjustable. Unplug the electrical connector, remove the two retaining screws and remove the TPS from the throttle body.

8   Install the new sensor, making sure it engages the throttle shaft correctly. Reconnect the electrical connector.

11 Mass Airflow (MAF) sensor - check and replacement

General description

Refer to illustration 11.1

Note: *If the following tests indicate that a sensor is good, and not the cause of a driveability problem or DTC, check the wiring harness and connectors between the sensor and the PCM for an open or short circuit. If no problems are found, have the vehicle checked by a dealer service department or other qualified repair shop.*

1   The mass airflow (MAF) sensor is installed in the air intake duct **(see illustration)**. This sensor uses a hot-wire sensing element to measure the molecular mass (or weight) of air entering the engine. The air passing over the hot wire causes it to cool, and the sensor converts this temperature change into an analog voltage signal to the PCM. The PCM in turn calculates the required fuel injector pulse width to obtain the necessary air/fuel ratio. A defective MAF sensor can cause surging, stalling, rough idle and other driveability problems. The OBD-II system can detect several different MAF sensor problems and set trouble codes to indicate the specific fault. If an OBD-II scan tool is not available, have the codes read by a dealer service department or other qualified repair shop.

Check

2   To check for power to the MAF sensor, disconnect the MAF sensor electrical connector.

3   Refer to the wiring diagrams in Chapter 12 and connect the positive (+) lead of your voltmeter to the B+ terminal of the harness connector; connect the meter negative (-) lead to the sensor connector ground terminal.

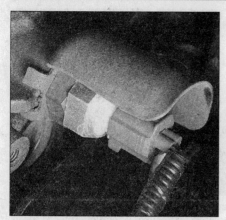

12.1 The knock sensor is installed in the lower forward area of the block on an OHC V6 engine

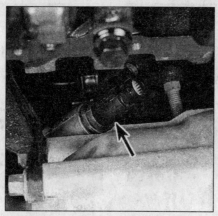

13.1 Location of the Vehicle Speed Sensor (VSS)

13.5 Remove the VSS and check for a pulsing ac voltage signal as you turn the drive gear

4   Turn the ignition On but do not start the engine. The meter should read more than 10 volts or close to battery voltage.

5   Reconnect the electrical connector and use straight pins or other suitable probes to backprobe the MAF signal (+) and ground (-) terminals with the voltmeter. Start the engine and check the voltage, it should be 0.5 to 0.7 volts at idle.

6   Increase the engine rpm. The signal MAF voltage should increase to about 1.5 to 3.0 volts. It is impossible to simulate driving conditions in the driveway, but it is necessary to watch the voltmeter for an increase in signal voltage as the engine speed is raised. The engine is not under load, but signal voltage should vary slightly.

7   If you suspect a defective MAF sensor, stop the engine and disconnect the MAF harness connector. Using an ohmmeter, probe the MAF signal (+) and ground (-) terminals. If the hot-wire element inside the sensor has been damaged, the ohmmeter will show an open circuit (infinite resistance).

8   If the voltage readings are correct, refer to the wiring diagrams and check the wiring harness for open circuits or a damaged harness. **Note:** *If MAF-related driveability problems continue but these general tests don't indicate a MAF fault, have the sensor tested by an experienced driveability technician. A MAF sensor can develop voltage signal problems that can't be seen on a voltmeter. The PCM can see such signal faults and a driveability problem will result.*

Replacement

Note: *The plastic MAF sensor body and the metal air duct on which it is mounted are an assembly that must be replaced as a unit. Do not try to separate the sensor body from the metal duct.*

9   Disconnect the electrical connector from the MAF sensor.

10   Remove the four nuts that secure the sensor to the air cleaner housing and remove the clamp that secures the sensor to the intake air duct.

11   Install and connect the new sensor.

12 Knock sensor - general information

Refer to illustration 12.1

1   A knock sensor is used on the OHC V6 to detect engine detonation, or pinging. The sensor produces a fluctuating output voltage which increases with the severity of the knock. The signal goes to the PCM, which will retard ignition timing to stop the detonation. The knock sensor is located on the forward side of the engine block under the exhaust manifold **(see illustration)**.

2   Knock sensor operation and any associated problems can be monitored best with an OBD-II scan tool. If your engine suffers from detonation or pinging, have it tested with the necessary equipment by an experienced driveability technician.

13 Vehicle Speed Sensor (VSS) - check and replacement

General description

Refer to illustration 13.1

Note 1: *If the following tests indicate that a sensor is good, and not the cause of a driveability problem or trouble code, check the wiring harness and connectors between the sensor and the PCM for an open or short circuit. If no problems are found, have the vehicle checked by a dealer service department or other qualified repair shop.*

Note 2: *On 2000 and later models, the sensor is called the Output Shaft Speed sensor, or OSS.*

1   The vehicle speed sensor (VSS) is pickup coil (variable-reluctance) sensor mounted on the transaxle case **(see illustration)**. It produces an AC voltage sine wave, the frequency of which is proportional to vehicle speed. The PCM uses the sensor input signal for several different engine and transmission control functions. The VSS signal also drives the speedometer on the

instrument panel. A defective VSS can cause various driveability and transmission problems. The OBD-II system can detect sensor problems and set trouble codes to indicate specific faults. If an OBD-II scan tool is not available, have the codes read by a dealer service department or other qualified repair shop.

Check

Refer to illustration 13.5

2   Refer to the wiring diagrams in Chapter 12 to identify the functions of connector terminals.

3   Disconnect the VSS connector and turn the ignition On but do not start the engine. Use a voltmeter to check for voltage between the sensor connector and ground as shown on the wiring diagrams. Approximately 1.5 volts should be present on one of the sensor wires with the key on and the engine off.

4   Remove the VSS from the car as described below.

5   Connect a voltmeter to the VSS, set the meter on the AC scale, and check for voltage pulses as you spin the sensor drive gear **(see illustration)**.

6   If no pulsing voltage signal is produced, replace the sensor.

Replacement

1996 to 1999 models

Refer to illustrations 13.9 and 13.10

7   Raise the vehicle and support it securely on jackstands.

8   Disconnect the electrical connector from the VSS.

9   Remove the hold-down bolt and clamp and remove the VSS from the transaxle **(see illustration)**.

10   Inspect the O-ring on the sensor **(see illustration)** and replace it if damaged. If you are installing a new sensor, use a new O-ring.

11   Installation is the reverse of removal.

2000 and later models

12   The OSS sensor is located on the top of the transaxle.

13.9 Removing the VSS from the transaxle

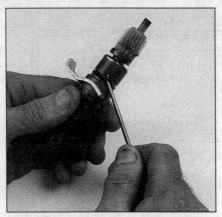

13.10 Inspect the sensor O-ring. Install a new one if damaged or if installing a new sensor

16.1 Location of the Transmission Range (TR) sensor

13   On either model of transaxle, raise the vehicle and support it securely on jackstands.
14   Disconnect the electrical connector for the OSS, located at the rear side of the transaxle, near the engine/transaxle juncture.
15   On AX4S transaxles, the OSS can be reached from underneath. Remove the bolt securing the plastic cover over the OSS, then unbolt and pull out the OSS.
16   On AX4N transaxles used with OHC engines, the OSS is located in the same position as on the AX4S, but access is from the passenger side. Refer to Chapter 2B and remove the crankshaft pulley, then refer to Chapter 5 and remove the alternator. The remainder of the procedure is the same as for the AX4S.

14   Power Steering Pressure (PSP) switch - check and replacement

General description

1   The power steering pressure (PSP) switch is a normally closed switch, mounted on the auxiliary actuator of the steering gear. When steering system pressure reaches a high-pressure setpoint, the PSP switch opens and sends a signal to the PCM that the PCM uses to maintain engine idle speed during parking maneuvers. The OBD-II system can detect switch problems and set trouble codes to indicate specific faults. If an OBD-II scan tool is not available, have the codes read by a dealer service department or other qualified repair shop.

Check

2   Check the operation of the PSP switch if the engine stalls during parking or if the engine idles continuously at high rpm.
3   Refer to the wiring diagrams at the end of this manual to identify the functions of connector terminals.
4   Disconnect the PSP switch connector and connect an ohmmeter to the terminals on the switch body.
5   Start the engine and let it idle.
6   Turn the steering wheel to point the front

wheels straight ahead and read the ohmmeter. It should indicate continuity of close to zero ohms.
7   Turn the steering wheel to either side and watch the ohmmeter. The PSP switch should open as the wheel nears the steering stop on either side, and the meter should indicate an open circuit (infinite resistance).
8   If the switch fails either test, replace it. If the switch is OK, troubleshoot the engine idle control operation if high idle speed or stalling problems continue.

Replacement

9   Raise the vehicle and support it securely on jackstands.
10   Disconnect the electrical connector from the switch and unscrew the switch from the auxiliary actuator on the steering gear.
11   Install and connect the new switch and lower the vehicle to the ground.
12   Refer to Chapter 10 and bleed air from the power steering system. Add fluid as required (see Chapter 1).

15   Brake On-Off (BOO) switch - check

General description

1   The brake on-off switch (also called the brake pedal position switch) tells the PCM when the brakes are being applied. The switch closes when brakes are applied and opens when the brakes are released. The switch is mounted on the brake pedal.
2   The brake light circuit is controlled by this switch, and burned-out bulbs or other circuit problems will cause the engine to idle roughly. Therefore, check the BOO switch operation when troubleshooting any rough-idle problems.

Check

3   Refer to the wiring diagrams at the end of this manual to identify the functions of connector terminals.

4   Disconnect the switch connector and connect your voltmeter positive (+) lead to the connector terminal that provides battery positive (B+) voltage to the switch. Connect the negative (-) meter lead to a good ground.
6   Turn the ignition On and read the meter. It should indicate more than 10 volts or close to battery voltage.
7   Connect an ohmmeter to the switch terminals and manually open and close the switch. The meter should alternate from continuity to an open-circuit reading.
8   Also check continuity from the switch to the brake light bulbs. Replace any burned-out bulbs or damaged wire looms.
9   Replacement of the switch is covered in Chapter 9.

16   Transmission Range (TR) sensor - check and replacement

General description

Refer to illustration 16.1

1   The Transmission Range (TR) sensor is mounted on the transaxle **(see illustration)** and senses the position of the gear selector as chosen by the driver. The TR sensor contains a series of resistors and switch contacts. Depending on the gear selector position, the sensor contacts route current through different combinations of resistors and produce voltage signals of different levels. The sensor sends these signals to the PCM, which uses them for a number of engine and transmission control operations.
2   The TR sensor input affects operation of the EGR system, idle speed control, and transaxle torque converter lockup. The sensor also takes the place of the neutral safety switch used on older automatic transmissions. If the gear selector is not in Park or Neutral, the TR sensor will not let the starter motor operate. The OBD-II system can detect sensor problems and set trouble codes to indicate specific faults. If an OBD-II scan tool is not available, have the codes read by a dealer service department or other qualified repair shop.

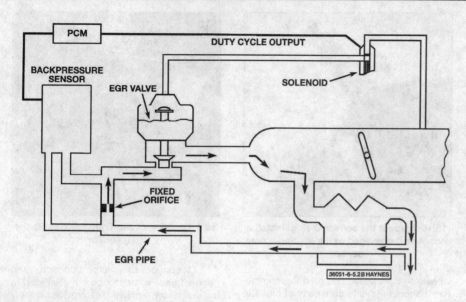

17.2a Typical differential pressure feedback EGR (DPFE) system

Check

3   If you suspect a problem with the TR sensor, check the connector for looseness and damaged terminals or wires.

4   Refer to the wiring diagrams at the end of this manual to identify the functions of connector terminals.

5   Disconnect the TR sensor connector and connect your voltmeter positive (+) lead to the connector terminal that provides battery positive (B+) voltage to the sensor. Connect the negative (-) meter lead to a good engine ground.

6   Turn the ignition On and read the meter. It should indicate more than 10 volts or close to battery voltage.

7   Disconnect the connector from the ignition coil pack to disable the ignition.

8   Crank the engine and use the voltmeter to verify that at least 9 volts is present at the appropriate connector terminal as shown on the wiring diagrams.

9   The preceding checks indicate whether or not voltage is available to the sensor with the ignition On and during cranking. If the sensor passes these tests but problems continue, have the system diagnosed by an experienced driveability technician.

17   Exhaust Gas Recirculation (EGR) system - check and component replacement

General description

Refer to illustrations 17.2a and 17.2b

1   Exhaust gas recirculation (EGR) systems on late-model vehicles have two equally important functions:

a) *EGR systems reduce oxides of nitrogen (NOx) emissions*

b) *EGR systems reduce engine detonation, or pinging*

Recirculating a small amount of exhaust back to the intake system reduces combustion temperatures because exhaust is a mixture of inert gases and does not contribute to the combustion process. Because high combustion temperature is a major factor in both NOx emissions and detonation, EGR effectively reduces both.

2   The PCM controls EGR flow rate by monitoring the pressure across a fixed metering orifice as exhaust passes through it. This kind of EGR system is called a differential pressure feedback (DPFE) system **(see illustration)**. The DPFE EGR system consists of the EGR valve, the EGR vacuum solenoid, the backpressure sensor **(see illustration)**, the PCM, the EGR pipe, and the various vacuum and pressure lines for the EGR system.

3   The EGR backpressure sensor monitors exhaust pressure both upstream and downstream from the fixed orifice. This backpressure comparison (or differential) measurement is converted to a varying voltage signal that the sensor sends to the PCM. The PCM controls the EGR vacuum solenoid with a varying duty cycle. The solenoid, in turn, regulates the amount of vacuum applied to the EGR valve. The DPFE system is more accurate than earlier systems because the PCM does not have to guess at the upstream EGR pressure to determine EGR flow rate as the engine operates under different conditions. The OBD-II system can detect several system problems and set trouble codes to indicate specific faults. If an OBD-II scan tool is not available, have the codes read by a dealer service department or other qualified repair shop.

System and component checks

4   Generally, the EGR system operates at part-throttle cruising speeds and, in some cases, during deceleration. EGR should not be present at idle or during full-throttle opera-

17.2b From left to right, these EGR system parts are the EGR valve (A) , the backpressure sensor (B) and the vacuum solenoid (C)

17.6 Check the vacuum line for leakage and looseness from the valve back to the port on the solenoid. Then check the vacuum line from the solenoid to the intake manifold

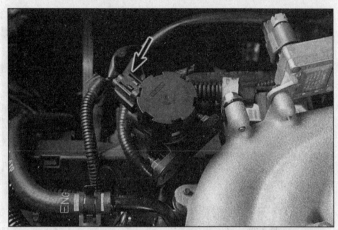

17.9 Disconnect the solenoid connector (arrow) and use a voltmeter to check for battery voltage on the specified wire with the ignition on

17.13 Disconnect the vacuum line (A) and the EGR pipe nut (B). Then remove the two valve mounting bolts (C)

tion. Too much EGR weakens combustion and causes the engine to run roughly or stall. Excessive EGR, or EGR operation at the wrong time, causes stalling after deceleration or at idle and surging at cruising speeds. In an extreme case, if the EGR valve stays open continuously, the engine may not run at all. Too little or no EGR allows combustion temperatures to get too high, which can cause detonation, engine overheating, and high NOx emissions. The following tests will help you pinpoint problems in the EGR system.

5   Refer to the wiring diagrams in Chapter 12 to identify circuit functions by wire color coding for the following tests. If the tests indicate that a component is good, and not the cause of a driveability problem or DTC, check the wiring harness and connectors between the component and the PCM for an open or short circuit. If no problems are found, have the vehicle checked by a dealer service department or other qualified repair shop.

EGR valve

Refer to illustration 17.6
6   Make sure the vacuum lines are in good condition and connected correctly **(see illustration)**. Check the vacuum connections at the valve, at the solenoid, and at the intake manifold.
7   Perform a vacuum leakage test by connecting a vacuum pump to the EGR valve. Apply a vacuum of 5 to 6 in. Hg to the valve. The vacuum pump should hold vacuum.
8   Remove the EGR valve as described below and clean the inlet and outlet ports with a wire brush or scraper. Remove an pieces of carbon from the valve seat and pintle that could hold the valve open and cause it to leak.

EGR control system

Refer to illustration 17.9
9   To check the EGR vacuum solenoid, disconnect the electrical connector **(see illustration)** and turn the ignition On but do not start the engine. Refer to the wiring diagrams to identify the B+ terminal on the

solenoid connector and check for battery voltage, which should be present.
10   Next, use an ohmmeter and check the resistance of the vacuum solenoid. It should be 20 ohms.
11   Check for reference voltage to the backpressure sensor **(see illustration 17.2b)**. Turn the ignition on but do not start the engine. Refer to the wiring diagrams and use a voltmeter to measure voltage on the harness side of the electrical connector at the VREF terminal. Voltage should be 5.0 ± 0.1 volts. If reference voltage is not correct, trace and repair the circuit from the solenoid to the PCM.
12   To check the operation of the EGR backpressure sensor, refer to the wiring diagrams and backprobe the correct connector terminals with your voltmeter. Check the signal voltage with the connector attached to the sensor and the engine running first while cold and then at warm operating temperature. With the engine cold there should be no EGR, and the voltage should be approximately 0.4 to 0.6 volts. As the engine warms up, open the throttle to about 2000 rpm and check the voltage again. At cruising rpm, sensor voltage should be about 1.5 to 2.5 volts.

Component replacement

Refer to illustrations 17.13, 17.16 and 17.17

EGR valve and pipe

Note: *The following illustrations show an EGR valve installation on an OHV V6 engine. Installation on an OHC V6 is similar.*
13   Disconnect the vacuum line from the EGR valve **(see illustration)**.
14   Disconnect the EGR pipe from the valve (the pipe on an OHC V6 has an upper flange attached to the valve with two small nuts and bolts).
15   Remove the bolts securing the EGR valve to the intake manifold.
16   Disconnect the backpressure sensor hoses from the small tubes on the EGR pipe **(see illustration)**.
17   Remove the EGR pipe from the exhaust manifold **(see illustration)**. Remove the EGR valve and gasket from the manifold. Discard the gasket.
18   Scrape all exhaust deposits and old gasket material from the EGR valve mounting surface on the manifold and, if you plan to use the same valve, from the mounting surface of the valve. Carefully remove carbon

17.16 Disconnect the backpressure sensor hoses from these two small tubes.

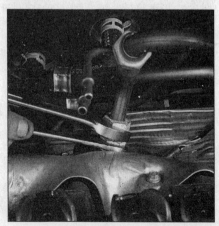

17.17 Hold the fitting on the exhaust manifold with one wrench and loosen the pipe coupling nut with another

17.21 Disconnect the electrical connector (A) and the vacuum connector (B)

18.3a The electric air pump is mounted down on the subframe

18.3b The OHV V6 has two diverter valves, one for the forward cylinder bank . . .

18.3c . . . and one for the rear bank

deposits from the valve port and pintle with a small screwdriver. **Caution:** *Do not try to wash the valve in solvent or sandblast it.*
19   If the EGR passage contains excessive deposits, clean it out with a small scraper and a vacuum. Make sure that all loose particles are removed to keep them from clogging the EGR valve or from being drawn into the engine.
20   Installation is the reverse of removal. Attach the EGR pipe nuts loosely at the valve and at the exhaust manifold until the EGR valve is tightened on the intake manifold. Then tighten the pipe fittings.

EGR vacuum solenoid

Refer to illustration 17.21
21   Disconnect the electrical connector and the vacuum hose connector from the solenoid **(see illustration).**
22   Remove the solenoid mounting screws and remove the solenoid.
23   Installation is the reverse of removal.

Backpressure sensor

24   Disconnect the electrical connector from the sensor **(see illustration 17.2b).**

25   Label and detach both vacuum hoses.
26   Remove the sensor mounting nuts and remove the sensor.
27   Installation is the reverse of removal.

---

18   Secondary air injection system - check and component replacement

General description

Refer to illustrations 18.3a, 18.3b and 18.3c
1   The secondary air injection system provides air to the exhaust manifolds during the first 20 to 120 seconds after startup. The system is controlled by the PCM, and operating time depends on engine temperature and the time since the engine was last shut down. Secondary air systems are used on California OHV V6 engines. The OHC V6 does not require a secondary air system.
2   Secondary air injection for a short time after startup serves several purposes. Most importantly, it provides extra oxygen to the catalytic converters to help heat them quickly. The extra air in the exhaust also aids

oxidation of carbon monoxide (CO) and hydrocarbon (HC) emissions, which are high immediately after startup until the catalyst heats to normal temperature.
3   The secondary air injection system consists of an electric air pump **(see illustration),** one or two vacuum-operated diverter valves **(see illustrations),** a relay to switch the air pump circuit, and a solenoid to control vacuum to the diverter valves. At startup, the PCM activates the relay to turn on the air pump. The PCM determines operating time based on engine temperature, speed, and other parameters. The PCM-controlled vacuum solenoid supplies manifold vacuum to the diverter valves. With high vacuum, the diverter valves direct air to the exhaust. With no vacuum at the diverter valves, the built-in check valves close to keep exhaust from flowing back to the air injection system.

System and component checks

Note: *Refer to the wiring diagrams in Chapter 12 to identify circuit functions by wire color coding for the following tests.*

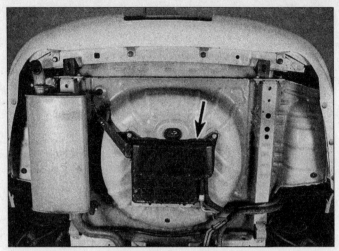

19.3a The vapor storage canister is under the vehicle, to the rear of the fuel tank (1996 through 2003 models)

19.3b Fuel tank pressure sensor

Electric air pump and relay

4   With the engine cold, disconnect the air line at one of the diverter valves, start the engine, and verify that fresh air is being pumped to the exhaust system. If no air is felt, continue checking the system.

5   With the engine cool, turn the ignition key On but do not start the engine. Use a voltmeter to check for battery voltage to the air pump.

6   Check for battery voltage to the pump relay. If battery voltage is not present, have the system diagnosed by an experienced driveability technician.

7   To check the operation of the electric air pump, disconnect the pump electrical connector and use jumper wires to apply battery voltage to the pump; it should operate.

8   Inspect the air pump and lines for damage, broken connectors or water that might have been gotten into the housing.

Diverter valves and vacuum solenoid

9   Inspect the vacuum lines and air hoses at the valves for damage and deterioration. Replace any that are defective.

10   With the engine cold, start the engine and disconnect the vacuum lines at the diverter valves. Verify that vacuum is present. If vacuum is not present, trace and repair the lines to the solenoid or have the solenoid tested by a qualified technician.

Component replacement

Electric air pump

11   Raise the front of the car and support it on jackstands. On 2000 and later models, remove the plastic pushpins and remove the radiator splash shield.

12   Disconnect the electrical connector from the air pump **(see illustration 18.3a)**.

13   Disconnect the inlet and outlet air hoses.

14   Remove the two nuts and one screw that hold the air pump to the subframe and

remove the pump from the car.

15   Installation is the reverse of removal.

Diverter valve

16   Disconnect the vacuum line, inlet air hose, and outlet air tube from the diverter valve.

17   Remove the mounting bolts and remove the valve from the engine.

18   If required, disconnect the air injection tube from the exhaust manifold.

19   Installation is the reverse of removal.

---

19   Evaporative emission control system - check and component replacement

---

General description

Refer to illustrations 19.3a, 19.3b and 19.3c

1   OBD-II diagnostic and emission control requirements have made evaporative emission control systems on late-model vehicles a bit more complex than on earlier models. Evaporative systems are checked by the OBD-II built-in monitors as explained earlier in this chapter and include provisions for external leak testing during emission inspections.

2   The evaporative emission control system traps and holds fuel vapors that would otherwise escape to the atmosphere during normal operation. Additionally, the evaporative system on California OHV V6 engines traps fuel vapors during refueling. The stored vapors are recycled to the intake system and added to the air/fuel mixture for combustion. Fuel vapors that escape from the vehicle by any means add to the overall HC emissions. Evaporative emission control systems prevent this.

3   The evaporative emission control system consists of:

a)   *Vapor storage canister, mounted under the rear of the car* **(see illustration)**.

19.3c The green plastic cap (arrow) identifies the leak test port

b)   *Canister purge valve, mounted in the engine compartment.*

c)   *Fuel tank pressure sensor* **(see illustration)**.

d)   *Vapor vent valve*

e)   *Vapor control valve*

f)   *Canister vent solenoid*

g)   *A test port for leak testing* **(see illustration)**.

The fuel tank, the filler pipe and cap, and the vapor lines and hoses complete the system.

4   The canister purge valve in the engine compartment is controlled by the PCM to regulate the purging of fuel vapor from the canister to the intake system.

5   The fuel tank pressure sensor is mounted on top of the fuel tank and monitors vapor pressure in the tank. The sensor sends a voltage signal to the PCM.

6   The vapor vent valve is mounted on top of the fuel tank and allows only vapor to enter the evaporative control system. The vent valve acts as a liquid separator to keep gaso-

19.21a Remove the vapor canister bracket bolts (arrows) at all four corners (1996 through 2003 models)

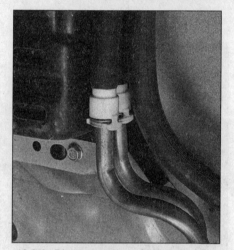

19.21b Disconnect the tube fittings from the canister hoses (1996 through 2003 models)

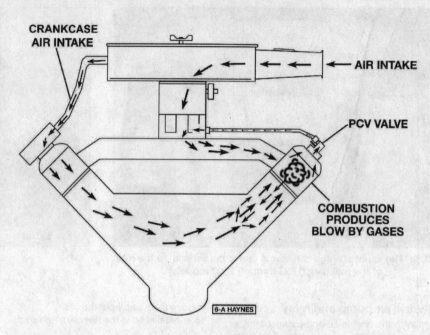

20.1 Gas flow in a typical PCV system

line out of the vapor lines and hoses.

7   The vapor control valve limits fuel tank volume during refueling on models with the OHV V6 engine.

8   The canister vent solenoid is mounted on the vapor canister and energized during the OBD-II monitor self-test and during externally activated system tests.

Check

9   The OBD-II system can detect several different evaporative emission control problems and set trouble codes to indicate a specific fault. If an OBD-II scan tool is not available, have the codes read by a dealer service department or other qualified repair shop.

General system checks

10   Poor idle, stalling, and poor driveability can be caused by an bad vapor vent valve or canister purge valve, a damaged canister, cracked hoses, or hoses connected to the wrong tubes. Fuel loss or fuel odor can be caused by fuel leaking from fuel lines or hoses, a cracked or damaged canister, or a defective vapor valve.

11   Inspect each hose attached to the canister for damage and leakage along its entire length. Repair or replace as necessary.

12   Inspect the canister for damage and look for fuel leaking from the bottom. If fuel is leaking or the canister is otherwise damaged, replace it.

13   To check for excessive fuel vapor pressure in the fuel tank, remove the gas cap and listen for the sound of pressure release. A more complete test can be done with an OBD-II scan tool. This will run a series of checks using the fuel tank pressure sensor and other output actuators to detect excessive pressure. Have the system diagnosed by a dealer service department or other qualified repair shop.

14   If excessive fuel tank pressure is detected, check the canister vapor hose and inlet port for blockage or collapsed hoses. Also inspect the vapor vent valve.

15   Refer to the wiring diagrams in Chapter 12 and use a voltmeter to check for voltage to the fuel tank vent valve. With the ignition key On and the engine not running, voltage should be more than 10 volts or close to battery voltage on the appropriate connector terminal. If battery voltage is not present, have the system tested by a dealer service department or other qualified repair shop.

Fuel tank pressure sensor

16   Refer to the wiring diagrams in Chapter 12 and use a voltmeter to check for reference voltage to the fuel tank pressure sensor **(see illustration 19.3b)**. With the ignition key On and the engine not running, reference voltage should be 5.0±0.1 volts. It may be difficult to reach the connector with the fuel tank in place. Find a location in the harness near the

tank to check for voltage without removing the sensor and fuel tank from the vehicle.

17   If reference voltage is available but you still suspect a sensor problem, further tests must be done with an OBD-II scan tool.

Component replacement

Vapor storage canister

Refer to illustrations 19.21a and 19.21b

18   Raise the rear of the car and support it on jack stands.

19   Disconnect the canister vent tube from the vent hose on the gas tank filler neck.

20   Disconnect the electrical connector(s) at the canister vent solenoid.

21   On 1996 through 2003 models, perform the following:

a) *Remove the canister bracket bolts and nuts* **(see illustration)**.

b) *Partially lower the assembly of the canister bracket and canister.*

c) *Label and disconnect all vacuum lines from the canister.*

d) *Disconnect the vent and purge lines from the canister* **(see illustration)**. *Refer to Chapter 4 for illustrations on disconnecting fuel line fittings.*

e) *Use a small prybar at the end opposite the vapor port to pry the canister out of its bracket.*

f) *Remove the vent solenoid and tube from the canister.*

22   On 2004 and later models, disconnect the dust box separator tube and the EVAP canister tube quick-connect fittings at the canister. Remove the canister mounting four bolts and remove the canister assembly.

23   If required, remove the canister vent solenoid from the canister.

24   Installation is the reverse of removal.

20.2 The PCV valve on an OHV V6 is installed in the rear valve cover. On an OHC V6, the valve is installed in an oil separator in the lower intake manifold.

21.1 Catalytic converters are the principal emission control devices on late-model vehicles

Fuel tank pressure sensor, vapor vent valve, and vapor control valve

25   Refer to Chapter 4 and remove the fuel tank for access to remove these parts.

20   Positive Crankcase Ventilation (PCV) system - check and component replacement

General description

Refer to illustrations 20.1 and 20.2

1   The positive crankcase ventilation (PCV) system reduces hydrocarbon emissions by scavenging crankcase vapors. It does this by circulating fresh air from the air cleaner through the crankcase, where it mixes with blow-by gases and is then rerouted through a PCV valve to the intake manifold **(see illustration)**.

2   The PCV system consists of the PCV valve **(see illustration)** and fresh-air filtered inlet lines to the crankcase. Additionally, the OHC V6 engine has an oil separator to which the PCV valve is attached.

3   To maintain idle quality, the PCV valve restricts the flow when intake manifold vacuum is high. Under abnormal operating conditions, the system allows excessive amounts of blow-by gases to flow back through the crankcase vent tube into the air cleaner to be consumed through the intake system.

Component check and replacement

4   Check the PCV valve hose and the crankcase ventilation hose for cracks, leaks and other damage. Disconnect the hoses from the valve cover and the intake manifold and check the inside for obstructions. If a hose is clogged, replace it.

5   Refer to Chapter 1 for other PCV system tests. If the PCV valve is clogged or otherwise not working properly, replace it, do not try to clean it.

21   Catalytic converters

Refer to illustration 21.1

General description

1   The exhaust system catalytic converter is the principal emission control device on all late-model vehicles. The three-way catalyst oxidizes carbon monoxide (CO) and hydrocarbons (HC) in the exhaust and reduces oxides of nitrogen (NOx) emissions. Chemical oxidation adds oxygen to HC and CO compounds and produces carbon dioxide (CO_2) and water vapor. Chemical reduction removes oxygen from NOx compounds and produces free nitrogen and oxygen that is then used in the oxidation process.

2   The models covered by this manual have two catalytic converters that are part of a welded assembly, along with the exhaust headpipes. The manufacturer calls this the "dual-converter Y-pipe assembly," or simply the "Y-Pipe" **(see illustration)**.

3   Refer to Chapter 4 for instructions on how to remove and replace the entire Y-pipe assembly.

4   If one or both catalytic converters fail, a muffler shop may be able to cut the old converters out of the system and weld in new ones. Otherwise, you must replace the entire Y-pipe assembly.

Notes

Chapter 7
Automatic transaxle

Contents

Specifications

Torque specifications
Ft-lbs (unless otherwise indicated)

Note: *One foot-pound (ft-lb) of torque is equivalent to 12 inch-pounds (in-lbs) of torque. Torque values below approximately 15 ft-lbs are expressed in inch-pounds, since most foot-pound torque wrenches are not accurate at these smaller values.*

Transaxle-to-engine bolts	39 to 53
Torque converter-to-driveplate nuts	20 to 33
Transmission range sensor	80 to 106 in-lbs

1   General information

These models use one of two electronic 4-speed automatic transaxles; the AX4N, renamed the 4F50N starting in 2001, and the AX4S. The main difference between the two is the internal design of the apply and hold devices used to perform automatic gear changes. Externally, both transaxles appear similar. To identify which transaxle is in your vehicle, look on the identification tag attached to the top of the bellhousing. The transaxle model is also stamped on the main valve body cover, which bolts onto the end of the unit. The end cover and the oil pan on some transaxles are stamped AXOD, which is an older name for the AX4S; the two are identical.

Shifting on these transaxles is controlled electronically. Utilizing data from the network of information sensors (see Chapter 6), the Powertrain Control Module (PCM) determines the best shift point for the particular driving situation. Shifts occur when the PCM grounds the electronic shift solenoids inside the transmission. No vacuum controls, TV cables or other mechanical devices are employed.

Because of the complexity and the special tools necessary, internal repair of automatic transaxles is not recommended for the home mechanic and should be performed by an automatic transmission specialist. Therefore, the information contained in this manual is limited to general information, diagnosis, linkage adjustments, and removal and installation procedures.

Depending on the expense involved in overhauling a faulty transaxle, it may be a better idea to simply replace it with a new or rebuilt unit. Your local dealer or transmission shop should be able to supply you with information concerning cost, availability and exchange policy. Regardless of how you decide to remedy a transaxle problem, you can often save a considerable expense by removing and installing the transaxle yourself.

2   Diagnosis - general

Note: *Automatic transaxle malfunctions may be caused by five general conditions: poor engine performance, improper adjustments, hydraulic malfunctions, mechanical malfunctions or malfunctions in the electronic control system. Diagnosis of these problems should always begin with a check of the basic items: fluid level and condition (Chapter 1), shift linkage adjustment, and secure mounting and installation. Next, perform a road test to see if the problem has been corrected or if more diagnosis is necessary. If the problem persists after the preliminary tests and corrections are completed, additional diagnosis should be done by a dealer service department or transmission repair shop specialist.*

Preliminary checks

1   Drive the vehicle to warm the transaxle to normal operating temperature.
2   Check the fluid level as described in Chapter 1:
  a) If the fluid level is too low, add enough fluid to bring the level within the designated area of the dipstick, then check for external leaks (see below).
  b) If the fluid level is too high, drain off the excess, then check the drained fluid for contamination by coolant. The presence of engine coolant in the automatic transaxle fluid indicates that a failure has occurred in the internal radiator walls that separate the coolant from the transmission fluid.
  c) If the fluid is foaming, drain it and refill the transaxle. Test drive, then recheck for coolant in the fluid and correct fluid level.
3   Check the engine idle speed. If the engine is malfunctioning, do not proceed with the preliminary checks until it has been repaired and runs normally.
4   Inspect the shift linkage for proper adjustment and smooth operation (Section 3).

Fluid leak diagnosis

5   Most fluid leaks are easy to locate visually. Repair usually consists of replacing a seal or gasket. If a leak is hard to find, the following procedure may help.
6   Identify the fluid to make sure it is transmission fluid, not engine oil, brake fluid, or some other liquid.
7   To pinpoint the source of the leak, drive the car several miles, then park it over a large sheet of clean cardboard. Locate the leak by determining the source of the fluid dripping onto the cardboard.
8   Carefully inspect the suspected component and the area immediately around it. Pay particular attention to gasket mating surfaces. A mirror is often helpful for finding leaks in areas that are hard to see.
9   If you still can't find the leak, clean the suspected area thoroughly with a degreaser or solvent, then dry it.

10   Drive the vehicle for several miles at normal operating temperature and varying speeds. After driving the vehicle, visually inspect the suspected component again.
11   Once the leak has been located, the cause must be determined before it can be properly repaired. If a gasket is replaced but the sealing flange is bent, the new gasket will not stop the leak. The bent flange must be straightened.
12   Before attempting to repair a leak, check to make sure that the following conditions are corrected or they may cause another leak. Some of the following conditions (a leaking torque converter, for instance) cannot be fixed without specialized tools and expertise. Such problems must be referred to a transmission shop or a dealer service department.

Gasket leaks

13   Check the cover pan and the oil pan periodically. Make sure all the bolts are installed and tight, but not overtightened. Be sure that the gasket is in good condition and the pan is flat. Dents in the pan may indicate damage to the valve body inside.
14   If the pan gasket is leaking, the fluid level may be too high, the vent may be plugged, the pan bolts may be too tight, the pan sealing flange may be warped, the sealing surface of the transaxle housing may be damaged, the gasket may be damaged, or the transaxle casting may be cracked or porous. If sealant instead of a gasket has been used between the pan and the transaxle case, it may be the wrong kind of sealant.

Seal leaks

15   If a transaxle seal is leaking, the fluid level may be too high, the vent may be plugged, the seal bore may be damaged, the seal itself may be damaged or improperly installed, the surface of the shaft that passes through the seal may be damaged, or a loose bearing may be causing excessive shaft movement.
16   Make sure the dipstick tube seal is in good condition and the tube is properly seated. Periodically check the area around the speed sensor for leakage. If transmission fluid is evident, check the O-ring for damage. Also inspect the side gear shaft oil seals for leakage.

Case leaks

17   If the case itself appears to be leaking, the casting is porous and will have to be repaired or replaced.
18   Make sure the oil cooler line fittings are tight and in good condition.

Fluid comes out vent pipe or fill tube

19   If this condition occurs, the transaxle is overfilled, there is coolant in the fluid, the case is porous, the dipstick is incorrect, the vent is plugged or the drainback holes are plugged.

3.3 Remove the nut (arrow) to separate the shift cable from the control lever on the transaxle

3   Shift cable - removal and installation

Warning: *The models covered by this manual have supplemental restraint systems (SRS), known as airbags. To avoid accidental deployment of the airbag and possible injury, always disconnect the battery ground (negative) cable, then the positive battery cable and wait two minutes before working near any of the impact sensors, steering column, or instrument panel (see Chapter 12). Do not use any electrical test equipment on any of the airbag system wires or tamper with them in any way.*
1   Set the parking brake securely and block the wheels. Be sure the vehicle cannot roll when taken out of Park.

Models with floor shifters

Refer to illustration 3.3

Shift lever and housing

2   Grasp the shift knob securely and pull up to remove it. Remove the center console (Chapter 11).
3   Disconnect the shift cable from the lever on the transaxle and the transaxle range selector lever **(see illustration)**.
4   Disconnect the ignition key interlock cable from the transaxle range selector lever and housing.
5   Remove the four retaining bolts and detach the shift lever and housing from the vehicle.
6   Installation is the reverse of removal. After installation, adjust the linkage (Section 4).

Shift cable

Removal

7   Remove the center console (Chapter 11).
8   If equipped with cruise control, disconnect the actuator cable.

9   Disconnect the shift cable from transaxle range selector lever.

10   Attach a length of wire, longer than the shift cable, to the range selector end of the shift cable.

11   Remove the nut and disconnect the shift cable from the manual control lever and bracket on the transaxle.

12   Push the rubber shift cable grommet free from the firewall; then slowly pull the cable through the firewall from the engine compartment. Make sure the length of wire does not pull through the dash.

13   Remove the nut and bolts securing the cable bracket to the transaxle and remove the bracket assembly.

Installation and adjustment

14   Disconnect the wire from the old shift cable and attach it to the new one. Then, attach the cable bracket to the transaxle and tighten fasteners securely

15   To install the cable, gently pull the wire to draw the cable through the firewall until the grommet can be inserted into the firewall. Work the grommet into place with a screwdriver.

16   Install the cable bracket and the carpeting.

17   Connect the shift cable to the transaxle control lever.

18   Install the center console, shift knob, and cruise control actuator cable.

19   Place the driver's gear selector lever in Drive. Have an assistant to hold it firmly in position.

20   Loosen the cable nut at the transaxle control lever and place the control lever in the Drive position (second detent from the rear position).

21   Tighten the cable nut and check the transaxle operation in each gear selector position.

Models with column shift

Shift cable removal

22   Remove the screws and lift off the upper steering column shroud. Disconnect the cruise control actuator cable if equipped. On 2000 and later models, remove the trim panel below the steering column, rather than the upper shroud.

23   Locate the ignition lock cylinder release pin access hole on the bottom of the lower steering column shroud. Insert an awl into the hole, push in on the pin to release it, turn the lock cylinder to the Run position, then remove the ignition lock cylinder from the steering column.

24   Remove the lower steering column shroud and the knee bolster from the instrument panel.

25   Rotate the shift indicator adjustment wheel clockwise to disengage the indicator cable end from the column lever. Pull the cable far enough through the adjuster so the assembly can hang clear of the steering column.

26   Refer to the instrument panel removal procedure in Chapter 3 and remove the steering column, disconnecting the shift

cable from the ball stud on the shift lever. On 2000 and later models, it isn't necessary to remove the instrument panel or steering column - there is access from the left side of the column to pry the cable off the ball-stud.

27   Attach a length of wire, longer than the shift cable, to the steering column end of the shift cable.

28   Remove the nut and disconnect the shift cable from the control lever and bracket on the transaxle.

29   Push the rubber shift cable grommet free from the firewall, then slowly pull the cable through the firewall from the engine compartment. Make sure the length of wire does not pull through the firewall.

30   On 1996 through 1999 models, remove the nut and bolts securing the cable bracket to the transaxle and remove the bracket assembly. On 2000 and later models, pull up the lock-tab at the shift cable bracket on the transaxle, then pull the cable from the bracket.

Shift cable installation and adjustment

31   Disconnect the wire from the old shift cable and attach it to the new one. Then, attach the cable bracket to the transaxle and gently pull the wire to draw the new cable through the firewall.

32   Complete the installation by connecting the cable, reattaching the steering column tube, fitting the indicator adjustment wheel, and attaching the shrouds.

33   Set the parking brake securely and block the wheels.

34   Place the driver's gear selector lever in Drive (models equipped with an Overdrive On/Off button on the shift lever) or OD (models not so equipped). Have an assistant hold it firmly in position.

35   Loosen the cable nut at the transaxle control lever and place the control lever in the second detent from the rear position (the "rear" position is actually when the end of the lever is moved as far to the left (driver's) side of the vehicle as it will go).

36   Tighten the cable nut and check the transaxle operation in each gear selector position.

---

4   **Transmission range sensor - removal and installation**

Note: *A special alignment tool is needed to adjust the range sensor. Read through this entire procedure and check on price and availability of the tool before deciding to do it yourself.*

Removal

Refer to illustration 4.2

1   Disconnect the battery ground (negative) cable and remove the air cleaner assembly. Then place the gear selector lever in Neutral.

2   Disconnect the transmission range sensor electrical connector **(see illustration)**.

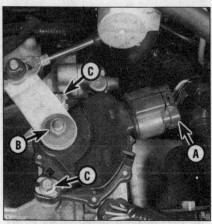

4.2 First disconnect the electrical connector (A), then remove the retaining nut (B), the lever and the two sensor mounting bolts (C) to replace the transaxle range sensor

3   Refer to Section 3 and disconnect the shift cable from the lever at the transaxle, then remove the retaining nut and the shift lever from the transaxle.

4   Remove the two retaining bolts and lift the range sensor off of the transaxle.

Installation

5   Make sure that the gear selector lever is in Neutral.

6   Slip the transmission range sensor onto the transaxle and loosely install the two mounting bolts.

7   Use a special alignment tool to adjust the position of the sensor. Then, tighten the bolts securely.

8   Connect the transmission range sensor electrical harness.

9   Install the manual control lever and tighten the nut securely.

10   Install the air cleaner assembly and reconnect the battery ground cable.

11   Verify that the engine starts only when the shift lever is in Park or Neutral positions.

---

5   **Automatic transaxle - removal and installation**

Note: *The engine and transaxle have a common mount and the engine must be supported when the transaxle or subframe is removed. This is done with a bar-type fixture that rests on the fender flanges. The engine is suspended from the fixture with brackets or chains so the transaxle can be removed. In addition, automatic transaxles are heavy and awkward to handle and a transmission jack should be used to remove and install the unit because the transaxle will not balance on a regular floor jack. Both the engine support fixture and a transmission jack can be rented from some auto parts stores and most equipment rental companies.*

5.5 Remove the retaining nut and lift the shift lever off the range sensor

5.6a To separate the fluid cooler lines from the transaxle, first pry the retainer clip off of the fitting with a small screwdriver . . .

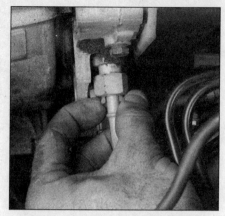

5.6b . . . then squeeze the plastic retaining clips in with your fingers and pull out on the line to separate it from the fitting

Warning: *Do not work or place any part of your body under the car when it is supported only by a jack. Jack failure could result in severe injury or death.*

Removal

Refer to illustrations 5.5, 5.6a, 5.6b, 5.7, 5.14 and 5.16

Note: *On some models it is necessary to remove the subframe before the transaxle can be removed from the car.*

1   Disconnect the negative battery cable, then the positive cable and remove the battery and battery tray from the car.

2   Refer to Chapter 4 and remove the air cleaner assembly.

3   Disconnect the transaxle electrical harness connector and the transmission range sensor electrical connector. On 2000 and later models, disconnect the power steering sensor connector and turbine shaft speed (TSS) sensor.

4   Disconnect the shift cable housing from the bracket on the transaxle.

5   Remove the retaining nut, then remove the shift lever from the transaxle **(see illustration)**.

6   Disconnect the fluid cooler lines from the transaxle **(see illustrations)**, then plug both the lines and the fittings to prevent contamination.

7   Fit the support fixture to the chassis and

attach it to the engine.

8   Loosen the wheel lug nuts, raise the vehicle and support it securely on jackstands.

9   Refer to Chapter 1 and drain the transaxle fluid. When the fluid has completely drained, reinstall the oil pan.

10   Remove the front wheels, then remove both driveaxles (see Chapter 8).

11   Unplug the four oxygen sensor electrical connectors, then refer to Chapter 4 and remove the exhaust system Y-pipe.

12   Refer to Chapter 5 and remove the starter motor.

13   Position a transmission jack under the transaxle and secure the transaxle to the jack. Use safety chains to secure the transaxle to the jack.

14   Remove the torque converter dust cover and mark one of the torque converter studs and the driveplate so they can be reinstalled in the same position **(see illustration)**.

15   Use a large socket and breaker bar on the crankshaft bolt at the front of the engine to lock the engine, preventing it from turning over, then remove the four torque converter nuts. Turn the engine over with the socket and bar for access to each nut.

16   Remove the lower transaxle-to-engine bolts **(see illustration)**.

17   Unbolt and remove the rear engine mount from the transaxle (Section 6) and the subframe connecting bolts and mounts. Carefully lower the subframe.

18   Pull the jack and transaxle back away from the engine, making sure the torque converter stays with the transaxle.

19   Slowly lower the jack to remove the transaxle from the car.

Installation

20   Place the transaxle on the transmission jack and secure it. Install the torque converter onto the transaxle, making sure it is fully seated (to do this, push the converter in while turning it. If the converter was not fully engaged, it will "clunk" into place. It may even "clunk" more than once). Then lightly coat the torque converter pilot hub with multi-purpose grease.

21   Roll the jack and transaxle into position and raise the jack until the transaxle aligns with the engine. Then push the jack and transaxle forward to mate it with the engine.

22   Position the torque converter so the mark on the driveplate lines up with the mark on the stud. Install the four torque converter nuts and tighten them evenly in stages to the torque listed in this Chapter's Specifications.

5.14 Make index marks on the torque converter driveplate and one of the mounting studs so the converter can be installed in the same position on assembly to maintain balance

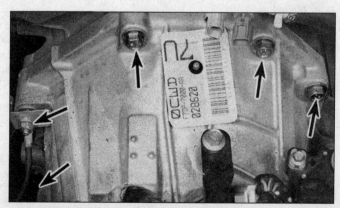

5.16 Remove the transaxle-to-engine bolts (not all bolts visible in this photo). Note that the bolt on the left also has a stud nut where the engine ground cable attaches

Use a large socket and breaker bar on the front crankshaft bolt to turn the engine over for access to each nut and to hold the engine when tightening them. Install the torque converter dust cover.

23   Install the transaxle-to-engine bolts and tighten them to the torque listed in this Chapter's Specifications.

24   Install the rear (left side) engine mount on the transaxle and tighten the bolts securely. Remove the transmission jack.

25   Install the starter motor and tighten the fasteners securely. Refer to Chapter 5 and attach the starter electrical connections.

26   Install the exhaust system Y-pipe. Connect the four oxygen sensor electrical connectors.

27   Refer to Chapter 8 and install both driveaxles and the wheels. Then, lower the vehicle.

28   Remove the engine support fixture.

29   Attach the transaxle fluid cooler lines.

30   Make sure the transmission range sensor is in the correct position (Section 4), then install the manual shift control lever and tighten securely.

31   Fit the shift cable onto the shift lever and bracket and tighten securely.

32   Plug in the transaxle electrical connectors and reinstall the air cleaner assembly.

33   Install the battery tray and battery. Connect the positive battery cable first, then the negative cable.

34   Refer to Chapter 1 and fill the transaxle with the specified fluid.

35   Road test, then recheck and correct fluid level and linkage adjustments.

6   Transaxle mount - inspection and replacement

Note 1: *The following procedure applies only to 1998 and earlier models. On 1999 and later models, the engine and transaxle must be removed as a single assembly from underneath the vehicle, using a special cradle, which is then rolled out from under the vehicle. This cradle is an expensive device, and can only be used under a vehicle that has been raised on a vehicle hoist, not jackstands. Engine removal on these models is therefore beyond the scope of the average home mechanic.*

Note 2: *The manufacturer refers to the mount that supports the engine and transaxle on the left-hand (driver's) side of the car as the "rear" engine and transaxle mount.*

Note 3: *Replacement of the front (right side) engine mounts is covered in Chapters 2A and 2C.*

Warning: *Do not work or place any part of your body under the car when it is supported only by a jack. Jack failure could result in severe injury or death.*

Inspection

Refer to illustration 6.1

1   You can inspect the engine and transaxle mount for damage or deterioration

6.1 The transaxle mount is accessible through the left wheel well

A) *Mount-to-transaxle bracket nut*
B) *Mount-to-frame bolts*

without removing the engine or the transaxle **(see illustration)**.

2   Disconnect the battery ground cable. Loosen the left front wheel lug nuts. Raise the car, support it on jackstands, and remove the left front wheel.

3   Place a hydraulic floor jack under the engine oil pan or the transaxle with a block of wood between the jack and the pan or transaxle to protect the pan. The exact jack placement will vary with the type of jack and the transaxle model. In any case, locate the jack so that it easily relieves the powertrain weight from the mount.

4   Slowly and carefully raise the jack slightly to take the powertrain weight off the mount.

5   Inspect the mount for damage, deterioration or separation. Use a flashlight and mirror to inspect the mount closely. Sometimes a rubber insulator that is separated from a bracket or bolt will not be apparent until engine weight is removed from the mount.

Removal

6   Remove the upper nut that holds the engine and transaxle mount to the support bracket attached to the rear (left side) of the engine and transaxle **(see illustration 6.1)**.

7   Remove the two through-bolts that hold the mount to its bracket on the left side of the subframe **(see illustration 6.1)**.

8   Raise the powertrain with the jack enough to fully unload the mount.

9   Remove the bolts and nuts that secure the support bracket to the transaxle.

10   Rotate the support bracket counterclockwise to disengage it from the upper stud on the engine and transaxle mount. Then remove the mount from the car.

Installation

11   Position the engine and transaxle mount on the car subframe.

12   Attach the support bracket to the transaxle; tighten securely.

13   Attach the engine and transaxle mount to the bracket on the subframe with two through-bolts; tighten securely.

14   Slowly and carefully lower the hydraulic jack until the powertrain weight is removed from the jack.

15   Attach the engine and transaxle mount to the support bracket with the nut on the

mount's upper stud; tighten securely.

16   Remove the jack from under the engine and transaxle.

17   Install the left front wheel and lower the car to the ground.

7   Shift lock system - general information and disabling

General information

1   This system provides a safety interlock that prevents the shift lever's movement out of Park unless the brake pedal is first depressed.

2   An actuator solenoid and module assembly, located on the lower portion of the steering column, locks the shifter in Park whenever it receives a signal that the ignition key is in the ON position. On models with floor shift, a cable connects the shifter to the interlock module at the steering column. When the module receives a signal from the Brake On-Off (BOO) switch that indicates the brake pedal is depressed, it unlocks the shifter so it can be shifted out of Park.

3   The most common failures in this system are the fuse, which also protects the cruise control deactivation circuit (see Chapter 12) and the BOO switch (see Chapter 9). A failure of the system will sometimes result in the shifter being permanently locked in Park. See Step 6 for the disabling procedure.

4   If the system is not operating, check the fuse first. If it's OK, the BOO switch may be the problem. If the BOO switch is not operating properly, the cruise control will also be affected (it will not deactivate during braking) and the brake lights might not be working.

5   If the BOO switch seems to be operating properly, take the vehicle to a dealer service department or other qualified shop, as this system requires special tools for complete diagnosis.

Disabling

6   If the shifter is locked in the Park position, even with the brake pedal depressed, apply the parking brake, turn the ignition key to LOCK, then remove the key.

7   Insert the key and turn it to OFF. Press the brake pedal.

8   Shift to Neutral, start the vehicle and select the desired gear.

Notes

Chapter 8   Driveaxles

Contents

Specifications

Driveaxle length (see illustration 4.35)

AX4N automatic transaxle
    Left side.. 18.35 inches (466 mm)
    Right side .... 22.17 inches (563 mm)
AX4S automatic transaxle
    Left side.. 18.35 inches (466 mm)
    Right side .... 23.56 inches (598 mm)

Lubricant specifications

High-temperature CV joint grease
    Inboard CV joint .... 16.75 oz (475 g)
    Outboard CV joint.. 6.3 oz (180 g)

Torque specifications

Ft-lbs
Driveaxle/hub nut.. 180 to 200
Wheel lug nuts .... See Chapter 1

1   General information

Power from the engine passes from the transaxle to the front wheels by two driveaxles, which are nearly equal in length. Each driveaxle consists of three sections: the inner constant velocity (CV) joint, the axleshaft, and the outer CV joint. The ends of the axleshaft have external splines that fit into internal splines on the CV joints. An internal snap-ring is used to hold the CV joints on the axleshaft. The outboard end of the outer CV joint has external splines that fit the hub to drive the wheels. The inner CV joint is a plunging design that allows for changes in shaft length as the wheels move up and down, and the outer CV joint is a caged-ball design that allows a constant torque transfer when the wheels turn during cornering. The CV joints are lubricated for life with special grease and are protected by rubber boots. Although no periodic lubrication is required, the rubber boots must be inspected regularly for cracks, holes, tears, and signs of leakage, which could lead to damage of the joints and failure of the driveaxle.

A lip seal, which is press fit into the transaxle case, rides on the inner CV joint housing for each driveaxle to prevent differential fluid leakage. Leaking differential seals are easily replaced with the driveaxle removed. Inspect the differential seals while servicing CV joints and replace any that are leaking or show signs of damage or wear.

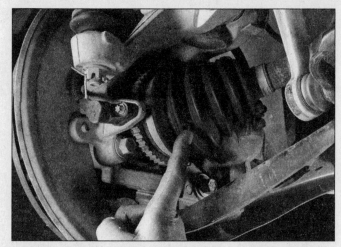

2.3 Periodically inspect the CV joint boots for cracks, tears, or other signs of damage

3.6 Use a two-jaw puller to push the driveaxle out of the hub

2   Driveaxles, constant velocity (CV) joints and boots - check

Refer to illustration 2.3

1   Inspect the driveaxles, CV joints and boots periodically and whenever the vehicle is raised for any reason. The most common symptom of driveaxle or CV joint failure is clicking or knocking noises when turning.

2   Raise the vehicle and support it securely on jackstands.

3   Inspect the CV joint boots for cracks, leaks and broken retaining bands **(see illustration)**. If lubricant leaks out through a hole or crack in the boot, the CV joint will wear prematurely and require replacement. Replace any damaged boots immediately (see Section 4) because the rotation of the axle forces the lubricant out of the joint, and a CV joint will quickly fail when operated without lubrication. It's a good idea to disassemble, clean, inspect and repack the CV joint whenever replacing a CV joint boot to ensure that the joint is not contaminated with moisture or dirt, which would cause premature CV joint failure.

4   Check the entire length of each axle to make sure there are no cracks, twists, bends, or other visible damage.

5   Grasp each axle and rotate it in both directions while holding the CV joint housings to check for excessive movement, indicating worn splines or loose CV joints.

6   If a boot is damaged or loose, remove the driveaxle as described in Section 3. Disassemble and inspect the CV joint as explained in Section 4. **Note:** *Some auto parts stores carry "split" replacement boots, which can be installed without removing the driveaxle from the vehicle. This is a convenient alternative; however, it's recommended that the driveaxle be removed and the CV joint disassembled and cleaned to ensure that the joint is free from contaminants such as moisture and dirt, which will accelerate CV joint wear.*

3.7 Hold the CV joint and pull the hub off it. Keep the axle supported as you continue to work; letting it hang free can damage the inner CV joint

3   Driveaxles - removal and installation

Warning: *Whenever any of the suspension or steering fasteners are loosened or removed they should be inspected and, if necessary, replaced with new ones of the same part number or of original equipment quality and design. Torque specifications must be followed for proper assembly and component retention.*

Removal

Refer to illustrations 3.6, 3.7 and 3.8

1   Remove the wheelcover and loosen the driveaxle/hub nut about 1/4-turn. Loosen the wheel lug nuts, raise the vehicle and support it securely on jackstands. Remove the wheel.

2   Remove the driveaxle/hub nut from the axle and discard it. To prevent the hub from turning as the nut is unscrewed, place a screwdriver or punch through the caliper and into a cooling vane in the brake disc.

3   Remove the nut holding the stabilizer

3.8 Use a large screwdriver or prybar (arrow) to carefully pry the inner CV joint out from the transaxle

bar link to the strut and swing the link out of the way (see Chapter 10, if necessary).

4   Remove the brake caliper and disc (see Chapter 9). Support the caliper with a piece of wire - don't let it hang by the hose.

5   Separate the lower control arm balljoint from the steering knuckle (see Chapter 10).

6   Using a two-jaw puller, push the driveaxle out of the hub **(see illustration)**.

7   Grasp the axleshaft in one hand and pull the hub and strut assembly out to separate the nose of the CV joint from the hub **(see illustration)**. Suspend the axle with a piece of wire or rest it on the control arm. Don't let it hang free because this can overextend and damage the inner CV joint.

8   Insert a prybar or large screwdriver between the inner CV joint housing and the transaxle case **(see illustration)**. Pry out just far enough to release the circlip. Be sure to seat the prybar on a solid surface and take care to avoid damaging the transaxle case.

9   Support the outer CV joint with one hand, grasp the axleshaft with your other hand, remove the support wire, and guide the driveaxle clear of the chassis.

4.6 Clamp the axleshaft in a vise, peel back the boot, and strike the inner race of the CV joint with a brass drift and hammer to dislodge it from the axle

4.11 Tilt the inner race far enough to remove the balls. Use a brass punch or a wooden dowel and hammer to reposition the inner race if it is difficult to move

Installation

10   Install a new circlip on the inner stub shaft splines. Fit one end of the circlip into the groove, then work around the shaft as you guide the clip into place. This prevents stretching the circlip.

11   Coat the differential seal lip with multi-purpose grease, align the splines of the inner CV joint with those of the differential side gear, then firmly grasp the inner CV joint housing and push to insert it into the transaxle. You should feel the circlip snap into place as it seats in the differential gear.

12   Pull out on the hub and strut assembly, align the splines of the outer CV joint with those of the hub, and push the outer CV joint stub shaft as far into the hub as possible by hand.

13   Fit the washer and thread a new driveaxle/hub nut as far as possible by hand. Never reuse the old retainer nut; these are a self-locking design that can only be used once.

14   Pry down on the lower control arm, align the lower balljoint stud with the steering knuckle, and slowly ease tension on the pry-bar as you guide the balljoint into position. Install and tighten the balljoint nut to the torque listed in the Chapter 10 Specifications.

15   Connect the stabilizer bar link to the strut, install the nut and tighten it to the torque listed in the Chapter 10 Specifications.

16   Immobilize the hub as described in Step 2 to keep the hub from turning while tightening the driveaxle/hub nut securely.

17   Install the wheel and lug nuts. Lower the vehicle and tighten driveaxle/hub nut to the torque listed in this Chapter's Specifications. Tighten the lug nuts to the torque listed in Chapter 1 Specifications.

18   Lower the vehicle, check the transaxle fluid level and top off as necessary (see Chapter 1).

19   Pump the brake pedal several times to bring the brake pads into contact with the disc before driving the vehicle.

4   Driveaxle boot replacement

Note: *If the CV joints are worn, indicating the need for an overhaul (usually due to torn boots), explore all options before beginning the job. Complete rebuilt driveaxles are available on an exchange basis, which eliminates much time and work. Whichever route you choose to take, check on the cost and availability of parts before disassembling the driveaxle. Also, individual CV joint parts are not available. If any damage is found, the entire CV joint must be replaced.*

1   Remove the driveaxle from the vehicle (see Section 3).

2   Place the driveaxle in a vise lined with wood so as not to mar the shaft. Make sure the vise jaws or wooden blocks do not contact the CV joint boot.

Outer CV joint and boot

Disassembly

Refer to illustrations 4.6, 4.11, 4.12, 4.13 and 4.14

3   Cut both of the boot retaining clamps with side cutters and remove them from the boot.

4   Slide the boot off the outer race and far enough down the shaft for clear access to the inside of the CV joint.

5   Reposition the axle in the vise so that the stub axle of the CV joint faces down at an angle and the inner race of the joint is exposed.

6   Carefully position a brass drift on the inner race of the CV joint. Then strike the drift a sharp blow with a hammer to dislodge the CV joint assembly from the axle **(see illustration)**. Don't let the CV joint fall as it comes off the shaft.

7   Remove the circlip from the axleshaft and discard it.

8   Remove the stop-ring, then slip the boot off the end of the axleshaft.

9   Check the grease for contamination by rubbing a small amount between your thumb and fingers. If you feel any grit in the grease,

it is contaminated and the joint needs to be completely disassembled, cleaned and inspected; continue with this disassembly sequence. If the grease feels smooth and free of grit, the joint is not contaminated and can be repacked and reinstalled with a new boot; skip ahead to the assembly sequence.

10   Mount the CV joint in a vise lined with wood so that the bearing assembly is facing up. Take care not to damage the dust shield or splines when clamping the joint in the vise.

11   Press down on one side of the inner race with your thumb so that the opposite side tilts up far enough to allow a ball bearing to be removed from the cage. If the joint is tight and the inner race is difficult to tilt, use a hammer and a brass punch or wooden dowel to tap it **(see illustration)**. Be careful not to strike the bearing cage; it can be damaged easily.

12   Pry the balls from the cage with a blunt screwdriver or wooden tool that will not scratch the surfaces on which the balls ride **(see illustration)**. Reposition the inner race to expose another ball and repeat this procedure as you remove the balls one at a time.

4.12 Lift the balls free of the cage. It may be necessary to pry them out with a screwdriver

4.13 Tilt the inner race and cage 90-degrees, align the windows in the cage with the lands of the outer race, then lift the cage and inner race up and out of the outer race

4.14 Align the inner race lands with the cage windows and rotate the inner race out of the cage

4.16a Inspect the inner race lands and grooves for pitting, scoring, scratches, dents, or any other signs of wear or damage . . .

4.16b . . . also inspect the cage for cracks, pitting and other signs of wear or damage. Shiny spots (arrow) are normal and do not affect operation

4.19 When assembled, the beveled edge of the inner race (arrow) must face out

4.20 Align the cage windows with the machined grooves of the inner and outer races. Then tilt the cage and inner race to insert the balls

13   With all of the balls removed from the cage, pivot the cage and inner race assembly 90-degrees, so that the ball windows of the cage align with the lands of the outer race **(see illustration)**.

14   Lift the cage and inner race out of the outer race. Then separate the two parts by tilting the inner race 90-degrees and removing it from the cage **(see illustration)**.

Inspection

Refer to illustrations 4.16a and 4.16b

15   Clean all of the components using a residue-free solvent, such as brake parts cleaner, to remove all traces of grease.

16   Inspect the cage and races for pitting, score marks, cracks and other signs of wear or damage. Shiny, polished spots are normal and will not adversely affect CV joint performance **(see illustrations)**. If the balls have worn a groove or indentation into the race, replace the CV joint.

17   Inspect each of the balls for signs of pitting, scoring, flaking, or discoloration due to overheating. Replace the CV joint if any damage is found.

Assembly

Refer to illustrations 4.19, 4.20, 4.22, 4.23 and 4.25

Note: *The tripod assembly for the inner CV joint cannot be removed from the axleshaft. Therefore, the inner CV joint boot must be installed onto the shaft from the outboard end. If the inner boot needs replacement, install it before you install the outer CV joint on the shaft.*

18   Apply a light coating of CV joint grease to the inner race. Then install it into the cage by reversing the technique described in Step 14.

19   Lightly coat the outer race with CV joint grease. Fit the inner race and cage assembly into the outer race by aligning the cage windows with the race lands and then pivoting the inner race into position. Note that one side of the inner race has a beveled edge machined into its surface near the splines. This bevel must face up and be visible when the inner race and cage are installed in the outer race **(see illustration)**.

20   Tilt the race and cage assembly and install the balls one at a time **(see illustration)**.

21   Wrap the splines of the axleshaft with tape to prevent damaging the boot, then slide the new clamp and boot onto the axleshaft. Remove the tape, install the stop-ring, and fit a new circlip into the groove on the axle.

22   Pack the CV joint with fresh grease. A tube of the proper grease is supplied with most replacement CV joints, and the tube contains the exact quantity needed to correctly pack the joint as listed in this Chapter's Specifications. Apply the grease through the splined hole in the inner race and pack the grease into the joint by inserting a wooden dowel through the splined hole and pushing it to the bottom of the joint **(see illustration)**. Repeat this procedure until the joint is completely packed, then spread any remaining grease evenly around the inside of the boot.

23   Clamp the axleshaft in the vise using wooden blocks to protect it. Position the CV joint on the end of the axleshaft, align the splines, and tap the joint onto the axle using a soft-faced hammer **(see illustration)**. Make sure the circlip snaps into place. You should not be able to pull the joint off the shaft after the circlip seats.

24   Wipe any excess grease from the out-

4.22 Apply grease through the splined hole, then insert a wooden dowel through the splined hole and push down - the dowel will force the grease into the joint

4.23 Line up the splines of the inner race with those of the axleshaft. Then use a soft-faced hammer to tap the CV joint onto the shaft until the inner race is seated against the stop-ring

4.25 Install the CV joint clamps and tighten them using special clamp-crimping pliers (available at most auto parts stores)

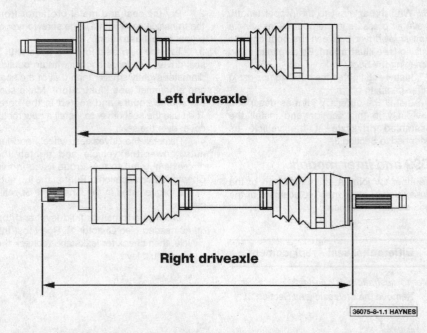

Left driveaxle

Right driveaxle

36075-8-1.1 HAYNES

4.35 The driveaxle standard length should be set to the dimension listed in this Chapter's Specifications before the boot clamps are tightened

side of the CV joint housing and from the inner sealing area of the boot. Slip the boot over the CV joint so that it fits into the sealing groove. Also make sure the inner end of the boot is seated in the groove of the axleshaft.

25 After the boot is positioned correctly, install the two retaining clamps. Special clamp-crimping pliers, available at most auto parts stores, are used to tighten the boot clamps **(see illustration)**.

Inner CV joint and boot 1996 through 1998

Disassembly

26 Remove the outer CV joint and boot (see Steps 3 through 8). Remove the boot retaining clamps and slide the boot toward the center of the axleshaft. **Note:** *The large retaining clamp used on the right-side inner CV joints is a special, reusable, low-profile design. Do not cut this clamp to remove it. A replacement is not provided with the boot. Use CV joint boot clamp pliers or an equivalent tool to remove and install this clamp.*

27 Mark the tripot housing and the axle so they can be returned to their original posi-

tions on reassembly. Then, slide the housing off of the axle and spider assembly.

28 Slide the boot off the outboard end of the axle to remove it.

Inspection

29 Clean old grease from the housing and spider assembly with a residue-free solvent, such as brake parts cleaner.

30 Carefully inspect the spider and tripot housing for scoring, pitting, excessive wear, and other damage. If any damage is found, replace the inner CV joint and axle assembly. **Note:** *The spider can't be removed from the axleshaft.*

Assembly

Refer to illustrations 4.35 and 4.36

31 Wrap the splines of the axleshaft with

tape to prevent damaging the boot, then slip the new boot into position on the axleshaft.

32 Apply a coat of CV joint grease to the inner surfaces of the tripot housing. Make sure the reference marks made in step 27 are aligned and insert the spider and axle assembly into the housing.

33 Pack the inner CV joint with CV joint grease by generously filling the housing and applying an even coat to the inside of the boot.

34 Wipe any grease from the outside of the housing, then fit the boot onto the housing making sure it seats in both the housing and axle seal grooves.

35 Adjust the length of the driveaxle to the dimension listed in this Chapter's Specifications **(see illustration)**.

4.36 After the axleshaft is set to the correct length, relieve air pressure from the inner CV joint boot by carefully lifting the edge with a blunt tool

5.2 Pry the seal from the transaxle case

36 With the axle set to the proper length, relieve air pressure in the boot by inserting a blunt screwdriver between the boot and the housing **(see illustration)**. Be careful to avoid damaging the boot.

37 Install and tighten the boot clamps using clamp-crimping pliers.

38 Install the outer CV joint as described previously in this section and install the assembled driveaxle in the vehicle as described in Section 3.

1999 and later models

The inner CV joint is an integral part of the driveaxle and, other than replacement of the boot, cannot be serviced.

---

5 Differential seal - replacement

Refer to illustrations 5.2 and 5.3

1 Remove the driveaxle (see Section 3).

2 Pry the seal and metal protector from the transaxle case with a large screwdriver or prybar **(see illustration)**.

3 Tap the new seal into the case with a seal driver, or a large socket with an outside diameter slightly smaller than that of the seal, and a hammer **(see illustration)**. Make sure the seal is square and seated in the bore. Then use the seal driver to install a new metal cover over the seal.

4 Reinstall the driveaxles, wheels and lug nuts. Lower the vehicle and tighten the driveaxle/hub nut to the torque listed in this Chapter's Specifications. Tighten the lug nuts to the torque listed in the Chapter 1 Specifications.

5 Check the transaxle fluid level and top off as needed (see Chapter 1). Road test the vehicle, then check for leaks and recheck the transaxle fluid level.

5.3 Drive the new seal into the transaxle housing with a large socket (arrow) or a seal driver - be careful not to cock the seal in the bore

Chapter 9   Brakes

Contents

Specifications

Brake fluid type	See Chapter 1

Disc brakes

Front brake disc	
Standard thickness	1.02 inch
Minimum thickness*	0.974 inch
Rear brake disc	
Standard thickness	0.55 inch
Minimum thickness*	0.50 inch
Brake disc thickness variation limit	0.0004 inch
Brake disc runout limit	0.0024 inch
Minimum brake pad thickness	See Chapter 1

Refer to the marks stamped on the disc - they supersede information printed here.

Drum brakes

Standard drum diameter	8.85 inch
Maximum drum diameter**	8.909 inch
Out-of-round limit	0.005 inch
Minimum brake lining thickness	See Chapter 1

**Refer to the marks stamped on the brake drum - they supersede information printed here.*

Torque specifications

Note: *One foot-pound (ft-lb) of torque is equivalent to 12 inch-pounds (in-lbs) of torque. Torque values below approximately 15 ft-lbs are expressed in inch-pounds, since most foot-pound torque wrenches are not accurate at these smaller values.*

	Ft-lbs (unless otherwise indicated)
Brake hose mounting bracket bolts	144 to 168 in-lbs
Brake hose-to-caliper bolt	
Front	
2005 and earlier	31 to 39
2006 and later	52
Rear	31 to 41
Brake tube connections	144 to 168 in-lbs
Caliper mounting bolts	
Front	23 to 28
Rear	23 to 25
Caliper mounting bracket bolts	65 to 87
Master cylinder-to-brake booster nuts	
1999 and earlier	16 to 21
2000 and later	24
Parking brake cable retaining bolts	132 to 168 in-lbs
Power brake booster-to-firewall nuts	16 to 21
Wheel cylinder bolts	108 to 156 in-lbs

2.4 Position the stationary end of the clamp on the flat of the caliper above the brake hose fitting and the screw end on the outer brake pad

2.5a Remove the lower caliper mounting bolt (lower arrow; the upper arrow points to the upper mounting bolt) . . .

1   General information and precautions

General information

All station wagons have disc-type front and rear brakes. Sedans with standard brakes have front disc brakes and rear drum brakes, while those with the optional Anti-lock Brake System (ABS) have four-wheel disc brakes. All brake systems are hydraulically operated and vacuum assisted.

Front and rear disc brakes are a single piston, floating caliper design. Rear drum brakes are a leading-trailing shoe design with a single pivot and dual-servo wheel cylinder.

Disc brakes automatically compensate for pad wear during use. The rear drum brakes have an automatic adjustment mechanism to compensate for wear.

The front brake pads on front-wheel-drive (FWD) vehicles wear faster than on a comparable rear-wheel-drive (RWD) vehicle. Therefore, FWD brake pads should be inspected frequently to prevent disc or caliper damage due to worn brake pads.

All models have a cable-actuated parking brake that operates the rear brakes.

The hydraulic system uses a dual master cylinder and diagonally split hydraulic circuits. In case of brake line or seal failure, half the brake system will still operate. Standard brake systems have a pressure control valve to reduce pressure to the rear brakes to limit rear wheel lockup during hard braking. The optional ABS electronically regulates hydraulic pressure to the wheels to prevent wheel lockup loss of control under hard braking. ABS is a sensitive and complex system; and servicing electronic or hydraulic components requires tools, equipment, and expertise beyond that of most home mechanics. Therefore, ABS repairs are not covered in this book.

Precautions

Use only brake fluid conforming to DOT 3 specifications.

Brake pads and linings contain fibers that are hazardous to your health if inhaled. When working on brake system components, carefully clean all parts with brake parts cleaner. Never allow the fine dust to become airborne.

Safety should be paramount when working on brake system components. All parts and fasteners must be in perfect condition. If not, replace them. Also, be sure all clearances and torque specifications are adhered to. If unsure about a certain procedure, seek professional advice. When finished working on the brakes, test them carefully under controlled conditions before driving the vehicle in traffic. Never drive a vehicle when you suspect a problem in the brake system until the fault is corrected.

2   Disc brake pads - replacement

Warning: *Disc brake pads must be replaced on both front wheels or both rear wheels at the same time - never replace the pads on only one wheel. Also, the dust created by the brake system may contain asbestos, which is hazardous to your health. Never blow it out with compressed air, and don't inhale any of it. Wear an approved filtering mask when working on the brakes. Do not, under any circumstances, use petroleum-based solvents to clean brake parts. Use brake system cleaner only.*
Note: *Work on one brake assembly at a time, using the opposite side brake assembly for reference if necessary.*

1   Remove the cap from the brake fluid reservoir, siphon off about two-thirds of the fluid into a container and discard it.

2   Loosen the wheel lug nuts, raise the vehicle and support it securely on jackstands.

Front

Refer to illustrations 2.4, 2.5a, 2.5b, 2.6, 2.9 and 2.11

3   Remove the front wheels and thoroughly wash the brake assembly with brake cleaner

2.5b . . . and pivot the caliper on the upper locating pin - tie a piece of wire to the caliper and a suspension component to hold the caliper out of the way

before beginning work. If you're checking the brake pads for wear, see Chapter 1.

4   Using a large C-clamp, push the piston back into the caliper bore **(see illustration)**. As the piston is depressed to the bottom of the caliper bore the fluid in the master cylinder will rise. Make sure it doesn't overflow, if necessary siphon off more fluid from the reservoir.

5   Remove the lower caliper mounting bolt, then use the upper locating pin as a pivot and swing the caliper up **(see illustrations)**. It may be necessary to carefully pry the caliper free with a screwdriver. If so, avoid prying on the caliper piston. Tie a piece of wire to the caliper and a suspension or body component to hold the caliper out of the way.

6   Remove the inner and outer brake pads from the caliper mounting bracket **(see illustration)**.

7   Check the brake disc carefully as outlined in Section 4. If machining is necessary, follow the procedure in Section 4 to remove the disc. **Note:** *Professionals recommend resurfacing the brake disc every time the brake pads are replaced.*

2.6 Remove the brake pads by lifting them out of the mounting bracket

2.9 Apply anti-squeal compound to the brake pad shims and install them onto the new pads

2.11 Fit the inner and outer brake pads onto the mounting bracket, make sure they are seated properly, then lower the caliper over them and install the caliper mounting bolt

2.14 When the upper mounting bolt is removed (arrow) the rear caliper will swing out of the way

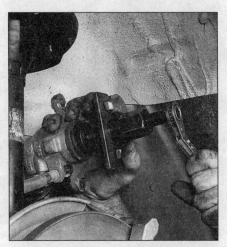

2.18a Turn the piston clockwise until it bottoms in the bore. Here a special caliper adjusting tool is being used

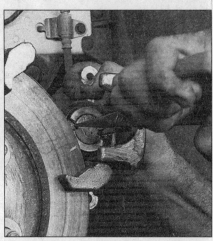

2.18b . . . but a pair of needle-nose pliers will work. Be sure to adjust the position of the piston so one of the notches on its face will align with the tab on the inner pad backing plate

8   If necessary, use a large C-clamp and a block of wood, to bottom the remainder of the caliper piston completely into the caliper bore.

9   Clean any dirt, rust, or debris from the brake pad contact areas of the caliper and mounting bracket with a wire brush. Attach the anti-squeal shims from the old brake pads onto the backs of the new brake pads **(see illustration)**.

10   Depress the caliper sliding pins to make sure they move freely in their bores. If the sliding pins do not move freely, remove the pins, then clean and lubricate them with high temperature grease **(see illustration 3.21)**.

11   Install the new brake pads into the caliper mounting bracket. Make sure the anti-rattle clip located in the caliper is correctly installed, then swing the caliper over the brake pads and onto the mounting bracket. It should fit easily over the new pads if the piston is completely depressed **(see illustration)**. Install the lower caliper mounting bolt and tighten it to the specified torque.

12   Repeat steps 3 through 11 for the

brake on the opposite side, then proceed to Step 25.

Rear

Refer to illustrations 2.14, 2.18a, 2.18b and 2.22

13   Remove the rear wheels and thoroughly wash the brake assembly with brake cleaner before beginning work. If you're checking the brake pads for wear, see Chapter 1.

14   With the parking brake released, detach the cable from the lever on the caliper **(see illustrations 3.5a, 3.5b and 3.5c)**. Remove the upper brake caliper mounting bolt from the caliper **(see illustration)**.

15   Pry the top of the caliper free of the mounting bracket, then use the lower locating pin as a pivot and swing the caliper down and away from the disc.

16   Remove the inner and outer brake pads from the mounting bracket **(see illustra-ion 2.6)**.

17   Check the brake disc carefully as outlined in Section 4. If machining is necessary,

follow the procedure in Section 4 to remove the disc. **Note:** *Professionals recommend resurfacing the brake disc every time the brake pads are replaced.*

18   Seat the caliper piston completely into the caliper bore by rotating it clockwise with a special caliper adjusting tool or similar instrument. Make sure one of the slots on the piston face are positioned to engage the tab on the inner brake pad backing plate **(see illustrations)**. **Note:** *When using needle-nose pliers to seat the piston, loosen the bleeder screw to allow fluid to be expelled from the caliper while seating the piston.*

19   Clean any dirt, rust, or debris from the brake pad contact areas of the caliper and mounting bracket with a wire brush.

20   Depress the caliper sliding pins to make sure they move freely in their bores. If the sliding pins do not move freely, remove the

2.22 Fit the new pads onto the mounting bracket, then swing the caliper into position

3.3 Remove the brake hose banjo fitting bolt (front caliper shown, rear caliper similar)

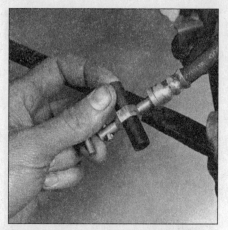

3.4 Using an appropriate size rubber hose, plug the brake line to prevent fluid leakage and system contamination

3.5a On rear calipers, compress the parking brake lever and spring with slip-joint pliers and use locking pliers to disconnect the cable from the lever

3.5b Use a screwdriver to pry the retainer clip (arrow) off of the parking brake cable . . .

pins, then clean and lubricate them with high temperature grease **(see illustration 3.21)**.

21　Fit the inner and outer brake pads onto the mounting bracket.

22　Make sure the anti-rattle clip located in the caliper is correctly installed, then swing the caliper up over the new pads and into position on the mounting bracket **(see illustration)**.

23　Clean the upper caliper mounting bolt, apply a drop of thread-locking compound to its threads, install the caliper mounting bolt, and tighten it to the specified torque.

24　Repeat steps 13 through 23 for the brake the opposite side then proceed to Step 25.

Final installation (front and rear)

25　When the new pads are in place and the caliper mounting bolts have been installed and properly tightened, install the wheels and lower the vehicle to the ground. **Note:** *If the brake hose was disconnected from the caliper for any reason, the brake system must be bled as described in Section 11.*

26　Fill the master cylinder reservoir with new brake fluid and slowly pump the brakes a few times to seat the pads against the disc.

27　Check the fluid level in the master cylinder reservoir one more time and then road test the vehicle carefully before driving it in traffic.

---

3 Disc brake caliper - removal, overhaul and installation

Warning: *Dust created by the brake system may contain asbestos, which is harmful to your health. Never blow it out with compressed air, and don't inhale any of it. Wear an approved filtering mask when working on the brakes. Do not, under any circumstances, use petroleum-based solvents to clean brake parts. Use brake system cleaner.*

Note: *If an overhaul is indicated (usually because of fluid leakage) explore all options before beginning the job. New or rebuilt calipers are available on an exchange basis, which makes this job quite easy. If you decided to rebuild the calipers, make sure*

that a rebuild kit is available before proceeding. Always rebuild the calipers in pairs; never rebuild just one of them.

Removal

Refer to illustrations 3.3, 3.4, 3.5a, 3.5b and 3.5c

1　Remove the cap from the brake fluid reservoir, siphon off two-thirds of the fluid into a container and discard it.

2　Loosen the wheel lug nuts, raise the vehicle and support it securely on jackstands. Remove the wheels.

3　Remove the banjo fitting bolt and detach the brake hose from the caliper **(see illustration)**. Discard the sealing washers - new washers should be used on installation. **Note:** *If you're just removing the caliper for access to other components, don't disconnect the hose.*

4　Plug the brake hose to keep contaminants out of the brake system and to prevent excessive fluid loss **(see illustration)**.

5　On rear calipers, use slip-joint pliers to depress the parking brake lever and relieve cable tension. Then, grip the end of the brake cable with locking pliers and disconnect the

3.5c . . . then pull the end of the cable free
of the caliper

3.7 With a block of wood to pad and
catch the piston, use low-pressure
compressed air to push the piston past
the seal. Keep your fingers out of the way

3.8 When the piston clears the seal, lift it
free of the caliper bore

3.9 Carefully pry the dust boot out of
the caliper

3.10 To remove the seal from the caliper
bore, use a plastic or wooden tool, such
as a pencil

3.11 Pry the pad anti-rattle clip loose from
the outside of the caliper housing, then
remove it from the inside

cable from the lever (see illustration). Then detach the parking brake cable retaining clip and remove the cable from the rear caliper (see illustrations).

6   Remove the caliper mounting bolts from the caliper (see illustration 2.5a and 2.14), lift the caliper free of the mounting bracket, and remove it from the vehicle (refer to Section 2 if necessary). If you're just removing the caliper for access to other components, support the caliper with a piece of wire - don't let it hang by the brake hose.

Overhaul
Front caliper
Refer to illustrations 3.7, 3.8, 3.9, 3.10, 3.11, 3.15, 3.16a, 3.16b, 3.17 and 3.18

7   Clean the outside of the caliper with brake cleaner or denatured alcohol. Place the caliper on a clean workbench. Position a wooden block or several shop rags in the caliper as a cushion; then use low-pressure compressed air to remove the piston from the caliper (see illustration). Use only enough air pressure to ease the piston out of the bore. **Warning:** *Never place your fingers in front of*

the caliper piston in an attempt to catch or protect it when applying compressed air; serious injury could occur.

8   When the piston is loose, remove the wooden block and lift the piston out of the caliper bore (see illustration).

9   Carefully pry the piston dust boot out of the caliper bore (see illustration).

10   Using a wood or plastic tool, remove the piston seal from the groove in the caliper bore (see illustration). Metal tools can damage the bore surface and prevent sealing.

11   Remove the caliper bleeder screw and the pad anti-rattle clip from the caliper (see illustration). Discard all rubber parts.

12   Clean the remaining parts with brake cleaner or denatured alcohol then blow them dry with compressed air. Also, make sure your hands are clean because any dirt or grease that enters the caliper can contaminate the system.

13   Carefully examine the piston for nicks and burrs and loss of plating. If surface defects are present, the parts must be replaced.

14   Check the caliper bore in a similar way. Light polishing with crocus cloth is permissible

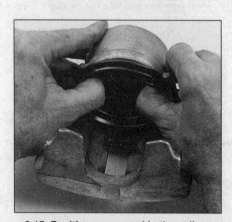

3.15 Position a new seal in the caliper
bore and install the boot, making sure
they seat in their grooves and are
not twisted

to remove light corrosion and stains. Discard the mounting bolts if corroded or damaged.

15   To assemble, lubricate the piston bore and seal with clean brake fluid. Position the seal in the lower groove and the flange of the new boot in the upper groove (see illustration).

3.16a Lubricate the piston, bore, and seal with fresh brake fluid or brake assembly lube. . .

3.16b . . . then fit the piston squarely into the caliper bore and push it into the seal by hand

3.17 Use a C-clamp and a block of wood to seat the piston to the bottom of the bore - work slowly and make sure the piston does not become cocked - it should slide in with very little resistance

3.18 Carefully guide the dust boot around the piston and into the groove

3.20 Press the brake pad anti-rattle clip into the caliper housing until it's fully seated

3.21 Clean the caliper sliding pins, then lubricate them with high temperature grease - make sure they move freely in their bores

16   Lubricate the piston with clean brake fluid, then insert the piston into the boot and push it squarely into the bore **(see illustrations)**.

17   When the piston is started into the bore, use a C-clamp and wood block to completely seat it in the caliper bore **(see illustration)**.

18   Make sure the dust boot is seated in the groove in the piston **(see illustration)** and install the bleeder screw.

Rear caliper

19   Overhauling the rear caliper is extremely difficult and requires several special tools which are quite expensive. If the rear caliper is leaking or malfunctioning, we recommend that you replace it with a new or rebuilt unit.

Installation

Refer to illustrations 3.20 and 3.21

20   Carefully inspect the anti-rattle clip for corrosion and damage. If damage is evident replace the clip. Install the anti-rattle clip onto the caliper housing **(see illustration)**.

21   Clean and lubricate the caliper sliding

pins **(see illustration)**.

22   Install the brake pads onto the caliper mounting bracket as described in Section 2.

23   Slip the caliper into position on the mounting bracket by fitting it over the brake pads. Apply a drop of thread-locking compound to each caliper mounting bolt. Thread the caliper mounting bolts into the caliper by hand, then tighten the bolt to the torque listed in this Chapter's Specifications.

24   On rear disc brakes, connect the parking brake cable end to the lever and secure the cable housing to the caliper with a new retaining clip.

25   Install the brake hose using new sealing washers, then tighten the bolt to the torque listed in this Chapter's Specifications.

26   Bleed the hydraulic system (Section 11).

27   Install the wheels and lower the vehicle, then tighten the wheel lug nuts to the torque listed in the Chapter 1 specifications.

28   After the job has been completed, firmly depress the brake pedal a few times to bring the pads into contact with the disc. Then, check and correct the brake fluid level.

4   Brake disc - inspection, removal and installation

Inspection

Refer to illustrations 4.3a, 4.3b, 4.4a and 4.4b

1   Loosen the wheel lug nuts, raise the vehicle and support it securely on jackstands. Remove the wheel and install two lug nuts to hold the disc in place.

2   Visually inspect the disc surface for score marks and other damage. Light scratches and shallow grooves are normal after use and may not be detrimental to brake operation. Score marks that are over 0.015 inch (0.38 mm) deep require refinishing by an automotive machine shop. Be sure to check both sides of the disc.

3   To check disc runout, install the wheel lug nuts to hold the disc tight against the hub (it may be necessary to install washers under the lug nuts). Then attach a dial indicator to the steering knuckle and locate the stem about 1/2-inch from the outer edge of the

4.3a Check the brake disc runout with a dial indicator. If the reading exceeds the maximum limit, the disc must be machined or replaced

4.3b If the disc is not to be resurfaced, use a swirling motion to remove the glaze from the disc with sandpaper or emery cloth

4.4a The minimum allowable disc thickness usually is stamped on the inside hub flange of the disc

disc **(see illustration)**. Set the indicator to zero and slowly turn the disc. The indicator reading should not exceed 0.003 inch (0.076 mm). If it does, the disc should be resurfaced by a machine shop. **Note:** *Professionals recommend resurfacing the brake discs regardless of the dial indicator reading to produce a smooth, flat surface that will eliminate brake pedal pulsations and other undesirable symptoms which are related to questionable brake discs.* At the very least, if you elect not to have the discs resurfaced, deglaze the brake pad surface with emery cloth or sandpaper (use a swirling motion, to ensure a non-directional finish) **(see illustration)**.

4   A disc must never be machined to a thickness under the specified minimum allowable thickness, which is stamped on the disc itself **(see illustration)**. You can check the disc thickness with a micrometer or vernier caliper **(see illustration)**.

Removal and installation
Refer to illustration 4.6

5   Remove the brake calipers and hang them out of the way (see Section 3). **Note:** *DO NOT disconnect the brake hose from the brake caliper.*

6   Remove the caliper mounting bracket bolts and lift off the mounting bracket **(see illustration)**.

7   Remove the wheel lug nuts that were put on to hold the disc in place and pull the disc from the hub. **Note:** *If equipped, remove the two disc retaining clips that attach the disc to the hub, then lift the disc off the hub.*

8   Installation is the reverse of removal. Make sure all mating surfaces are clean and tighten all fasteners to their specified torque values.

---

5   Brake drum - removal, installation and inspection

Warning: *The dust created by the brake system may contain asbestos, which is hazard-*

ous *to your health. Never blow it out with compressed air, and don't inhale any of it. Wear an approved filtering mask when working on the brakes. Do not, under any circumstances, use petroleum based solvents to clean brake parts. Use brake system cleaner, only.*

Removal and installation

1   Loosen the wheel nuts, raise the rear of the vehicle and support it securely on jackstands. Block the front wheels; then remove the rear wheel and release the parking brake.

2   Remove and discard any brake drum retaining clips from the wheel studs. These simply hold the drum in place on the assembly line.

3   Pull the drum straight out to clear the studs. If the drum does not want to slip off, the brake shoe adjuster may need to be loosened. To loosen, remove the inspection hole cover plug from the backing plate. Insert a screwdriver or brake tool through the inspection hole to disengage the adjusting lever;

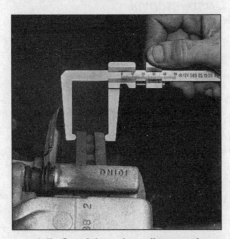

4.4b Special vernier calipers and micrometers with pointed ends that will fit into wear grooves are available for measuring brake disc thickness

then back off the adjuster screw star wheel with another screwdriver.

4   To install, slip the drum over the brake shoes and onto the studs.

5   Install the wheel and lower the vehicle.

Inspection
Refer to illustration 5.6

6   Check the drum for cracks, score marks, deep grooves and signs of overheating of the shoe contact surface. If the drums have blue spots, indicating overheated areas, they should be replaced. Also, look for grease or brake fluid on the shoe contact surface. Grease and brake fluid can be removed with brake system cleaner, but the brake shoes must be replaced if they are contaminated. Surface glazing, which is a glossy, highly polished finish, can be removed with sandpaper or emery cloth. **Note:** *Professionals recommend resurfacing the drums whenever a brake job is done. Resurfacing eliminates the possibility of out-of-round drums. If the drums are worn so much that they can't be resur-*

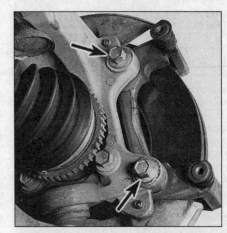

4.6 Remove the the caliper mounting bracket bolts (arrows) (front disc brake shown, rear disc similar)

5.6 The maximum allowable diameter is cast into the drum

6.3 If present, remove the retainers holding the brake drum to the hub

6.4a To retract the brake shoes, remove the rubber plug from the backing plate (arrow) . . .

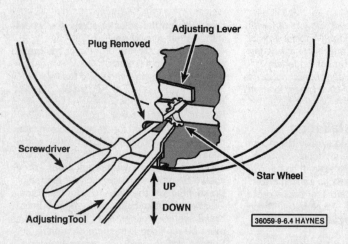

6.4b . . . then use a screwdriver to push the adjusting lever off the adjuster star wheel and another screwdriver to turn the star wheel (typical shown)

6.5a Remove glaze from the drum surfaces with sandpaper or emery cloth

faced without exceeding the maximum allowable diameter, which is cast into the drum **(see illustration)**, *they must be replaced.*

6 Drum brake shoes - replacement

Warning: *The brake shoes must be replaced on both rear wheels at the same time - never replace the shoes on only one wheel. Also, brake system dust is harmful to your health. Never blow it out with compressed air and don't inhale any of it. Do not, under any circumstances, use petroleum-based solvents to clean brake parts. Use brake system cleaner only. Whenever the brake shoes are replaced, the return and hold-down springs should also be replaced. Due to the continuous heating/cooling cycle that the springs are subjected to, they lose their tension over a period of time and may allow the shoes to drag on the drum and wear at a much faster rate than normal.*

Drum removal
Refer to illustrations 6.3, 6.4a and 6.4b

1   Remove about two-thirds of the brake fluid from the master cylinder reservoir.
2   Loosen the wheel lug nuts, raise the rear of the vehicle and support it on jackstands. Block the front wheels and remove the rear wheels from the vehicle.
3   Remove the retainers holding the drum to the hub, if present **(see illustration)**. Discard the retainer(s) - it isn't necessary to reinstall them.
4   Grasp the brake drum and pull it off. If the drum is stuck, remove the rubber plug behind the backing plate and loosen the brake adjuster star wheel with a small screwdriver or equivalent **(see illustrations)**.

Inspection
Refer to illustrations 6.5a and 6.5b

5   Check the drum for cracks, score marks, deep grooves and signs of overheating of the shoe contact surface. If the drums have blue spots, indicating overheated areas, they should be replaced. Also, look for grease or

6.5b Drum maximum diameter markings

6.8a Before doing any work on the rear brakes, wash the assembly with brake system cleaner

6.8b Use a pair of needle-nose pliers to remove the upper spring

6.8c Remove the brake shoe adjusting lever

6.8d Using a hold-down spring tool, remove the leading shoe's hold-down spring

6.8e Pull the leading shoe away and remove the adjuster assembly

6.8f Release the lower spring and remove the leading shoe

brake fluid on the shoe contact surface. Grease and brake fluid can be removed from the drum with denatured alcohol or brake cleaner, but the brake shoes must be replaced if they are contaminated. Surface glazing, which is a glossy, highly polished finish, can be removed from the drum with sandpaper or emery cloth **(see illustration)**. Note: *Professionals recommend resurfacing the drums whenever a brake job is done. Resurfacing will eliminate the possibility of out-of-round drums. If the drums are worn so much that they can't be surfaced without exceeding the maximum allowable diameter* **(see illustration)**, *then new ones will be required.*

6   Inspect the wheel cylinder for fluid leakage as described in Chapter 1.

7   Inspect the surface of the brake shoes for cracks, contamination from grease, and wear and compare their thickness to the Chapter 1 Specifications.

Shoe replacement

Refer to illustrations 6.8a through 6.8q
Note: *The wheel hub is removed for clarity.*

8   Follow the accompanying photos **(see**

illustrations 6.8a through 6.8q) for the actual shoe replacement procedure. Be sure to stay in order and read the information in the caption under each illustration.

9   Once the new shoes are in place, turn

the adjuster until the diameter of the shoe assembly is just smaller than the inner diameter of the brake drum. **Note:** *Work on only one side of the vehicle at a time. The left and right adjusters are different, with a right-hand*

6.8g Use the tool to remove the hold-down spring on the trailing shoe

6.8h Pull the parking brake cable end out of the end of the lever with pliers

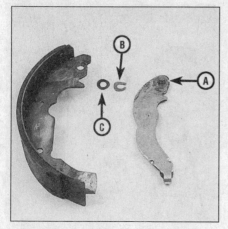

6.8i Pry the old horseshoe clip (B) from the old shoe - grease the pin (A) of the lever and assemble it to the new trailing shoe with the wave-washer (C) and a new horseshoe clip

6.8j Squeeze the new clip over the lever's pin

6.8k Clean the backing plate and apply high-temperature brake grease at the points indicated

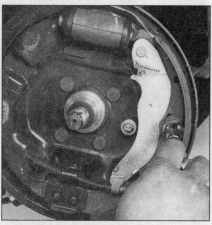

6.8l Connect the parking brake cable to the lever, then install the trailing shoe and hold-down spring

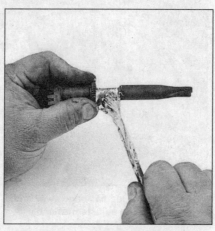

6.8m Clean the threads of the adjuster and lubricate it with high-temperature brake grease

6.8n Install the adjuster and the new leading shoe

6.8o Secure the leading shoe with its hold-down spring

6.8p Install the adjuster lever (A) and hook the upper spring (B) into the hole in the top of the adjuster lever

6.8q Hook the lower spring into the hole in the trailing shoe from the backside, then into the hole in the leading shoe

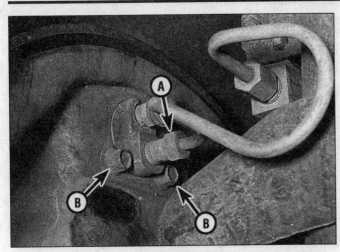

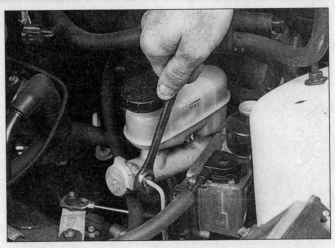

7.5 Disconnect the brake line fitting (A) and remove the two wheel cylinder bolts (B), then lift the cylinder off of the backing plate

8.3 Use a flare-nut wrench to loosen the master cylinder brake line fittings

thread for the right side and left-hand thread for the left side. The socket ends are marked R and L, and the right-side nut has two machined grooves, while the left side nut has only one.

10 Install the brake drum. Insert a narrow screwdriver or brake adjusting tool through the adjustment hole and turn the star wheel until the brakes drag slightly as the drum is turned **(see illustrations 6.4a and 6.4b)**.

11 Turn the star wheel in the opposite direction until the drum turns freely. Keep the adjuster lever from contacting the star wheel or it won't turn.

12 Repeat the adjustment on the opposite wheel.

13 Install the plug in the backing plate access hole.

14 Install the wheels and lower the vehicle. Tighten the lug nuts to the torque listed in the Chapter 1 Specifications.

15 Pump the brake pedal several times and top off the master cylinder with brake fluid, if necessary (see Chapter 1). Check brake operation carefully before driving the vehicle in traffic.

---

7   Wheel cylinder - removal and installation

Refer to illustration 7.5

Note: *If an overhaul is indicated by fluid leakage or faulty operation, we recommend that you replace the wheel cylinder with a new or rebuilt unit. Never replace only one wheel cylinder, always replace both at the same time.*

1 Raise the rear of the vehicle and support it securely on jackstands.

2 Remove the brake drum (Section 5) and the brake shoes (Section 6).

3 Remove all dirt and foreign material from around the wheel cylinder with brake cleaner.

4 Disconnect the brake line. Do not pull the brake line away from the wheel cylinder.

5 Remove the wheel cylinder mounting

bolts and pull the cylinder off of the brake line and the backing plate **(see illustration)**. Plug the line to prevent fluid loss and contamination.

6 To install, place the wheel cylinder in position and make sure it aligns with the fluid line.

7 Connect the fluid line fitting, then install the bolts and tighten them to the torque listed in this Chapter's Specifications. Tighten the fitting securely.

8 Install the brake shoes and the brake drum (Section 6).

9 Bleed the brakes (Section 11).

10 Refill the master cylinder with brake fluid and pump the pedal several times. Lower the vehicle and check brake operation before driving the vehicle in traffic.

---

8   Master cylinder - removal and installation

Caution: *Brake fluid will damage paint. Cover all body parts and be careful not to spill fluid during this procedure.*

Removal

Refer to illustrations 8.3 and 8.5

1 Disconnect the cable from the negative battery terminal.

2 Pump the brake pedal several times to relieve vacuum from the booster. Place rags under the brake line fittings and have caps or plastic bags ready to cover the ends of the fluid lines after they are disconnected. **Note:** *On later models, the air intake tube may have to be removed (see Chapter 4).*

3 Loosen the brake line fitting nuts on the master cylinder. To prevent rounding off the flats on these nuts, use a flare-nut wrench that wraps around the fitting **(see illustration)**.

4 Pull the brake lines away from the master cylinder slightly and plug the ends to prevent leakage and contamination.

5 Disconnect the brake warning light switch electrical connector, then remove the two master cylinder mounting nuts **(see illustration)**.

6 Slide the master cylinder off the studs and remove it from the vehicle.

Installation

7 Whenever the master cylinder is removed, the complete hydraulic system must be bled. The time required to bleed the system can be reduced if the master cylinder is filled with fluid and bench bled before it is installed on the vehicle.

8 To bench bleed a master cylinder, insert threaded plugs of the correct size into the cylinder outlet holes and fill the reservoirs with brake fluid. Support the master cylinder in a vise so that brake fluid will not spill during the bench-bleeding procedure.

9 Loosen one plug at a time, starting with the rear outlet port, which is closest to the booster. Push the piston assembly into the bore to force air from the master cylinder. To prevent air from being drawn back into the

8.5 Remove the nuts (arrows) securing the master cylinder to the power brake booster

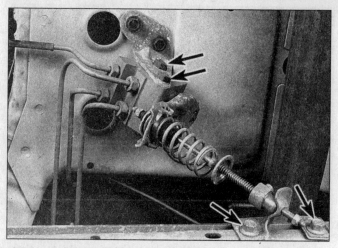

9.3 Use a flare-nut wrench to loosen the brake line fittings, then remove the bolts (arrows) securing the proportioning valve to the frame and the lower suspension arm

10.3 Brake hoses are supplied as an assembly that includes the line connection fitting and mounting bracket (front brake hose shown, rear brake hose similar)

cylinder, replace the plug before allowing the piston to return to its original position.

10   Stroke the piston three or four times for each outlet to ensure that all air has been expelled.

11   Because high pressure is not used in the bench-bleeding procedure, an alternative to the removal and replacement of the plugs is available:

   a) *Before pushing in on the piston assembly, remove one of the plugs completely.*

   b) *Before releasing the piston, put your finger tightly over the hole to keep air from being drawn back into the master cylinder.*

   c) *Wait several seconds for the brake fluid to be drawn from the reservoir to the piston bore; then repeat the procedure.*

   d) *When you push down on the piston it will force your finger off the hole and allow air inside to be expelled. When only brake fluid is ejected from the hole, replace the plug and go on to the other port.*

12   Carefully install the master cylinder by reversing the removal steps.

13   Refill the master cylinder with brake fluid and install the reservoir cap, then bleed the brakes (Section 11).

9   Proportioning valve - removal and installation

Sedan

Refer to illustration 9.3

1   Sedan models from 1996 through 2000 are equipped with a load sensing proportioning valve that is located at the rear of the vehicle above the rear suspension arm. Raise the rear of the vehicle and support it securely on jackstands.

2   Loosen the brake line fitting nuts on the proportioning valve. To prevent rounding off the flats on these nuts, use a flare-nut wrench that wraps around the fitting.

3   Remove the bolts that hold the proportioning valve to the frame and the lower suspension arm **(see illustration)**, carefully pull the hydraulic lines out of the valve, and remove the valve.

4   Plug the fluid lines to prevent fluid loss and contamination. The proportioning valve is not serviceable and must be replaced if defective.

5   Installation is the reverse of removal.

Station wagon

6   Station wagon models are equipped with a fixed type proportioning valve which is mounted at the front of the vehicle below the master cylinder and brake booster assembly. Raise the front of the vehicle and support it securely on jackstands.

7   Loosen the brake line fitting nuts on the proportioning valve. To prevent rounding off the flats on these nuts, use a flare-nut wrench that wraps around the fitting.

8   Remove the bolt that secures the proportioning valve to the frame rail, then carefully pull the hydraulic lines out of the valve, and remove the valve.

9   Plug the fluid lines to prevent fluid loss and contamination. The proportioning valve is not serviceable and must be replaced if defective.

10   Installation is the reverse of removal.

10   Brake hoses and lines - inspection and replacement

Inspection

1   About every six months, with the vehicle raised and supported securely on jackstands, the rubber hoses that connect the steel brake lines with the front and rear brake assemblies should be inspected for cracks, chafing of the outer cover, leaks, blisters, and other damage. These are important and vulnerable parts of the brake system and inspection

10.4 On front brakes, the bracket that attaches the brake hose to the strut is also part of the hose assembly. Remove the mounting bolt (arrow)

should be thorough and complete. A light and mirror will help for a thorough check. If a hose shows any of the above conditions, replace it with a new one.

Replacement

Flexible hose

Refer to illustrations 10.3 and 10.4

2   Clean all dirt away from the ends of the hose and place a drain pan under the work area.

3   Disconnect the brake line from the hose fitting using a flare-nut wrench. The hose, fitting, and mounting bracket are supplied as an assembly **(see illustration)**. Be careful not to bend the bracket or line. If necessary, soak the connections with penetrating oil.

4   On front brakes, unbolt the hose bracket from the suspension strut **(see illustration)**.

5   Remove the bolt attaching the hose bracket to the frame and detach the hose and bracket.

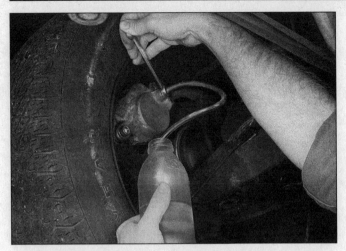

11.8 To bleed the brakes, connect one end of a hose to the bleeder screw and submerge the other end in brake fluid - air forced from the system creates bubbles that can be seen in the container and hose as the pedal is depressed (all air must be expelled before moving to the next wheel)

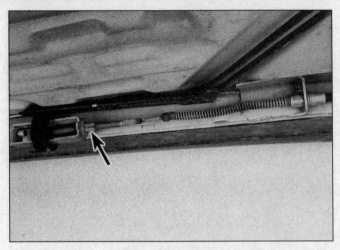

12.3 Use pliers to keep the cable from twisting while you turn the adjusting nut (arrow) on the parking brake cable

6   Disconnect the hose from the caliper, discard the two sealing washers, and plug the caliper port (see Section 3).

7   Attach the new hose to the fluid line using a flare-nut wrench and a backup wrench.

8   Fit the bolts that hold the hose brackets to the frame and strut on front brake hoses and tighten to the torque listed in this Chapter's Specifications.

9   Connect the brake hose to the caliper, using new sealing washers.

10   Carefully check to be sure that the suspension or steering components do not rub or contact the hose in any way. Have an assistant push up and down on the vehicle and also turn the steering wheel from lock to lock during inspection.

11   Bleed the brake system (Section 11).

Metal brake lines

Warning: *When replacing brake lines, be sure to use the correct parts. Never use copper tubing for any brake system components. Purchase genuine steel brake lines only. Copper tubing cannot withstand the high pressures of the brake system, and it may work-harden from vibration and break while driving.*

12   Prefabricated brake line, with the tube ends already flared and fittings installed, is available at auto parts stores and dealers. These lines also may be available already bent to the proper shapes.

13   When installing the new line, make sure it is supported securely in the brackets and has plenty of clearance between moving or hot components. Always start the fittings on both ends before tightening.

14   After installation, check the master cylinder fluid level and add fluid as necessary. Bleed the brake system (Section 11) and test the brakes carefully before driving the vehicle in traffic.

11   Brake hydraulic system - bleeding

Refer to illustration 11.8

Warning: *Wear eye protection when bleeding the brake system. If fluid contacts your eyes, immediately rinse them with water and seek medical attention.*

1   Bleeding the hydraulic system is necessary to remove any air that enters the system as a result of removal and installation of a hose, line, caliper, or cylinder. Use only the specified fluid, or extensive system damage could result. It will be necessary to bleed the system at all four brakes if air has entered the system due to low fluid level or if the brake lines have been disconnected at the master cylinder.

2   If a brake line was disconnected only at one wheel, only that caliper or wheel cylinder needs to be bled.

3   If a brake line is disconnected at a fitting between the master cylinder and any of the brakes, that part of the system served by the disconnected line must be bled.

4   Remove any residual vacuum from the power brake booster by applying the brake several times with the engine off.

5   Remove the master cylinder reservoir cover and fill the reservoir with brake fluid. Reinstall the cover. **Note:** *Check the fluid level often during the bleeding operation and add fluid as necessary to prevent the level from falling low enough to allow air into the master cylinder.*

6   Have an assistant on hand, as well as a supply of new brake fluid, an empty clear plastic container, a length of clear plastic or vinyl tubing to fit over the bleeder screw and a wrench to open and close the bleeder screw.

7   Beginning at the right rear wheel, loosen the bleeder screw slightly; then tighten it to a point where it is snug but can still be loosened quickly and easily.

8   Place one end of the tubing over the bleeder screw and submerge the other end in brake fluid in the container **(see illustration)**.

9   Have an assistant pump the brakes a few times to get pressure in the system, then lightly hold the pedal down.

10   While the pedal is held down, open the bleeder screw until brake fluid begins to flow. Watch for air bubbles to exit the submerged end of the tube. When the fluid flow slows after a couple of seconds, tighten the screw and have your assistant release the pedal.

11   Repeat Steps 9 and 10 until no more air is seen leaving the tube; then tighten the bleeder screw and proceed to the left front wheel, the left rear wheel and the right front wheel, in that order, and perform the same procedure. Check the fluid supply in the master cylinder reservoir frequently.

12   Refill the master cylinder with fresh fluid at the end of the operation. Never use old brake fluid. It contains moisture, which will deteriorate the brake system components.

13   Check the operation of the brakes. The pedal should feel solid when depressed, with no sponginess. If necessary, repeat the entire process. **Warning:** *Do not drive the vehicle if you doubt the effectiveness of the brake system.*

12   Parking brake - adjustment

Refer to illustration 12.3

1   Raise the vehicle and support it securely on jackstands. Block the front wheels to prevent the vehicle from rolling.

2   Make sure the parking brake is completely released.

3   Working under the car, hold the cable with pliers to keep it from turning as you tighten the adjusting nut until the rear brakes drag slightly when the wheels are rotated **(see illustration)**. Turn the nut in the opposite direction until there is no drag.

13.6 Disconnect the cable housing from the parking brake bracket, then unhook the cable end from the clevis (arrow)

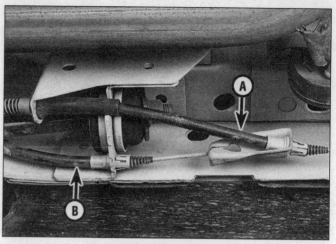

13.10 Depress the cable retaining clip and disconnect the right-rear cable (A) from the equalizer and the frame bracket, then disconnect the left-rear cable (B) from the bracket and separate it from the equalizer

13.13a To remove a rear cable with drum brakes, depress the tangs on the cable housing retainer (arrows) and push the retainer through the backing plate

13.13b To remove a rear cable with disc brakes, use slip-joint pliers to compress the lever and spring (A), unhook the cable end from the lever (B), remove the retaining clip (C) and then slip the cable off the caliper

4   Lower the vehicle and check the operation of the parking brake.

13   Parking brake cables - replacement

1   Raise the rear of the vehicle and support it securely on jackstands. Release the parking brake completely.

Front cable

Refer to illustration 13.6

2   Loosen the parking brake cable adjusting nut **(see illustration 12.3)**.
3   Disconnect the threaded end of the front cable from the rear parking brake cable adjuster.
4   Working inside of the vehicle, remove the left side kick panel; then pull the carpet from the panel. Depress the tangs of the

cable housing bracket retainer using a 13-mm box wrench and remove the cable and housing from the bracket.
5   Push the cable grommet up and out of the floor pan.
6   Disconnect the cable end from the clevis on the pedal control assembly **(see illustration)**.
7   Working under the vehicle, pull the cable assembly out through the floor pan hole.
8   Installation is the reverse of removal. Adjust the cable as described in Section 12.

Rear cables

Refer to illustrations 13.10, 13.13a and 13.13b

9   Loosen the parking brake cable adjusting nut **(see illustration 12.3)**.
10   Working at the rear of the vehicle, dis-

connect the cables from the cable equalizer and frame brackets **(see illustration)**.
11   On drum brakes, remove the rear wheel and brake drum (refer to Section 5). On disc brakes, remove the wheel.
12   Disconnect the end of the parking brake cable from the parking brake lever (see Section 6 for drum brakes; see Section 3 for disc brakes).
13   With drum brakes, depress the tangs on the cable housing retainer and push the cable through the brake backing plate. With disc brakes, remove the retaining clip and separate the cable from the caliper **(see illustrations)**.
14   Remove the bolts, one on the left cable and three on the right, attaching the cable assembly to the chassis.
15   Installation is the reverse of removal. Adjust the cable as described in Section 12.

14   Power brake booster - removal, installation and adjustment

1   The power brake booster requires no special maintenance apart from periodic inspection of the vacuum hose and the case.
2   The brake booster is not serviceable. If a problem develops, install a new or rebuilt unit.

Removal

Refer to illustrations 14.7 and 14.8

3   Disconnect the cable from the negative terminal of the battery.
4   Disconnect the vacuum hose from the check valve at the power brake booster.
5   Loosen the air cleaner assembly and the cruise control actuator and cable and move them off to the side. On 2001 models, disconnect the shift control cable and its bracket at the transmission (see Chapter 7), and remove the two nuts at the firewall securing

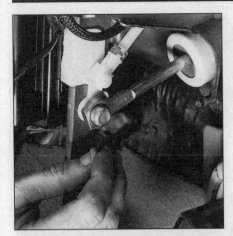

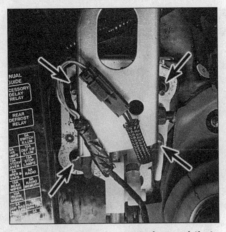

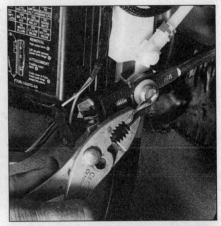

14.7 Remove the retaining clip, nylon washer, and the power booster pushrod from the brake pedal pin, then slide the brake light switch off the pedal arm

14.8 Remove the four nuts (arrows) that attach the booster to the firewall

15.3 Unplug the connector, remove the retaining clip and nylon washer, then slide the booster pushrod off the pedal pin just enough to allow switch removal

the vacuum distribution block and set the hoses and block aside for clearance to remove the brake booster.

6   Remove brake master cylinder (see Section 8).

7   Working in the passenger compartment under the steering column, unplug the wiring connector from the brake light switch, then remove the pushrod retaining clip and nylon washer from the brake pedal pin. Remove the brake light switch (see Section 15). Slide the booster pushrod off the pin **(see illustration)**.

8   Remove the nuts attaching the brake booster to the firewall **(see illustration)**. Then carefully detach the booster from the firewall and lift it out of the engine compartment.

Installation

9   Place the booster into position on the firewall and tighten the mounting nuts. Connect the pushrod and brake light switch to the brake pedal. Install the retaining clip in the brake pedal pin.

10   Install the master cylinder on the booster,

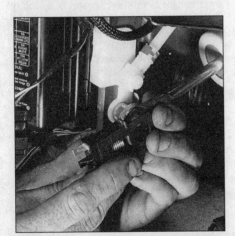

15.4 Slide the brake light switch down to remove it

tighten the nuts to the specified torque, and bleed the hydraulic system (Section 11). **Note:** *Some brake boosters have an adjustable pushrod which should be checked before installing the master cylinder (see Step 13).*

11   Secure the air cleaner and cruise control actuator; reconnect the vacuum hose and battery.

12   Carefully check the operation of the brakes before driving the vehicle in traffic.

Adjustment

13   Some brake boosters have an adjustable pushrod. Pushrods lengths are usually set at the factory and should not require adjustment but should be checked as a matter of precaution.

14   Some common symptoms caused by a misadjusted pushrod include dragging brakes (if the pushrod is too long) or excessive brake pedal travel accompanied by a groaning sound from the brake booster (if the pushrod is too short).

15   To check the pushrod length, unbolt the master cylinder from the booster and move it to one side. It is not necessary to disconnect the hydraulic lines, but be very careful not to bend them.

16   Block the front wheels, apply the parking brake, and place the transaxle in Park or Neutral.

17   Start the engine and measure the distance that the pushrod protrudes from the master cylinder mounting surface, while exerting a force of approximately five pounds to seat the pushrod in the booster. The rod measurement should be 15/64-inch. If not, adjust it by holding the knurled portion of the pushrod with pliers and turning the end with a wrench.

18   When the adjustment is complete, reinstall the master cylinder and check for proper brake operation before driving the vehicle in traffic.

15   Brake light switch - removal and installation

Removal

Refer to illustrations 15.3 and 15.4

1   Remove the under-dash panel.

2   Locate the switch near the top of the brake pedal and disconnect the wiring harness.

3   Remove the switch retaining pin and the white nylon washer from the brake pedal pin, then slide the brake light switch and pushrod off far enough for the outer hole of the switch to clear the pin **(see illustration)**.

4   Slide the switch down to remove it **(see illustration)**.

Installation

5   Position the switch so it straddles the pushrod and the slot on the inner side of the switch rests on the pedal pin. Slide the pushrod and switch back onto the pin, then install the nylon washer and retaining pin.

6   Reconnect the wiring harness.

7   Install the under-dash panel.

8   Check the brake lights for proper operation.

16   Anti-lock Brake System (ABS) - general information

Some models are equipped with an Anti-lock Brake System (ABS). The ABS system is designed to maintain vehicle steerability, directional stability and optimum deceleration under severe braking conditions and on most road surfaces. It does so by monitoring the rotational speed of each wheel and controlling the brake line pressure to each wheel during braking. This prevents the wheel from locking-up and provides maximum vehicle controllability.

16.2 The ABS hydraulic control unit/brake control module is located in the left front corner of the engine compartment

16.6a ABS front wheel sensor location (arrow)

Hydraulic control unit (HCU)

Refer to illustration 16.2

The hydraulic control unit **(see illustration)** is located in the left front corner of the engine compartment. It consists of a brake pressure control valve block, a pump motor and a hydraulic control unit reservoir with a fluid level indicator assembly.

During normal braking conditions, brake hydraulic fluid from the master cylinder enters the hydraulic control unit through two inlet ports and passes through four normally open inlet valves, one to each wheel.

When the ABS control module senses that a wheel is about to lock up, the control module closes the appropriate inlet. This prevents any more fluid from entering the affected brake. If the module determines that the wheel is still decelerating, the module opens the outlet valve, which bleeds off pressure in the affected brake.

Wheel sensors

Refer to illustrations 16.6a and 16.6b

The ABS system uses four "variable-reluctance" sensors to monitor wheel speed ("reluctance" is a term used to indicate the

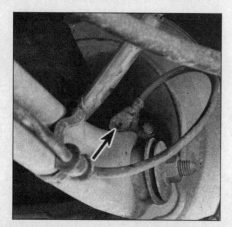

16.6b ABS rear wheel sensor location (arrow)

amount of resistance to the passage of flux lines - lines of force in a magnetic field - through a given material). Each sensor contains a small inductive coil that generates an electromagnetic field. When paired with a toothed sensor ring which interrupts this field as the wheels turn, each sensor generates a low-voltage analog (continuous) signal. This voltage signal, which rises and falls in proportion to wheel rotation speed, is continuously sampled (monitored) by the control module, converted into digital data inside the module and processed (interpreted).

The front wheel sensors **(see illustration)** are mounted in the steering knuckle in close proximity to the toothed sensor rings, which are pressed onto the the outer CV joint housings. The rear wheel sensors **(see illustration)** are mounted in the caliper mounting plate or the wheel spindle and the sensor rings are pressed onto the rear wheel hubs.

Brake control module

The brake control module is also mounted in the left front corner of the engine compartment (it's an integral part of the HCU). The control module is the "brain" of the ABS system. The module constantly monitors the incoming analog voltage signals from the four ABS wheel sensors, converts these signals to digital form, processes this digital data by comparing it to the map (program), makes decisions, converts these (digital) decisions to analog form and sends them to the hydraulic control unit, which opens and closes the front and/or rear circuits as necessary.

The module also has a self-diagnostic capability which operates during both normal driving as well as ABS system operation. If a malfunction occurs, a red "BRAKE" warning indicator or an amber "CHECK ANTI-LOCK BRAKES" warning indicator will light up on the dash.

a) *If the red BRAKE light glows, the brake fluid level in the master cylinder reservoir has fallen below the level established by the fluid level switch. Top up the reservoir and verify that the light goes out.*

b) *If the amber CHECK ANTI-LOCK BRAKES light glows, the ABS and, if equipped, Traction Assist, have been turned off because of a symptom detected by the module. Normal power-assisted braking is still operational, but the wheels can now lock up if you're involved in a panic-stop situation. A diagnostic code is also stored in the module when a warning indicator light comes on; when retrieved by a service technician, the code indicates the area or component where the problem is located. Once the problem is fixed, the code is cleared. These procedures, however, are beyond the scope of the home mechanic.*

Diagnosis and repair

Warning: *If a dashboard warning light comes on and stays on while the vehicle is in operation, the ABS system requires immediate attention!*

Although a special electronic ABS diagnostic tester is necessary to properly diagnose the system, the home mechanic can perform a few preliminary checks before taking the vehicle to a dealer who is equipped with this tester.

a) *Check the brake fluid level in the reservoir.*

b) *Verify that the control module electrical connector is securely connected.*

c) *Check the electrical connectors at the hydraulic control unit.*

d) *Check the fuses.*

e) *Follow the wiring harness to each wheel and check that all connections are secure and that the wiring is not damaged.*

If the above preliminary checks do not rectify the problem, the vehicle should be diagnosed by a dealer service department or other qualified repair shop. Due to the rather complex nature of this system, all actual repair work must be done by the dealer service department or repair shop.

Chapter 10
Suspension and steering systems

Contents

Specifications

Torque specifications

	Ft-lbs

Front suspension

Strut upper mounting nuts	22 to 29
Strut-to-steering knuckle pinch bolt	72 to 97
Damper shaft nut	39 to 53
Control arm-to-frame	
1996 to 1999	
Front bolt	57 to 75
Rear bolt	72 to 97
2000 and later	
Front bolt	98
Rear bolt	85
Hub/bearing-to-steering knuckle bolts	61 to 78
Steering knuckle-to-balljoint pinch bolt nut	50 to 67
Stabilizer bar bracket-to-frame	22 to 29
Stabilizer link-to-stabilizer bar	
1996 to 2000	35 to 46
2001 and later	59
Stabilizer link-to-strut	57 to 75
Subframe (cradle)-to-body bolts	57 to 75

Torque specifications (continued)

Ft-lbs (unless otherwise indicated)

Note: *One foot-pound (ft-lb) of torque is equivalent to 12 inch-pounds (in-lbs) of torque. Torque values below approximately 15 ft-lbs are expressed in inch-pounds, since most foot-pound torque wrenches are not accurate at these smaller values.*

Rear suspension

Sedan
Shock absorber upper nut	19 to 25
Stabilizer bar bracket	25 to 33
Strut-to-spindle pinch bolt	50 to 67
Control arm mounting nuts	50 to 67
Tension strut mounting nuts	35 to 46
Upper arm-to-body bolts	73 to 97
Hub and bearing assembly retaining nut	188 to 254

Wagon
Shock absorber upper nut	19 to 25
Shock absorber-to-spindle nut	50 to 67
Stabilizer bar bracket-to-arm	14 to 19
Stabilizer bar link-to-body	44 to 59
Lower arm-to-spindle	50 to 67
Lower arm-to-body	40 to 52
Tension strut mounting nuts	35 to 46
Hub and bearing assembly retaining nut	190 to 255

Steering system

Axle shaft retaining nut	170 to 202
Intermediate shaft-to-steering column shaft nuts	17 to 20
Intermediate shaft-to-steering gear input shaft bolt	31 to 37
Power steering hose-to-gear fitting	25 to 30
Steering gear mounting bolt nuts	72 to 97
Steering wheel-to-steering shaft	
1996 to 1999, nut	25 to 34
2000 through 2003, pinion bolt	156 in-lbs
2004 and later, bolt	30
Tie-rod end-to-steering knuckle*	35 to 46
Wheel lug nuts	85 to 105

Tighten to the minimum specified torque, then align the next castellation in the nut with the cotter pin hole by further tightening.

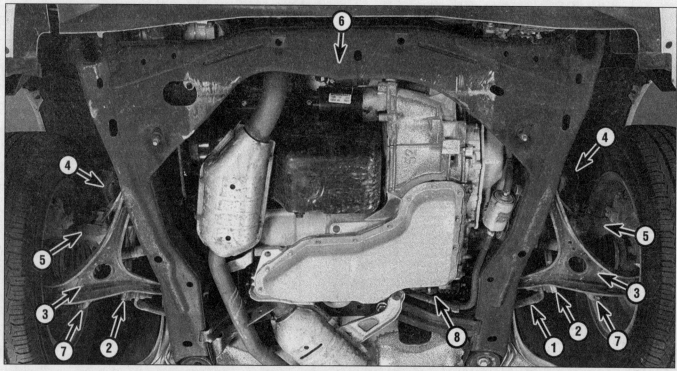

1.1 Front suspension and steering components

1	Stabilizer bar	4	Strut and coil spring assembly	7	Tie-rod end
2	Stabilizer bar link	5	Steering knuckle and hub assembly	8	Steering gear
3	Control arm	6	Subframe		

1.2 Rear suspension components (sedan)

1	Stabilizer bar	3	Control arms	5	Spindle
2	Strut and coil spring assembly	4	Tension strut		

1   General information

Refer to illustrations 1.1 and 1.2

The front suspension on these models is a MacPherson strut design **(see illustration)**. The steering knuckle on each side is located by a lower control arm. A stabilizer bar connects the left control arm to the right control arm, minimizing body lean during cornering.

The rear suspension on sedans uses MacPherson struts **(see illustration)**. Lateral movement is controlled by two parallel arms on each side, with longitudinal tension struts between the body and the rear spindles. Body lean is controlled by a stabilizer bar.

The rear suspension on station wagons consists of upper and lower control arms (one each per side), coil springs, tension struts (one per side), shock absorbers, spindles and a stabilizer bar.

The rack-and-pinion steering gear is located behind the engine and transaxle on the subframe. The gear actuates the steering arms, which are integral with the steering knuckles. All models covered by this manual have power steering as standard equipment. The steering column is connected to the steering gear through an articulated intermediate shaft. The steering column is designed to collapse in case of an accident.

Note: *These vehicles use a combination of*

standard and metric fasteners on the various suspension and steering components, so it would be a good idea to have both types of tools available when beginning work.
Warning 1: *Do not work or place any part of your body under the vehicle when it is supported only by a jack. Jack failure could result in severe injury or death.*
Warning 2: *Whenever any of the suspension or steering fasteners are loosened or removed they must be inspected and if necessary, replaced with new ones of the same part number or of original equipment quality and design. Torque specifications must be followed for proper assembly and component retention. Never attempt to heat, straighten or weld any suspension or steering component. Instead, replace any bent or damaged part with a new one.*

2   Front stabilizer bar - removal and installation

Refer to illustrations 2.2 and 2.4
Note: *This procedure requires two floor jacks.*

Removal

1   Loosen the front wheel lug nuts on both wheels. Raise the front of the vehicle and support it securely on jackstands placed

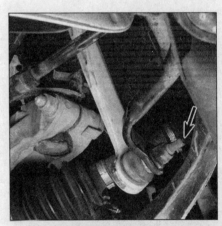

2.2 To separate the link from the stabilizer, use an 8 mm wrench on the hex-head end of the ballstud (arrow) to keep it from turning while loosening the retaining nut

under the reinforced area behind the subframe. Remove the front wheels.
2   Disconnect the stabilizer bar link from the strut and the stabilizer bar **(see illustration)**. If only the stabilizer bar is to be removed, it is not necessary to disconnect the link from the strut bracket.
3   Remove the steering gear-to-subframe nuts and push the steering gear up off of the subframe (Section 22).

4   Place a floor jack under each side of the rear of the subframe. Remove the two rear subframe bolts and slowly lower the jacks a little at a time until the stabilizer bar bracket bolts are accessible **(see illustration)**.

5   Remove the stabilizer bar bracket bolts and pry the U-brackets off the bushings. The bushings can now be removed from the stabilizer bar, if desired, without removing the bar from the vehicle. If it is necessary to remove the bar, carefully guide it out from between the subframe and the body.

Installation

6   Clean the stabilizer bar in the area where the bushings ride. Position the bar on the subframe and fit the bushings over the bar in their approximate locations. Rubber lubricant can be used on the inside of the bushings to help them slide onto the bar more easily. Do not use a petroleum-based lubricant, which would cause the bushing rubber to deteriorate.

7   Push the U-brackets over the bushings and install the bolts, tightening them to the torque listed in this Chapter's Specifications.

8   Raise the subframe until it contacts the floorpan, then install the subframe bolts, tightening them to the torque listed in this Chapter's Specifications.

9   Attach the stabilizer bar link to the strut bracket and the bar. Tighten the nuts to the torque listed in this Chapter's Specifications.

10   Install the wheels and wheel nuts. Lower the vehicle and tighten the nuts to the torque listed in the Chapter 1 Specifications.

---

3   Control arm (front) - removal and installation

Refer to illustrations 3.2, 3.3 and 3.4

Removal

1   Loosen the wheel lug nuts on the side to be dismantled, raise the front of the vehicle, support it securely on jackstands, and remove the wheel.

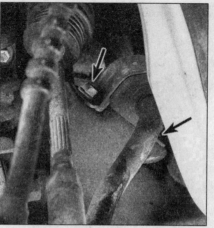

2.4 Support each side of the rear of the subframe with a floor jack, remove the two rear subframe mounting bolts, then lower the jacks just enough for access and remove the stabilizer bar bracket bolts (arrows)

2   Remove the lower balljoint nut. Separate the balljoint from the control arm with a balljoint separator tool **(see illustration)**.

3   Remove the control arm front mounting bolt and nut **(see illustration)**.

4   Remove the rear mounting bolt and nut, then remove the control arm from the vehicle **(see illustration)**.

Installation

5   Place the control arm into position on the subframe; then install the front and rear mounting bolts and nuts and tighten to the torque listed in this Chapter's Specifications.

6   Guide the balljoint stud into the control arm. Install the balljoint nut and tighten it to the torque listed in this Chapter's Specifications.

7   Install the wheel and the wheel nuts, lower the vehicle and tighten the lug nuts to the torque listed in the Chapter 1 Specifications.

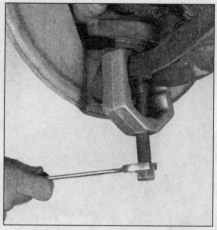

3.2 Remove the nut and use a balljoint separator to disconnect the lower balljoint from the control arm

---

4   Front strut assembly - removal and installation

Refer to illustration 4.2

Removal

1   Loosen the wheel lug nuts. Raise the vehicle and support it securely on jackstands placed under the subframe, then remove the front wheel.

2   Loosen, but do not remove the three strut upper mounting nuts **(see illustration)**.

3   Remove the speed sensor wiring guide clip and the brake hose bracket from the strut.

4   Disconnect the stabilizer bar link from the bracket on the strut.

5   Remove the steering knuckle (see Section 6).

6   Support the strut and remove the three upper strut mounting nuts from the tower.

7   Carefully guide the strut and spring assembly out of the wheel well. If the strut unit or coil spring is to be replaced, proceed to Section 5.

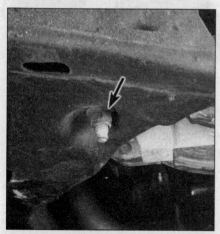

3.3 Two bolts attach the control arm to the subframe. Remove the front nut and bolt first (arrow)

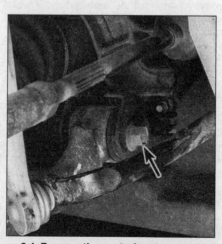

3.4 Remove the control arm rear nut and bolt (arrow), then lift the control arm out from the chassis

4.2 Begin strut removal by loosening, but not removing, the strut upper mounting nuts

5.3 Install spring compressors and tighten them in increments, alternating from side to side, until the spring force is released from the bearing and seat assembly

5.4 When the spring is compressed, remove the damper shaft nut. Use a Torx socket to keep the damper shaft from turning while loosening the nut

Installation

8   To install the strut, place it in position with the studs extending up through the shock tower. Install and loosely tighten the nuts.
9   Install the steering knuckle (see Section 6).
10   Connect the stabilizer bar link to the strut, tightening the nut to the torque listed in this Chapter's Specifications.
11   Connect the wiring clip and the brake hose bracket to the strut.
12   Tighten the three upper strut-to-shock tower mounting nuts to the torque listed in this Chapter's Specifications.
13   Install the wheel and lug nuts and lower the vehicle. Tighten the wheel lug nuts to the torque listed in the Chapter 1 Specifications.

5   Strut/shock absorber or coil spring - replacement

Refer to illustrations 5.3, 5.4, 5.5 and 5.6
1   If the strut assemblies show the telltale signs of wear (leaking fluid or loss of dampening capability) explore all options before beginning any work. The strut damper units are not serviceable and must be replaced if a problem develops. **Warning:** *Disassembling a strut is dangerous. Use only a high-quality spring compressor, which can be rented at most auto parts stores or equipment yards. Carefully follow all instructions furnished by the tool manufacturer or serious injury could result.*
2   Remove the strut and spring assembly as described in Section 4 (front) or Section 10 (rear). Mount the strut assembly in a vise with the jaws of the vise clamping onto the bracket for the stabilizer bar link.
3   Following the tool manufacturer's instructions, install the spring compressor on the spring and compress it enough to relieve all pressure from the spring seat **(see illustration)**. This can be verified by wiggling the spring.
4   Use a T-50 Torx socket to hold the damper shaft while loosening the shaft nut **(see illustration)**. Remove the nut and the concave washer.

5   Lift the bearing and seat assembly and upper mount off of the upper shaft **(see illustration)**. Check the bearing in the spring seat for smooth operation and replace it if necessary. **Warning:** *Never put your head or hands over or near the ends of the spring.*
6   Carefully remove the compressed spring assembly **(see illustration)**. Set the compressed spring in a safe place, where it cannot cause injury or damage if the tool breaks or comes loose.
7   Slide the dust boot, washer, and rubber jounce bumper off the shaft.
8   Assemble the strut beginning with the jounce bumper, dust boot, washer and spring, then the spring seat and bearing cap top mount assembly. Note that the larger concave washer is installed below the mount.
9   Install the upper shaft nut and tighten it to the torque listed in this Chapter's Specifications while holding the shaft with the Torx socket.
10   Install the strut and spring assembly on the vehicle as explained in Section 4 (front) or Section 10 (rear).

5.5 Lift the bearing and seat assembly off the end of the shaft

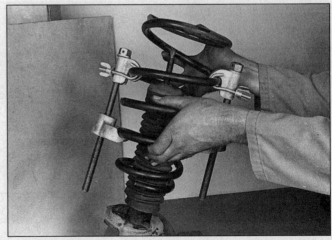

5.6 Remove the compressed spring. Use extreme caution when handling the spring

6   Steering knuckle and hub - removal and installation

Refer to illustrations 6.4, 6.7 and 6.8

Warning: *Brake system dust may contain asbestos, which is harmful to your health. Never blow it out with compressed air and don't inhale any of it. Do not, under any circumstances, use petroleum-based solvents to clean brake parts. Use brake system cleaner only.*

Removal

1   Remove the hubcap and loosen the driveaxle/hub nut. Loosen the wheel nuts, raise the vehicle and support it securely on jackstands. Remove the wheel.

2   Refer to Chapter 9 and remove the brake caliper and support it with a piece of wire. Remove the brake disc from the hub.

3   Detach the tie-rod end from the steering knuckle (see Section 26).

4   Remove the ABS wheel speed sensor mounting bolt, then move the sensor out of the way **(see illustration)**.

5   Detach the control arm from the steering knuckle (see Section 3).

6   Remove the driveaxle/hub nut and push the driveaxle from the hub with a two-jaw puller (see Chapter 8).

7   Mark the relationship of the strut to the steering knuckle **(see illustration)**. This will simplify assembly.

8   Remove the strut-to-steering knuckle pinch bolt **(see illustration)**.

9   Wiggle the knuckle and hub assembly off the strut. If it is stuck, tap the assembly off the strut with a brass hammer.

10   If necessary, remove the hub and bearing from the steering knuckle (see Section 7).

Installation

11   If it was removed, install the hub and bearing (see Section 7).

12   Install the knuckle and hub assembly onto the end of the strut, aligning the blade on the strut with the pinch joint in the knuckle. Align the index mark made in Step 7.

13   Install the strut-to-steering knuckle pinch bolt, but do not tighten it at this time.

14   Refer to Chapter 8 and install the driveaxle into the hub.

15   Pull down on the control arm and insert the balljoint stud into the steering knuckle. Install the balljoint nut and tighten it to the torque listed in this Chapter's Specifications.

16   Tighten the strut-to-knuckle pinch bolt to the torque listed in this Chapter's Specifications.

17   Attach the tie-rod end to the steering knuckle arm (see Section 26).

18   Install the brake disc and caliper (see Chapter 9).

19   Install the driveaxle/hub nut and tighten it securely, but not fully yet.

20   Install the wheel and lug nuts. Lower the vehicle and tighten the lug nuts to the torque listed in the Chapter 1 Specifications. Tighten the driveaxle/hub nut to the torque listed in the Chapter 8 Specifications. Pump the brake pedal several times to reseat the brake pads.

7   Hub and bearing assembly (front) - removal and installation

Removal

1   Remove the hubcap and loosen the driveaxle/hub nut. Loosen the wheel nuts, raise the vehicle and support it securely on jackstands. Remove the wheel.

2   Refer to Chapter 9 and remove the brake caliper and support it with a piece of wire. Remove the brake disc from the hub.

3   Detach the tie-rod end from the steering knuckle (see Section 26).

4   Remove the ABS wheel speed sensor mounting bolt, then move the sensor out of the way **(see illustration 6.4)**.

5   Detach the control arm from the steering knuckle (see Section 3).

6   Remove the driveaxle/hub nut and push the driveaxle from the hub with a two-jaw puller (see Chapter 8).

6.4 Remove the mounting bolt (arrow) and pull the ABS wheel speed sensor out of the knuckle

7   Remove the three hub and bearing bolts from the back of the steering knuckle. If the hub/bearing sticks in the knuckle, pry it free.

Installation

8   Clean the area on the steering knuckle where the hub/bearing assembly seats.

9   Position the hub/bearing on the steering knuckle and install the bolts, tightening them to the torque listed in this Chapter's Specifications.

10   The remainder of installation is the reverse of removal. Tighten the balljoint stud nut and the tie-rod end nut to the torque values listed in this Chapter's Specifications. Tighten the wheel lug nuts to the torque listed in the Chapter 1 Specifications. Tighten the driveaxle/hub nut to the torque listed in the Chapter 8 Specifications.

8   Rear coil spring (wagon) - removal and installation

Removal

1   Loosen the wheel lug nuts, raise the vehicle and support it securely on jackstands. Remove the wheel.

6.7 Paint an index mark on the strut where it meets the steering knuckle as a reference for position on assembly

6.8 Remove the strut-to-steering knuckle pinch bolt (arrow)

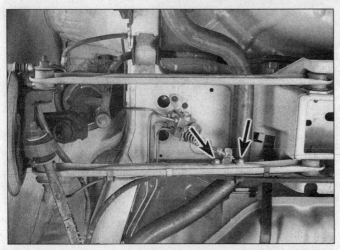

10.3 Remove the bolts (arrows), then separate the proportioning valve control rod from the control arm

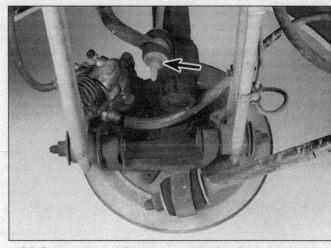

10.5 Remove the stabilizer bar mounting brackets, then remove the nut and bushing (arrow) to separate the bar from the link

2   Position a floor jack under the outer end of the suspension lower arm and raise it slightly.

3   Attach a coil spring compressor tool to the spring and tighten it so the spring is slightly compressed.

4   Unbolt the brake hose bracket from the frame.

5   Unbolt the stabilizer bar bracket from the suspension lower arm.

6   Remove the shock absorber lower mounting nut and bolt.

7   Wire the upper arm and spindle to the frame to prevent it from dropping down.

8   Detach the spindle from the lower arm (see Section 14).

9   Slowly lower the floor jack and remove the compressed spring. Set the spring in a safe place. **Warning:** *Keep the ends of the spring pointed away from your body.* Remove the lower insulator from the lower arm.

Installation

10   Inspect the spring insulators for damage and replace them if necessary. Check the spring for distortion and heavy nicks, which will warrant replacement.

11   Push the spring insulator into the lower arm. Place the upper insulator on top of the coil spring. Guide the coil spring into place, making sure it seats properly on the lower arm.

12   Raise the lower arm into position while guiding the upper end of the coil spring into place.

13   Connect the lower arm to the spindle, making sure the marks on the adjusting cam and the lower arm are lined-up. Don't fully tighten the bolts yet.

14   Remove the coil spring compressor from the spring.

15   The remainder of installation is the reverse of removal. Raise the lower arm to simulate normal ride height and tighten the bolts/nuts to the torque listed in this Chapter's Specifications.

16   Install the wheel and lug nuts. Tighten the lug nuts to the torque listed in the Chap-

ter 1 Specifications. Have the wheel alignment checked and, if necessary, adjusted.

9   Rear shock absorber (wagon) - removal and installation

Removal

1   Loosen the wheel lug nuts, raise the rear of the vehicle and support it securely on jackstands. Block the front wheels and remove the rear wheels.

2   Position a floor jack under the lower control arm and raise it slightly, just enough to support some of the weight. **Warning:** *The jack must remain in this position throughout the entire procedure.*

3   Remove the rear compartment access panel, then loosen the shock absorber upper mounting nut. If the nut is rusted or extremely tight, apply penetrating oil and allow it to soak in for a few minutes. It may also be necessary to clamp a pair of locking pliers onto the damper shaft to prevent it from turning. Do not use pliers on the shaft if the shock is going to be reinstalled. Remove the nut, washer, and rubber insulator bushing.

4   Remove the lower shock absorber mounting bolt and nut, then compress the shock absorber to remove it. **Note:** *A considerable amount of effort is required to compress the gas-filled shock for removal.*

Installation

5   Install a new washer and insulator bushing onto the shock absorber shaft, then insert the top of the shock through the opening in the vehicle body.

6   Push up on the shock to compress it until the lower bracket aligns with the mounting hole on the suspension arm. Install the lower mounting bolt and nut and tighten it to the torque listed in this Chapter's Specifications.

7   Install the upper rubber insulator bushing, washer, and nut. Tighten the nut to the torque listed in this Chapter's Specifications.

8   Install the wheel and lug nuts. Lower the

vehicle and tighten the lug nuts to the torque listed in the Chapter 1 Specifications.

10   Rear strut assembly (sedan) - removal and installation

Refer to illustrations 10.3 and 10.5

Removal

1   Refer to Chapter 11 and remove the trim panel from the parcel shelf in the passenger compartment. Then loosen, but do not remove, the three strut retaining nuts.

2   Loosen the rear wheel lug nuts, raise the rear of the vehicle and support it securely on jackstands, block the front wheels, and remove the rear wheels.

3   On 1996 to 2000 models, remove the bolts that attach the brake proportioning valve to the suspension arm **(see illustration)**.

4   Disconnect the brake hose bracket from the strut, then position the hose out of the way.

5   Remove the stabilizer bar bracket from the body, then remove the nut and washer to separate the stabilizer bar from the link **(see illustration)**.

6   Remove the tension strut-to-spindle nut, washer and bushing (see Section 11). Move the spindle assembly to the rear far enough to free the tension strut from the spindle.

7   To prevent damaging the brake line and hose when the shock is removed, tie the spindle and brake assembly to the chassis using wire.

8   Remove the spindle-to-strut pinch bolt.

9   Use a screwdriver to spread the pinch joint slightly to loosen the bond between the spindle and strut.

10   Wiggle the knuckle and hub assembly off of the strut. If it is stuck, gently tap the assembly off the strut using a brass hammer.

11   Remove the three upper mounting nuts and lift the strut assembly from the vehicle. Be careful not to let the assembly fall out as the upper mounting nuts are removed.

Installation

12   Fit the stabilizer bar link into the shock absorber bracket, install the washer and nut, and tighten to the torque listed in this Chapter's Specifications.

13   Guide the strut assembly up into the wheel well, inserting the three mounting studs into the holes in the shock tower, then start the three upper retaining nuts by hand. Do not tighten the nuts at this time.

14   Align the blade on the back side of the strut with the pinch joint slot on the spindle and insert the strut into the spindle.

15   Remove the wire installed to secure the spindle and brake, install the pinch bolt and tighten it to the torque listed in this Chapter's Specifications.

16   Pull back on the spindle and insert the tension strut into position. Install the bushing, washer, and nut. Tighten the nut to the torque listed in this Chapter's Specifications.

17   Attach the stabilizer bar to the stabilizer bar link and fit the brackets to attach the bar to the chassis. Tighten all of the fasteners to the torque listed in this Chapter's Specifications.

18   Connect the brake hose bracket to the strut and tighten the bolt securely.

19   Position the proportioning valve rod on the suspension arm, then install and tighten the attachment bolts.

20   Tighten the three upper mounting nuts to the torque listed in this Chapter's Specifications. Install the trim panel.

21   Install the wheel, lower the vehicle, and tighten the lug nuts to the torque listed in the Chapter 1 Specifications.

11   Rear tension strut and bushings (sedan) - removal and installation

Refer to illustration 11.2

Removal

1   Loosen the wheel nuts. Raise the rear of the vehicle and support it securely on jackstands. Block the front wheels and remove the rear wheels.

2   Remove the nut that attaches the tension strut to the spindle **(see illustration)**. Use a wrench on the flat area of the tension strut to keep it from turning. Make a note of the washer and bushing arrangement for reference on assembly.

3   Remove the nut that attaches the tension strut to the body. Again, keep the strut from turning by holding it with a wrench on the flat portion. Keep the front bushings separate from the rear bushings; they are different.

4   Pull the spindle and strut assembly toward the rear of the vehicle to free the tension strut. At the same time, pull the tension strut from the front mount and remove it from the vehicle. **Note:** *If the spindle and strut can't be pulled back far enough to remove the tension strut, loosen the strut/shock absorber upper mounting nuts.*

Installation

5   Check the rubber bushings for cracks and wear. Replace them if necessary.

6   Place the concave washers and inner bushings on the ends of the tension strut, with the dished portion of each washer toward the center.

7   Insert the tension strut, with inner washers and bushings in place, into the body mount. Assemble the bushing, washer, and nut onto the strut, but do not tighten the nut at this time.

8   Pull the spindle and suspension strut assembly back, then insert the front of the tension strut into the spindle. Assemble the bushing, washer, and nut onto the strut. Tighten both the spindle and body attachment nuts to their specified torque.

9   Install the wheel and lug nuts and lower the vehicle to the ground. Tighten the lug nuts to the torque listed in the Chapter 1 Specifications.

10   If they were loosened, tighten the strut upper mounting nuts to the torque listed in this Chapter's Specifications.

12   Rear tension strut and bushings (wagon) - removal and installation

Note: *The rear wheel alignment should be checked and adjusted whenever the rear tension strut or bushings are removed or replaced.*

Removal

1   Loosen the wheel lug nuts, raise the rear of the vehicle and support it securely on jackstands. Block the front wheels, and remove the rear wheels.

2   Remove the nut that attaches the tension strut to the spindle. Use a wrench on the flat area of the tension strut to keep it from turning. Make a note of the washer and bushing arrangement for reference on assembly. On 2000 and later models, use a jack under the lower control arm to put some upward tension on the rear suspension, then remove the lower shock absorber bolt and the lower control arm-to-spindle bolt.

3   Remove the nut that attaches the tension strut to the body. Again, keep the strut from turning by holding it with a wrench on the flat portion. Keep the front bushings separate from the rear bushings - they are different.

4   Pull the spindle and strut assembly toward the rear of the vehicle to free the tension strut. At the same time, pull the tension strut from the front mount and remove it from the vehicle. On 2000 and later models, pull the spindle from the lower control arm enough to get the tension strut out.

Installation

5   Place the washers and inner bushings on the ends of the tension strut.

6   Insert the front end of the tension strut into the body mount. Assemble the bushing,

11.2 Remove the tension strut nut (arrow)

washer, and nut onto the strut but do not tighten the nut at this time.

7   Pull the spindle and strut assembly back, then insert the end of the tension strut into the spindle. Assemble the bushing, washer, and nut onto the strut. Tighten both the spindle and body attachment nuts to the torque listed in this Chapter's Specifications.

8   Install the wheel and lug nuts and lower the vehicle to the ground. Tighten the lug nuts to the torque listed in the Chapter 1 Specifications.

9   Have the rear wheel alignment checked and, if necessary, adjusted.

13   Rear wheel spindle (sedan) - removal and installation

Refer to illustration 13.5

Removal

1   Loosen the wheel lug nuts, raise the rear of the vehicle and support it securely on jackstands. Block the front wheels and remove the rear wheel.

2   Disconnect the brake hose bracket from the strut.

3   Separate the strut from the spindle (Section 10).

4   If the vehicle has rear disc brakes, remove the brake caliper and hang it out of the way with a piece of wire, then remove the brake disc, disc splash shield, wheel hub, and wheel speed sensor. If the vehicle has drum brakes, remove the brake drum, wheel hub (see Section 15), and brake backing plate. Hang the brake assembly out of the way on a piece of wire. Refer to Chapter 9 for brake part removal procedures.

5   Remove the nuts and bolts that attach the suspension control arms to the spindle **(see illustration)**.

6   Detach the tension strut from the spindle (see Section 11).

7   Remove the spindle-to-strut pinch bolt.

8   Pull the spindle to the rear far enough to clear the tension strut; then slide it off the strut. If necessary, tap the spindle off the strut with a brass hammer.

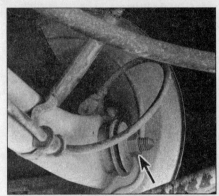

13.5 Remove the control arm-to-spindle nut (arrow), push the bolt in as far as possible, and slide the control arm off the end of the bolt

Installation

9   Inspect the tension strut bushings for cracks, deformation and signs of wear. Replace them if necessary.
10   Install, but do not tighten, the suspension arm bolts to the holes on the spindle.
11   Place the spindle on the tension strut end; then push it up onto the strut. Align the gap in the pinch joint with the blade on the strut. Insert the spindle-to-strut pinch bolt and tighten it finger tight.
12   Install the outer tension strut bushing, washer and new nut. Do not tighten the nut at this time.
13   Place the control arms onto the spindle bolts, fit the bushings, install the washers and new nuts. Tighten the nuts by hand.
14   Place a jack under the spindle and raise it to simulate normal ride height.
15   Tighten the control arm-to-spindle nuts to the torque listed in this Chapter's Specifications.
16   Tighten the tension strut nut to the torque listed in this Chapter's Specifications.
17   Tighten the strut-to-spindle pinch bolt to the torque listed in this Chapter's Specifications.
18   Assemble the brake to the spindle (see Chapter 9).
19   Attach the brake hose bracket to the strut.
20   Install the wheel and lug nuts. Lower the

vehicle and tighten the lug nuts to the torque listed in the Chapter 1 Specifications. Pump the brake pedal several times to seat the pads or shoes before driving the vehicle.

14   Rear wheel spindle (wagon) - removal and installation

Removal

1   Loosen the wheel nuts, raise the rear of the vehicle and support it securely on jackstands, block the front wheels, and remove the rear wheels.
2   Place a floor jack under the lower arm and raise it slightly. **Warning:** *The jack must remain in this position throughout the entire procedure.*
3   Disconnect the brake hose bracket from the frame.
4   If the vehicle has rear disc brakes, remove the brake caliper and hang it out of the way with a piece of wire, then remove the brake disc, disc splash shield, wheel hub, and wheel speed sensor. If the vehicle has drum brakes, remove the brake drum, wheel hub (see Section 15), and brake backing plate. Hang the brake assembly out of the way on a piece of wire. Refer to Chapter 9 for brake part removal procedures.
5   Detach the tension strut from the spindle (see Section 12).
6   Remove the upper balljoint retaining nut; separate the balljoint from the spindle using a balljoint separator.
7   Mark the relationship of the adjusting cam to the rear suspension arm. This will ensure correct rear wheel alignment after reassembly. Remove the nuts and bolts attaching the suspension arm to the spindle.
8   Remove the spindle from the vehicle.

Installation

9   Position the spindle onto the tension strut and suspension arm; make sure all the bushings are in place.
10   Install the suspension arm-to-spindle bolts but do not tighten the bolts at this time.
11   Insert the upper balljoint stud through the spindle opening, then install the nut and tighten it to the torque listed in this Chapter's Specifications.

12   Make sure the floor jack is supporting the suspension at approximately the normal ride height, then tighten the suspension arm bolts to the torque listed in this Chapter's Specifications.
13   Tighten the tension strut nut to the torque listed in this Chapter's Specifications.
14   Assemble the brake to the spindle (see Chapter 9).
15   Attach the brake hose bracket to the frame.
16   Install the wheel, lower the vehicle, and tighten the lug nuts to the torque listed in the Chapter 1 Specifications. Pump the brake pedal several times to seat the pads or shoes before driving the vehicle.

15   Hub and bearing assembly (rear) - removal and installation

1   These models have sealed rear wheel bearings which do not require maintenance. The bearing assemblies should be replaced when they become noisy or develop excessive play.
2   Loosen the wheel lug nuts, raise the rear of the vehicle and support it securely on jackstands. Block the front wheels and remove the rear wheels.
3   If the vehicle has disc brakes, remove the brake caliper and hang it out of the way with a piece of wire, then remove the brake disc (see Chapter 9). If the vehicle has drum brakes, remove the brake drum (see Chapter 9).
4   Remove the grease cap from the center of the hub. Discard the cap.
5   Remove and discard the hub retaining nut and remove the hub and bearing assembly from the spindle.
6   Installation of the hub and bearing assembly is basically the reverse of removal. Tighten a new hub retaining nut to the torque listed in this Chapter's Specifications and install a new grease cap. Be sure to pump the brake pedal several times to seat the pads or shoes before driving the vehicle.

16   Rear suspension control arms (sedan) - removal and installation

Refer to illustrations 16.3 and 16.5

Removal

1   Loosen the wheel lug nuts, raise the rear of the vehicle and support it securely on jackstands. Block the front wheels and remove the rear wheel.
2   On 1996 to 2000 models, remove the bolts attaching the brake proportioning valve to the suspension arm **(see illustration 10.3)**.
3   Detach the parking brake cable from the suspension arm **(see illustration)**.
4   Remove the nut and washer that retains the suspension control arm to the spindle.
5   Trace around the adjustment cams on the inboard control arm mounts with paint or

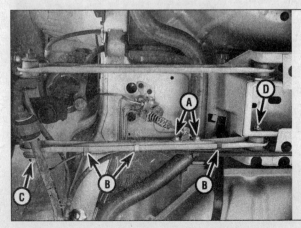

16.3 Rear suspension arm details (sedan models)

A   *Proportioning valve bolts*
B   *Parking brake cable clips*
C   *Control arm-to-spindle nut and bolt*
D   *Control arm-to-body nut and bolt*

16.5   Mark the position of the control arm adjustment cams (arrows) as an installation reference before removing the mounting bolt and nut

19.2   Remove the nut (arrow) that attaches the stabilizer bar to the link on both sides of the vehicle

a felt-tip pen to mark their position for assembly. Remove the nut and bolt that attach the suspension arm to the body **(see illustration)**.

6   Remove the suspension control arm from the car.

Installation

7   If you're installing either left side suspension arm or the front right side control arm, position the arm with the offset facing up and the flanged side toward the rear. If the right side rear suspension arm is being installed, the offset must also face up, but the flanged side must face the front of the vehicle.

8   Place the suspension arm in position and install the arm-to-body bolt; do not tighten it at this time. Make sure the adjustment cams are lined-up with the marks you made in Step 5.

9   Connect the suspension arm to the spindle and install the washer and nut. Don't tighten the nut fully at this time.

10   Raise the spindle with a floor jack to simulate normal ride height. Tighten the suspension arm-to-body nut(s) and the arm-to-spindle nut(s) to the torque listed in this Chapter's Specifications.

11   Connect the parking brake cable to the suspension arm.

12   Install and tighten the bolts that attach the brake proportioning valve to the suspension arm.

13   Install the wheel and lug nuts and lower the vehicle. Tighten the lug nuts to the torque listed in the Chapter 1 Specifications.

14   Drive the vehicle to an alignment shop to have the rear wheel alignment checked and, if necessary, adjusted.

17   Rear suspension upper arm (wagon) - removal and installation

Removal

1   Loosen the wheel nuts, raise the rear of

the vehicle and support it securely on jackstands, block the front wheels, and remove the rear wheel.

2   Support the lower suspension arm with a floor jack. **Warning:** *The jack must remain in this position throughout the entire procedure.*

3   Remove the bolt attaching the brake hose bracket to the frame.

4   Remove the upper balljoint nut, then separate the balljoint from the suspension arm with a balljoint removal tool.

5   Remove the nuts attaching the upper suspension arm to the body.

6   Remove the suspension arm-to-body bolts and lift the arm from the vehicle.

Installation

7   Place the upper suspension arm in position on the vehicle. Install the bolts and nuts, but don't fully tighten them at this time.

8   Install the upper balljoint into the suspension arm and tighten the nut to the torque listed in this Chapter's Specifications.

9   Raise the floor jack to simulate normal ride height and tighten the upper suspension arm-to-body nut and bolt to the torque listed in this Chapter's Specifications.

10   Fit the brake hose bracket to the frame, then install and tighten the bolt.

11   Install the wheel and lug nuts. Lower the vehicle and tighten the lug nuts to the torque listed in the Chapter 1 Specifications.

12   Drive the vehicle to an alignment shop to have the rear wheel alignment checked and, if necessary, adjusted.

18   Rear suspension lower arm (wagon) - removal and installation

Removal

1   Perform Steps 1 through 9 of Section 8 and remove the coil spring.

2   Remove the lower arm-to-frame nut and bolt and remove the arm.

Installation

3   Position the lower arm in the mounting bracket and install the bolt and nut with the bolt head facing the front of the vehicle. Do not tighten the nut at this time.

4   Install the coil spring (see Steps 10 through 15 of Section 8).

5   Install the wheel and lug nuts. Lower the vehicle and tighten the lug nuts to the torque listed in the Chapter 1 Specifications.

6   Drive the vehicle to an alignment shop to have the rear wheel alignment checked and, if necessary, adjusted.

19   Rear stabilizer bar and links (sedan) - removal and installation

Refer to illustrations 19.2 and 19.3

1   Raise the rear of the vehicle and support it securely on jackstands. Block the front wheels.

2   Remove the nut, washer, and bushing that attach the stabilizer bar to the link on both sides of the vehicle **(see illustration)**.

19.3   Remove the bolts (arrow) that attach the stabilizer bar brackets to the body on both sides of the vehicle, then remove the bar

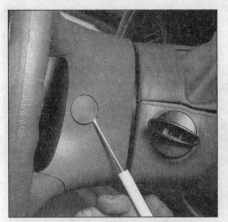

21.3a Pry off the two trim covers on the back of the steering wheel, remove the nuts, and lift the airbag module away from the steering wheel . . .

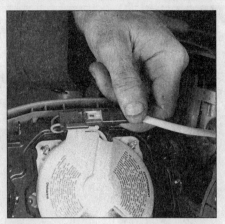

21.3b . . . then disconnect the electrical connector and remove the airbag module

21.4 Remove the Torx-head bolt that attaches the steering wheel to the steering column

3   Remove the bolts attaching the stabilizer bar brackets to the body **(see illustration)** and lift the stabilizer bar from the vehicle.
4   Remove the nut attaching the stabilizer bar link to the strut; then remove the link from the vehicle.
5   Inspect the bracket and link bushings for wear, hardness, and cracking. Replace bushings if necessary. Be sure to inspect the link upper bushings as well.
6   Installation is the reverse of removal. Tighten the fasteners to the torque listed in this Chapter's Specifications.

20   Rear stabilizer bar and links (wagon) - removal and installation

1   Raise the rear of the vehicle and support it securely on jackstands placed under the lower suspension arms (this is necessary to relieve the tension from the stabilizer bar links. Block the front wheels. Shake the vehicle to make sure it is firmly supported by the jackstands.
2   Remove the nuts and bolts attaching the stabilizer bar brackets to the lower suspension arms.

3   Clean any dirt and debris off the ends of the stabilizer bar, then slide the brackets off the bar.
4   Remove the bolts attaching the stabilizer bar link to the body, then remove the bar and links from the vehicle.
5   Slide the bushings and link assemblies off the bar and inspect them for deterioration. Replace any worn parts.
6   Installation is the reverse of removal. Be sure to tighten the fasteners to the torque listed in this Chapter's Specifications.

21   Steering wheel - removal and installation

Refer to illustrations 21.3a, 21.3b, 21.4, 21.5a and 21.5b
Warning: *The steering wheel contains an airbag with a backup power supply that will trigger the device in case of a vehicle electrical failure. This backup power supply must be completely discharged before removing the steering wheel to prevent accidental deployment of the airbag, which may result in serious injury and damage to the steering wheel, column, and dash panel. Because an explosive*

device is used to inflate the airbag, it may be best to have any services requiring the removal of the steering wheel performed by a dealer service department or other qualified shop.

1996 to 1999 models, and 2004 and later models
Note: *Appearance and/or fastener types and electrical connector types may vary among the two different model year vehicles in this procedure, but the same steps are followed. Be sure to keep note of any changes and install all components in the order they were in before removal.*

Removal
1   Disconnect the negative battery cable, then disconnect the positive battery cable.
2   **Warning:** *Wait at least one full minute after the battery is completely disconnected before proceeding. This is necessary to allow the backup power supply for the airbag to dissipate.*
3   From the back side of the steering wheel, pry off the two caps, then remove the two nuts that attach the airbag module to the steering wheel **(see illustration)**. Remove the airbag module by slowly pulling it straight back. When the module clears the steering wheel, disconnect the wiring harness connector and lift the airbag module off the steering wheel **(see illustration)**. **Warning 1:** *When handling the airbag module, carry it with the trim side facing away from your body. Set the airbag aside in a safe location, with the trim side facing up.* **Warning 2:** *On 2004 and later models, there is more than one electrical connector at the airbag module. Be sure to mark the proper location of each connector before removal to aid in reinstallation. These connections MUST be connected in the right order and not be reversed when installing.*
4   Remove the steering wheel retaining bolt **(see illustration)**.
5   Make an index mark on the steering wheel and the end of the steering shaft to use as a reference on assembly **(see illustration)**. Use a steering wheel puller to separate the wheel from the shaft **(see illustration)**. Take

21.5a Mark the relationship of the steering wheel to the steering shaft

21.5b Use a steering wheel puller to separate the steering wheel from the steering column - DO NOT hammer on the wheel or shaft in an attempt to remove it

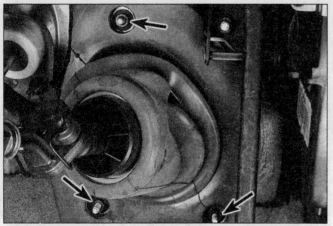

22.2 Remove the nuts (arrows) attaching the steering column boot to the firewall, pull back the boot, and disconnect the intermediate shaft-to-steering gear coupler

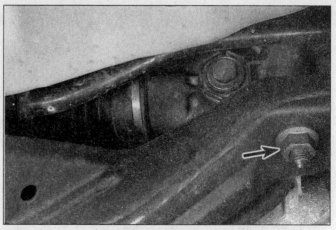

22.8 Two nuts and bolts attach the steering gear to the subframe (arrow). Remove the nuts and push the bolts up through the subframe

care to avoid damaging the sliding contact for the airbag when removing the wheel. Carefully guide the sliding contact wiring through the steering wheel as you remove the wheel from the shaft.

Installation

6   Align the index mark on the steering wheel hub with the mark on the shaft and slip the wheel onto the shaft. Carefully guide the wiring for the airbag sliding contact through the steering wheel as you slip the wheel onto the steering shaft.
7   Install the mounting bolt and tighten it to the torque listed in this Chapter's Specifications.
8   Plug in the electrical connector and install the airbag module. Tighten the screws to the torque listed in this Chapter's Specifications.
9   Connect the positive battery cable, then connect the negative battery cable.

2000 through 2003 models

10   On these models, the steering wheel is not retained to the steering shaft by a conventional nut, but by a pinion shaft/bolt behind the wheel. The steering wheel is removed as a unit with the airbag module attached behind it.
11   **Warning:** *Wait at least one full minute after the battery is completely disconnected before proceeding. This is necessary to allow the backup power supply for the airbag to dissipate.*
12   Position the steering wheel in the straight-ahead position.
13   Remove the rectangular plastic access panel (on the right side of the steering wheel) with a thin-bladed tool.
14   Disconnect the electrical connectors for the airbag module and the horn/accessory connector(s).
15   The pinion shaft, which is visible after the plastic access panel is removed, has a longer head than a standard bolt. Using a socket and ratchet, loosen the pinion bolt 20

to 30 full revolutions. If the wheel does not pull off easily, continue turning the pinion shaft bolt until it does.
16   Pull the steering wheel from the column, taking care to feed the electrical connectors and wires through the upper column as the wheel is removed.
17   Installation is the reverse of the removal procedure. **Warning:** *Make sure the wiring is carefully fed through as the wheel is installed, and not pinched during the installation. Tighten the pinion to the torque value listed in this Chapter's Specifications.*

22   Steering gear - removal and installation

Refer to illustrations 22.2, 22.8 and 22.16
Warning 1: *The steering wheel contains an airbag with a backup power supply that will trigger the device in case of a vehicle electrical failure. This backup power supply must be completely discharged before removing the steering wheel to prevent accidental deployment of the airbag, which may result in serious injury and damage to the steering wheel, column, and dash panel. Because an explosive device is used to inflate the airbag, it may be best to have any services requiring the removal of the steering wheel performed by a dealer service department or other qualified shop.*
Warning 2: *Make sure the steering shaft is not turned while the steering gear is removed or you could damage the airbag system. To prevent the shaft from turning, place the ignition key in the LOCK position or thread the seat belt through the steering wheel and clip it into place.*
Note: *This procedure requires two floor jacks.*
1   Disconnect the negative battery cable, then disconnect the positive battery cable.
Warning: *Wait at least one full minute after the battery is completely disconnected before proceeding. This is necessary to allow the backup power supply for the airbag to dissipate.*

2   From inside the car, remove the nuts attaching the steering column boot to the firewall on 1996 to 1999 models **(see illustration)**. Then, pull the boot back to expose the intermediate shaft coupling. Mark the intermediate shaft, the steering gear input shaft and the steering column shaft so they can be reassembled in the same position. On 2000 and later models, the pinch bolt is accessed through the engine compartment after removing the air cleaner assembly and the engine anti-roll bar (se Chapter 2). Turn the steering wheel to the right a half-turn to expose the pinch bolt.
3   Remove the pinch bolt from the intermediate shaft coupling, then center the steering wheel and turn the key to the Off position, and finally, separate the intermediate shaft from the steering gear.
4   Loosen the lug nuts on both front wheels. Raise the vehicle and support it on jackstands. Place the jackstands under the reinforced area behind the engine cradle (subframe). Jackstand position must allow enough room for the engine cradle to drop down to remove the steering gear.
5   Block the rear wheels and remove both front wheels.
6   Refer to Chapter 4 and disconnect the exhaust oxygen sensor electrical connectors, then remove the exhaust system Y-pipe.
7   Detach the tie-rod ends from the steering knuckle (see Section 26).
8   Remove the two steering gear mounting nuts from under the engine cradle (subframe) **(see illustration)**.
9   Place a floor jack under each side of the rear of the engine cradle and raise it just high enough to support the weight of the drivetrain. Then remove the two rear engine cradle subframe mounting bolts.
10   Slowly lower the floor jacks until there is about four inches of clearance between the cradle and the body.
11   Separate the push-pins from the power steering hose bracket and remove the heat shield. Then remove the power steering hose bracket.

22.16 Once everything is disconnected from the steering gear, carefully guide it out of the chassis through the left side wheel opening

23.5 Remove the power steering pump and bracket from an OHV V6 engine as an assembly

12   Remove the left side stabilizer bar link. Refer to Section 2.

13   Disconnect the electrical connector for the auxiliary actuator on the steering gear.

14   Push the steering gear up to dislocate the mounting bolts from the holes; then rotate the gear to gain access to the fluid-pressure and return hose fittings on the gear.

15   Place a drain pan under the steering gear, then disconnect the two hose fittings at the gear and allow the unit to drain.

16   Rotate the steering gear forward to bring the input shaft out of its hole in the firewall; then carefully guide the steering gear out the left side wheel well (see illustration).

17   Installation is the reverse of removal. Be sure to connect the positive battery cable first and the negative battery cable second. Tighten all mounting fasteners to the torque values listed in this Chapter's Specifications. Bleed the power steering system as explained in Section 25. Drive the car to an alignment shop to have the front wheel alignment checked and adjusted.

23   Power steering pump assembly - removal and installation

Refer to illustrations 23.5 and 23.6

Removal

1   Disconnect the cable from the negative terminal of the battery.

2   Refer to Chapter 3 and remove the coolant expansion tank.

3   Place a drain pan under the power steering pump. Remove the drivebelt (Chapter 1) and the alternator on models with an OHV V6 engine (see Chapter 5) (see illustration).

4   Remove the pressure and return hoses from the pump and allow the fluid to drain. Plug the hoses and the pump ports to prevent contaminants from entering the pump or system.

5   For an OHV V6 engine, remove the idler pulley from the pump support and the bracket mounting bolt located under the tensioner mounting. Then remove the nuts from

the two pump bracket mounting studs and lift the bracket and pump assembly from the engine (see illustration). For an OHC V6 engine, remove the three pump mounting bolts and lift the pump off of the engine.

6   Remove the pulley nut from the pump shaft. Then use a power steering pump pulley puller to remove the pulley from the pump (see illustration). Note: *On some 2000 and later models, it is necessary to remove the power steering pump pulley in-vehicle, then unbolt and remove the pump from the engine.*

Installation

7   Press the pulley onto the pump shaft using a pulley installation tool. The pulley should fit onto the shaft so the front of the hub is flush with the end of the shaft, but no further.

8   For an OHV V6 engine, assemble the pump in the mounting bracket and install it onto the engine. For an OHC V6 engine, bolt the pump to the engine.

9   Connect the hoses to the pump, make sure they are not twisted or out of position, and tighten the fittings securely.

10   Reinstall the cooling system expansion

tank, then refer to Chapter 1 and fill and bleed the cooling system.

11   Install the rest of the parts in the reverse order of removal.

12   Fill the power steering reservoir with the recommended fluid and bleed the system following the procedure described in Section 25.

24   Power steering hoses - replacement

Refer to illustrations 24.3 and 24.8

1   Disconnect the battery negative cable.

2   Refer to Chapter 1 and remove the drivebelt.

3   Place a drain pan under the power steering pump, then disconnect the hose to be replaced from the pump (see illustration) and allow the fluid to drain. Plug the hose and the pump port to prevent contaminants from entering the pump or system.

4   Raise the vehicle and support it securely on jackstands.

5   From underneath, remove the splash shield and disconnect any brackets or tie-wraps that hold the hose to the body.

23.6 Special tools are used to remove and install the power steering pump pulley

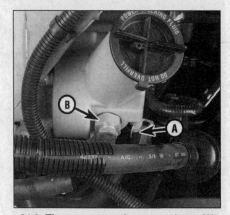

24.3 The power steering return hose (A) connects to the pump with a hose clamp, while the pressure hose (B) has a threaded fitting

24.8 Replace the power steering fluid filter, located in the return line, whenever contaminants have circulated in the system

6   Disconnect the hose to be replaced from the steering gear and plug the hose and the steering gear port. A crows-foot wrench may be needed for access to some hose fittings.
7   Allow the fluid to drain, then work the hose out of the engine compartment.
8   Replace the power steering fluid filter on the return hose along with the hose or any time contaminants have entered the system **(see illustration)**.
9   Installation is the reverse of removal. Keep the hoses and ports plugged until you are ready to connect the fittings and make sure the fittings are clean.
10   Fill the power steering reservoir with the recommended fluid and bleed the system following the procedure described in Section 25.

25 Power steering system - bleeding

1   Anytime a power steering fluid line has been disconnected, the power steering sys-

tem must be bled to remove all air and obtain proper steering performance.
2   With the front wheels in the straight ahead position, check the power steering fluid level and, if low, add fluid until it reaches the Cold mark on the dipstick.
3   Start the engine and allow it to run at fast idle. Slowly turn the steering wheel from side to side several times without hitting the stops. This works the air out of the system. Check the fluid level in the reservoir and add fluid as needed while bleeding.
4   When the air is worked out of the system, return the wheels to the straight ahead position and check the fluid level again.
6   Road test the vehicle to be sure the steering system is working normally and free of noise.
7   Recheck the fluid level to be sure it is up to the Hot mark on the dipstick while the engine is at normal operating temperature. Refer to Chapter 1 and add fluid if needed.

26 Tie-rod ends - removal and installation

Refer to illustrations 26.2a, 26.2b and 26.4

Removal

1   Loosen the wheel nuts, raise the front of the vehicle and support it securely on jackstands. Block the rear wheel, and set the parking brake. Remove the front wheel.
2   Hold the tie-rod with a pair of pliers and break the jam nut loose with a wrench **(see illustration)**. Back-off the jam nut and mark the position of the tie-rod end on the tie-rod with paint **(see illustration)**.
3   Remove and discard the cotter pin, then loosen the nut on the tie-rod end ballstud.
4   Separate the tie-rod end from the steering knuckle with a puller **(see illustration)**.
5   Remove the nut, detach the tie-rod end from the steering knuckle and unscrew the tie-rod end from the tie-rod.

Installation

6   Thread the tie-rod end onto the tie-rod to the marked position and insert the tie-rod ballstud into the steering knuckle arm. Tighten the jam nut securely.
7   Install the nut on the stud and tighten it to the torque listed in this Chapter's Specifications. Install a new cotter pin.
8   Install the wheel, lower the vehicle, and tighten the lug nuts to the torque listed in the Chapter 1 Specifications.
9   Have the alignment checked by a dealer service department or an alignment shop.

27 Steering gear boots - replacement

1   Loosen the wheel nuts, raise the front of the vehicle and support it securely on jackstands. Block the rear wheels and set the parking brake. Remove the front wheel.
2   Detach the tie-rod end from the steering knuckle, then remove the tie-rod end from the tie-rod (see Section 26). Also remove the jam nut.
3   Remove the steering gear boot clamps

26.2a Loosen the tie-rod end jam nut . . .

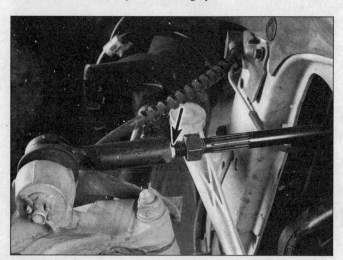

26.2b . . . and mark the position of the tie-rod end on the tie-rod

26.4 A puller is used to separate the tie-rod end from the steering knuckle

and slide the boot off the tie-rod.

4   Before installing the new boot, wrap the threads and serrations on the end of the steering rod with tape to prevent damage to the small end of the new boot during installation.

5   Slide the new boot into position on the steering gear until it seats in the groove in the steering rack and install new clamps.

6   Remove the tape and install the tie-rod end (see Section 26).

7   Install the wheel and lug nuts, lower the vehicle and tighten the lug nuts to the torque listed in the Chapter 1 Specifications.

8   Have the alignment checked by a dealer service department or an alignment shop.

28   Wheels and tires - general information

Refer to illustration 28.1

All vehicles covered by this manual are equipped with metric-sized fiberglass or steel-belted radial tires **(see illustration)**. Use of other size or type of tires may affect the ride and handling of the vehicle. Don't mix different types of tires, such as radials and bias belted, on the same vehicle as handling may be seriously affected. It's recommended that tires be replaced in pairs on the same axle, but if only one tire is being replaced, be sure it's the same size, structure and tread design as the other.

Because tire pressure has a substantial effect on handling and wear, the pressure on all tires should be checked at least once a month or before any extended trips (see Chapter 1).

Wheels must be replaced if they are bent, dented, leak air, have elongated bolt holes, are heavily rusted, out of vertical symmetry or if the lug nuts won't stay tight. Wheel repairs that use welding or peening are not recommended.

Tire and wheel balance is important to the overall handling, braking and performance of the vehicle. Unbalanced wheels can adversely affect handling and ride characteristics as well as tire life. Whenever a tire is installed on a wheel, the tire and wheel should be balanced by a shop with the proper equipment.

29   Wheel alignment - general information

Refer to illustration 29.1

A wheel alignment refers to the adjustments made to the wheels so they are in proper angular relationship to the suspension and the ground. Wheels that are out of proper alignment not only affect vehicle control, but also increase tire wear. The alignment angles normally measured are camber, caster and toe-in **(see illustration)**. Toe-in is the only angle normally adjusted on the front or the

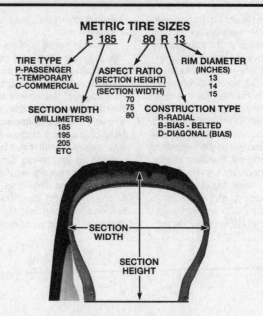

28.1 Metric tire size code

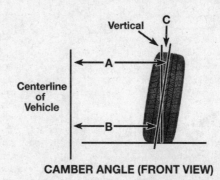

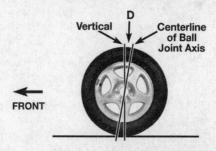

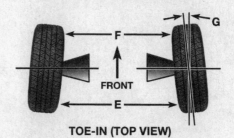

29.1 Front end alignment angles

A minus B = C (degrees of camber)
D = caster angle (degrees)

E minus F = toe-in (measured in inches)
G = toe-in (expressed in degrees)

rear. The other angles should be measured to check for bent or worn suspension parts. If required, the front camber and caster can be adjusted, but only after modifying the alignment plate on the strut tower. The rear camber can also be adjusted, but it requires modifying the mounting bolt holes for the inner ends of the rear suspension arms.

Getting the proper wheel alignment is a very exacting process, one in which complicated and expensive machines are necessary to perform the job properly. Because of this, you should have a technician with the proper equipment perform these tasks. We will, however, use this space to give you a basic idea of what is involved with a wheel alignment so you can better understand the process and deal intelligently with the shop that does the work.

Toe-in is the turning in of the wheels. The purpose of a toe specification is to ensure parallel rolling of the wheels. In a vehicle with zero toe-in, the distance between the front edges of the wheels will be the same as the distance between the rear edges of the wheels. The actual amount of toe-in is normally only a fraction of an inch. On the front end, toe-in is controlled by the tie-rod end position on the tie-rod. On the rear end, it's controlled by a cam on the inner end of the rear suspension arm (sedan models) or a cam on the lower arm-to-spindle front mounting bolt (wagon models). Incorrect toe-in will cause the tires to wear improperly by making them scrub against the road surface.

Camber is the tilting of the wheels from vertical when viewed from one end of the vehicle. When the wheels tilt out at the top, the camber is said to be positive (+). When the wheels tilt in at the top the camber is negative (-). The amount of tilt is measured in degrees from vertical and this measurement is called the camber angle. This angle affects the amount of tire tread which contacts the road and compensates for changes in the suspension geometry when the vehicle is cornering or traveling over an undulating surface.

Caster is the tilting of the front steering axis from the vertical. A tilt toward the rear is positive caster and a tilt toward the front is negative caster.

Chapter 11 Body

Contents

1 General information

These models have a unibody construction, with front and rear frame side rails incorporated into the floor pan. The unibody supports the body structure, front and rear suspension systems, and other mechanical components. The drivetrain is supported by a subframe, which bolts to the unibody structure.

Certain body components are particularly vulnerable to accident damage and can be unbolted and repaired or replaced. These bolt-on parts include the body moldings, bumpers, doors, hood, and trunk lid or station wagon lift gate.

This chapter includes only general body maintenance practices and body panel repair procedures that are within the scope of the home mechanic.

2 Body - maintenance

1   The condition of the vehicle body is very important because the resale value depends a great deal on it. Repairing a neglected or damaged body is much more difficult than repairing mechanical components. The hidden areas of the body, such as the wheel wells, frame, and engine compartment, are equally important although they do not require attention as frequently as the rest of the body.

2   It is a good idea to have the underside of the body steam cleaned once a year, or every 12,000 miles. This removes all traces of dirt and oil so that the chassis, body, and frame can be inspected carefully for rust, damaged brake lines, frayed electrical wires, damaged cables and other potential prob-

lems. The suspension components should be lubricated after steam cleaning; refer to Chapter 1.

3   At the same time, clean the engine and the engine compartment with a steam cleaner or water-soluble degreaser.

4   The wheel wells should be given close attention because undercoating can peel away, and stones and dirt thrown up by the tires can chip the paint and allow rust to set in. If rust is found, clean the surrounding area down to bare metal and apply an anti-rust paint.

5   External body panels should be washed about once a week. Wet the vehicle thoroughly to soften the dirt, then wash it down with a soft sponge and plenty of clean soapy water. If the dirt is not washed off, it can wear down the paint.

6   Remove spots of road tar or asphalt

with a soft cloth and a commercial tar remover, which is available at auto parts stores.

7   To protect the paint and exterior finish, wax the body and chrome trim once every six months. If a chrome cleaner is used to remove rust from any chrome plated parts, remember that the cleaner also removes part of the chrome so use it sparingly.

3   Vinyl trim - maintenance

Never clean vinyl trim with detergents, caustic soap, or petroleum-based cleaners. Mild detergent, such as dish soap, and water works fine. Use a soft brush to clean dirt that may be ingrained in the vinyl. Wash the vinyl as often as the rest of the vehicle.

After cleaning, applying a high-quality rubber and vinyl protectant improves appearance and helps prevent oxidation and cracks. The protectant also can be applied to weather-strips, vacuum lines, rubber hoses, and the tires. Rubber parts often fail as a result of chemical degradation. Keeping them clean and coated with protectant can extend their life.

4   Upholstery and carpets - maintenance

1   Remove the floor mats and clean the interior of the vehicle at least once every three months. Vacuum the upholstery and carpets to remove loose dirt and debris.

2   Leather upholstery requires special care. Remove stains with warm water and a very mild soap solution, such as saddle soap. Use a clean, damp cloth to remove the soap; then wipe again with a dry cloth. Never use alcohol, gasoline, solvent, or any petroleum product to clean leather upholstery.

3   After cleaning, treat leather upholstery with a leather wax. Never use car wax on leather upholstery. Use rubber and vinyl protectant to treat interior vinyl trim.

4   In areas where the interior of the vehicle is subject to bright sunlight, cover leather seats with a sheet if the vehicle is to be left out for any length of time.

5   Body repair - minor damage

See photo sequence

Repair of minor scratches

1   Repairing a superficial scratch that does not penetrate the paint down to the metal of the body is fairly simple. Lightly rub the scratched area with a fine rubbing compound to remove loose paint and built-up wax. Then, thoroughly rinse the area with clean water.

2   Apply touchup paint to the scratch with a small brush. Continue to apply thin layers of

paint until the surface of the paint in the scratch is level with the surrounding paint. Allow the new paint at least two weeks to completely dry and harden. Then blend it into the surrounding paint by rubbing with a very fine rubbing compound. Finally, apply a coat of wax to the scratch area.

3   A scratch that has penetrated the paint and exposed the metal of the body, possibly causing the metal to rust, requires a different repair technique. Remove all loose rust from the bottom of the scratch with a pocket knife, then apply rust-inhibiting paint to prevent the formation of rust in the future. Coat the scratched area with glaze-type filler, available at auto parts stores, using a rubber or nylon applicator. If needed, the filler can be mixed with thinner to provide a very thin paste, which is ideal for filling narrow scratches. Before the glaze filler in the scratch hardens, wrap a piece of smooth cotton cloth around the tip of a finger. Dip the cloth in thinner and quickly wipe it along the surface of the scratch. This ensures that the surface of the filler is slightly hollow. Once the filler dries completely, the scratch can be painted as described earlier in this section.

Repair of dents

4   The first step in repairing a dent is to pull the metal out until the affected area is as close to its original shape as possible. Completely restoring the metal to is original shape is impossible because the metal in the damaged area has been stretched from the impact. Try to bring the level of the dent up to a point about 1/8-inch below the level of the surrounding metal. Where the dent is very shallow, it is not worth trying to pull it out at all.

5   If the back of the dent is accessible, it can be gently hammered out from behind using a soft-faced hammer. When using this method, place a block of wood and hold it firmly against the opposite side of the metal. The wooden block absorbs the hammer blows to keep the metal from stretching.

6   If the dent is in a section of the body that has double layers of sheet metal, or is inaccessible from behind, a different technique is required. Drill several small holes through the metal inside the damaged area in deepest sections of the dent. Then, partially install long, self-tapping screws into the holes. Run the screws in just deep enough for them to get a good grip in the metal. Grip the screw heads with locking pliers and pull out to remove the dent. Start at the center, or deepest point of the dent and work your way toward the edges. Avoid pulling the metal out too far because the screws leave a slightly raised ridge around the drill holes.

7   The next stage of repair is to remove the paint from the damaged area and from an inch or so of the surrounding metal. This can be done using either a wire brush or sanding disk and a drill motor, or by hand with sandpaper. Prepare the metal by making score marks on the surface of the bare metal with a

screwdriver or the tang of a file. This provides a good grip for the filler material. To complete the repair, see the subsection on filling and painting later in this section.

Repair of rust holes or gashes

8   Remove all paint from the area and from an inch or so of the surrounding metal using either a sanding disk or wire brush mounted in a drill motor or by hand using sandpaper.

9   After the paint is removed, you can determine the severity of the corrosion and decide whether to replace the whole panel or repair it. New body panels are not as expensive as most people think, and it is often quicker to install a new panel than to repair large areas of rust.

10   Remove all trim pieces except those that can act as a guide to the original shape of the damaged body, such as headlamp trim rings. Use metal snips or a hacksaw blade to remove any loose metal or sections that are severely rusted. Carefully hammer in the edges of the hole to create a slight depression for the filler material.

11   Use a stiff wire brush to remove the powdery rust from the surface of the metal. If the back of the rusted area is accessible, wire brush it as well, then treat it with rust-inhibiting paint.

12   Block the hole in some way to provide a backing for the filler. This can be done with sheet metal riveted or screwed into place or by stuffing the hole with wire or nylon mesh.

13   Once the hole is blocked, the area is ready to be filled and painted.

Filling and painting

14   Although many types of body fillers are available, body repair kits that contain filler paste and a tube of resin hardener are best suited for this kind of repair work. A wide, flexible plastic or nylon applicator is needed to obtain a smooth and contoured surface finish on the filler material. Mix up a small amount of filler on a clean piece of wood or cardboard. Use the hardener sparingly and carefully follow the instructions on the package, otherwise the filler will set incorrectly.

15   Apply the filler paste to the prepared area with the flexible applicator. Draw the applicator across the surface of the filler to achieve the desired contour and to keep the surface level. Once the contour approximates the original shape, stop working the filler. Continuing will cause the filler to stick to the applicator. Apply the filler in thin layers and allow it to sit about 20 minutes between coats. Repeat the process until the level of the filler is just above the surrounding metal.

16   After the filler has hardened, remove the excess with a body file. Then, use progressively finer grades of sandpaper to obtain the desired finish. Start with a 180-grit paper and work down to 600-grit wet-or-dry paper. Wrap the sandpaper around a flat rubber or wooden block to keep the working surface completely flat. Keep wet-or-dry paper wet by dipping or rinsing it in clean water as you

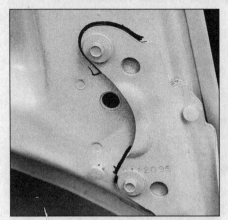

8.2 Draw alignment marks on the hood around the hinge flanges and bolts before removal so they can be reinstalled in the same position

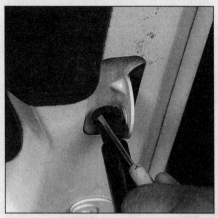

8.3 Use a screwdriver to pry out the retaining clip; then disconnect the hood support strut

8.10 Adjust the position of the front of the hood by turning the two outer bumper stops on the radiator support in or out to change their height

work. This ensures a very smooth finish in the final stage.

17   After sanding, the repair area should be surrounded by a ring of bare metal, which in turn should be encircled by the finely feathered edge of good paint. Rinse the repair area with clean water until all of the dust produced by the sanding operation is gone.

18   Spray the entire area with a light coat of primer to reveal any imperfections in the surface of the filler. Repair the imperfections with fresh filler paste or glaze filler; then smooth the surface with sandpaper again. Repeat this spray-and-repair procedure until you are satisfied that the surface of the filler and the feathered edge of the paint are perfect. Rinse the area with clean water and allow it to dry completely.

19   The repair area is now ready for painting. Spray painting must be done in a warm, dry, windless and dust-free atmosphere. These conditions are easy to create if you have access to a large indoor work area, but if you are forced to work outdoors, you should pick the day very carefully. When working indoors, douse the floor in the work area with water to settle the dust. If the repair area is confined to one body panel, mask off the surrounding panels. This helps to minimize the effects of a slight paint color mismatch. Trim pieces, such as chrome strips or door handles also need to be masked off or removed. Use masking tape and several thickness of newspaper to mask parts and adjacent areas.

20   Before spraying, shake the paint can thoroughly, then spray a test area until the spray painting technique is mastered. Cover the repair area with a thick coat of primer. The thickness should be built up using several thin layers of primer rather than one thick one. Use 600-grit wet-or-dry sandpaper to sand the surface of the primer until it is very smooth. While doing this, keep the work wet by thoroughly rinsing it with water. Periodically rinse the wet-or-dry sandpaper as well. Allow each coat of primer to dry before spraying additional coats.

21   Spray the top coat in a similar manner; build up the thickness with several thin layers of paint. Begin spraying in the center of the repair area and use a circular motion to work out from there. Paint the entire repair area and about two inches of the surrounding original paint. Remove all masking material 10 to 15 minutes after spraying the final coat of paint. Allow the new paint at least two weeks to harden. Then use a very fine rubbing compound to blend the edges of the new paint into the existing paint. Finally, apply a coat of wax.

6   Body repair - major damage

1   Major body damage must be repaired by an auto body shop equipped to perform unibody repairs. These shops have the specialized equipment and expertise to do the job properly.

2   When damage is extensive, the body must be checked for proper alignment or the handling characteristics of the vehicle may be adversely affected, which can cause other components to wear quickly.

3   Because all of the major body parts, such as the hood, fenders, and doors, are separate and replaceable units, any seriously damaged parts should be replaced rather than repaired. Often, replacement parts can be found in a wrecking yard at considerable savings over the cost of new parts.

7   Hinge and lock - maintenance

Lubricate the hinges and latch assemblies on the doors, hood, and trunk every 3000 miles, or every three months, whichever comes first. Apply a few drops of light oil or lock lubricant. Lubricate door latch striker plates with a thin coat of grease to reduce wear and ensure free movement. Lubricate the inside door and trunk lock mechanisms with graphite lubricant spray.

8   Hood - removal, installation and adjustment

Refer to illustrations 8.2, 8.3, and 8.10

Note: The hood is heavy and awkward to remove and install. At least two people should do this job.

1   Open the hood and cover the cowl area of the body and fenders with blankets or pads to protect the paint and sheet metal as the hood is lifted off.

2   Trace alignment marks around the edges of the hood hinges and mounting bolts with a felt-tip pen to provide an alignment reference for installation (see illustration).

3   Have an assistant support the hood, then pry off the hood support retaining clips with a small screwdriver (see illustration). Then disconnect the upper ends of the hood support struts.

4   Remove the hinge-to-hood mounting bolts.

5   With the help of an assistant, carefully lift the hood clear of the body.

6   To install the hood, lift it into position with the help of an assistant; then loosely fit the mounting bolts.

7   Align the hinge and bolt reference marks; then tighten the bolts. Install the hood support struts and check the alignment.

8   The hood can be adjusted fore-and-aft and side-to-side by loosening the two hood-to-hinge bolts at each hinge. Reposition the hood and tighten the bolts.

9   To raise or lower the rear of the hood, loosen the hinge-to-body bolts. Raise or lower the hinge as necessary to make the hood flush with the surrounding panels. Then tighten the hinge-to-body bolts.

10   Raise or lower the front of the hood by adjusting the two outer bumper stops on the radiator support; the two inner bumpers are not adjustable. To adjust, grasp the rubber portion of the bumper stops and turn them in or out to reposition them (see illustration).

These photos illustrate a method of repairing simple dents. They are intended to supplement *Body repair - minor damage* in this Chapter and should not be used as the sole instructions for body repair on these vehicles.

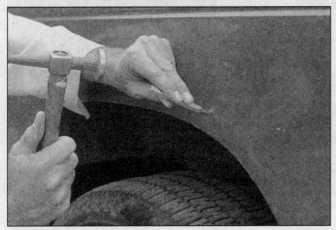

1 If you can't access the backside of the body panel to hammer out the dent, pull it out with a slide-hammer-type dent puller. In the deepest portion of the dent or along the crease line, drill or punch hole(s) at least one inch apart . . .

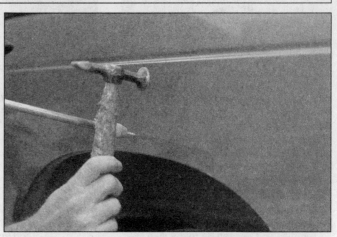

2 . . . then screw the slide-hammer into the hole and operate it. Tap with a hammer near the edge of the dent to help 'pop' the metal back to its original shape. When you're finished, the dent area should be close to its original contour and about 1/8-inch below the surface of the surrounding metal

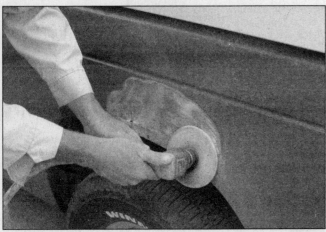

3 Using coarse-grit sandpaper, remove the paint down to the bare metal. Hand sanding works fine, but the disc sander shown here makes the job faster. Use finer (about 320-grit) sandpaper to feather-edge the paint at least one inch around the dent area

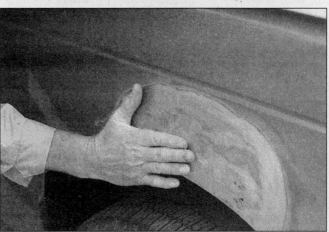

4 When the paint is removed, touch will probably be more helpful than sight for telling if the metal is straight. Hammer down the high spots or raise the low spots as necessary. Clean the repair area with wax/silicone remover

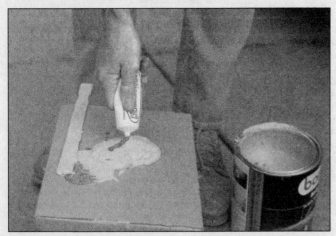

5 Following label instructions, mix up a batch of plastic filler and hardener. The ratio of filler to hardener is critical, and, if you mix it incorrectly, it will either not cure properly or cure too quickly (you won't have time to file and sand it into shape)

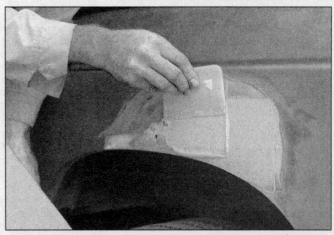

6 Working quickly so the filler doesn't harden, use a plastic applicator to press the body filler firmly into the metal, assuring it bonds completely. Work the filler until it matches the original contour and is slightly above the surrounding metal

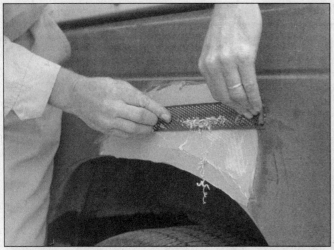

7   Let the filler harden until you can just dent it with your fingernail. Use a body file or Surform tool (shown here) to rough-shape the filler

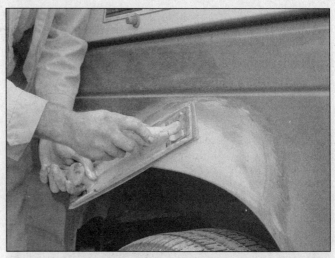

8   Use coarse-grit sandpaper and a sanding board or block to work the filler down until it's smooth and even. Work down to finer grits of sandpaper - always using a board or block - ending up with 360 or 400 grit

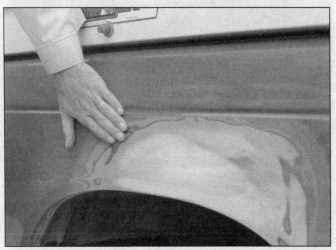

9   You shouldn't be able to feel any ridge at the transition from the filler to the bare metal or from the bare metal to the old paint. As soon as the repair is flat and uniform, remove the dust and mask off the adjacent panels or trim pieces

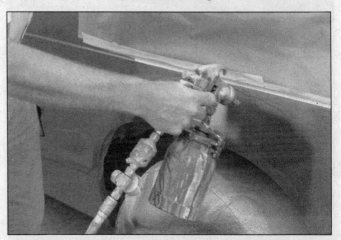

10   Apply several layers of primer to the area. Don't spray the primer on too heavy, so it sags or runs, and make sure each coat is dry before you spray on the next one. A professional-type spray gun is being used here, but aerosol spray primer is available inexpensively from auto parts stores

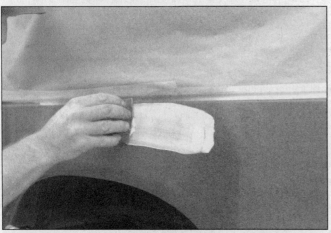

11   The primer will help reveal imperfections or scratches. Fill these with glazing compound. Follow the label instructions and sand it with 360 or 400-grit sandpaper until it's smooth. Repeat the glazing, sanding and respraying until the primer reveals a perfectly smooth surface

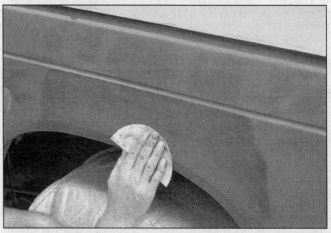

12   Finish sand the primer with very fine sandpaper (400 or 600-grit) to remove the primer overspray. Clean the area with water and allow it to dry. Use a tack rag to remove any dust, then apply the finish coat. Don't attempt to rub out or wax the repair area until the paint has dried completely (at least two weeks)

9.3 Remove the single screw (arrow) at the top of the wheel well that connects the two fender liner halves to the body

9.4 Three of the four plastic push pins that attach the fender liner to the frame are visible in this photo (arrows)

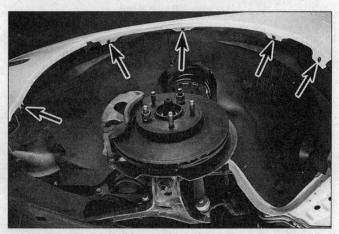

9.5 Remove the screws (arrows) attaching the liner to the fender, then pull the liner out of the wheel well

10.1 Draw alignment marks around the hood release latch mounting flange as a reference for assembly

9   Front fender liner - removal and installation

Refer to illustrations 9.3, 9.4, and 9.5

Warning: *Do not work or place any part of your body under the car when it is supported only by a jack. Jack failure could result in severe injury or death.*

1   Raise the front of the vehicle and support it securely on jackstands. Then, remove the appropriate front wheel.

2   From underneath the vehicle, remove the single screw attaching the fender liner to the radiator air deflector.

3   Remove the single screw at the top center of the fender liner that attaches the two halves of the liner to the body **(see illustration)**.

4   Remove the four plastic push pins that attach the fender liner to the body **(see illustration)**. To remove the pins, carefully pry them up with a small screwdriver, then use needle-nosed pliers to pull the pins from the fender liner.

5   Remove the screws that attach the fender liner to the fender **(see illustration)**. On 2000 and later models, remove the plastic

pushpins securing the front portion of the rocker panel molding, then remove the molding to allow removal of the rear half of the fender liner.

6   Firmly grasp the sides of the fender liner, pull it away from the fender well, and lower it from the vehicle.

7   To install, position the liner in the wheel well and install the four attachment screws. Fit the push pins in place, then push the centers in until they lock. Install the top center screw and lower air deflector screw. Fit the wheel and tire, lower the vehicle, and tighten the wheel nuts securely.

10   Hood release latch and cable - removal and installation

Refer to illustrations 10.1, 10.3, and 10.7

Latch

1   Mark the latch position by tracing around it with a felt-tip pen **(see illustration)**.

2   Remove the two retaining bolts, and lift the latch off of the support.

3   Disconnect the cable from the back of

the latch by squeezing the cable locking tangs with pliers **(see illustration)**, then slip the ball end of the cable out of the latch.

4   To install, connect the cable to the latch, fit the latch to the support, align the latch to the positioning mark, then fit and tighten the bolts.

10.3 Remove the latch mounting bolts, turn the latch over, and disconnect the cable by squeezing the lock tangs with pliers

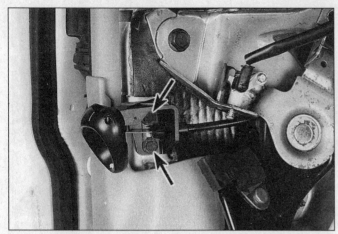

10.7 Remove the left kick panel; then remove the two hood cable release bracket attachment bolts (arrows)

11.1 Remove the two door check rod mounting bolts and wrap the end of the disconnected check rod to prevent damaging the paint

Cable

5   Working in the engine compartment, remove the latch and disconnect the cable as described above.

6   Attach a piece of thin wire, heavy string, or fishing line about eight feet long to the latch end of the cable.

7   Working in the passenger compartment, remove the left kick panel for access to the cable. Then remove the two cable mounting bracket retaining screws **(see illustration)** and carefully pry the sealing grommet out of the dash panel.

8   Pull the cable through into the vehicle interior, being careful not to pull the wire all the way through as well. Attach the wire or string to the new cable Then pull the wire from the engine compartment to guide the cable into position.

9   Connect the cable to the latch and install the latch as described above. Then install the mounting bracket in the passenger compartment.

11 Door - removal, installation, and adjustment

Refer to illustration 11.1, 11.4a, and 11.4b

Note: *Doors are heavy and awkward to remove and install. At least two people should do this job.*

1   Remove the two bolts that attach the check-rod assembly **(see illustration)**. Then wrap the end of the check rod with a rag to avoid scratching the paint.

2   Disconnect the wiring harness connector leading to the door. The connector on the driver's front door is secured with a screw. Peel back the rubber boot for access. On rear doors, remove the trim panel for access to the electrical connectors (Section 15).

3   Mark the position of the door hinge retaining bolts with paint or a felt-tip pen.

4   Have an assistant support the door, remove the hinge-to-door retaining bolts **(see illustrations)** and lift the door off the hinges.

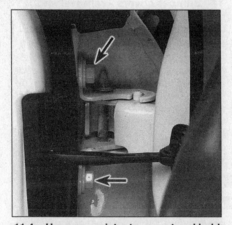

11.4a Have an assistant support and hold the door and remove the two upper hinge mounting bolts (arrows) . . .

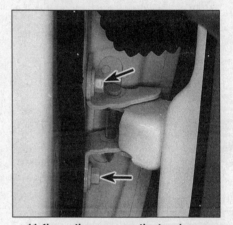

11.4b . . . then remove the two lower hinge mounting bolts (arrows) and lift off the door

5   To install, place the door up to the hinges, have an assistant hold it position, and install the bolts finger tight. Adjust the door until all of the bolts are in their marked positions, then tighten the bolts securely.

6   The door hinge mountings are enlarged and elongated for door alignment adjustment **(see illustration)**. To adjust the door position, loosen the bolts and nuts slightly and move the door to the desired position with a padded pry bar. Tighten the bolts securely and close the door to check the fit. Repeat the procedure until the door fits properly.

12 Trunk lid - removal, installation, and adjustment

Refer to illustrations 12.1 and 12.5

Note: *The trunk lid is heavy and awkward to remove and install. At least two people should do this job.*

1   Open the trunk lid and trace index marks around the hinge with paint or a felt-tip pen **(see illustration)**.

2   Have an assistant support the trunk lid,

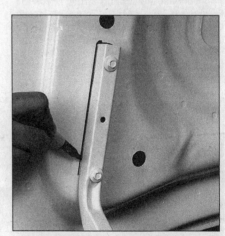

12.1 Make alignment marks on the trunk lid hinge mounting flange to ensure reinstallation in the same position

then loosen and remove the four lid-to-hinge bolts.

3   Lift the trunk lid clear of the hinges and remove it from the vehicle.

4   To install, lift the trunk lid into position,

have an assistant hold it in place, fit the hinge bolts, align the index marks, then tighten the bolts securely.

5   The trunk lid can be aligned by shifting it fore-and-aft and from side-to-side. Height adjustments are made at the hinge end by loosening the hinge screws and raising or lowering the trunk lid and at the outer edge by adjusting the bumper stops (**see illustration**).

6   Adjust the trunk lid for an even and parallel fit in the opening and for a flush fit with the surrounding panels. Be careful not to distort or mar the trunk lid or surrounding body panels.

13   Station wagon liftgate - removal, installation, and adjustment

Note: *The liftgate is heavy and awkward to remove and install. At least two people should do this job.*

1   Open the liftgate and support it in the open position.

2   Remove the trim panels covering the hinge mounts on the upper corners of the liftgate and unplug any electrical connectors.

3   Trace index marks around where the hinges attach to the body with paint or a felt-tip pen.

4   Disconnect the upper ends of the liftgate support struts by prying the spring clips off with a small screwdriver.

5   Have an assistant support the liftgate, then remove the bolts and nuts that attach the hinges to the body. Do not loosen or remove the Torx-head bolts. These are used to align the hinge assembly on the body.

6   To install, place the liftgate in position, have an assistant hold it, install the bolts, align the index marks, and tighten the bolts securely.

7   Connect the support struts, check the fit, and adjust as needed. To adjust, loosen the hinge-to-body bolts, shift the liftgate to the desired position, and tighten the bolts. Repeat the procedure until the gap between the liftgate and surrounding panels is even, then fit the trim panels.

12.5 Turn the trunk lid bumper stops to adjust the height so, when closed, the trunk lid is even with the rear fenders

14   Bumper covers - removal and installation

Note: *The bumper cover can be easily removed and replaced, but the support structure (bumper) behind the cover is spot welded to the body. Spot welds must be drilled out, the support pried off, and the weld area ground down to ensure a flush fit for the new part. Because these procedures require special equipment and skills, they are not detailed here*

Warning: *Do not work or place any part of your body under the car when it is supported only by a jack. Jack failure could result in severe injury or death.*

1   Raise the vehicle, support it securely on jackstands, then remove either the front or rear wheels depending upon which bumper is to be removed.

2   Disconnect the electrical harness connectors from the turn signal and side marker lamps.

Front

Refer to illustrations 14.4, 14.7, and 14.8

3   Open the hood and remove both head-

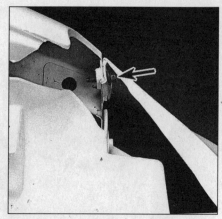

14.4 Remove the headlamp assemblies to reach the two hidden bumper cover-to-body screws. One screw (arrow) faces the front and the other (not shown) faces up

lamp assemblies (see Chapter 12).

4   Remove the screws inside the headlamp opening, one on each side, that attach the bumper to the fender (**see illustration**).

5   Working under the vehicle, remove the radiator air deflector panel. On models with fog lamps, disconnect the electrical connectors at the fog lamps.

6   Remove both inner fender liners as described in Section 9.

7   Remove the nuts, one on each side, that attach the bumper cover to the fenders (**see illustration**).

8   Working under the hood, remove the five bolts that secure the bumper cover to the radiator support (**see illustration**). On 2000 and later Taurus models, remove the four push pins securing the grille, then the push pins securing the bumper cover to the grille opening. On 2000 and later Sable models, the bumper cover is secured to the grille opening with clips.

9   With the help of an assistant, slide the bumper cover forward to remove it from the support structure.

10   Installation is the reverse of removal.

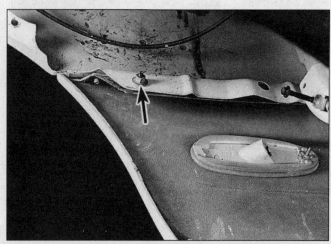

14.7 Remove the inner fender liner for access to the nut that attaches the bumper cover to the fender (arrow)

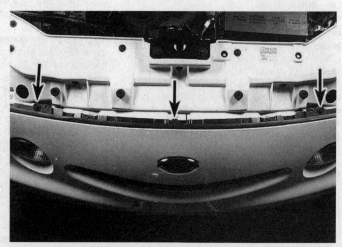

14.8 Remove the bolts attaching the bumper cover to the radiator support (arrows). The two outer bolts are not shown in this photo

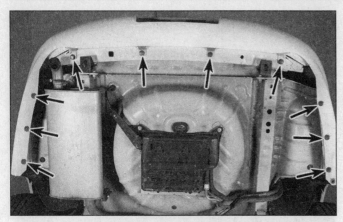

14.13 The bottom of the rear bumper cover attaches to the body with 10 plastic push pins

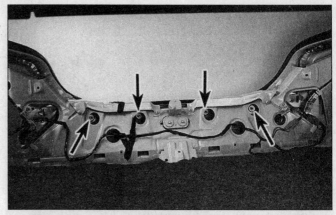

14.15 Eight rear bumper cover attachment nuts, four across the back (arrows) and two on either side, are removed from inside the trunk

Rear

Refer to illustrations 14.13 and 14.15

Note: *The following illustrations show a Sedan. Bumper cover removal on station wagons is similar.*

11   Working inside the right side wheel well opening, disconnect the fuel filler overflow hose from the bumper cover. Remove the screws and nut that attach the bumper cover to the quarter panel and the splash shield.

12   Working inside the left side wheel well opening, remove the screws and nut that attach the bumper cover to the quarter panel and the splash shield.

13   Working underneath the vehicle, remove the 10 push pins along the lower edge of the bumper cover **(see illustration)**. To remove the pins, carefully pry them up with a small screwdriver, then use needle-nose pliers to pull the pins out.

14   From inside the trunk, remove the scuff plate and the left and right side trim panels.

15   Remove the eight nuts that attach the bumper cover to the body **(see illustration)**. On 2000 and later Taurus models, there are only six nuts.

16   With the help of an assistant, slide the bumper cover back to remove it from the support structure.

17   Installation is the reverse of removal.

15   Door trim panel - removal and installation

Refer to illustrations 15.2, 15.5, 15.6a, 15.6b, and 15.8

1   Disconnect the battery ground (negative) cable.

2   Carefully pry off the trim cover behind the inside door pull handle **(see illustration)**.

3   Remove the plug covering the screw at the bottom of the door pull pocket, then remove the screw.

4   On 1996 to 1999 models and later models with optional Mach 40 speakers, remove the speaker grille cover at the lower front corner of the window, if equipped, by gently squeezing in on the sides to disengage the lock tabs, then lifting it off. On 2000 and later models, remove the five panel mounting screws: two along the bottom, two below the armrest, one each at the front edge and read edge, and one at the top-rear of the panel. The rear door panels on these models have only two screws, along the bottom.

5   Insert a large screwdriver, small pry bar, or trim-clip tool between the door panel and the door and gently lift out to disengage the clips one at a time along the bottom and sides of the trim panel **(see illustration)**. On

15.2 Carefully pry out and remove the trim panel behind the door pull handle

2000 and later models, there are push pins instead of clips.

6   With the clips disengaged, swing the bottom of the door panel out and reach behind the panel to disconnect the electrical connectors for the power windows, locks, mirrors and, on 2000 and later models, the speakers **(see illustrations)**.

7   Lift the panel straight up to remove it from the door.

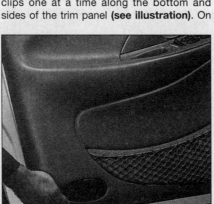

15.5 Use a screwdriver or a trim clip tool to pry the door trim panel clips out of the sheet metal

15.6a Once the clips are loose, swing the bottom of the door trim panel out from the door . . .

15.6b . . . then reach behind the panel to disconnect the electrical wiring to the window, lock, and mirror

15.8 A plastic watershield is glued onto the door to protect the trim panel. Remove it by carefully peeling it back

16.3 Remove the two bolts (arrows) that secure the handle assembly to the inside of the door

8   For access to the inner door, carefully peel back the plastic watershield **(see illustration)**. To install, place the watershield in position and press it into place.

9   Before installation, install any push pins or clips that may have come out during removal in the door panel.

10   Plug in any electrical connectors and lower the top of the panel into position in the door; then push the front edge straight in to engage the guide pins.

11   Press the door panel into place until the all clips and push pins are seated. Install the retaining screw and the cover plug. On 2000 and later models, replace the seven panel screws.

12   Replace the speaker grille and snap the door release cover panel back into place (1996 to 1999 models).

13   Reconnect the negative battery cable.

16   Door handle, lock cylinder and latch - removal and installation

1   Raise the door window, remove the door trim panel as described in Section 15 and carefully peel back the watershield.

Outside handle and lock cylinder

Refer to illustrations 16.3 and 16.6

2   Apply tape around the outside of the door, around the handle area, to prevent scratching the paint as the handle is removed.

3   From inside the door, remove the two screws securing the handle assembly **(see illustration)**. On models with keyless entry, disconnect the electrical connector.

4   Carefully pull the door handle assembly out of the door far enough for access to the control rod(s).

5   On front doors, unclip the lock cylinder control rod. On all doors, rotate the handle assembly to disconnect the handle control rod.

6   To disconnect the lock cylinder from the handle assembly, remove the clip **(see illustration)**.

7   Installation is the reverse of removal.

Door latch

8   On front doors, remove the screw attaching the door latch control rod to the door. On 2000 and later models, drill out the rivet securing the interior door handle, then pull the handle forward and set it aside.

9   Unclip all control rods from the latch assembly, if possible. Note that in some cases the rod may need to be detached at its other end. In cases where the rod has a Z-shaped bend where it goes through the arm on the latch, it is usually best to wait until the latch is loose (Step 11), then rotate the latch assembly free of the rod.

10   Using a 1/4-inch drill bit, drill out the pop-rivet attaching the power door lock motor to the door, then disconnect the electrical connector and remove the lock motor from the door.

11   Disconnect the Door Ajar electrical connector from the latch. On 2000 and later models, remove the glass channel bolt, then the two bolts securing the center glass support bar. Remove the bar.

12   Remove the three screws at the rear of the door, then carefully withdraw the latch assembly from inside the door.

13   Installation is the reverse of removal. Use a sheet-metal screw to reattach the power door lock actuator.

Door inside handle

14   Remove the screw holding the latch control and link to the door.

15   Using a 1/4-inch drill bit, drill out the pop-rivet holding the inside handle to the door.

16   Remove the plastic cover that's over the cable at the latch end.

17   Detach the latch control link and remove the handle from the vehicle.

18   Installation is the reverse of removal. Use a sheet-metal screw in place of the pop-rivet.

17   Outside mirror - removal and installation

Refer to illustration 17.4

1   Remove the door trim panel and speaker grille as described in Section 15.

2   Remove the two screws from the speaker grille backing plate.

3   For power mirrors, disconnect the wiring harness connector and wiring guide clips.

4   Remove the three mirror mounting nuts and pull the mirror out to remove it **(see illustration)**.

5   To install, guide the wiring through opening and follow the removal steps in reverse.

18   Center console - removal and installation

1996 to 1999 models

1   Use a small screwdriver to carefully pry up the front of the cup holder; then grasp the cup holder and lift it off the console.

2   Open the ashtray cover and move the gear selector lever to the Drive 1 position.

3   Firmly grasp the front panel of the console and pull it back to disengage the retaining clips. Disconnect the electrical connectors and lift off the front panel.

4   Open the armrest, remove the two storage compartment attachment screws and lift out the storage compartment.

5   Remove the two screws that attach the console to the center of the instrument panel.

6   Pull the lower front corners of the console straight out to disconnect the push-clip fittings.

7   Remove the four bolts attaching the console to the front mounting bracket in the

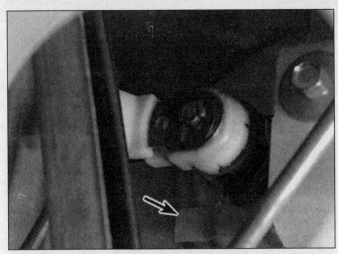

16.6 To disconnect the lock cylinder from the handle assembly, remove this clip (arrow)

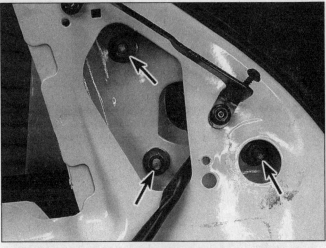

17.4 Three nuts (arrows) attach the outside mirror to the door

cup holder area and the two bolts at the rear mounting bracket in the storage compartment area.

8   Lift the console up and remove it from the vehicle.

9   To install the console, follow the removal procedure in reverse.

2000 and later models

10   On models with optional CD changer in the console, pry up the changer cover, then remove the four screws and the changer.

11   Open the storage bin and remove the four console bolts at the bottom.

12   Using a flat-bladed tool, remove the trim panel around the shifter.

13   Remove the two bolts, one near the center on each lower side, then lift out the console.

14   Installation is the reverse of the removal procedure.

19   Door window glass - removal, installation and adjustment

Removal

1   Remove the door trim panel, watershield, and speaker grill cover as described in Section 15.

2   Lower the window and remove the felt window channel molding by carefully pulling it out by hand.

3   Remove the inner door weatherstrip from the door flange by pulling it out.

4   On front doors, lower the glass for access to the two glass-to-retaining bracket rivets. Drill the rivets out with a 1/8-inch drill bit. On rear doors, place a block of wood

under the glass to support it while removing the rivets.

5   On front doors, loosen the door glass stabilizer retaining nut and remove the rear mounting bolt on the front window run channel. Remove the glass by tipping it forward and then lifting it from the door through the door belt opening toward the outside.

6   On rear doors, remove the glass bracket and lift the glass up through the door belt molding and remove it from the door.

Installation

7   Make sure the plastic spacers and retainer are installed on the glass.

8   Lower the glass into position in the door making sure it is seated in the top run channel.

9   Position the glass in the bracket and secure it with rivets. On front windows only, two 1/4-20 by 1-inch bolts and 1/4-20 nuts can be used in place of rivets to secure the glass to the bracket. Tighten the nuts securely.

10   Install the door weather-strip, adjust the window, and tighten the front channel run bolt securely.

Adjustment

11   Lower the glass approximately two to three inches from the fully up position.

12   Place one hand on each side of the glass and pull it back fully into the B-pillar glass run.

13   Set the stabilizer so that it slightly touches the window glass and tighten the bracket nut securely.

14   Cycle the glass several times to make sure it fits properly and moves freely in the channels.

15   Reassemble the door trim by reversing the disassembly procedure.

20   Parcel shelf - removal and installation

1996 to 1999 models

1   Remove the rear seat. First, push back on the front center section of the rear seat cushion to release the clips, then lift the cushion up and out of the vehicle. Remove the two lower bolts attaching the rear seat back, raise the bottom of the cushion, remove the two upper attachment bolts, and lift the cushion out of the vehicle.

2   Pull up the rear of the door scuff plate where it overlaps the upper quarter trim panel, grasp the trim panel, and pull it away from the body.

3   Remove the parcel shelf panel by pulling it forward while lifting up.

4   Reverse the disassembly order to install the parcel shelf.

2000 and later models

5   On models with high-mounted stop light in the parcel shelf, remove the light by lifting up at the rear to disengage the clip, then pull the light forward. Disconnect the electrical connector.

6   Remove the rear seat as in Step 1.

7   Use a flat-bladed trim tool to remove the upper corner trim panels and slide the panels forward along the shoulder belts,

8   Pry up the center of the push pins and remove the parcel shelf.

9   Reverse the disassembly order to install the package shelf.

Notes

Chapter 12
Chassis electrical system

Contents

1   General information

The electrical system is a 12-volt, negative-ground system. Power for the lights and all electrical accessories is supplied by the battery, which is charged by the alternator (generator).

This chapter covers repair and service procedures for the various electrical components not associated with the engine. Information on the battery, alternator, ignition system, and starter motor is in Chapter 5.

When portions of the electrical system are serviced, disconnect the negative battery cable from the battery to prevent electrical short circuits and possible system damage or fire.

2   Electrical troubleshooting - general information

A typical electrical circuit consists of an electrical component, any switches, relays, fuses, fusible links or circuit breakers related to that component, and the wiring and connectors that link the component to the battery and to the chassis. To help you pinpoint an electrical circuit problem, wiring diagrams are included at the end of this Chapter.

Before troubleshooting any electrical circuit, study the appropriate wiring diagrams to get a complete understanding of what makes up that individual circuit. For example, trouble spots often can be isolated by noting if other components related to the circuit are operating properly. If several components or circuits fail at one time, chances are the problem is in a fuse or ground connection, because several circuits are often routed through the same fuse and ground connections.

Electrical problems usually result from simple causes, such as loose or corroded connections, a blown fuse, a melted fusible link, or a failed relay. Inspect all fuses, wires and connections in a problem circuit before troubleshooting the circuit.

The basic tools for electrical troubleshooting include a circuit tester or voltmeter (a 12-volt bulb with a set of test leads also can be used), a continuity tester (which includes a bulb, battery and set of test leads), and a jumper wire to bypass electrical switches and connections, preferably with a circuit breaker incorporated. Use the diagrams to plan where you will connect your test equipment to pinpoint the trouble spot before trying to locate the problem.

Voltage checks

Voltage checks should be performed if a circuit is not working properly. Connect one lead of a circuit tester to either the negative battery terminal or a known good ground. Connect the other lead to a connector in the circuit being tested, preferably nearest to the battery or fuse. If the bulb of the tester lights, voltage is present, which means that the part of the circuit between the connector and the battery is okay. Continue checking the rest of the circuit in the same way. When you reach a point at which no voltage is present, the problem lies between that point and the last test point with voltage. Most of the time the problem can be traced to a loose connection. **Note:** *Remember that some circuits receive voltage only when the ignition key is in the Accessory or Run position.*

Short-circuit check

One way to find a short to ground in a circuit is to remove the fuse and connect a voltmeter across the fuse terminals. With all circuit switches off, there should be no voltage present in the circuit. Move the wiring harness from side to side while watching the meter. If the meter suddenly indicates battery voltage, there is a short to ground somewhere in the area where you wiggled the harness, probably where the insulation has rubbed through. The same test can be performed on each component in the circuit, even a switch.

You can substitute a 12-volt test light for the voltmeter, but the bulb may light very dimly, depending on the voltage drop of other devices in the circuit. A voltmeter is a more reliable test instrument.

Ground check

Perform a ground test to check whether a component is properly grounded. Disconnect the battery and connect one lead of a self-powered test light, known as a continuity tester, to a known good ground. Connect the other lead to the wire or ground connection being tested. If the bulb goes on, the ground is good. If the bulb does not go on, the ground is not good.

Continuity check

A continuity check is done to determine if there are any breaks in a circuit, or if it is conducting electric current properly. With the circuit off (no power in the circuit), use a self-powered continuity tester to check the circuit. Connect the test leads to both ends of the circuit. If the test light comes on, the circuit is conducting current properly. If the light doesn't come on, there is a break somewhere in the circuit. The same procedure can be used to test a switch, by connecting the continuity tester to the switch terminals. With the switch turned on, the test light should come on.

Open-circuit check

When diagnosing for possible open circuits, it is often hard to locate them by sight because oxidation or terminal misalignment can be hidden by the connectors. Merely wiggling a connector on a sensor or in the wiring harness may correct the open circuit condition. Remember this when an open circuit is indicated when troubleshooting a circuit. Intermittent problems may also be caused by oxidized or loose connections.

Electrical troubleshooting is simple if you remember that all electrical circuits are paths for current to flow from the battery, through the wires, switches, relays, fuses and fusible links to each electrical component (light bulb, motor, etc.) and to ground, from where it flows back to the battery. Any electrical problem is an interruption in normal current flow to and from the battery.

3   Connectors - general information

Refer to illustration 3.5

1   Most electrical connections on these vehicles are made with multiwire plastic connectors. The mating halves of many connectors are secured with locking clips molded into the plastic connector shells. The mating halves of large connectors, such as some of those under the instrument panel, are held together by a bolt through the center of the connector.
2   When separating the halves of a mated connector, don't pull on the wiring harness. You may damage the individual wires and terminals inside the connector. A broken or separated wire or terminal can be hidden by the connector shell and create an open circuit that is very hard to find.
3   To separate a connector with locking clips, use a small screwdriver to pry the clips apart carefully. Then separate the connector halves, pulling only on the shells. Look at the connector closely before trying to separate the halves. Often the locking clips are engaged in a way that is not immediately clear. Additionally, many connectors have more than one set of clips.
4   Each pair of connector terminals has a male half and a female half. When inserting a test probe into a male terminal, be careful not to distort the terminal opening. Doing so can lead to a poor connection and corrosion at that terminal later. When you look at the end view of a connector in a diagram, be sure to understand whether the view shows the harness side or the component side of the connector. Connector halves are mirror images of each other, and a terminal shown on the

3.5   To backprobe a connector, insert small, sharp probes (such as straight-pins) into the back of the connector along side the desired wires until they contact the metal terminal inside - connect your meter leads to the probes (this allows you to test a functioning circuit)

right side end view of one half will be on the left side end view of the other half.
5   It is often necessary to take circuit voltage measurements with a connector connected. Whenever possible, carefully insert the test probes of your meter into the rear of the connector shell to contact the terminal inside. This kind of connection is called "backprobing" **(see illustration)**.

4   Fuses and fusible links - general information and replacement

Refer to illustrations 4.1a, 4.1b and 4.3

1   The vehicle electrical circuits are protected by a combination of fuses, circuit breakers, and fusible links. All models covered by this manual have two fuse blocks, one primarily for low-current fuses under the left side of the instrument panel, and a power distribution box for high-current fuses in the engine compartment, next to the battery **(see illustrations)**.
2   The fuse block in the passenger compartment contains compact fuses with blade terminals, as well as some relays. These all can be replaced easily by hand. The power distribution box in the engine compartment contains high-current fuses and relays, along with the main megafuse that protects the entire electrical system.
3   If an electrical component fails, always check the fuse first. The best way to check the fuses is with a test light. Check for power at the exposed terminal tips of each fuse while it is installed in the fuse box. If power is present at one side of the fuse but not the other (with the ignition key On), the fuse is blown. A blown fuse can also be identified by inspecting the connection visible through the

4.1a   The passenger compartment fuse block is located under the driver's side of the instrument panel - fuse identification and instructions are on the cover

clear plastic body of the fuse **(see illustration)**.
4   Be sure to replace blown fuses with the correct type. Fuses of different ratings are physically interchangeable, but only fuses of the proper rating should be used. Replacing a fuse with one of a higher or lower value than specified can be dangerous. Each electrical circuit needs a specific amount of protection. The amperage value of each fuse is molded into the fuse body.
5   If the replacement fuse immediately fails, don't replace it again until you identify and fix the cause of the problem. In most cases, the cause will be a short circuit in the wiring caused by a broken or deteriorated wire.
6   The vehicles covered by this manual do not have traditional fusible links, which are sections of wire smaller than the circuit wiring they protect and designed to melt under unsafe, high-current conditions. Instead, these vehicles have high-current maxifuses in the engine compartment power distribution box. These maxifuses are often considered to be "cartridge fusible links." You can inspect and replace a blown maxifuse just like any other fuse.
7   In addition to the maxifuses, the entire vehicle electrical system is protected by a 175-ampere megafuse, installed in one end of the power distribution box. **(see illustration 4.1b)**. If the megafuse fails, the alternator (generator) field will be disabled. To replace the megafuse, remove the center bolt from the fuse holder, remove the fuse holder from the end of the box, and replace the megafuse.

5   Circuit breakers - general information

1   All models covered by this manual do not have separate circuit breakers. All circuits

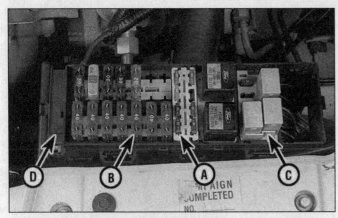

4.1b The power distribution box is located in the engine compartment is next to the battery - it contains miniaturized fuses (A), maxifuses (cartridge-type fusible links) (B) and relays (C) - the 175-ampere megafuse is located at one end (D)

4.3 A blown fuse (left) is easily identified by inspection

are protected by a combination of fuses and maxifuses described in section 4.

2   The headlamp switch has a built-in circuit breaker, as required by Federal motor vehicle safety standards. This circuit breaker is an automatic resetting type, but it can't be tested or serviced separately from the complete headlamp switch assembly. Similarly, each power window motor contains an integral circuit breaker that can't be serviced separately from the motor.

6   Relays - general information and testing

General information

1   Several electrical circuits in the vehicle, such as the electronic engine control system, the fuel pump, horns, starter, fog lamps, and others use relays to switch high current to system components. Relays use a low-current control circuit to open and close a high-current power circuit. If the relay is defective, the circuit load will not operate properly. Most of the relays are in the fuse blocks described in section 4. If you suspect a faulty relay, you can remove it and test it using the procedure below. Alternatively, have the relay tested by a dealer service department or a repair shop. Defective relays must be replaced.

2   Most of the relays used in these vehicles are often called "ISO" relays, which refers to the International Standards Organization. The terminals of ISO relays are numbered to indicate their usual circuit connections and functions.

Testing

Refer to illustration 6.5

3   Refer to the wiring diagram for the circuit to determine the proper connections for the relay you're testing. If you can't determine the correct connection from the wiring diagrams, however, you may be able to deter-

mine the test connections from the information that follows.

4   Two of the terminals are the relay control circuit and connect to the relay coil. The other relay terminals are the power circuit. When the relay is energized, the coil creates a magnetic field that closes the larger contacts of the power circuit to provide power to the circuit loads.

5   Terminals 85 and 86 are normally the control circuit **(see illustration)**. If the relay contains a diode, terminal 86 must be connected to battery positive (B+) voltage and terminal 85 to ground. If the relay contains a resistor, terminals 85 and 86 can be connected in either direction with respect to B+ and ground.

6   Terminal 30 is normally connected to the battery voltage (B+) source for the circuit loads. Terminal 87 is connected to the ground side of the circuit, either directly or through a load. If the relay has several alter-

nate terminals for load or ground connections, they usually are numbered 87A, 87B, 87C, and so on.

7   Use an ohmmeter to check continuity through the relay control coil.

a) *Connect the meter according to the polarity shown in illustration 6.5 for one check; then reverse the ohmmeter leads and check continuity in the other direction.*

b) *If the relay contains a resistor, resistance should be the specified value with the ohmmeter in either direction.*

c) *If the relay contains a diode, resistance should be the specified coil resistance value with the ohmmeter in the forward polarity direction. With the meter leads reversed, resistance should be lower.*

d) *If the ohmmeter shows infinite resistance in both directions, replace the relay.*

8   Remove the relay from the vehicle and

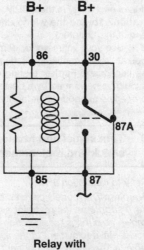
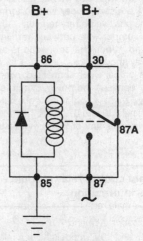

Relay with internal resistor   **Relay with internal diode**

38026-12-5.2a HAYNES

6.5 Typical ISO relay designs, terminal numbering, and circuit connections

7.1a The CCRM module is mounted next to the battery on 1996 and 1997 models

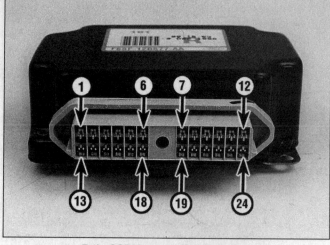

7.1b CCRM terminal identification

1	Electric cooling fan power (low)	14	Low speed fan signal from PCM
2	Electric cooling fan power (low)	15	Ground
3	Battery power	16	Air conditioning compressor clutch ground
4	Battery power	17	High speed fan signal from PCM
5	Inertia fuel shut-off	18	Fuel pump relay ground
6	Electric cooling fan power (high)	19	Not used
7	Electric cooling fan power (high)	20	Not used
8	Battery power	21	Air conditioning clutch signal to PCM
9	Not used	22	Wide-open throttle signal to PCM
10	Battery power	23	Power to air conditioning compressor clutch
11	Battery power		
12	Battery power to PCM	24	Power to PCM
13	Battery power		

8.1 The flasher for the turn signals and the hazard lights is mounted on a bracket under the left side of the instrument panel

use the ohmmeter to check for continuity between the relay power circuit terminals. There should be no continuity between terminal 30 and 87 with the relay de-energized.
9   Connect a fused jumper wire to terminal 86 and the positive battery terminal. Connect another jumper wire between terminal 85 and ground. When the connections are made, the relay should click.
10   With the jumper wires connected, check for continuity between the power circuit terminals. Now, there should be continuity between terminals 30 and 87.
11   If the relay fails any of the above tests, replace it.

7   Constant control relay module - general information

Refer to illustrations 7.1a and 7.1b
1   The 1996 and 1997 models have a relay assembly called the Constant Control Relay Module (CCRM). The CCRM is mounted next to the battery and contains the EEC power relay, the fuel pump relay, the low-speed fan control relay, the high-speed fan control relay, and the solid-state air conditioning

relay (see illustrations).
2   The CCRM is serviced only as an assembly, the relays inside are not replaceable individually. To test the separate operation of each relay in the CCRM. Refer to illustration7.1b and the wiring diagrams at the end of this chapter.
3   Use your voltmeter or ohmmeter to test operation and continuity of the power circuits as necessary. Further testing of the CCRM should be performed by a dealership or other properly equipped repair facility.

8   Turn signal and hazard flasher - check and replacement

Refer to illustration 8.1
Warning: *The models covered by this manual have supplemental restraint systems (SRS), known as airbags (see Section 28). To avoid accidental deployment of the airbag and possible injury, always disconnect the negative battery cable, then the positive battery cable and wait two minutes before working near any of the impact sensors, steering column, or instrument panel. Do not use any electrical test equipment on any of the airbag system*

wires or tamper with them in any way.
1   The turn signal and hazard flashers are controlled from a single electronic flasher, mounted to a brace under the instrument panel (see illustration). On 2000 and later models, the flasher is mounted in the passenger compartment fuse panel.
2   When the flasher unit is working properly, you can hear an audible click during its operation. If the turn signals fail on one side or the other and the flasher unit does not make its characteristic clicking sound, a faulty turn signal bulb is indicated.
3   If both turn signals fail to blink, the problem may be due to a blown fuse, a faulty flasher, a broken switch, or a loose or open connection. If a quick check of the fuse box indicates that the turn signal fuse has blown, check the wiring for a short before installing a new fuse.
4   To replace the flasher, simply disconnect the three-wire connector and remove the single screw that holds the flasher to its bracket.
5   Make sure that the replacement unit is identical to the original. Compare the old one to the new one before installing it.
6   Installation is the reverse of removal.

Turn Signal
and
Hazard Switch

Wiper
and
Dimmer Switch

9.5a Multifunction switch terminal identification guide - 1996 through 2003 models

9 Steering column switches - check and replacement

Warning: *The models covered by this manual have supplemental restraint systems (SRS), known as airbags (see Section 28). To avoid accidental deployment of the airbag and possible injury, always disconnect the negative battery cable, then the positive battery cable and wait two minutes before working near any of the impact sensors, steering column, or instrument panel. Do not use any electrical test equipment on any of the airbag system wires or tamper with them in any way.*

Multifunction switch
Refer to illustrations 9.5a, 9.5b, 9.5c, 9.5d, 9.5e, 9.5f, 9.5g, 9.5h, 9.5i and 9.5j

1   The multifunction switch is located on the left side of the steering column. It incorporates the turn signal, headlamp dimmer,

Turn Signal	Hazard warning	Continuity between
Neutral	OFF ON	11 and 4 6 and 10 1 and 11
Left	OFF	1 and 10; 1 and 8
Right	OFF	1 and 2; 1 and 5

36075-12-9.5b HAYNES

9.5b Turn signal and hazard switch continuity chart - 1996 to 1999

Turn Signal	Hazard Warning	Continuity Between
Neutral	Off On	1 and 11, 9 and 10, 9 and 2 4 and 11, 6 and 8, 6 and 5 6 and 10, 6 and 2
Left	Off	6 and 8
Right	Off	6 and 5

36075-12-9.5c HAYNES

9.5c Turn signal and hazard switch continuity chart - 2000 through 2003 models

Switch positions	Continuity between
Flash to Pass hold lever in this position	5 and 7 2 and 3
High beam	2 and 5
Low beam	2 and 3

36075-12-9.5d HAYNES

9.5d Headlamp dimmer switch continuity chart - 1996 through 2003 models

and windshield wiper and washer functions into one switch.

2   Disconnect the negative battery cable, then the positive cable and wait two minutes before proceeding any farther.

3   Tilt the steering wheel to its lowest position and remove the key release lever. Remove the lock cylinder (see Section 11). Refer to Chapter 11 and remove the lower steering column trim cover and the steering column covers.

4   Disconnect the electrical connectors, remove the retaining screws then detach the switch from the steering column.

5   Use an ohmmeter or self-powered test light and the accompanying charts to check for continuity between the indicated switch terminals with the switch in each of the specified positions **(see illustrations)**. If the continuity isn't as specified, replace the switch.

6   Installation is the reverse of removal.

Cruise control switches
Refer to illustration 9.9

7   Disconnect the negative battery cable, then the positive cable and wait two minutes before proceeding any further.

Switch positions	Test terminals	Ohmmeter readings (+ or - 10%)
Wiper OFF	1 and 4	47.6 K-ohms
Wash OFF	4 and 6	103.3 K-ohms
Intermittent	1 and 4	11.3 K-ohms
Low	1 and 4	4.08 K-ohms
High	1 and 4	0-ohms
Wash ON Wiper OFF	4 and 6	0-ohms
Delay control knob @ maximum position	4 and 6	103.3 K-ohms
Delay control knob @ minimum position	4 and 6	3.3 K-ohms

36075-12-9.5e HAYNES

9.5e Windshield wiper switch continuity chart - 1996 through 2003 models

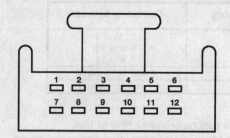

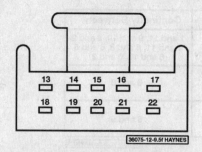

Turn signal	Hazard warning	Continuity on ohmmeter
Neutral	ON	13 and 14; 13 and 2; 13 and 15; 13 and 5; 16 and 20
Neutral	OFF	16 and 2; 16 and 17; 21 and 22
Left	OFF	13 and 14; 13 and 2
Right	OFF	13 and 15; 13 and 17

9.5g   Turn signal and hazard switch chart - 2004 and later models

9.5f   Turn signal, hazards, headlamps and dimmer switch terminals - 2004 and later models

Switch positions	Test terminals	Ohmmeter readings
High beam	10 and 9	Continuity
Low beam	12 and 9	Continuity
Flash to Pass	12 and 9; 10 and 11	Continuity

9.5h   Headlamp switch continuity check - 2004 and later models

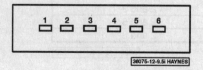

9.5i   Windshield wiper terminal designations - 2004 and later models

Switch positions	Test terminals	Ohmmeter readings
Wash ON	5 and 2	Continuity
Wiper OFF	6 and 5; 1 and 5; 4 and 5	No continuity
Wiper Low	6 and 5; 4 and 5	Continuity
Wiper High	6 and 5; 1 and 5; 4 and 5	Continuity
Intermittent Interval 1	5 and 4	Continuity
Interval 2	3 and 5; 5 and 4	Continuity
Interval 3	3 and 5	Continuity
Interval 4	6 and 5; 3 and 5	Continuity
Interval 5	6 and 5	Continuity
Mist ON	6 and 2	Continuity

9.5j   Windshield wiper continuity chart - 2004 and later models

8   Refer to Chapter 10 and remove the driver's side airbag module.

9   Disconnect the electrical connections for each switch from the steering wheel **(see illustration)**.

10   Remove the two Torx screws that hold each switch to the steering wheel.

11   Installation is the reverse of removal.

10   Ignition switch - check and replacement

Refer to illustrations 10.5, 10.7a, 10.7b, 10.7c, 107d and 10.7e

Warning: *The models covered by this manual have supplemental restraint systems (SRS), known as airbags (see Section 28). To avoid accidental deployment of the airbag and possible injury, always disconnect the negative battery cable, then the positive battery cable and wait two minutes before working near any of the impact sensors, steering column, or instrument panel. Do not use any electrical test equipment on any of the airbag system wires or tamper with them in any way.*

1   The ignition switch is mounted below the steering column. To check the switch it must first be removed.

2   Disconnect the negative battery cable, then the positive cable and wait two minutes before proceeding any farther.

3   Turn the ignition key lock cylinder to the Run position.

4   Refer to Chapter 11 and remove the driver's side knee bolster and the lower steering column cover. On 2000 and later models,

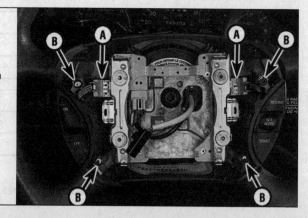

9.9   Disconnect the switch connectors (A) from the steering wheel - remove the screws (B) that secure the switches to the wheel

10.5 Disconnect the harness connector from the ignition switch

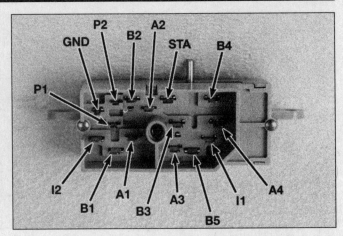

10.7a Check the ignition switch terminals for continuity in each of the indicated positions - 1995 through 2005 models

Switch positions	Continuity between
ACC	B1 and A1
LOCK	no continuity
OFF	no continuity
RUN	B1 and A1; B2 and A2 B3 and A3; B4 and A4 B5 and I1
START	B1 and I2; B4 and STA B5 and I1; P1 and GND P2 and GND

36075-12-10.7c HAYNES

10.7b Ignition switch continuity chart - 1996 through early 2005 models

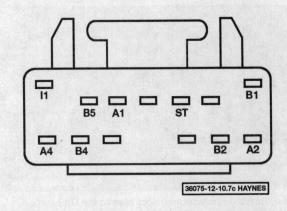

36075-12-10.7c HAYNES

10.7c Ignition switch terminal designations - late 2005 models

remove the two bolts and the wire-rod reinforcement behind the lower steering column cover.
5   Remove the screws that hold the switch under the instrument panel. Then remove the center bolt that secures the connector to the switch **(see illustration)**.

6   Disengage the ignition switch from the actuator pin and remove the switch from the vehicle.
7   Using an ohmmeter or self-powered test light and the accompanying illustrations, check for continuity between the indicated switch terminals with the switch in each of the indicated

positions **(see illustrations)**. If the continuity isn't as specified, replace the switch.
8   Make sure the actuator pin slot in the new ignition switch is in the Run position **(see illustration 10.7b)**.
9   Place the new switch in position on the actuator pin and install the retaining screws.

Switch positions	Continuity between
ACC	B5 and A1
LOCK	no continuity
OFF	no continuity
RUN	B1 and A1; B2 and A2 B5 and I1 ; B4 and A4
START	B5 and I1; B4 and STA

36075-12-10.7d HAYNES

10.7d Ignition switch continuity chart - late 2005 models

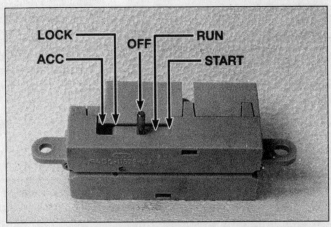

10.7e Ignition switch position details

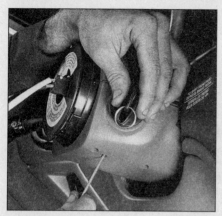

11.3 To remove the ignition lock cylinder, turn the key to the Run position, push in on the release tab with a punch, and pull the cylinder straight out

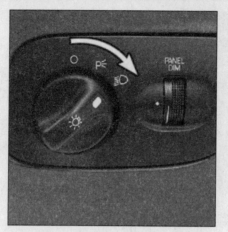

12.2 Turn the headlamp switch On, then pry the knob off

12.4 Turn the knob 180 degrees and reinstall it on the switch stem

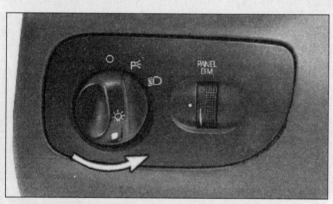

12.5a Turn the knob counterclockwise to the Off position . . .

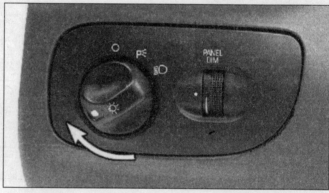

12.5b . . . then turn it clockwise to retract the lock

It may be necessary to move the switch back and forth to line up the screw holes.

10   The rest of the installation is the reverse of removal. Check for proper operation of the ignition switch in the lock, start and accessory positions.

11   Ignition lock cylinder - removal and installation

Refer to illustration 11.3
Warning: *The models covered by this manual have supplemental restraint systems (SRS), known as airbags (see Section 28). To avoid accidental deployment of the airbag and possible injury, always disconnect the negative battery cable, then the positive battery cable and wait two minutes before working near any of the impact sensors, steering column, or instrument panel. Do not use any electrical test equipment on any of the airbag system wires or tamper with them in any way.*

Removal

1   Disconnect the negative battery cable, then the positive cable and wait two minutes before proceeding any further.
2   Turn the ignition key lock cylinder to the Run position.

3   Insert an 1/8-inch pin punch, or similar tool, into the hole at the bottom of the steering column cover surrounding the lock cylinder. Depress the punch while pulling out on the lock cylinder to remove it from the column housing **(see illustration)**.

Installation

4   Depress the retaining pin on the side of the lock cylinder and rotate the ignition key lock cylinder to the Run position.
5   Install the lock cylinder into the steering column housing, making sure it's fully seated and aligned in the interlocking washer.
6   Rotate the key back to the Off position. This allows the retaining pin to extend itself back into the locating hole in the steering column housing.
7   Turn the lock to ensure that operation is correct in all positions.
8   The remainder of installation is the reverse of removal.

12   Instrument panel switches - check and replacement

Warning: *The models covered by this manual have supplemental restraint systems (SRS),*

known as airbags (see Section 28). To avoid accidental deployment of the airbag and possible injury, always disconnect the negative battery cable, then the positive battery cable and wait two minutes before working near any of the impact sensors, steering column, or instrument panel. Do not use any electrical test equipment on any of the airbag system wires or tamper with them in any way.

Headlamp switch

Refer to illustrations 12.2, 12.4, 12.5a, 12.5b, 12.6, 12.7a, 12.7b, 12.7c and 12.7d
1   Disconnect the negative battery cable, then the positive cable and wait two minutes before proceeding any farther.
2   Turn the headlamp switch On and pull the knob out **(see illustration)**. **Note:** *Steps 2 through 5 apply only to 1996 to 1999 models.*
3   Insert a small screwdriver blade into the slot at the base of the knob and release the locking tab. Then pull the knob off.
4   Turn the knob 180 degrees and reinstall it on the switch stem **(see illustration)**.
5   Rotate the knob counterclockwise to the Off position **(see illustration)**. Then turn it clockwise as far as possible and hold it to retract the locking tab on the back of the switch **(see illustration)**. Pull the switch straight out of the instrument panel.

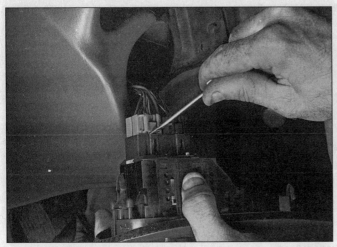

12.6 Disconnect the electrical connector and remove the switch

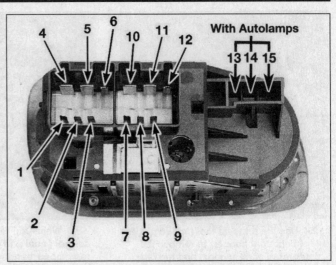

12.7a Headlamp switch terminal identification guide, 1996 to 1999

Switch positions	Test terminals	Ohmmeter readings
OFF	4 and 5; 10 and 11	open circuit
PARK	4 and 5	closed circuit
ON	4 and 5; 10 and 11	closed circuit
Dimmer knob rotated to full left position	6 and 7	closed circuit
Dimmer knob rotating right from the full left position	1 and 12	varied resistance
Autolamp knob rotated from off to full delay position	10 and 15	varied resistance from 3 K to 200 K-ohms
Autolamp knob rotated to off position	10 and 14	open circuit
Autolamp knob rotated to all other positions	10 and 14	closed circuit

36075-12-12.7b HAYNES

12.7b Headlamp switch continuity chart, 1996 to 1999

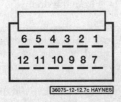

36075-12-12.7c HAYNES

12.7c Headlamp switch terminal
identification guide, 2000 and later models

SWITCH POSITION	CONTINUITY BETWEEN
Headlight	9 and 8, 11 and 12
Park	11 and 12
Off	None
Auto lamp, On	7 and 8
Dimmer	1 and 4, varied resistance
Fog Lamps, On	2 and 5

36075-12-12.7d HAYNES

12.7d Headlamp switch continuity chart, 2000 and later models

12.9 Remove the remote trunk release
switch by prying it from the
instrument panel

6   Unplug the electrical connector and remove the switch **(see illustration)**. On 2000 and later models, use a small screwdriver in the slot below the switch to pry the switch out of the instrument panel, then disconnect the electrical connector.

7   Following the accompanying illustrations, check for continuity as indicated, with the switch in each position **(see illustrations)**. If the switch fails any of the tests, replace the switch.

8   Installation is the reverse of removal.

Remote trunk release switch

Refer to illustration 12.9

9   Use a small screwdriver to release the locking tab on each side of the switch and carefully remove the trunk release switch from the instrument panel **(see illustration)**.

10   Unplug the electrical connector and remove the switch from the vehicle.

11   Using an ohmmeter, check for continuity across the two switch terminals with the button depressed and no continuity with the button released. If the switch fails the test, replace the switch.

12   Installation is the reverse of removal.

**13.4 Use the removal tool (or two pieces
of bent coat hanger) to remove the
integrated control panel and the radio**

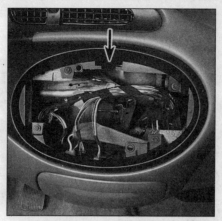

**13.5 When you reinstall the integrated
control panel and the radio, be sure the
rear support engages the rail inside the
instrument panel (arrow)**

**13.7 The rear chassis unit for the radio is
behind a trim panel on the left side of the
trunk in a sedan or under the spare tire in
a station wagon**

13   Radio and speakers - removal and installation

Warning: *The models covered by this manual
have supplemental restraint systems (SRS),
known as airbags (see Section 28). To avoid
accidental deployment of the airbag and possible injury, always disconnect the negative
battery cable, then the positive battery cable
and wait two minutes before working near any
of the impact sensors, steering column, or
instrument panel. Do not use any electrical
test equipment on any of the airbag system
wires or tamper with them in any way.*

1   Disconnect the negative battery cable,
then the positive cable and wait two minutes
before proceeding farther.

Radio and integrated control panel
Refer to illustrations 13.4 and 13.5

2   The radio is part of the integrated control panel, along with the air conditioning
controls, and is removed as an assembly. On
2000 and later models, the optional CD
changer is located either in the floor console
or in the trunk.

3   The integrated control panel is retained
in the instrument panel by special clips.
Releasing these clips requires a set of Ford
radio removal tools (available at auto parts
stores). You also can use two short lengths of
coat hanger wire bent into U-shapes as a
substitute. Insert the tools about 1-1/2 inches
into the holes at the edges of the panel until
you feel the internal clips release.

4   With the clips released, push outward
simultaneously on both tools and pull the
assembly out of the instrument panel, disconnect the electrical and vacuum connectors,
and remove the unit from the vehicle **(see
illustration)**.

5   Install the control panel by plugging in
the electrical connectors, then sliding the unit
into the instrument panel until the rear support engages the upper support rail and the
clips snap in place **(see illustration)**.

Rear chassis unit
Refer to illustration 13.7

6   The rear chassis unit of the radio is
mounted in the trunk on sedans and under the
spare tire on station wagons. Working on a
sedan, remove the left-hand trim panel in the
trunk. On 1996 to 1999 wagons, remove the
spare tire. On 2000 and later wagons, the unit
is behind the right quarter panel, and on six-
passenger models, it is in the center console.

7   Disconnect the antenna cable and other
connectors from the chassis unit **(see illustration)**.

8   Remove the nuts or screws that secure
the unit and remove it from the vehicle.

9   Installation is the reverse of removal.

Speakers

Door mounted
Refer to illustrations 13.11, 13.12 and 13.14

10   Each door contains a pair of radio
speakers, a small one mounted in the sail
panel by the side-view mirror and a large one
mounted low in the door.

11   Remove the speaker grille from the door
(see illustration).

12   Remove the two speaker retaining
screws, disconnect the wiring harness, and

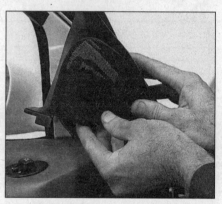

**13.11 Detach the speaker grille
from the door**

remove the speaker **(see illustration)**.

13   To remove the lower door speaker, refer
to Chapter 11 and remove the door trim panel.

14   Remove the four speaker retaining
screws, disconnect the wiring harness, and
remove the speaker **(see illustration)**.

15   Installation is the reverse of removal.

Rear quarter panel mounted

16   If your vehicle has speakers in the rear
quarter panels, refer to Chapter 11 and

**13.12 Remove the retaining screws,
disconnect the speaker wiring and remove
the speaker**

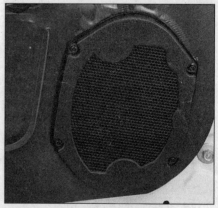

**13.14 Typical lower door
speaker installation**

14.4a Remove the antenna mast from a fixed antenna

14.4b The antenna base retaining nut can be removed using a pair of snap-ring pliers or similar tool

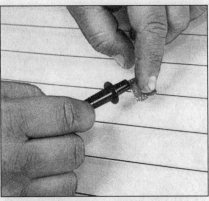

15.5 When measuring the voltage at the rear window defogger grid, wrap a piece of aluminum foil around the positive probe of the voltmeter and press the foil against the heating element with your finger

remove the rear seat and the rear quarter trim panels for access to the speakers.

17   Remove the speaker retaining screws, withdraw the speaker, unplug the electrical connector and remove the speaker from the vehicle.

18   Installation is the reverse of removal.

Package shelf mounted

19   If your vehicle has speakers in the rear package shelf, refer to Chapter 11 and remove the rear seat and package shelf for access to the speakers.

20   Remove the speaker retaining screws, withdraw the speaker, unplug the electrical connector and remove the speaker from the vehicle.

21   Installation is the reverse of removal.

14   Antenna - removal and installation

Refer to illustrations 14.4a and 14.4b

1   A fixed-type antenna is standard equipment on all models while an automatic power antenna is offered as optional equipment.

2   Working on a sedan, remove the left-hand trim panel in the trunk. On a wagon, remove the spare tire.

3   Disconnect the antenna cable from the radio chassis unit in the rear of the vehicle.

4   To remove a fixed antenna, remove the antenna mast and the base retaining nut from outside the vehicle **(see illustrations)**. Then remove the nuts or screws that secure the antenna inside and remove it from the vehicle.

5   To remove a power antenna, remove the antenna nut from outside the vehicle. Then disconnect the wiring harness from the antenna motor inside the vehicle and remove the nuts or screws that secure the antenna assembly.

6   For either antenna, installation is the reverse of removal.

15   Rear window defogger - check and repair

1   The rear window defogger consists of a number of horizontal heating elements baked

onto the inside surface of the glass. Power is supplied through 40-ampere fuse number 7 in the power distribution box in the engine compartment. The heater is controlled by the instrument panel switch and the generic electronic module (GEM).

2   A small break in an element can be repaired without removing the rear window.

Check

Refer to illustrations 15.5, 15.6 and 15.8

3   Turn the ignition switch and defogger system switches On.

4   Using a voltmeter, place the positive probe on the defogger grid positive terminal and the negative probe on the ground terminal. If battery voltage is not indicated, check the fuse, defogger switch and related wiring. If voltage is indicated, but all or part of the defogger doesn't heat, proceed with the following tests.

5   When measuring voltage during the next two tests, wrap a piece of aluminum foil around the tip of the voltmeter positive probe and press the foil against the heating element with your

finger **(see illustration)**. Place the negative probe on the defogger grid ground terminal.

6   Check the voltage at the center of each heating element **(see illustration)**. If the voltage is 5 to 6 volts, the element is okay. If the voltage is 0 volts, the element is broken between the center of the element and the positive end. If the voltage is 10 to 12 volts the element is broken between the center of the element and ground. Check each heating element.

7   If none of the elements are broken, connect the negative probe to a good chassis ground. The reading should stay the same, if it doesn't the ground connection is bad.

8   To find the break, place the voltmeter negative probe against the defogger ground terminal. Place the voltmeter positive probe with the foil strip against the heating element at the positive side and slide it toward the negative side. The point at which the voltmeter deflects from several volts to zero is the point where the heating element is broken **(see illustration)**.

15.6 To determine if a heating element is broken, check the voltage at the center of each element. If the voltage is 5 to 6 volts, the wire is unbroken; if the voltage is 0 volts, the element is broken between the center of the element and the positive end; if the voltage is 10 to 12 volts, the element is broken between the center of the element and ground

15.8 To find the break, place the voltmeter negative probe on the defogger ground terminal, place the voltmeter positive probe with the foil strip against the heating element at the positive side and slide it toward the negative side. The point at which the voltmeter deflects from several volts to zero is where the element is broken

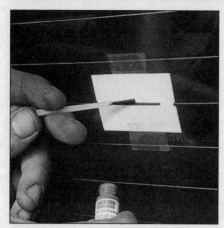

15.14 To use a defogger repair kit, apply masking tape to the inside of the window at the damaged area, then brush on the conductive coating

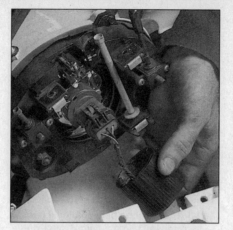

16.2 Rotate the headlamp bulb retainer counterclockwise and remove it from the bulb holder

16.3 Disconnect the wiring harness and pull the bulb holder (arrow) and bulb out of the headlamp housing

Repair

Refer to illustration 15.14

9   Repair the break in the element using a repair kit specifically for this purpose, such as Dupont paste No. 4817 (or equivalent). The kit includes plastic conductive epoxy.

10   Before repairing a break, turn off the system and allow it to cool for a few minutes.

11   Lightly buff the element area with fine steel wool; then clean it thoroughly with rubbing alcohol.

12   Use masking tape to mask off the area being repaired.

13   Thoroughly mix the epoxy, following the kit instructions.

14   Apply the epoxy material to the slit in the masking tape, overlapping the undamaged area about 3/4-inch on either end **(see illustration)**.

15   Allow the repair to cure for 24 hours before removing the tape and using the system.

16   Headlamp - bulb replacement

Refer to illustrations 16.2 and 16.3

Caution: *Halogen-gas-filled bulbs are under pressure and may shatter if the surface is scratched or the bulb is dropped. Wear eye protection and handle the bulbs carefully, grasping only the base. Do not touch the surface of the bulb with your fingers because the oil from your skin could cause it to overheat and fail prematurely. If you do touch the bulb surface, clean it with rubbing alcohol.*

Note: *On some models, the integrated relay control module or the constant control relay module may be in the way of the left headlamp. If so, remove the module from its mounting and move it out of the way.*

1   Open the hood. On 2000 and later models, refer to Section 17 and remove the headlamp housing.

2   Turn the plastic retainer counterclock-

wise to remove it from the bulb socket **(see illustration)**.

3   Unplug the connector from the rear of the bulb holder **(see illustration)**.

4   Carefully remove the bulb holder and bulb from the headlamp housing by pulling it straight out.

5   Without touching the glass with your bare fingers, insert the new bulb and holder into the headlamp housing.

6   Plug in the electrical connector and install the retainer. Test headlamp operation, then close the hood.

17   Headlamp - housing removal, installation and lamp adjustment

Refer to illustration 17.2

Note: *The headlamps must be aimed correctly. If adjusted incorrectly, they could blind oncoming motorists and cause fatal accidents. The headlamps should be checked for proper aim every 12 months and any time a*

new bulb is installed or front-end body work is done. The following procedure is an interim method that will provide temporary adjustment until the headlamps can be adjusted by a properly equipped shop.

1   To remove the headlamp housing, ensure that the headlamp switch is Off. Then open the hood.

2   On 1999 and earlier models remove the headlight housing screws from the top of the housing and loosen the pinch bolt **(see illustration)**. On 2000 and later models, remove the one bolt, near the grille opening, and pry up the two retaining rods at the outboard end of the headlamp housing.

3   Pull the housing outward, disconnect the electrical connector from the headlamp bulb and remove the housing from the vehicle.

4   Installation is the reverse of removal.

5   Adjust the headlamps with the vehicle parked level, the gas tank half full, and no heavy load in the vehicle.

6   Turn the headlamps on. Check the bubble in the built-in level. If the bubble is within four graduations of zero, leave well enough alone.

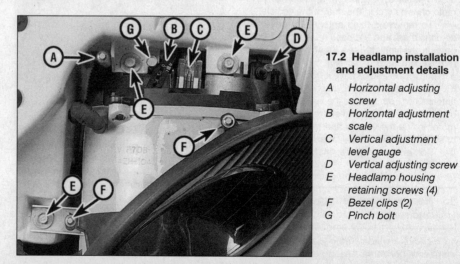

17.2 Headlamp installation and adjustment details

A   Horizontal adjusting screw
B   Horizontal adjustment scale
C   Vertical adjustment level gauge
D   Vertical adjusting screw
E   Headlamp housing retaining screws (4)
F   Bezel clips (2)
G   Pinch bolt

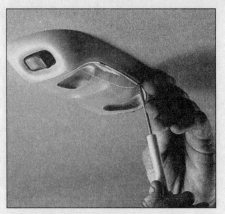

18.2a Pry the lens off the dome lamp housing . . .

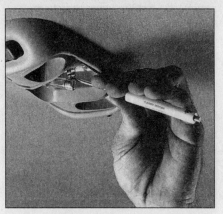

18.2b . . . and remove the bulb with a small screwdriver

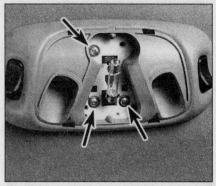

18.2c Install the new bulb into the clip terminals - to remove the lamp housing from the roof, remove the three screws (arrows)

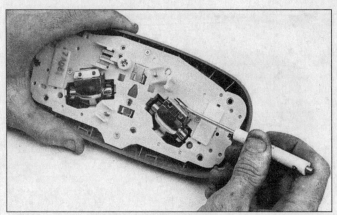

18.5 Press the reflector locking tab on the back of the housing and remove the reflector

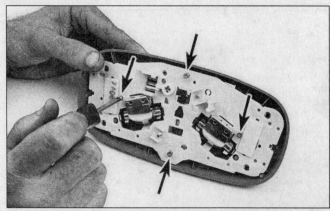

18.7 Remove the four screws (arrows) that hold the two halves of the housing together

7   If the bubble is not within four graduations of zero, turn the vertical adjuster until the bubble is in the orange area of the gauge.

8   For left-to-right adjustment, turn the horizontal adjuster until the angle gauge is at 0-degrees.

9   Turn off the headlamps and close the hood.

10   Have the headlamps adjusted by a dealer service department or service station at the earliest opportunity.

18 Bulb replacement

Interior dome and map lamps

Refer to illustrations 18.2a, 18.2b, 18.2c, 18.5 and 18.7

1   The overhead dome lamp housing contains the dome lamp and two map lamps. On a vehicle with a sunroof, this lamp housing also holds the sunroof switches. The dome lamp is lit when any door is opened and when the instrument panel dimmer control is turned to the detented UP position.

2   To replace the cartridge bulb for the dome lamp, pry the lens off the housing, use a small screwdriver to remove the bulb, and install the new bulb into the clip terminals **(see illustrations)**.

3   To replace a map lamp bulb, remove the three screws that hold the lamp housing to the roof **(see illustration 18.2c)**. On 2000 and later models, the housing is retained, without screws, by two clips.

4   Lower the housing from the roof and unplug the connector.

5   Use a small screwdriver to press the locking tab that retains the reflector on the back of the housing and remove the reflector **(see illustration)**.

6   Pull the bulb out of the clip terminals. Use a screwdriver, if necessary, to pry the bulb out.

7   If necessary to replace either the front or the back of the housing, remove the four screws that hold the two parts together **(see illustration)**.

8   Installation is the reverse of removal. **Note:** *The overhead lamp bulbs in an assembly with the sunroof controls and the bulbs in the station wagon cargo area lamp housing are replaced similarly to the dome and map bulbs.*

Interior courtesy lamps

Refer to illustration 18.11

9   Courtesy lamps in the doors and under the instrument panel, light when a door is opened.

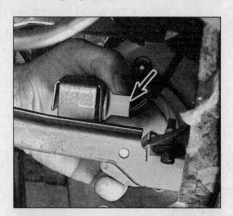

18.11 Twist the bulb holder (arrow) to remove it from the lamp housing under the instrument panel 18.14 Remove the

10   To replace a bulb for a door lamp, pry the lamp lens out of the door with a screwdriver at the notch in the front of the lens, then replace the bulb.

11   To replace a bulb under the instrument panel, twist the bulb housing to align the tabs and remove it from its bracket **(see illustration)**.

12   Remove the bulb by pulling it straight out of the socket. Install the new bulb by pressing it in.

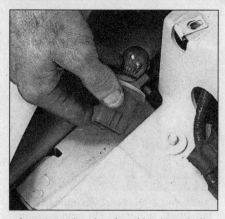

front turn signal and parking lamp bulb and socket

18.15 Remove the housing retaining screws (arrow) from the rear of the housing)

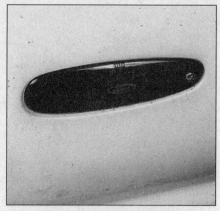

18.17a Side-marker lenses are secured by one screw and a tab on the lens

18.17b Remove the socket from the lens to replace the bulb

18.20a Typical rear finish panel inside the trunk of a sedan model

Front turn signal and parking lamps

Refer to illustrations 18.14 and 18.15

13   Remove the headlamp housing (see Section 17).
14   Twist the bulb socket a quarter turn counterclockwise, then remove the bulb and socket from the housing **(see illustration)**.
15   To detach the lamp housing, use an 8-mm swivel socket and remove the two screws located on the rear of the housing **(see illustration)**.
16   Installation is the reverse of removal. Check and aim the headlamps, as needed, after reinstalling the housing.

Front and rear side-marker lamps

Refer to illustrations 18.17a and 18.17b

17   To replace a side-marker bulb, remove the one screw from the lens and remove the lens **(see illustrations)**.
18   Replace the bulb and reinstall the lens.

Tail lamps, rear turn signals, brake lamps, backup lamps and license plate lamps

Refer to illustrations 18.20a, 18.20b, 18.20c, 18.22a and 18.22b

19   On the different sedan and station wagon models, some of the rear lamps are in the deck lid, others are in the rear of the body. All of the bulbs are replaced from inside the rear trunk compartment or cargo area.
20   Working in the sedan trunk or wagon cargo area, detach the plastic pins and clips that secure the rear finishing panels that must be removed for access to any lamp, then remove the panel from the vehicle **(see illustrations)**. On sedan models, remove the nuts securing the tail lamp housing (Taurus models have four nuts, Sable models have three). On wagon models, two screws secure the tail lamp housing.

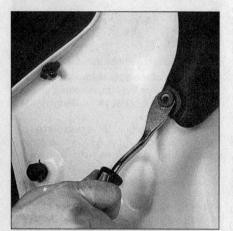

18.20b Pry out the clips to remove the necessary panels

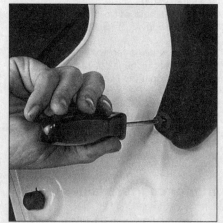

18.20c Press the clips back into place to reinstall the panel

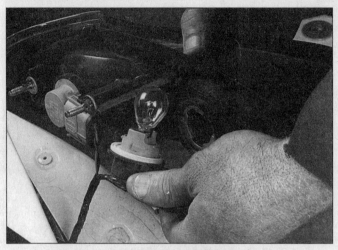

18.22a Turn the socket counterclockwise to remove it from the housing

18.22b Install a new bulb and reinstall the socket into the lamp housing

21   Carefully pull the tail lamp housing out for access to the bulbs.

22   Twist the bulb socket a quarter turn counterclockwise and remove the bulb from the housing **(see illustrations)**.

23   Install the new bulb and reinstall any trim panels that were removed.

High-mounted brake lamp

24   The high-mounted brake light bulbs can be reached from the trunk or cargo area. On 2000 and later sedans, pull the housing forward to detach it from the parcel shelf; on wagon models, remove the interior trim panel at the top of the liftgate to expose the four nuts securing the housing.

25   Twist the bulb socket a quarter turn counterclockwise, then remove the bulb from the housing and replace the bulb. **Note:** *On LED equipped housings, the entire housing must be replaced if the unit is faulty.*

Fog lamps (2002 and later models)

26   Raise the front of the car and support it on jack stands.

27   Working under the vehicle, remove the air deflector panel.

28   Disconnect the electrical connector from the socket, then remove the bulb from the fog lamp housing and replace the bulb

29   Install the air deflector panel.

Instrument cluster lamps

30   Remove the instrument cluster for access to the instrument cluster lamp bulbs (see Section 22).

---

19   Daytime running lamps (DRL) - general information

The daytime running lamp (DRL) system (if equipped) lights the headlamps whenever the engine is running. The only exception is with the engine running and the parking brake

engaged. After the parking brake is released, however, the headlamps will stay on as long as the ignition switch is on, even if the parking brake is later reapplied.

The DRL system supplies reduced power to the headlamps to prolong headlamp life and to reduce brightness for daytime use.

---

20   Wiper motor - check and replacement

Check

Refer to illustration 20.3

Note: *Refer to the wiring diagrams at the end of this Chapter to identify circuit functions by wire color coding for the following tests.*

1   If the wipers work slowly, make sure the battery is in good condition and fully charged (Chapter 1). If the battery is in good condition, check for binding linkage. Lubricate or repair the linkage as necessary. If the wipers still operate slowly, check for loose or corroded connections, especially the ground connection. If all connections are okay, replace the motor.

2   If the wipers fail to operate when activated, check the fuse. If the fuse is okay, connect a jumper wire between the wiper motor ground terminal and ground, then retest. If the motor works now, repair the ground connection.

3   If the motor still doesn't work, turn the wiper switch to the LO and the HI positions and check for voltage at the motor **(see illustration)**. If voltage is present at the motor, remove the motor and test it off the vehicle with fused jumper wires from the battery. If the motor now works, check for binding linkage as explained in step 1 above. If the motor still doesn't work, replace it.

4   If voltage is not present at the motor, check for voltage at the Generic Electronic Module (GEM), which controls the wipers. If voltage is present at the module but not at the motor, check the wiper switch for continuity (see Section 9). If the switch is okay, the GEM may be bad.

5   If the interval (delay) function is inoperative, check the continuity of all the wiring between the wiper switch and control module. If the wiring is OK, check the resistance of the delay control knob of the multifunction

20.3 Wiper motor terminal identification

1   *Battery positive (B+) voltage for park position*
2   *Battery positive (B+) voltage for run position*
3   *Ground*
4   *High speed return*
5   *Low speed return*

20.9 The wiper assembly is located underneath the cowl vent screen

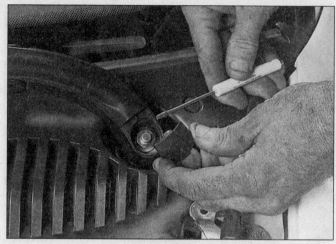

20.11 Pry the plastic caps off the wiper arm ends

switch. If the delay control knob is okay, the GEM may be bad.

6   If the wipers do not park but stop at the position they are in when the switch is turned off, check for voltage at the park feed wire of the wiper motor connector when the wiper switch is off but the ignition is on **(see illustration 20.3)**. If no voltage is present, trace and repair the park circuit to the ignition switch or the fuse.

7   If the wipers won't shut off unless the ignition is off, disconnect the wiring from the wiper control switch. If the wipers stop, replace the switch. If the wipers keep running, a limit switch in the motor is defective; replace the motor.

8   If the wipers won't retract below the cowl line, check for mechanical obstructions in the wiper linkage or on the vehicle body that would prevent the wipers from parking. If there are no obstructions, check the wiring between the switch and motor for continuity. If the wiring is okay, replace the wiper motor.

Replacement
Refer to illustrations 20.9, 20.11, 20.13, 20.14, 20.15 and 20.16

9   The wiper motor and mechanism are underneath the cowl vent screen **(see illustration)**.

10   Turn the ignition switch On and turn the wiper switch to Low speed. When the wiper arms are pointing straight up the windshield, turn the ignition Off.

11   Use a small screwdriver to pry the plastic caps off the wiper arm mounting ends **(see illustration)**.

12   Disconnect the negative battery cable.

13   Remove the small retaining nut from each wiper arm **(see illustration)** and remove the wiper arms.

14   Remove the cowl screen by turning the eight plastic retainers 1/4 turn counterclockwise. Then remove the six screen retaining clips **(see illustration)**. On 2000 and later models, remove the four bolts securing the wiper arm mounting bar to access the wiper motor.

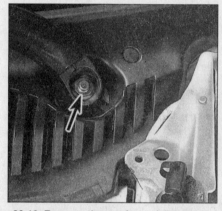

20.13 Remove the nut (arrow) from each wiper arm

15   Disconnect the electrical connector from the wiper motor and remove the four screws that secure the motor and mechanism to the cowl **(see illustration)**. Remove the motor and drive mechanism.

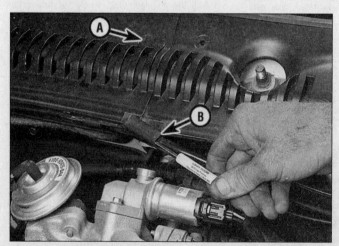

20.14 Turn the eight plastic retainers (A) 1/4 turn counterclockwise, then remove the six clips (B)

20.15 Disconnect the electrical connector (A) and remove the four motor retaining screws (B)

20.16 Remove the nut from the motor shaft (A) and the three screws (B) that hold the motor to the drive mechanism

21.1 The windshield washer reservoir is located in the right front fender well

11   The remainder of installation is the reverse of removal.

22 Instrument cluster - removal and installation

Refer to illustrations 22.3, 22.7, 22.8, 22.9 and 22.10

Warning: *The models covered by this manual have supplemental restraint systems (SRS), known as airbags (see Section 28). To avoid accidental deployment of the airbag and possible injury, always disconnect the negative battery cable, then the positive battery cable and wait two minutes before working near any of the impact sensors, steering column, or instrument panel. Do not use any electrical test equipment on any of the airbag system wires or tamper with them in any way.*

1   Disconnect the negative battery cable, then the positive cable and wait two minutes before proceeding any further.

2   Remove the integrated control panel (see Section 13).

3   Remove the four screws that secure the instrument cluster trim panel on 1996 to 1999 models **(see illustration)**. On 2000 and later models, remove the center instrument panel section that is behind the integrated control panel, remove the headlight switch, then remove the two screws above the instrument cluster and one to the right of the steering column, then remove the instrument cluster trim panel, which is the full length of the dash on these models.

4   Remove two retaining screws from the upper steering column cover and remove the cover.

5   Tilt the steering wheel to its lowest position and remove the trim panel.

6   Detach the transmission range indicator cable from the gear selector tube in the steering column.

7   Remove four screws that hold the cluster in the instrument panel and pull the cluster forward from the instrument panel **(see illustration)**.

8   Reach behind the cluster and disconnect

16   The wiper drive mechanism is not serviceable, but the motor can be replaced. To replace the motor, remove the operating arm nut from the motor shaft. Then remove the three screws that hold the motor to the drive mechanism **(see illustration)**.

17   Reinstall the wiper mechanism into the cowl and connect the electrical connector. **Caution:** *Before reinstalling the wiper arms and blades, turn the ignition On and turn the wiper switch to either LO or HI, then turn the wiper switch OFF. This lets the motor to cycle to the park position, which will avoid damage to the arms and drive mechanism.*

18   Install the wiper pivot arms, ensuring that the blade tip aligns with the park reference mark at the base of the windshield.

19   Ensure that the wiper blade is fully seated on the wiper arm before operating the wipers.

20   The remainder of the installation is the reverse of removal.

21 Windshield washer reservoir and pump - removal and installation

Refer to illustration 21.1

1   The windshield washer reservoir is underneath the right front fender. Its filler cap is directly behind the cooling system expansion tank **(see illustration)**. The washer pump is pressed into a sealing grommet toward the bottom of the reservoir.

2   On 1996 to 1999 models, refer to Chapter 3 and remove the expansion tank from the engine compartment.

3   Disconnect the electrical connector from the washer reservoir.

4   Remove the two nuts in the engine compartment near the air conditioner accumulator that hold the reservoir to the body.

5   Raise the vehicle and support it on jackstands.

6   Refer to Chapter 11 and remove the front half of the right front fender splash shield.

7   Remove the screw at the top of the reservoir that holds the reservoir to the inner fender.

8   Disconnect the hose connectors from the bottom of the reservoir and let it drain into a suitable container.

9   Remove the pump by pulling it out of the grommet at the bottom of the reservoir.

10   When reinstalling the pump, lubricate the inside diameter of the sealing grommet with a soap-and-water solution to ease pump installation.

22.3 These two screws at the top and two more at the bottom retain the trim panel to the instrument panel

22.7 Remove the screws (arrows) at both sides of the instrument cluster

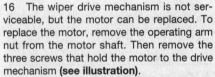

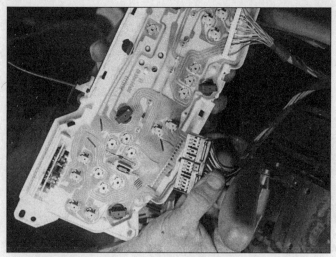

22.8 Disconnect two connectors to remove the cluster

22.9 Remove the screws (arrows) to remove the lens from the cluster

two electrical connectors **(see illustration)**.

9   To replace the instrument cluster lens, remove the screws and separate the lens from the cluster **(see illustration)**.

10   To replace any lamp bulb in the cluster, turn the bulb holder on the back of the cluster counterclockwise and remove the bulb **(see illustration)**.

11   Installation is the reverse of removal.

23 Horn - check and replacement

Check

Refer to illustration 23.1

1   The high-pitched horn is mounted on the left-hand forward part of the subframe. The low-pitched horn is on the right side of the subframe **(see illustration)**.

2   Before starting any other electrical troubleshooting, check the horn fuse.

3   To test either horn, disconnect the electrical connector and connect battery positive (+) voltage directly to the horn terminal with a jumper wire. If the horn doesn't sound, con-

nect another jumper wire from the horn to the subframe. If the horn still doesn't sound, replace it.

4   If the horn does sound, check for voltage at the terminal when the horn button is pressed. If voltage is present at the terminal, check for a bad ground at the horn.

5   If voltage is not present at the horn, check the relay in the power distribution box. (section 7).

6   If the relay is okay, check for voltage to the relay power and control circuits in the power distribution box; repair as necessary.

7   If both relay circuits are receiving voltage, press the horn button and check the circuit from the relay to the horn button for continuity. If there is no continuity, check the circuit for an open. If there is no open circuit, Check for an open or short circuit from the horn button to ground. If all parts of the circuit are okay, replace the horn button.

Replacement

8   To replace either horn, disconnect the electrical connector and remove the horn bolt

(see illustration 23.1).

9   Installation is the reverse of removal.

24 Cruise control system - description and check

1   The cruise control (or speed control) system maintains vehicle speed with a servo motor which is connected to the throttle linkage by a cable. The system consists of the servo motor, the brake switch, control switches, and a relay. Most features of the system require special testers and diagnostic procedures that are beyond the scope of this manual. Listed below are some basic checks that can be used to locate general problems.

2   Locate and check the fuse (see Section 4).

3   The brake pedal position (BPP) switch (or stop lamp switch) deactivates the cruise control system. Have an assistant press the brake pedal while you check the stop lamp operation.

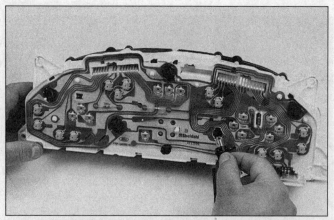

22.10 Turn the bulb holder counterclockwise to remove and replace any instrument cluster lamp bulbs

23.1 Unplug the connector (A) and remove the bolt (B) to replace a horn

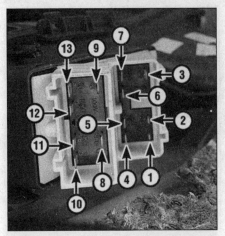

25.12a Master window switch terminal identification, 1996 to 1999 models

1   Power from accessory delay relay
2   Ground
3   Window lockout control
4   Right rear motor feed
5   Right rear motor feed
6   Left rear motor feed
7   Left rear motor feed
8   Ground
9   Power from accessory delay relay
10   Right front motor feed
11   Right front motor feed
12   Power from one-touch window
     down relay
13   GEM input

4   If the stop lamps don't light or don't turn off, fix the problem and retest the cruise control.

5   Refer to Chapter 4 and inspect the cruise control cable connections at the throttle body. Verify that the cable is not broken or binding. Repair the cable and linkage as required.

6   The cruise control system gets a vehicle speed signal from the vehicle speed sensor (VSS) in the transaxle. Refer to Chapter 6 and test the VSS signal.

7   Check the operation of the cruise control switches on the steering wheel (Section 9).

8   Test drive the vehicle to see if the cruise control is now working. If it isn't, take it to a dealer service department or an automotive electrical specialist for further diagnosis.

25   Power window system - description and check

Refer to illustrations 25.12a and 25.12b

1   The power window system operates electric motors in the doors to lower and raise the windows. The system consists of the control switches, the motors, regulators, glass mechanisms, and associated relays and wiring.

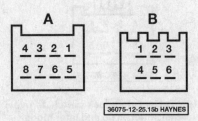

25.12b Master window switch terminal identification, 2000 and later models

B4   Power from accessory delay relay
B2   Ground
A2   Right rear motor feed
B3   Right rear motor feed
B5   Left rear motor feed
B6   Left rear motor feed
A6   Driver's motor feed
A7   Driver's motor feed
      A3 Right front motor feed
A4   Right front motor feed
A8   GEM input

2   The power windows can be lowered and raised from the master control switch by the driver or by remote switches at the individual windows. Each window has a separate motor which is reversible. The position of the control switch determines the motor polarity and therefore the direction of operation.

3   The circuit is protected by fuses. Each motor also has an internal circuit breaker to prevent one stuck window from disabling the whole system.

4   The power window system will only operate when the ignition switch is On. A delay relay lets the system continue to operate for 45 seconds after the ignition is turned off, however. A window lockout switch at the driver's control switch can be used to disable the switches at the other windows. Always check these switches before troubleshooting a window problem.

5   The following procedures are general in nature, so if you can't find the problem using them, take the vehicle to a dealer service department or other repair facility. Refer to the wiring diagrams at the end of this chapter to identify circuit functions by wire color coding for the following tests.

6   If the power windows won't operate, check the fuses first. **Note:** *If a wire breaks, it is most often in the portion of the harness between the body and the door. Opening and closing the door fatigues the wires and may cause one to break.*

7   If only the rear window and right front window are inoperative, or if the windows only operate from the master control switch, check the window lockout switch for continuity in the unlocked position. Replace it if it doesn't have continuity.

8   Check the wiring between the switches and the fuse panel for continuity. Repair the

wiring, if necessary.

9   If only one window (other than the driver's window) is inoperative from the master control switch, try the other control switch at the window.

10   If the same window works from one switch, but not the other, check the inoperative switch for continuity.

11   If the switch tests okay, check for a short or open in the circuit between the switch and the window motor.

12   If one window is inoperative from both switches, remove the trim panel from the door and check for voltage at the switch **(see illustrations)** and at the motor while the switch is operated.

13   If voltage is reaching the motor, refer to Chapter 11 and disconnect the glass from the regulator. Move the window up and down by hand while checking for binding and damage. Also check for binding and damage to the regulator. If the regulator is not damaged and the window moves up and down smoothly, replace the motor. If there's binding or damage, lubricate, repair, or replace parts as necessary.

14   If voltage isn't reaching the motor, check the wiring for continuity between the switches and motor. Refer to the wiring diagrams at the end of this chapter. Check circuit relays for proper connections and operation.

15   Test the windows after you are done to confirm proper repairs.

26   Power door lock and keyless entry system - description and check

Power door lock system

Refer to illustrations 26.6a and 26.6b

1   The power door lock system consists of the switches, relays, motors, a fuse, and wiring. Diagnosis can be limited to simple checks of the wiring connections and motors for minor faults.

2   Power door lock systems are operated by motors (or actuators) in the doors. The lock switches have two operating positions, lock and unlock. On models with keyless entry, the switches activate a module which in turn applies voltage to the door lock motors. On models without keyless entry, the switches activate the door lock motors directly.

3   If you can't locate a problem using the following general steps, consult a dealer service department or other repair facility. Refer to the wiring diagrams at the end of this chapter to identify circuit functions by wire color coding for the following tests.

4   Always check the circuit fuse in the power distribution box first.

5   Operate the door lock switches in both directions with the engine off. Listen for the click of the door lock motor or relay operating.

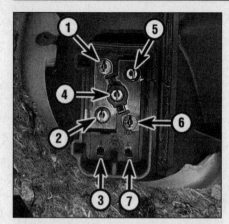

**26.6a Driver's door lock switch terminal
identification, 1996 to 1999 models**

1   *Not used*
2   *Door lock input*
3   *Power from accessory delay relay*
4   *Ground*
5   *Door unlock input*
6   *Not used*
7   *Lamp ground*

6   If there is no click, check for voltage at
the switches **(see illustrations)**. If no voltage
is present, check the wiring between the fuse
block and the switches for shorts and opens.
7   If voltage is present but no click is heard,
test the switch for continuity. Replace it if
there is no continuity in both switch positions.
8   If the switch has continuity but the motor
or relay doesn't click, check the wiring
between the switch and the motor for continuity. Repair the wiring if there is no continuity.
9   If all but one lock operates, refer to
Chapter 11 and remove the trim panel from
the door and check for voltage at the motor
while the lock switch is operated. One of the
wires should have voltage in the lock position; the other should have voltage in the
unlock position. **Note:** *If a wire breaks, it is
most often in the portion of the harness
between the body and the door. Opening and
closing the door fatigues the wires and may
cause one to break.*

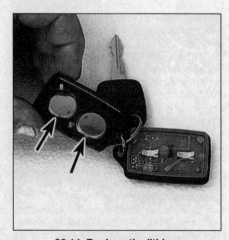

**26.14 Replace the lithium
batteries (arrows)**

36075-12-26.6b HAYNES

**26.6b Driver's door lock switch terminal
identification, 2000 and later models**

1   *Lamp ground*
2   *Door lock input*
3   *Power from accessory delay relay*
4   *Ground*
5   *From instrument cluster*
6   *Not used*
7   *GEM input*
8   *Not used*

10   If the inoperative motor is receiving voltage, replace the motor.

Keyless entry system
Refer to illustrations 26.13 and 26.14
11   The keyless entry system consists of a
remote control transmitter that sends a coded
infrared signal to a receiver in the trunk that
operates the door lock system.
12   Replace the transmitter batteries when
the red LED light on the side of the case
doesn't light when the button is pushed.
13   Use a small screwdriver to carefully separate the case halves **(see illustration)**.
14   Replace the two 3-volt 2016 lithium batteries **(see illustration)**.
15   Snap the case halves together.

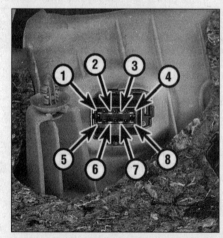

**27.7a Mirror control switch terminal iden-
tification, 1996 to 1999 models**

1   *Power*
2   *Not used*
3   *Left mirror horizontal movement*
4   *Right mirror motor input*
5   *Ground*
6   *Right mirror horizontal movement*
7   *Right mirror vertical movement*
8   *Left mirror vertical movement*

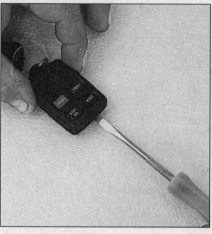

**26.13 Use a small screwdriver to separate
the transmitter halves**

27 Electric side-view mirrors -
     check and replacement

Check
Refer to illustrations 27.7a and 27.7b
1   Power-operated outside rear-view mirrors are standard equipment. Heated mirrors
are optional. Each mirror has a two-way
motor that moves the glass up and down, as
well as left and right.
2   The control switch has a selector portion
that sends power to the left or right side mirror.
With the ignition on but the engine off, lower
the windows and operate the mirror control
switch through all functions (left-right and up-
down) for both the left and right side mirrors.
3   Listen carefully for the sound of the
motors running in the mirrors.
4   If you can hear the motors but the mirror
glass doesn't move, there is probably a problem with the drive mechanism inside the mirror. Remove and disassemble the mirror to
locate the problem.
5   If the mirrors don't operate and no sound
comes from the mirrors, check the fuse.

36075-12-27.7b HAYNES

**27.7b Mirror control switch terminal
identification, 2000 and later models**

1   *Ground*
2   *Not used*
3   *Right mirror horizontal movement*
4   *Left mirror horizontal movement*
5   *Not used*
6   *Motor input*
7   *Left mirror vertical movement*
8   *Right mirror vertical movement*

28.1 The airbag diagnostic module is mounted under the instrument panel (1996 and 1997 models) or under the center console (1998 models)

28.2a The airbag module is connected to the coil assembly by a wiring harness running through the steering wheel

6   If the fuse is okay, remove the mirror control switch from its mounting without disconnecting the wires attached to it. Turn the ignition on and check for voltage at the switch. There should be voltage at one terminal. If no voltage is present at the switch, check for an open or short in the wiring between the fuse panel and the switch.

7   If voltage is present at the switch, disconnect it. Check the switch for continuity in all operating positions (see illustrations). If the switch does not have continuity, replace it. **Note:** *If a wire breaks, it is most often in the portion of the harness between the body and the door. Opening and closing the door fatigues the wires and may cause one to break.*

8   Reconnect the switch. Locate the wire going from the switch to ground. Leaving the switch connected, connect a jumper wire between this wire and ground. If the mirror works normally with this wire in place, repair the faulty ground connection.

9   If the mirror still doesn't work, remove the mirror and check the wires at the mirror for voltage. Check with ignition on and the mirror selector switch on the appropriate side. Operate the mirror switch in all its positions. There should be voltage at one of the switch-to-mirror wires in each switch position (except the neutral, "off," position).

10   If voltage is not present in any switch position, check the wiring between the mirror and switch for opens and shorts.

11   If voltage is present, remove the mirror and test it off the vehicle with jumper wires. Replace the mirror if it fails this test.

Replacement

12   The mirror glass snaps onto the motor mechanism. To remove the glass, rotate the mirror inward so that the outside edge is as far out of the housing as possible.

13   Grasp the outboard corner of the glass and pry it off the motor.

14   If the mirror is heated, disconnect the heater connector.

15   To install a new mirror, connect the heater if so equipped and place the glass over the motor mechanism.

16   Press inward until the snaps engage the motor.

17   To replace the control switch, refer to Chapter 11 and remove the left front inside door panel.

18   Press the lock tabs on the switch body inward and push the switch out of the back of the door panel. Then disconnect the connector.

19   To remove an entire mirror assembly, remove the inner trim from the door sail panel and remove the radio speaker (see Section 13).

20   Remove two screws from the cover and disconnect the wiring to the mirror.

21   Remove the three nuts that secure the mirror assembly to the door and remove the mirror.

22   Installation is the reverse of removal.

---

28   Airbag - general information

Refer to illustrations 28.1, 28.2a, 28.2b and 28.6

1   All models have a supplemental restraint system (SRS), more commonly called an airbag. This system is designed to protect the driver and the front seat passenger from injury in case of a frontal collision. The system consists of an airbag module in the center of the steering wheel and another in the right side of the instrument panel, two crash sensors at the front of the vehicle, and a diagnostic module. The diagnostic module is mounted on the bulkhead, under the center of the instrument panel on 1996 and 1997 models or under the center console on 1998 and later models (see illustration). On 2000 and later model years, some models are also

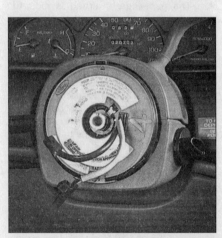

28.2b The steering wheel coil assembly transmits electrical power to the airbag module

equipped with side-impact airbags, which are mounted in the exterior-facing side of the front seats, near the driver/passenger shoulder level.

Airbag modules

Steering wheel (driver's airbag)

2   The airbag inflator module contains a housing that holds the airbag and the inflator unit. It is mounted in the center of the steering wheel. The inflator is mounted on the back of the housing over a hole through which gas is expelled to inflate the bag almost instantly when an electrical signal is sent from the system. A coil assembly on the steering column under the module carries this signal to the module (see illustrations).

3   This coil assembly can transmit an electrical signal regardless of steering wheel position. The igniter in the airbag converts the electrical signal to heat and ignites the sodium azide and copper oxide powder to produce nitrogen gas, which inflates the bag.

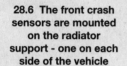

28.6 The front crash sensors are mounted on the radiator support - one on each side of the vehicle

Instrument panel (passenger's airbag)

4   The passenger's airbag is mounted above the glove compartment and identified by the letters SRS for "supplemental restraint system." It consists of an inflator containing an igniter, a bag assembly, a reaction housing, and a trim cover.

5   The airbag is larger that the steering-wheel-mounted unit and is supported by the steel reaction housing. The trim cover is textured and painted to match the instrument panel and has a molded seam that splits when the bag inflates. As with the steering-wheel-mounted airbag, the igniter electrical signal converts to heat, converting sodium azide and iron oxide powder to nitrogen gas to inflate the bag.

Sensors

6   On 1996 and 1997 models, the system has three sensors, two crash sensors at the front of the vehicle **(see illustration)** and a

safing sensor inside the airbag diagnostic module. The sensors are pressure-sensitive switches that complete an electrical circuit during an impact of sufficient G force. The electrical signal from these sensors is sent to the module, which then completes the circuit and inflates the airbags. On 1998 models, all the sensors are incorporated in the diagnostic module. On 1999 and later models, there are four crash sensors. One is in the diagnostic module, one at the front of the vehicle behind the bumper, and one each under the driver's and passenger's seats.

Diagnostic module and warning lamp

7   The electronic diagnostic module supplies the current to the airbag system in a collision, even if battery power is cut off. The module checks the system every time the vehicle is started, causing the instrument panel AIRBAG lamp to light then turn off if the system is operating properly. If there is a fault in the system, the lamp will light and stay on,

flash, or the dash will make a beeping sound. If this happens, the vehicle should be taken to a dealer immediately for service.

Disabling the system

8   Whenever working near the steering wheel, steering column, or other parts of the airbag system, disarm the system as follows:

a) *Turn the ignition key to the Lock position and remove the key.*

b) *Disconnect the cable from the negative battery terminal, then disconnect the cable from the positive battery terminal. Wait 2 minutes for the electronic module backup power supply to be depleted.*

Enabling the system

9   After completing the repairs enable the airbag system as follows:

a) *Make sure the ignition switch is in the Off position.*

b) *Connect the positive battery cable to the positive battery terminal, then connect the negative cable to the negative battery terminal.*

29 Wiring diagrams - general information

Because it isn't possible to include all wiring diagrams for every year and model covered by this manual, the following diagrams are those that are typical and most commonly needed.

Before troubleshooting any circuits, check the fuses to make sure they're in good condition. Make sure the battery is fully charged and check the cable connections.

When checking a circuit, make sure that all connectors are clean with no broken or loose terminals. When unplugging a connector, do not pull on the wires. Pull only on the connector housings themselves.

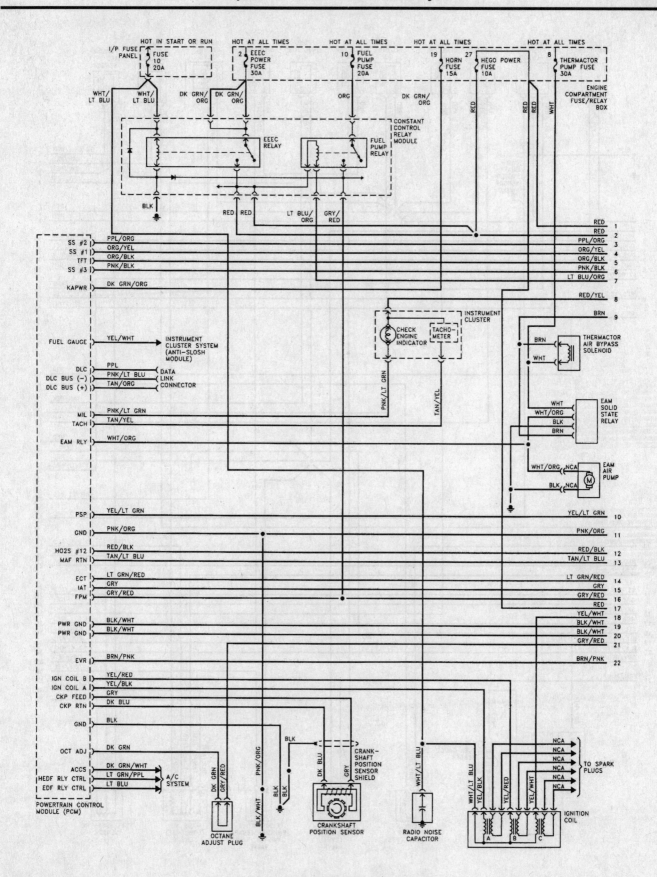

Typical engine control system (1 of 3)

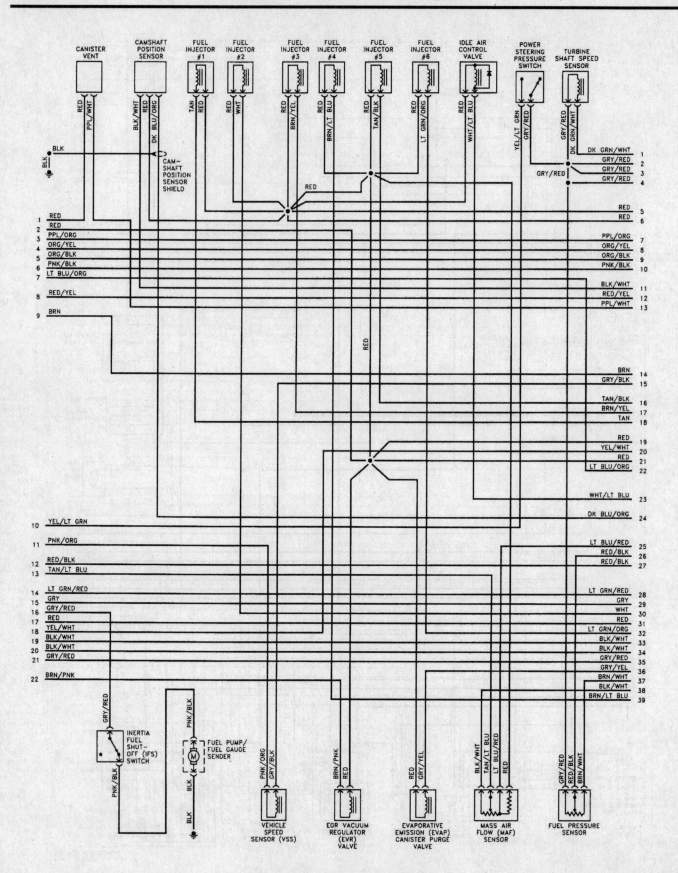

Typical engine control system (2 of 3)

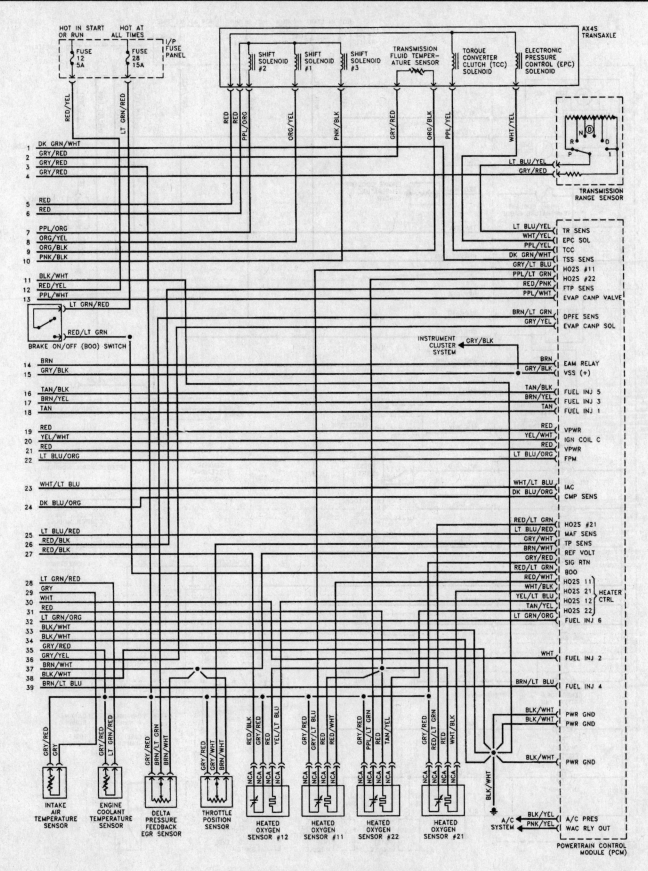

Typical engine control system (3 of 3)

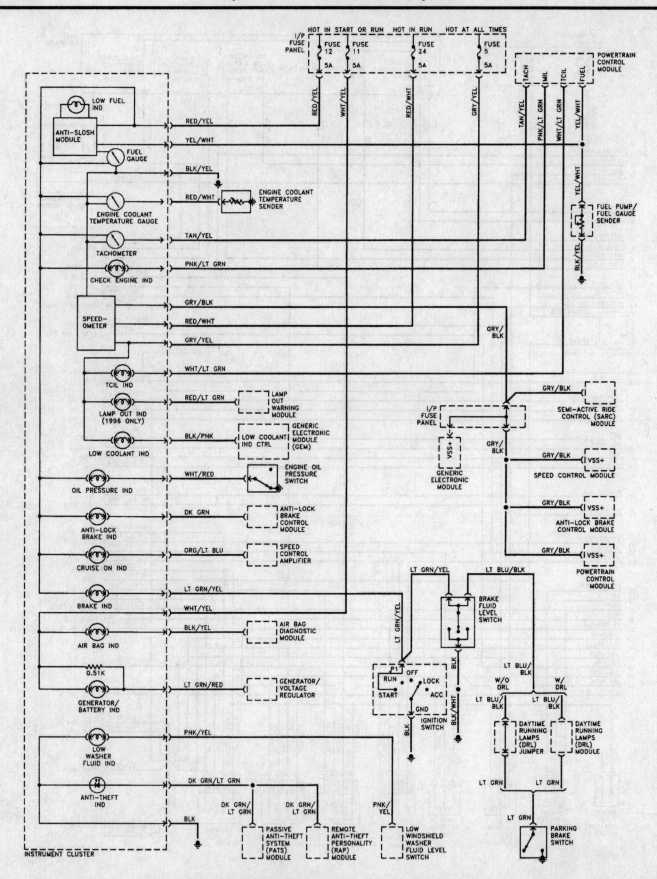

Typical instrument panel warning lights and gauge system

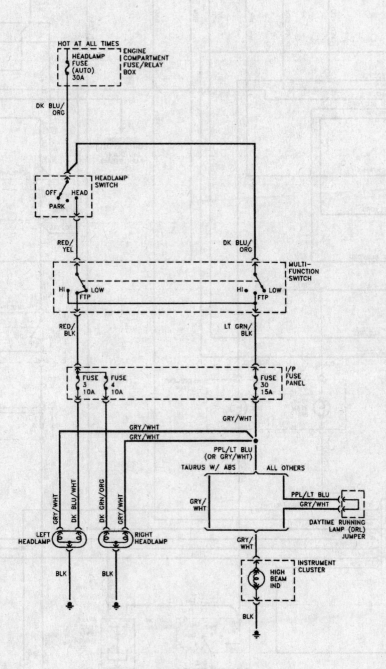

Typical headlight system - without Daytime Running Lights

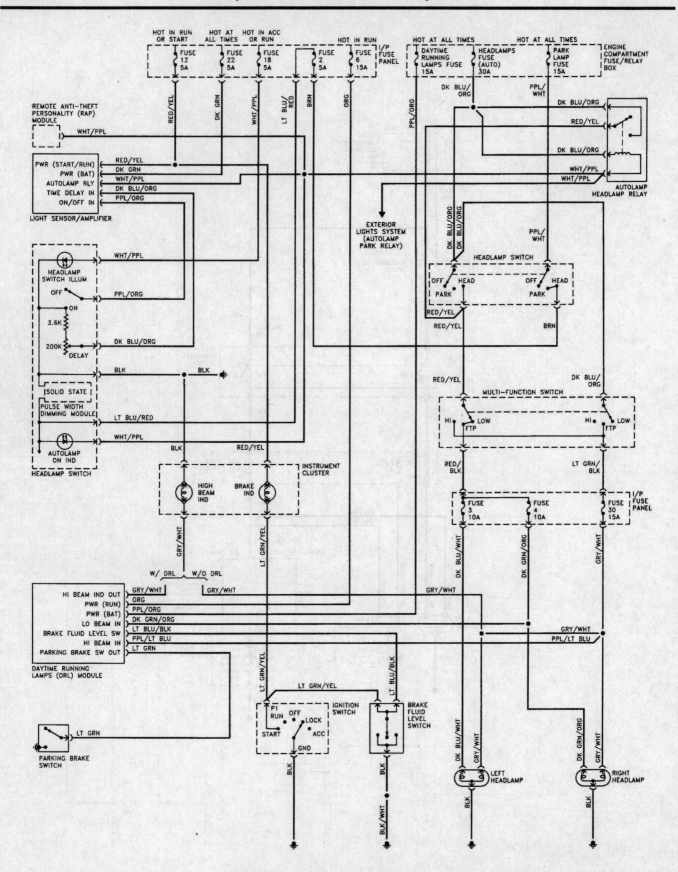

Typical headlight system - with Daytime Running Lights

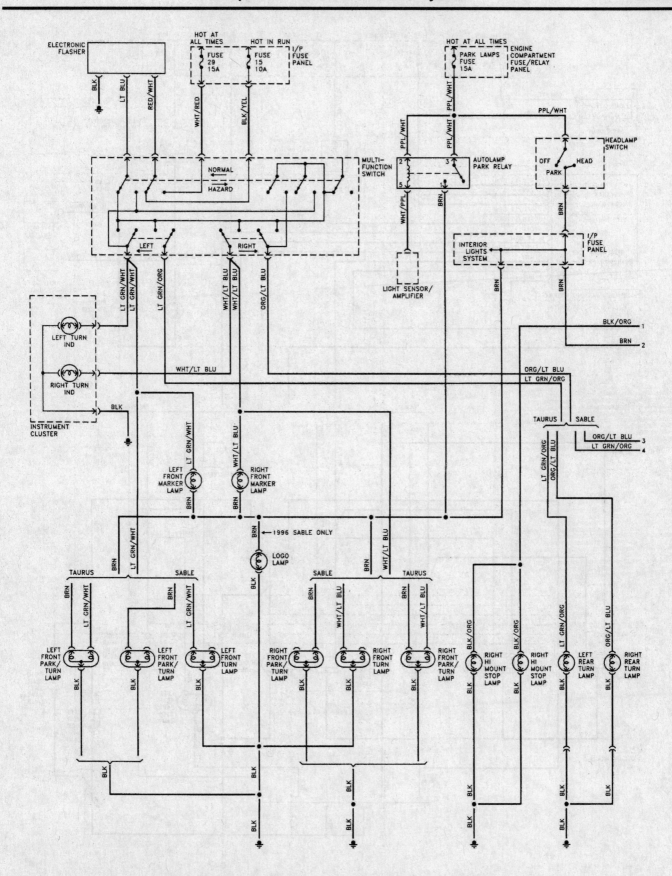

Typical exterior lighting system - sedan models with Lamp Out Warning (1 of 2)

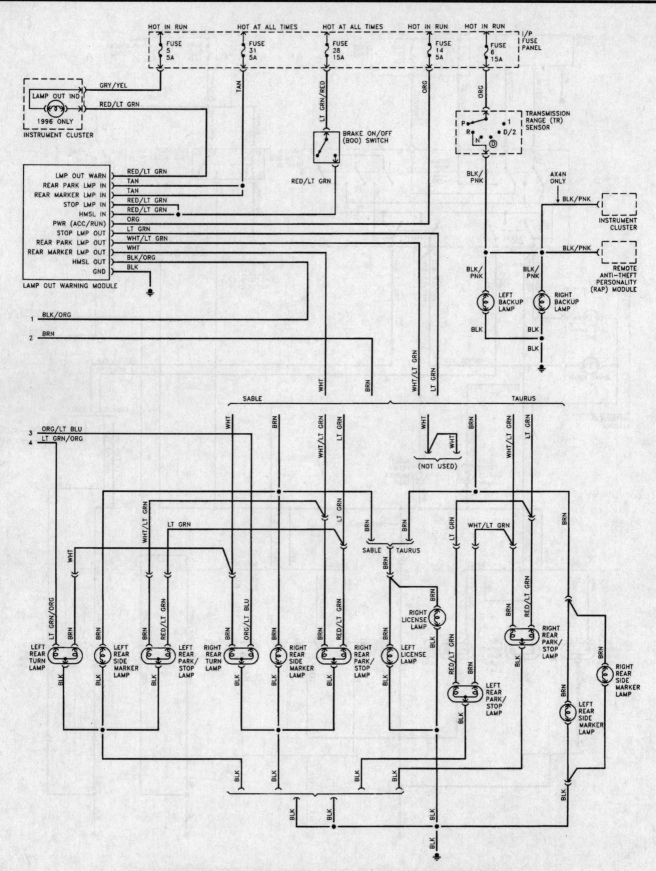

Typical exterior lighting system - sedan models with Lamp Out Warning (2 of 2)

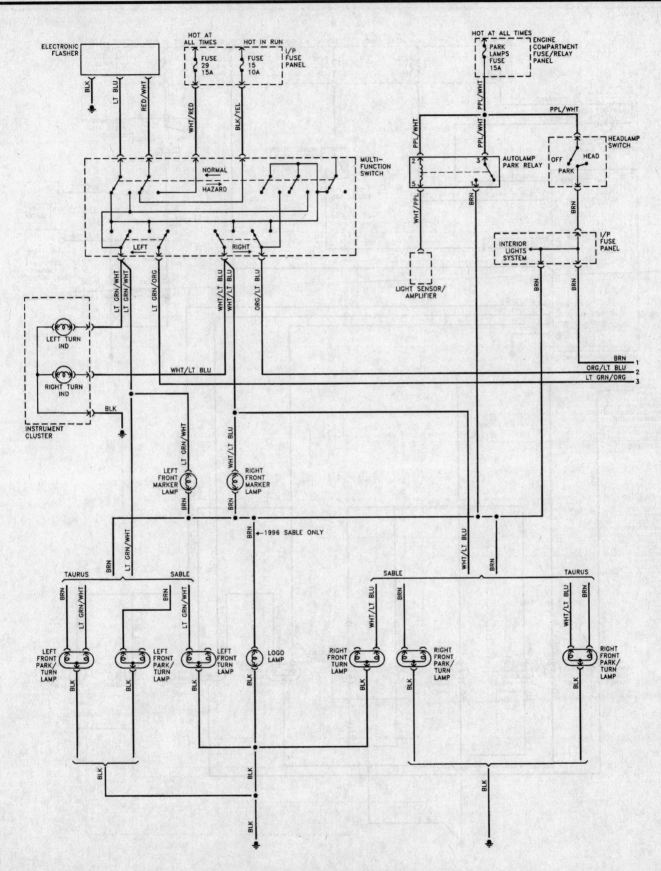

Typical exterior lighting system - wagon models with Lamp Out Warning (1 of 2)

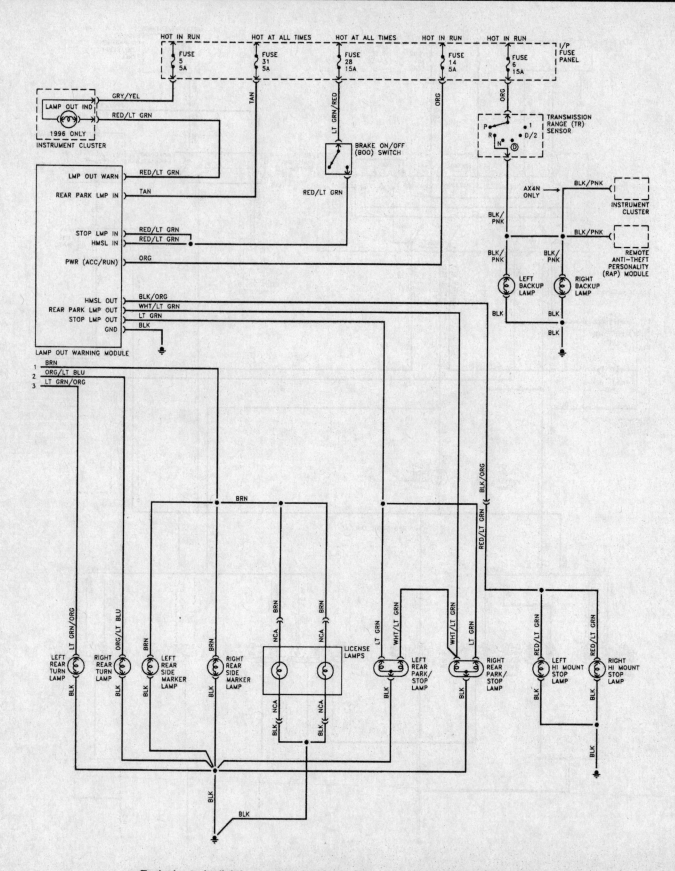

Typical exterior lighting system - wagon models with Lamp Out Warning (2 of 2)

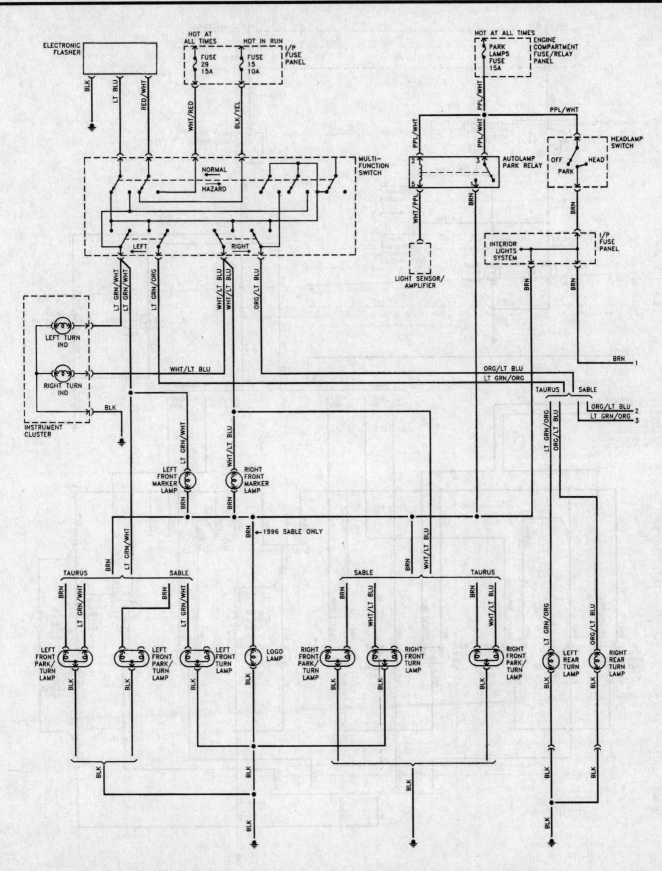

Typical exterior lighting system - sedan models without Lamp Out Warning (1 of 2)

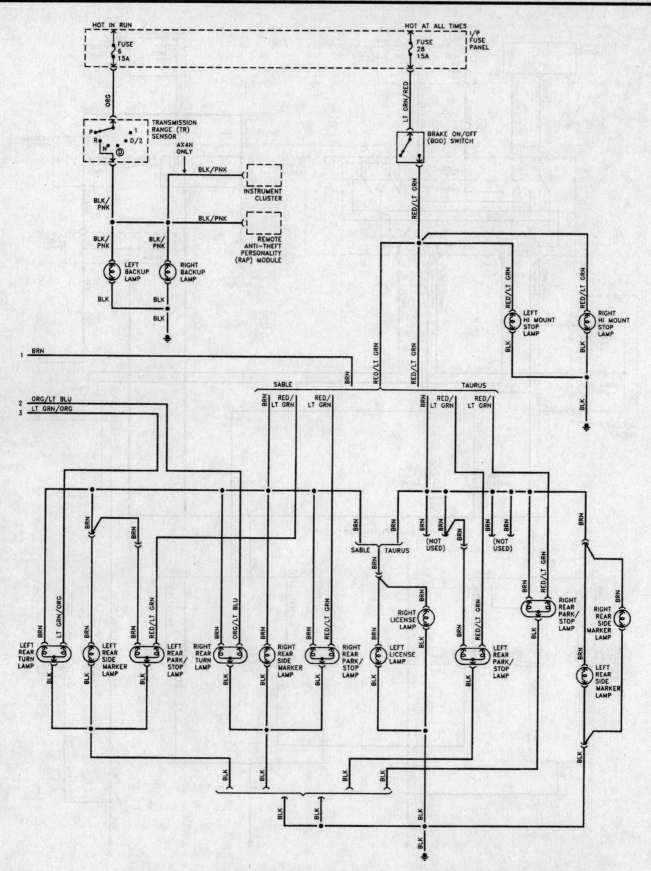

Typical exterior lighting system - sedan models without Lamp Out Warning (2 of 2)

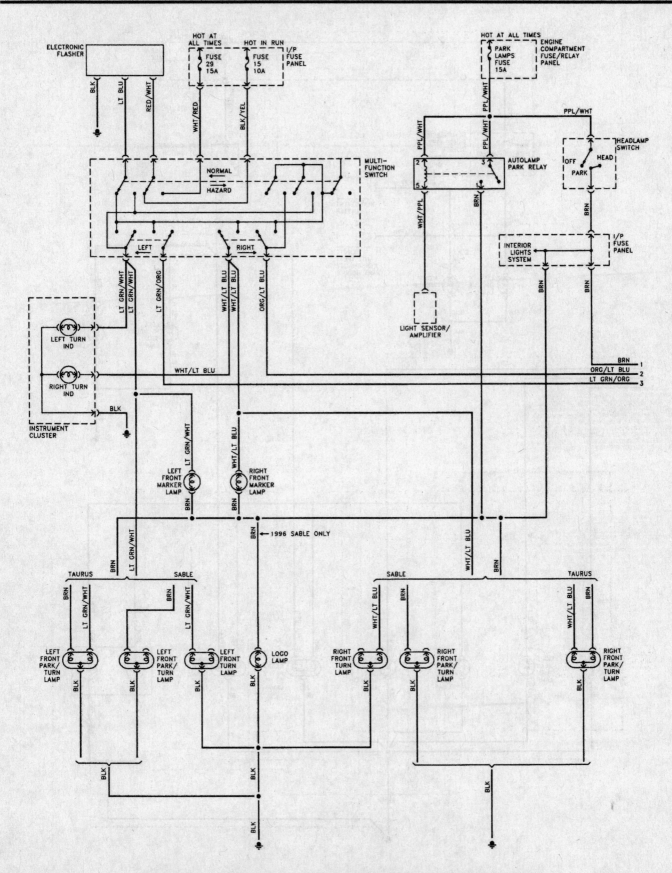

Typical exterior lighting system - wagon models without Lamp Out Warning (1 of 2)

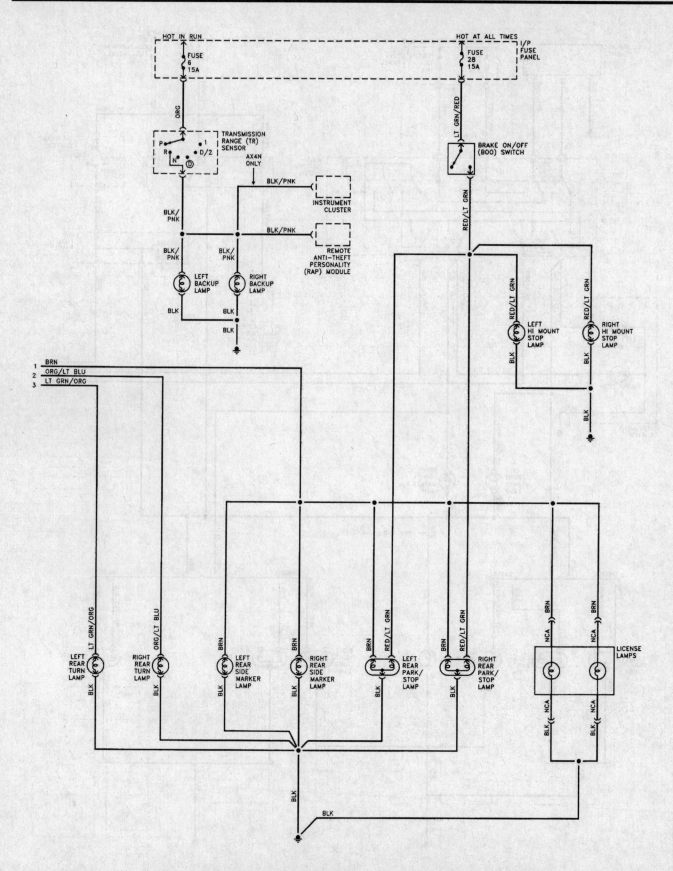

Typical exterior lighting system - wagon models without Lamp Out Warning (2 of 2)

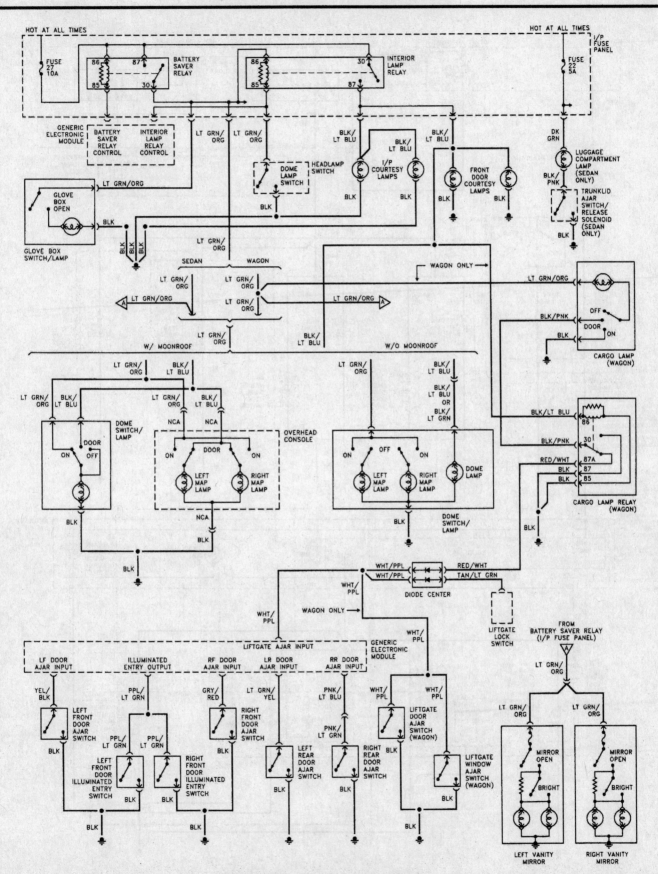

Typical courtesy and dome lamp system

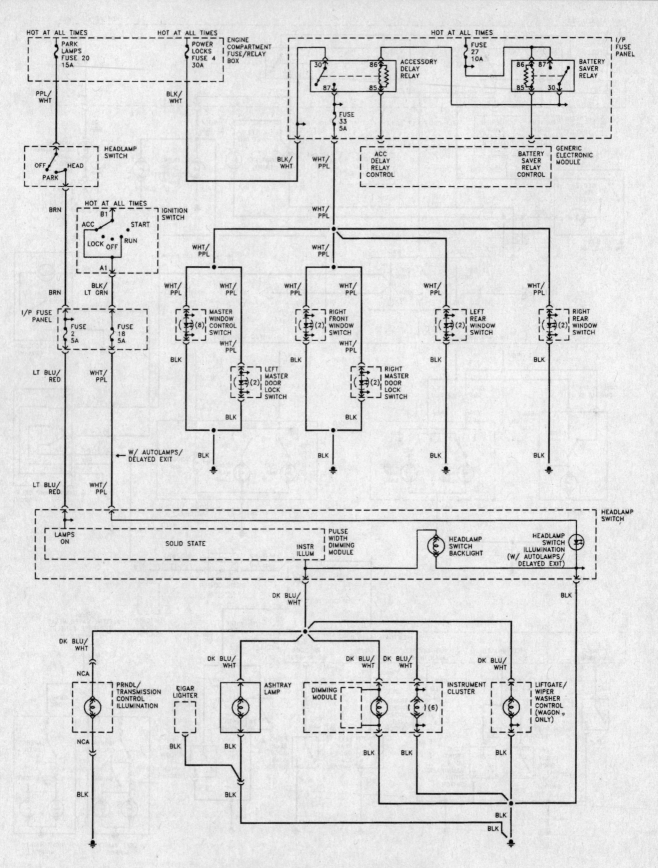

Typical instrument panel illumination lamp system

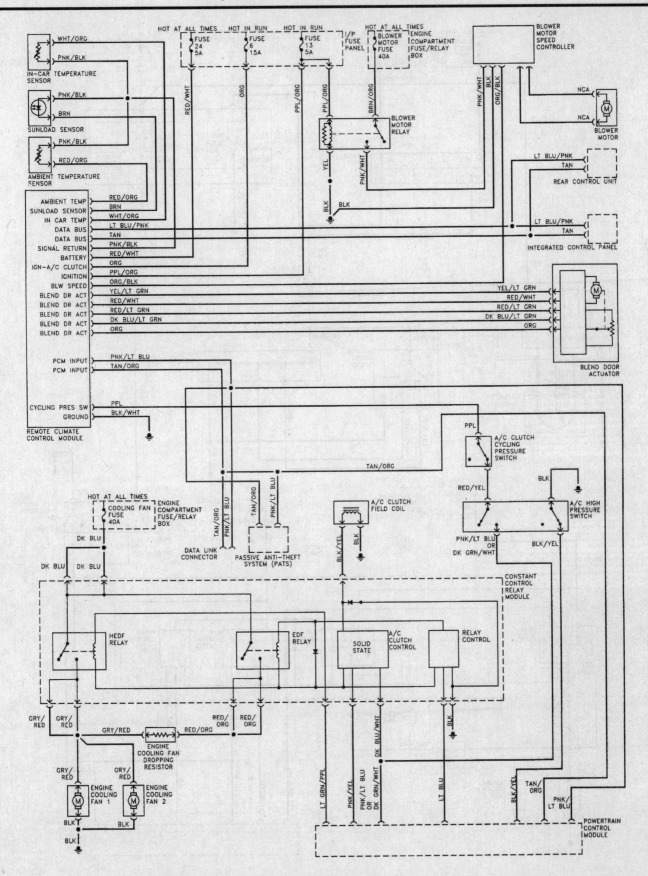

Typical automatic heating and air conditioning system and engine cooling fan system

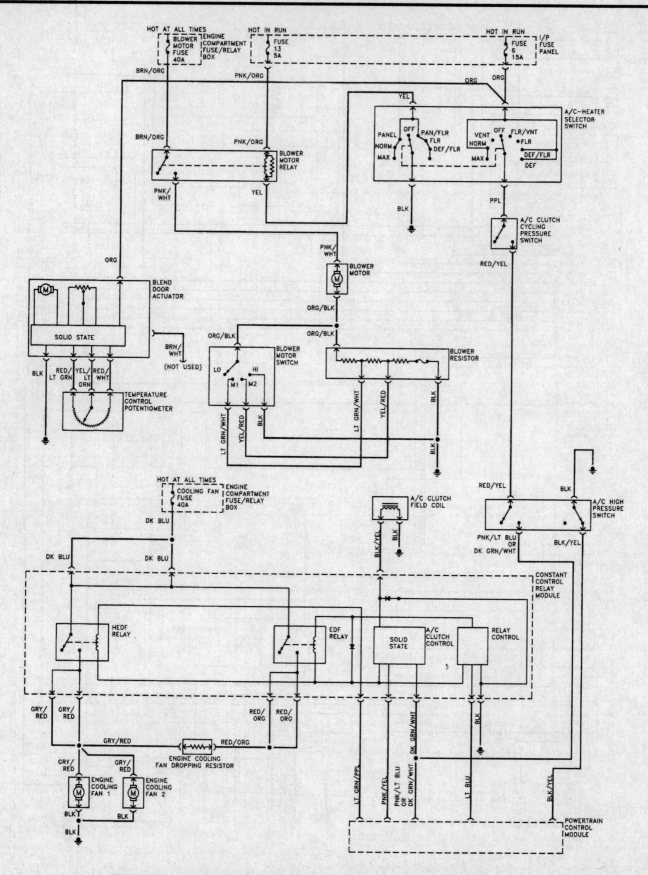

Typical manual heating and air conditioning system and engine cooling fan system

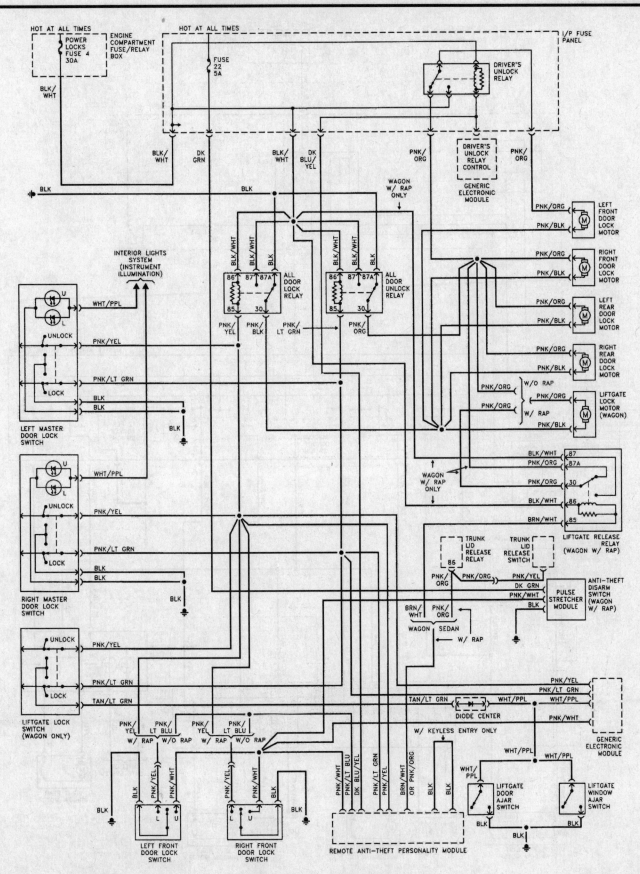

Typical power door lock system

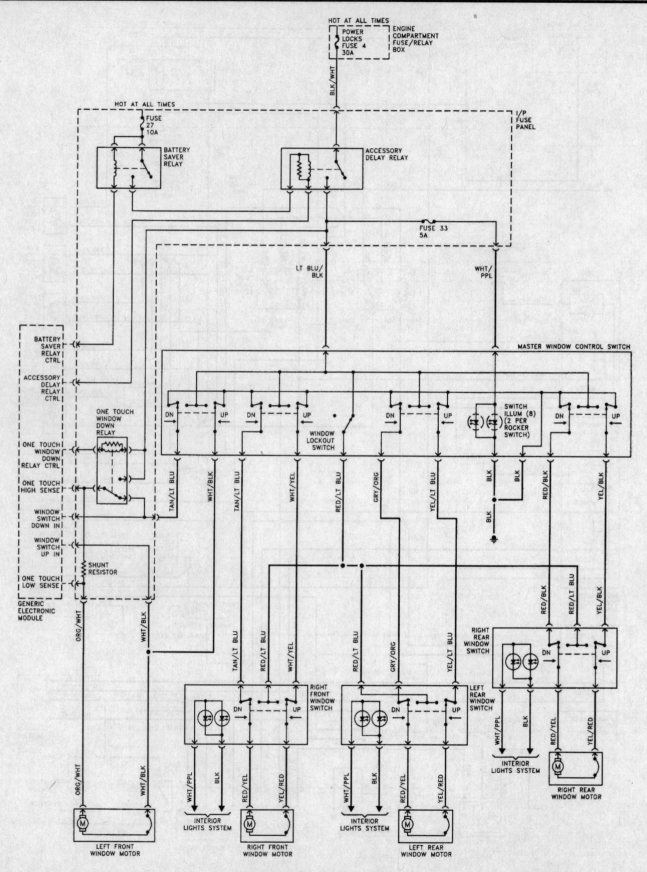

Typical power window system

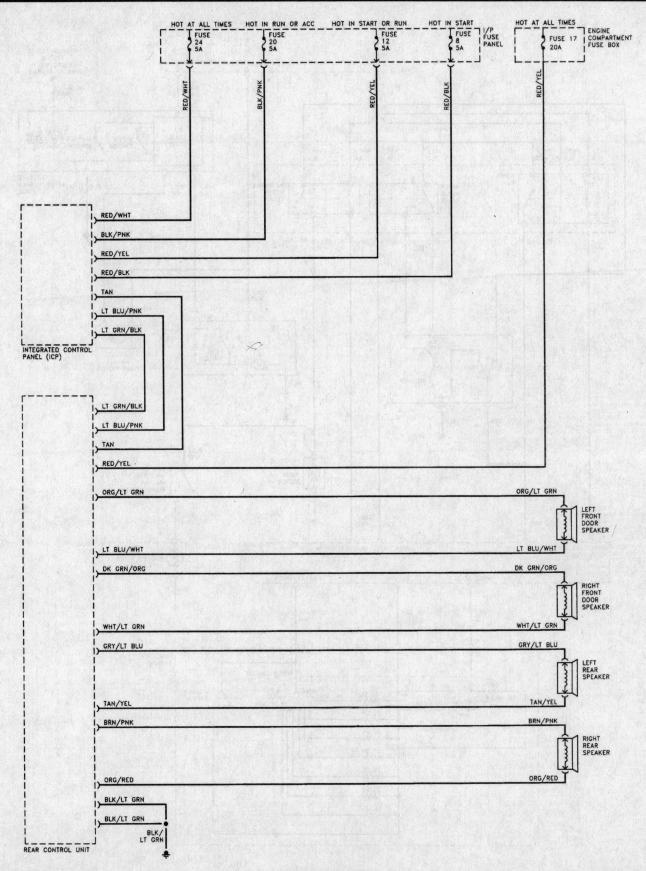

Typical audio system

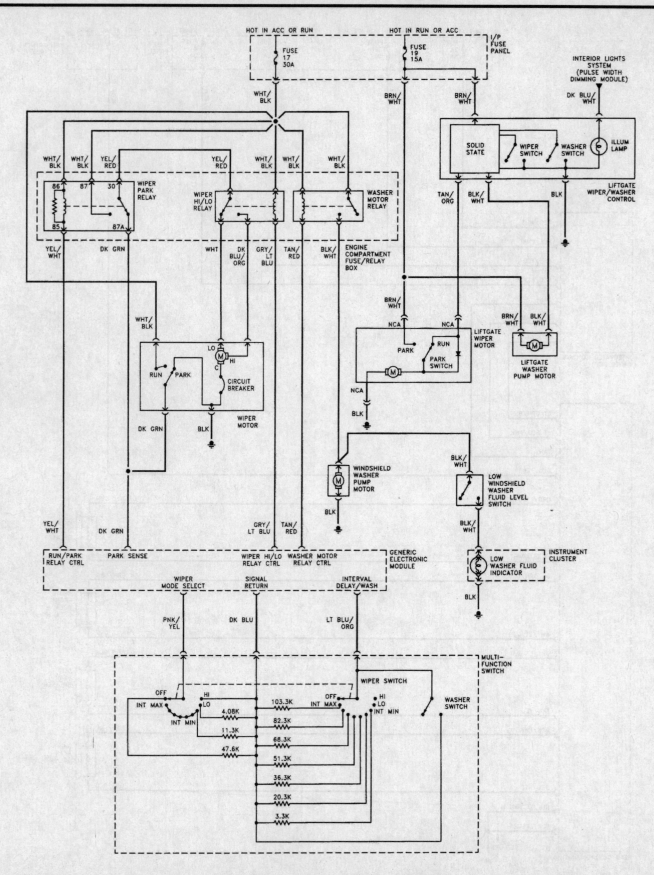

Typical windshield wiper and washer system

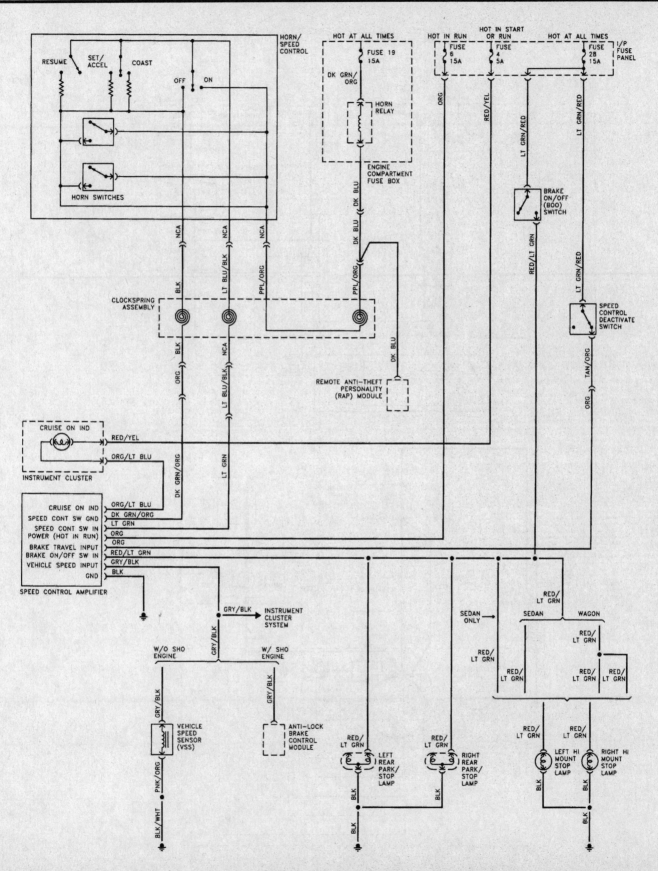

Typical cruise control system

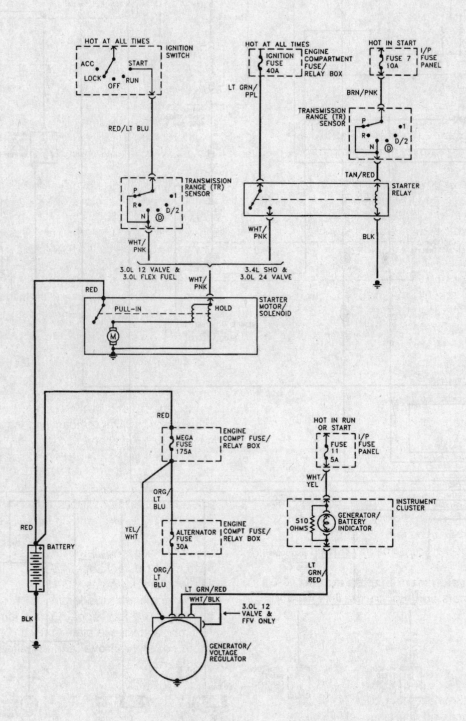

Typical starting and charging systems

Index

Haynes Automotive Manuals

NOTE: If you do not see a listing for your vehicle, consult your local Haynes dealer for the latest product information.

ACURA
12020 Integra '86 thru '89 & Legend '86 thru '90
12021 Integra '90 thru '93 & Legend '91 thru '95
Integra '94 thru '00 - see HONDA Civic (42025)
MDX '01 thru '07 - see HONDA Pilot (42037)
12050 Acura TL '99 thru '08

AMC
Jeep CJ - see JEEP (50020)
14020 Concord/Hornet/Gremlin/Spirit '70 thru '83
14025 (Renault) Alliance & Encore '83 thru '87

AUDI
15020 4000 all models '80 thru '87
15025 5000 all models '77 thru '83
15026 5000 all models '84 thru '88
Audi A4 '96 thru '01 - see VW Passat (96023)
15030 Audi A4 '02 thru '08

AUSTIN
Healey Sprite - see MG Midget (66015)

BMW
18020 3/5 Series '82 thru '92
18021 3 Series including Z3 models '92 thru '98
18022 3-Series incl. Z4 models '99 thru '05
18023 3-Series '06 thru '10
18025 320i all 4 cyl models '75 thru '83
18050 1500 thru 2002 except Turbo '59 thru '77

BUICK
19010 Buick Century '97 thru '05
Century (front-wheel drive) - see GM (38005)
19020 Buick, Oldsmobile & Pontiac Full-size (Front wheel drive) '85 thru '05
19025 Buick, Oldsmobile & Pontiac Full-size (Rear wheel drive) '70 thru '90
19030 Mid-size Regal & Century '74 thru '87
Regal - see GENERAL MOTORS (38010)
Skyhawk - see GM (38030)
Skylark - see GM (38020, 38025)
Somerset - see GENERAL MOTORS (38025)

CADILLAC
21015 CTS & CTS-V '03 thru '12
21030 Cadillac Rear Wheel Drive '70 thru '93
Cimarron, Eldorado & Seville - see GM (38015, 38030, 38031)

CHEVROLET
10305 Chevrolet Engine Overhaul Manual
24010 Astro & GMC Safari Mini-vans '85 thru '05
24015 Camaro V8 all models '70 thru '81
24016 Camaro all models '82 thru '92
Cavalier - see GM (38015)
Celebrity - see GM (38005)
24017 Camaro & Firebird '93 thru '02
24020 Chevelle, Malibu, El Camino '69 thru '87
24024 Chevette & Pontiac T1000 '76 thru '87
Citation - see GENERAL MOTORS (38020)
24027 Colorado & GMC Canyon '04 thru '10
24032 Corsica/Beretta all models '87 thru '96
24040 Corvette all V8 models '68 thru '82
24041 Corvette all models '84 thru '96
24045 Full-size Sedans Caprice, Impala, Biscayne, Bel Air & Wagons '69 thru '90
24046 Impala SS & Caprice and Buick Roadmaster '91 thru '96
Impala '00 thru '05 - see LUMINA (24048)
24047 Impala & Monte Carlo all models '06 thru '11
Lumina '90 thru '94 - see GM (38010)
24048 Lumina & Monte Carlo '95 thru '05
Lumina APV - see GM (38035)
24050 Luv Pick-up all 2WD & 4WD '72 thru '82
Malibu - see GM (38026)
24055 Monte Carlo all models '70 thru '88
Monte Carlo '95 thru '01 - see LUMINA
24059 Nova all V8 models '69 thru '79
24060 Nova/Geo Prizm '85 thru '92
24064 Pick-ups '67 thru '87 - Chevrolet & GMC
24065 Pick-ups '88 thru '98 - Chevrolet & GMC
24066 Pick-ups '99 thru '06 - Chevrolet & GMC
24067 Chevy Silverado & GMC Sierra '07 thru '12
24070 S-10 & S-15 Pick-ups '82 thru '93
24071 S-10, Sonoma & Jimmy '94 thru '04
24072 Chevrolet TrailBlazer, GMC Envoy & Oldsmobile Bravada '02 thru '09
24075 Sprint '85 thru '88, Geo Metro '89 thru '01
24080 Vans - Chevrolet & GMC '68 thru '96
24081 Full-size Vans '96 thru '10

CHRYSLER
10310 Chrysler Engine Overhaul Manual
25015 Chrysler Cirrus, Dodge Stratus, Plymouth Breeze, '95 thru '00
25020 Full-size Front-Wheel Drive '88 thru '93
K-Cars - see DODGE Aries (30008)
Laser - see DODGE Daytona (30030)
25025 Chrysler LHS, Concorde & New Yorker, Dodge Intrepid, Eagle Vision, '93 thru '97
25026 Chrysler LHS, Concorde, 300M, Dodge Intrepid '98 thru '04
25027 Chrysler 300, Dodge Charger & Magnum '05 thru '09
25030 Chrysler/Plym. Mid-size '82 thru '95
Rear-wheel Drive - see DODGE (30050)
25035 PT Cruiser all models '01 thru '10
25040 Chrysler Sebring '95 thru '06, Dodge Stratus '01 thru '06, Dodge Avenger '95 thru '02

DATSUN
28005 200SX all models '80 thru '83
28007 B-210 all models '73 thru '78
28009 210 all models '78 thru '82
28012 240Z, 260Z & 280Z Coupe '70 thru '78
28014 280ZX Coupe & 2+2 '79 thru '83
300ZX - see NISSAN (72010)
28018 510 & PL521 Pick-up '68 thru '73
28020 510 all models '78 thru '81
28022 620 Series Pick-up all models '73 thru '79
720 Series Pick-up - see NISSAN (72030)
28025 810/Maxima all gas models, '77 thru '84

DODGE
400 & 600 - see CHRYSLER (25030)
30008 Aries & Plymouth Reliant '81 thru '89
30010 Caravan & Ply. Voyager '84 thru '95
30011 Caravan & Ply. Voyager '96 thru '02
30012 Challenger/Plymouth Saporro '78 thru '83
Challenger '67-'76 - see DART (30025)
30013 Caravan, Chrysler Voyager, Town & Country '03 thru '07
30016 Colt/Plymouth Champ '78 thru '87
30020 Dakota Pick-ups all models '87 thru '96
30021 Durango '98 & '99, Dakota '97 thru '99
30022 Durango '00 thru '03, Dakota '00 thru '04

30023 Durango '04 thru '09, Dakota '05 thru '11
30025 Dart, Challenger/Plymouth Barracuda & Valiant 6 cyl models '67 thru '76
30030 Daytona & Chrysler Laser '84 thru '89
Intrepid - see Chrysler (25025, 25026)
30034 Dodge & Plymouth Neon '95 thru '99
30035 Omni & Plymouth Horizon '78 thru '90
30036 Dodge and Plymouth Neon '00 thru '05
30040 Pick-ups all full-size models '74 thru '93
30041 Pick-ups all full-size models '94 thru '01
30042 Pick-ups full-size models '02 thru '08
30045 Ram 50/D50 Pick-ups & Raider and Plymouth Arrow Pick-ups '79 thru '93
30050 Dodge/Ply./Chrysler RWD '71 thru '89
30055 Shadow/Plymouth Sundance '87 thru '94
30060 Spirit & Plymouth Acclaim '89 thru '95
30065 Vans - Dodge & Plymouth '71 thru '03

EAGLE
Talon - see MITSUBISHI (68030, 68031)
Vision - see CHRYSLER (25025)

FIAT
34010 124 Sport Coupe & Spider '68 thru '78
34025 X1/9 all models '74 thru '80

FORD
10320 Ford Engine Overhaul Manual
10355 Ford Automatic Transmission Overhaul
11500 Mustang '64-1/2 thru '70 Restoration Guide
36004 Aerostar Mini-vans '86 thru '97
Aspire - see FORD Festiva (36030)
36006 Contour/Mercury Mystique '95 thru '00
36008 Courier Pick-up all models '72 thru '82
36012 Crown Victoria & Mercury Grand Marquis '88 thru '10
36016 Escort/Mercury Lynx '81 thru '90
36020 Escort/Mercury Tracer '91 thru '02
36022 Escape & Mazda Tribute '01 thru '11
36024 Explorer & Mazda Navajo '91 thru '01
36025 Explorer/Mercury Mountaineer '02 thru '10
36028 Fairmont & Mercury Zephyr '78 thru '83
36030 Festiva & Aspire '88 thru '97
36032 Fiesta all models '77 thru '80
36034 Focus all models '00 thru '11
36036 Ford & Mercury Full-size '75 thru '87
36044 Ford & Mercury Mid-size '75 thru '86
36045 Ford Fusion & Mercury Milan '06 thru '10
36048 Mustang V8 all models '64-1/2 thru '73
36049 Mustang II 4 cyl, V6 & V8 '74 thru '78
36050 Mustang & Mercury Capri '79 thru '93
36051 Mustang all models '94 thru '04
36052 Mustang '05 thru '10
36054 Pick-ups and Bronco '73 thru '79
36058 Pick-ups and Bronco '80 thru '96
36059 Pick-ups & Expedition '97 thru '09
36060 Super Duty Pick-up, Excursion '99 thru '10
36061 F-150 full-size '04 thru '10
36062 Pinto & Mercury Bobcat '75 thru '80
36066 Probe all models '89 thru '92
Probe '93 thru '97 - see MAZDA 626 (61042)
36070 Ranger/Bronco II gas models '83 thru '92
36071 Ford Ranger '93 thru '11
Mazda Pick-ups '94 thru '09
36074 Taurus & Mercury Sable '86 thru '95
36075 Taurus & Mercury Sable '96 thru '05
36078 Tempo & Mercury Topaz '84 thru '94
36082 Thunderbird/Mercury Cougar '83 thru '88
36086 Thunderbird/Mercury Cougar '89 thru '97
36090 Vans all V8 Econoline models '69 thru '91
36094 Vans full size '92 thru '10
36097 Windstar Mini-van '95 thru '07

GENERAL MOTORS
10360 GM Automatic Transmission Overhaul
38005 Buick Century, Chevrolet Celebrity, Olds Cutlass Ciera & Pontiac 6000 '82 thru '96
38010 Buick Regal, Chevrolet Lumina, Oldsmobile Cutlass Supreme & Pontiac Grand Prix front wheel drive '88 thru '07
38015 Buick Skyhawk, Cadillac Cimarron, Chevrolet Cavalier, Oldsmobile Firenza Pontiac J-2000 & Sunbird '82 thru '94
38016 Chevrolet Cavalier/Pontiac Sunfire '95 thru '05
38017 Chevrolet Cobalt & Pontiac G5 '05 thru '11
38020 Buick Skylark, Chevrolet Citation, Olds Omega, Pontiac Phoenix '80 thru '85
38025 Buick Skylark & Somerset, Olds Achieva, Calais & Pontiac Grand Am '85 thru '98
38026 Chevrolet Malibu, Olds Alero & Cutlass, Pontiac Grand Am '97 thru '03
38027 Chevrolet Malibu '04 thru '10
38030 Cadillac Eldorado & Oldsmobile Toronado '71 thru '85, Seville '80 thru '85, Buick Riviera '79 thru '85
38031 Cadillac Eldorado & Seville '86 thru '91, DeVille & Buick Riviera '86 thru '93, Fleetwood & Olds Toronado '86 thru '92
38032 DeVille '94 thru '05, Seville '92 thru '04
Cadillac DTS '06 thru '10
38035 Chevrolet Lumina APV, Olds Silhouette & Pontiac Trans Sport '90 thru '96
38036 Chevrolet Venture, Olds Silhouette, Pontiac Trans Sport & Montana '97 thru '05
GM Full-size RWD - see BUICK (19025)
38040 Chevrolet Equinox '05 thru '09
Pontiac Torrent '06 thru '09
38070 Chevrolet HHR '06 thru '11

GEO
Metro - see CHEVROLET Sprint (24075)
Prizm - see CHEVROLET (24060) or TOYOTA (92036)
40030 Storm all models '90 thru '93
Tracker - see SUZUKI Samurai (90010)

GMC
Vans & Pick-ups - see CHEVROLET

HONDA
42010 Accord CVCC all models '76 thru '83
42011 Accord all models '84 thru '89
42012 Accord all models '90 thru '93
42013 Accord all models '94 thru '97
42014 Accord all models '98 thru '02
42015 Accord '03 thru '07
42020 Civic 1200 all models '73 thru '79
42021 Civic 1300 & 1500 CVCC '80 thru '83
42022 Civic 1500 CVCC all models '75 thru '79
42023 Civic all models '84 thru '91
42024 Civic & del Sol '92 thru '95
42025 Civic '96 thru '00, CR-V '97 thru '01, Acura Integra '94 thru '00
42026 Civic '01 thru '10, CR-V '02 thru '09
42035 Odyssey models '99 thru '10
Passport - see ISUZU Rodeo (47017)

42037 Honda Pilot '03 thru '07, Acura MDX '01 thru '07
42040 Prelude CVCC all models '79 thru '89

HYUNDAI
43010 Elantra all models '96 thru '10
43015 Excel & Accent all models '86 thru '09
43050 Santa Fe all models '01 thru '06
43055 Sonata all models '99 thru '08

INFINITI
G35 '03 thru '08 - see NISSAN 350Z (72011)

ISUZU
Hombre - see CHEVROLET S-10 (24071)
47017 Rodeo, Amigo & Honda Passport '89 thru '02
47020 Trooper '84 thru '91, Pick-up '81 thru '93

JAGUAR
49010 XJ6 all 6 cyl models '68 thru '86
49011 XJ6 all models '88 thru '94
49015 XJ12 & XJS all 12 cyl models '72 thru '85

JEEP
50010 Cherokee, Comanche & Wagoneer Limited all models '84 thru '01
50020 CJ all models '49 thru '86
50025 Grand Cherokee all models '93 thru '04
50026 Grand Cherokee '05 thru '09
50029 Grand Wagoneer & Pick-up '72 thru '91
50030 Wrangler all models '87 thru '11
50035 Liberty '02 thru '07

KIA
54050 Optima '01 thru '10
54070 Sephia '94 thru '01, Spectra '00 thru '09, Sportage '05 thru '10

LEXUS
ES 300/330 - see TOYOTA Camry (92007) (92008)
RX 330 - see TOYOTA Highlander (92095)

LINCOLN
Navigator - see FORD Pick-up (36059)
59010 Rear Wheel Drive all models '70 thru '10

MAZDA
61010 GLC (rear wheel drive) '77 thru '83
61011 GLC (front wheel drive) '81 thru '85
61012 Mazda3 '04 thru '11
61015 323 & Protegé '90 thru '03
61016 MX-5 Miata '90 thru '09
61020 MPV all models '89 thru '98
Navajo - see FORD Explorer (36024)
61030 Pick-ups '72 thru '93
Pick-ups '94 on - see Ford (36071)
61035 RX-7 all models '79 thru '85
61036 RX-7 all models '86 thru '91
61040 626 (rear wheel drive) '79 thru '82
61041 626 & MX-6 (front wheel drive) '83 thru '92
61042 626 '93 thru '01, & MX-6/Ford Probe '93 thru '02
61043 Mazda6 '03 thru '11

MERCEDES-BENZ
63012 123 Series Diesel '76 thru '85
63015 190 Series 4-cyl gas models, '84 thru '88
63020 230, 250 & 280 6 cyl sohc '68 thru '72
63025 280 123 Series gas models '77 thru '81
63030 350 & 450 all models '71 thru '80
63040 C-Class: C230/C240/C280/C320/C350 '01 thru '07

MERCURY
64200 Villager & Nissan Quest '93 thru '01
All other titles, see FORD listing.

MG
66010 MGB Roadster & GT Coupe '62 thru '80
66015 MG Midget & Austin Healey Sprite Roadster '58 thru '80

MINI
67020 Mini '02 thru '11

MITSUBISHI
68020 Cordia, Tredia, Galant, Precis & Mirage '83 thru '93
68030 Eclipse, Eagle Talon & Plymouth Laser '90 thru '94
68031 Eclipse '95 thru '05, Eagle Talon '95 thru '98
68035 Galant '94 thru '10
68040 Pick-up '83 thru '96, Montero '83 thru '93

NISSAN
72010 300ZX all models incl. Turbo '84 thru '89
72011 350Z & Infiniti G35 all models '03 thru '08
72015 Altima all models '93 thru '06
72016 Altima '07 thru '10
72020 Maxima all models '85 thru '92
72021 Maxima all models '93 thru '01
72025 Murano '03 thru '10
72030 Pick-ups '80 thru '97, Pathfinder '87 thru '95
72031 Frontier Pick-up, Xterra, Pathfinder '96 thru '04
72032 Frontier & Xterra '05 thru '11
72040 Pulsar all models '83 thru '86
72050 Sentra all models '82 thru '94
72051 Sentra & 200SX all models '95 thru '06
72060 Stanza all models '82 thru '90
72070 Titan pick-ups '04 thru '10, Armada '05 thru '10

OLDSMOBILE
73015 Cutlass '74 thru '88
For other OLDSMOBILE titles, see BUICK, CHEVROLET or GM listings.

PLYMOUTH
For PLYMOUTH titles, see DODGE.

PONTIAC
79008 Fiero all models '84 thru '88
79018 Firebird V8 models except Turbo '70 thru '81
79019 Firebird all models '82 thru '92
79025 G6 all models '05 thru '09
79040 Mid-size Rear-wheel Drive '70 thru '87
Vibe '03 thru '11 - see TOYOTA Matrix (92060)
For other PONTIAC titles, see BUICK, CHEVROLET or GM listings.

PORSCHE
80020 911 Coupe & Targa models '65 thru '89
80025 914 all 4 cyl models '69 thru '76
80030 924 all models incl. Turbo '76 thru '82
80035 944 all models incl. Turbo '83 thru '89

RENAULT
Alliance, Encore - see AMC (14020)

SAAB
84010 900 including Turbo '79 thru '88

SATURN
87010 Saturn all S-series models '91 thru '02
87011 Saturn Ion '03 thru '07

87020 Saturn all L-series models '00 thru '04
87040 Saturn VUE '02 thru '07

SUBARU
89002 1100, 1300, 1400 & 1600 '71 thru '79
89003 1600 & 1800 2WD & 4WD '80 thru '94
89100 Legacy all models '90 thru '99
89101 Legacy & Forester '00 thru '06

SUZUKI
90010 Samurai/Sidekick/Geo Tracker '86 thru '01

TOYOTA
92005 Camry all models '83 thru '91
92006 Camry all models '92 thru '96
92007 Camry/Avalon/Solara/Lexus ES 300 '97 thru '01
92008 Toyota Camry, Avalon and Solara & Lexus ES 300/330 all models '02 thru '06
92009 Camry '07 thru '11
92015 Celica Rear Wheel Drive '71 thru '85
92020 Celica Front Wheel Drive '86 thru '99
92025 Celica Supra all models '79 thru '92
92030 Corolla all models '75 thru '79
92032 Corolla rear wheel drive models '80 thru '87
92035 Corolla front wheel drive '84 thru '92
92036 Corolla & Geo Prizm '93 thru '02
92037 Corolla models '03 thru '11
92040 Corolla Tercel all models '80 thru '82
92045 Corona all models '74 thru '82
92050 Cressida all models '78 thru '82
92055 Land Cruiser FJ40/43/45/55 '68 thru '82
92056 Land Cruiser FJ60/62/80/FZJ80 '80 thru '96
92065 Matrix & Pontiac Vibe '03 thru '11
92070 MR2 all models '85 thru '87
92075 Pick-up all models '69 thru '78
92076 Pick-up all models '79 thru '95
92076 Tacoma, 4Runner & T100 '93 thru '04
92077 Tacoma all models '05 thru '09
92078 Tundra '00 thru '06, Sequoia '01 thru '07
92079 4Runner all models '03 thru '09
92080 Previa all models '91 thru '95
92081 Prius '01 thru '08
92082 RAV4 all models '96 thru '10
92085 Tercel all models '87 thru '94
92090 Sienna all models '98 thru '09
92095 Highlander & Lexus RX-330 '99 thru '07

TRIUMPH
94007 Spitfire all models '62 thru '81
94010 TR7 all models '75 thru '81

VW
96008 Beetle & Karmann Ghia '54 thru '79
96009 New Beetle '98 thru '11
96016 Rabbit, Jetta, Scirocco, & Pick-up gas models '75 thru '92 & Convertible '80 thru '92
96017 Golf, GTI & Jetta '93 thru '98, Cabrio '95 thru 02
96018 Golf, GTI & Jetta '99 thru '05
96019 Jetta, Rabbit, GTI & Golf '05 thru '11
96020 Rabbit, Jetta, Pick-up diesel '77 thru '84
96023 Passat '98 thru '05, Audi A4 '96 thru '01
96030 Transporter 1600 all models '68 thru '79
96035 Transporter 1700, 1800, 2000 '72 thru '79
96040 Type 3 1500 & 1600 '63 thru '73
96045 Vanagon air-cooled models '80 thru '83

VOLVO
97010 120, 130 Series & 1800 Sports '61 thru '73
97015 140 Series all models '66 thru '74
97020 240 Series all models '76 thru '93
97040 740 & 760 Series all models '82 thru '88

TECHBOOK MANUALS
10205 Automotive Computer Codes
10206 OBD-II & Electronic Engine Management
10210 Automotive Emissions Control Manual
10215 Fuel Injection Manual, '78 thru '85
10220 Fuel Injection Manual, '86 thru '99
10225 Holley Carburetor Manual
10230 Rochester Carburetor Manual
10240 Weber/Zenith/Stromberg/SU Carburetor
10305 Chevrolet Engine Overhaul Manual
10310 Chrysler Engine Overhaul Manual
10320 Ford Engine Overhaul Manual
10330 GM and Ford Diesel Engine Repair
10333 Engine Performance Manual
10340 Small Engine Repair Manual
10345 Suspension, Steering & Driveline
10355 Ford Automatic Transmission Overhaul
10360 GM Automatic Transmission Overhaul
10405 Automotive Body Repair & Painting
10410 Automotive Brake Manual
10415 Automotive Detailing Manual
10420 Automotive Electrical Manual
10425 Automotive Heating & Air Conditioning
10430 Automotive Reference Dictionary
10435 Automotive Tools Manual
10440 Used Car Buying Guide
10445 Welding Manual
10450 ATV Basics
10452 Scooters 50cc to 250cc

SPANISH MANUALS
98903 Reparación de Carrocería & Pintura
98904 Manual de Carburador Modelos Holley & Rochester
98905 Códigos Automotrices de la Computadora
98906 OBD-II & Sistemas de Control Electrónico del Motor
98910 Frenos Automotriz
98913 Electricidad Automotriz
98915 Inyección de Combustible '86 al '99
99040 Chevrolet & GMC Camionetas '67 al '87
99041 Chevrolet & GMC Camionetas '88 al '98
99042 Chevrolet Camionetas Cerradas '68 al '95
99043 Chevrolet/GMC Camionetas '94 al '04
99048 Chevrolet/GMC Camionetas '99 al '06
99055 Dodge Caravan/Ply. Voyager '84 al '95
99075 Ford Camionetas y Bronco '80 al '94
99076 Ford F-150 '97 al '09
99077 Ford Camionetas Cerradas '69 al '91
99088 Ford Modelos de Tamaño Mediano '75 al '86
99089 Ford Camionetas Ranger '93 al '10
99091 Ford Taurus & Mercury Sable '86 al '95
99095 GM Modelos de Tamaño Grande '70 al '90
99100 GM Modelos de Tamaño Mediano '70 al '88
99106 Jeep Cherokee, Wagoneer & Comanche '84 al '00
99110 Nissan Camionetas & Pathfinder '80 al '96
99118 Nissan Sentra '82 al '94
99125 Toyota Camionetas y 4-Runner '79 al '95

Over 100 Haynes motorcycle manuals also available

7-12

Haynes North America, Inc., 861 Lawrence Drive, Newbury Park, CA 91320 • (805) 498-6703 • http://www.haynes.com